JUDICIAL RECOURSE TO FOREIGN LAW

The University of Texas at Austin, Studies in Foreign and Transnational Law
General Editors: Sir Basil Markesinis and Dr Jörg Fedtke

The *UT Studies in Foreign and Transnational Law* series aims to publish books covering various aspects of foreign private, criminal, and public law as well as transnational law. This broad ambit of the series underlines the editors' belief that in a shrinking world there is a growing need to expand our knowledge of other legal orders – national or supranational – and to publish books discussing comparative methodology and not merely describing foreign systems.

Also in the series:
The French Civil Code, J.-L. Halpérin, transl. T. Weir

Forthcoming titles
The Protection of Human Rights in German and English Law, J. Fedtke & C. O'Cinneide
Italian Private Law, G. Alpa & V. Zenovich
International Negotiation in the 21st Century, A. Plantey

JUDICIAL RECOURSE TO FOREIGN LAW

A New Source of Inspiration?

Sir Basil Markesinis and Dr Jörg Fedtke

with commentary by

Laurie Ackermann, formerly Justice of the South African Constitutional Court
President Aharon Barak, Israel Supreme Court
Professor Dr Brun-Otto Bryde, German Constitutional Court
M. Guy Canivet, First President of the Cour de cassation, France
Sir Sydney Kentridge KCMG, QC
Professor Christof Rozakis, Vice President, Court of Human Rights, Strasbourg
Judge Konrad Schiemann, Court of the European Communities, Luxembourg

University of Texas at Austin,
Studies in Foreign and Transnational Law
Sir Basil Markesinis and Dr Jörg Fedtke, General Editors

First published 2006
by UCL Press
The name of University College London (UCL) is a registered trade mark
used by UCL Press with the consent of the owner

UCL Press is an imprint of the Taylor & Francis Group, an informa business

Taylor & Francis
2 Park Square, Milton Park, Abingdon, Oxon, OX14 4RN, UK

Published in the USA
by Routledge · Cavendish
270 Madison Ave, New York, NY 10016

Typeset in Sabon by Newgen Imaging Systems (P) Ltd., Chennai, India
Printed and bound in Great Britain by
Antony Rowe Ltd, Chippenham, Wiltshire

British Library Cataloguing in Publication Data
A catalogue record for this book is available from the British Library

Library of Congress Cataloging in Publication Data
A catalog record for this book has been requested

ISBN 10: 1–84472–159–0
ISBN 13: 978–1–84472–159–7

Contents

COMMENTARY BY OUR INVITED JUDGES

Preface

This book began life as the *Eason Weinmann Lecture* which the first of us delivered at the Tulane Law School on 2 March 2005 under the title *The Judge as Comparatist*. When, after the lecture, the request was made to turn the 'elementary' notes (which are remarkably close to the present table of contents) into a fully fledged article for the November issue of the *Tulane Law Journal* it became obvious that this was a task that went beyond the ability of one person, especially if it were to be achieved with the requisite degree of thoroughness and also within such a short period of time. The difficulty was further accentuated by the breadth of the treatment which, it is believed, for the first time covers private as well as public law and roves over no less that seven major jurisdictions covering a huge amount of material, as attested by over 700 (often long) footnotes. So Dr Jörg Fedtke was invited to participate in this venture and the article (and now the book which draws on it) became co-authored works.

Transforming the article (which appeared in the Journal a few months ago) into a book has given us the opportunity to adapt, modify, and correct the original version in many ways. But we have gone much further than just re-writing passages, smoothing edges, or filling gaps and also added new material – increasing the (already long) article to twice its original size. This new material appears mainly in Chapters 1, 4, and 5, and is partly aimed to set our thesis against the wider (and highly controversial) debate about the limits of judicial adjudication. It also touches upon the crucial but hitherto unexplored theme of judicial mentality and how this can help or hinder recourse to foreign ideas. The result of these labours should be a fuller and more polished discussion of our topic set against its proper legal and *political* setting.

The word 'political' in the previous paragraph was italicised since the book makes a special point to address its legal topics within their proper political context. This, in turn, raises and addresses the dangers that accompany comparative law as well as those attributed to judicial creativity. Though we are conscious of the fact that in what we say in this book we will not have calmed the fears of those who are, as a matter of deeply held convictions, reluctant to use foreign law for guidance and inspiration, we are at least declaring our awareness that their fears are often linked to political beliefs about the proper role of judges and their ability to subvert popular opinion. We have thus paid particular attention to the constitutional debates in the United States which have, in turn, been influenced by political conceptions prevailing in that country over a wide variety of topics (some of which touch upon the limits of judicial review while others are connected with the even wider issue of America's role and obligations in the troubled world of today). We thus go to great pains to present our material against the background of local political debates and also stress, we believe for the first time, what we call the 'time factor' in comparative borrowings. The effect of this factor is that with the passage of time, societies change. Obstacles in the movement of ideas, even of an institutional nature once considered insurmountable, thus fall by the wayside one after the other as the 'pressures' to reach similar solutions grow. Still, the multiplicity of factors which make difficult to attain the degree of international judicial dialogue we wish to see remain undeniable and we conclude these sections of our book (Chapters 4 and 5) by assigning to 'mentality' a role as a major obstacle (if less quantifiable as some of the more known, institutional constraints). After years if not centuries of bias, enmity, and misunderstandings – some deliberate – it will take time to alter the impact of this factor.

The text of this book was delivered to the publisher early in October 2005, a mere seven months after the lecture took place, so it was impossible to pay sufficient attention to a collection of stimulating essays published earlier in the same year by Professor Michael Ignatieff of Harvard University under the title *American Exceptionalism and Human Rights*[1] (for brevity's sake henceforth referred to as the *Ignantieff Essays*). The essays, written mainly by Professors from Harvard, Yale, and Princeton, have a largely liberal hew with which we generally agree and which compliments, indeed in many respects elaborates, much more distinctly and eloquently than we have done points that featured in the Eason Weinemann Lecture and now appear mainly in our first and concluding chapters. Though we have managed to include (rather late in the day) sporadic references to these essays (especially where they seem to back our views as 'outsiders') here we wish to make three general observations that stem from the *Ignatieff Essays* and help set our own book apart.

First, in our work we take the discussion about access to foreign law and ideas a step further by discussing private as well as public law and asking the question to what extent the views expressed in the public law, especially in the context of human rights, may be affecting and 'infecting'

[1] Princeton University Press (2005).

the practice of American courts even when it comes to private law issues. We deliberately use the word 'infect' because we feel that there are signs that this 'indifference' or (even) 'hostility' to foreign law, found in the domain of public law and statutory interpretation, may (as part of American 'exceptionalism') be spilling over to private law and Common law (as contrasted to statutory) kind of reasoning. To the extent that this is true, we find it even less justifiable when it happens in the area of private law given a distinctly different pattern of behaviour by American courts in the past as well as the fact that modern commercial realities seem, to us at least, to suggest the very opposite as the right way forward.

Second, though as stated we tend to share on the whole the more liberal slant of the *Ignatieff Essays*, in our view they underplay the impact that some extreme academic positions (and court decisions) advocated by the so-called radical liberal left of the academic spectrum may have had in *provoking* the counter-revolution of the conservative right.[2] In our opinion, it is this section of political opinion which, in political and economical matters, now seems to have gained the upper hand in the United States, though a number of recent liberty-enhancing decisions suggests that it is still (narrowly) loosing on the legal front. For us, and to all non-American readers less directly involved in these 'internal' fights, this quest for a better understanding of the opposing sides is essential for appreciating the motivation behind the legal arguments. For lawyers, this is a fascinating new dimension which calls for closer co-operation with political scientists.

We regard the above points as important since the aim of our book is the study of foreign law and comparative methodology (and the two are not the same). This means that we are not merely interested in describing what happens in other systems (first step); nor, even, trying to explain it by setting it into its proper setting (second step – always done better with the help of experts from other disciplines); but also going all the way and discovering *where* and *how* and *why* foreign law can be put to some more practical use by a potentially 'receiving' system. Since we do not believe in the manufacturing of synthetic supra-national rules and then imposing them on national systems where they clash with fundamental local values and beliefs, we have tried to identify, albeit very tentatively, the underlying similarities in the systems under review, noted as often as we could the dangers of over-estimating them (as well as getting the foreign system wrong), and suggested 'entry points' or 'soft spots' where a growing degree of 'commonness' seems to be emerging, allowing (if not

[2] Professor Cass Sunstein's contribution is among those which stress this point and implies that 'American exceptionalism may wax and wane according the political fortunes of conservatism and liberalism, evangelicanism and secularism.'

encouraging) more cross-border fertilisation. The words used, both here and in the book as a whole, have thus been chosen with as much care as possible since we are more than aware of how excited the debate has been and how easily it can become emotional and thus get derailed.

In this book we have tried hard to contribute, however modestly, to the need to find common ground between radically differing views about the desirability of judicial discourse across national borders. The search for a synthesis and compromise did not, however, make us feel obliged to conceal our own views over a whole range of issues. On the contrary, we voiced them firmly, especially in the concluding chapter, because we felt that it would be useful to American academics and judges to know how 'friendly' outsiders felt about American 'exceptionalism' in its present phase. But it requires no stressing that our criticism of currently pursued policies in no way diminishes our often proclaimed admiration for a great country, populated by kind, generous, and proud people many of whom have become friends during long years of professorial visits at various centres of learning.

A third and final general point must be made about one of our main messages compared with that found in the *Ignatieff Essays*.

The reasons for the American exceptionalism may be many. Professor Ignatieff summarises them in his helpful opening essay; and his learned colleagues elaborate on different aspects of these multiple explanations.[3] Ignatieff and his collaborators, approaching their main theme from many angles, explain why all these reasons, individually and collectively, may explain American exceptionalism (and, on occasion, even find a good word to say about it). For all the reasons they give, as well as the fact that mono-causal explanations in science, law, and political life are rarely convincing, studying these essays represents a helpful corrective to any theory which chooses to emphasise a single explanation for the contemporary disdain felt in some circles for nuanced politico-legal dialogue. Yet, on the whole, we feel that the current American position owes much of its *sui generis* insular and even arrogant posture to the reality and the *illusion* of global power which at this historical juncture – mainly since the end of the cold war – America holds as a monopoly. In that sense we are placing special emphasis on one factor and attempting

[3] Ignatieff gives the headings: *realism* (exceptional global power since 1945; we beg to differ; the exceptional really began after the end of the cold war when it became unique); *cultural* (he refers here, among others, to statements such as Winthrop's vision of the Massachusetts Bay Colony which we, too, mention in Chapter 5 – though we note that its admonitory/religious tone became political and quasi imperialist since the Reagan years); *institutional*; and *political* (which includes references to such notions as evangelical conservatism and the way it has influenced a variety of political decisions ranging from abortion to the war in Iraq).

to trace its impact on various parts of the law. This may need a few words of explanation.

The reason why we italicised 'illusion' of power is because we recall vividly the inconsistency in the debates prior to the invasion of Iraq and, before that, the post-9/11 reactions to the plague of our times – terrorism – and, before that, the creation of the International Criminal Court, and, before that, the Kyoto Protocol and so on. The list is growing and underlines the diverging views between the United States and some of its more traditional allies.

As far as Iraq is concerned, what is striking is how firm the belief (of the so-called experts) was in the presence of weapons of mass destruction (and their geographical 'reach') – fears since proved unjustified – but also on the (justified) conviction on how easy it would be to subdue the inhuman regime of the unspeakable opponent (whom, however, the principal invading forces had themselves once aided). The discussion and thinking of what would follow the toppling of the regime was, on the other hand, minimal; and from subsequent official acknowledgements we now know that it was sketchy at best. One can only speculate about the reasons for this (apparent) omission; but it is permissible to think that the belief in the show of force – let us not forget the code name of the operation was 'Shock and Awe' – was so great that it must have minimised in the minds of the planners the real problems that still plague them. The world was thus brainwashed with stories about American troops entering the rose-strewn road to Baghdad and welcomed by the liberated population.

It is for public international lawyers and not us to decide whether the above (along with the accompanying record of non-compliance with UN resolutions) provided sufficient justification in law for a pre-emptive invasion of another country. We suspect that on this the verdict is probably quite one-sided and not one that would favour those who thought that right was on the side of might. Be that as it may, the fact is that the image of the welcomed liberators did not, alas, materialise; and without trying to assess, which we cannot, whether the whole operation was worth the cost in lives and money and helped contain (or, on the contrary, increase) international terrorism, we note that mere – brutal – power (force sounds more accurate) was not enough to solve the problem that mobilised it in the first place. What, in other words, we had here was an 'illusion' that power could solve problems, an 'illusion' that propelled forward America and its closer allies. The reality proved different and not altogether a pleasant one. As the book is about to go to the press we are concerned to hear the same noises being repeated, in this case about Iran.

Now, if this suggests that mere power and its display and use does not, of itself, solve problems of this magnitude, it follows, we believe, that thinking and talking to one another has a vital role to play. Self-sufficiency is not possible, even against the background of immense technological superiority, quite apart from the fact that history shows us that monopoly of power does not last. Consensus building may have its advantages (as the elder President Bush discovered); and consensus building comes through talking, understanding, and give and take. It is this wider context of give and take that applies to the whole spectrum of human activities, and now we are back to law: a system that ignores it, sooner rather than later will become poorer for it. Most of the major legal systems of the world have got this message; but what about America?

The answer brings up a paradox. For, despite appearances, in the area of *contemporary* law the need for dialogue and give and take is, in some respects, stronger in the ambivalent America that denies it. For in this domain the world at large is realising that while America is a huge storehouse of legal ideas, it no longer is the only one. To put it differently, the monopoly in military and technological superiority does not extend to legal superiority. For whether we are talking of patterns of federalism, models of human rights, accident compensation, or corporate, financial, or competition models for trade and business, newcomers in the field of 'advanced legal systems' or 'emerging democracies' have more directions to turn to for guidance and help than those who appeared on the world scene some 100 years before them. If America wishes to be the guiding 'beacon on the hill' (to change somewhat the well-known image), it will have to talk, convince, and then 'export' ideas and not just decide unilaterally how other nations should be governed. Though these legal dialogues are, in most respects, at a much lower level of importance than the wider political dialogues that determine the course of world events, they can be very important for both cultural and commercial reasons.

These approaches to international legal problems can be informed by one of two mindsets.

The first starts with the pronoun 'I' or 'ours'. 'Our' law, 'our' views, 'our' system, 'our' way of running the economy are not only the best; they are also the ones others 'should' adopt. The reverse mindset is based on the more humble and intellectually attractive view that we all stand to learn from one another (which does not mean that, at the end of the day, we must or, necessarily, can adopt each others' ideas and rules). This applies to public law, where so much constitution-building has to be done in so many parts of the world (Iraq included); and it is, arguably, even more strongly needed in the areas of private and especially commercial law where enhanced communication, trade, and information mean that people have to work more with one another. In other words, the days when America could impose its constitutional model upon defeated 'enemies' have gone. If such 'receptions' (and we have difficulty using this term when force is involved) are to work, the work will have to be done in a more selective and nuanced way.

In what one could broadly call the business/commercial realm, the current dominance of the Anglo-Saxon model is due to the fact that the three crucial elements – language, the financial institutions, and the law – have all been largely Anglo-American. Yet even in the area of international corporate and financial law, potential borrowers may be faced with interesting variants from countries such as Canada or Australia (to mention but two) as well as the need to make local adaptations and, we submit, mitigate the excesses associated with the Wall Street economic ethos. Here, as well, the monopoly of American ideas may thus not be as unshakable as it appears, and that has its own consequences. For weaken the legal leg of the tripod that supports the Anglo-Saxon commercial/business/financial model and what is left of it will become unstable.

So, ultimately, this book turns around one theme: there is no monopoly of wisdom. An exchange of ideas is not just desirable but also essential provided it respects certain rules and boundaries. These can vary from the very important need to take into account widely prevalent local sensibilities (though we also suggest that, with the passage of time, the internationalisation of tastes and habits and patterns of behaviour is making such movement of ideas much easier than was the case a few decades ago), to learning how to present a foreign idea to a national court or legislator in order to make its acceptance more attractive. Legal convergence may not be an easy subject to describe, let alone accept; but denying its occurrence is not a realistic alternative even if it keeps the odd academic in business.

What we say in this book must thus be read in conjunction with an earlier book written by the first of us, entitled *Comparative Law in the Courtroom and the Classroom: The Story of the Last Thirty Five Years*, where much emphasis was laid on the need to 'package' foreign law in a manner which makes its use possible by lawyers coming from another country or culture. This is because one book compliments the other though, again, agreement is not likely to be forthcoming from all quarters on the ideas contained in both. Yet someone has to do something about comparative law in the twenty-first century since, in our view, our subject went through a stale phase (roughly in the 1970s and 1980s) and is still suffering, either as a result of the suffocating (but happily weakening) embrace of Roman law or, conversely, as a result of flirting with trendy modernism which deprives it of all practical utility. So, the time has come to try out new ways of presenting the subject in a way that can be *useful* to both practitioners (including judges and legislators) and students.

One last point about the emphasis of our book. This is, on the whole, an examination of the role that judges can and should play in the twenty-first century. The focus on the judiciary was determined by the title of the lecture which is the origin of this book. Though its title has now been altered, the focus on judges remains unchanged and this for three reasons.

The first is a paradox and one which needs to be looked at in a comparative perspective. Judges are and meant to be apolitical. Yet much of what we say shows how this is one of those areas of the law where political ideas have combined with more traditional legal reasoning to produce the attitudes and results we study in this book. Though we explore this phenomenon in a number of jurisdictions, it is most prominent in contemporary America and thus, towards the end of the book, our message acquires strong political dimensions. However much we may regret this – and as pure lawyers we do – it was inevitable if a realistic attempt was to be made to understand and explain to non-American lawyers the current situation in the United States.

Second, what we say about judges and their use of foreign law largely also applies to legislators as well. For both need to know the foreign law, both need to have the similarities stressed and the differences explained, and both need to have the foreign law suitably 'packaged' so that it can be used by them if, where and when circumstances require this. For neither judges nor legislators are interested in foreign law just for the fun of it but only if they can be convinced that it could be of some practical use to them and shown how this can be done. In our work in the classroom and, more so, in the courtroom, comparative law serves a distinctly utilitarian purpose.

Finally, we focus on judges because we believe that they can turn out to be one of the greatest stimulants for the revival of comparative law (as legislators turned out to be approximately 100 years ago when modern comparative law was, essentially, born). For if it became known that judges will listen to – even welcome – foreign ideas, practitioners would then be forced to cater for this need. This, in turn, would require them to work with academics so as to obtain from them the kind of information they need in order to make foreign law appear relevant and useful to the court. The result would thus benefit all the sides of the legal profession, giving them a new optic to their common problems and forcing them into co-operation with one another by asking them to do what each can do best. This is the reason why, at the end of the book, we also propose a sequel looking at 'the judge as hero' – a strange omission from Carlyle's famous lectures given that he was writing at the dawn of what may well have been the most heroic and, certainly, the most learned period of English judicial history. The envisaged trilogy, if it is ever completed, would thus look at what judges do (and can do) from the new angle – the globalisation of ideas – which the many existing books discussing their role and duties have not hitherto attempted to do. For state borders have become porous, and this change cannot leave the law and the judiciary untouched for long.

Special Acknowledgements

After the manuscript of the article was submitted to the *Tulane Law Review* early in May 2005 the Editors of the Journal asked the first of the authors to invite judges to comment on the text of the lecture. Ten were approached and, despite the fact that the invitation was extended just as the summer holiday was about to begin, eight generously agreed to take part in the discussion of this important topic. They are, in alphabetical order, Laurie Ackermann, formerly of the South African Constitutional Court; Professor Aharon Barak, President of the Supreme Court of Israel; Bundesverfassungsrichter Professor Dr Brun-Otto Bryde; M. Guy Canivet, Premier Président de la Cour de cassation; Sir Sydney Kentridge QC, formerly part-time Judge at the South African Supreme Court; Lord Phillips of Worth Mattravers, Master of the Rolls, Royal Court of Justice, England; Professor Dr Christos Rozakis, Judge and Vice President of the European Court of Human Rights, Strasbourg; and Judge Konrad Schiemann, of the Court of the European Communities in Luxembourg. Unfortunately (for us) the subsequent elevation of Lord Phillips to the position of Lord Chief Justice of England and Wales obliged him to withdraw from this venture. Our loss is the gain of the English legal system as a whole so we offer him best wishes in his new and difficult task. To those who have stayed the course, we also extend deep-felt thanks for the confidence they showed towards us as well as for enriching through their participation the prestige of this project.

The first of the authors also wishes to record his personal indebtedness for the friendship and assistance that all of the above have given him over the years. Grateful and sincere thanks are also due from both of us to our Texas colleague Professor Douglas Laycock, FAAAS, for many helpful comments on an early version of the text of the Tulane article (and also for permission to use verbatim some of his many and carefully crafted sentences without the use of inverted commas) as well as Ms Meredith Byars, the Chief Editor of the *Tulane Law Review* and her team for supervising with supreme efficiency and courtesy the appearance of these pieces in her Journal a mere five months after the lecture was delivered.

The lecture would not have taken place but for Professor Thanassis Yiannopoulos's invitation to deliver it at Tulane, part of his unceasing efforts to promote his Institute's international reputation the world over. We know from experience how much work such events require if they are to go well and it was the impressive efficiency of Ms Janice Sayas, the Institute's Secretary, which ensured, yet again, the smooth functioning of this prestigious series of lectures. But the greatest thanks go to Ambassador and Mrs John Griffen Weinmann who are not simply invaluable friends of the Tulane Law School but, by backing their eponymous Institute of Comparative Law, are making an enormous and very tangible contribution towards keeping alive the Law School's old and invaluable connection with the civil law systems. Only the most enlightened of Ambassadors can realise fully the significance of 'talking to one another' – especially in a world which is both shrinking and becoming more dangerous by the minute. These papers discuss how this new reality may be affecting legal thinking, sometimes for better and sometimes for the worse.

3 October 2005
Names-day of Saint Dionysius, first Athenian converted
to Christianity on the site of the old Athenian Supreme Court

Basil Markesinis
Jörg Fedtke

PS: As is the case with most of our books, the research for this one, as well, was carried out at the Tarlton Law Library of The University of Texas at Austin, brilliantly managed and constantly updated over the years by its Director Professor Roy Mersky. But the expression of general thanks to him and his most obliging staff would not do justice to Mr Jon Pratter, the Foreign and International Law Librarian. For our debt to him is enormous as he has constantly supplied us with copies of books, articles, and other materials wherever our highly peripatetic lives happened to take us. The expression of thanks is, in such circumstances, an inadequate way of repaying our debt to him, though admitting our admiration for the extent of his knowledge in our chosen field of research may explain our long-standing belief that research librarians should often be seen as quasi co-authors of the books written by those who profit from their services.

Table of Cases

American cases

Supreme Court

Other cases

Canada

United Kingdom

European Court of Justice

European Court of Human Rights

France

Cour de cassation

Germany

Federal Constitutional Court

Reichsgericht

Bundesgerichtshof

Bundesarbeitsgericht

Oberlandesgerichte and lower courts

South Africa

Other systems

Australia

Cyprus

India

Israel

Namibia

Zambia

Zimbabwe

Chapter 1: Setting the Scene

1. Preliminary observations

Acoustically, 'globalisation' is an unattractive word. For some, the images it tends to conjure up may not be much better. In economic terms many would associate it with multi-nationals. Depending on underlying political beliefs, that might in turn prompt thoughts of contemporary economic imperialism, while to others these terms might even bring to mind the kind of riots one reads about whenever the leaders of the G8 countries meet. Culturally, the word may also imply a disappearance of national differences in tastes, fashions, and even attitudes towards matters as varied as aesthetic and moral values. Again, some may regret this diminution of cultural diversity, while others may, in specific areas at least, see advantages in this convergence. Lawyers, too, are not immune from the changes this phenomenon is bringing in its wake, though being (invariably) less imaginative than artists and less bold than businessmen, one might be tempted to argue that they have reacted to, rather than helped shape it. Only a few of them have thought of using the law as an instrument for social change; and that certainly has its problems, especially if it means using judges to effect these changes.

'Lawyers' is a broad term. It covers those who work in multi-national firms, those who do (or are meant to be doing) in academic cloisters the basic thinking that lies behind the daily humdrum, those working in the public sphere (e.g. as law reformers for governments and legislators, or as decision-makers in the various areas of public administration), and those who act as judges and resolve disputes – mechanically or imaginatively.

Arguably, the first group has been the one most alert to these changes. But its members deal with them only in specific practical contexts and without any attempt (or even the ability) to see them – let alone place them – in a wider and co-ordinated scheme of things. Despite some fascinating developments in legal practice, which would merit closer analysis,[1] harmonisation and unification of the law is thus taking

[1] Think, e.g., of internet companies working towards standardised contractual solutions for their truly global commercial activities.

place in a spasmodic manner, itself indirectly contributing to a different kind of diversity and, even, new problems.[2] Academics are mostly timid by nature; and a fair number of them these days have, as far as the real world is concerned, placed themselves in the margins by allowing their writings to reflect various issues of political correctness rather than try and serve the real world. This has, in turn, often led them to advocate interest in systems and topics which the real users of the law (the first and third groups) have little time for[3] or on which research can, for technical reasons, be impossible. In purely academic terms, such projects may be defensible. Writing about these subjects may also be fashionable. With few exceptions, however, it tends to diminish the influence of those who opt for them in the real world of practice, business, law reform and the like. This book deals with the fourth group, namely, judges.[4]

Most in this category, especially those operating in the common law world, are anything but timid in character, though some may prefer an isolated and, certainly, a low profile existence, which is quite a different matter. But in their professional pronouncements, they are (and should be) cautious, mainly because of reasons of impartiality and democratic legitimacy. For though most systems would nowadays accept, with varying degrees of emphasis, that judges *do* make new law, most lawyers (and ordinary people) would agree that this should be more in the nature of bringing the law up-to-date with societal beliefs rather than *shaping* these beliefs before they have been accepted by society itself.[5] In this book, we are dealing with the first aspect of this issue not the second; but even in this form this is a topic that is particularly sensitive in the United States, though this does not mean that it is ignored elsewhere.

---

[2] See, for instance, Walter van Gerven, 'Community and National Legislators, Regulators, Judges, Academics and Practitioners: Living Together Apart?' in: B. S. Markesinis (ed), *Law Making, Law Finding and Law Shaping: The Diverse Influences* (1997), pp 13–35.

[3] See, e.g., N. Demleiter, 'Challenge, Opportunity and Risk: An Era of Change in Comparative Law', (1998) 46 *Am. J. Comp. L.* 647, 653; Hugo Mattei, 'An Opportunity not to be Missed: The Future of Comparative Law in the United States', (1998) 46 *Am. J. Comp. L.* 709, 711, note 7.

[4] We are conscious of the fact that in this paper we do not look at legislators and law reformers, an omission partly prompted by lack of space but also justified by the fact that some of the things that we say about judges would also be relevant and be taken into account by legislators. This admission also implies that we acknowledge and, indeed, welcome the interaction that takes place between all these types of 'lawyers' but prefer to focus on the category which could these days be seen both in the common law and civil law systems (as well as transnational courts) to be playing a crucial role in the globalisation of ideas of justice.

[5] A famous English judge, the late Lord Devlin, expressed this well extra-judicially when he distinguished between 'activist' lawmaking (designed to keep the law in pace with change in the consensus) and 'dynamic' lawmaking (designed to generate change in the consensus); see 'Judges and Lawmakers', (1976) 39 *MLR* 1 ff.

The literature on judges and their role is huge, and we do not intend to re-examine it here. Our concern is to look at the 'judge as a comparatist' – the title of the lecture on which this book is based – a role not hitherto openly ascribed to him. Yet judges across the globe are gently entering into this marginalised area of the law curriculum; and the present authors are among those who welcome this timid innovation. Indeed, they wish to encourage it for the additional reason that they believe that, if the trend gains strength, it will encourage academics to broaden their horizons and reflect on the internationalisation of law in their books on national law even more openly than they have hitherto done.[6] We believe that practitioners might also benefit from such a move since it is bound to enhance the range of arguments available to them and even their critical ability to understand their own law. This predilection of both authors must not, however, obscure the real difficulties that retard (if not obstruct) their aim. The purpose of this book has had to be met by the production of a fairly long text and many footnotes (perhaps too many for the liking of English lawyers but enough to please the Germans and Americans).[7] Yet its wish to look at the practices of more than one system and to provide one more building block in the revival of the study of foreign law and comparative methodology could not begin to be achieved without giving the reader access to the raw material on which the thesis stands or falls. But the authors of the book should be the first to state that they are moving in dangerous territory and therefore, at best, can only hope to move the debate a slight step forward.

What accounts for the difficulties we are alluding to is the fact that, at its core, the outcome of the debate we are engaging in is largely one of political beliefs; and the one thing that globalisation has not yet managed to achieve is harmonisation on this score. Indeed, the Americans, who have been largely behind this globalisation movement, have in law proved to be anxious to exclude themselves from treaties they have helped negotiate and, even, shunned cross-boarder judicial dialogues. The current political climate in the United States may have something to do with this phenomenon which we explore from many different angles in various parts of this book. Yet even in this, the most sensitive part of any legal analysis, one cannot ignore how political and economic decisions

---

[6] A good example of this can be seen in the 27th edn (1998) of the classic English textbook *Anson's Law of Contract* undertaken by Professor (now Mr Justice) Jack Beatson. Though the current 28th edn (2002) has changed somewhat its approach, the not-that-distant previous edition was remarkable in its presentation of the English law of contract (almost) in isolation from the considerable and increasing influences of European directives, international conventions, and multi-national projects bringing about or suggesting important transformations of traditional, national-based law.

[7] The topic has given rise to at least one study – A. Grafton, *The Footnote* (1997) – which may amuse as well instruct.

(e.g. accepting Turkey into the European Union if, among other things, it modernises its criminal code; enhancing trade with China if it improves its human rights record; allowing former eastern block countries to become members of organisations such as the European Union or NATO if they make changes to their form of governance) are nowadays overtly linked to legal changes being made at national level. These changes may affect such varied areas as human rights, family law, national criminal codes, harmonisation of currency or tax laws, the unification of rules applying to commercial transactions with an international element, and the like. The re-unification treaty of the two Germanys, incorporated in a large and complex set of documents, even contained provisions about the survival of the more liberal abortion laws found in East Germany, but for a limited period of time only. More about all this further down.

2. How judges speak

In an elegant piece of scholarship, written 30 years ago and dedicated to the most learned (yet, possibly, not the most influential) of British comparatists, the predecessor of the first of the present authors in the Chair of Comparative Law at the University of Oxford compared 'Courts and Codes in England, France and Soviet Russia'.[8] In his view, the distinctive features of the common law judicial style are given away by the 'four dialogues' that take place in the process of arriving at a decision. The first he called the dialogue between Bench and Bar; the second was the dialogue among the Bench (one should add: conducted in calmer tone in England than in the United States); the third was the dialogue with the past (by which the learned author meant the consideration and refinement of precedent); and, finally, the dialogue with the future (where, for instance, we find what Professor Sir Neil MacCormick has described the 'consequentialist' type of arguments such as the notion of 'floodgates', which figures in common law but not in civil law decisions).[9] What is immediately noticeable by its absence is the dialogue with (living) academics, perhaps because this was forbidden in England until the Practice Statement of the House of Lords of 1966.

But this dialogue *is* visible in American decisions;[10] and it has helped both Bench and academics. For historical reasons[11] this dialogue is even

---

[8] Bernhard Rudden, 'Courts and Codes in England, France and Soviet Russia' (1974) 48 *Tulane L. Rev.* 1010 ff.

[9] *Legal Reasoning and Legal Theory* (1978), pp 129 ff.

[10] See, e.g., *Bonbrest v Kötz*, 65 F Supp. 138 DDC 1946, 140.

[11] Succinctly explained by the late Jack Dawson in his Cooley Lectures entitled *The Oracles of the Law* (reprinted 1978).

more prominent in German judgments.[12] This is the 'dialogue' which we wish to expand to include foreign ideas and notions (developed both by academics and judges). If such an aim was unthinkable when the Emeritus Professor of Comparative Law at the University of Oxford penned his thoughts it no longer was when his successor took over. Though controversial and not without its difficulties, judges the world over are already attempting to engage in it.

How this is done in various legal systems (openly or clandestinely, boldly or hesitantly) will be discussed in the next chapter. In Chapter 3 we will look at those situations where the dialogue with foreign law is most appropriate, while in Chapters 4 and 5 we will examine and try to address some of the most common fears expressed against the use of foreign law. In the sixth and final chapter we shall attempt to wrap things up by focusing especially on some American issues and make an attempt to prophecy the future, providing some suggestions of our own to what we predict will become an ever more pressing and frequently addressed issue, even if its resolution does not follow the path we will recommend.

Before turning to these issues, however, we wish to stress our preference for the terms 'dialogue' and 'intellectual interaction' rather than 'borrowing', which we see as a narrow and more direct application of foreign law. Equally, we caution against the attempt to try and 'transplant' or use foreign notions and concepts. We do this for two reasons. First, because concepts and notions are often radically different and can thus discourage the natural idea of an intellectual dialogue. Indeed, concepts and notions attract definitional and linguistic difficulties, especially as one tries to find the foreign equivalent for one's own notion or concept. Second, because the idea of transplantation, though successful in some systems and at some times, itself carries with it the danger of subsequent 'rejection' and is perhaps one of the most difficult operations lawyers can attempt to perform. To put all this differently, in accord with most comparatists, we are not even envisaging the possibility that foreign law could be used as *binding precedent* by judges but rather as a source of *inspiration*, especially when national law is dated, unclear, or contradictory. Quite obviously, then, in this book we are not talking about foreign law as applicable law where the rules of conflict of laws so require. Nor, indeed, are we talking of *public*[13]

[12] For interesting statistics see H. Kötz, *Essays in Honor of John Henry Merryman* (1990), pp 183 ff.

[13] We italicise the word since, unlike other colleagues who use the words 'international law' somewhat loosely to cover public international law *as well as* foreign law, we are here excluding from our purview public international law. *Roper v Simmons*, reviewed by Professor Sarah Cleveland in the *Washington Post* of 20 March 2005 and examined towards the end of this book, thus had nothing to do with 'international law' but with the utility (and permissibility) of foreign law helping re-shape internal norms – in that instance the Eighth Amendment.

international law rules which may (in different ways[14]) have become part of national law. Nor, finally, are we thinking of law that a court of one nation state has to apply because it is bound by the decisions of some supra-national court (which may, itself, have used foreign law in order to shape its own decisions) though, occasionally, we will refer to the two European transnational courts and the use they make of comparative law.

If, statistically speaking, the number of cases where the need for what we are advocating as desirable is likely to be quite small, we nonetheless feel this is equally likely to occur with greater frequency. Yet, though the number of instances where this need arises is small, their significance is considerable. Moreover, in times of rapid social change life is constantly producing new problems (or placing old solutions under investigation) and it is here, once again, where comparison is most likely to offer maximum benefit. We submit that only persons with totally closed minds can seriously question this assertion. This means that much of what we say about the utility of studying foreign law may be appropriate not only for new democratic states and their constitutional courts (which are often starving for inspiration or legitimisation) but also for those systems which have respectable histories to look back upon.

This last point is stressed since it has been almost consistently underestimated or ignored in comparative studies (or studies about the movement of foreign ideas from one state to another). We call it the 'time factor'. This opaque phrase refers to the undoubted fact that values and ideas change over time. Unlike the Roman jurists, who stated their rules in a seemingly atemporal manner, citing each other and their predecessors as if nothing had happened between the second century BC (when these ideas began to acquire special interest) and the second century AD (when they reached their peak), we live in times where everything – from politics, regimes, *mores*, and tastes – changes rapidly. This rapid change means that what was once firmly rooted in one system, and not acceptable to another, may also be subject to change. This is a crucial underlying theme of this essay. It is picked up here and there whenever appropriate and, we feel, in the long run favours those who, like us, believe that a purely national interpretation of the law will not be sustainable for long.

---

[14] Note, for instance, ss 39(1) (b) and (c) of the South African Constitution of 1996 (discussed in more detail below), according to which the courts of the land '*may* consider foreign law' but '*must* consider international law' when interpreting the national Bill of Rights.

3. Judicial creativity

a) Preliminary observations

It has, for a long time now, been widely believed and strongly argued that the judge cannot substitute his personal moral judgments for the rules of the constitution (or whatever lesser text he is called upon to interpret). In recent times this argument has resurfaced, especially in the United States, with considerable vigour in the context of judicial review as conservative writers have reacted, in part to some extreme statements made by academics (and more rarely judges)[15] belonging to the other end of the political spectrum. More importantly, this debate has been fed by a series of liberty-enhancing judgments of the US Supreme Court, mainly in the 1960s but also in the 1970s, which the more traditional section of the community has found un-appealing if not down right wrong and provocative. For them, the main answer to this (new) trend was to restrict the scope of judicial interpretation; and in the United States this came with a substantial increase in the politicisation of the appointment of judges. If this shift at times gives the impression that the debate is becoming more technical in nature there is no escaping the fact that it is firmly based on politics.

This debate has inexorably been linked to the question where the judges can seek to find justifications for judgments which purport to 'revise' the constitutional text; but this is where it also touches upon our subject. Obviously, the starting point is the text itself; but if it is clearly dated, unclear, or (more typically) a widely phrased provision susceptible to different interpretations,[16] in which quarters can guidance be sought for its adaptation or extension? And how far can this process of 're-formulating' a constitution go without it ceasing to be 'interpretation' and becoming constitutional redrafting through the back door? It is in this context that the permissibility of using foreign law has surfaced as an issue of contention, and our looking at the wider picture in this chapter is only intended to help place the comparative discussion of this book into its proper context.

---

[15] E.g., Justice William J. Brennan, Jr., speech delivered at a symposium organised by the Georgetown University on 12 October 1985 and reprinted as 'The Great Debate: Interpreting Our Written Constitution', 11 *The Federalist Society* 1986.

[16] According to Sir John Elliott, *Richelieu and Olivares* (1984) at p 30, Cardinal Richelieu was 'acutely sensitive to the possibilities of language as an instrument of power'. The founder of the modern French State (and the *Académie Française*) is reputed to have said once 'get any man to write down any ten words and I can find a way to hang him'. Two hundred years later, another great statesman, Otto von Bismarck, was also notoriously good with exploiting the inherent ambiguity of words both for the purposes of declaring war or destroying his political enemies. Though judges do not pursue such dark aims, they are no less sensitive to the possibilities that language offers them so it is entirely utopian to deny them creative powers. The real question thus is where one draws the limits.

In one sense at least this battle was to be expected. For it is difficult to separate this entire debate about the limits of adjudication from the basic notion of democratic legitimacy and even the doctrine of separation of powers. On the other hand it has also been long recognised – in the United States this has been referred to as the 'Madisonian dilemma' – that there are some things that a majority cannot do to a minority, and a balance thus has to be struck between these competing principles. This dilemma is also obvious in other systems; and since we cannot mention them all, suffice it to refer to one – the German – where it takes the form of a potential conflict between the *Rechtsstaatsprinzip* (which, unlike the English rule of law, is regarded as the theoretical foundation of, *inter alia*, substantive human rights and thus minority protection) and the constitutionally equally important principle of democracy. So it is in this context, whatever the precise notions or words used, that much of the modern debate about judicial interpretive freedom has arisen; and if this includes the right to go beyond the original understanding of the drafters of a constitution, what principle should guide it *lest it otherwise gets completely out of control*? For the idea that the interpreter '(S)imply beats the text into a shape which will serve his own purpose'[17] may be many things (including literature) but, to most European jurists at least, it is not law. Indeed, it could be seen as the surrender of law to anarchy.

In the United States this debate has given rise to a huge academic literature which, to our knowledge, remains unequalled (in volume at least) when compared to the other systems we study in this book. Germany is, in fact, the only country that comes close; and despite the fact that the style and tone of writing is very different to that encountered in the United States, a plausible case can be made that in Germany one can find the precursors of most current American philosophical schools (though by this we are not suggesting that the latter have directly copied or adapted the former).[18] Moreover, one should add that in the United States those on the liberal 'revisionist' side have outnumbered the traditionalists in their own country. Their work (unlike that of the traditionalists) also comes in various shades, ranging from modest, indeed intellectually interesting proposals,[19] to outright admissions that constitutional interpretation is

---

[17] Sanford Levinson, 'Law as Literature', (1982) 60 *Texas L. Rev.* 373 at 385.

[18] For an excellent summary of this proposition see Winfried Brugger, 'Legal Interpretation, Schools of Jurisprudence, and Anthropology: Some Remarks from a German Point of View', (1994) 42 *Am. J. Comp. L.* 395 at 404–5 and note 22.

[19] For instance, Alexander Bickel, *The Least Dangerous Branch. The Supreme Court at the Bar of Politics* (1962); John Ely, *Democracy and Distrust. A Theory of Judicial Review* (1980).

little more than an overt political judgment.[20] Happily, for the purposes of this book we do not have to dwell on this rich literature but can restrict ourselves to three comments suitable to a work with overt comparative but not constitutional law aims.

First, to Europeans and (perhaps) others who are non-Americans, the debates in the United States are remarkable for their novel ideas as well as the intemperate language that can sometimes creep into these pieces. This, of course, has the consequence that as one 'thesis' (extremely phrased) provokes equal extremism in its 'antithesis', the study of the law easily slides into the formulation of subjective preferences – themselves at times quite eccentric (to put it mildly), to European minds at least.[21]

---

[20] For instance, Professor Mark Tushnet, 'The Dilemmas of Liberal Constitutionalism', (1981) 42 *Ohio St. L. J.* 411 at 424. His later piece 'The Possibilities of Comparative Law', (1999) 108 *Yale L. J.* 1225 ff comes closer to what we would regard as a legal analysis though (as we explain in Chapter 4) this, too, contains proposals which may jar the European legal mind. Professor Tribe's prolific work has been deemed to fall into this category of 'law as politics', at any rate by his intellectual opponents. Thus, see Richard Posner, 'The Constitution as Mirror: Tribe's Constitutional Choices', (1986) 84 *Mich. L. Rev.* 551 at 567 where he states that Tribe's 'method is to use the skills of a lawyer to make political choices for society in the name of a fictive constitution, as if the Supreme Court really were a superlegislature and government by lawyers has, at last, arrived'. In this context one notes with interest how American jurists seem to have discovered belatedly Carl Schmitt's 1932 treatise *Der Begriff des Politischen* (probably since it was translated into English by George Scwhab in 1976 under the title *The Concept of the Political*). Ironically, his advocacy and radical application of the politicisation of law may now be dazzling American jurists, even of the 'left', who probably remain unaware of the extent of Schmitt's (at times outrageous) support for the Nazi regime. Three other books of Schmitt have also, belatedly, been translated into English. They are: *Political Theology* (1985), *The Crisis of Parliamentary Democracy* (1986), and *Political Romanticism* (1986).

[21] We are thinking here of some of Professor Duncan Kennedy's pronouncements found in Louis B Schwartz, 'With Gun and Camera', (1984) 36 *Stan. L. Rev.* 413 ff, from which comes this eccentric set of thoughts:

> (H)e [Kennedy] announced [at a public lecture] his thesis that 'illegitimate hierarchies' should be abolished and proposed that the Harvard Law School initiate the action by establishing a single salary for everyone from janitor to dean and rotating each member of the community through each job. He gaily waved aside suggestions that, however competent the janitor might be in jurisprudence, the dean might be totally at a loss with a blocked toilet. Almost as intriguing were his proposals that the tenure system be abolished, that admission to the Law School be by lot, and that classroom discussion be restructured to allow more time for poor or unprepared students to be heard. Upon my inquiry, he acknowledged good-naturedly that he did not select his research assistants by lot and that there would be a certain amount of difficulty in persuading law firms, judges, faculty appointment committees, government agencies, and community legal services to hire by lot.

The European (mainly German) literature, on the other hand, even when it echoes strong political, moral, or societal concerns, tends to be sombrely phrased, continuously attempting to combine the legal with the political under the guise of canons of interpretation or 'theories'. To the scientific mind this has its attractions; but then it was the great German who also warned that all theories are 'grey'.[22]

The second observation is that, in this atmosphere, it becomes extremely difficult to discuss the issue of international judicial dialogue between the United States and the rest of the world unless, of course, one takes the view that some at least (maybe much?) of what appears in its legal literature has no or little relevance in the real world of decision-making. That this is so despite the aforementioned fact that American theories find their parallels in Germany is deeply troubling. In the end, it forced us to adopt a bifurcated approach in the formulation of our (tentative) conclusions, treating the United States on the one hand[23] and the world's other systems on the other. In the meantime, however, we content ourselves with one tentative observation. Constitutional law, always closely linked to politics, now seems to be so dominated by that branch of human knowledge that – in the United States at least – it is progressively stripped of much of its legal, doctrinal, content. For those legal scholars who remain attached to the doctrinal examination of the law (though not isolated from the realities of life), comparison with systems becomes more than merely desirable. An attempt by American jurists to familiarise themselves with the great European legal literatures (French, German, Italian, etc.) would greatly enrich the level of discourse in the United States.[24]

Third and finally, we note that if the language and argumentation in the United States has often bordered on what we, on the other side of the Atlantic, would regard as eccentric, the underlying issues are often very similar. Thus, the so-called Madisonian dilemma (as already shown above in the German context) is not unknown to us who work on the eastern side of the Atlantic; nor are we impervious to the need to find pragmatic

---

22 Goethe, *Faust II*, 2038–9 ('Grau, teurer Freund, is alle Theorie, Und grün des Lebens goldner Baum:' Grey, my dear friend, is all that theory is, and green the golden tree of Life.).

23 This fits perfectly with the central theme found in a collection of Essays recently edited by Professor Michael Ignatieff under the title *American Exceptionalism and Human Rights* (2005) to which we shall be referring in several parts of this book even though it appeared at a time when the writing of this text was almost completed.

24 One of the American scholars who, in our view, constantly strikes the right balance in tone as well as praise/critique of the American system is Professor Mary Ann Glendon; see, for instance, her piece on 'Rights in the Twentieth-Century Constitutions', (1992) 59 *U. Chi. L. Rev.* 519 ff.

principles to determine the limits of judicial creativity and not merely rely on legal dogma. Our difficulty as authors of this book has thus been to find ways to reinvigorate judicial dialogue between both sides of the Atlantic, despite these differences in culture and form of stylistic expression which makes dialogue difficult. For notwithstanding some recent liberal decisions of the US Supreme Court and a recent flurry of public talks in various European fora by some of its liberal members, we feel that the current overall political climate in the United States is making this task more not less difficult to achieve. If the existing (and future) vacancies in the US Supreme Court are filled with 'conservative' jurists, then this dialogue will become yet more difficult and, perhaps, even dry out. Thoughts such as these have forced us in our conclusions to go beyond pure law and try and link legal attitudes to political views of the currently dominant ruling class, adopting a pessimistic view which, it must be stressed, the liberal judges of the American Supreme Court certainly do not share.

A few more related thoughts can be penned down at this point.

In addressing the above issues, the doctrine of sovereignty of the legislative body may also have to be linked to yet one further question – 'has the constitution, itself, given in some cases judges the right to decide issues which, through accident or design, it did not address itself?' We shall return to this particular issue below though we also raise it here since it is essential once one leaves the American scene and tries to look at our main topic from the perspective of other constitutions. The possibility that the 'grundnorm' may encourage transnational study does not seem to have occupied American constitutionalists at all since they have been so absorbed by their indigenous model which, though not introvert when adopted, has become so since then. Thus, when two Texas scholars observed that '(T)raditionally, American constitutional scholarship has been deep, but not at all wide',[25] we think they were probably pondering over missed opportunities for enriching indigenous law (to which we, too, have alluded above) and not the equally serious danger of a future decrease in the influence of American legal ideas abroad (though that, as well, will come if the current insular attitudes win the day).

A further point worth noting is that the general question with which we are here concerned is, at its most sensitive, found in human right cases. Indeed, in recent times this has been the most 'fashionable' part of constitutional law. Nonetheless, the proper way to interpret statutes has occupied American jurists trying to fix the frontiers of other areas of

---

[25] William E. Forbath and Lawrence Sager, 'Comparative Avenues in Constitutional Law: An Introduction', (2004) 82 *Texas L. Rev.* 1653 at 1669.

constitutional law since the debate about the limits of statutory interpretation has developed tentacles which reach out to embrace other topics, besides human rights. The constitutional debate is, therefore, seen as part of a wider problem which, especially in the United States, has been linked to the absence of developed rules of statutory (as distinct to common law) interpretation.[26] Nor has the dispute stopped there. For, in turn, it has led scholars to place part of the blame for this 'gap' upon the American university system; and it was only a matter of time before American comparatists would step into the fray and draw comparisons with the position in Europe – and here especially Germany where, in matters of statutory interpretation, one finds a well-developed theory which ensures workable rules as well as the internal consistency of the law.[27]

For all their strengths, American law schools have thus not yet made a significant contribution to this problem of statutory interpretation. Interestingly enough some prominent American judges as well as academics admit as much.[28] And this deficiency may also owe much to another feature of the American educational system: the Socratic way of teaching. This is another huge and controversial subject which cannot be discussed here. Yet one of its consequences is relevant to our theme so it has to be mentioned, albeit briefly.

The Socratic method of teaching is a very time-consuming form of instruction. The price one has to pay for it is most often noticed by foreign visitors to US law schools who discover, often to their dismay, how huge chunks of constitutional law (or, come to that, any other core subject) are omitted from most courses. The usual (defensive) answer – that law schools are keen to teach young lawyers how to think and less concerned to cover the entire syllabus – has some force to it but then only to a point. For our purposes, however, another consequence of teaching law in this way can be seen to exact an even higher price.

---

26 See Henry M. Hart, Jr. and Albert M. Sacks in William N. Eskridge, Jr. and Philip P. Frickey (eds), *The Legal Process* (1994), p 1169: 'The hard truth of the matter is that American courts have no intelligible, generally accepted, and consistently applied theory of statutory interpretation.' Roscoe Pound, 'The Formative Era of American Law' in *The Life of the Law* (1964), p 59: 'The Common law (...) in comparison with the civil law, [has always been] awkward and none too effective in deciding on the basis of legislative texts.' Cass R. Sunstein, Book Review, *New Republic*, 11 March 1991, p 35: 'Our understanding of constitutional interpretation remains in a primitive state'.

27 Mary Ann Glendon, 'Comment', in Antonin Scalia, *A Matter of Interpretation. Federal Courts and the Law* (1997), pp 95 ff.

28 Mary Ann Glendon, op. cit. note 27, pp 96–7, citing a 1992 Harvard Law School curriculum committee report admitting that 'We [at Harvard] teach the first year required program almost without regard to the coming of the regulatory state, and without recognition that statutes and regulations have become the predominant legal sources of our time.'

Thus, the effect that 'fragmented' knowledge has on methodology, including interpretation, has yet to be assessed fully. American law students thus often face considerable difficulty in appreciating that the law is a 'seamless web' and, in later years, as practitioners or judges they fail (or give the impression of failing) to strive for even a modicum of internal consistency. Such omissions, coupled with the fact that which parts of a subject are actually chosen for discussion in class depends on changing fashions, mean that American lawyers are rarely taught the entire area of constitutional law and thus never really are impressed with the need to interpret provisions in a way which sees the relevant constitution as an integral text. In Germany, by contrast, students in their first semester will not only hear that the Basic Law is regarded as a holistic unit (*Einheit der Verfassung*) but that statutory interpretation in any particular area of the law will have to take into account and strive for the inner consistency of the whole legal order (*Einheit der Rechtsordnung*). Both principles are firmly established and dicta to that effect abound in German court decisions in every part of the legal system.

Additionally, and we raise this since Justice Scalia has made it a key point of his essay *A Matter of Interpretation. Federal Courts and the Law*,[29] American students receive little or no instruction on statutory interpretation. But without this, and relying (mainly) on common law interpretative techniques, how can one even begin the search for an underlying principle (or principles) which would provide workable parameters for the task of judicial adjudication? The huge variation in responses is reflected in the academic literature and, we submit, is of only limited use to judges looking for an alternative to 'originalism'. Naturally, Justice Scalia, has been quick to pick this point up in his extra-judicial writings.

b) Judicial adjudication in systems with developed techniques of statutory interpretation

The significance of the above comments becomes obvious when the situation in the United States is compared with systems which have developed sophisticated norms of statutory interpretation. Since Germany is one of the systems discussed in this book and, in this matter at least, can lay claim to have the oldest rationally developed rules on the subject, we focus on this system – though we also readily admit that much of what is said here has been followed by other Continental European

[29] Published by the Princeton Press in 1997.

systems.[30] The ambit of the comparison may thus be wider than it may appear from the fact that we are only talking about German law.

The basic rules of German statutory interpretation are quickly summarised. They can be traced back to Friedrich Carl von Savigny's work in 1840[31] where the great jurist formulated three cannons of interpretation: (a) textual or grammatical (which relies on the analysis of words and phrases contained in a specific provision); (b) systematic, structural, or contextual (which seeks to interpret single norms with respect to their position within the overall framework of a statute and their relationship to other provisions); and (c) historical (which focuses on the historical background of a piece of legislation). To these three, a fourth was added later known as the teleological or purposive interpretation (which seeks to discover the underlying aim of a provision, taking into account the intentions of the lawgiver). These techniques were devised for the interpretation of statutory *private law* (since this dominated legal studies at that time) but are generally held to apply to public law, as well.[32] More recently, constitutional lawyers such as Professor Peter Häberle have also advocated comparative law as a fifth method of interpretation;[33] but as we shall note in Chapter 2, very limited practical use has thus far been made of this technique despite the fact that it is frequently mentioned in academic literature.

Yet a constitution is a special document, paramount in the hierarchy of laws, strongly political in nature,[34] and with a large amount of open-ended clauses.[35] So, in addition, as Konrad Hesse, a former and highly respected Justice of the German Constitutional Court (*Bundesverfassungsgericht*,

---

30 The literature is huge. For Germany we mention, indicatively, Konrad Hesse, *Grundzüge des Verfassungsrechts der Bundesrepublik Deutschland* 2 II 1 (20th edn 1999); Winfried Brugger, *Rundfunkfreiheit und Verfassungsinterpretation* (1991), pp 4–10. For accounts in English see Magiera, 'The Interpretation of the Basic Law', in: Christian Starck (ed), *Main Principles of the German Basic Law* (1983), pp 89, 91–3.

31 *Das System des heutigen Romischen Rechts*, Vol. I, s 33 (1840), especially at pp 213–14.

32 Ingo von Münch, *Staatsrecht I* (6th edn, 2000), pp 11 ff; Ekkehart Stein, *Staatsrecht* (16th edn, 1998), pp 35 ff. See also the recent book by Aharon Barak, *Purposive interpretation in law* (2005).

33 Peter Häberle, *Rechtsvergleichung im Kraftfeld des Verfassungsstaates* (1992), pp 27 ff.

34 Constitutional law is thus even coined 'political law' by some; see, e.g., Ulrich Karpen, 'Auslegung und Anwendung des Grundgesetzes', *Hamburger Rechtsstudien* Heft 74 (1987), pp 43/44.

35 A point of considerable importance for the relationship between judges exercising constitutional review and the 'democratic' legislator. On this see Professor Jutta Limbach's comments in *Das Bundesverfassungsgericht als politischer Machtfaktor*, Humboldt Forum Recht 1996, Beitrag 12. What makes her views so interesting is the fact that she was, until recently, (the first woman) President of the German Constitutional Court.

FCC) put it, the following additional interpretative ideas must be employed:[36]

> (1) Each interpretation must support the unity of the constitution. (2) In cases of tension or conflict, the principle of practical concordance must be used to harmonize conflicting provisions. (3) All governmental organs must respect the functional differentiation of the constitution, that is, their respective tasks and powers in the separation of powers scheme. (4) Each interpretation must try to create an integrative effect with regard to both the various parties of a constitutional dispute as well as to social and political cohesion. (5) Each interpretation shall attempt to optimize all the aforementioned elements.

These additional principles of constitutional interpretation in Germany could be amplified somewhat in the following way for while they retain their legal clothing and language, they also make room for other human sciences (such as politics and economics) to enter into the process of adjudication.

First, the Basic Law is perceived as a unit, and single provisions are interpreted so as to avoid conflicts with other parts of the text.[37] This, in itself, makes it less easy for a judge to embark on a personal ideological fancy. Established interpretative techniques can thus act – to a certain degree – as a brake on judicial adventurism.

---

[36] Summarised by Brugger (op. cit. note 18) at 398–9.

[37] The Constitutional Court, as early as 1951, described this approach in the *Südweststaat*-decision (BVerfGE 1, 14 at p 32) in the following way:

> A single constitutional provision cannot be regarded in isolation and interpreted by itself. Every provision is related to the meaning of the other provisions of the Basic Law, which constitutes a single intrinsic unit. Every provision is subject to certain basic constitutional principles and fundamental decisions which follow from the overall content of the text. (...) As a consequence, every constitutional norm must be interpreted in a way which is consistent with these fundamental principles and basic decisions of the constitutional legislator.

For another example see the extract of the *Gleichbereichtigungs*-decision (1953) of the *Bundesverfassungsgericht* in Appendix (...). Cf. the above with the views expressed by Professor Mark Tushnet in 'The Possibilities of Comparative Constitutional Law', op. cit. note 20 at pp 1287 ff, where he asserts that the speeches of some of the Founding Fathers of the American Constitution would support a similar approach in the United States (e.g. Hamilton) while others (e.g. Madison) seemed to emphasise more the unsystematic character of the compromises. We are not sure that this necessarily means that by seeing a constitution as a product of compromise rather than principle one is prevented from trying to interpret it in a unifying and integrated manner. But we raise the possibility here not to discuss it but in order to draw a contrast with the position in Germany.

Second, this 'logical-teleological unity'[38] of the Basic Law is closely connected to the concept of a so-called objective order of values (*objektive Wertordnung*) according to which the framers of the 1949 Constitution made a number of basic value choices. The most important elements of this constitutional 'vision' are contained in the notion of the so-called 'free democratic basic order' (a phrase found in several provisions of the Basic Law[39]) and include human dignity, fundamental rights, popular sovereignty, separation of powers, the legality of public administration, a multiparty system, and the legitimacy of political opposition.

This content of the 'free democratic basic order' was not expressly defined in the German Constitution but has rather emerged over time through a series of key decisions of the *Bundesverfassungsgericht*. Both the content of this constitutional *leitmotiv* and the way in which it was (and continues to be) developed is thereby crucial in our current context. For the interpretative technique – regarding the Basic Law as a closely woven unit of interrelated provisions – cannot, by itself, be expected to limit successfully the danger of individual judges or courts from introducing their subjective considerations in judgments and, possibly, thwarting the will of the democratic legislator. However, *in combination* with the 'objective' order of values (gleaned from specific provisions of the German Constitution such as Arts 1 and 20 BL and, more importantly, developed over a substantial period of time by a number of courts and through their respective judicial and extra-judicial dialogues with politicians and academics), the method may in fact have proved quite successful. For it meant that changes to the constitutional edifice have only occurred in the most gradual of ways, and only within the framework of the established techniques and values – some of which are, in fact, 'untouchable' even by the unanimous decision of the constitutional legislator.[40]

Moreover, the influence of single judges of the *Bundesverfassungsgericht* is further reduced by their limited time on the bench. Many judges do not even serve the statutory maximum of twelve years before reaching the age limit of 68,[41] which is quite a contrast to the American situation where currently the three most senior justices of the Supreme Court – Chief Justice William Rehnquist, John Paul Stevens, and Sandra Day O'Connor – have each served 33, 30, and 24 years respectively (the latter having, at

---

[38] Johan Kruger, 'Towards a new interpretative theory', in: Johan Kruger/Brian Currin, *Interpreting a Bill of Rights* (1994), p 127.

[39] See Arts 10(2), 11(2), 18, 21(2) and 91(1) BL for references to the *freiheitliche demokratische Grundordnung*.

[40] See Art 79(3) BL.

[41] See § 4 *Bundesverfassungsgerichtsgesetz*.

the time of completion of this manuscript, submitted her resignation from the court).[42]

The (relatively) higher 'turnover' of judges in Germany increases the number of views which contribute to the gradual development and growth of German constitutional law and, consequently, weakens the impact of single voices in the Federal Constitutional Court. The fact that dissenting opinions, though possible, remain less usual in the practice of the Court may also contribute to this altogether different scenario, as does the fact that candidates require overwhelming political support in one of the two legislative chambers, which alternately elect them with a two-third-majority.

Third, every provision of the Basic Law must be given an interpretation which maximises its effect. This is especially true for the fundamental rights contained in Arts 1 to 19 of the Basic Law. If in doubt, therefore, German courts must 'choose the interpretation which is capable of offering the strongest protective effect.'[43] This has, in a number of cases, led the Constitutional Court to opt for a generous interpretation of particular human rights provisions.[44] Despite the occasional highly controversial judgment[45] the Court has, as we shall

---

[42] There is more to these figures than the text, above, suggests. For the German constitutional judges not only serve for shorter periods of time but also enter and leave the court at a younger age than their American counterparts. Of the current members of the Court, six were born before the end of the Second World War. The oldest member is Justice Hans-Joachim Jentsch (born in 1937). Five members were born in the 1950s. Aged 51, Justices Reinhard Gaier, Udo di Fabio, and Rudolf Mellinghoff are the youngest members of the Court. Half of the judges of the Court will have studied law at universities in the late 1960s or early 1970s. The average age at present is 59. By contrast, the members of the US Supreme Court were born in 1920 (Stevens), 1924 (Rehnquist), 1930 (O'Connor), 1933 (Ginsburg), 1936 (Scalia and Kennedy), 1938 (Breyer), 1939 (Souter), and 1948 (Thomas). The average age at present is 71. That most of the justices serving at the moment in the German *Bundesverfassungsgericht* were 'products' of the turbulent and/or exciting 1960s (readers may react differently on the term they wish to use) must have had some impact on their wider outlook and must thus be relevant to the 'mentality' issue which we discuss in greater detail in Chapter 4, section 11. Also potentially interesting is the fact that close to one-third of the total number of judges who have served on the court since its creation have been academics. Likewise, five out of eight of the Court's presidents have been academics – one of them, Professor Herzog, later also becoming Federal President of Germany.

[43] BVerfGE 39, 1 at p 38.

[44] See, e.g., BVerfGE 32, 54 ff where the Court interpreted Art 13 BL, which protects the inviolability of the home, to cover also premises used for business activities.

[45] Such as the *Kruzifix*-decision, which banned Christian crosses from Bavarian classrooms; see BVerfGE 93, 1 ff.

note below, nevertheless avoided some of what one might call 'the excesses' of its American counterpart. This is no mean feat given that the German Constitutional Court is more easily and more frequently asked to adjudicate on disputes than its American counterpart.[46]

Third, constitutionally questionable laws will pass judicial scrutiny if they are reasonably capable of an interpretation which does not exceed the limits imposed by the Basic Law so they be interpreted 'in conformity with the Constitution' (*verfassungskonforme Auslegung*).[47] This is less than a presumption in favour of constitutionality of legislation for all it does is merely to open the door for judges to *consider* whether the language of a statute actually permits an interpretation which is in accordance with the Basic Law.[48] In the United Kingdom the Human Rights Act 1998 contains a similar guideline for courts and tribunals interpreting rights established by the European Convention on Human Rights.[49]

---

[46] Unlike its US counterpart, the Court is concerned both with concrete and abstract review and is far more restricted in its ability to reject hearing cases. The latter point is particularly problematic in the area of individual constitutional complaints, which amount to over 5,000 applications each year. More importantly, the FCC has long been 'discovered' by the political opposition of the day. Parties from all sides of the political spectrum have tried to shift issues ranging from the deployment of armed forces in Somalia (BVerfGE 89, 38 ff) to the ratification of Chancellor Willy Brandt's so-called Eastern Treaties with Moscow and Warsaw of 1972 (BVerfGE 40, 141 ff). A particularly striking case was the attempt to force the Federal Government to negotiate the release of Hanns-Martin Schleyer, former President of the German Confederation of Industry, taken hostage by terrorists in Germany in 1977 (BVerfGE 46, 160 ff). Though in all these cases the Court acted pragmatically and deferred to the executive, the possibility of it being seized of such disputes is not without consequences and marks clearly the current German desire to subject, where possible, even political action to legal rules. As Professor Rupert Scholz (himself a member of the conservative Christian Democratic Party and minister in the Federal Government under the former Chancellor Helmut Kohl) points out: 'The more legislation and politics are "juridified" by the courts [because they are forced to decide increasingly "political" issues], the higher the danger of a "politicized" justice system.' See Rupert Scholz, *Deutschland – In guter Verfassung?* (2004), p 189. Despite this warning, the system has survived and, we submit, is increasingly admired – largely due to the restraint and pragmatism of the judges of the Court who have, on the whole, avoided the danger of taking over the roles of either the legislature and the executive. This, however, does not imply that in their judgments they have avoided political controversy.

[47] See, e.g., BVerfGE 69, 1 at p 55.

[48] See Ingo von Münch, Vorbemerkungen zu Art 1–19, in: Ingo von Münch/Philip Kunig, *Grundgesetz-Kommentar* (5th edn, 2000), Vorb. Art 1–19, no 66.

[49] Section 3(1) HRA thus declares: 'So far as it is possible to do so, primary legislation and subordinate legislation must be read and given effect in a way which is compatible with the Convention rights.'

The difficulty in such cases lies in distinguishing (unacceptable) legislative court activity from (acceptable) interpretation.[50] The ideal aim is, obviously, to strike a balance between judicial power to interpret – and, perhaps, even invalidate – legislation and respect for the will of the popularly elected legislator. Needless to say, the approaches taken to this issue may vary from system to system and be dictated by the wording of their respective constitutional texts.[51]

Though, as stated, the literature on this topic is enormous, three further lesser points must be mentioned here.

First, it is widely accepted that none of the German criteria of interpretation occupies a preponderant position. Having said this, one may add that the historical interpretation seems less crucial; most certainly it has never mustered the strong support which 'originalism' has attracted in the United States. The German Constitutional Court has thus emphasised that the method only serves to confirm a result already achieved with the help of other interpretative principles or to deal with last doubts which cannot otherwise be overcome. In the words of the Constitutional Court, '(T)he subjective understanding of the legislative organs or of particular individuals concerning the meaning of a certain provision is not decisive.'[52]

---

[50] In *Poplar Housing and Regeneration Community Association Ltd. v Donoghue*, [2002] QB 48 at 73 Lord Woolf CJ thus observed:

> Section 3 does not entitle the court to *legislate* (its task is still one of *interpretation*, but interpretation in accordance with the direction contained in section 3). (...) The most difficult task which courts face is distinguishing between legislation and interpretation. Here practical experience of seeking to apply section 3 will provide the best guide. However, if it is necessary in order to obtain compliance to radically alter the effect of the legislation this will be an indication that more than interpretation is involved.

[51] The Human Rights Act (not a grundnorm but an ordinary Act of Parliament) in s 19(1) (a) decides this issue in favour of the legislator. A Minister of the Crown in charge of a Bill in either House of Parliament is thus required to make a statement to the effect that in his view the provisions of the Bill are compatible with the Human Rights Act (so-called 'statement of compatibility') but can also opt to 'make a statement to the effect that although he is unable to make a statement of compatibility the government nevertheless wishes the House to proceed with the Bill' – in other words, to enact legislation which openly infringes the rights found in the European Convention. Judges, on the other hand, may declare provisions 'incompatible' with the Human Rights Act but are nevertheless bound to apply the law to the case at hand since they do not have the power to set aside legislation (s 4). As the recent dispute over the compatibility of the Terrorism Act 2001 has shown, there are, however, strong *political* checks and balances which give far more weight to such a 'judicial declaration of incompatibility' than is apparent from the text of the Human Rights Act; and the long-term results achieved under this regime may, in many cases, turn out to be quite similar to those found under a supreme constitution.

[52] See BVerfGE 1, 299 at p 312.

It should also be pointed out that 'historical interpretation' in Germany and 'originalism' in the United States are overlapping but by no means identical concepts. Historical interpretation will not only search for the subjective intent of the framers of a particular constitutional norm *but also take into consideration its subsequent development* through court decisions, public discussion, and academic research. Within this method, the current meaning of a provision is thus determined with regard to a *historical process* – much like analysing the annual circles of a tree – rather than seen as a snapshot taken at one particular (if admittedly important) historical moment. The promulgation of the Basic Law did not, as Professor Ekkehart Stein has repeatedly pointed out, 'bring the historical development to an end', and historical interpretation in Germany will try to take into account political, economical, sociological, and technological changes which have occurred since the initial constitutional debates of Herrenchiemsee and Bonn in 1948/1949 and which may impact on the contemporary understanding of the text.[53] Beyond differences in detail, it is thus generally accepted that law – and especially constitutional law – must respond to the contemporary political situation and be interpreted, within reasonable limits, to reflect changed factual circumstances and social values. Without this flexibility, a constitution will lose its persuasive force and, eventually, either have to be updated through a formal revision or, in the worst case, be disregarded.

Second, though none of the four original cannons of interpretation is, formally, given any priority, the purposive interpretation could be said to be of particular importance. In practice, German judges resort to all four in turn and also cumulatively. If a particular result passes all tests, the case is, obviously, an easy one; if it meets some but becomes stuck on others, the difficulties are greater. This brings us to our third point.

German (no less than American) jurists admit that a political text has to be approached in a different manner than ordinary texts.[54] The generally acknowledged additional requirements for constitutional interpretation were given earlier on and it is widely accepted that they have managed to keep the immense growth of German constitutional

---

[53] Stein (op. cit. note 31) at p 40.

[54] Professor Donald Kommers has thus assembled a fine collection of statements made by judges of the *Bundesverfassungsgericht* which clearly indicate that the members of the Court are highly aware of the ambiguous nature of their task, located on the borderline between law and politics; see Donald P. Kommers, *The Constitutional Jurisprudence of the Federal Republic of Germany* (2nd edn, 1997), pp 43–5. This is also discussed by the distinguished German political scientist Klaus von Beyme in *Der Gesetzgeber* (1997), pp 310 ff. For a more recent German contribution to the topic see Rupert Scholz (op. cit. note 46) at pp 183 ff.

case law and theory within parameters which are both coherent and legal rather than political, sociological, and amorphous. This is because the Constitutional Court and, it would seem, those other European courts modelled after it,[55] have been pragmatic rather than dominated by principles (legal or otherwise). Alexander Bickel's idea that '(N)o good society can be unprincipled; and no viable society can be principle-ridden'[56] is thus not just a beautifully crafted aphorism; it seems to fit German interpretative techniques perfectly. A current member of the German Constitutional Court expressed a variation of this idea in the following manner:[57]

> A constitutional court will probably be able to make the greatest contribution to a new democratic system when the political system exhibits sufficient democratic and rule-of-law elements to accept decisions of a court constraining powerful political actors but retains so many traces of pre-democratic traditions that it can benefit from the court's guidance. The power a court acquires in this situation is, however, also dependant on its own strategic behaviour. It can hardly win an all out confrontation with the political actors in a yet unsettled constitutional situation. On the other hand, with too deferential a behaviour it will lose credibility and become disfunctional as a check on the abuse of governmental power.

The above points, taken together and then combined with another fact (to which we shall return below), namely, the very regular legislative updating of the German Constitution, may help explain why what is an acute problem in the United States is much less visible in German case law. The rules of statutory interpretation are thus fairly clear: the main issue is to instruct lawyers on how to use them, and this begins at law school – avoiding, as stated, one of Justice Scalia's major complaints as formulated in his above-mentioned essay on interpretation.

Finally, it should also be mentioned that the rules of statutory and constitutional interpretation briefly described above have by no means *excluded* conflicts between judges and the legislator in Germany.[58] The Constitutional Court in particular has thus been criticised as an

---

[55] For instance Hungary.

[56] Op.cit. note 19, p 64.

[57] Justice Brun-Otto Bryde, 'Constitutional Courts in Constitutional Transition' in F. Van Loon and K. Van Aeken (eds), *60 maal recht en 1 maal wijn, Liber Amicorum Prof. Dr. Jean van Houtte* (1999), pp 235–6.

[58] For Thomas Ellwein, a distinguished political scientist, these conflicts were mainly the result of a failure of the political actors in Germany to resolve contentious issues themselves – such as the reform of military service (the right not to serve in the armed forces), the deployment of troops outside the NATO area, or abortion – and chose, instead, to leave it to the Federal Constitutional Court to take the final decision. See Ellwein/Jesse, *Der überforderte Staat* (1994), p 135. To this list, Jutta Limbach adds the much criticised taxation cases BVerfGE 93, 121 and 93, 165; see Jutta Limbach (op. cit. note 35).

'alternative legislator' (*Ersatzgesetzgeber*) despite the use of these interpretative methods and the development of different levels of judicial scrutiny – ranging from strict review in human rights issues to the acceptance of more legislative discretion in areas such as economical development, environmental protection, and, more generally, decisions involving a prognosis of uncertain future developments (*Prognoseentscheidungen*).

The *Bundesverfassungsgericht* has reacted to this criticism by adopting its own theory of judicial restraint in highly political matters.[59] Thus, it might, for example, in borderline cases refrain from striking down a particular piece of legislation for the time being but indicate that legislative action is required if the norm is to pass future scrutiny by the Court.[60] These more intricate aspects of constitutional litigation go far beyond our immediate concern here but do suggest that finding an appropriate balance between a powerful court and the democratic legislator may require more sophisticated methods than mere adherence to the original intent of the drafters of a constitution. That is not to say that the 'Madisonian dilemma' has been successfully resolved in Germany (it has not);[61] but the quest for a coherent system of statutory interpretation has at least provided a number of stepping stones which promise to lead in the right direction. Additionally, as we explain below, many of the 'far reaching' and controversial decisions can be explained as decisions which *ran ahead of the legislator* in defining the details of

---

59 See BVerfGE 36, 1 at p 14; Brun-Otto Bryde, *Verfassungsentwicklung* (1982), pp 147 ff. For a very critical analysis of this effort to devise a workable formula (both in Germany and the United States) see Jutta Limbach (op. cit. note 35). Ernst Benda, President of the *Bundesverfassungsgericht* between 1971 and 1983, sees 'judicial restraint' as a state of mind rather than a precise legal formula. The Court must thus exercise its constitutional functions to the full but should, with a view to the division of powers principle, not *expand* them; see Ernst Benda, 'Constitutional Jurisdiction in West Germany' (1981) *Columbia Journal of Transnational Law* 1 at 11 ff. In this context it is important to note that the Federal Constitutional Court *must* hear and decide cases appropriately filed with the Court and will have more latitude to reject applications only in dealing with individual constitutional complaints (through the use of 'screening committees' composed of three judges).

60 Examples of refraining to intervene with decisions of the Executive were given in note 46, above.

61 Adolf Arndt, a prominent jurist and politician in the first two decades of the Federal Republic, concluded that any country with a powerful system of judicial review will encounter this difficulty because 'control of political power is, inevitably, itself power' (*Kontrolle der Macht ist notwendig selber Macht*); see Adolf Arndt, *Das Bild des Richters* (1957), pp 8, 12. Helmut Simon, Justice of the Bundesverfassungsgericht in the 1970s and 1980s, confirms this view with regard to the Basic Law by emphasising that the German Constitution had 'decided the age-old conflict between political power and the law in favour of the law'; see Helmut Simon, 'Verfassungsgerichtsbarkeit' in Benda/Maihofer/Vogel (eds), *Handbuch des Verfassungsrechts* (2nd edn, 1994), p 1137 at 1661.

newly created rules (instead of leaving this task to the political legislator) *but were not leading public opinion*. This distinction, however, is a fine one; and not every scholar and judge may share it.

c) Devising a wider model of constitutional adjudication

We have said something about the wider implications of our topic to show that it is highly complex; and its complexity is enhanced by it being inter-linked to other important issues – a good example as any of the point made earlier on about the law being a seamless web. The complexity of the subject is, however, further increased when one tries to examine judicial adjudication (and the permissible recourse to foreign law), as we are here, from a worldwide comparative perspective. For the variety of approaches to what are otherwise increasingly common concerns is formidable. The little we said about German law has already brought into the open the differences which exist between this system and American law; it also makes the presentation of this topic difficult (if not impossible), especially within the short confines of a sub-section of an introductory (albeit important) chapter.

Yet, the question of statutory interpretation (and how, indirectly, it can also affect a court's attitude to foreign law) is highly relevant to what we discuss in this book, which is the role of the judge (not only the American judge) as comparatist. Our aim in discussing it in the first chapter, as part of the general background for what follows, is thus to suggest (very tentatively) an 'over-arching' model or scheme that informs the reader of how some systems have dealt with these problems (and, perhaps, to explain divergent solutions or concerns by attributing them in part to the local norms of statutory construction and judicial adjudication). The emphasis of this 'over-arching' model has *not* been on detail (and the shades of diverging attitudes in how to handle the main question) but on coming up with wider parameters which can accommodate within them most systems for the purposes of, at least, starting a meaningful comparison. Even beginning to achieve this aim, in however rudimentary a manner, would be of some use even to national lawyers in so far as it could show them how the 'Madisonian dilemma' is addressed in other systems which thereby avoid to a large extent (though never entirely) the 'law and feminism', 'law and literature', or 'law and philosophy' arguments which often colour (if not even overshadow) legal discourse in the United States. One possible way of providing this framework for further comparison is offered below by discussing the possible approaches under three headings. Despite the rich variety of constitutional contexts which dictate or enable different interpretative techniques, we think the rules (and judicial attitudes) can, without too much straining, fall into one of three categories.

Category one cases involve situations where the judges have been left free by their constitution to fill such gaps or make necessary adaptations to their basic text. Freedom here stems from the fact that the constitutional legislator has deliberately left a particular point to be solved by the courts and refused to address it himself or has, for whatever reason, remained silent about the matter. Freedom also includes the right to choose the sources from which inspiration can be drawn. Alternatively, a country may not have a written constitution (England, for instance), or only possess specific constitutional texts (Israel), and the question then must be asked how this different constitutional background affects our main question. Though these variations in the background do not alter the general position that the judge applies the law and not his own views, the background *can* affect the latitude given to him when performing his interpretative functions. The detailed and highly structured German Constitution is not the same as two relevant constitutional acts in contemporary Israel.

Category two comprises cases where the judges are not meant to defy the legislative/democratic will found in a constitution or other statutes but have given the impression (through their decisions) of having done so. Category two types of cases are the ones which take judicial creativity to its *permissible* limits. Quantitatively speaking, they may also provide the bulk of the disputed cases. This material represents a reality which, however much academics and judges may wish to criticise, cannot be denied. What is called for is an attempt to explain or rationalise this case law by fitting it into an acceptable definition of judicial adjudication. On balance we feel that the rationalisation which offers most promise must be sought in the idea that the judge, depending on the 'wider context' of his constitutional environment, must be taken to be empowered to update his text. Crucially, we include in this term – 'wider context' – the frequency with which the legislator has, himself, updated the constitutional document in question. For we believe that where legislative revisions are frequent, the case for judicial creativity has, in practice, been less obvious than where the text, out of reverence or technical reasons, has proved to be immutable.

As a general reaction, in the second type of cases, our sympathies do not lie with the 'Scalia's of the world', though we do agree with the learned Justice that once we abandon clear rules of interpretation (and his originalism, despite the difficulties it presents to those who have recourse to it, can be said to have this (relative) advantage) we are then confronted with the difficulty of having to decide where to draw the line. Drawing the lines between category two and category three type of cases can be difficult; but drawing lines between permissible and impermissible is what lawyers do and, in the end, public opinion sooner or later determines whether the correct limits may have been overstepped and a 'correction' is needed.

Category three, finally, contains the most extreme and 'suspect' examples of judicial creativity where, following Lord Devlin's idea, the judge is no longer attempting to ensure that the constitutional text is in touch with public opinion but is, instead, trying to shape it himself.

Let us look at these three categories in greater detail.

(i) Category one

South Africa, which openly constitutionalised comparative law as a method of constitutional interpretation in 1993, falls into this category.

The initial decision to 'open' *in principle* the South African legal system to outside influence was *not* made by judges but by the political leaders engaged in the legal, economical, and social reconstruction of the country following the end of the apartheid era. Section 35(1) of the 1993 Constitution thus invited courts of law to have regard to comparable foreign case law when interpreting the fundamental rights contained in the third chapter of the document.[62] It is also worthwhile emphasising that this provision mentioned foreign case law as a *possible* (but by no means *binding*) source of inspiration while at the same time also creating a much closer link with international law (which was given binding force).

This distinction is in line with one of the main themes of this book, namely, that foreign solutions (however persuasive they may seem to be or however close their resemblance to national law) can never *bind* the national judge who remains entirely free to reject them or to use them either as an inspiration or as a model for his own approach. The provision is, nevertheless, a clear constitutional mandate for South African courts to look abroad. It also distinguishes the South African set-up from that found in the United States and may to a large extent explain the different judicial attitudes towards the matter under investigation. This different position of 'principle,' however, does not eliminate tensions between 'unelected' judges and 'elected' legislators, a point that has much troubled conservative American judges and lawyers. For they exist in South Africa as much as they do in most other democratically organised societies and, in one sense, may even be stronger here due to the fairly recent abolition of the principle of parliamentary sovereignty and the introduction of a supreme and judicially enforceable constitutional

---

[62] Section 35(1) of the 1993 Constitution declares:

> In interpreting the provisions of this Chapter a court of law shall promote the values which underlie an open and democratic society based on freedom and equality and shall, where applicable, have regard to public international law applicable to the protection of the rights entrenched in this Chapter, and may have regard to foreign case law.

framework. It does, however, prevent comparative law from being drawn into the political quagmire surrounding the wider relationship between judges and legislators.

In the latter part of the above-mentioned norm also lies hidden a more subtle invitation to look abroad. This is the duty to promote 'the values which underlie an open and democratic society based on freedom and equality' enshrined in s 35 (and, later, in s 39 of the 1996 Constitution) which, itself, requires a standard by which to measure the emerging new South African legal order. Indeed, it is not surprising that South African judges have frequently chosen precisely *this* wording as a starting point for *comparative* reflections.[63]

This approach can be contrasted with the German legal system which has both influenced the constitutional development in South Africa and, in earlier times, had, itself, experienced the need to make a fresh start after a period of unprecedented political, social, economic, and military upheaval. For the draftsmen of the German Basic Law envisaged a society based on a set of core values, which Art 21(2) BL[64] summarises as 'the free democratic basic order' (*freiheitlich-demokratische Grundordnung*).[65]

Like the South African notion of an 'open and democratic society', this expression is not defined in the constitutional text and is thus in need of interpretation. The similarity, however, ends there. For the subtle difference in wording sets the scene for a completely different approach in practice. Thus, the South African text refers to 'an' open and democratic society (inviting some form of comparison) while the German phrase clearly calls for adherence to 'the' free democratic basic order *as established by the Basic Law, itself*. German judges have thus seldom ventured beyond this boundary. The leading case of the *Bundesverfassungsgericht* dealing with the *freiheitlich-demokratische Grundordnung*, relevant not only for the purposes of Art 21(2) BL but also for the determination of the protective scope of important fundamental rights such as freedom of speech (Art 5 BL) and freedom of

---

[63] Take, e.g., the passage from the *Ferreira*-decision of the Constitutional Court discussed in more detail below, where Ackermann J turns to Canadian, US, and German law in order to establish 'the norms that apply in other open and democratic societies based on freedom and equality'. See *Ferreira v Levin NO and Others*, 1996 (1) BCLR 1 at [72].

[64] See note 39, above.

[65] The notion is also the focal point of Art 18 BL (dealing with the forfeiture of certain fundamental rights if someone abuses these to combat the free democratic basic order) and Art 87a(4) BL (which entitles the Federal Government to use not only police but also military force to defend the free democratic basic order within the country if no other solution is available).

assembly (Art 8 BL),[66] demonstrates this difference for it defines the concept only by reference to the *German* legal order.

There is, of course, no doubt that the two provisions – German and South African – discussed here perform quite different functions in their respective constitutional environments. The South African norm contains a rule for the *interpretation* of the fundamental rights enshrined by the 1993 Constitution while Art 21(2) BL provides a basis for the banning of unconstitutional political parties by the Federal Constitutional Court. The different *perspectives* of both Constitutions nevertheless become apparent at this point. For the Basic Law is very much focused on the *national* context,[67] and German judges have usually developed the fundamental constitutional principles and values from *within* the framework established in 1948/1949. South Africa, on the other hand, was conceived from the outset as a more permeable legal order, conscious of and open to the ideas of a legal world *outside* its political borders.

A third observation concerns the scope of application of the South African provision. Interestingly, it provides a basis for comparative work in an area of the law which seems, by its very nature, to be closely connected to the intrinsic values of any society (and may thus *a priori* appear to be 'national' in character) – human rights. There are a number of reasons why the political leaders responsible for the peaceful transition from the 'old' apartheid regime to the 'new' South Africa not only used comparative law *themselves* when drafting the two Constitutions of 1993 and 1996, but also felt that the judiciary (which survived this legal revolution in much the same composition) should be alerted to the rich bounty of foreign experience available to courts venturing into the uncharted waters of South African human rights protection. This, again, marks a difference with the (much older) American Constitution and thus calls for special attention.

Apart from differences in 'age' (which, itself, has important consequences), some of the reasons that led the South Africans to adopt a more open approach have already been indicated. The new regime's lack of constitutional experience has often been mentioned – sometimes overstressed – by American writers. But there are others which are just as noteworthy, even if they have received inadequate attention.

---

[66] For further discussion see, e.g., Karl Doehring, 'The Special Character of the Constitution of the Federal Republic of Germany as a Free Democratic Basic Order' in Ulrich Karpen (ed), *The Constitution of the Federal Republic of Germany* (1988), pp 25 ff (at pp 29 ff). Doehring thus describes the free democratic basic order as 'the basis of the entire constitutional system' (at p 33).

[67] Despite the initial Allied influence on the country and the desire of most Germans to embrace not only economical but also legal, political, and social principles of leading western societies in the decades following the end of the Second World War.

Among them we include the close cultural and academic ties which, in various ways, South Africa had enjoyed since its inception with different legal cultures. At this point we only wish to emphasise that most of these considerations apply equally to the other parts of the 1993 and 1996 Constitutions which do *not* deal with human rights issues – and yet the same political leaders chose to limit the foreign search for inspiration to human rights and *not* to authorise expressly the courts to look abroad in cases pertaining to other matters.[68] This difference has, however, not affected legal practice. South African judges have worked comparatively when dealing with cases unrelated to human rights; and references to foreign law can be found, for example, in decisions dealing with the provincial legislative competences under the 1993 Constitution.

But it may be more than a coincidence that South African judgments have been at their 'comparative best' when discussing human rights disputes, and we feel that there is, indeed, some merit in the general distinction that both Constitutions draw between certain subject-matters when it comes to the use of foreign ideas in the courtroom. The attempt to develop a rough compass for the use of comparative law by judges must therefore not be restricted to the two groups of constitutional norms identified by the South African legislator (human rights and what Germans call *Staatsorganisationsrecht*, that is, all other constitutional rules pertaining to the structure and functioning of a state). Other areas of the law where comparative work is more or less useful must be included in such a system, which should also try to identify different shades *within* the larger categories such as human rights protection, general constitutional norms, administrative law, or contract and torts.

We will return to this issue below but here note that this wider question has also been raised in two forms in the United States, mainly by those who oppose the use of foreign law by American judges. The first is, why have comparative ideas been used to enlarge or extend existing rights and not to restrict them?[69] The second is why have courts resorted to foreign ideas in some subjects and not others? Our quick answer to both questions is consistent with the tenor of this book and the haphazard nature of litigation which does not depend on a pre-arranged plan. As a matter of principle, however, the answer to both these questions should be the same: no a priori restriction should be imposed on the possibility of entertaining a dialogue with foreign ideas. For what is determinative is not the area of the law where comparison is

---

[68] E.g., the legislative process or questions of federalism. In both of these areas there was, incidentally, considerable foreign influence on the drafting process.

[69] Something which has caused concern to a number of American academics; see, for instance, Michael D. Ramsay, 'International Materials and Domestic Rights: Reflections on Atkins and Lawrence', 98 *Am. J. Int'l L.* 69 at 76–7. We return to this issue in Chapter 6.

contemplated or how the foreign idea is going to be used to 'affect' local law but the 'superiority' *and* 'tansplantability' of the foreign idea when considered as an alternative to the local model. This would mean – to take but one of the examples which most exercise American scholars – that if the European tendency to weigh speech versus reputation was not favoured in America, American courts would not be in any way bound to follow it. After all, this is not an approach that has met with a unified approach among legal systems; and many courts which require weighing consciously incline on favour of speech (even if they do not do so in the absolutist manner which the First Amendment seems to require). The 'weight' of foreign authority on the American position would thus not be as overwhelming as it is on other matters (e.g. the death penalty). But this way of looking at things does not mean that a dialogue with other systems should, by definition, be excluded if the end result might be to restrict rather than enlarge a particular freedom.

We also note that s 35(1) of the 1993 Constitution was expressly *confirmed* by the framers of the 1996 Constitution who opted for the same rule of interpretation[70] after more than two years of experience with a newly created Constitutional Court – a court which had shown, on the whole, a 'comparative appetite' that must surely have exceeded the expectations of even the most open-minded politicians. Within the South African context, the continued use of the comparative method by judges is thus not an aberration forced upon the system for a limited transitional period by truly exceptional circumstances but rather an informed and permanent choice of the constitutional legislator. We stress this again given how many American commentators have been quick to attribute the South African recourse to foreign and comparative law to the 'youth and inexperience' of the 'new' regime. As the time passes, this explanation of the South African open-mindedness would thus appear to loose its force.

Finally, it is worth noting that – despite the often very detailed and almost 'contractual' style of drafting – conspicuous gaps or ambiguities were left in the South African Constitution of 1993, for example regarding the death penalty and the (horizontal) application of human rights in the private sphere (*Drittwirkung*). The political parties involved in the drafting process clearly left a number of highly controversial topics for the (then future) Constitutional Court to decide in order to reach an agreement within the prescribed period of time.[71] Though most certainly a result of political pragmatism, this technique basically accepts (if only as the lesser evil in the face of a political deadlock) that judges do have a

[70] See s 39 of the 1996 Constitution, which again invites courts, tribunals, or forums to consider foreign law when interpreting the Bill of Rights.

[71] For more details on this point see the discussion of three South African cases in Chapter 2, below.

pivotal role to play in the decision of fundamental constitutional questions – a position equally acknowledged, as explained above, by the German legislator in respect to the financial compensation for infringements of the *allgemeines Persönlichkeitsrecht*. Many post-conflict societies seeking to establish new constitutional structures will resort to the same method (the future constitution of Iraq is likely to feature quite a number of such 'open issues'), and judges in these systems will thus have greater latitude in the development of their respective legal orders. This may have long-term effects on the relationship between the legislator and the judiciary, and it is perhaps no surprise that the German Constitutional Court – itself the product of a fundamental restructuring of the German legal order – is regarded as one of the most powerful courts around.

(ii) Category two

Judicial creativity is not unknown in Germany. Yet this system has not, as stated earlier on, experienced the same difficulties found in the United States though it has had its share of controversies. This may be partly due to its fairly sophisticated interpretative rules of statutory construction discussed above (even though they do not command uniform acceptance in the way they are to be applied), and partly due the pragmatic manner in which it has exercised its (theoretically) very extensive powers. However, we also believe that two other factors exist which can account for this state of affairs.

The first is that Germany has had a more frequent updating of its constitutional text than, say, the United States which is still saddled with an almost sacred[72] but old text. The rate of constitutional amendment is roughly nine times as high than it has been in the United States.

The second is the fact that many of the so-called bold decisions can, ultimately, be seen as *updating the law* (instead of or ahead of the legislature) but not trying to lead *society* in a new direction favoured by a minority, albeit a vociferous one.[73] In this section we must therefore look

---

[72] George Fletcher, 'Three Nearly Sacred Books in Western Law,' (2001) 54 *Arkansas L. Rev.* 1 ff.

[73] This may be a fine distinction to make but it is, we feel, a valid one nonetheless. For judges may and, indeed, have at times (correctly) sensed a changing mode in societal values which, however, a multitude of factors have stopped from being reflected in the constitution or ordinary laws. If the judge gets this change of mood right, his judgment will survive even if in the process he has, through his judgment, shaped the legal contours of the development himself instead of leaving it to the legislator. This does not make his decision any less controversial; certainly academic commentators are more than likely to seize upon such opportunities and criticise the courts. But in political terms, the decision will survive; and after the passage of a certain period of time, it may even come to be seen as wise. The two German cases we discuss in the text that follows could fall under this heading; and that is why we discuss them under this category and not the next.

at German law, then compare it with American law, and then briefly compare some American attitudes to their English counterparts.

The *Brokdorf*-decision,[74] the first of the Constitutional Court concerning Art 8 BL, is thus full of obiter dicta and reads more like a commentary on the freedom of assembly than a court judgment. It has had a major impact on the interpretation of all subsequent legislation in this area of the law by administrative courts and some academic commentators even see the rushed enactment of a new law regulating public assemblies, passed just days before *Brokdorf* was published, as a desparate 'pre-emptive strike' of the Federal Government designed to counteract the impression that it was being led by the courts.[75]

The *Volkszählungs*-decision,[76] a judgment concerning the national census law of 1982 which had attracted an incredible number of 1,310 individual constitutional complaints, laid crucial foundations of data protection law in Germany which remain relevant to the present day.

In *Volkszählung*, the Court developed a new *dimension* of the general right to the development and protection of individual personality, this wider right having already been sanctioned some 30 years earlier. This so-called right to informational self-determination has become the cornerstone of individual protection against both the State and private entities collecting and processing personal information. Handed down only days before the beginning of the emotionally charged Orwellian year 1984, and even hailed as the 'invention of a new basic right',[77] the decision specifically raised the issue of new technological developments which – unforeseen by the fathers of the Basic Law – demanded an appropriate constitutional answer and corresponding safeguards in ordinary legislation. The law, one could thus argue, was thus no longer in touch with technological changes and a slowly evolving public concern about their consequences. Without underestimating the importance of the decision, it can be seen as a development of the earlier creation of the general right to one's personality which was, itself, an outgrowth of the constitutional texts.

In such circumstances the court could and did act, even if in setting the new legal parameters of the problem and the required protection it was innovative if not controversial. With a view to the specific requirements set out by the Federal Constitutional Court concerning the technical conditions of a constitutionally acceptable form of processing personal data, Professor Spiros Simitis – at the time data protection Ombudsman in Hesse – declared that the Court had, with *Volkszählung*, opened 'a new

---

[74] BVerfGE 69, 315 ff of 14 May 1985.

[75] See K. Kühle, NJW 1985, 2379 ff.

[76] BVerfGE 65, 1 ff of 15 December 1983. The case is discussed in detail by Professor Spiros Simitis in NJW 1984, 398 ff.

[77] See *Frankfurter Allgemeine Zeitung* of 17 December 1983, p 12.

chapter of data protection law in Germany'.[78] And, as in *Brokdorf*, subsequent legislation was heavily influenced by the judgment – to the point of words and phrases from the text re-appearing as 'building-blocks' of federal and *Länder* statutes. But that is the point we are making: this can be seen as guiding the legislator by doing what society needed (or, at the very least, was ready to accept) but not leading society in the direction the judges might wish it to go.

On a different front, the revision of the family section of the Bürgerliches Gesetzbuch (BGB) offers a protracted example of judicial creativity which has often been *contra legem* but not contrary to the changing public opinion on the underlying subject. But cannot this development, too, be ultimately explained (and indeed justified!) by the fact that the ordinary legislator had ignored the will of the constitutional legislator to adapt the older Code (of 1900) so as to make it meet the requirements of the new and supreme constitutional text of 1949? The Basic Law, itself, clearly called for conflicts between any legal provision and Art 3(2) BL – establishing equality between man and woman – to be resolved by 31 March 1953; and Art 117(1) BL even went on to declare that provisions contravening this new basic constitutional principle would lose their legal force after that date.[79] In the light of the legislative inactivity of Chancellor Adenauer's conservative government, which failed to utilise the time provided by this sunset clause to adapt several provisions of the BGB which accorded the husband/father a superior position in family relationships, it seems that the courts – rather than the ordinary legislator – were in conformity with the Basic Law. In such cases it took less courage for judges to take the initiative[80] out of the hands of the political majority since they were reflecting a 'changing' consensus in society. So these were not cases where the courts were running ahead of public opinion but rather giving effect to the ignored

---

[78] See S. Simitis, KritV 1994, 121 at 124 and discussed in English by the same author in his 'Reviewing Privacy in an Informational Society' (1986) 135 *Univ. Penn. L. Rev.* 797 ff.

[79] 'Law which is inconsistent with paragraph (2) of Article 3 of this Basic Law shall remain in force until adapted to that provision, but not beyond March 31, 1953.' A leading decision of the *Bundesverfassungsgericht* in this context is BVerfGE 3, 225 ff, where the Court refused to accept any extension of this deadline even in highly complex areas such as the financial settlement between spouses in cases of divorce.

[80] It is easy to forget that at that time (early 1950s) the German Government and Parliament had many more pressing problems to face among which one must include the rebuilding of the ruined German economy, the provision of much-needed housing, and the coping with the almost daily problems posed to Germany (and its new allies) by an aggressive Soviet regime.

wishes of the constitutional legislator of a few years earlier and correctly assessing society's responsiveness to a changing world.[81]

The creation of the general right of personality is another example of a series of *contra legem* interpretations which one encounters in German private law. But, though criticised at the time, can they not also be justified in a similar way? A series of decisions, finding plaintiffs infringed in various aspects of their private lives but left without compensation due to the traditionally restrictive approach of the BGB in the question of non-pecuniary loss, held that this constitutionally protected value (the *allgemeines Persönlichkeitsrecht*, derived from Art 1 and 2 BL) could not remain unprotected in the private sphere. Compensation in money was thus, eventually, awarded contrary to § 253 BGB. And have they not been subsequently legitimized through legislative reform or constitutional acquiescence? In the *Soraya*-case the Federal Constitutional Court, itself, admitted that in exceptional cases the courts can draw their justification from the wider and evolving legal order; and as this case law shows, the German courts did, indeed, draw inspiration from American case law.[82] A crucial extract of the decision of the Constitutional Court deserves quoting not only because it has subsequently been used (sparingly it must be admitted)[83] to justify decisions in other parts of the law but also because it represents in our view a very balanced position regarding the limits of judicial creativity. The Court thus said:[84]

> Occasionally, the law can be found outside the positive legal rules erected by the State; this is law which emanates from the entire constitutional order and which has as its purpose the 'correction' of written law. It is for the judge to 'discover' this law and through his opinions give it concrete effect. The Constitution does not restrict judges to apply statutes in their literary sense when deciding cases put before them. Such an approach assumes a basic completeness of statutory rules which is not attainable in practice. (...) The insight of the judge may bring to light certain values of society (...) which are implicitly accepted by the constitutional order but which have received an insufficient expression in statutory texts. The judge's decision can help realize such ideas and give effect to such values.

---

[81] In this context it is interesting to note that the bad economic conditions prevailing in East Germany forced that country to use women in its workforce and by doing this had to recognise to them a greater 'right' to work than West Germany did at that time as well as give them greater freedom to terminate early pregnancies. Studying these differences of the two Germanys of yesterday is now only of academic interest except in so far as they can reveal how legal rules are often responses to societal needs.

[82] This is the American law of privacy before it and the law of defamation were stunted by *New York Times v Sullivan* 376 U.S. 254, 84 S. Ct. 719 (1964).

[83] For instance, Bundesarbeitsgericht of 12 June 1992, BAGE 70, 337 ff.

[84] BVerfGE 34, 269 ff of 14 February 1973.

The above statement could in our view, be seen, as lending some support to our thesis, namely, that the judge was more attune with the changing feelings of society and this not because his antennae were more sensitive than those of the legislator but because he was freer to respond to these changed feelings, being less 'intimidated' by the reaction of the Press.

This instance of judicial activism (in the way described above) was, by the way, eventually openly accepted by the legislator who, in the course of a substantial reform of German tort law in 2002, chose not to incorporate the *allgemeines Persönlichkeitsrecht* into the BGB because of the well-established, balanced, and flexible solutions developed by the courts over the past decades! Additionally, if somewhat cynically, one could add that the contemporary legislator, more harassed by the modern Press than his predecessor, may have felt more comfortable in leaving the law to lie as it was shaped by the courts than attempting to rationalise it himself.

The one situation where judicial creativity, though well-intended, may not have reflected properly the views of a divided population[85] and, in any event, undoubtedly provoked an open constitutional crisis with the German executive and legislature, was when it produced the very rich case law amplifying the rather mundanely phrased § 242 BGB (the famous good faith clause).[86] Notwithstanding once again the fact that Germany had, at the time, an inactive legislator,[87] one can argue that in this case the Imperial Supreme Court (the *Reichsgericht*) took matters into its own hands too boldly and went too far.[88]

So could it not be said (on the basis of this admittedly bird's eye view of some leading but disputed decisions) that in most of the instances included in our second category the judge was *not* imposing his personal opinions, let alone substituting his personal moral views for those found in the legislative texts, but merely giving expression to changes which had taken place in society – but which, for a multitude of reasons, had not yet found their way into the law, itself? And could it not further be said that

---

85 It almost certainly did not represent the views of most financial experts who saw in the decisions of the *Reichsgericht* rules that added to the inflationary pressures of the period.

86 Discussed in detail by B. S. Markesinis, Hannes Unberath, and Angus Johnson, *The German Law of Contract. A Comparative Treatise* (2nd edn, 2006), Chapter 7.

87 Until the *Aufwertungsgesetz* of 15 July 1925 allowed owners of land to extinguish their mortgages by paying a sum of money amounting to 25 per cent of the value of the mortgage in gold marks. But the Act applied only to some types of transaction and thus did not displace all the case law.

88 The literature is vast but see Kübler, 'Der deutsche Richter und das demokratische Gesetz', 162 *AcP* 1963, 114–15. The financial aspects which precipitated the legal crisis are superbly discussed by Elster, *Von der Mark zur Reichsmark* (1928). An account in English can be found in Graham, *Exchange, Prices and Production in Hyper Inflation: Germany, 1920–1923* (1930).

(subsequent) legislative approval legitimised the role for future updating forays (provided these were attempted within limits)?

If this kind of interpretation were to prove acceptable – and we certainly feel it is arguable – would it not thereby justify the distinction suggested above between two types of judgments: the first *leading societal opinion* when, clearly, this remains divided or opposed to the proposed new developments, the second *innovating in legal terms* (at the, perhaps temporary, expense of the legislator) but in order to bring an outdated constitutional text or other law in line with wider changes that require this adaptation? If such distinctions appear to some as being too fine, one must counter such an objection by reminding the unconverted that at times of 'transition' clear and unbending rules are not always the best answer for the problems that come before the courts.

The above observations lead to the following thought. Could any of these ideas prove usable in the United States? In an increasingly polarised society it may be difficult to find a common middle ground if, as is likely, neither side wishes to budge from its respective positions. Yet what we suggest may be worth attempting, albeit tentatively, even if the drawing of parallels across continents and cultures ignores concealed dangers. Yet, without underestimating these dangers, we nevertheless feel that, in essence, this is what is happening in the United States in those cases which figure in the discussion that follows in the subsequent chapters. Prominent among them is the issue of the death penalty; and the ways devised to mitigate the rigour (as we see it) of the original text by having recourse to the content of the Eighth Amendment. That not every American lawyer likes this does not put in doubt the fact that it is happening. Moreover, one could see it as nothing more than a way of bringing an old text up-to-date on those aspects of major issues which lie 'at the fringes' and over which a once adamant society may now be starting to soften up.

Nor does such an interpretation question Justice Scalia's objections in *Roper* (on which we express no view) that the current Court is now willing to use its own judgment and detect social change even on the basis of slight empirical evidence, no longer requiring signs of 'massive or demonstrable change'. If the test has, indeed, come to be applied in a laxer manner, it does not mean it is a bad one to begin with; all it may need is tightening up (which, arguably, is why in *Roper*[89] Justice O' Connor did not agree with the majority).

It is because the American Constitution falls into the precise opposite category than, say, the South African, that we cannot place it in the first category of cases. But can we (beyond the death penalty cases) slot

---

[89] 125 S. Ct. 1183, 1209 ff.

judicial activism in the United States into this second category of cases where an explanation (or rationalisation) can be found for such interpretations along the lines earlier suggested for some of the German instances of judicial creativity? We think this is arguable, for instance in the case of the decisions enhancing the rights of the accused in criminal trials (even though they caused a furore when they were decided), though we note, once again, how originalism makes this attempt to find a common ground nearly impossible.

Consider, for instance, the following sentence of Justice Scalia alluding to the technique currently in fashion to avoid imposing the death sentence (undoubtedly allowed by the Constitution) by relying on the Eighth Amendment:[90]

> (…) when people come to believe that the Constitution is not a text like other texts; that it means, not what it says or what it was understood to mean, but what it should mean, in light of the 'evolving standards of decency, that mark the progress of a maturing society' – *well, then they will look for qualification other than impartiality, judgment, and lawyerly acumen on those whom they select to interpret it.*

Now, while the wisdom of Justice Scalia's originalism has been doubted or attacked from many quarters, which include scholars[91] who are in principle sympathetic to his right-wing tendencies, this statement reveals consequential beliefs which have not, it seems to us, been addressed by others nor can be left unquestioned. Here then are some of our doubts which emerge from Justice Scalia's text cited above and which are best explained against the background of a Supreme Court decision which he, himself, regards as a sign of these modern, unfortunate tendencies.

A case that Justice Scalia sees typical of the trend he condemns is *Maryland v Craig*,[92] the facts of which had to deal with a criminal prosecution for sexual abuse of a young child. Because of the widely shared conviction that confronting her with her assailant would be highly traumatising, the child was allowed to testify only in the presence of the prosecutor, the defence counsel, and with judge, jury, and the defendant watching over closed circuit camera. This decision was upheld by the Supreme Court despite the language of the Sixth Amendment which clearly states that in 'all criminal prosecutions the accused shall enjoy the right to be confronted with the witnesses against him.' Justice Scalia feels that 'confront' meant (and still means) 'face to face'; and if this causes

---

[90] *A Matter of Interpretation* (op. cit. note 28) at p 46 (italics supplied).

[91] For instance, judges of the 'right' – e.g., Richard A. Posner, 'What Am I, A Potted Plant? The Case Against Strict Constructionism', 197 *The New Republic* 1987, 23 – and historians – e.g., Gordon S. Wood, 'Comment', in: Antonin Scalia (op. cit. note 28), pp 49 ff.

[92] 497 U.S. 836 (1990).

extra pressure on the witness, in this case the little girl victim of the assault, so much the better since the 'major purpose of this provision was to induce *precisely* that pressure (...) [for] it is difficult to accuse someone to his face when you are lying.'[93]

Though there are other cases where judicial creativity seems to have been over-stretched (and we include such cases in our third category), the instant decision does not strike us as being one of them. We thus see Justice Scalia's criticism as unconvincing and the example we discussed as one that reveals his originalism at its weakest.

We would thus see this case as falling in what we call the second category, not the third (discussed below). Of course, one could say that child abuse is a phenomenon that existed in the eighteenth century and, indeed, Justice Scalia was quick to point this out. So did, however, inter-spousal rape (and a host of other sexual or physical behaviour) which was tolerated more in the eighteenth century than (happily) it is today. But the science of understanding the human mind is also more developed these days and it can be shown beyond reasonable doubt that the human, especially young mind, can be traumatised by insensitive behaviour. This is why courts the world over have come to accord infants a different treatment and enhanced protection in all sorts of aspects when they are involved in trials[94] and one would be very hard-pressed to attribute this to 'European leftist' tendencies. The narrow interpretation of the American constitutional text, such as is favoured by the learned Justice, thus seems to us to brush aside totally important changes in attitudes, psychology, and medicine for the sake of remaining consistent with a theory. Indeed, it is noteworthy to remind our readers that the learned Justice was forced to admit that the result reached by his court would, probably, meet with the approval of the (American) electorate – an admission which, incidentally, shows how right Justice O' Connor was to maintain (in a different context[95]) that:

> We should not be surprised to find congruence between domestic and international values, especially where the international community has reached clear agreement. (...) At least, the existence of an international consensus of this nature can serve to confirm the reasonableness of a consonant and genuine American consensus.

In our view the example also shows that whereas American public opinion may (on this issue) have altered in line with worldwide opinion,

---

[93] Op. cit. note 28, p 44.

[94] Other countries have thus enacted specific legislation dealing with these difficult cases. In Germany, for instance, § 58a of the Code of Criminal Court Procedure (*Strafprozeßordnung*) protects victims under the age of 16 by requiring their testimony to be videotaped in the absence of the accused.

[95] 125 S. Ct. 1183, 1216.

the texts have remained unaltered given the near-impossibility to pass amendments to the Federal Constitution. In this case, therefore, judicial intervention is not frustrating the democratic element of any country but, actually, *expressing* it. For this is not one of those marginal or divisive kind of cases that fall into the third category and in which greater judicial cautions may be strongly advisable.

So should all these merits be cast aside for the sake of fidelity to the original understanding when this is so obviously now outdated and democratic (i.e. based on popular vote) reform could be obtained? Justice Scalia obviously thinks that the reply is 'yes' for, otherwise, the dreadful consequences he describes at the end of his passage will ensue. For our part we see them as being more in the nature of a rhetorical flourish.

Yet even if dismissed as a flourish, the passage about 'lack of impartiality, judgment and lawyerly acumen' raises one last point: was it general in its application or addressed only to the American scene? If the first, it could be seen to 'catch' in its amplitude many a great judge of England, Germany, or South Africa, and, as such, would rank only mildly below Professor Bork's broad-brush description of those who take a different view from his as 'faux intellectuals'. Justice Scalia, however, does not often leave his flanks unguarded. The results he fears are thus more likely to be predictions of what could happen (is happening?) in the American scene. In this case, however, it is for our American readers to decide if his comments were unnecessarily broad if not even offensive.

Justice Scalia's criticism of the interpretative techniques of his liberal opponents is also premised on his belief that statutory interpretation in the United States has unfortunately got out of control as a result of being influenced by the common law and its methods. There is little doubt that one can cite cases where his Court has gone too far; and the courts of other countries have also been bold to the point of truly challenging the prerogatives of legislatures.[96] But the danger of following Justice Scalia's prescribed solution is that the reverse could now occur; and even though he denies that he seeks to achieve this,[97] originalist-type of thinking (informed by the same underlying conservative philosophy) could spread to common law areas of the law.

We develop and address this concern of ours in other parts of the book. Here, however, we note that Justice Scalia's interpretive techniques

---

96 A series of German cases frequently discussed in this context concern questions of social security law and taxation where the German Constitutional Court has relied on human rights provisions (equality and the protection of marriage and family) to invalidate legislative reforms – with serious repercussions for the federal budget. For details see Hans D. Jarass and Bodo Pieroth, *Grundgesetz für die Bundesrepublik Deutschland* (6th edn 2002), Art 6 nos 17 ff.

97 Op. cit. note 28, p 13.

apply to all statutes alike. When he talks of the Constitution being a text like other texts we see him as suggesting that it should be subjected to the same kind of statutory interpretation as any other written enactment. If, indeed, he is saying that (and reading his texts we are left with the impression that this is not an aspect of the debate he has considered in sufficient detail), then we invite our readers to compare this with the following dicta of Lord Bingham (which come from the most recent Privy Council decision on the death penalty). In *Matthews*[98] the learned judge thus said that:

> [The Privy Council] has of course recognised that the provisions of any constitution must be interpreted with care and respect, paying close attention to the terms of the constitution in question. But it has also brought to its task of constitutional adjudication a broader vision, *recognizing that a legalistic and over literal approach to interpretation may be quite inappropriate when seeking to give effect to the rights, values and standards expressed in a constitution as these evolve over time.*

The italicised words emphasise the crucial difference with the 'originalists'. Lord Bingham also gives an attractive twist to his argument when he invokes more than the 'time factor' to justify the need for his 'updating' interpretive techniques and, in this sense, his judgment could be of use to those in the United States who feel instinctive sympathy with his position for it addresses the point we said is missing from the Scalia line of argument. He thus states:

> The task of expounding a constitution is crucially different from that construing a statute. A statute defines present rights and obligations. It is easily enacted and as easily repealed. A constitution, by contrast, is drafted with an eye to the future. Its function is to provide a continuing framework for the legitimate exercise of governmental power and, when joined by a Bill or Charter of Rights, for the unremitting protection of individual rights and liberties. Once enacted, its provisions cannot easily be repealed or amended. It must therefore be capable of growth and development over time to meet new social, political and historical realities often unimagined by its framers. The judiciary is the guardian of the constitution and must, in interpreting its provisions, bear this consideration in mind. Professor Paul Freund expressed the idea aptly when he admonished the American courts 'not to read the provisions of the Constitution like a last will and testament lest it become one'.[99]

What we have said thus far has focused mainly on American ideas since not only they seem very different (in degree if not in subject matter) from

---

[98] *Charles Matthew v The State* [2004] 3 WLR 812, at p 543

[99] 2004 WL 1372517, at p 8.

those found in Europe (or elsewhere) but also because these differences help those who believe differently to re-examine the validity of their own beliefs. But we have also opposed Scalia's underlying assumptions since we do not subscribe to the view that in modern democracies judges deliberately set out to impose their views on moral or other issues instead of applying the law. Certainly, we are not aware of a single English or German judge who has invoked foreign law to achieve this aim. The question, however, remains, whether these judges have only invoked foreign law when it padded up the view already reached on different grounds? The *impression* we have is that most judges remain open to argument; and in at least one *comparative* case – *A & Others v NBA*[100] – we have it from the pen of the very judge who decided it[101] that 'he was very much swayed first one way and then the other as the argument and evidence continued and developed.'

(iii) Category three

Here one must place the most adventurous types of judicial interpretation which, in Lord Devlin's scheme of things (which we find appealing irrespective of one's national legal background), cannot be seen as updating an old text by bringing it into conformity with societal changes already in place but, on the contrary, pushing society in a particular direction which is ahead of majority opinion and, to say the least, controversial. Many commentators might also place here part at least of the case law of the Barak Court;[102] but we know little about the wider socio-political context of Israel and, having only limited linguistic access to its materials, we feel unable to pronounce further on this case law. We note, however, that within the United States it has found both admirers and severe critics and we, knowing the judge personally, have the highest regard for his ability.

In this category, too, one could place some of the most 'adventurous' decisions of the US Supreme Court which are more susceptible to criticism for a kind of liberalism which is shared only by a minority of the population. *If* we are right in this appreciation – and we stress the 'if' as foreign observers must do in such cases – the 'extremity' of the thesis will explain the 'extremity' of the antithesis. Not everyone who lives in

---

[100] [2001] 3 All ER 289.

[101] Mr Justice Burton, in his note published in Guy Canivet, Mads Andenas, and Duncan Fairgrieve (eds), *Comparative Law Before the Courts* (2004), at p 81.

[102] The decisions of the Israeli Supreme Court concerning 'standing' and 'justiciability' seem to be among the most controversial in so far as they appear to have vastly extended the Court's power to control every aspect of Israeli life.

such a polarised society may see this, but those interested in civilised legal discourse will note it with despair.

We readily agree that a main difficulty with the approach we favour is that it provides no widely shared or clear criterion to tell us when the extension is permissible (because it represents an 'updating' interpretation in a way that already commands the respect of a sizeable part of the population) and when its results touch on the unacceptable because they have, through 'interpretation', gone beyond what one calls the 'core' of a constitutional text, representing the desired agenda of a minority, even if organised and vociferous. Does equating, for instance, 'political speech' (which, we understand, was what the First Amendment was originally meant to protect) with other forms of self-expression which help 'define' an individual go a step too far? In abstract terms one could argue in both ways; but it is the concrete examples that have resulted from this move that have 'shocked'. An 'originalist' or textualist approach (and here we are not placing the word in inverted commas in order to indicate that we are not using the term in its American sense but applying it in the context of *any* constitutional text) has the advantage that it may reduce such uncertainties.

Yet it would be difficult to deny that the world is far too complex a place to succumb to simplifying formulae, however convenient they may at times be; and a distinguishing search based on the common sense of the community could be a workable if pliable criterion.[103] The German Constitutional Court, a valuable source of information about the thoughts of judges on this matter, has thus emphasised that the separation of powers certainly precluded

> courts from assuming authority which the Constitution clearly allocates to the legislator. Article 20(3) BL binds the judiciary to law and justice. It would contradict this principle if the courts were to shift their role in applying the law [*Normanwender*] to a position involving the creation of law [*normsetzende Instanz*] – objectively releasing them from the abovementioned restrictions of law and justice. These constitutional principles do not, however, prohibit the judge from developing the law. *In the light of the increasing pace of societal change and the limited ability of the legislator to react to this change, as well as the open-ended language of many legal provisions, adaptation of the existing law to changed circumstances must, on the contrary, be regarded as a function of the judicial branch.*[104]

The italicised section at the end would seem to point in the direction preferred by Lord Devlin and, we think, that also supported by eminent

[103] In this we thus have some sympathy with Professor Bork's criticism of Justice Harlan's speech in the Supreme Court's decision in *Cohen v California* 403 U.S. 15, at p 25 (1971).

[104] BVerfGE 96, 394 ff.

French judges. But though satisfying in principle, it does not really resolve the difficulty of distinguishing between an interpretation which brings a text up-to-date with societal thinking and one which tries to lead it.

Though not unconscious of the dangers of rules that leave it to individual judges or courts to make such distinctions, we favour them because we find them less worrying than the broad-brush approach with which 'conservative' American lawyers have dismissed all the innovative work of their Supreme Court from the 1950s onwards.

Thus, the expansion of the equal protection clause to strike down legal entitlements between legitimate or illegitimate children,[105] the exclusion of evidence wrongfully obtained,[106] and the expansion of rights given to arrested persons,[107] or the abolition of racial segregation in schools have been condemned with equal vehemence as decisions enlarging the application of the First Amendment to protect pornography,[108] obscenity,[109] or hate speech.[110] In our view the first line of cases enjoy much wider popular support than the second and though severely criticised soon after they were decided, they have survived the passage of time.

In any event, the American experience and literature becomes less convincing when transplanted to other systems without due consideration of their own particularities. It is, for instance, far-fetched, over-simplifying, and in some cases plainly wrong to argue, as Professor Bork has done,[111] that

> (...) in the United Kingdom, the primary proponents of adopting a written constitution and the power of judicial review of legislation are the Labour Party and intellectuals. *The reasons are obvious. That development would shift a great deal of power from the British electorate to judges who would better reflect the leftist agendas of Labour intellectuals. Cultural and political victories would then be achieved in the courts that could not be achieved in Parliament.*

---

105 *Levy v Lousiana*, 391 U.S. 68 (1968).

106 *Mapp v Ohio*, 367 U.S. 643 (1961).

107 *Miranda v Arizona*, 384 U.S. 436 (1966).

108 *United States v Playboy Entertainement Group, Inc.*, 529 U.S. 803 (2000).

109 *Cohen v California*, 403 U.S. 15 (1971).

110 *Brandenburg v Ohio*, 395 U.S. 444 (1969).

111 *Slouching Towards Gomorrah. Modern Liberalism and American Decline* (revised paperback edition 2003), p 97. The sections from the quotation italicised by us represent comparative law at its least informed not least because so many English writers with left-wing sympathies have repeatedly accused the English judiciary for being deeply conservative if not reactionary! See, for instance, Professor John Griffith's controversial book *The Politics of the Judiciary* (5th edn, 1997) and J. Conaghan and W. Mansell, *The Wrongs of Tort* (1994).

We are reluctant to criticise the American law beyond what we have stated above lest we, in turn, commit the errors we have attributed to some of those with whom we find ourselves in disagreement. But it might be worth adding as a kind of postscript that all these issues have not been uniquely American and that something may be learned from the way other systems have coped with them.

Thus, removing the stigma from illegitimacy (with all its economic as well as moral consequences) was, understandably, a hot issue when it first figured prominently in France during the revolutionary debates in eighteenth century but had become a well overdue change by the 1960s when it happened in most other systems as well. It seems equally accepted that the judicial activity of the 1950s, both in Germany and the United States, can no longer be seen as a challenging measure leading society down a leftist path but as a credible judicial attempt to modernise the law in the face of legislative inactivity caused by a variety of reasons.

On the other hand, discovering 'basic speech principles' in cases such as *United States v Playboy Entertainment Group Inc.*[112] seems as far-fetched as is the American tendency to refuse even to attempt to draw lines between political speech and other forms of self-expression which would appear to have little social value. And if this type of case does not fall clearly on the wrong side of judicial activism – and undoubtedly many a learned lawyer in the United States has expressed his opinion to the contrary – what about the attempt to get judges to introduce social welfare legislation in the face of consistent doubt by the majority of Americans? To be sure, learned commentators have tried to argue that if only one had the 'right' kind of judges one could have tipped the scales in favour of such rights – sometimes referred to as the second generation of human rights.[113] But that is precisely the kind of situation where we would be asking judges to perform the unenviable and, in terms of separation of powers, impermissible role of legislators.

German constitutional law, on the other hand, seems to have avoided extreme positions and taken a more nuanced approach to many of these issues. No single human right (with the exception of human dignity, which is used sparingly) is sacrosanct but rather subject to various levels of protection, depending on the particular individual and societal interests involved in a conflict. Free speech, for example, is accorded a

---

[112] 529 U.S. 803 (2000).

[113] See, for instance, Cass R. Sunstein, 'Why Does the American Constitution Lack Social and Economic Guarantees?' in Michael Ignatieff (op. cit. note 23), pp 90–110 and, in greater detail, in *The Second Bill of Rights* (2004); see also Mary Ann Glendon, op. cit. note 24, explaining why this is so but also pointing out how even European Constitutions which contain such articles have treated their contents as programmatic rather than legally enforceable.

high degree of protection due to its pivotal importance for the functioning of democracy. Within the ambit of this right, however, different shades exist, and pornography, commercial advertisement, 'mainstream' entertainment, art, or contributions to the political discourse (to name only some of the possible categories which may fall under this heading) will carry more or less weight if in conflict with public or other private interests.

The protection of minors, explicitly mentioned in Art 5(2) BL, will thus restrict the freedom of broadcasters to show pornographic or overly violent productions at times when children are likely to watch generally accessible programmes – despite the fact that such films enjoy free speech protection *in principle*. If, on the other hand, technical barriers such as pay-tv allow parents to control what children see, the result will be different. Courts will resolve most of these conflicts on the justification stage of their human rights analysis, and it is thus no surprise that the case law concerning the principle of proportionality (involving precisely this type of flexible balancing of interests) is particularly rich in Germany.

Finally, German constitutional law features a number of other characteristics which determine the results reached by the FCC and affect the relationship between the Court and the legislator.

Article 5 BL thus not only protects the right to express and disseminate freely opinions in the form of speech, writing, and pictures, but also contains a separate provision establishing freedom of art, scholarship, research, and teaching.[114] Each dimension has its own scope of protection and level of judicial scrutiny. Any behaviour found to lie outside these provisions (or any other specifically mentioned human right) will still enjoy constitutional protection under Art 2(1) BL (the general right to free development of the personality), but it is here that the Court will allow the legislator the widest margin of appreciation when enacting law which limits individual freedom. And even within the closer confines of Art 5(1) of the Constitution, general laws not designed to limit freedom of speech specifically or suppress specific opinions but rather meant to protect other sufficiently important societal interests will survive judicial scrutiny. It is here that the famous *Wechselwirkungslehre*, which attempts to strike a balance between such interests and free speech, comes into play, and legislation regulating pornography[115] or outlawing incitement of hate against parts of the population,[116] as well as the disparagement of the State and its symbols[117] has survived constitutional

[114] Which, in some respects, enjoys even greater protection – but that is another matter!

[115] BVerfGE 47, 109 ff (*Bestimmtheitsgebot*-decision).

[116] BVerfGE 90, 251 ff (*Auschwitzlüge*-decision).

[117] BVerG NJW 1985, 264 ff; BVerfG NJW 1995, 2521 ff.

review.[118] Many have criticised this development, arguing that Art 5(2) BL – a qualified constitutional limitation clause – is slowly degenerating into the simple requirement that any restriction of the freedom of speech be based on formally enacted legislation (a requirement already established by Art 19 BL for any restriction of basic human rights).[119] Looking at the balanced approach German courts have taken in other areas of the law such as the freedom of the press[120] and, later, pornography,[121] we doubt that things have come quite that far.

A drawback of the German approach briefly outlined above is that since the outcome is fact-sensitive, it may encourage constitutional litigation – something which the 'cheapness' of going to court in Germany makes even more likely.[122] For the Germans, of course, this is seen as price 'worth paying' in the interests of democracy though judges from other systems might fear this effect. Certainly the English would probably see this as an unworkable solution within their own environment, the most cynical among them going a step further and seeing in these figures yet another example of the extravagance of the German welfare system which is making the once-mighty German economy groan.

Once again, therefore, one cannot but be alert to the need to be cautious and relative and not allow one's enthusiasm for internationalism to lead one to ignoring local realities. We re-examine this topic from a wider angle in Chapter 4, below. In the meantime, however, we mention that Germany has had its own (if, perhaps, smaller) share of difficulties in identifying the borderlines between legislator and the (constitutional)

---

[118] For details see Jörn Ipsen, *Staatsrecht II: Grundrechte* (8th edn 2005), pp 136 ff; D. Kommers (op. cit. note 54), pp 424 ff.

[119] See, e.g., Herbert Bethge in: Michael Sachs (ed), *Grundgesetz Kommentar* (3rd edn, 2003), Art 5 no 142 ff.

[120] See the points raised in this context in B. S. Markesinis, Colm O'Cinneide, Jörg Fedtke, and Myriam Hunter-Henin, 'Concerns and Ideas About the Developing English Law of Privacy (And How Knowledge of Foreign Law Might Be of Help)' (2004) 52 *Am. J. Comp L.* 133 ff.

[121] See BVerfGE 83, 130 ff (*Mutzenbacher*-decision) of 27 November 1990, where the Court upheld the constitutional complaint of the publisher of a new edition of the story 'Josefine Mutzenbacher. Die Lebensgeschichte einer Wiener Dirne, von ihr selbst erzählt' (a pornographic text dating back to early twentieth century Vienna). The book had previously been rated as 'highly dangerous' by the relevant public authority on the basis of a restrictive interpretation of legislation protecting minors (*Gesetz über die Verbreitung jugendgefährdender Schriften und Medieninhalte*).

[122] The low cost of litigation is not only a fact; it is also a reason for a growing willingness to fight in court for paultry sums. Thus the German Federal Ministry of Justice recently published statistics according to which the amount of cases with less than £200 in dispute (less than $360) have increased by 11 per cent from 230,000 in 2002 to 257,000 in 2003. During the same period money spent on legal aid increased by 20 per cent. In England most of these cases would not even reach the courts!

judge.[123] To a large extent, however, we are inclined to attribute this German result to the pragmatism and good sense of the judges sitting on the *Bundesverfassungsgericht*.

To conclude, in our view it is this 'third type of cases' which provoke the greatest discussion. More importantly, however, we note that it is dicta in some of these American decisions[124] which 'feed the counter-reaction' and give the left/right debate its often virulent language. This makes intelligent discourse difficult and prevents any attempt to find a via media. But we say no more on the above since we are conscious of the dangers of outsiders pontificating on another nation's internal politics and morals.

4. How 'common' are our common values?

These days reference to common values is very common, especially in the political context. Politicians are among those who make such references, especially when they wish to 'cement wobbly alliances' or demonstrate how what they stand for differs from what they oppose. It is thus right to say that England and the United States are more bonded than ever in their common (political) ventures, which, of course, is true. But political talk is vague, often deliberately so; and what is embodied in treaties or international declarations can become problematic when analysed by judges who may be called upon to interpret such documents.[125] It is at

---

123 Thus, in the first of several abortion cases of the *Bundesverfassungsgericht*, two judges (Rupp-von Brünneck and Simon) expressed their deep concern for the (in their – minority – view) too proactive role of the Court, which should not intervene in cases where the legislator had, after a highly controversial and lengthy public debate, eventually opted for a certain solution. Judges, according to this position, should make very careful use of their power to strike down legislation duly passed by parliament and only intervene if 'the legislator has completely overlooked a certain constitutional value or chosen measures which obviously counteract such a value' (BVerfGE 39, 1 at pp 72/73). The approach of the majority – which in this case clearly went beyond a constitutional analysis of the challenged statute (developing detailed conditions under which abortion was to be regarded legally acceptable and demanding criminal sanctions or equally severe measures for all other cases) – would endanger the balance established by the Basic Law between the democratic legislator and a court empowered to scrutinise parliamentary legislation.

124 'One man's vulgarity ... is another's lyric': *Cohen v California*, 404 U.S. 15, 25 (1971). To us, as outsiders, once again the dates of the 'thesis' help explain the appearance of the 'antithesis' some ten plus years later.

125 See Professor Cass Sunstein's views in Michael Ignatieff, op. cit. note 23, at pp 90, 101 ff where he maintains that many of the international documents (such as the Universal Declaration of Human Rights) were 'debated and signed with little attention to the question of judicial enforcement, which was of course not contemplated'. If such an approach is applied to other documents referring to 'common values' then what are the judges who are one day called upon to apply them to make of this attitude? Is it fair to blame them if they try to give effect to such statements? Or are we to expect them, as well, to treat them as cavalierly – as some of the bureaucrats who draft them and some of the politicians who sign them seem to?

this stage that talk about common values becomes an over-generalisation, especially once one begins to look at the constitutional and institutional differences that separate the various systems. The Devil is in the detail; and when this detail is legal the Devil can have a field day! These differences can be important if not crucial when one is thinking of legal transplants, legal harmonisation, or even legal unification. Thus, in his *Roper* dissent, Justice Scalia seized upon the difference in rules (if not in general values) and, it is submitted, did so with great effect. One must thus be slow when talking of common values, let alone common rules. Here is the relevant part of his judgment attacking the myth of communality of rules (if not of values) between English and American law.[126] It shows how an advocate can see differences where the politician (or philosopher) sees similarities.

> The Court's special reliance on the laws of the United Kingdom is perhaps the most indefensible part of its opinion. It is of course true that we share a common history with the United Kingdom, and that we often consult English sources *when asked to discern the meaning of a constitutional text written against the backdrop of 18th-century English law and legal thought.*[127] If we applied that approach today, our task would be an easy one. As we explained in (...), the 'Cruell and Unusuall Punishments' provision of the English Declaration of Rights was originally meant to describe those punishments 'out of [the Judges'] Power' – that is, those punishments that were not authorized by common law or statute, but that were nonetheless administered by the Crown or the Crown's judges. Under that reasoning, the death penalty for under-18 offenders would easily survive this challenge. The Court has, however – I think wrongly – long rejected a purely originalist approach to our Eighth Amendment, and that is certainly not the approach the Court takes today. Instead, the Court undertakes the majestic task of determining (and thereby prescribing) *our* Nation's *current* standards of decency. It is beyond comprehension why we should look, for that purpose, to a country that has developed, in the centuries since the Revolutionary War – and with increasing speed since the United Kingdom's recent submission to the jurisprudence of European courts dominated by continental jurists – a legal, political, and social culture quite different from our own. If we took the Court's directive seriously, we would also consider relaxing our double jeopardy prohibition, since the British Law Commission recently published a report that would significantly extend the rights of the prosecution to appeal cases where an acquittal was the result of a judge's ruling that was legally incorrect. (...) We would also curtail our right to jury trial in criminal cases since, despite

[126] *Roper v Simmons*, 125 S. Ct.1183 (2005) at pp 1227 ff (references omitted).

[127] The section italicised by us is, of course, consistent with Scalia's originalism but the 'limitation' would not meet with the approval of those judges and scholars who do not share his wider philosophy. Nonetheless, it is indicative of an advocate who does not lower his guard at any point.

> the jury system's deep roots in our shared common law, England now permits all but the most serious offenders to be tried by magistrates without a jury.

It would be wrong to allow oneself to go down the route of comparing the English and American solutions on the points Scalia touches in order to demonstrate that one system is better than another. What, instead, will suffice is to note that, if such differences exist between systems like the English and American which belong to the same legal family, one can imagine how many more differences and difficulties of reconciliation will arise when one is comparing legal systems that belong to different legal families (e.g. common and civil law or mixed jurisdictions), let alone different cultures and religious backgrounds such as China and the Islamic world. The more interesting point to explore is to what extend the growing respect for human values (an undoubted phenomenon of the last 30 years or so of recent legal and political history) can, in certain cases, become an agent for overturning these (in nature) more technical but (in substance) just as important differences in the legal rules.

Thus, there can be little doubt that many of the core rules found in England, France, and Germany – to mention but three countries only – differ substantially as far as notions of democracy, judicial review, and human rights are concerned. Despite their undisputed similarities, European legal cultures are thus still far apart in many ways, and judges who have to determine (and then utilise) the common constitutional traditions of these 25 societies face a truly daunting task. One does not have to go into real detail to note this. Even basic rules of democracy, accepted in one country, would cause problems in another; and we are always talking only of Europe and not venturing further afield.

To give but one example, it could be argued that the undiluted winner-takes-all election system to the House of Commons currently in operation in the United Kingdom would not pass constitutional scrutiny by the German Constitutional Court for lack of compliance with the idea that every vote should have equal weight.[128] Likewise, to give another illustration, the English are accustomed to – and in their majority endorse – the principle of parliamentary supremacy, and would have great difficulty in accepting the powers of judicial review accorded to the judges of the German *Bundesverfassungsgericht*. If the worst comes to the worst (as it seemingly happened in the recent House of Lords decision concerning the Terrorism Act of 2001[129]), English judges can only declare laws enacted by Parliament as 'incompatible' with the Human Rights Act of 1998. The final word in the matter will be uttered in Westminster. With its system of

---

128 Article 38 of the Basic Law of 1949.

129 *A (FC) v Secretary of State for the Home Department*, [2004] UKHL 56.

limited abstract review exercised by the *Conseil constitutionnel* before the law comes into effect, France takes middle ground on this question. But would the French (or the English) accept the profound impact of human rights protection as it has developed in Germany over the past 50 years – forcing the state to justify its activities in areas as diverse as zoning, the introduction of a duty to wear safety belts in motorised traffic, the use of administrative fees levied from university students, or the enactment of laws forcing citizens to keep dogs on a leash? The more we go into such details, the more we find differences. Denying them would be intellectually dishonest. But this does not mean that the international dialogue we advocate in this book looses its value or becomes less pressing. There are two reasons why this is not so.

First, these common or shared values must, already, be used by supranational courts to shape treaty law that applies to more than one state. The question, then, arises how rules are distilled from these common values? How are (local, regional, or national) variations reconciled or ignored? And what are the wider advantages of such intellectual exercises? Could they, even, provide for a more nuanced analysis (and, if undertaken, better justification) of economic sanctions or military interventions on the basis of human rights considerations?

Second, we believe that the answers to these questions can also be of great relevance where the comparative exercise is undertaken in a national context by a national court seeking *inspiration* rather than *binding precedents* (or being obliged to apply treaty law binding its own country). This second reason is the one which forms the subject of our book, so little will be said about it in this introduction; but here are some few words about the first, which is not really part of our enquiry but whose resolution has some bearing on our subject.

Take, for instance, Art 6(1) of the Treaty of Maastricht (1992) which emphasises 'liberty, democracy, respect for human rights and fundamental freedoms, and the rule of law' as being 'common to the Member States'. Look, also, at the Charter of Fundamental Rights of the European Union[130] which solemnly declared eight years later in its Preamble the 'spiritual and moral heritage' of the Member States, claiming that

> the Union is founded on the indivisible, universal values of human dignity, freedom, equality and solidarity.

According to this document, the European Union

> contributes to the preservation and to the development of these common values while respecting the diversity of the cultures and traditions of the peoples of Europe as well as the national identities of the Member States

---

[130] Document 2000/C 364/01.

> and the organisation of their public authorities at national, regional and local levels.

Finally, the Charter refers to

> the rights as they result, in particular, from the constitutional traditions and international obligations common to the Member States.

These references to a *common heritage* and *constitutional traditions common to the Member States* indicate the official belief that the 25 independent nations currently forming the European Union share common ground despite their national identities and that this common ground is an important point of reference for the EU as a separate legal system.[131]

Do European judges really have to worry about this?

One could, for instance, argue that the Preamble of the Charter of Fundamental Rights exerts even less practical influence than the various human rights provisions of the document themselves. The rights enumerated in the Charter are, after all, *not* judicially enforceable.

The response to this argument is twofold.

First, the judges of the European Court of Justice (ECJ) may, in future years, have to apply and interpret a European Constitution which contains rights based, apparently, on these common values. Indeed, the Charter is already used by this Court as an *interpretative* tool in the resolution of human rights disputes today.

Second, however uncertain the fate of the Draft European Constitution may be – and after the French and Dutch referenda the text (as it now stands) seems to be as good as dead – Art 6(1) of the EU Treaty (a core provision of European law) likewise calls for an interpretation of the 'fundamental rights *common* to the Member States'. These rights are regarded as general principles of Community law or, rather, from these widely recognised national laws the court has *creatively* used those most compatible with the aims of the Treaties to fashion the so-called general principles of Community law which have such an impact on its decisions. But what, then, *are* these rights, and what *is* their precise legal content in the eyes of Europeans today? To take two topical and closely related examples – are identity cards an infringement of individual freedom (overwhelmingly regarded with suspicion in the United Kingdom but

---

131 One could add here Art 2 of the Draft Constitution (CIG 87/04), which declares:

> The Union is founded on the values of respect for human dignity, freedom, democracy, equality, the rule of law and respect for human rights, including the rights of persons belonging to minorities. These values are common to the Member States in a society in which pluralism, non-discrimination, tolerance, justice, solidarity and equality between women and men prevail.

accepted, in principle, in Germany and France)? And is observation with CCTV cameras acceptable under data protection principles (there are currently an estimated 7 million cameras in operation in the United Kingdom today whereas public opinion in Germany and Austria still regards this technology as the incarnation of the Orwellian state, and security legislation thus far imposes tight restrictions on their use)? Only a comparative survey, it seems, can provide an answer to these important questions. In the meantime, one adds the idea that current German 'sensitivities' to some of these issues can easily be linked to that country's experience during the Nazi period and the fact that Germany's post-War friends never ceased to remind her of it.

Thus, the emphasis on mutual values, often stressed in this work, cannot obscure this opposite reality. Our task thus becomes one of finding the acceptable medium of taking into account this (proclaimed) common background in shaping our national rules but not to the point where transplantation, unification, or copying are seen as aims *in themselves*. For pragmatism is an attribute of durable justice.

In the light of the above we would like to add three concluding comments.

First, we must not forget that some of the much-criticised decisions of the Court of Justice of the European Communities and the European Court of Human Rights are, to a certain extent, the result of the language used in international treaties and conventions involving human rights protection. If – in this case – European legislators (and they are *not* 'unelected bureaucrats in Brussels' but the elected top representatives of the Member States) create the impression of a common European cultural heritage, they should not be surprised if judges – called upon to interpret and apply these *legal* texts – later take their cue from phrases such as 'universal values' or 'common constitutional traditions' when deciding conflicts that must inevitably arise. Which places the ball squarely back into the court of those politically responsible for – and, apparently, experienced in – the drafting of such texts.

Second, a judicial consensus of sorts seems to be emerging that the utilisation of the shared principles in legal disputes does not mean a total 'head count' nor the formulation of rules which represent the minimum common denominator of the specific rules we find in each system included in one's survey. For national law, dicta to that effect are given in the next chapter showing that senior English judges at least do not believe that either of these approaches is valid or convincing. As far as the Court of the European Communities is concerned an old but classic statement of the exercise involved leaves not doubt of what has to be done; and it ties in perfectly with the English dicta. Thus in *Hoogovens v*

High Authority,[132] Advocate General Lagrange described the essence of the evaluative approach in the following terms:

> (...) the case law of the Court, in so far as it invokes laws (as it does to a large extent) to define the rules of law relating to the application of the Treaty, is not content to draw on more or less arithmetical 'common denominators' between the different national solutions, but chooses from each of the Member States those solutions which, having regard to the objects of the Treaty, appear to be the best[133] or, if one may use the expression, the most progressive. That is the spirit (...) which guided the Court hitherto.

Finally, the shaping of the rule must not stop there but must also show some sensitivity to whatever national rules or practices may thus be seriously affected by this interpretive creation of a new rule. Lagrange did not allude to this but (a) that was not necessary in his case nor (b) had the ECJ (or, come to that, the Strasbourg Court), in those days, become as 'intrusive' into national law as it has become since.

The point considered here can be particularly dangerous in the area of human rights law where long-established practices may be sacrificed to this judicial creation of 'synthetic' new rules.[134] In England we experienced this not that long ago in the *Osman*[135] ruling and its attack on the use of the common law notion of 'duty of care' to create, essentially, large swathes of tort immunity. Though some of us dislike the blunderbuss kind of operation of the notion of duty of care, fact is that the *Osman* ruling caused uproar in England and this, in turn, 'forced' the Court in Strasbourg to back-peddle. A similar reaction occurred in France when the European Court of Human Rights in its *Fontaine*[136] and *Kress*[137] rulings declared that the posts of *Avocat Général* in the *Cour de cassation*

---

[132] Case 14/61 [1962] ECR 253, at 283–4.

[133] In another case – Case 5/71 *Zuckerfabrik Schöppenstedt v Council* [1971] ECR 975, at 989 – the German AG Roemer argued that particular regard should be had of 'the best elaborated national rules'.

[134] Something which may also be occurring in the current attempts to draft a European Code of Private Law without taking into account the different economic philosophies that underlie the current European codes and statutes governing private law. This clash between the 'Anglo-Saxon' and French 'social' models was recently catapulted into the open following the inability of the European Heads of State and Prime Ministers to agree upon a budget for the European Union. Only ivory-tower academics or Commission-employed bureaucrats in pursuit of their own agendas can allow themselves to loose so completely contact with the feelings of the European electorate. Note that this point is also made (more elegantly and more obliquely) by President Canivet in the quotation of his which we reproduce at the end of this chapter.

[135] Osman *v* United Kingdom, (1998) ECHR 101 of 28 October 1998.

[136] Case of 8 July 2003.

[137] Case of 7 June 2001.

and that of *Procureur de la République* in the *Conseil d' Etat* run counter to Art 6 of the European Convention of Human Rights.

We cite these French decisions not only because, like the *Osman* case, they caused national protest – showing that French attitudes towards Strasbourg are not that different from the English. Yet they also received a strong rebuff from the First President of the *Cour de cassation* who is a known internationalist. His views deserve to be quoted in full not only because of the beauty of the language used (admittedly largely lost in our translation) but mainly because the wider lesson they contain is relevant to the theme discussed in this book. For judicial dialogue aims to broaden horizons, increase awareness of alternative options, give new angles to looking at common problems and, occasionally, assists to harmonise responses where such harmonisation is needed. It is not there, however, to disturb deeply held national convictions and practices unless by quoting these foreign ideas one finds further support for national trends. In other words, we see in his formulation what we have proposed at the outset of our book as a possible way of reconciling national differences and eventually developing normative rules about the proper use of the comparative method. But to return to M. Canivet's statement, he observed:

> This [entire] dispute illustrates the contrast between the abstract formalism of human rights and the reality of historical traditions. This is an old debate, at least as old as that over human rights. Can we endanger what is dear to our history in the names of disembodied principles running roughshod over traditions, habits and existing realities in the name of an ideal? The rights of man, from their first appearance at the end of the 18th century, were accused of ignoring concrete realties in the name of abstract principles [citation of Burke]. And one could already discern emerging a disagreement between the English attachment to pragmatism and the French preference for the tabula rasa. To be honest, it is no longer a mater of conflict between [these] cultures but, rather, a clash, on the one hand, between a long-established and prestigious culture and, on the other, a non-culture, an aggregate of many national legal cultures. Even though many European lawyers feel that they share something in common with one another, they do not have the same feelings towards the Strasbourg case law that they nourish towards their home grown culture. Indeed, in some extreme cases, jostled by such attitudes, national lawyers are thus forced to react by adopting nationalistic positions denying the legitimacy of the European judge. In this way Europe succeeds in bringing closer to us the agony of globalisation. For can we ever be satisfied by a synthetic culture? National culture is alive with stories, symbols, traditions, which is another way of saying a shared consciousness. For by being omnipresent it needs not to be proclaimed. To articulate it risks proving fatal to it for it would be tantamount to admitting that it is threatened. Article 6 of the Convention of Human Rights is not, therefore, the antidote, a way of ridding the law of its impurities, but a solvent of national legal cultures. If

> people that do not have myths are left in the cold, the globalisation that follows the clash of these two ways of thinking will lead us to a world which may attain some peace through trade but which will have become glacial. This example of convergence enforced from the top thus presents us with a paradox of globalisation. For as legal cultures slowly integrate into their systems the principles of superior values, the more the local pockets of resistance tend to develop.

This wise warning provides an appropriate conclusion to an introductory chapter the aim of which is to set the scene for what follows in this book. For in a summary way it underscores two realities. First, that the subject studied in this monograph is one which spreads its tentacles across many branches of the law of many legal systems which few lawyers can master in any truly satisfactory manner. Second, it suggests that whereas globalisation is a phenomenon which is undeniably with us today, it must be handled in a way that does not run roughshod over local sensibilities – a danger which may go back as far as the Universal Declaration of Human Rights of 1948, which attempted not only to create a common standard of human rights protection for a single continent but rather the whole planet.[138]

These days, we have ample political examples to show how wise is this warning and how high is the price that those who ignore it have to pay. What is happening on the political scene could also happen to transborder legal discourse if it, too, is not handled with caution and sensitivity. The wisdom of the common law lies largely in the fact that it knows that the best way to move forward is to move incrementally, avoiding unnecessary generalisations. Pragmatism can have its advantages over volatile, if sometimes understandable, enthusiasm;[139] and this applies to enthusiasms that create as well as destroy.

---

[138] For different cultural perspectives on issues such as criminal law, family law, women's rights, socio-economic rights, and the attempt to 'universalize' Western-style democratic practices see Daniel A. Bell, *East Meets West* (2000).

[139] An insight occasionally even shared by the ECJ (for example in its recent *Omega*-decision, discussed in detail in Chapter 3, involving the banning of so-called laserdromes on the basis of human dignity in Germany).

Chapter 2: A Quick Glance at Seven Jurisdictions

1. As a matter of principle: to do or not to do? the ambivalence of the United States

Since this text evolved from a lecture delivered in the United States it is, perhaps, only appropriate to remain faithful to the original scheme and begin by asking this general question in the context of that country. But there is a further reason why it is best to begin in this way. For America these days illustrate perfectly the ambivalence its lawyers seem to have towards the issue. Whether this is part of what a recent collection of essays[1] described as 'American Exceptionalism' and, indeed, whether it has been a semi-permanent feature of the American scene or not, is not a matter to be discussed here. Our thesis is that the United States is currently going through an acute paroxysm. But, at the same time, the multiple objections levied against the idea of foreign borrowings can also help highlight some of the difficulties that confront other systems, as well. Finally, we set the scene by starting with the United States because here one encounters some of the strongest pronouncements against even attempting the exercise; and the tone of the American debates can, at times, be surprisingly strident.

Prominent among American judges who take this view is Justice Antonin Scalia, a jurist known for views which are as strongly held as they are re-iterated with (admirable) consistency and undeniable power. Thus, in *Lawrence v Texas*,[2] referring to submissions that other systems had decriminalised sodomy between consenting adults in private, he said:

> Constitutional entitlements do not spring into existence because some States choose to lessen or eliminate criminal sanctions on certain behaviour. Much less do they spring into existence, as the Court seems to believe, because foreign nations decriminalize conduct. (...) *The Court's discussion of these foreign views (...) is therefore meaningless dicta. Dangerous dicta, however, since 'this court (...) should not impose foreign moods, fads or fashions on Americans.*

---

[1] Michael Ignatieff (ed), *American Exceptionalism and Human Rights* (2005), on which see our brief comments in the Introduction.

[2] 123 S. Ct. 2472.

It is the italicised end of the quotation that will arrest the attention of the foreign reader.[3] And yet it is the opening statement that holds the key to the Scalia doctrine, gives it coherence, and also earns it its opponents. For, paraphrasing it, it states that contemporary law reform in the United States and, a fortiori, in foreign countries cannot change the original understanding of the US Constitution. For Scalia, the originalist,[4] believes that, whether he is dealing with the Constitution or with federal statutes, he is interpreting a legal text, enacted at a particular time and place. To understand it and apply it all he needs to know is the understanding of the text at the time of its enactment by the polity entitled to enact it. With such a starting point, the possibility of foreign law casting any light on the enactment in question is not

---

[3] For how we speak often says much about how we think, and Justice Scalia's adoption of Justice Thomas' words – 'foreign moods, fads or fashions' taken from *Foster v Florida*, 537 U.S. 990, n (2002) – talks volumes of how he perceives the 'values' that are currently shaping the case law of foreign courts, many of which are comparable in standing to his own not only in form but also in achievements. That Justice Scalia is, indeed, using these words in a pejorative manner can be seen from his earlier dictum in *Atkins*, 536 U.S. at 347–8, where he wrote: 'Equally irrelevant are the practices of the "world community", whose notions of justice are (*thankfully*) not always those of our people (...)' (italics added). Other jurists of the American 'right' have used even more vivid language to express their dislike of European criticism of American 'insularity'. Thus Robert Bork, *Coercing Virtue: The Worldwide Rule of Judges* (revised edn, 2003), pp 2–16 refers to academics like us (arguing for an open mind) as socialist, anti-religious, 'faux intellectuals (...) [hoping] to outflank American legislatures by [imposing] liberal views on the United States', while at pp 24–5 he describes the European reaction to Justice Kennedy's reluctance to cite foreign law as 'insolent browbeating'. That Professor Bork was never confirmed to the Supreme Court may, conceivably, explain in part such vitriolic hyperbole even though the strength and sincerity of his beliefs is well documented in his many books. But the greatest irony must surely be that the judge he defended for siding with the majority in *Stanford v Kentucky* and refusing to take into account foreign law gave the majority decision in *Roper* which invoked foreign law as a supplementary reason for the changed outcome! This, indeed, must be more than ironical. For it must also offer a good example of how the 'time factor' – discussed in several sections of this essay – can, over time, change attitudes and legitimise the use of foreign law, reversing old practices. The Bork polemic can be found (with some repetition) in his two other main books: *The Tempting of America. The Political Seduction of the Law* (1990) and *Slouching Towards Gomorrah. Modern Liberalism and American Decline* (1996). Their richness in ideas seems matched by a richness in invective and indignation which will provide European lawyers, more accustomed to restrained legal (and legalistic) discourse, interesting insights into the politicisation of the contemporary American legal debate. It is a matter of speculation how much of this – in substance and in tone – may, one day, cross over to the 'old Continent'.

[4] Justice Scalia's views can be found in his many judgments but have also been expounded in summary form in his following writings: *A Matter of Interpretation: Federal Courts and the Law* (Princeton University Press 1997); 'The Rule of Law as a Law of Rules', (1989) 56 *U. Chi. L. Rev.* 1175 ff; and 'Originalism: The Lesser Evil', (1989) 57 *U. Cin. L. Rev.* 849 ff. Some of his underlying theories also come through in 'Assorted Canards of Contemporary Legal Analysis', (1990) 40 *Case W. Res. L. Rev.* 581 ff.

possible; indeed, his approach precludes foreign law before one even gets to other reasons which make him (and other fellow jurists on the 'right'[5]) hostile towards foreign ideas.[6] The points made above may represent an American 'problem'; but to the extent that they also touch upon the question 'can a judge allow his personal moral view influence his judgement?' they acquire a wider significance. We touched up the wider aspects of this question in Chapter 1; and will return to this issue later on (in both Chapters 4 and 5).

In *Stanford v Kentucky*[7] the point was whether the death sentence could be carried out on a defendant who was 17 years old at the time he

---

[5] We have, in this book, used the labels 'right' and 'left' to describe the political leanings of judges or academics because they seem to crop up so often in American writings (and discussions). But for reasons that we need not discuss here we find them unsatisfactory and note with pleasure that they are going out of fashion in Europe where parties with realistic ambitions to power have come to realise that they can only attain it if they occupy the moderate centre ground.

[6] Though a jurist, Justice Scalia is thus part of a wider 'political movement' and the question non-American lawyers will ask themselves is 'why would a political movement commit to such a formalist theory of interpretation?' The answer seems to be clear – entirely for domestic reasons. For those who adhere to this ideology strongly dislike many of the liberty-enhancing decisions of the Warren Court (their bête noir in particular is *Roe v Wade*, which they think has no roots in the Constitution). Of course there are theories by which *Roe* is derived from the Constitution, but the right utterly rejects those theories. So, the problem the right diagnosed was unbridled judicial discretion leading to constitutionalising the political preferences of the left. Their remedy was simple – to end judicial discretion and tie judicial power to a narrow and formalist theory of interpretation. So, if the Founding Fathers of the Constitution had not said something, the judges could not do it either. These observations are, of course, trite knowledge for American lawyers. But foreign observers of the American constitutional scene must realise the need to understand American constitutional writings and the wider political debates taking place in that country in order to understand properly American decisional law. This, in itself, is a reason why foreign admirers of American legal institutions should be slow in trying to introduce them into their systems before having carefully checked their transplantability. We discuss these dangers of comparative law in section 6, below. For a very different conception of the judicial role see G. Canivet (op. cit. note 5) at p 41, where the senior French judge considers it to be 'un des aspects essentiels du rôle du juge (...) d'assimiler le progress et l'innovation en ne dédaignant pas d'ouvrir le débat judicaire à la modernité (...).' See also his elegant contribution to the *Mélanges Jean Buffet* entitled 'L imagination du juge' (co-authored with Professor Nicolas Molfessis of the University of Paris and published by Petites affiches in 2004). German law, as explained in Chapter 1, would accept the judges' right to interpret texts in a way that brought them in line with current societal thinking (assuming formal constitutional revision had not taken place), though occasionally (as stated in Chapter 1) constitutional courts have run ahead of their times (thereby attracting both praise and criticism). Lord Devlin's discussion of this topic in 'Judges and Lawmakers', (1976) 39 *MLR* 11 ff contains thoughts and ideas that also apply to other systems, though less so to the United States.

[7] 492 US 361 (1989), 369 n 1.

committed a murder (and other crimes). Delivering the opinion of the Court in this (and a similar case heard at the same time), Justice Scalia refused to hold that the carrying out of the death sentence amounted to cruel and unusual punishment violating the Eighth Amendment, *inter alia* on the grounds that '(...) it is American conceptions of decency [sic] that are dispositive.'[8] This observation was made in dismissing the contention made by petitioners (and various *amici*) that the sentencing practices of other nations could indicate that a particular practice was so widespread as to occupy a place not only among American mores but also, text permitting, being capable of becoming part of American practice. Incidentally, to a foreign observer the use of the words 'American conceptions of decency' are, given the issue in this case, arguably unfortunate; and the peremptory dismissal of this argument in a mere (short) footnote underscores the learned Justice's hostility to the notion that an idea commonly shared by many democracies could have any relevance in the American adjudicatory process. If the point had to be addressed, it could be relegated to a mere footnote. Yet 13 years later another Court[9] seemed to reject Justice Scalia's indifference to the sentencing practices of other countries and took the view that 'within the world community, the imposition of the death penalty for crimes committed by mentally retarded offenders is overwhelmingly disapproved', thus banning executions in such cases as being contrary to the Eighth Amendment.

---

[8] This last sentence strikes us as ambiguous. The majority in that case had made evolving standards of decency central to the Eighth Amendment. In *Stanford*, however, Scalia was writing for the Court, and not just for himself, so he had to work within precedent. Given his general outlook (as sketched above) it would be surprising if he actually welcomed the 'evolving standards of decency' standard. Arguably, therefore, his real standard is in the preceding paragraph – 'those modes or acts of punishment that had been considered cruel and unusual at the time that the Bill of Rights was adopted'. But assuming that evolving standards matter (either because he is willing to make an exception here or because he was stuck with it unless he gave up the majority opinion) he says they must be confined to American standards. This does get him to a square choice between American and European views, somewhat insulated from his general interpretative theory. If we are right in the preceding analyses, this would lend some support to our view that an independent hostility to foreign law is *also* at work. But it is also consistent with another strand of Justice Scalia's interpretive theory – when text and original understanding are too open-ended, one should interpret them in the light of American constitutional tradition. This is another, less satisfactory, way of looking to the voters, instead of judges deciding for themselves. And if it is traditional practice among voters and elected officials that matters, then, of course, it must be *American* voters and elected officials.

[9] *Atkins v Virginia* 536 U.S. 304, 316 n 21 (2002).

If Justices Scalia,[10] Thomas, and Kennedy have, at various times, expressed views such as the above,[11] the Chief Justice (though usually bracketed with the right) has made utterances that go both ways.[12] On the other hand, the so-called liberal Justices have expressed the opposite views, both in judicial opinions and extra-judicially, so the strength of their convictions must be deemed more serious and also indicative of the fact that the US Supreme Court could (unlikely, one would add at present) change its position sometime in the near future.

Thus, in *Printz v U.S.*,[13] Justice Breyer, after citing European practices, added that:

> Of course, we are interpreting our own Constitution, not those of other nations, and there may be relevant political and structural differences between their systems and our own. (...) But their experience may nonetheless cast an empirical light on the consequences of different solutions to a common problem – in this case the problem of reconciling central authority with the need to preserve the liberty-enhancing autonomy of a smaller constituent entity.

In *Atkins v Virginia*,[14] Justice Stevens stressed in a note that used evidence of widespread foreign practices that although this was

> by no means dispositive, their consistency with the legislative evidence lends further support to our conclusion that there is consensus among those who have addressed the issue.

---

[10] The strength of Justice Scalia's views is even more evident in his 'Commentary', 40 St. Louis U. L. J. 1119 ff where, referring to *United States v Alvarez-Machain*, 504 U.S. 655 (1992), he wrote '[there] we held that the United States' resort to self-help, even if a "shocking" [sic] violation of [public] international law, was not our concern (...).' The litigation there arose with the kidnapping of a Mexican citizen by the US authorities for a crime committed in Mexico, who then insisted that he should be extradited back to Mexico for trial by his own courts in accordance with an existing US–Mexican treaty.

[11] To them we must add Judge Richard Posner's more fully argued (extra-judicial) objections in his 'No thanks, we already have our own laws', 2004-AUG *Legal Affairs* 40. His views are considered more fully below in section 4.

[12] In favour of an open approach: 'Constitutional Courts – Comparative Remarks' in Kirchhof/Kommers (eds), *Germany and its Basic Law* (1993), p 412; contra in *Atkins v Virginia*, 306 US 304, 321 (2002). On the other hand, in *Washington v Glucksburg*, 521 U.S. 702, 710 and n. 8, 718 n 16 (1997), he referred to a decision of the Supreme Court of Canada upholding a ban on assisted suicide and observed that 'in almost every western democracy it is a crime to assist a suicide.' Would such an implicit acknowledgement of world practice had occurred if the outcome had been the other way? It is submitted that the Chief Justice's views display the kind of pragmatism that would allow him to invoke foreign practice if it supported the ideological position he favoured in any particular case.

[13] 521 US 898, 977 (1997).

[14] 536 US 304, 316 n 21 (2002).

As a result of such thinking (and evidence), the execution of mentally retarded criminals was seen as being prohibited by the Eighth Amendment.

Justice Ruth Bader Ginsburg seems to have sided with the same school of thought, both judicially[15] and extra-judicially,[16] while Justice Sandra Day O'Connor, moderately positioned on the right of the Court, has, on this issue, joined the liberal call for open-mindedness but has only done so extra-judicially and in essays that bear visibly the characteristics of an opening speech rather than a rigorous presentation of a scholarly position.[17]

The ambivalence of these dicta is further enhanced when one takes into account the fact that, occasionally, even an 'anti-foreign law' judge may, himself, have recourse to the 'condemned' practice. Thus, Justice Scalia, so extreme in his dislike of foreign law and yet so powerful by virtue of the strength of his convictions, in his dissent in *McIntyre v Ohio Elections Commission* himself invoked Australian, Canadian, and English law in the mid-1990s when dealing with the question whether the source of an election campaign leaflet opposing a school tax levy proposed in Ohio should be revealed to the public. He wrote:

> The third and last question relevant to our decision is whether the prohibition of anonymous campaigning is effective in protecting and enhancing democratic elections. In answering this question no, the Justices of the majority set their own views – on a practical matter that bears closely upon the real-life experience of elected politicians and not upon that of unelected judges – up against the views of 49 (and perhaps all 50 ...) state legislatures and the Federal Congress. We might also add to the list on the other side the legislatures of foreign democracies: Australia, Canada, and England, for example, all have prohibitions upon anonymous campaigning. See, e.g., Commonwealth Electoral Act 1918, § 328 (Australia); Canada Elections Act, R.S.C., ch. E-2, § 261 (1985); Representation of the People Act, 1983, § 110 (England). How is it, one must wonder, that all of these elected legislators, from around the country and around the world, could

---

[15] See *Grupo Mexicano de Desarrollo, S.A. v Alliance Bond Fund, Inc.*, 527 U.S. 308, 336–7 (1999) where (along with Justices Stevens, Souter, and Breyer) she dissented from the Court's static conception of equitable remedial authority. In that case the Court was asked (but refused) to apply the principles of the *Mareva* injunctions, fashioned by the English courts since the seminal judgment of Lord Denning in *Mareva Compania Naviera S.A. v Int'l Bulkcarriers S.A.*, 2 Lloyd's Rep. 509 (C.A. 1975).

[16] 'Looking beyond our borders: The value of a comparative perspective in constitutional adjudication', 40 *Idaho L. Rev.* 1 ff.

[17] Thus, see 'Broadening our Horizons: Why American Lawyers must learn about Foreign Law', 45 SEP *Fed. Law* 20 and 'Keynote Address', Proceedings of the 96th Annual Meeting of the American Society of International Law, (2002) *Am. Soc'y Int'l L.* 348, 350.

> not see what six Justices of this Court see so clearly that they are willing to require the entire Nation to act upon it: that requiring identification of the source of campaign literature does not improve the quality of the campaign?[18]

How can a judge who denounces so strongly references to foreign law when opposing moves to decriminalise sodomy or restrict the application of the death penalty *nonetheless* invoke foreign examples himself when taking a tough line on political campaigning? It would be too crass to accuse the learned Justice of intellectual opportunism, not least since intelligent men tend to cover up well the tracks of such conduct and here there is not the slightest evidence of covering up. More in line with the general thrust of this essay would thus be to argue that judges are *selective* in their use of foreign law, making use of it in some areas but not in others. This way of explaining such quotes is, in fact, more than a hypothesis; it is a way of formulating the challenge (for us and others interested in the topic) of discovering *normative* rules that can help identify those areas where recourse to foreign law is desirable, and even necessary, from those where it is not. We will return to this problem later, particularly in Chapter 3 of this book.

In the light of the above one thing is clear: the growing academic literature in America has not surprisingly taken a mixed, if not, on the whole, a hostile view to the issue, and the question is to what extent have academics and the judicial protagonists considered in depth the practice of other courts. As stated, our intention is to review how these issues have been handled in other systems and then examine in Chapter 3 the type of situations where recourse to foreign law seems to us desirable. Chapter 4 will then bring to a close this part of the enquiry by addressing the dangers that stem from the use (or misuse) of foreign law, leaving it to Chapter 5 to bring the discussion to its conclusion.

For convenience's sake we have placed some of the major legal systems into four categories: those which do not seem to favour recourse to foreign law (already briefly discussed in this section); those who have recourse to it, but do not admit it openly; those which do so openly; and, finally, those who do it not only openly but almost as a regular practice. Before we turn to them, however, we must touch upon one or two important issues which run through our narrative.

The case law of the last two categories or groups of countries (i.e. those which openly cite foreign law) raises issues of particular interest which are only now beginning to be addressed. The first and paramount of these is to find out whether the citing judge looks at foreign law because he genuinely feels it may contain an idea that may help shape his

---

18 *McIntyre v Ohio Elections Commission*, 514 U.S. 334 at 381/382.

own law or whether he has recourse to foreign law simply because he believes that by contrasting it with what he already knows foreign ideas will help sharpen his own perception of the problem. Though the first frame of mind often leads to accepting a foreign rule more than the second (which may, after consideration, decide to reject it), they are both 'intellectually' worthy of attention and should be contrasted with a third way of using foreign material, which is usually a mere 'padding' for a judgment already reached on other grounds.

Resolving the first issue can, in turn, raise others such as: 'Why has the judge looked at foreign law?' 'Was he prompted (or simply not prohibited) by his own legal order?' 'Why does the citing judge choose one system rather than another?' 'Is there anything that bars a judge from using foreign law in one type of case but not another?' 'Can judges seek their models in different systems depending on their subject matter?' And 'can judges stray away from their genealogical ancestors as a result of modern realties more linked to commerce, finance, and politics than language, history, and culture?'

In what follows we address some of these issues, conscious of the fact that all deserve more attention than we can give them in the space of a short monograph. We also attempt to analyse the problem in as wide a manner as possible, so we look at two systems in each category but (for reasons of space) do so only briefly. The rich footnotes should, however, aid those of the readers who wish to find out more for themselves.

2. Using (overtly or covertly) foreign law: the experience in six further systems

a) *Doing it but not admitting: the examples of Italy and France*

(i) Italy

Italian courts are among those which do not cite academic authorities in their judgments, be they of national or international origin. Indeed, such citation is prohibited by Art 118.3 of the Rules Concerning the Application of the Code of Civil Procedure (1942). This, however, does not mean that Italian judges do not consult academic literature. Indeed, there is emerging (and, arguably, widespread) consensus that in the field of private and commercial law[19] some important national innovations

[19] Unlike their French counterparts, Italian administrative courts seem to have thus far shown little interest in foreign law, having instead shown a preference 'towards a hand-made, domestic product'. On this see Aldo Sanduli, 'The Use of Comparative Law Before the Italian Public Law Courts', in Guy Canivet, Mads Andenas, and Duncan Fairgrieve (eds), *Comparative Law Before the Courts* (2004), pp 165, 175.

have been the result of extra-judicial meetings and exchanges between judges and academics, an exchange process which is aided by the healthy state of comparative law studies at university level (more about this at the end of this sub-section). The development of the particular Italian heading of damage known as *danno biologico*,[20] pioneered by the regional courts of Genoa, may owe its origins to such exchanges with the academic world;[21] and the Italian law of privacy may also owe its present form to international influences.

Though this unofficial evidence suggests that this interest extends to foreign law and literature, it is important to note that it has not been documented in a fully reliable manner. Among the academics who have supported this view we find Professor Alessandro Somma, whose work cites instances where such influences appear in the judgements.[22] It has to be admitted that they are not numerous.

This academic belief that foreign ideas lie hidden behind judicial opinions which are silent (or, at least, inconclusive) as to their (foreign) sources of inspiration has, even more recently, received further support by one of Italy's most prolific and widely read scholars, Professor Guido Alpa. Thus, chapter 1.5 of a recently published monograph[23] is entitled 'The Use of Foreign Law by Judges'. This title is, in itself, both revealing and, perhaps, a sign of the times. In it our colleague provides a series of wide-ranging illustrations which show Italian law changing under the influence of foreign ideas. Intriguingly, Professor Alpa also implies that these borrowings are evident from the decisions, themselves. But since he writes in the Continental European tradition, giving references in his footnotes mostly to academic writings and less so to decisional law, we have not been able to verify whether the linkage has been 'open' or can be surmised only by local experts. More unfortunate is the fact that one cannot discuss how Italian judges have used the foreign ideas, for example, as supplementary arguments or as a testing ground for the validity of their own solutions, and from which system these ideas have been mostly borrowed. Thus, if the above practice means that Italian courts cannot be placed (as their South African or Canadian sister courts are) among the leaders of the world in the use of foreign law and ideas, it does suggest that the practice of looking abroad may, nonetheless, be

---

[20] Explained and discussed in B. S. Markesinis, Michael Coester, Guido Alpa, and Augustus Ullstein, *Compensation for Personal Injury in English, German and Italian Law* (CUP 2005), chapters 1 and 2.

[21] For further details see Markesinis/Coester/Alpa/Ullstein, ibid, pp 84 ff.

[22] *L'uso giursprudenziale della comparazione nel diritto interno e comunitario* (2001).

[23] *Tradition and Europeanization in Italian Law* (2005).

growing. More important, for long-term developments, is the fact that Italian authors are beginning to feel the need to discuss this phenomenon, more than they did in the past.

Indeed, the Italian scene changes dramatically if we shift our attention to academically proclaimed interest in foreign law and this may, indirectly, explain the slow awakening of Italian judges to the possibilities offered by comparative methodology. For, if the judicial references to foreign law and ideas are poor and of little if any value to potential 'borrowers', the overall state of *academic* comparative studies in Italy is among the healthiest in Europe – if not the world. This is in no small measure due to the efforts of such 'grand-masters' of the subject as the late Professor Gino Gorla and, more recently, Professor Rodolfo Sacco – a tradition continued and even expanded by scholars such as (the late) Mauro Cappelletti (especially in the domain of civil procedure), Antonio Gambaro, Maurizio Lupoi, Guido Alpa, and Mario Bussani (to mention but a few). Individually, and along with others, the above have generated a healthy Italian school of comparatists which has extended its reach to include the United States and Germany, and in productivity terms (and, arguably, originality) surpasses what one finds in other countries such as England and France. Since the academic side of comparative law is not, however, part of this essay's main focus we leave the discussion of their work for another occasion, noting simply the fact that the foundations for future growth of comparative law are well established in this country of fertile legal minds.

(ii) France

French law, likewise, belongs to this category, the judgments of France's superior civil (and, to a lesser extent, administrative) courts being known for their brevity. Indeed, citing academic authority in a judgment as a reason for the solution reached by the court would be a ground for a *pourvois* (legal challenge) before the *Cour de cassation*![24] The current First President of the *Cour de cassation*, M. Guy Canivet, has no doubt

---

24 Though the Conseil d' Etat – the supreme administrative court of the country – has shown a greater willingness to cite foreign law and, recently, broken with tradition and cited in one of its opinions a judgment of the English High Court; see CE No 260768 of 29 October 2003. For more details of this developing story see M. Justice Roger Errera's account in 'The Use of Comparative Law Before the French Administrative Law Courts', in Guy Canivet, Mads Andenas, and Duncan Fairgrieve (op. cit. note 19) at pp 153 ff.

that this is [the?][25] main reason why French courts have not used foreign law overtly. He puts his idea in this way:[26]

> En France, la Cour de cassation et les autres juridictions son *structurellement* contraintes, par le style d'écriture traditionnel de l'arrêt à phrase unique et l'impossibilité de l'explication interprétative de la règle, à ne pas se referrer *expressément* aux droits étrangers dans le corps meme de l' arrêt.

Yet, as the last seven words of the First President's text suggest, what the French judgments conceal as a result of a long historical tradition, the *conclusions* of the *avocats généreaux* (who advise the *Cour de cassation* but do not take part in the drafting of the actual judgment and have no vote on it) increasingly make clear. These documents, longer and replete with references to the earlier case law of the Court *and* to academic literature, show clearly the dialogue between judges and academics, mainly the French *arrêtistes*, who tend to flesh out (and praise or criticise) the decisions of the Court. Along with the report produced by the *juge-raporteur* (i.e. the judge chosen by the panel to write the first draft of the proposed opinion) these texts are, nowadays, published with greater frequency than they were in the past; and, under the inspiration of M. Canivet, have been encouraged to reveal a growing interest in foreign law. Indeed, we are told that these reporters are nowadays *expected* to consult foreign law when preparing their recommendations, and the *Service de documentation et d'études* of the Court (currently headed by M. le Conseiller Alain Lacabarats) has been set up to assist in this exciting new development. Additionally, M. Canivet has both described and strongly supported this trend in a number of extra-judicial statements made while the guest of learned societies[27] or in contributions published in various Festschriften.[28] The controversial but fascinating

---

[25] The first of the authors, in a lecture to be delivered at the French Academy in March 2006 and entitled 'Auto-suffisance nationale ou arrogance internationale? Le droit étranger et les notions contemporaines de justice devant le juge américain et le juge français' questions whether this is the only reason why French lawyers in general have, on the whole, shied away from the use of foreign law. He there suggests that French academics and their State-run infrastructure may account for a degree of 'ethnocentricity' which resembles the current American introversion even though it stems from different reasons. Many French academics have the courage to admit these shortcomings; see, for instance, Olivier Moréteau, 'Ne tirez pas sur le comparatiste', Dalloz 2005, no 7, pp 452 ff.

[26] Op. cit. note 5 at p 45 (our emphasis).

[27] See 'The Use of Comparative Law Before the French Private Law Courts', in Guy Canivet, Mads Andenas, and Duncan Fairgrieve (op. cit. note 19) at pp 181 ff.

[28] For instance, 'Le role du juge dans un monde en mutation' in: *Claire L'Heureux-Dubé à la cour suprème du Canada 1987–2002* (2003), 25 ff; 'La convergence des systèmes juridique du point de vue du droit privé français', *European Review of Private Law*, Vol 11, no. 1 (2003), pp 50 ff; 'La convergence des systèmes juridiques par l'action du juge', *Mélanges Xavier Blanc-Jouvan* (2005), pp 11 ff.

Perruche litigation,[29] which dealt with claims of wrongful birth and wrongful life (and was eventually overruled by hastily drafted legislation supported by diverse, mainly religious, interest groups), gives some interesting insights into this new and developing trend.[30] Overall, however, the French courts, though showing signs of being influenced by foreign ideas, have not yet acquired a leadership position in this area of the law. In part, this may be due to what, at least to us, seems to be a lack of dedicated and focused study of foreign law by the present generation of French academics.[31] This is further accentuated by the brevity and style of the judicial decisions. The most obvious clues as to foreign influences come from decisions which have been forced to adapt national law as a result of the dictates of European directives.[32]

b) Doing it openly: England and Germany

England and Germany belong to this category; and, again, they must be looked at separately.

(i) England

Since approximately the mid-1970s onwards, British judges have taken to writing articles with an ever-growing comparative element. Originally, the impetus was provided by the European Convention on Human Rights, which, though England helped draft and ratified in 1951, was not incorporated into national law until the Human Rights Act 1998 (which came into effect in 2000). Though understandably of unequal quality, these pieces (unlike most of the extra-judicial pronouncements of their American counterparts, which tend to be short opening addresses at conferences or legal meetings) are article-sized essays (of the usual English length of between 8,000 to 10,000 words) and are well supported by notes and references. For completeness sake we thus refer the reader indicatively and in passing to the writings of Lord Scarman,[33] Lord

---

[29] See JCP, 13 December 2000, No 50, 2293 ff.

[30] For a comparative discussion of the decision see B. S. Markesinis, 'Réflexions d'un comparatiste anglais sur et à partir de l'arrêt Perruche', *RTD civ.* (1), 77–102.

[31] Though the work of Professor Mireille Delmas-Marty of the *Collège de France*, especially in the area of comparative criminal law, deserves special mention.

[32] Sometimes even going beyond what the directives require. For illustrations see the discussion of Guy Canivet, 'La convergence des systèmes juridiques du point de vue du droit privé français', *European Review of Private Law* (2003), 50, 53.

[33] His seminal Hamlyn Lectures *English Law – the New Dimension* (1974) could be credited for having started this whole debate in its contemporary form.

Woolf,[34] Lord Bingham,[35] Lord Browne-Wilkinson,[36] Lord Steyn,[37] Lord Hoffmann,[38]Mr Justice Laws,[39] Mr Justice Sedley,[40] Lord Justice Schiemann (now Judge Schiemann at the European Court of Justice)[41] and, indeed, the former Lord Chancellor, Lord Irvine of Lairg.[42] In England the trend of publishing judicial speeches is, if anything, gaining strength and may well be a phenomenon without parallel in Europe, Germany excepted.

Much more important, however, has been the trend that has gained momentum since the early 1990s for judges to invoke foreign law as supporting/supplementary evidence of what they are trying to achieve. Though not numerically significant, this (newer) trend is noteworthy not only for the detail which the citation has, at times, achieved, but also for the fact that it has attracted the support of some of Great Britain's most academically minded judges such as Lords Goff, Woolf, Bingham, Steyn, and others. Thus, among the cases citing foreign law and academic authority about foreign law – and we do not include in this list decisions referring to foreign law in the process of construing international conventions or because conflicts rules made this obligatory – we note the following which have appeared in the space of the last 10 years: *White v Jones*;[43] *Henderson v Merrett Syndicates Ltd.*;[44] *Hunter & Others v*

---

[34] E.g., the Hamlyn Lectures *Protection of the Public: A New Challenge* (1990). See also his F. A. Mann Lecture entitled 'Droit Public – English Style', [1995] *Public Law* 57 ff.

[35] 'The European Convention on Human Rights: Time to Incorporate', The Denning Lecture, reprinted in Richard Gordon and Richard Wilmot-Smith (eds), *Human Rights in the United Kingdom* (1996), pp I–II; 'Should there be a Law to Protect Rights of Personal Privacy?' [1996] *European Human Rights Law Review*, 450 ff.

[36] 'The Infiltration of a Bill of Rights', [1992] *Public Law* 397 ff.

[37] A number of his public speeches recently appeared in book form under the title, *Democracy Through Law: Selected Speeches and Judgments* (2004).

[38] 'A Sense of Proportion' in F. Jacobs and M. Andenas (eds), *Community Law in English Courts* (1998).

[39] 'The Ghost in the Machine: Principle in Public Law', [1989] *Public Law* 27 ff; 'Is the High Court the Guardian of Fundamental Constitutional Rights?' [1993] *Public Law* 59 ff; 'Law and Democracy', [1995] *Public Law* 72 ff.

[40] 'The Sound of Silence: Constitutional Law Without a Constitution', (1994) in *Law Quarterly Review* 270 ff; 'Human Rights: A Twenty-First century Agenda', [1995] *Public Law* 386 ff.

[41] 'Recent German and French influences on the development of English law' in Reiner Schulze and Ulrike Seif (eds), *Richterrecht und Rechtsfortbildung in der Europäischen Rechtsgemeinschaft* (2003), pp 189 ff.

[42] 'Judges and Decision-Makers: The Theory and Practice of *Wednesbury* Review', [1996] *Public Law* 59 ff.

[43] [1995] 2 AC 207.

[44] [1995] 2 AC 145.

Canary Wharf Ltd.;[45] *Barry v Midland Bank plc*;[46] *Co-operative Insurance Society Ltd v Argyll Stores (Holdings) Ltd*[47] *McFarlane v Tayside Health Board*;[48] *Arthur JS Hall & Co. v Simons*;[49] *Michael Douglas, Catherine Zeta-Jones, Northerm and Shell plc. v Hello! Ltd.*;[50] *Greatorex v Greatorex*;[51] *Alfred McAlpine Construction Ltd. v Panatown Ltd.*;[52] *A and Others v National Blood Authority*;[53] *Campbell v Mirror Group Newspapers Ltd.*;[54] *Fairchild v Glenhaven Funeral Services Ltd.*;[55] *The Starsin*,[56] and, most recently, *JD (FC) v East Berkshire Community Health NHS Trust and others*.[57] For high courts with a small load of annually published judgements, especially if compared with Continental European jurisdictions, this is, if not a record, certainly a promising trend.

Elation must, however, be kept in check. For in most of these cases the use of the foreign law was 'supplementary' and, on the whole, 'supportive' of the main thrust of the *English* argument. On the other hand, in some cases – for example, *White v Jones* and *Fairchild v Glenhaven* – recourse to foreign ideas was extensive, in breadth as well as depth, and was accompanied by dicta of considerable utility to anyone applying the method in practice. Moreover, in this list of cases we have not included decisions, usually of the Privy Council, dealing with constitutional/criminal law matters (and often the availability of the death penalty in Caribbean states)[58] where the citation of foreign law has been both extensive and much more integrated in the judgment,

---

45 [1997] AC 655.

46 [1998] 1 All. E. R. 805.

47 [1998] AC 1.

48 [2000] 2 AC 59.

49 [2000] 3 WLR 543.

50 [2000] EWCA Civ 353.

51 [2000] 1 WLR 1970.

52 [2001] 1 AC 518.

53 [2001] EWHC QB 446; [2001] 3 All E.R. 289.

54 [2002] EWCA Civ 1373.

55 [2002] 1 AC 32.

56 [2003] UKHL 12.

57 [2005] UKHL 23.

58 See, for instance, *Pratt v Attorney General for Jamaica*, [1994] 2 AC 1; *Reyes v The Queen*, [2002] 2 AC 235, and *Charles Matthew v The State*, No 12 of 2004 [2004] WL 1372517.

forming an integral and decorative part of it.[59] But to return to the private law decisions mentioned above, noticeable in particular are three points.

First is the sophistication of some of the citations. In the *Fairchild* case we find, probably, the best example of what Professor McCormick has called 'substantive' rather than merely 'passing' citation – that is, an example where 'the citing judge[s] elaborate on the specific content of the cited case[s] [or material]'.[60] Thus, two of the five judges in that case – Lords Bingham and Roger of Earlsferry – gave us references to the German practitioners' commentary of *Palandt* (a 'difficult' book even for German lawyers to use) as well as the *Motive* of the BGB (i.e. the preparatory works that justified and explained the decisions adopted by the authors of the German Civil Code).

Second, in the *Fairchild* case it was their Lordships (and not Counsel) who took the initiative and asked to be addressed on the solutions adopted by civilian law systems. But they do not simply use the information they personally had but, quite properly (if one may say so) asked Counsel to extend their research and argument beyond the traditional consideration of Commonwealth and American authority and to advise them on the attitudes prevalent in civilian systems. The source of this new 'interest' is thus as notable as the fact that by asking Counsel to give their views in open court on this foreign jurisprudence, the British judges avoided the complaint voiced by Justice Scalia in the recent American case of *Roper* (discussed in greater detail in Chapter 5) to the effect that in that latter case foreign law was never subjected to open and critical discussion in the courtroom. At a lower but no less interesting level, the same occurred in the blood-contamination case of *A and Others v National Blood Authority*,[61] in many respects a model of 'comparative law in action'.

---

[59] For the period 1972–93, Peter de Cruz thus identified in English court decisions 40 references to American cases, 35 to Australian cases, 34 to Canadian cases, and 27 to decisions from New Zealand, while mentioning that Continental European systems have rarely been cited despite Britain's accession to the European Community in 1972. He points out, however, that 'such citations would only be made if the need arose to consider a foreign law as in a conflict of laws situation', which is not our primary point of interest here. See Peter de Cruz, *Comparative Law in a Changing World* (2nd edn, 1999), no 8.5.7. It is also interesting to contrast these findings with the series of more recent references to Continental European law beginning in the mid-1990s.

[60] Peter McCormick, 'What Supreme Court Cases Does the Supreme Court Cite?: Follow-up Citations on the Supreme Court of Canada, 1989–1993', *Supreme Court Law Review*, vol. 7(2d) 451, at p 459 (1996).

[61] [2001] EWHC QB 446; [2001] 3 All E.R. 289.

Third, their Lordships were in some of these cases made aware of the fact that the major legal systems of the world were not in accord as to which solution to adopt. Thus, in the *Henderson* case they weighed the respective merits of French and German law on the question of cumulation of contractual and tortious remedies (broadly speaking, the first prohibits it, the second allows it), consulted the relevant literature, and finally came down in favour of the German (and American) view. In the *Fairchild* case, faced with even greater diversity, Lord Bingham warned:[62]

> Development of the law in this country [the UK] can not of course depend on a head count of decisions and codes adopted in other countries around the world, often against a background of different rules and traditions. The law must be developed coherently, in accordance with principle, so as to serve, even-handedly, the ends of justice. If however a decision is given in this country which offends one's basic sense of justice, and if consideration of international sources suggests that a different and more acceptable decision would be given in most other jurisdictions, whatever their legal tradition, this must prompt review of the decision in question.

And in the *McFarlane* case Lord Steyn expressed the same idea in a manner which is particularly relevant to the thesis of this paper when he argued that

> (...) the discipline of comparative law does not aim at a poll of the solutions adopted in different countries. It has the different and inestimable value of sharpening our focus on the weight of competing considerations.[63]

These observations merit special attention since they address an objection often raised by those opposed to the use of foreign law. Typically, this objection is phrased either in the form of, for example, 'why cite German and not French law?' or 'how do we know that what is cited is accurate and/or up to date?' Each of these questions can justify long replies but here are some brief reactions[64] to them. A variant of the above is now emerging in American decisions and academic literature and asks the question 'why look at foreign systems in one type of problem and not in others?'

With regard to the first, one must come to accept that the chances of foreign courts using the case law of major and established systems are far greater than of having recourse to the outpourings of 'lesser' courts. The answer is determined not only by the fact that some systems have,

---

62 Op. cit. note 5 at p 66.

63 [2000] 2 AC 59 at 81.

64 Brief, for we return to these understandable worries and discuss them in greater detail in Chapter 4.

traditionally, acted as 'parent' systems for most others but also because some courts have, over a long period of time, earned their place as opinion formers whose views are worthy, at the very least, of serious consideration. But more modern courts can 'earn their spurs' (as the Constitutional Court of South Africa clearly demonstrates) while what we called – without any intent to offend – 'lesser' systems have also occasionally been able to innovate in a way that deserves attention. At the end of the day, however, one must not ignore the very pragmatic argument that language limitations may restrict the extent of these 'fishing expeditions' though, as is explained below, the growing number of electronically available material is enlarging the availability of foreign primary material.

The second (and very valid) fear is addressed in greater detail below in Chapter 4 while the third and last question is also mentioned towards the end of this book.

(ii) Germany

The presentation of German law calls of an introduction of its own for in terms of geographical spread it has not rivalled either the common law or French law. Language difficulties as well as an inchoate suspicion or even dislike of things German has also not helped this system in modern times achieve the geographical radiance it deserves. And yet, its long pedigree and its undoubted intellectual robustness has earned it not just admirers the world over but also increased attention in some quarters. Though England has been slow to take up this challenge, South African courts, as we shall see below, have met it head on and greatly benefited from it.

The relationship with America is more complex, indeed in some respects intriguing for the links are mainly of an academic rather than judicial kind. Its traces can thus be found mainly in the American legal literature and, this is one of its intriguing aspects, more often in the works of political scientists whose work has a bearing on constitutional law than lawyers, proper. The revived interest in the work of Carl Schmitt, a brilliant German scholar severely compromised by his pro-Nazi and overtly anti-Semitic tendencies, is one example and was briefly touched upon in Chapter 1. This American interest in German 'theorising' is returned by German Constitutional Court judges, for their writings and (if not as frequently as one would wish) judgments display a keen interest in American law. These observations are made here solely to link the account that follows with what was said in the first chapter about American constitutional theorising and how mirrored this is in the German literature. German federalism is another example where one finds a (mutual) interest and, even, potential competition for 'new' countries seeking to imitate one or the other model. On the other hand, the truly amazing case law of the German Federal Constitutional Court on human rights issues remains to be discovered.

In matters of private law, the current attempts to produce a European private code (the *von Bar*-project) or establish commonly prevailing principles of tort law (the European Group on Tort Law headed by, *inter alia*, Professors Helmut Koziol from Vienna and Ulrich Magnus from Hamburg) are basically in 'German' hands, though one must also mention the 'Trento Project' run mainly from Italy. The above examples, mentioned indicatively, thus strengthen our view, expressed here and elsewhere, that in matters of pure university scholarship there is little doubt that Italian and German comparatists dominate the scene.

But let us now turn to specifics.

In German law and practice[65] we note a picture similar in mentality but dissimilar in emphasis and intensity than that found in England. What follows, which to some extent draws on the research of German colleagues, again focuses on the 'true' types of comparative law (i.e. *not* those where the court is 'obliged' by the nature of the subject or rules of conflict to look at foreign law). One must also note that in Germany the plethora of different, specialised courts means that one must distinguish between the practices of each of them. For practical purposes, however, what is of most interest are the FCC and the Federal Supreme Court (*Bundesgerichtshof*, BGH, which decides cases in the areas of private and criminal law).

In an article published some 20 years ago Professor Ulrich Drobnig identified seven decisions of the *Bundesgerichtshof*, one decision of the Federal Administrative Court (*Bundesverwaltungsgericht*), and two decisions of the *Bundesverfassungsgericht* resorting to foreign law.[66] Writing in 2000, that is, 14 years later, Professor Hein Kötz pointed to seven additional decisions of the *Bundesgerichtshof* and concluded that the voluntary use of the comparative method is still confined to exceptional cases in Germany.[67] These decisions referred to issues of tort law,[68] family

---

[65] In this section we draw heavily on our material which first appeared in B. S. Markesinis, *Comparative Law in the Courtroom and the Classroom. The Story of the last Thirty-Five Years* (2003), chapter 3.

[66] U. Drobnig, 'Rechtsvergleichung in der Deutschen Rechtsprechung', (1986) 50 *RabelsZ* 610, 611.

[67] H. Kötz, 'Der Bundesgerichtshof und die Rechtsvergleichung' in Heldrich and Hopt (eds), *50 Jahre Bundesgerichtshof, Festgabe der Wissenschaft, Band II* (2000), p 842.

[68] Infringement of personality rights: BGHZ 35, 363 ff (of 1961); BGHZ 39, 124 ff (of 1963); BGHZ 131, 332 ff (of 1995); BVerfGE 34, 269 ff (of 1973). Compensation for damage suffered in the course of dangerous sports activities: BGHZ 63, 140 ff (of 1974). Wrongful life: BGHZ 86, 240 ff (of 1983). Rescue doctrine: BGHZ 101, 215 ff (of 1987). Claims based on tort if the requirements of claims based on sales contracts are precluded: BGHZ 101, 337 ff (of 1987). Duty of a tortfeasor to pay compensation although the victim continues to be paid by an employer during sick leave on the basis of § 616 BGB: BGHZ 21, 112 ff (of 1956).

law,[69] labour law,[70] criminal law,[71] and administrative law.[72] Interestingly enough, Professor Bernhard Aubin, writing in 1970,[73] argued that the Imperial Supreme Court had been more open to the use of comparative material than its republican successor.[74] Thus, 17 decisions, handed down between 1909 and 1928, made use of foreign legal material, a large number of these cases dealing with issues related to limited liability companies.[75]

In another study on the use of foreign material in cases involving only constitutional law issues, Professor Jörg Manfred Mössner counted 24 decisions of the *Bundesverfassungsgericht* which had recourse to comparative law. To these he adds two further decisions from State constitutional courts, two decisions of the *Bundesgerichtshof*, and one decision of the *Landgericht* Lübeck.[76] All of these decisions involved a 'voluntary' use of comparative law and dealt with the interpretation of basic concepts of the German Constitution with the help of foreign material.[77]

---

69 BVerfGE 36, 146 ff (of 1973).

70 BGHZ 24, 214 ff (of 1957).

71 BGHSt 1, 293 ff (of 1951); BGHSt 9, 385 ff (of 1956); BGHSt 32, 345 ff (of 1984); BGHSt 38, 214 ff (of 1992); BGHSt 44, 308 ff (of 1998).

72 BVerwGE 12, 42 ff (of 1961).

73 B. Aubin, 'Die Rechtsvergleichende Interpretation autonom-internen Rechts in der deutschen Rechtsprechung', (1970) 34 *RabelsZ* 458 ff.

74 English and American lawyers (judges and academics) were also more comparatively minded during the nineteenth century, especially its second half, than most of their successors were during the middle years of the twentieth century. One reason of this may have been the effects of the First and, even more so, the Second World War. But this may explain only the reduction in interest in German law, and the whole subject still awaits a more comprehensive examination.

75 RGZ 74, 276 ff (of 1910); RGZ 77, 152 ff (of 1911); RGZ 79, 332 ff (of 1912); RGZ 80, 385 ff (of 1912); RGZ 82, 116 ff (of 1913); RGZ 84, 419 ff (of 1914); RGZ 123, 102 ff (of 1928).

76 J. M. Mössner, 'Rechtsvergleichung und Verfassungsrechtsprechung', (1974) AöR 193 ff.

77 Parliamentary system: BVerfGE 1, 144 ff (of 1952) on parliamentary procedures concerning money bills; BVerfGE 1, 208 ff (of 1952) on election principles; OVGE 12, 470 ff on the participation of cabinet members in parliamentary commissions of inquiry; BVerfGE 4, 144 ff (of 1955) and BVerfGE 32, 157 ff (of 1971) on the expenses of MPs. Social state principle (*Sozialstaatsprinzip*): BVerfGE 1, 97 ff (of 1951). Division of powers: BVerfGE 3, 225 ff (of 1953); BGHZ 10, 266 ff (of 1953) and LG Lübeck NJW 1953, 907 ff. Definition of political treaties within the meaning of Article 59(2) Basic Law: BVerfGE 1, 372 ff (of 1952). Prohibition of political parties: BVerfGE 5, 85 ff (of 1956). Extradition: BVerfGE 4, 299 ff (of 1955) and BVerfGE 18, 112 ff (of 1964). Adjudication of law enacted by the Allies during their occupation of Germany after 1945 (so-called *Besatzungsrecht*): BVerfGE 2, 181 ff (of 1953). Analogous application of time limits:

Just as interesting is to see which (foreign) legal systems served as models for inspiration for the German courts. In the decisions looked at by Mössner, the United States headed the list with nine examples. It was followed by Switzerland with eight, France with four, the United Kingdom with three, Austria with three, Italy with two, and the Netherlands, Norway, and Sweden each having one. The International Court of Justice was also used in one instance. Eleven cases referred to 'foreign experience' in general without identifying a particular country.[78]

These statistics suggest that courts seem more willing to look at systems outside Germany's own (private law) legal family when dealing with constitutional issues than they are in matters pertaining to private law (where comparative material is more often taken from Austria and Switzerland).[79] This would suggest that the language barrier may play a part in this 'reluctance' to consult foreign material but that it is by no means an insurmountable obstacle. Especially in the early years of the Constitutional Court language proved less of an inhibiting factor since a substantial minority of these justices had either studied or taught in the United States and England or lived there as political refugees.

The studies also indicate that German courts use the comparative method with caution, in some instances even with an undesirable (one might add: unexpected) degree of uncertainty. Many comparative observations are thus left undocumented, with decisions often referring vaguely 'to the situation in other legal systems' without further qualification,[80] or making use of unspecified quotations.[81] Given the German punctiliousness this is a somewhat surprising practice and may suggest lack of confidence on the part of the citing judge in the thoroughness and reliability of his understanding of foreign law.

BVerfGE 4, 31 ff (of 1954). Validity of penal judgments pronounced in the absence of the accused: BVerfGE 1, 332 ff (of 1952) and BGH NJW 1965, 1146 ff. Right of members of the press to give evidence in criminal proceedings concerning treason: BVerfGE 20, 162 ff (of 1966). Freedom of expression: BVerfGE 1, 198 ff (of 1951). Nature of laws dealing with press delicts (State laws, not federal criminal law): BVerfGE 7, 29 ff (of 1957). Family law: BVerfGE 10, 59 ff (of 1959). Freedom of artistic opinion: BVerfGE 30, 173 ff (of 1971). Freedom of occupation: BVerfGE 7, 377 ff (of 1958) and BVerfGE 21, 245 ff (of 1967). Constitutional complaint (*Verfassungsbeschwerde*): BVerfGE 1, 97 ff (of 1951).

78 Mössner, op. cit. note 76, p 228.

79 Drobnig, op. cit. note 66, p 626. We, may, by the way, be faced with a similar pattern in South Africa which in public law matters seems to have been more adventurous than it has when dealing with private law.

80 Mössner has counted 11 unspecified comparative arguments in 29 decisions. These decisions frequently use phrases such as 'the development of this area of law in other countries' or refer to 'international developments'.

81 One example is the unspecified quotation of Cardozo in the famous *Lüth*-decision of the *Bundesverfassungsgericht* (BVerfGE 7, 198 at p 208).

Equally understandable, but perhaps also surprising, is a certain degree of 'mistrust' of material which comes from a different legal family. This is obvious in one of the early leading 'wrongful life' decisions where the *Bundesgerichtshof* mentioned English and US case law but cautioned against an unqualified reliance on this material. After emphasising the absence of comparable German cases the Court thus stated:

> It appears that foreign experience, *which can already be of only limited value to national law because of the different legal foundations* [in other countries], can be found in England and the United States.[82]

The BGH noted that the claim of the child against the doctor had been rejected in *McKay v Essex Health Authority and Another*,[83] and that legislation in Great Britain, passed a few years earlier,[84] had, similarly, excluded claims of this nature. On the other hand, concerning US law the *Bundesgerichtshof* was, arguably, less accurate in its use of foreign law – citing *Curlender v Bio-Science*[85] as a decision awarding compensation to the child but failing to mention the subsequent decision of *Turpin v Sortini*,[86] which had overruled *Curlender* and given the child 'special' damages only. Nonetheless, the most surprising (indeed disappointing) feature of the decision is the suspicion shown by the BGH towards foreign, especially non-Germanic law. We stress this since the issue before the Court was not one that depends for its solution on a specific legal provision of the German Civil Code but deals with a wider philosophical issue that transcends state borders (and even religious beliefs), and thus makes legal borrowing instructive – if not even necessary.

By contrast the *Bundesverfassungsgericht* has, as already stated, shown itself more open to comparative law *in general* (and, again, we note a certain parallel with South Africa). Commenting in December 1953 on the rapid development of family law by German courts over the preceding eight months,[87] the FCC thus expressly included comparative

---

[82] BGHZ 86, 240 at p 250 (our emphasis).

[83] [1982] 2 WLR 890.

[84] Congenital Disabilities (Civil Liability) Act 1976.

[85] 106 Call. App. 3d 811, 165 Cal. Rptr. 477 (1980).

[86] 31 Cal. Rptr. 3rd 220, 643 P. 2d 954 (1982).

[87] This judicial 'hyperactivity' was caused by the fact that the Federal Parliament had failed to adapt all provisions of the Civil Code which contravened the principle of equality established by the Constitution of 1949. Article 117 had given the Federal Parliament up until 31 March 1953 to do this and when the date passed without this task being accomplished, the Federal Supreme Court began to unpick one provision of the Civil Code after the other and re-fashion the law on a case law basis. For an account in English see B. S. Markesinis and S. Enchelmeier, 'The Applicability of Human Rights as between Individuals under German Constitutional Law', in B. S. Markesinis (ed), *Always on the Same Path. Essays in Foreign Law and Comparative Methodology* (2001), Vol. II, chapter 8.

law in its list of accepted and well-proven judicial techniques. The judgment stated:

> The courts have quite rightly not seen it as their task to completely restructure the area of matrimonial and family law. They have rather felt themselves bound by the existing laws insofar as they are not incompatible with Article 3(2) BL. On this basis, a number of issues could easily be resolved by the judges through the adoption of quite obvious solutions. In all other cases, courts have made use of the tried and tested judicial techniques, i.e. legal interpretation and the closing of gaps in the law, *also with help of the comparative method*, and have taken into particular consideration the essentially unanimous demands concerning the equality of man and woman – crucial also for the purposes of legal interpretation – which have been voiced in the discussion over the past five decades.[88]

This clear, if brief, endorsement of comparative work by German judges is one of the rare cases in which the *Bundesverfassungsgericht* has actually indicated – in abstract terms – a position on the *methodological* status of foreign law in German judgments. This may be surprising (especially in the light of the open discussions about the merits and dangers of comparative law in contemporary US, English, and South African judgments). Yet, in part at least, it can be explained by the different style of German decisions, which are traditionally focused on the solution of a case and will not often feature abstract methodological discussion, for example on the role of foreign law in the work of a court. One must also bear in mind that the general 'climate' in 1953 regarding comparative law was, the world over, certainly a different one than it is today.

The famous *Spiegel*-decision of 1966[89] – politically a highly controversial case which also led to divided opinions within the Court – offers more insights into the use of the method by the FCC. Here, four judges referred to foreign material in answering the question whether members of the Press can refuse to give evidence in criminal proceedings involving treason and opted against such a right. Drawing on papers presented at an international conference on the legal position of the Press in criminal proceedings,[90] the Court stated:

> The German and Swiss contributors concluded that the right [of members of the Press] to refuse to give evidence should recede if information is [itself] gained through criminal conduct or if the criminal proceedings in question involve one of the (political) offences identified by the law. This corresponds to the legal approaches found in other democratic countries [reference to Swiss law omitted].

---

88 BVerfGE 3, 225 at p 244 (our emphasis).

89 BVerfGE 20, 162 ff.

90 Organised by the *Gesellschaft für Rechtsvergleichung* barely a year earlier.

> It can hardly be the aim of the Basic Law to tolerate an abuse of the freedom of the Press, a great liberal achievement designed to further a more objective approach to politics through the free and public debate of responsible citizens, in order to obstruct inquiries into serious crimes directed against the security of the State and its free basic order. Such far-reaching interpretations of Press freedom must also have a negative effect on the trustworthiness of the Federal Republic within an integrated alliance such as NATO, where all other members, despite the fact that their legal orders are based on essentially the same intellectual-historical traditions, regard a far more intensive protection of military secrets as something perfectly natural.[91]

This argument, which not only drew parallels to other (unspecified) 'democratic countries' – only Switzerland was mentioned by name – but also made a highly *political* case for a solution compatible with the approaches adopted by Germany's military partners, was openly rejected by the other four judges of the Senate. Interestingly, their criticism was not directed against the use of comparative law *as such* but rather at the slim factual foundation on which the comparative argument was based in this particular case. They thus pointed out:

> A comparison with the legal systems of other democratic countries is equally incapable of providing convincing arguments against the opinion presented here if this comparison is reduced to the existence or absence of one particular legal provision and fails to evaluate the other legal system as a whole – such as England and the federal law of the United States, which do not grant a right to refuse to give evidence to any profession – or to take into consideration court decisions or the democratic convictions of these societies in general.[92]

The passage indicates that the depth of comparative analysis conducted behind a court's closed doors and eventually culminating in a forceful reference to 'other' legal systems in the final draft of a judgment may in fact often not be state-of-the-art in methodological terms. We will return to this problem – and how it could be overcome by closer co-operation between judges and academics – when discussing the various real or perceived dangers of using foreign law in Chapter 3.

Finally, it seems noteworthy that over 80 per cent of the decisions identified by Mössner (in 1973), Drobnig (in 1986), and Kötz (in 2000) were delivered by the *Bundesgerichtshof* and the *Bundesverfassungsgericht* between 1951 and 1974; only three decisions with comparative input were identified over the past 14 years. Subject to further analysis

---

[91] At pp 220/221.

[92] At p 208. The lack of a coherent comparative methodology in court decisions is also noted by Drobnig, op. cit. note 66, p 625.

(especially of constitutional and labour law cases), this could be an indication that the use of comparative arguments has become less frequent in German court decisions over the past three decades than was the case in earlier times. This would suggest a development which is directly in opposition with what we find in England and other countries (such as Israel and South Africa).

A convincing explanation for this recent decline would certainly require more research than was possible for us to conduct at this stage. Yet it seems that the 'ups and downs' of comparative law in German courtrooms may be due more to the influence of individual judges or special historical circumstances rather than to any wider reason connected with the use of comparative law in courts. This interpretation may appear to provide an 'easy' way out of this dilemma; but it is supported by the study of Aubin, who identifies three (partially overlapping) 'waves' of decisions with comparative input. The first covers the years 1910 to 1924, with a sequence of six decisions of the *Reichsgericht* on limited liability companies within five years alone, and two further decisions on § 7 Road Traffic Act[93] and family law[94] (all eight decisions focusing on Austrian law). The second phase is between 1920 and 1928, with four *Reichsgericht* decisions on § 315 BGB,[95] trademarks,[96] insolvency law,[97] and § 138 BGB[98] (these decisions involve French, English, and Swiss law). The third period covers 1951 to 1961 and has a total of 11 decisions on private, criminal, and public law issues.[99] The same explanation would also be compatible with a thesis we tentatively put forward at the end of this paper which sees in exceptional individuals – be they politicians, legislators, judges, or academics – a crucial factor for innovation, be it political or legal.

Closer analysis of the material provided by our German colleagues also reveals that *Bundesgerichtshof* decisions with comparative input, though less numerous, are fairly evenly distributed over the decades (with a decline in the area of private law beginning only in the 1990s) whereas by far the most 'comparative' *Bundesverfassungsgericht* decisions were handed down in the first decade of the FCC's existence. After this initial flurry of comparative interest, the number of Constitutional Court judgments making references to foreign law dropped abruptly by

[93] RGZ 91, 269 ff (of 1917).

[94] RGZ 109, 243 ff (of 1924).

[95] RGZ 99, 105 ff (of 1920).

[96] RGZ 103, 359 ff (of 1921).

[97] RGZ 120, 205 ff (of 1928).

[98] RGZ 123, 102 ff (of 1928).

[99] See Aubin, op. cit. note 73, pp 463 ff.

approximately 66 per cent, putting the FCC on par with the rate of the BGH. This particular decline of cases involving constitutional issues is likely to find its explanation in the fact that the *Bundesverfassungsgericht* was still developing its jurisprudence in the early days of the Federal Republic. Called to interpret a new constitutional document born under the watchful eyes of the United States, Great Britain, and France, it seems quite logical that the Court would be particularly open to the experience of western democracies in the initial post-War phase. If this is, indeed, the answer (or part of it) then this could prove a pattern that may be followed by other (new) courts (such as the South African Constitutional Court) as their local jurisprudence grows in diversity and sophistication. On the other hand, it is worth noting the continued vitality of comparative law in the Canadian courts.

The German Constitutional Court has also used comparative law on at least one occasion falling into this period and done so in order to justify a constitutional provision which *distinguishes* the Federal Republic from its western neighbours.

In the famous KPD-case of 1956, where the FCC banned the West German Communist Party on the basis of Art 21(2) BL,[100] the unanimous judgment thus held:[101]

> So it is no coincidence that the liberal democracies of the West do not have provisions banning political parties comparable to Art 21(2) BL, which was equally unknown to the Weimar Constitution of 1919 and the contemporary constitutions of the German States. The constitutional logic of these [Western] democracies – which equally, it must be noted, lack the strong legal institutionalisation and protection of political parties as offered by the Basic Law – lies in the fact that citizens are free or, as under the Italian Constitution of 1947, even encouraged to form political parties without limitation, and that the risk of a party opposing the existing constitutional order is consciously accepted; in cases of extreme danger to the existence of the State criminal sanctions will be brought to bear against the responsible individuals. This approach may be due to the optimistic conception that the best guarantee for a free democratic State lies in the

---

[100] Article 21 BL currently declares:

(1) The political parties participate in the forming of the political will of the people. They may be freely established. Their internal organization shall conform to democratic principles. They shall publicly account for the sources of their funds and for their assets. (2) Parties which, by reason of their aims or the behavior of their adherents, seek or impair or destroy the free democratic basic order or to endanger the existence of the Federal Republic of Germany shall be unconstitutional. The Federal Constitutional Court decides on the question of unconstitutionality. (3) Details will be regulated by Federal legislation.

[101] BVerfGE 5, 85 at pp 135/136.

> views of its citizens; where there are free elections, the fight against hostile political parties can and should express itself in the denial of votes. These parties are thus excluded from influencing the political future of the State in a way consistent with the logic of democracy. During the Weimar Republic political parties could operate unfettered in Germany and fight against State institutions in every possible form although courts had ascertained that they were aiming for the violent abolition of the existing order and its replacement by their own constitutional concepts.

At the same time, the judges were also eager to find some foreign experience which could help 'soften' this seemingly harsh German approach. The same Court thus continued:

> Recent developments have, however, shown that free democracies can equally not ignore the practical and political problems of excluding parties from public life which are hostile to the constitutional order if the threat to the State reaches a certain level of intensity. The solutions are not always the same. If the hostility of a certain party towards the constitutional order can already be safely concluded from historical experience, parties might sometimes already be prohibited by the constitution, itself (e.g., the Fascist Party in Italy); more often – aside from interventions on the basis of criminal law, which are limited to extreme cases – administrative action against parties hostile towards the constitution will be authorised by special statutes or on the basis of general constitutional powers. The Communist Party was thus prohibited in France and Switzerland in 1939 and 1940 by government regulations. In the United States the party was required to register in order to allow public authorities to efficiently monitor its activities as a subversive organisation.

It should also be noted that German judges use comparative arguments mainly to support solutions they already seem to have reached by traditional ways of reasoning; foreign material is thus often mentioned only as a supportive addition.[102] In this sense, the practice of the German judges seems to be comparable to their British counterparts.

Our final observation, on matters already touched upon at various points of this chapter, concerns the influence of history on constitutional interpretation and, more specifically, the use of comparative methodology by judges.

In the first chapter of this book we argued that the German approach to statutory interpretation is more developed than that found in other systems – certainly the American. This may explain the fact that the German Constitutional Court, while not having avoided controversy

---

[102] Dölle, 'Der Beitrag der Rechtsvergleichung zum deutschen Recht', in: *Hundert Jahre Deutsches Rechtsleben (Festschrift Deutscher Juristentag), Band* 2 (1960), 19, 37; Kötz, op. cit. note 67, p 835; Mössner, op. cit. note 76, p 220; Aubin, op. cit. note 73; p 470.

itself,[103] may have not divided its citizens as much (or as often) as its American counterpart has done. On the matter of recourse to foreign law and ideas, the German rules of statutory interpretation do not, however, seem to have had any effect internally, partly perhaps because those who advocated recourse to foreign ideas failed, in practice, to carry judicial opinion with them. For the analysis of German case law presented in this chapter has shown that the open use of comparative law is still a fairly rare event, both within and outside the area of constitutional litigation. Thus, though more willing to look abroad in the first years of its existence, even the FCC has, apparently, adjusted its initial outlook to the more national perspective of the *Bundesgerichtshof*.

Whatever the reasons, and clearly many could be invoked, this is quite surprising given the historical circumstances under which the Basic Law was drafted in the late 1940s – and, indeed, even earlier. For there can be no doubt that foreign ideas exerted much influence on German thinking ever since American constitutionalism inspired the discussions in the *Frankfurter Paulskirchenversammlung* of 1848/1849.[104] Though less conspicuous in the Constitution of Weimar (1919), this influence survived both World Wars and, if at all, was further strengthened by the conditions laid down in the *Frankfurt Documents* for the eventual Allied approval of the Basic Law drafted in 1948/1949. For at that time, though refraining from an open prescription of particular provisions, the victorious allies made it clear that the new West German Constitution should be democratic, provide for a federal type of governmental structure (including the distribution of financial resources to the various levels and, more specifically, the allocation of police powers to the *Länder*), and should contain guarantees of individual rights and freedoms.[105] Even if historical analysis is only given the status of an additional tool and not regarded as the main method in statutory interpretation, one would therefore expect to find more comparative law in German courtrooms, especially in constitutional cases.

The answer to this riddle may, again, lie in the existence of much comparative work hidden 'behind the scenes'. Professor Alexander Somek has thus drawn attention to the influence of American thinking on judges like Gerhard Leibholz and Konrad Hesse in the development of

---

[103] As we stress ourselves in various parts of this book by making references to specific decisions of the Constitutional Court.

[104] For more detailed information see Helmut Steinberger, 'American Constitutionalism and German Constitutional Development' in Louis Henkin and Albert J. Rosenthal (eds), *Constitutionalism and Rights* (1990), pp 199 ff.

[105] See the text of the *Frankfurt Documents* in JöR 1951, 1 ff.

the German equality doctrine,[106] an influence confirmed by some German observers and also alluded to ourselves in the first chapter when referring to the extra-judicial writings of some contemporary German Justices.[107] Though giving this 'comparative account' some credit, Somek himself thereby challenges the view that German law has, beyond the initial identification of two levels of judicial scrutiny, indeed gone through more than a superficial phase of 'Americanisation', and that the (German) principle of proportionality could provide a better matrix for the understanding of German case law in this area.[108]

This is certainly not the place to dwell on the intricacies of the German equal protection doctrine and its possible roots in US law. The degree of borrowing or, to put it in a more interesting way, the degree of resemblance or difference is, in our view, incapable of being set out clearly in a few lines since the reality is very nuanced. We do, however, submit that the true potential of comparative law in practice (beyond the inevitable influence that the experience or knowledge of individual judges must have) lies in the *open* discussion of specific points of law rather than the 'hidden' use of foreign doctrine in general. This, we believe, is the importance of the emerging trend (faint though it may be) in the recent English cases discussed above; and it is even more noteworthy in the Canadian and South African approaches, to which we now turn our attention.

c) *Wide-ranging use of foreign law: Canada and South Africa*

The Constitutional Court of South Africa and the Supreme Court of Canada have been active in and (in their respective jurisdictions) commended, not criticised the frequent use of foreign law. But since the latter is rather better known in the United States than the former, they will, for reasons of space, receive unequal treatment in this chapter.

---

[106] See Konrad Hesse, 'Der Gleichheitssatz in der neueren deutschen Verfassungsentwicklung', 109 Archiv des offentlichen Rechts 1984, 174 at pp 188 ff; Gerhard Leibholz, *Die Gleichheit vor dem Gesetz: Eine Studie auf rechtsvergleichender und rechtsphilosophischer Grundlage* (1959), pp 36–8 and 79–81.

[107] Former Justice Dieter Grimm (a regular visitor to the Yale Law School) and Justices Hoffmann-Riem and Brun-Otto Bryde are examples of contemporary judges who are fluent English speakers, have strong links with the United States and, as former law professors, have despite their judicial duties maintained an active presence on the scholarly/academic front.

[108] See Alexander Somek, 'The deadweight of formulae: What might have been the second Germanization of American equal protection review', 1 *U. Pa. J. Const. L.* 284 at 296.

(i) Canada

There are many reasons why Canada presents a particular interest for our enquiry. We offer four (though others could easily be added).[109]

First we note that Canada's mixed cultural background, politically a cause for many internal disagreements, in cultural terms prepared Canadians for an open and multi-cultural approach to law.[110] Those scholars who have studied comparatively the Canadian and American systems thus, not surprisingly, find that the Canadian courts are more prone to a 'dialogic' model rather than adopt the role favoured by American courts (especially strong, it would seem, during the Rehnquist era) of 'enforcers' of the internal constitutional order – a position which, almost inevitably, carries with it the idea of internal self-sufficiency.[111]

Second, we note that from about the mid/late-1980s Canada has experienced an important *shift*[112] towards US law, this almost universally being attributed to the introduction of the Charter of Rights and Freedoms and the perceived need to seek inspiration from the United States.[113]

This 'shift' of a legal system from its genealogical ancestors to 'new players' on the international scene has been little studied in comparative

---

[109] For instance, one could enquire to what extent the contemporary influx of American ideas was facilitated by the fact that some of the Canadian judges who had most recourse to it had studied in the United States. Though the evidence may be inconclusive – see, for instance, Peter McCormick, 'The Supreme Court of Canada and American Citations 1945–94: A Statistical Overview', 8 (2d) *Supreme Court Law Review* 527, esp pp 535 ff (1997) – the wider point deserves to be borne in mind since we argue that the presence of German law in South Africa may have benefited from the fact that Germany pursued an active cultural policy of prosilitisation during the apartheid years when many young South African scholars may have found it difficult to pursue further studies in countries such as the United States and Britain.

[110] Fifty-nine per cent of the population is English-speaking, 23 per cent speak French, 4 per cent are Aboriginal, and 13 per cent belong to identifiable minorities.

[111] Chief among these scholars is Professor Sarah Harding in 'Comparative Reasoning and Judicial Review', (2003) 28 *Yale J. Int. L.* 409, drawing on the work of such notable comparatists as Professor Patrick Glenn.

[112] We italicise here the word 'shift' for, if statistical studies of citing practices of the Canadian Supreme Court are to be believed, the shift has taken the form of looking at US case law but not, necessarily, following it. Thus, if we look at all Charter cases decided between 1984 (the year of its introduction) and 1995 we see that out of 702 such cases four, only, followed US law, 30 refused to follow it, but 668 of them chose to consider it. To us, this does not indicate slavish imitation (nor subversion of internal law or values to foreign law) but healthy curiosity. For details see C. L. Ostberg, Matthew E. Wetstein, and Craig R. Ducat, 'Attitudes, Precedents and Cultural Change: Explaining the Citation of Foreign Precedents by the Supreme Court of Canada', (2001) 34 (2) *Canadian Journal of Political Science*, 377 at 394.

[113] See, for instance, *Rahey v The Queen*, [1987] 1 S.C.R. 588 (*per* Justice La Forest); *The Queen Simmons v*, [1988] 2 S.C.R. 495 at 516 (*per* Brian Dickson CJ); *The Queen v Elshaw*, [1991] 3 S.C.R. 24 at 57 (*per* Justice Claire L'Heureux-Dubé).

law, even though one can imagine other countries in the 'old' world (e.g. Spain – moving away from the French Code) or the 'new' world (e.g. Brazil – being drawn into the American orbit and away from its Portuguese origins) experiencing similar gravitational pulls. We raise here briefly two issues for future consideration since a longer discussion would detract us from our main theme.

The first is what accounts for this re-orientation: economic, commercial, or political factors? Second, are these systems 'shifting' towards one other system or are they being 'eclectic' in their choices, moving, for instance, towards American law in such areas as commercial and trade law but towards German law in others (e.g. constitutional law or models of federalism)?

The point is not fanciful since there is intriguing evidence from countries whose courts are 'great citers' that shows that such bifurcated tendencies may already exist.[114] But the question still remains how they should be explained.

Third, the Canadian universalism – and statistics demonstrate[115] that their courts cite not only English, Commonwealth, and American case law but also civilian systems (beyond the obvious interest in French law) – has continued after the novelty of the Charter made such consideration of foreign experiences necessary. This is an important point to grasp, for it may neutralise the interpretation often advanced by 'introverted' lawyers to the effect that new courts (or new bills of rights) are the main reason which promote an interest in foreign law and that 'mature' systems do not need such additional sources of inspiration. The Canadian universalism may thus demonstrate the confident state of an eclectic mind which does not see in transnational judicial *dialogues* a threat to national individuality or an impoverishment of the local legal culture but, on the contrary, a source of constant inspiration and reinforced judicial legitimacy.

Finally, in the previous sentence we italicised the word 'dialogue' because in the reception of American law in Canada, from about the mid-1980s onwards, we see no slavish adoption of its solutions nor, indeed, the opposite, that is, a closing of the eyes towards the large (and sometimes menacing) Southern neighbour[116] but an opportunity for a

---

114 Canadian courts for instance still, apparently, cite British cases more than American in matters of private law (tort, family, property), though the later system gains a clear lead in the human rights area. Likewise, South African courts retain for historical reasons the predilection to cite Roman–Dutch law in matters of private law but display a wider reach in matters of public law.

115 Thus, during the period 1984–95, 35.7 per cent of citations in decisions of the Canadian Supreme Court were to United States courts, 55 per cent to British, 5.9 per cent to Commonwealth, and 3.4 to foreign and international.

116 For statistical evidence for both of these propositions see C. L. Ostberg, Matthews E. Wetstein, and Craig R. Ducat, op. cit. note 112 at pp 393–4.

genuine dialogue in search for inspiration. Indeed, some Canadian judges[117] may now be suggesting that the main source of inspiration for Canadian judges can come from the decisions of the Warren and Burger Courts, and that the current, more 'introverted' case law of the Rehnquist court may be proving less exciting. For those American lawyers who take (justified) pride at the contribution their law has made to the legal systems of other countries this may be a warning of possible side effects of the current attitude towards foreign law. To put it differently, it is permissible to speculate whether, notwithstanding past practice,[118] in the years to come foreign courts may turn more and more towards those sister courts which prove themselves to be the richest source of inspiration while at the same time openly fashioning solutions that are exportable and do not depend – and are clearly stated not to depend – on the text of one constitution alone, however famous (and old[119]) it may be.

(ii) South Africa

Among the countries we have chosen to include in this survey South Africa is today certainly located at the very top end of the scale as far as the use of comparative law is concerned. In our attempt to shed some light on the role of the judge as comparatist, the frequent references to foreign legal ideas that feature so prominently in South African judgments thus merit close attention. Indeed, court decisions of this country are a showcase for comparative law *in action*, providing exceptional insights into the opportunities, dangers, and practical difficulties inherent to comparative law.

---

[117] See, e.g., Claire L'Hereux-Dubé, 'The Importance of Dialogue: Globalisation and the International Impact of the Rehnquist Court', (1998) 34 *Tulsa L. J.* 15. It would be wrong if the uninitiated reader were to attribute this 'reserve' towards a conservative court as being motivated by the author's French background, not only given her admirable sense of independence of mind but also, and perhaps more importantly, the fact that among Canadian judges she is the fourth most frequent citer of American material; see Peter McCormick, op. cit. note 109, p 536.

[118] Described eloquently by Anthony (now Lord) Lester in 'The Overseas Trade in the American Bill of Rights', (1988) 88 *Columb. L. Rev.* 537 ff.

[119] Though English Common lawyers feel special reverence for antiquity, age (in this instance) may not be a point of unalloyed strength for the American Constitution. For, as Lord Diplock observed nearly 25 years ago, 'decisions of the Supreme Court of the United States on that country's Bill of Rights, whose phraseology is now 200 years old, are of little help in construing provisions of (...) modern Commonwealth constitutions which follow broadly the Westminsiter model' (*Ong Ah Chuan v Public Prosecutor* [1981] AC 648, 669). These sentiments are shared by Canadian (and other) judges and may well pose a long-term threat to American intellectual imperialism.

1. Preliminary observations

Before turning to three particular cases which serve to illustrate how foreign material has been used (and sometimes not used) by South African courts, a few preliminary points should be made. Notable among them is a methodological observation about the way we have approached the task of presenting the peculiarities of South Africa within such a short confine. We have thus chosen to present the South African approach to comparative law in a way that differs methodologically from that adopted to highlight some key features of the position taken by German and Canadian lawyers for the following reasons.

The geographical and (in some respects) cultural proximity of Canada with the United States determined how we would present the Canadian law since it has coloured much of the comparative debate in this country, especially after the introduction of the Charter of 1983. Would Canada follow the case law of the US Supreme Court? Would it, indeed, be overwhelmed by it? Would the English links weaken as a result, or even reach vanishing point? And what about the French factor within the wider range of debates? Inevitably, these questions spawned a fair number of Canada-related questions as well as specific American–Canadian comparisons. We also noted a useful stream of statistical surveys which proved, as stated in the preceding sub-section, that the situation actually reached in Canada is much more subtle than the above questions originally led most commentators to expect.

We could have followed the same way in presenting South African law and, indeed, in what follows we provide the kind of information about the use of foreign material found in South African judgments which we also gave in the Canadian section. On the whole, however, we have chosen to present the rich South African material in a different manner, and this for three reasons.

First, because though much has been written about the South African death penalty case (in the United States especially), little is really known[120] about the constitutional *evolution* experienced by that country in the mid-1990s and, especially, the constitutionalisation of comparative law under the 1993[121] and 1996[122] Constitutions (already discussed in some detail in Chapter 1, above). In contrast with what we find in the United States, this constitutional background helps explain the willingness (if not need) of South African judges to make use of foreign material. But if this may help explain in part the differences with the

---

120 See, however, Albie Sachs, 'Constitutional Developments in South Africa', (1996) 28 *N.Y.U.J. Int.'l L. & Pol.* 695 ff.

121 Republic of South Africa Constitution Act 200 of 1993.

122 Republic of South Africa Constitution Act 108 of 1996.

United States, it does not fully address the other wider concern of the American right, that is, the judge's ability to use his own moral perceptions in order to shape local law.

Second, and relatedly, this gradual evolution was achieved through a subtle and complex interplay of legislator and judge and is a key to the understanding of the judicial attempts to use foreign law to shape contemporary South African law. To our knowledge, this has thus far not been adequately discussed, at any rate outside the contours of South Africa itself.

Finally, while South Africa has, *in the area of private law*, remained largely loyal to its original 'dual' cultural background (common law and Roman–Dutch law) along lines similar to those found in Canada, in the area of constitutional law and, more specifically, human rights law it has revealed an intriguing (some would say surprising) interest in not only American but also German constitutional law. Whereas one could almost call the first interest 'natural', the interest in German law raises a host of sub-issues of its own. What promoted the interest? How was it sustained? How was the language barrier overcome? Will it continue in the future? Once again, therefore, these factors cannot (and should not) be ignored when discussing excerpts from leading South African judicial opinions, and for this reason we provide a brief outline of the historical developments which have shaped the current constitutional regime before coming to the cases, themselves. We thus begin with some less well-known details particularly relevant to our discussion.

2. The historical background

Providing a brief outline of the country's most recent constitutional history is important for it is here that one will find some explanations which may hold out lessons for others. This survey, however, will also show how South Africa was particularly open for legal transplants due to special conditions which may not readily be found elsewhere.

The competing political parties, while restructuring the country's new legal order in the 1990s, agreed on a two-staged reform process. This led to the negotiation of the so-called Interim Constitution (1993/1994) and – following the first free elections in May 1994 – the final 1996 Constitution. Both documents were strongly influenced by foreign constitutional ideas, the German *Grundgesetz* of 1949 proving one important source.[123] Among the systems (and legal instruments) which

[123] From the German side in particular one finds parts of the bill of fundamental rights, the concept of the constitutional state (*Rechtsstaat*), a specialised constitutional court (as opposed to the American Supreme Court model), and a number of federal features pertaining to, *inter alia*, the distribution of legislative competence between the central and provincial levels as well as the concept of 'co-operative government' (*kooperativer Föderalismus*).

influenced the framers we find the United States, Canada, India, Namibia, the European Union, and the European Convention on Human Rights.

The degree of German influence is quite remarkable given that Germany was the only country outside the common law world and the English-speaking legal community which received such attention from the framers of the new South African constitutional order. This remarkable reception of foreign ideas was mainly fostered by political parties and individual influential academics offering legal advice to the Multi-Party Negotiating Process (MPNP) at Kempton Park (outside Johannesburg) in 1993 and, subsequently, the newly elected Parliament (convened as a Constitutional Assembly between 1994 and 1996). As the cases discussed below show, the South African judiciary was (and also remains) the third main catalyst in this development. The above suggests, once again, that the 'human' factor – personal contacts – can play a more significant part in the exchange of ideas than has hitherto been acknowledged by the academic literature. This, of course, is but an aspect of the wider issue which has occupied historians for ages: do single actions of personalities really shape the course of history? As a general rule the answer must surely lie in a synthesis of the two preconditions, that is, the charismatic leader appearing at the right point in time.

The reasons why German constitutional law proved to be such a successful model are of interest in the context of this book. Thus, parts of the German fundamental rights doctrine had already found their way into South Africa prior to the political changes in Pretoria, having permeated its borders via the Constitutions of Bophuthatswana[124] and Namibia. The Supreme Court of South Africa, exercising final judicial authority in Bophuthatswana until 1982 and in Namibia as late as 1990, found itself confronted with cases of constitutional review many years before the first judgements of South African courts were handed down following the enactment of the 1993 Constitution. These judgements referred to German law on more than one occasion and were discussed in South Africa, fuelling the local fundamental rights debate and opening the doors for further German influence in the subsequent constitution-making process.

A second reason can be found in the fact that a number of (mostly Afrikaans-speaking) academics found opportunities for comparative studies in Germany at a time when academic institutions in other countries seemed closed to South African scholars due to the political quarantine imposed on that country. On the constitutional level, the inclusion of the *Rechtsstaatsprinzip* in the preamble of the 1993

---

124 A so-called homeland with its own constitution, regarded as independent by South Africa at the time, though internationally never recognised as such.

Constitution (inserted literally 'overnight' on the initiative of Professor François Venter) and the reception of Art 12 BL (occupational freedom) on advice of the late Professor Etienne Mureinik in 1996 are, perhaps, the most remarkable direct results of this 'personal' connection between the two countries.

Close personal links between judges in South Africa may also have had a positive effect on the awareness of and knowledge about foreign law in the country. At least one distinguished judge, the late Justice Ismail Mahomed – initially a practicing advocate in Johannesburg – thus became judge and eventually President of the Lesotho Court of Appeal before being appointed to the Supreme Court of Namibia (where he later became Chief Justice and was involved in some of the leading constitutional and administrative law judgements of that Court). In 1994, Mahomed became Deputy President of the new South African Constitutional Court. Laurie Ackermann, too, served both on the Lesotho Court of Appeal and the Namibian Supreme Court prior to his appointment to the Constitutional Court of South Africa. The Namibian Court in particular is thereby known for its use of comparative law following the independence of the country in 1990. The close linguistic relationship between Afrikaans and German must also have served as an important bridge for legal ideas; many key German terms (such as *Rechtsstaat, Wechselwirkung, Wesensgehalt, Drittwirkung*, or *Bundestreue*) are often not even translated by South African courts and academics.

Other factors explaining the role of German law during the negotiation process included the international reputation of the *Grundgesetz* and the support rendered by the German government, political parties, politically affiliated foundations, and academic institutions to the emerging new state. Finally, one could point out that a legal system (the German) that had itself been confronted in the post-War period with a traumatic past, must have appeared as especially relevant to a country struggling to put behind it its own tormenting experience with apartheid.[125]

---

[125] It is important to point out that the importation of foreign ideas and notions was neither wholesale nor always long-lasting. As far as the German side is concerned, some elements such as the *Rechtsstaatsprinzip*, the interpretative 'reading down' of constitutionally challenged statutes in the course of legal disputes (*verfassungskonforme Auslegung*), the 'indirect' or 'radiating' effect of fundamental rights in the private sphere (*mittelbare Drittwirkung der Grundrechte*), parts of the property clause, and the explicit protection of the essential content of a fundamental right (*Wesensgehaltsgaratie*) were discarded after the transitional period and partly substituted by doctrines already developed in South Africa prior to 1993. Other elements such as the establishment of a specialised court for constitutional matters and parts of the *Bundesrat* model found their way into the 1996 Constitution, albeit in a strongly modified form. Yet again other items (such as the constitutional freedom of occupation, the application of certain fundamental rights to juristic persons, and parts of the limitation clause) today closely resemble their German counterparts.

As indicated above, the South African judiciary exerted much influence on these legal transplants and today still continues to play an exceptional role in the use of foreign ideas. The Constitutional Court in particular (itself a legal transplant) has repeatedly referred to foreign material in order to shape the country's new and developing body of constitutional doctrine. Judges have thereby not restricted themselves to foreign case law; references to foreign legislation and, more importantly, to academic work feature prominently in many judgments. This demarcates a clear break with the past, when South African judges 'did not value academic writing highly',[126] and is a change initially necessitated by the absence of South African precedents in this field of law.

Scrutinising Supreme Court and Constitutional Court judgements between July 1994 and August 1998, one of us thus counted no less than 1,258 references to the decisions of American, Canadian, British, German, European, and Indian courts alone.[127] In view of the language barrier, the strong influence of German law on South Africa thereby calls for some explanation, and our research has shown that most of this effect is due to translations of court judgements made available through the work of a limited number of (often non-German!) academics.[128] Basic comparative work of this kind is obviously one important key, which enables South African judges to take advantage of German ideas, especially in the area of human rights. A precondition is thereby the open-minded approach, which some judges (such as Justice Laurie Ackermann) take towards the use of foreign material.

---

[126] Susan Scott, 'Evaluation of security by means of movables: Problems and possible solutions. Section C: Codification of the law of cession', (1997) *Tydskrif vir Hedendaagse Romeins-Hollandse Reg* 633 at 638.

[127] Jörg Fedtke, *Die Rezeption von Verfassungsrecht. Südafrika 1993–96* (Nomos Verlagsgesellschaft, Baden-Baden 2000), p 446.

[128] See, e.g., the death penalty case of the South African Constitutional Court mentioned earlier. In *Makwanyane*, the Court referred to the *Grundgesetz* and various judgements of the *Bundesverfassungsgericht* mainly with the help of two American sources: Donald Kommers, *The Constitutional Jurisprudence of the Federal Republic of Germany* (1989) and David Currie, *The Constitution of the Federal Republic of Germany* (1994). Kommers and Currie are thus cited three and five times respectively by the Court. Professor Dieter Grimm (at that time a member of the German Constitutional Court) is also cited twice – but for one of his *English* publications, namely, 'Human Rights and Judicial Review in Germany' in Beatty (ed), *Human Rights and Judicial Review: A Comparative Perspective* (1994), pp 267 ff. Original German sources (judicial and academic) are referred to only indirectly. The judgements of the *Bundesverfassungsgericht* were accessed through the works of Kommers and Currie; and a reference to Maunz/Dürig, *Grundgesetz* (one of the leading commentaries on the German Basic Law) can also be found 'via' Currie. This and other such cases, which we do not cite because of lack of space, confirm the validity of one of the theses of this article: academics can help judges, thus not only ensuring better co-operation between the different parts of the legal profession but also promoting the use of foreign law.

3. Comparative law in South African courtrooms

Turning now to three particular cases, our aim is to show how South African judges have actually made use of their constitutional mandate to look abroad. The order in which we discuss these three cases is not arbitrary. It reflects the degree of difference in wording and content between the relevant South African provisions on the one hand and, on the other, their foreign counterparts.

In the first case, a foreign solution is thus proposed although the text of the 1993 Constitution and the background material of the drafting process offer no indication that its framers had in any way discussed such a possibility. The foreign idea (which would have amounted to a judicial legal transplant) is rejected by the majority of the Constitutional Court.

This is different in the second case. Here, there are clear signs that the political parties negotiating the constitutional settlement of 1993 had already contemplated various solutions found abroad. For political reasons, the agreement eventually found was highly ambiguous, and in interpreting this text it made good sense for the judges to apply their minds to the arguments put forward in the drafting process. Comparative law suggested itself as a valuable method.

The last case concerned a legal transplant, which the legislator took from Germany for very specific reasons. The texts of the 1996 Constitution and the Basic Law are nearly identical on this point, and comparative law, it seems, would have offered an ideal methodological framework within which to interpret the South African provision. The potential value of foreign experience is clearly the highest in this last case, and yet the Court did not look in any detail at the historical background of the South African provision or seek the insights German law could have provided. For reasons explained below, we believe that this was a missed opportunity, but also concede that the working conditions of judges (e.g. time constraints, library resources, research staff, and the opportunity to discuss the wider background of cases with experienced colleagues) differ strongly on the various levels of a legal system. Lower courts – as in this case – may thus not be adequately equipped to take advantage of comparative law even if the preconditions for the use of the method are ideal.

The first South African case which we present here provides an excellent example of the second 'judicial dialogue' identified by Bernhard Rudden – the dialogue between judges – when it comes to the use of foreign law.

In *Ferreira*,[129] the court dealt with the statutory duty of company employees to disclose confidential business information under circumstances specified by section 417 of the South African Companies

---

[129] *Ferreira v Levin NO and Others*, 1996 (1) BCLR 1.

Act[130] *notwithstanding* the risk that this information might incriminate them and subsequently be used as evidence in criminal proceedings. Ackermann J proposed to expand the protective scope of s 11(1) of the 1993 Constitution[131] to include (beyond the limits of the constitutional text) a *general* right to freedom. After referring to Sir Isaiah Berlin and the opinion of Dickson CJC in the Canadian case *R. v Big M Drug Mart*,[132] he defined this freedom as the right of individuals not to have obstacles to possible choices and activities placed in their way by the State.[133]

Ackermann J justified this interpretation (1) by emphasising the vast number, extent, and variety of limitations which had been placed on the personal freedom of citizens under the *apartheid* regime; (2) by reference to the values underlying an 'open and democratic society based on freedom and equality';[134] and (3) by arguing that the new constitutional order required the State to justify any limitation of the citizens' freedoms. A broad interpretation of s 11(1) would help to create a 'culture of justification', while comparative experience had shown that it would not subject the courts to a flood of frivolous complaints or unduly restrict State legislation.[135]

Despite references to foreign legal systems such as the United States and Canada, Ackermann J developed these ideas and addressed possible objections to his proposal in this part of the opinion primarily within the framework of *South African* constitutional law and the country's *own* history.

He then, however, focused his attention to foreign law and analysed in great detail Canadian, US, and German experience, as well as the International Covenant on Civil and Political Rights and the European Convention on Human Rights. These reflections were introduced by the following passage, which seems to indicate that Ackermann J was using comparative law mainly (but not exclusively) to *support* a result reached through other means. He thus wrote:

> It is appropriate to consider whether comparable foreign case law would lead to a different conclusion. Direct comparison is of course difficult and needs to be done with circumspection because the right to personal freedom is formulated differently in the constitutions of other countries and in the

---

130 Act 61 of 1973.

131 Entitled 'freedom and security of the person'. The provision grants everyone the right 'to freedom and security of the person, which shall include the right not to be detained without trial'.

132 (1985) 13 C.R.R. 64.

133 At no 54.

134 At no 50.

135 At no 61 ff.

> international and regional instruments. Nevertheless, s 33(1) of our Constitution enjoins us to consider, *inter alia*, what would be 'justifiable in an open and democratic society based on freedom and equality' and s 35(1) obliges us to promote the values underlying such a society when we interpret Chapter 3 and encourages us to have regard to comparable case law. In construing and applying our Constitution, we are dealing with fundamental legal norms which are steadily becoming more universal in character. When, for example, the United States Supreme Court finds that a statutory provision is or is not in accordance with the 'due process of law' or when the Canadian Supreme Court decides that a deprivation of liberty is not 'in accordance with the principles of fundamental justice' (...) we have regard to these findings, not in order to draw direct analogies, but to identify the underlying reasoning with a view to establishing the norms that apply in other open and democratic societies based on freedom and equality.[136]

This, then, is a good example of the open-minded approach that many South African judges take when dealing with questions of national law – societies which broadly operate on the basis of a similar set of values are taken as an additional point of reference in order to determine the validity of their own solution. What is surprising, though, is the amount of space invested for this purpose (judges in other countries such as Germany, the United States or England would – at most – add a throwaway line or a footnote indicating that their solution is confirmed by the approaches found abroad). We thus suspect that Ackermann J's reflections served an *additional* purpose beyond mere confirmation 'whether comparable foreign case law would lead to a different conclusion', and the final paragraph dealing with the interpretation of s 11(1) indicates that foreign ideas are indeed part of his *ratio decidendi*.[137]

The attempt to expand s 11(1)[138] was, admittedly, difficult. Neither the text of the 1993 Constitution nor the negotiations at Kempton Park indicate that the political parties contemplated the introduction of any such right; and only during the later work of the Constitutional Assembly do we find references to a broad residual right in the positions of the African National Congress and the Freedom Front.[139]

---

[136] At no 72.

[137] At no 90, Ackermann J includes these ideas in his 'end result'.

[138] Along the lines, e.g., of the German *allgemeine Handlungsfreiheit*. This notion, derived from Art 2(1) BL, provides a residual right to individual self-fulfilment (*freie Entfaltung der Persönlichkeit*) subject to the rights of others and subject to the constitutional order and morality. Article 2(1) BL is a general clause establishing freedom from *any* kind of State intervention but plaintiffs will only invoke the provision successfully in the absence of a more specific fundamental right.

[139] Constitutional Assembly, Theme Committee 4, *Schematic Report on Freedom and Security of the Person* of August 1995, at 2.2.1 and 2.2.2.

These textual differences between the 1993 Constitution and its foreign counterparts are an important counter-argument for the majority of the Court. Though in agreement with Ackermann J that the relevant provision of the Companies Act *is* unconstitutional (though for different reasons), Chaskalson P felt the need to explain why s 11(1) should be interpreted primarily as a protection of the *physical* integrity of every person. For this purpose, he, too, relied on comparative evidence:

> This is how a guarantee of 'freedom (liberty) and security of the person' would ordinarily be understood. It is also the primary sense in which the phrase, 'freedom and security of the person' is used in public international law. The American Declaration of the Rights and Duties of Man, the International Covenant on Civil and Political Rights, the European Convention for the Protection of Human Rights and Fundamental Freedoms, and the African Charter on Human and People's Rights, all use the phrase 'liberty and security of the person' in a context which shows that it relates to detention or other physical constraints. Sieghart notes that although '(...) all the instruments protect these two rights jointly in virtually identical terms, they have been interpreted as being separate and independent rights,' and that the European Commission of Human Rights and the European Court of Human Rights have found that what is protected is 'physical liberty' and 'physical security.' There is nothing to suggest that the primary purpose of section 11(1) of our Constitution is different.[140]

He then emphasised the differences in wording between the foreign constitutions specifically discussed by Ackermann J,[141] and responded to the arguments drawn from US, Canadian, and German law. Focusing particularly on the *Lochner*-decision of the US Supreme Court, Chaskalson P noted the dangers of a broad interpretation of s 11(1) for the workload of the courts and rejected (at least for the time being) the solution proposed by Ackermann J.

Three points are worth emphasising in this context.

First, Ackermann J emerged from this judicial dialogue with some success *despite* the rejection of his approach by the majority of the Court. The opinion of Chaskalson P concedes that the text could be interpreted differently in other factual circumstances, and O'Regan J already took a

---

140 At no 170.

141 At no 175 he thus notes:

> Reference is made in the judgment of Ackermann J to the manner in which the courts have construed the Constitutions of the United States of America, Canada and Germany. It is important to appreciate – as Ackermann J is at pains to point out – that these Constitutions are formulated in different terms, and the rights protected under them are not dealt with in the same way as the rights protected in Chapter 3 of our Constitution are.

middle ground in the subsequent *Bernstein*-decision of 1996.[142] Ackermann J's interpretation could thus still bear fruit in the future.[143]

Second, Chaskalson P did not reject the solution proposed by Ackermann J *simply because it was strongly influenced by foreign law*. Both sides used comparative law to argue their respective positions.

Finally, Ackermann J's approach would have amounted to a full legal transplant, not just an expansion or development of the law on the basis of constitutional principles already contained in the 1993 text. This 'free-standing' use of comparative law in the courtroom must be particularly controversial as judges who venture into hitherto uncharted constitutional waters inevitably slip into a highly legislative function.

This last aspect is different in our second South African case, which is the decision of the Constitutional Court in *Du Plessis and Others v De Klerk and Another*[144] dealing with the horizontal effect of constitutional rights. In contrast to the question of a residual right to freedom, which was not discussed in any detail at Kempton Park, the issue of a possible 'Drittwirkung' led to one of the most heated debates between so-called anti-horizontalists and those in favour of the application of fundamental rights and freedoms in the private sphere. The outcome of this political conflict was a highly ambiguous constitutional text, which avoided the clear language proposed, for example, by the Technical Committee on Fundamental Rights, a body responsible for the scientific support of the politicians discussing the issue.

With respect to the use of foreign law, the Constitutional Court's position was thus different from *Ferreira* in at least two respects. First,

---

142 *Bernstein and Others v Bester NO and Others*, 1996 (4) BCLR 449 (CC). O'Regan J thus wrote:

> Section 11(1), however, will protect a residual area of freedom. I do not believe that this residual scope of the right should be interpreted as broadly and generously as possible. To this extent I disagree, respectfully, with Ackermann J. I also disagree, respectfully, with Mokgoro J that the right to freedom in section 11(1) should be limited to physical freedom. It is likely, given the clear entrenchment of freedoms such as expression, belief and association, that the residual scope of section 11(1) will largely concern physical freedom, but I am unconvinced that it should be limited to physical freedom.

143 A historical interpretation of s 12 of the 1996 Constitution would thus have to consider the following passage in the *Explanatory Memorandum* of the Technical Committee to Theme Committee 4 (of 9 October 1996): 'The right to freedom refers in this context to physical deprivation of liberty, not other dimensions of freedom which are protected by other rights, e.g., freedom of assembly, religion, conscience, speech etc.' (at p 35 note 2). A major concern of the majority in *Ferreira*, the strict requirements for a limitation of s 11(1), has, on the other hand, been mitigated by Constitutional Assembly's sole reliance on a general limitation clause in the 1996 Constitution.

144 1996 (3) SA 850.

the Court could simply not avoid deciding the issue, which had been left open by the Multi-Party Negotiating Process in 1993. Here, we encounter a similarity with the well-known death penalty dispute,[145] which was equally left for the courts to resolve. In both cases, South African judges were thus given a mandate by the political process – a mandate, one could argue, not only to apply traditional *judicial* but also *legislative* techniques, which must surely include the use of comparative law. Second, the judges had to deal with an ambiguous textual framework which was already influenced by comparative arguments raised by politicians and academics alike.[146] Instead of conjuring up a new element (as Ackermann J in *Ferreira*), the Court was thus, in a way, merely completing a puzzle, many parts of which were already foreign in origin.

Taking into account this legislative background, it is thus no surprise that *Du Plessis* is probably one of the most comparative judgments ever published. Foreign law also had exceptional impact on the reasoning of the judges because the issue at hand – the *inter partes* application of fundamental rights – has, at one time or the other, riddled most societies with a system of human rights protection.[147] As Kentridge J emphasises in the leading opinion at no. 8 of the judgment:

> The question whether Chapter 3 of the Constitution (Fundamental Rights) has only a 'vertical' application or has in addition a 'horizontal' application has been the subject of considerable debate by commentators on the Constitution. There have been similar debates, both academic and judicial, in other countries with constitutional Bills of Rights.

And at no. 32:

> The 'horizontality' issue has arisen in other countries with entrenched Bills of Rights and the parties have supplied us with a wealth of comparative material both judicial and extra-judicial, for which we are grateful.

Before embarking on an extensive analysis of US, Irish, Canadian, and German law, as well as the work of Chief Justice Barak in Israel,

---

145 *The State v Makwanyane and Mchunu* (Case No. CCT/3/94 of 6 June 1995).

146 See, e.g., the 5th, 6th, and 7th Reports of the Technical Committee of Fundamental Rights (dating 11 June 1993, 15 July 1993, and 29 July 1993); South African Law Commission, *Project 58: Group and Human Rights – Interim Report* (1991); Annél van Aswegen, 'The Implications of a Bill of Rights for the Law of Contract and Delict', [1995] *South African Journal on Human Rights* 50 ff; Johan de Waal, 'A Comparative Analysis of the provisions of German Origin in the Interim Bill of Rights', [1995] *South African Journal on Human Rights* 1 ff; Erika de Wet, 'A German perspective on the constitutional enforceability of children's and labour rights in the interim bill of rights with special reference to *Drittwirkung*', [1996] Tydskrif vir Hedendaagse Romeins-Hollandse Reg 577 ff.

147 Stephen Gardbaum describes the issue as 'currently one of the most important and hotly debated in comparative constitutional law'; see 'The "Horizontal Effect" of Constitutional Rights', [2003] 102 *Michigan Law Review*, 387 ff at 388.

Kentridge J nevertheless emphasised the need to bear in mind the specific characteristics of the South African setting:

> There can be no doubt that the resolution of the issue must ultimately depend on an analysis of the specific provisions of the Constitution. It is nonetheless illuminating to examine the solutions arrived at by the courts of other countries. The Court was referred to judgments of the courts of the United States, Canada, Germany and Ireland. I would not presume to attempt a detailed description, or even a summary, of the relevant law of those countries, but in each case some broad features are apparent to the outside observer. A comparative examination shows at once that there is no universal answer to the problem of vertical or horizontal application of a Bill of Rights.[148]

It would be superfluous to provide a full reconstruction of the judgment in this article and interested readers are, instead, referred to the original text. We do, however, wish to stress two points.

First, we find again – as in *Ferreira* – a balance between a line of reasoning which focuses on the provisions of the 1993 Constitution and the discussion of foreign ideas. The latter are thereby not only used to *confirm* a 'South African' solution; references to Canadian and German law show that some foreign ideas were actually used to *shape* the result in *Du Plessis*. Kentridge J thus describes remarks on considerations of policy cited from the opinion of McIntyre J in *Dolphin Delivery* as 'fully applicable to Chapter 3 of our own Constitution',[149] and explains that the German approach to the interpretation of private law by a specialised constitutional court is of particular interest to South Africa. We thus find the following passage at no. 60 of the judgment:

> The model of indirect application or, if you will, indirect horizontality, seems peculiarly appropriate to a judicial system which, as in Germany, separates constitutional jurisdiction from ordinary jurisdiction. This does not mean that the principles evolved by the German Constitutional Court must be slavishly followed. They do however afford an example of how the process of influencing the common law may work in practice.

A second element which specifically enhanced the influence of German law on the thinking of some judges is the close genealogical relationship between South African law and the German legal system. The provisions of the 1993 Constitution relevant in *Du Plessis* may not have been *direct* legal transplants (we will deal with such a transplant in our last example from South African case law), but there *was* certainly substantial influence of German legal thinking on the work of the Multi-Party Negotiating Process related to the question of *Drittwirkung*. This

---

[148] At no 33.

[149] At no 58.

thinking continued to exert its influence in *Du Plessis*. One can see this clearly from the following passage from the opinion of Ackermann J:

> That the drafters of our Constitution had recourse to or were influenced by certain features of the GBL in drafting our Constitution is evident from various of its provisions. The marked similarity between the provisions of section 35(3), enjoining courts '[i]n the interpretation of any law and the application and development of the common law and customary law' to 'have due regard to the spirit, purport and objects of [Chapter 3]', and the indirect horizontal application of the basic rights in the GBL in German jurisprudence cannot, in my view, simply be a coincidence. It provides a final powerful indication that the framers of our Constitution did not intend that the Chapter 3 fundamental rights should, save where the formulation of a particular right expressly or by necessary implication otherwise indicates, apply directly to legal relations between private persons.

Finally, we wish to point out that the use of comparative law was not uncontroversial in *Du Plessis*. In dissenting with the majority of the Court (which opted for an indirect application of fundamental rights in the private sphere), Kriegler J emphasised the unique character of the South African constitutional arrangements, and cautioned against too much reliance on foreign experience. At no. 127 he thus wrote:

> It is therefore no spirit of isolationism which leads me to say that our Constitution is unique in its origins, concepts and aspirations. Nor am I a chauvinist when I describe the negotiation process which gave birth to that Constitution as unique; so, too, the leap from minority rule to representative democracy founded on universal adult suffrage; the Damascene about-turn from executive directed parliamentary supremacy to justiciable constitutionalism and a specialist constitutional court, the ingathering of discarded fragments of the country and the creation of new provinces; and the entrenchment of a true separation and devolution of powers. Nowhere in the world that I am aware of have enemies agreed on a transitional coalition and a controlled two-stage process of constitution building. Therefore, although it is always instructive to see how other countries have arranged their constitutional affairs, I do not start there. And when I do conduct comparative study, I do so with great caution. The survey is conducted from the point of vantage afforded by the South African Constitution, constructed on unique foundations, built according to a unique design and intended for unique purposes.

And at no. 144 he continued:

> Nor does the advent of the Constitution (...) warrant the wholesale importation of foreign doctrines or precedents. To be true we are to promote values not yet rooted in our traditions and we must have regard to applicable public international law. We are also permitted to have regard to foreign case law. But that does not amount to a wholesale importation of doctrines from foreign jurisdictions.

We accept this criticism, which has also featured in the opinions of judges in other legal systems. At the same time, we believe that our survey has shown the colleagues of Kriegler J to be fairly balanced in their use of foreign law. The *Ferreira*-decision in particular is an example where the majority of the Constitutional Court carefully weighed the comparative arguments put forward by Ackermann J – only to reject them with a view to the specific features of South African constitutional law. A second criticism of Kriegler J seems to be, however, more substantial. At no. 147 of the *Du Plessis*-decision he thus remarked:

> I find it unnecessary to engage in a debate with my colleagues on the merits or demerits of the approaches adopted by the courts in the United States, Canada or Germany. That pleases me, for I have enough difficulty with our Constitution not to want to become embroiled in the intricacies of the state action doctrine, Drittwirkung and the like.

Kriegler J is referring here to the basic precondition of any comparative exercise, which is adequate knowledge about foreign law. He later further elaborates this point in the *Bernstein* case,[150] criticising the depth of comparative analysis as conducted in South African courtrooms. Again we feel that both *Ferreira* and *Du Plessis* do not fall foul of the standards rightly invoked by Kriegler J, though our next case does show that especially lower courts may have difficulties in this respect. We will thus return to this problem when addressing the dangers of using foreign law under s 6 below.

Our last example from South Africa serves to illustrate the special importance of comparative law in situations where courts have to deal with legal transplants. These can take place on different levels of a legal system and for a variety of reasons. More than a decade ago, Alan Watson declared that 'borrowing from another system is the most common form of legal change',[151] and it seems as if the demise of the former socialist systems in Eastern Europe, the ambition of many countries to join the European Union and to develop active commercial relationships with the United States, as well as the democratisation of many societies, accompanied by the concerted effort to improve human rights protection around the world, have further strengthened the trend towards a global spread of legal ideas. Legal transplants are thereby not only the result of decisions made by national legislators but also – if not as frequent – a product of judicial activity. Borrowing is, therefore, often justified by the quality of a given foreign solution. Other, at times overlapping, reasons include: the harmonisation of law within the framework of international agreements; the influence of new or attractive political concepts; special

---

150 Op. cit. note 148.

151 Alan Watson, *Legal Origins and Legal Change* (1991), p 73.

economic, judicial, or cultural ties between societies;[152] the general influence that many 'parent' legal systems continue to exert on their former colonies;[153] or, finally, demands of donor countries calling for the observance of democratic standards and respect for human rights by nations receiving from them development aid.[154] The unequal distribution of economic power creates further incentives for the introduction of changes based on foreign commercial law, and military intervention followed by the reconstruction of societies on the basis of 'imported' legal principles has re-emerged, it seems, as yet another scenario favouring legal transplants.

The transplantation of law is, of course, a dynamic process. The initial phase involves the identification of an appropriate model and (in most cases) more or less comprehensive adjustments of the chosen material in order to merge it successfully with the existing rules of the borrowing system. Even mere translation will thus often increase the differences between the original and the imitated provision.

But what about the further development of foreign ideas once they have found their way into their new legal and factual environment? The borrowing system is not in any way bound by the interpretation of the model provision in its country of origin and the courts are thus free to ignore (or take into account) the case law and academic literature available in that system. That said, not even the strongest critics of comparative law in the courtroom could deny that there are, indeed, good reasons for judges to look at this foreign material. For lawyers operating in a legal system which attaches importance to the legislative intent, a comparison can not only help to show why a particular foreign model was chosen; by highlighting possible differences between that model and the own national variant, the meaning of one's own law may also become clearer. More importantly, foreign case law dealing with a very similar (or even identical) provision will be likely to display a range of possible solutions for disputes with a similar factual background. At the end of the day, that does not absolve judges from forming their own opinion; it may, however, expand the 'argumentative horizon' for the solution of their case and thus, sometimes, even save precious court time.

Let us now look more closely at one particular legal transplant and its subsequent fate in a South African courtroom.

As pointed out above, a number of ideas were taken from the German Basic Law in the process of reconstructing the South African

---

[152] One such close relationship which has led to a number of mutual influences is that between Germany and Austria.

[153] Zweigert/Kötz, *Introduction to Comparative Law* (3rd edn, 1998), pp 65 ff.

[154] Decalo, 'The Process, Prospects and Constraints of Democratization in Africa', [1992] *African Affairs* 7, 16 ff.

constitutional order between 1993 and 1996. The right to freedom of trade, occupation, and profession guaranteed by s 22 of the 1996 Constitution was thereby drafted on the basis of the German *Berufsfreiheit* protected by Art 12(1) BL. It is not always easy to identify legal transplants, but in this instance the South African provision seems to be a straightforward candidate. A simple textual comparison immediately reveals the close relationship. Both norms establish the right to choose freely an occupation or profession, and allow the practice of such activities to be regulated by law. Both systems restrict the protective scope of this right to nationals. Here, then, is the text of the two provisions:

Table 2.1 Freedom of occupation in Germany and South Africa

Article 12(1) BL[155]	**Section 22 of the 1996 Constitution**
[1]All Germans shall have the right freely to choose their occupation or profession, their place of work, and their place of training.[2] The practice of an occupation or profession may be regulated by or pursuant to a law.	[1]Every citizen has the right to choose their trade, occupation or profession freely.[2] The practice of a trade, occupation or profession may be regulated by law.

When one moves to details, three differences become apparent.

The German text includes a reference to the place of training and specifies that the practice of an occupation or profession may also be regulated pursuant to a law. In South Africa, trade is singled out as a separate category of protected activity. Closer analysis shows, however, that these differences in wording are not substantial. The term 'occupation' (*Beruf*) is generally acknowledged to mean any permanent activity designed to create and safeguard the economical basis of earning a livelihood in Germany and covers all forms of commercial activity including trade. The choice of a place of training is thereby clearly not more than a sub-category of the right to choose freely an occupation for which such training is necessary or desirable. Finally, the ability of the South African executive to regulate the practice of a trade, occupation,

[155] Translation by Tomuschat/Curry in: Press and Information Office of the Federal Government, *Basic Law for the Federal Republic of Germany* (1998). The German text of Art 12(1) BL declares: 'Alle Deutschen haben das Recht, Beruf, Arbeitsplatz und Ausbildungsstätte frei zu wählen. Die Berufsausübung kann durch Gesetz oder auf Grund eines Gesetzes geregelt werden'.

or profession *pursuant* to a law is contained in the right to regulate *by* law. As in Germany, laws which meet the constitutional requirements of a limitation can authorise the executive to take further action within the limits of the empowering statute.

This prima facie evidence that the South African provision was, indeed, drafted along the lines of the German model is further strengthened by a contextual analysis of the South African Bill of Rights. The 1996 Constitution relies on a general limitation clause contained in s 36.[156] A similar provision was included in s 33 of the 1993 Constitution, but was accompanied there by a number of additional, specific ('internal') limitation clauses located within the various human rights provisions themselves (much in the style of the German *Grundgesetz*, which does not contain a general limitation clause). These superfluous 'internal limitation clauses' were omitted in 1996. The right to freedom of trade, occupation, and profession, however, a latecomer in the drafting process which substituted the right to economic activity introduced in 1993, obviously retained in its second sentence the first part of the special limitation clause which the draftsmen had found in its German counterpart. This second sentence seems to be redundant for the purposes of simply limiting the right safeguarded by s 22 (which is already possible on the basis of the general limitation clause[157]) and can only be explained in one of two ways. Either it is an editorial error, which is rather unlikely given the omission of the words 'or pursuant to [a law]' in preliminary drafts of the text and the careful deletion of the other internal limitation clauses contained in the 1993 Constitution. Alternatively, it is a sign that the draftsmen attached some significance to the difference between the *choice* (mentioned in the first sentence of the provision) and the *practice* of a trade, occupation, or profession (expressly subjected to a limitation by law in the second sentence). And sure enough – it is precisely *this* distinction which characterises Art 12(1) BL and has influenced the approach of German courts when dealing with

---

156 Section 36 Republic of South Africa Constitution Act 1996 declares:

> (1) The rights in the Bill of Rights may be limited only in terms of law of general application to the extent that the limitation is reasonable and justifiable in an open and democratic society based on human dignity, equality and freedom, taking into account all relevant factors, including – (a) the nature of the right; (b) the importance of the purpose of the limitation; (c) the nature and extent of the limitation; (d) the relation between the limitation and its purpose; and (e) less restrictive means to achieve this purpose. (2) Except as provided in sub-s (1) or in any other provision of the Constitution, no law may limit any right entrenched in the Bill of Rights.

157 This is also pointed out by Ignus Rautenbach and E. F. J. Malherbe, *Constitutional Law* (2nd edn, 1998), p 328 ('the clause does not seem to serve any purpose').

the interpretation of that provision. Depending on the quality of a legislative or administrative measure, different levels of judicial scrutiny are thereby applied with respect to limitations of the *choice* (mentioned in the first sentence) as opposed to the *practice* of an occupation or profession (mentioned in the second sentence).

Finally, the German origin of s 22 is also confirmed by contemporary accounts of the drafting process. Peter Leon, one of the experts intimately involved in the negotiations leading to both Constitutions, recalls that the stalemate between those in favour of giving the State more latitude to engage in the socio-economic reconstruction of the country and those who stressed the protection of individual freedom, property, and economic activity was overcome by a proposal of the late Professor Etienne Mureinik, who pointed to the German approach as a possible compromise.[158]

This German origin of s 22 was acknowledged in the South African decision *City of Cape Town v Ad Outpost (Pty) Ltd*,[159] a case where the plaintiff (a commercial firm) challenged a municipal by-law placing restrictions on the use of billboards for commercial purposes by relying, *inter alia*, on the protection offered by the freedom of trade, occupation, and profession. Said the court:

> Section 22 appears to be modelled on Article 12(1) of the German Basic Law which provides that all Germans have the right freely to choose their occupation and profession, their place of work, study or training. The practice of an occupation may be regulated by law. The German courts have interpreted Article 12 to provide a considerable amount of constitutional protection for commercial activities. Thus in the Pharmacy case 7 BVerfGE 377 Article 12(1) was interpreted to empower the legislator to regulate the practice as well as the choice of an occupation. Regulations dealing with the latter are greatly circumscribed by the article. The practice of an occupation which is the relevant issue in the present case may be 'restricted by *reasonable* regulations predicated on considerations of the common good.' In short an uncritical application of German jurisprudence would afford some assistance to respondent's attempt to attack the by-law in terms of section 22 of the Constitution.

As pointed out above, German constitutional doctrine does, indeed, differentiate between the *choice* and the *practice* of an occupation, establishing a higher level of judicial scrutiny for limitations of the former. But (as correctly indicated in the South African judgment) *both*

---

[158] Peter Leon, 'A Personal Perspective on Etienne Mureinik's Contribution to South Africa's Final Constitution', (1998) *South African Journal of Human Rights* 201, 203.

[159] *City of Cape Town v Ad Outpost (Pty) Ltd and Others*, 2000 (2) *BCLR* (Butterworths Constitutional Law Reports) 130 (C) at 141F.

types of limitation are subject to the principle of proportionality, which is regarded as a basic constitutional safeguard often derived from the rule of law but which is not found in the text of the Basic Law, itself. Under German law, limitations such as the restrictions imposed by the *City of Cape Town* regarding billboards would thus have to be capable of achieving the legislative or administrative aim (*Geeignetheit*), they would have to be the mildest means by which this aim can be achieved (*Erforderlichkeit*), and they would have to be reasonable when balancing the adverse effects of the measure on the individual citizen with the positive effects on the public interest (*Verhältnismäßigkeit*). The different structure of the South African Constitution, which constitutionalised the principle of proportionality as part of its *general* limitation clause, led the South African judge to a different result regarding the appropriate standard of judicial scrutiny in this case. The Court thus continued:

> However for Mr Heunis' [counsel for the company] submission to be accepted, a similar approach will be required to be followed to interpret section 22. There is always a great danger in the uncritical employment of foreign law in the process of domestic interpretation. Notwithstanding that Article 12 and section 22 are similar in wording the latter must be interpreted in the context of the South African constitutional text and its own pedigree. (...) The purpose of section 22 would thus appear to be to ensure that regulations which control a citizen's right to choose a trade and occupation or profession should be implemented in a rational manner.

When it comes to limitations of the practice of a trade, occupation, or profession, South African authorities therefore only need to show a *rational connection* between the desired measure and a legitimate public interest. According to this interpretation, the special internal limitation clause taken from the Basic Law – *specifically introduced, as shown above, in an attempt to strike a balance between necessary State intervention and the protection of the individual on the basis of the German model*[160] – thus leads to a much lower level of protection for the individual. The regulation of commercial practice is not even subject to a proportionality analysis, which is only activated (on the basis of the general limitation clause) if South African authorities wanted to limit the *choice* of a trade, occupation, or profession. The flexible and sliding scale of judicial scrutiny – which determines the specific character of the German model and which formed the basis of the political compromise in South Africa during the negotiation process in 1996 – is thus exchanged for an all-or-nothing approach which draws a rigid line between these two types of limitation.

---

160 In which the *importance* of the public interest and the *degree of danger* to this interest play a crucial role in the application of the principle of proportionality.

The differences in the interpretation of the two provisions are even more profound when it comes to the application of the South African norm to juristic persons. In *City of Cape Town v Ad Outpost (Pty) Ltd*, the respondent – a legal entity – could not even *invoke* successfully the protection offered by the freedom of trade, occupation, and profession. Dismissing s 22 of the 1996 Constitution as a possible defence in this case, the Court explained:

> In my view section 22 introduces a constitutional protection to be enjoyed by individual citizens as opposed to juristic bodies. The right ensures that each citizen will have the right to choose how to employ his or her labour and skills without irrational governmental restriction. It is not a provision which should be extended to the regulation of economic intercourse as undertaken by enterprises owned by juristic bodies which might otherwise fall within the description of economic activity. For this reason I do not consider that section 22 is of any assistance to respondents in the present case.

This is a surprisingly brief discussion of a very difficult and in practice highly relevant question which has been the subject of much academic writing and case law in Germany. Comparative work would thus have revealed that Art 12 BL offers *full* protection to juristic persons formed under German law. This is especially important because s 8(4) of the 1996 Constitution – dealing with the application of human rights to juristic persons in South Africa – is, again, a *legal transplant* based on the *German* approach. Thus the two texts read as follows:

Table 2.2 Juristic persons in Germany and South Africa

Article 19(3) BL	**Section 8(4) of the 1996 Constitution**
Basic rights also apply to domestic corporations to the extent that the nature of the right permits	A juristic person is entitled to the rights in the Bill of Rights to the extent required by the nature of the rights and the nature of that juristic person.

Under these circumstances, the arguments which led German constitutional doctrine to expand the scope of protection to legal entities when it comes to commercial activity must surely have been of interest to the South African judge confronted with the very same question. This is especially true since a textual analysis of the 1996 Constitution *itself* raises serious doubts concerning the restrictive approach of the South African court, which is to a large extent focused on the term *citizen*. In all other cases, the Bill of Rights of the 1996 Constitution thus refers to citizenship only where the framers of the Constitution tried to identify rights which are granted to *citizens* and not to *aliens*. These are rights which can obviously not be exercised by a juristic person – political rights (including the right to form, participate in the activities of, or recruit members for, a political party; the right to free, fair, and regular elections; and the right to vote and to stand for public office),[161] the right not to be deprived of citizenship,[162] the right to enter, to remain in, and to reside anywhere in the Republic; and the right to a passport.[163] Clearly, s 22 does *not* belong to this group. The reference to 'citizens' is therefore likely to be an editorial error resulting from the translation of the German model, which indeed refers to 'all Germans' – distinguishing (as does the 1996 Constitution in the instances mentioned above!) between *German* natural and juristic persons and *aliens*. A comparative analysis could have clarified this wider background and, perhaps, led to a different outcome of the case.

At this point we feel, again, the need to emphasise that foreign law can never be a binding guideline for the national judge – not even in the case of closely related legal transplants. In this instance, therefore, the South African courts are not in any way bound by a virtual German 'copyright' concerning the interpretation of their 'own' freedom of occupation enshrined in the 1996 Constitution. On the contrary, the different socio-economic parameters prevalent in both countries actually call for a very careful assessment of the transplanted solution and can, perhaps, justify an interpretation which gives South African authorities more latitude in the regulation of economic activity and/or restricts the right to natural persons. But we also feel that comparative law *can* provide important additional angles from which to analyse the local legal system. Especially in the case of legal transplants, the method can lead to a more informed result, and we see no reason why it should be restricted to the legislator. Here, the German model was chosen for specific reasons by the framers of the 1996 Constitution, and we have serious doubts whether the solution adopted by the Court regarding the low level of justification required for a limitation of the practice of a trade, occupation, or profession can be reconciled with the original intent of the Constitutional Assembly. The application of the right to juristic persons is, perhaps, a different matter. In the absence of a clear constitutional answer, the judge was bound to apply s 8(4) of the 1996 Constitution in order to determine whether the respondent was entitled

161 Section 19.

162 Section 20.

163 Section 21.

to invoke the freedom of occupation, taking into account both the nature of the right and the nature of the juristic person in question. Employing the very same approach, German experience could have been of particular interest in this context, and would certainly have facilitated a more profound discussion of this important question. The South African result could *still* have been different, but a comparative analysis would have at least revealed that the choice of the term 'citizen' in the text of the 1996 Constitution is probably just a coincidence resulting from the translation of the German text and not an informed choice of the legislator.

A final note should be added to complete the story of this legal transplant. As pointed out in the essay by Laurie Ackermann,[164] the Constitutional Court had, in late 2004/early 2005 the opportunity to deal with the interpretation of s 22 of the 1996 Constitution. In that case[165] – involving the introduction of specific requirements for the dispensation of medicines by medical practitioners (rather than pharmacists) – Justice Ngcobo, delivering the judgement of the Court, again reflected on the close similarity between the South African provision and its German counterpart. Without referring to that case, the Court in essence confirmed the position already indicated in *City of Cape Town v Ad Outpost (Pty) Ltd* by distinguishing between choice and practice of a profession (as in Germany) and requiring a *reasonable* (i.e. proportionate) limitation in the first but only an *objectively rational* regulation in the second alternative. This marks, as explained above, an important difference to the German model. Interestingly, though, Justice Ngcobo leaves open a back door through which the Court could, in the future, still introduce a stricter form of inquiry:

> [93] That said, however, the scope of permissible regulation that we adopt here is not entirely inconsistent with the German approach. It recognises that it is not always possible to draw a clear line of distinction between regulation that affects the practice of a profession on the one hand and one that affects choice on the other. It requires that where, objectively viewed, the regulation of the practice of a profession impacts negatively on choice such regulation must be tested under section 36(1). Such regulation does not fall within the purview of section 22, and must therefore meet, amongst other requirements, the standard of reasonableness, of which proportionality analysis is an important component. The same standard must be met where the regulation of the practice of a profession limits any of the rights in the Bill of Rights. However where, as here, the regulation,

---

164 See p 283.

165 *The Affordable Medicines Trust and Others v The Minister of Health of the Republic of South Africa and Others*, Case CCT 27/04 of 11 March 2005.

objectively viewed, does not impact negatively on choice, it need only satisfy the rationality test. In the result, restrictions on the right to practise a profession are subject to a less stringent test than restrictions on the choice of a profession.

Finally, it seems remarkable that the question whether the first and second applicants (both legal entities!) could at all rely on s 22 of the 1996 Constitution was not discussed with a single word. Only the third applicant in this case was a natural person. The underlying assumption made by the Court (that juristic persons such as the Affordable Medicines Trust and the National Convention on Dispensing *can* indeed rely on the protection granted by that provision) certainly confirms the position presented in this chapter. Comparative arguments, however, would have provided a better foundation for the development of the law in this respect.

Chapter 3: When Should Such Dialogue Take Place?

1. When the court has to discover 'Common principles of law'

At first blush one would certainly expect a court which operates in an international setting – especially when it is, by its very composition, multi-national in character – to work comparatively. A distinction should be made, however, according to the rules which judges sitting on such bodies apply. These can fall into one of two categories.

In the first, they form an *independent* system of law, which has little or no connection to other (national or international) legal orders. Here, comparative law will have the same appeal (strong or weak) as it does in any other national courtroom. In the second category, these rules can have direct textual or contextual links to other systems of law, either by explicit references to particular features of these systems or by deriving much of their implicit logic from such law. A court working with rules which fall into the latter category will be likely to benefit from comparative work.

The European Union may arguably be the best legal order to analyse under this heading. Its roots go back to the European Coal and Steel Community of 1951, which was initially conceived by its six founding Member States to fulfil a very limited purpose. By 2006 the European Union has, however, developed into a union of 25 nations, and the Communities exert substantial influence on their national law in areas as diverse as agriculture, environmental protection, social security, human rights, data protection, monetary policy, and, most importantly, issues related to the free movement of goods, persons, services, and capital. Some estimate that as much as 60 percent of the national law in EU Member States is today directly or indirectly influenced by European legislation.

Such a development does not, of itself, necessarily change the character of the rules applied in an international organisation; and despite the additional competences transferred to the European level over the past decades, Community law could still aim at far-reaching (or even complete) independence from the law of its Member States.

It seems, however, that Europe is *not* a one-way street; and this forms the second aspect of Community law. For here we see it not as an autonomous system but one which has to draw its nourishment from the Member States. The thesis that the European Court of Justice cannot ignore the law of the Member States can be illustrated in at least three (additional)[1] ways.

First, the Treaties themselves sometimes refer directly to national law. This is, for example, the case with Art 288 EC Treaty, which determines that the Community shall, in the case of non-contractual liability, make good any damage caused by its institutions or by its servants in the performance of their duties 'in accordance with the general principles common to the laws of the Member States'.

Second, both primary and secondary Community legislation is influenced by rules of municipal law and makes use of legal terminology which has a common content in the various national legal systems. The use of common (national) terms in EU legislation is an indication that judges applying EU law should at least seek guidance in national law when ascertaining the precise meaning of particular rules in their judgments.[2]

Third, judges applying EU law encounter the same difficulties as their national colleagues when it comes to gaps in the law. Judges confronted with open questions are likely to find possible answers in the law of the Member States and should make use of these 'national treasuries'.[3]

Has the ECJ, then, used comparative law as a tool? If so, to what extent has the method influenced the development of specific principles of Community law or the outcome of particular cases?

On the surface of ECJ judgements one finds little evidence of comparative work; open references to the national law of the Member States are, on the whole, far and few. An expert on the subject has put it in this way: 'National law influences are sometimes overt but more often

---

[1] We stress 'additional' for in Chapter 1, section 3, we referred briefly to the development of the general principles of Community law, focusing largely on the legal values shared by the Member States.

[2] Though one must, of course, also bear in mind that Community law serves a *separate* overall purpose which is different from national law and can thus call for different interpretations.

[3] This view is shared, e.g., by Koen Lenaerts, 'Interlocking Legal Orders or the European Union Variant of E Pluribus Unum' in Guy Canivet, Mads Andenas, and Duncan Fairgrieve (eds), *Comparative Law Before the Courts* (2004), pp 99 ff; Jürgen Gündisch/Sigrid Wienhues, *Rechtsschutz in der Europäischen Union* (2nd edn, 2003), p 182; Hans-Werner Rengeling and Peter Szczekalla, *Grundrechte in der Europäischen Union* (2004), pp 262/263; Christian Calliess, 'Grundlagen, Grenzen und Perspektiven europäischen Richterrechts', [2005] NJW 929 at 932.

covert and indirect'.[4] The *Alegra*-decision[5] is one exception. Confronted with the question whether an individual administrative act, which has given rise to a subjective right, may be revoked by a public authority (an issue not addressed by EU law), the Court gave a detailed analysis of the law as applied in the Member States. It said:

> The possibility of withdrawing such measures is a problem of administrative law, which is familiar in the case-law and learned writing of all the countries of the Community, but for the solution of which the Treaty does not contain any rules. Unless the Court is to deny justice it is therefore obliged to solve the problem by reference to the rules acknowledged by the legislation, the learned writing and the case-law of the Member Countries.[6]

After this interesting introduction, which explains the use of the comparative method by reference to the notion of *justice*, the Court then turned to examine briefly the law of the various Member States. It stated:

> 'It emerges from a comparative study of this problem of law that in the [then] six Member States an administrative measure conferring individual rights on the person concerned cannot in principle be withdrawn, if it is a lawful measure; in that case, since the individual right is vested, the need to safeguard confidence in the stability of the situation thus created prevails over the interests of an administration desirous of reversing its decision. This is true in particular of the appointment of an official.

If, on the other hand, the administrative measure is illegal, revocation is possible under the law of all the Member States. The absence of an objective legal basis for the measure affects the individual right of the person concerned and justifies the revocation of the said measure. It should be stressed that whereas this principle is generally acknowledged, only the conditions for its application vary.

French law requires that the withdrawal of the illegal measure should be pronounced before the expiry of the time-limit for instituting legal proceedings and, if proceedings have been instituted, before judgment is delivered; with certain small differences, Belgian, Luxembourg, and Netherlands laws seem to follow similar rules.

German law, on the other hand, does not set any time-limit for the exercise of the right of revocation, except where such a time-limit is laid down by a special provision. Thus Art 13 of the *Bundesbeamtengesetz* (Federal Law Governing Civil Servants) allows the withdrawal of an

---

[4] Takis Tridimas, *The General Principles of EC Law* (2001), p 353. On the other hand, earlier on (at p 15) he also gives an excellent summary of the areas where German and French law have made their influence most strongly felt.

[5] Joined Cases 7/56, 3/57 to 7/57.

[6] At p 55.

appointment only within a period of six months. However, it is generally acknowledged that unduly late withdrawal, occurring considerably later than the date on which withdrawal could have been pronounced, is contrary to the principle of good faith (*Treu und Glauben*). In this connection, case law and learned writing found themselves also upon the concepts of waiver (*Verzicht*) and of forfeiture (*Verwirkung*) of the right of revocation.

Italian law is particularly clear on the question. Any administrative measure which is vitiated by lack of competence, infringement of the law, or abuse of powers (*eccesso di potere*) may be annulled ex tunc by the administrative authority which issued it, irrespective of the individual rights to which it might have given rise. Such withdrawal may be declared at any time (*in qualsiasi momento*); thus there is no time-limit prescribed for withdrawal. However, according to learned writing and case-law, unduly late withdrawal can constitute abuse of powers; measures which have been in force for a long time (*fatti avvenuti da lunga data*) should be kept in force, even if they were contrary to the law, unless overriding reasons require their withdrawal in the public interest.

Thus the revocability of an administrative measure vitiated by illegality is allowed in all Member States.'[7]

In the above decision, therefore, the Court openly used national law to develop Community law.[8] The same was done in *Hauer*, where the ECJ analysed the different approaches found in the limitation of constitutionally protected property rights.[9] Here, the Court also reiterated its view on the importance of human rights already developed in *Internationale Handelsgesellschaft*[10] and *Nold*,[11] and said that

> (...) fundamental rights form an integral part of the general principles of the law, the observance of which it ensures; that in safeguarding those rights, the Court is bound to draw inspiration from constitutional traditions common to the Member States, so that measures which are incompatible with the fundamental rights recognised by the Constitutions of those States are unacceptable in the Community.[12]

---

[7] At pp 55/56.

[8] More recent examples include Case T-43/90, *Diaz Garcia v European Parliament* [1992] ECR II-2619 and Case T-85/91, *Khouri v Commission* [1992] ECR II-2637.

[9] Case 44/79, *Liselotte Hauer v Land Rheinland-Pfalz* [1979] ECR 3727, 3746.

[10] [1970] ECR 1125.

[11] [1974] ECR 491.

[12] At no 15.

This is clear evidence that comparative law has a role to play in defining the standard by which the ECJ will measure possible human rights infringements.[13]

More often, however, judgments merely give a general indication that the Court has indeed engaged in comparative work. This can, for instance, be seen in *Industrial Diamonds Supplies v Riva*[14] where the ECJ analysed how national legal systems distinguish between 'ordinary' and 'extraordinary' appeals. Without specifying individual systems or their respective approaches in any detail, the Court thus explained that:

> (I)t follows from a comparison of the legal concepts of the various Member States of the Community that although in some States the distinction between 'ordinary' and 'extraordinary' appeals is based on the law itself, in other legal systems the classification is made primarily or even purely in the works of learned authors, while in a third group of States this distinction is completely unknown.[15]

Finding that on this point national laws are not in agreement with one another, the Court then went on to develop its own definition of an 'extraordinary' appeal.

Other decisions show that national solutions are sometimes only described in the *facts* but do not feature openly in the *reasons* given by the Court. The *Defrenne*-decision[16] of 1976 is such a case. *Defrenne* is also worth mentioning because the ECJ had actually asked the Commission – involved in the dispute – to provide comparative material.

A first result of our analysis thus suggests that the ECJ does not frequently adopt an *open* use of comparative law. Traces of foreign law, however, often compelling, do exist (albeit couched in general language) and they suggest that some degree of comparative work has taken place behind the scenes. A survey of the opinions of the Advocates General reinforces this view. Indeed, much in the tradition of the French *avocats généreaux*, these conclusions contain fairly regular references to national law and its interpretation and application in the Member States of the

---

[13] Other examples of a use of comparative law by the Court are the development of the liability of Community institutions in damages (see, e.g., the opinion of the Advocates General in *Aktien-Zuckerfabrik Schoppenstedt v Council*, Case 5/71 [1971] ECR 975 and *Kampffmeyer v Commission*, Cases 5, 7 and 13–24/66 [1967] ECR 245) and the judgments in *R v Secretary of State for Transport, ex p Factortame Ltd*, Case C-213/89 (1990) and *Brasserie du Pêcheur SA v Germany*, Case C-46/93 (1996) dealing with the liability of national authorities for breach of national law with a view to establishing their liability for breach of EC law.

[14] Case 43/77.

[15] At no 22.

[16] *Gabrielle Defrenne v Société anonyme belge de navigation aérienne Sabena*, Case 43/75.

Union. A.G. Roemer thus expressly stated that the Court has to 'call upon the law of the different Member States in order to arrive at a meaningful interpretation of (...) Community law'.[17]

Other examples, such as the detailed discussions of Member State law by A.G. Lagrange in *Associazione Industrie Siderurgische Italiane (ASSIDER) v High Authority of the European Coal and Steel Community*[18] and *Compagnie des Hauts Fourneaux de Chasse v High Authority of the European Coal and Steel Community*[19] confirm the point. There can thus be little doubt that the comparative work contained in the much fuller opinions of the Advocates General has influenced the shorter – and indeed sometimes cryptic – judgments of the Court.

The influence of national legal traditions is also secured through the composition of the ECJ, itself, since every Member State is entitled to nominate one of the 25 judges sitting on the Court. This must result in an ongoing comparative judicial dialogue, which is supported by the ECJ's own legal research unit. To facilitate the work of the Court, this unit produces substantial comparative reports on the law as applied in the various Member States; and the library in Strasbourg could be called a 'repository' of national Member State law.

Though the above indicates that comparative law *is* a highly relevant tool in the work of the ECJ two questions remain. First, has national law influenced the results reached by the Court *beyond* the limited ways outlined above? Second, why has the method not been used more openly in the judgments *themselves*?

The principle of proportionality is a very clear example of national law actually influencing the jurisprudence of the ECJ and, subsequently, the legal approach in other Member States. Rooted in the German notion of the *Rechtsstaatsprinzip*,[20] proportionality (or *Verhältnismäßigkeit*) is a core unwritten principle of German constitutional law. To pass judicial scrutiny, any state action affecting the rights of individuals must comply with three requirements: (1) The public aim, itself, has to be constitutional, and the measure *capable* of reaching the desired aim in practice; (2) the measure also has to be *necessary* in the sense that no equally effective but less infringing alternative exists; and (3) the public interest in reaching the aim has to outweigh the interest of the affected individual in the unlimited exercise of constitutionally acknowledged or otherwise protected rights. This last aspect of the principle calls for a complex balancing of conflicting values, which should, ideally, be reconciled so as to give each interest full constitutional recognition.

---

17 *Netherlands Government v High Authority of the ECSC*, [1954–6] ECR 103, Case 6/54.

18 Case 3/54, [1954–6] ECR 63.

19 Case 2/57, [1957–8] ECR 199 at 203–5.

20 A concept frequently equated with the rule of law.

The main area in which the principle of proportionality has exerted its influence in German law is the protection of fundamental rights, and it is here, also, that it first appeared as a concern on the European stage. In the famous *Internationale Handelsgesellschaft* case of 1970,[21] German judges felt that a Community system of deposits connected to export licenses was incompatible with the freedom of action, the freedom of occupation, and the principle of proportionality as protected by the Basic Law. The Court asked the ECJ for a ruling on the validity of the Community measure.

In dealing with the reference, the ECJ first found that Community measures could only be judged in the light of Community law. The Court stated that[22]

> (R)ecourse to the legal rules or concepts of national law in order to judge the validity of measures adopted by the institutions of the Community would have an adverse effect on the uniformity and efficacy of Community law.

This passage clearly distinguished the legal order of the Community from national constitutional law. Avoiding the apparent tension between the protection of the individual under German constitutional guarantees and the lack of a comparable regime on the European level the Court, nevertheless, went on to say that[23]

> an examination should be made as to whether or not any analogous guarantee inherent in Community law has been disregarded. In fact, respect for fundamental rights forms an integral part of the general principles of law protected by the Court of Justice. The protection of such rights, whilst inspired by the constitutional traditions common to the Member States, must be ensured within the framework of the structure and objectives of the Community.

Here the Court is, clearly, trying to build a bridge between its own jurisprudence and the traditions of the Member States. It is, however, a 'fortified' bridge. The gatekeepers on the Community side are the qualifiers 'traditions *common* to the Member States' and the 'structures and objectives of the *Community*'.

Scrutinising the legality of the system of deposits attacked by the German plaintiff with a view to these *analogous guarantees inherent in Community law*, the ECJ was obviously inspired by the German notion of *Verhältnismäßigkeit* and applied, in essence, the same criteria. Taking

---

[21] Following a preliminary reference from the Administrative Court Frankfurt am Main; see note 10, above.

[22] Case 11/70, *Internationale Handelsgesellschaft mbH v Einfuhr- und Vorratsstelle für Getreide- und Futtermittel* [1970] ECR, 1125 ff at para 3.

[23] Ibid, at para 4.

the relevant Thirteenth Recital of the Preamble to Regulation 120/67 as a point of departure, the Court thus found that (1) the contested system was designed to meet an important Community objective involving 'heavy financial responsibilities for the Community and the Member States', and that the measure was capable of reaching that aim; (2) that less infringing alternatives such as, for example, a mere declaration of exports and unused quota would 'be incapable of providing the competent authorities with sure data on trends in the movement of goods' and (3) that the financial loss for the plaintiff did not 'constitute an amount disproportionate to the total value of the goods in question and of the other trading costs'.

The judgment contains no indication that the Court relied on a principle of German law. It was, however, a preliminary reference from a *German* administrative court which questioned the validity of a Community measure by invoking, *inter alia*, the *German* concept of proportionality. And the ECJ was clearly trying to avoid a gap between the standard of human rights protection in this *particular* Member State on the one hand and the Community on the other.

Though clothed in different words, this 'discovery' of an 'integral part of the general principles of law protected by the Court of Justice' is *technically* nothing else than judicial borrowing. When compared to the other examples of legal transplants discussed in the South African context, above, the only differences seem to be the absence of a constitutional text in the borrowing system[24] and, more importantly, the fact that foreign – Member State – law is, apparently, not 'borrowed' at all but rather 'inherent in Community law'.

There are, however, some crucial differences lurking below the surface of the straightforward text of a judgment such as *Internationale Handelsgesellschaft*. The Community and its Member States are linked much closer to each other than South Africa is to the various legal systems it has chosen to borrow from. The South African Constitution invites judges to look at other 'open and democratic societies based on freedom and equality' – in the words of the ECJ 'the constitutional traditions common to the Member States'. In South Africa, this is a one-sided process, and the national judges are free in their decision to engage in comparative thinking. In Europe, transplants such as the adoption of the principle of proportionality are far more complex since the game currently involves 26 players (25 Member States and the Community). The decision of the ECJ to adopt a certain approach found in national law inevitably has a knock-on effect on all other Member States, and it is interesting to note that the notion of *Verhältnismäßigkeit* has spread, in

24 The Treaties and secondary Community law, however, fulfil a very similar function.

some cases, not only to those parts of Member State law which are subject to Community influence but also to purely national law.[25] More important is the fact that the ECJ is not entirely free to engage in this exchange of ideas. The well-known further case history of *Internationale Handelsgesellschaft*[26] shows that the tensions between the constitutional traditions of Member States and the autonomous and supreme legal order of the Community can force the ECJ to seek a compromise. Despite earlier indications that fundamental rights would start to play a more important role in the jurisprudence of the ECJ, German judicial resistance to the supremacy of a Community lacking (from the FCC's point of view) adequate protection for the individual citizen affected by Community law forced the Court to develop its human rights jurisprudence. This development was largely based on comparative law, not only involving legal ideas drawn from the Member States but also, increasingly, from the case law of the European Court on Human Rights in Strasbourg.

The example of proportionality thus shows that national law has provided significant input when it comes to the development of core principles of Community law. A more detailed analysis is likely to produce even more evidence of this, though it can sometimes be very difficult, as stated above, to discern truly original 'Community law' from judicial borrowing.

A more recent case shows that comparative law is also utilised to identify the substantive content of Community human rights. In *Omega Spielhallen- und Automatenaufstellungs-GmbH v Oberbürgermeisterin der Bundesstadt Bonn*,[27] a company operating a so-called laserdrome had challenged an administrative order of the local police authority prohibiting the use of sub-machine-gun-type laser targeting devices and sensory tags fixed to jackets worn by players and designed to 'play at killing people'.[28] In making this decision, the German authorities were guided by their concern for human dignity. The Federal Administrative

---

[25] See, e.g., G. de Búrca, 'The Influence of European Legal Concepts on UK Law: Proportionality and Wednesbury Unreasonableness' [1997] *European Public Law*, 561 ff.

[26] Leading to the *Solange I*-decision of the *Bundesverfassungsgericht* (BVerfGE 37, 271 ff). For an English translation of the case see the website of the Institute of Global Law, University College London, at www.ucl.ac.uk/laws/global_law/cases/german/bverfg/bverfg_29may1974.html.

[27] Case 36/02 of 14 October 2004.

[28] Cases of this kind may seem strange to many Americans (and, indeed, many Europeans). Handed down by a new post-War generation of judges, they are part and parcel of the profound changes (and sometimes even paranoia) Germany has experienced after 1945. 'Killing for fun', as the local police authority in Bonn called it, is thus still associated with the atrocities of the Third Reich, prompting administrative authorities and courts to intervene. The closer the resemblance with reality (human beings as targets instead of images in video games and the like), the greater the likelihood of State

Court, eventually confronted with the issue, referred to the ECJ the question whether a common legal conception in all Member States (in this case regarding human dignity) was a precondition for one of those States to restrict, at its discretion, the provision of certain goods or services protected by the EC Treaty. The preliminary reference was deemed necessary because the plaintiff had entered into a franchise agreement with the British producer of the laser equipment and had argued, *inter alia*, that the prohibition order infringed his freedom to provide services under Art 49 EC. In dealing with the issue, Advocate General Stix-Hackl first argued that

> an established restriction on freedom to provide services cannot immediately be justified by the protection of specific fundamental rights guaranteed by the Constitution of a Member State. It is also necessary to examine the extent to which the restriction can be justified on grounds acknowledged in Community law, such as the safeguarding of public policy.

---

intervention. The important comparative aspects of this case are discussed in the text, above; but an anecdotal addendum might offer its own, no less important, illumination of the difficulties which comparatists must surmount. Our readers, especially the non-Americans, may thus be interested to read the reactions of a senior and well respected American jurist to the facts of the *Omega* case. He thus wrote to one of us:

> This is the sort of ruling that makes Americans think the Europeans are daft. In the United States, the game is called laser tag. There is also a low tech version called paintball, in which the gun shoots a sphere that bursts on impact and leaves a splotch of paint on the target. Laser tag is more sophisticated, because when you get 'shot', your own laser is disabled for a time; you can't shoot back while you are 'dead'. I'm sure there are anti-gun and anti-violence parents who don't let their kids play these games. But it seems bizarre to believe that kids won't play such games with or without technology. When I was a child (…), we played endless games of army, cowboys and Indians, and cops and robbers, shooting away with pretend guns and having frequent arguments about who shot first and who was therefore dead. I remember thinking as a kid that this needed something like paintball, to resolve those arguments. And then, my own kids discovered paintball and laser tag.

We cite this text, partly because the first of us has more sympathy with its point made in the letter than the second but, mainly, because it shows how it can also condition the reactions and attitudes of subsequent generations shaping their outlook. 'Mentality', as the source of human attitudes towards particular issues (including the use of foreign ideas), is explored in section 10 of the next chapter. If there is a wider moral to this story, it seems simple enough: people (and this includes, of course, jurists) from different countries often misunderstand one another because they know so little about each other. Thus, if American attitudes often seem strange to Europeans, the opposite is also true. The aim of those comparatists who, like us, wish to encourage international dialogue and reciprocal learning must always go beyond the presentation of the foreign law and cover also its explanation before, finally, proceeding to consider if, where, and how reconciliation is possible. Some may see in this an added difficulty in engaging in comparative law, it is; but it is also an incomparable intellectual challenge!

> A common conception among the Member States on the matter of protecting public order is not a precondition for such a justification.

She then conducted a comparative survey of the approaches to human dignity found in the Member States, because

> if such an examination should show that the restrictive national measure concerned is based on an evaluation of national protection of fundamental rights that reflects general legal opinion in the Member States, a corresponding requirement of protection could (also) be inferred from Community protection of fundamental rights – which would mean, methodologically speaking, that it would no longer be necessary to examine whether the national measure is to be considered a justified, because permissible, exception to the fundamental freedoms enshrined in the Treaty, but (...) 'how the requirements of the protection of fundamental rights in the Community can be reconciled with those arising from a fundamental freedom enshrined in the Treaty'.[29]

The ECJ followed this reasoning, stating:

> (I)t should be recalled (...) that, according to settled case-law, fundamental rights form an integral part of the general principles of law the observance of which the Court ensures, and that, for that purpose, the Court draws inspiration from the constitutional traditions common to the Member States and from the guidelines supplied by international treaties for the protection of human rights on which the Member States have collaborated or to which they are signatories. The European Convention on Human Rights and Fundamental Freedoms has special significance in that respect (...).
>
> As the Advocate General argues (...), the Community legal order undeniably strives to ensure respect for human dignity as a general principle of law. There can therefore be no doubt that the objective of protecting human dignity is compatible with Community law, it being immaterial in that respect that, in Germany, the principle of respect for human dignity has a particular status as an independent fundamental right.
>
> Since both the Community and its Member States are required to respect fundamental rights, the protection of those rights is a legitimate interest which, in principle, justifies a restriction of the obligations imposed by Community law, even under a fundamental freedom guaranteed by the Treaty such as the freedom to provide services (...).[30]

This juxtaposition of Advocate General Stix-Hackl's opinion and the Court's decision in *Omega* shows that the formula so frequently found in ECJ judgments – that the Court 'draws inspiration from the

---

[29] At no 72 of the opinion.

[30] At nos 33 ff.

constitutional traditions common to the Member States' – is in fact often a code for comparative work previously conducted by the Advocate Generals. Moulded into a corpus of Community law by the ECJ, the lines between national ideas thereby eventually fade and, over time, disappear.

The area of *autonomous* EU law is nevertheless likely to be substantial. A *sui generis* legal order, the Community is characterised by its very own political aims and economical objectives, practical difficulties, and legal values. These distinguish it from national law, and European judges will often develop their *own* solutions by reference to the increasing corpus of legal and extra-legal material by now available on the supra-national level (e.g. Intergovernmental Conferences, declarations of Community institutions such as the European Parliament, and documents like the European Charter of Fundamental Rights).

Notwithstanding the above, we would still expect the influence of the Member States to be more visible, and it is here that tactical considerations may come into play. For many years the Court has had to fight for recognition vis-à-vis the Member States, and too much comparative work or at least a highly visible use of the method could have been interpreted as a sign of the Court's insecurity, jeopardised its position in the many conflicts the ECJ had to survive, and put in question the autonomous nature of Community law. Open reliance on one particular national model also bears the danger of alienating other Member States, and can draw the Court into undesirable political discussions as to why a particular legal solution was found by reference to one country and not another.[31]

Finally, as with any national system of law, we must again stress the importance of the time factor. Fifty years into its existence, the European Union has matured into a highly developed and increasingly autonomous system of law. This has clearly reduced the need for comparative considerations, though new developments and concepts – such as the accession of further countries, the introduction of a coherent regime of human rights protection, or the principle of subsidiarity – are more than likely to result in a renaissance of national legal influence on Community law. Given the necessary resources (especially judicial time), the ECJ may thus again, as in its early days, make more use of the comparative method. Stronger and more confident than it was two or three decades

---

31 This is indicated by Hans-Wolfram Daig, 'Zu Rechtsvergleichung und Methodenlehre im Europäischen Gemeinschaftsrecht' in Festschrift Zweigert (1981), pp 395 ff at pp 411 ff.

ago, the Court might even attempt to do this more openly. The South African experience also indicates that dissenting opinions, not possible under the current procedural arrangements of the ECJ, can be of particular value in the context of comparative law. The understanding and acceptance of the Court's jurisprudence on the national level would improve substantially, we believe, if the ECJ were to discard the image of a 'unanimous oracle' and revealed the difficult (and often controversial) judicial dialogue which the identification of common principles and values must surely involve.

2. When local law presents a gap, ambiguity, or is in obvious need of modernisation, and guidance would be welcome

Two English decisions illustrate this point. The first is *Greatorex v Greatorex*;[32] but since one of us has already discussed it extensively elsewhere,[33] we shall concentrate on the second one, namely *Derbyshire County Council v Times Newspaper Ltd*.[34]

Derbyshire was a defamation case. It had to resolve a disagreement between two decisions of earlier lower courts as to whether a local authority, itself (as distinct from its individual councillors), could sue in defamation for allegations of inefficiency or corruption. In *Manchester Corp v Williams*,[35] the Divisional Court had taken the view that a municipal corporation could not, itself, bring an action for libel in respect of an allegation of 'bribery and corruption', but the later (and much criticised[36]) decision of the Queen's Bench Division in *Bognor Regis v Campion*[37] held that

> (J)ust as a trading company has a trading reputation which it is entitled to protect by bringing an action for defamation, so (...) the plaintiff as a local

---

[32] [2000] 1 WLR 1970.

[33] Basil Markesinis, *Comparative Law in the Courtroom and the Classroom. The Story of the Last Thirty-Five Years* (2003), chapters 2 and 4.

[34] [1992] 1 QB 770; CA 790; [1993] AC 534. The Court of Appeal decision in our view is more interesting in so far that it is also more honest than the decision in the House of Lords in admitting that its outcome was largely influenced by developments at the European level.

[35] [1891] 1 QB 94.

[36] See, especially, Tony Weir, '*Local Authority v Critical Ratepayer* – A Suit in Defamation', [1972] *CLJ* 238 – an essay unique for its conciseness, incisiveness, and immoderation!

[37] [1972] 2 QB 169.

> government corporation have a 'governing' reputation which they are equally entitled to protect in the same way (...).[38]

For years readers of practitioners' textbooks were offered technical ways of reconciling these two decisions. One of the most respected of these books in fact sided with the newer decision of what was, technically speaking, an inferior court (inferior to the one which had decided the old one) predicting its eventual confirmation by the highest court of the land.[39] The decision of the Court of Appeal in *Derbyshire* must have thus come as a surprise, as was its open and courageous admission that this issue could no longer be decided simply on tort grounds without taking into account Art 10 of the European Convention on Human Rights. The decision, in other words, was the English equivalent to *New York Times v Sullivan*[40] in so far as it constitutionalised the English law of defamation (though one would have to wait a few more years before the assessment offered in the text were to be truly confirmed by the coming into force of the Human Rights Act 1998.

In this light, it had to be seen as being affected by Art 10 ECHR even though it had not, at the time, been incorporated into English law.[41] Lady Justice Butler-Sloss's judgement in particular contains useful dicta as to when English courts can obtain guidance from foreign or international material. She thus said:

> (...) where the law is clear and unambiguous, either stated as the Common law or enacted by Parliament, recourse to Article 10 is unnecessary and inappropriate (...). But where there is an ambiguity, or the law is otherwise unclear or so far undeclared by an appellate court, the English court is not only entitled but, in my judgment, obliged to consider the implications of Article 10.[42]

The House of Lords confirmed this result (by rejecting the appeal of the local authority),[43] but via a different reasoning in so far as Lord Keith expressly stated that he saw no reason to refer to Art 10 of the Convention.[44] Instead, as so often happens in Britain's highest court, an attempt was made to argue that the Common law was always as efficient in protecting speech but merely proceeded in a different *methodological*

---

38 [1972]2 QB 169 at p 175.

39 Carter Ruck, *Libel and Slander* (4th edn, 1992), p 73.

40 376 US 254, 82 S. Ct. 710 (1964).

41 Though the United Kingdom ratified the Convention in 1951.

42 [1992] 1 QB 790, at p 830.

43 [1993] AC 534.

44 Ibid at p 551.

manner.[45] Nonetheless, comparative law was not avoided but merely restricted to supporting authorities from US[46] and Commonwealth courts.[47] This preference for taking into account the experience of systems whose language we share is entirely understandable though in this case and, indeed, in others, it fails to show sufficient sensitivity to local conditions (in this case the United States and its First Amendment) which may not be replicated in the borrowing system and may thus lead its lawyers to misunderstand what they are copying. Thus, though Lord Keith even borrowed the expression 'chilling effect' (which is widely used in American law but was until then uncommon in the English context), he made little reference to the First Amendment and the extent to which this has shaped the American law of defamation since *New York Times Co. v Sullivan*.[48] Though this might not have been fatal for the purposes of the litigation at hand, ignoring this (different) background factor can 'inhibit' the use of American law in other areas of the law (such as our presently emerging law of privacy), given that in England we are now (as a result of the Human Rights Act 1998) obliged to weigh the competing rights contained in Arts 8 and 10 of the Convention and not forced to give preference to speech over reputation or dignity. English law is thus,

---

[45] Reference is thus often made to Law Goff's judgment in *A-G v Guardian Newspapers Ltd (no2)* [1990] 1 AC 109, 280, where the learned judge said, *inter alia* (at p 283),

> (...) I wish to observe that I can see no inconsistency between English law on this subject [speech rights] and Article 10 of the European Convention on Human Rights. This is scarcely surprising, since we may pride ourselves on the fact that freedom of speech has existed in this country perhaps as long as, if not longer than, it has existed in any other country in the world. The only difference is that, whereas Article 10 of the Convention, in accordance with its avowed purpose, proceeds to state a fundamental right and then to qualify it, we in this country (where everybody is free to do anything, subject only to the provisions of the law) proceed rather upon an assumption of freedom of speech, and turn to our law to discover the established exceptions to it.

Cf. Lord Bingham's more cynical and, it is submitted, more convincing observation: 'If in truth the Common law as it stands were giving the rights of United Kingdom citizens the same protection as the Convention – across the board, and not only in relation to Article 10 – one might wonder why the United Kingdom's record as a Strasbourg litigant was not more favourable'. See 'The European Convention on Human Rights: Time to Incorporate', in Richard Gordon and Richard Wilmot-Smith (eds), *Human Rights in the United Kingdom* (1996), pp 1, 9.

[46] *City of Chicago v Tribune* 139 NE 86 (1923) and *New York Times Co. v Sullivan*, 376 US 254 (1964).

[47] *Hector v A-G of Antigua and Barbuda*, [1990] 2 AC 312, PC; *Die Spoorbond v South African Railways*, 1946 AD 999.

[48] 376 US 254 (1964).

on this point, different from American law and the ability to read the texts of the latter should not lull us into believing that they can be transplanted across the Atlantic without further thought.

What was said above about English law could be argued also about American law though here, at any rate as far as constitutional interpretation is concerned, we immediately run into the difficulties caused by the wider American dispute about the limits of judicial interpretation. Those, in particular, who subscribe to the 'original understanding' doctrine feel unable to interpret the constitutional document by going beyond discovering the original intent (or, as it is said these days, understanding) of its drafters. The difficulty which, at any rate, non-American lawyers have with this approach is what happens when no such intent can be discovered. The constitutional text, for instance, is silent on the much debated issue of abortion. Does that mean constitutional reform or, in its absence (and everyone knows how difficult this is to achieve), judicial paralysis? From our experience of teaching in the United States we realise that no amount of reasoning is likely to budge those lawyers who take this 'conservative' view though we do not hide our sympathies for the more 'open' view, championed by Justices such as Breyer,[49] O'Connor, and Ginsburg, who believe, like us, that an open consideration of alternatives can only help fashion a more workable and contemporary solution. And, in any event, this must be more than permissible in those areas of (mainly) private law where the real or imaginary obstacles that emanate from the constitutional text and the intentions of (its comparatively minded) draftsmen are of no or little relevance. Nor, by the way, is the idea that State legislators can act as an acceptable palliative since the race relations decisions of the 1960s and 1970s were needed to remedy precisely this kind of State inactivity.

3. When a problem is encountered in many similar systems and it is desirable to have a harmonised response

The case of *Fairchild v Glenhaven*[50] was an asbestos litigation case. The claimants, who had worked for various companies and while doing so were exposed to asbestos dust, could not identify, on the balance of probabilities, where exactly they had been exposed to the fibres. On a strict application of the 'but for' test no defendant would be held liable but the House of Lords, reversing the Court of Appeal, held this not to be

49 Evidenced, for instance, not only in his many judgments but also in his peroration in 'Constitutionalism, Privatization, and Globalization', 21 *Cardozo L. Rev*. 1045, 1061.

50 [2002] 1 AC 32.

equitable. From a comparative point of view the opinions of Lords Bingham and Rodger of Earlsferry present the greater interest. The first runs to 30 pages, of which nine are devoted to foreign law; the second is 23 pages, of which about five considered non-English material. The space devoted to the examination of foreign law is not the only interesting feature of the decision; nor should this be sought in the fact that, in addition to Commonwealth authority, these judges also considered Roman, German, French, Dutch, and Norwegian law. *How* they came to do so, the reasons *why* they did so, the *kind of materials* they used, and the comments made in passing are just as important. We must look briefly at all of these points.

First, the non-Commonwealth material was, as Lord Rodger informs us,[51] supplied by Counsel at the Lordships' request:

> The material provides a check, from outside the Common law worlds, that the problem identified in these appeals is genuine and is one that requires to be remedied.

This reveals their Lordships as being as open-minded as their Canadian or South African counterparts; it also shows them fully conscious of the fact that this material is treated as a source of ideas, as a way of confirming their hunch that English law needs fine-tuning, and is not seen as being in any way binding authority. The last point, though obvious, needs to be stressed since opponents of the use of foreign law often impute to its advocates the desire to make it somehow binding on national judges, which is patently not the case.[52]

Second, and more relevant to the present sub-section, is the reason for undertaking such a wide comparative exercise. It was given above by Lord Rodger when he noted that the problem before the national court is one that has been confronted by many others as well. The similarity of the problem, coupled with the growing similarity in socio-economic environments (at any rate among developed nations), may call for a similarity in legal outcome notwithstanding undoubted differences in language and legal techniques. The First President of the French Cour de cassation seems to agree; and his views, read in conjunction with the views of the Scottish Law Lord, lend support to the argument that in

---

[51] Ibid at p 169, no 165.

[52] The above also (partly) answers the argument put forward by Professor Levinson which, in its barest outline, is this: 'If the foreign law is the same why bother with it; and if it's different, we do not need it.' Levinson, however, does make a limited use of foreign law whenever it performs an empirical function. On all this see 'Looking Abroad When Interpreting the US Constitution: Some Reflections' in (2004) 39 *Texas Int'l L. J.* 353 ff.

these types of cases recourse to comparative law is permissible. In a lecture delivered in London M. Canivet thus said:

> Citizens and judges of States which share more or less similar cultures and enjoy an identical level of economic development are less and less prone to accept that situations which raise the same issues of fact will yield different results because of their differences in the rules of law to be applied (...). There is [thus] a trend, one might even say a strong demand, that compatible solutions are reached, regardless of the differences in the underlying applicable rules of law.[53]

In *Fairchild* Lord Bingham echoed the same kind of thoughts though, significantly, he was willing to incorporate them in his judicial opinion. He thus wrote:

> If (...) a decision is given in this country which offends one's basic sense of justice, and if consideration of international sources suggests that a different and more acceptable decision would be given in most other jurisdictions, *whatever their legal tradition*, this must prompt anxious review of the decision in question.

We have italicised four words from the above quotation because to us they illustrate how a consciousness is *gradually* developing (among all save the most timorous of academics), minimising the traditional divide between Common law and civil law.

Third, we attach particular importance to the kind of materials used by the British judges to inform themselves about foreign law. For, in addition to 'focused' textbook discussions of foreign law (instead of the old, René David-type of treatises on *Les Grands Systèmes de Droit Contemporain*) the citations also included references to such practitioner's books as *Palandt*, specific judicial decisions of foreign courts (available in translated form[54]), and even the *Motive* of the BGB, which were not just cited but *used* to discover the policy reasons which justified the partial abandonment of the 'but for' test.[55] These, we

---

[53] The text is reproduced in Mads Andenas and Duncan Fairgrieve, 'Introduction: Finding a Common Language for Open Legal Systems', in Guy Canivet, Mads Andenas, and Duncan Fairgrieve (eds), op. cit. note 3, p xxvii at p xxxi.

[54] Nearly 1,000 leading French and German decisions now appear in translated form (some with up-dating notes) in the website of the Institute of Global Law of University College London, addressing a traditional complaint that foreign material is not available in the English language.

[55] Roman law texts were also cited by Sir Sidney Kentridge QC, Counsel for the claimants, but that is understandable given that his origins and most of his career were South African as well as the fact that he was addressing one judge – Lord Rodger – who is a champion of Roman law. It is, however, also noteworthy that Lord Rodger, while citing the Roman law material, was also quick to switch his main attention to the German material which he admitted was 'more instructive' (ibid at p 169, no 167).

submit, are significant observations in so far as they support the views advanced by one of us *in extenso*,[56] that what makes foreign law usable is (a) its relevance and (b) its helpful 'packaging'.

Finally, it is worth reminding readers of Lord Bingham's point that when one is undertaking a broad research exercise it is likely that the various systems will not reveal a unanimity in results. In such cases, of course, one does not undertake a 'head count' but learns how to differentiate between systems. Broadly speaking, this can be done in two ways.

The first is by placing more emphasis on systems that belong to the same legal family. The second is by looking more attentively at the major legal systems, that is, the ones from which most others have in one way or another sprung from, paying less attention to less dominant derivatives. This last observation, however, should not be taken to suggest that a smaller system never has anything to offer the comparatist. For even these derivative systems on occasion (and for reasons of their own) can innovate in interesting ways. Thus, the Greek Civil Code, which for obvious historical reasons has been closely linked to German law (enacted as it was less than 50 years after its German prototype), includes an interesting general provision which deals with the protection of human dignity and personality which has no parallel in the German BGB.

4. When foreign experience (aided by empirically collected evidence) help disprove locally expressed fears about the consequences of a particular legal solution

Three examples (among many) can be discussed here; and it must be stressed from the outset that this heading covers the use of foreign law in an empirical way which even those who oppose recourse to it would appear to accept. This, then, could be one of the most fertile areas of further growth of judicial exchanges since, by itself, it intrudes least into the domain of local values and only wishes to demonstrate how a particular solution has worked in practice in another country. This is how one of the authors who accepts this type of use of foreign law – Professor Sanford Levinson – has put it (when discussing Justice Scalia's views in the context of the death penalty and regulation of homosexual expression). He said:

> It really depends whether one is trying to place such issues within the context of expressing basic social values about the importance of retributive punishment (...) and condemning 'unconventional' sexual expression. If one

[56] B. S. Markesinis, op. cit. note 33.

> is behaving as a legal anthropologist manqué, which is at least one way of understanding the 'fundamental values' enterprise, then the central task is indeed trying to figure out what constitutes a particular society's way of expressing values in the world. It is almost by definition *this* society and *not* one elsewhere that is the centre of our inquiry (...). Things [however] get far more complicated if we view these not so much in *expressive* terms, reflecting our basic values, but rather far more *instrumentally*. Consider, for example, the proponent of capital punishment who speaks not of revenge but, rather, its deterrent effect and concomitant saving of lives, or the opponent of gays in the military who emphasizes the ostensible effects on military cohesion of accepting gays (...) into the armed forces. Given that these latter assertions are entirely *empirical* in their thrust, they call for an entirely different response from those that are only *expressive*.[57]

The three topics we would like to include in this section would come under the second of Professor Levinson's categories. All come from English law, which has opposed both the extension of privacy rights and patient rights (in the technical area of medical information before the patient's consent to treatment can be deemed to have been validly given), and has also had a tendency to provide extensive (some argue excessive) protection to statutory bodies against suits for damages flowing from their negligent conduct. In our view, and subject to some important provisos concerning the use and presentation of the material collected, in all of these cases the fears of English courts are not substantiated by foreign experience. We therefore believe English law would benefit from the empirical use of foreign information that could disprove this particular kind of fear that has gripped the English judicial psyche. We shall look at these three instances under separate headings while admitting that our thoughts – brief because of the lack of space – are only meant to provide starting points for further enquiries along the lines we recommend here.

a) Liability of statutory bodies

The very latest judgment of the House of Lords in *JD (FC) v East Berkshire Community Health NHS Trust and others*[58] touches on this point which, in the not too distant past, brought English law into collision with the European Court of Human Rights.[59] The dispute, in

57 Op. cit. note 52 at 363–4.

58 [2005] UKHL 23.

59 For a comparative (English, French, and German) discussion of the substantive issues see B. S. Markesinis, J. B. Auby, D. Coester-Waltjen, and S. F. Deakin, *Tortious Liability of Statutory Bodies. A Comparative and Economic Analysis of Five English Cases* (1999). For an additional Anglo-American perspective see B. S. Markesinis and Adrian R. Stewart, 'Tortious Liability for Negligent Misdiagnosis of Learning Disabilities: A Comparative Study of English and American Law' (2001) 36 *Texas Intern.'l L. J.* 427 ff.

the words of Lord Bingham of Cornhill, the Senior Law Lord, was whether

> the parent of a minor child falsely and negligently said to have abused (...) the child may recover (...) damages for negligence against a doctor or social worker who, discharging professional functions, has made false and negligent statement, if the suffering of psychiatric injury by the parent was a foreseeable result of making it and such injury has in fact been suffered by the parent.

The question, as is so often the case in such disputes, turned upon whether the social worker or doctor owed a duty of care towards the parents. Invoking, directly and indirectly, the usual fear of opening the floodgates, the House of Lords, agreeing with the Court of Appeal, rejected the existence of a duty of care. The appellants' attempt to overturn the judgment of the Court of Appeal, which had gone against them, failed.

Now, in England the presence or absence of a duty of care depends on a number of (often repetitive) policy criteria, the most notorious (and ambiguous) of which (and not replicated in American tort law) is that it has to be 'fair, just and reasonable' for the judge to find such a duty. The 'floodgates' fear invariably makes this unfair, unjust, and unreasonable; and plaintiffs thus have their case 'nipped in the bud' without any evidence being called or the facts properly investigated.

In the *Berkshire* case, Lord Bingham, consistent with early opinions of his,[60] was the only judge who dissented from this view. He laid great emphasis on the fact that the law in the area had evolved in recent years – partly as a result of decisions of the European Court of Human Rights, which had shown 'that [the application of an exclusionary rule (...) may lead to serious breaches of Convention rights'. He also referred to French and German law to suggest that neither of these systems had suffered from allowing such claims. Once again, the open-mindedness of this learned judge impresses as much as his wider reading and common sense. But is this not also a perfect topic for comparative empirical research to show whether other equally advanced systems of equally industrialised societies have suffered from the rule which so frightened the highest English court? It is with this aspect of the case that we deal here; and we believe that it offers excellent opportunities for empirical research in order to prove or disprove the validity of these fears.

The truth of the matter is that the research here needed requires the collaboration of practitioner and academic, for only the latter can furnish

---

[60] 'If [the child/claimant] can make good her complaints (a vital condition, which I forebear constantly to repeat), it would require very potent considerations of public policy (...) to override the rule of public policy which has first claim on the loyalty of the law: that wrongs should be remedied.' *M. v Newham London Borough Council and X v Bedfordshire County Council* [1994] 2 WLR 55, at 532. A German case with very similar facts (BGH NJW 2005, 68 ff) had no doubt that in this case liability would be imposed.

the former with the information he needs to support any comparative arguments in court. And collecting and shifting this raw material is not easy. For if one takes Germany as an example one sees that such claims have invariably been allowed to be brought before a court but that few succeed in practice.[61] Lest it be objected that even this is too much for any legal system to digest (since it can take up much court time and effort) one should then enquire how many of these claims were actually dismissed summarily without the exaggerated costs and delays of a full and lengthy trial. And, finally, one should check the level of awards – and if one does, one will find that these are substantially lower in these types of cases than those one would find in cases of medical malpractice or traffic accidents. If that is, indeed, the case – and this summary is only meant to whet the appetite of the reader as to how the research should proceed – should not the answer then lie in the law of damages rather than be found through the use of the blunt instrument of duty of care? Lord Bingham touched upon these points in his judgment; and for those interested, we provide new ideas of how the evidence about foreign law should be marshalled, analysed, and then used. That this needs patience, careful research, and collaborative action is beyond doubt. But this way of providing the empirical data could also dispel the (justified) fears[62] concerning the danger of producing misleading information about foreign law. Lord Bingham not only opened up these possibilities to inquisitive researchers and broad-minded practitioners, but also proved again that imaginative judges are the exception; those who prefer to hide behind opaque concepts, the rule. If *Berkshire* represents another example of a missed opportunity to reflect about the law more widely, it also shows to those who like us believe in international dialogue how much ground still has to be covered before such dialogue becomes routine.

b) Privacy[63]

English law has always protected aspects of human privacy and done so by using (not always successfully) a miscellany of (mostly) mediaeval

---

[61] Useful raw data can be found in Bundesministerium der Justiz (ed), *Zur Reform des Staatshaftungsrechts* (1976), pp 161, 197; Infratest Burke Rechtsforschung, *Zur Reform des Staatshaftungsrechts, Tabellarische Ergebnisse (1993–5)* (1999), Tables B 4.1, K 4, L 4.1, T 1 (though this material needs 'packaging' before it can acquire meaningful significance for an English court).

[62] Expressed convincingly by Justice Scalia in *Roper v Simmons* 125 S. Ct. 1183, 1222 ff.

[63] For a brief comparative discussion of Anglo-American law see Markesinis and Deakin, *Tort Law* (5th edn, 2003 by Simon Deakin, Angus Johnston, and Basil Markesinis), pp 701–39 (the American part written by Professor David Anderson of The University of Texas at Austin).

torts (such as nuisance[64] and trespass[65]) and procedures (invoking, for instance, the wardship jurisdiction[66]), as well as a growing number of criminal procedures. But in a world experiencing an increasing ability to collect, collate, and disseminate information,[67] this casuistic approach has been seen as inadequate by some courts[68] as well as officially commissioned reports,[69] though also defended by others.[70]

It is submitted that in this debate the real opposition has come from sections of the Press anxious to exploit political misbehaviour (amounting in some cases to crimes) as well as the usual titillating stories associated with the entertainment world. But this desire to keep the reporting of such incidents, which could often increase newspaper circulation and thus provide enhanced earnings, has been shrouded behind arguments about the ability and the desirability to create a tort of privacy. Some of these arguments are as old as the so-called tort itself and are linked to the understandable wish to protect privacy without stunting free speech. Others have been associated with the real and imaginary difficulties of defining privacy rights,[71] as if the current English attempts to solve the problems coming before the courts through an ever-expanding notion of confidentiality[72] avoid such uncertainties. Here we are not concerned with the merits of the above argument[73] but with the more pragmatic fear that recognition of the right of privacy would open the floodgates of litigation.

To counter this argument the first of us attempted to collect all published decisions of Germany's highest courts on this subject during the

---

64 *Bernstein v Skyviews & General Ltd* [1978] QB 479; *Khorasandjian v Bush*, [1993] QB 727, reversed by the House of Lords in *Hunter & Others v Canary Wharf*, [1997] 2 WLR 684.

65 *Gordon Kaye v Andrew Robertson and Sport Newspaper Ltd* [1991] FSR 62.

66 *Re X* [1984] 1 WLR 1422.

67 Prophetically foreshadowed in the United States by the famous Warren and Brandeis article 'The Right of Privacy' (1890) 4 *Harv. L. Rev*. 193 ff.

68 *Gordon Kaye v Andrew Robertson and Sport Newspaper Ltd* [1991] FSR 62, per Bingham L.J. (as he then was).

69 Lord Chancellor's Department and the Scottish Office, *Infringement of Privacy: A Consultation Paper* (1993).

70 For instance Mummery, LJ in *Wainright v Home Office* [2002] 3 WLR 405, 419.

71 In England this argument was invoked strongly by the Report of the Committee on Privacy, chaired by Sir Kenneth Younger and published in 1972, and succeeded in stunting all further discussion for nearly twenty years.

72 Favoured in cases such as *A v B plc and Another* [2002] 2 All ER 545 and *Naomi Campbell v MGN* [2003] 2 WLR 80.

73 Discussed in detail in B. S. Markesinis, C. O'Cinneide, J. Fedtke, and M. Hunter-Henin, 'Concerns and Ideas about our Developing Law of Privacy (And how Knowledge of Foreign Law Might be of Help)' (2004) 52 *The Amer. J. Comp. L*. 133 ff.

last 20 years.[74] The total figures hardly justified concerns, especially when seen against the background of (a) the higher volume of litigation in Germany as compared to England; (b) the cheapness of having resort to the courts in Germany as compared to the high cost of litigation in England; and (c) the real (or alleged) 'mentality' differences between the two nations, the citizens of the latter apparently being much less willing than the citizens of the former to have recourse to litigation. Interestingly enough, the overall belief of the first of us that a recognition of a privacy right would not result in unmanageable litigation was also confirmed by a report prepared by a committee set up by Lord Chancellor Mackay.[75] In the light of the above, would it not be prudent to submit such comparative evidence to a court and invite it to test the material and then to draw the appropriate conclusions? As we shall note in the next section, empirical study of foreign systems may be equally relevant to other cases where the floodgates argument is raised in order to protect other interests.

c) *Informed consent*

To the question of how much information must be disclosed to the patient before his consent to medical treatment can be legally valid three answers are possible. Interestingly, they depend on the philosophical attitude one takes towards patients' and doctors' rights (to determine how much they reveal); but it is also, indirectly, affected by fears that a pro-patient position could generate 'defensive' medicine and a flood of claims. Are such fears backed by real evidence?

The first possible answer to our problem is found in English law; and it basically leaves the decision to 'a responsible body of medical men skilled in that particular art'. This is known as the *Bolam* test[76] and is the most paternalistic of all.

One reason why English law takes such a conservative view was given by Lord Denning in *Whitehouse v Jordan*[77] and, as already hinted,

---

[74] B. S. Markesinis and H. Unberath, *The German Law of Torts. A Comparative Treatise* (4th edn, 2002), pp 476–8.

[75] Op. cit. note 69.

[76] *Bolam v Friern Hospital Management Committee* [1957] 1 WLR 582. This test was, essentially, re-affirmed by four out of five law lords in *Sidaway v Royal Bethlehem Hospital Governors* [1985] 1 AC 871. The tone of the judgment was set by Lord Diplock who insisted that medical opinion remained 'determinative' in such matters. This can be seen in the next important case – *Gold v Haringey Area Health Authority* [1988] QB 481 – where the Court of Appeal overruled a more pro-plaintiff judgment by Schiemann J (see [1987] 1 FLR 125) by insisting that 'the Judge was not free, as he thought, to form his own view of what warning and information ought to have been given, irrespective of any body of responsible medical opinion to the contrary' (per Lloyd LJ at p 490).

[77] [1980] 1 All ER 650, at 658.

it is connected with the fear of increased malpractice litigation. Decisions such as *Bolitho*[78] would suggest that a shift of emphasis is nowadays taking place in English law, which the new Human Rights Act 1998 (and the growing 'rights culture' it is generating) can only accelerate further (another example of 'constitutionalisation' of private law?).

This English position is rejected by most Common law jurisdictions, which adopt the so-called doctrine of informed consent – taking the view that the doctor must disclose as much information as a reasonable patient would require to make an informed choice, and frequently add, for good measure, that the doctor 'should not lightly make the judgment that the patient does not wish to be fully informed'.[79]

Germany, however, may yet be the most illustrative example for the purposes of disproving these floodgate fears. Both positions outlined above have been rejected by many decisions of Continental European systems on the grounds that they violate the patient's right of self-determination.[80] This position has, as stated, been forcefully stressed by German courts which, in the light of the recent past, have been only too conscious of the dangers of ignoring human dignity and not preventing unwarranted medical interferences with the body and health of human beings. Thus, from the beginning of the post-War period, courts have stressed that 'proper respect for the patient's right of self-determination will further rather than damage the patient's trust in his doctor', and 'to respect the patient's own will is to respect his freedom and dignity as a human being'.[81] Consequently, the principle of full disclosure is repeatedly stressed;[82] and in one case, involving *diagnostic* treatment, the court took the view that even a 0.5 per cent chance of a particular risk occurring should be disclosed![83] In the case of *therapeutic* operations disclosure will be geared to the patient's individual circumstances such as his level of understanding,[84] and even the attending doctor's degree of experience.[85] The urgency of the situation is also a factor that can be

---

[78] *Bolitho (Deceased) v City & Hackney HA*, [1998] AC 232.

[79] *F v R* (1983) 33 SASR 189, at 193. The same ideas are, essentially, found in many American jurisdictions – see, e.g., *Canterbury v Spence*, 464 F 2d 772 (1972) and *Crain v Allison*, 443 A. d 558 (1982) – as well as in Canada (see *Reibl v Hughes* [1980] 2 SCR 880 and *White v Turner*, 120 DLR 3d 269).

[80] Giesen, *International Medical Malpractice Law* (1988). Though dated, this text gives a good overview of Continental European systems in comparative juxtaposition with Anglo-American law.

[81] BGHZ 29, 46, 53–6. See also BGHZ 90, 96, 103.

[82] See BGH VersR 1980, 428, 429; NJW 1984, 1397 ff.

[83] OLG Hamm VersR 1981, 68 ff.

[84] BGH NJW 1980, 633 ff.

[85] OLG Köln VersR 1982, 453 ff.

taken into account;[86] and even the defence of 'therapeutic privilege' (no revelation of risks since a patient might not be able to 'handle' adverse news) has been treated with caution, as a decision of the BGH of 28 November 1957 clearly shows.[87] This case law has not abated, there being, over the past years, a constant drip of BGH decisions clarifying difficult related issues. But for a court that delivers around 1,000 motivated judgments per annum, two or even three decisions per year is a drip, not a flood;[88] and this remains so even though the number of disputes at first instance level raising such points probably runs into a few hundred (but in a system that copes with over 1,500,000 writs per year issued before its two lower tiers of courts).[89]

The sketch of the German position may provide both an interesting contrast with English (and even American law) as well as an illustration of how current rules may have been shaped in part by a country's particular political history. But it also serves a further purpose in so far as it shows that such a libertarian or pro-patient view has *not* resulted in the realisation of the fears that haunt the English courts. Indeed, we have not been able to find any statistical evidence in Germany to support this fear. A glance at the published decisions of the BGH indirectly supports our argument – even though one can find, almost on an annual basis, one or two decisions dealing with these (or closely related) issues. This may sound high in countries such as England, accustomed to something in the order of 60 (civil) appeals per annum being heard by the House of Lords. Yet in a country where litigation is (relatively) cheap and the supreme court delivers so many motivated judgments per annum it is statistically insignificant (even if it suggests that courts at lower levels probably hear more such cases). At the very least, therefore, further empirical studies are needed before a conclusive view can be expressed. In the meantime,

---

86 BGH VersR 1972, 153 ff.

87 See BGHSt 11, 111, 114 and compare similar statements in *Meyer Estate v Rogers*, (1991) 6 CCLT 2d 114.

88 For recent examples see BGH NJW 2001, 2798 ff (extent of duty to inform about the risks of an operation of intervertebral discs); OLG München VersR 2002, 717 ff (consultation of a young mother of Turkish origin about the consequences of a sterilisation); and BGH NJW 2003, 2012 ff (timely information of the patient on remote medical risks resulting from an operation of a slipped intervertebal disc) – confirming and expanding BGH NJW 1985, 1399 ff and BGH NJW 1998, 1784 ff.

89 For a dated (but broadly speaking still relevant discussion see B. S. Markesinis, 'Litigation-mania in England, Germany and the United States: are we so very different?' in *Foreign Law and Comparative Methodology. A Subject and a Thesis* (1977), p 438, especially pp 453 ff. As the statistics cited in the above piece show, Germany presents another significant difference with the United States and England: a much larger percentage of actions commenced end up by a full judgment.

however, it is submitted that such evidence could properly be submitted before any foreign court contemplating the relaxation of local rules in favour of patients' rights with the caveat that full and precise information is still lacking.

5. When the foreign law provides 'additional' evidence that a proposed solution has 'worked' in other systems

The decision of the House of Lords in *Hunter v Canary Wharf* (a nuisance case),[90] relying for additional support on BGHZ 88, 344 ff, offers a good illustration. For this reason foreign law was also taken into account in *McFarlane v Tayside Health Board*,[91] a case involving a claim for damages regarding the costs of healthy child born after a failed vasectomy.[92]

6. When the statute that is interpreted comes from another legal system or has its origins in an international instrument

Our third South African case discussed in the previous section involved a legal transplant from Germany, and it is here that the comparative method may be most effective. *City of Cape Town v Ad Outpost* is, of course, a rare example where a judge had to interpret a provision that was literally translated and incorporated (with only minor changes) by the South African legislator from another system into his own national law. Other, less direct examples such as the constitutionalisation of the (uncodified) German notion of 'co-operative government'[93] and the so-called constitutional state principle mentioned in the Preamble of the 1993 Constitution could, however, be added to this list. Finally, South African judges were confronted with a complete 'system change' by the country's shift from the principle of parliamentary sovereignty to the enactment of a supreme constitution and full judicial review of legislation. Compared to more specific legal transplants such as the use of Art 12 BL in s 22 of the 1996 Constitution, this was a far more profound change. Moreover,

---

[90] [1997] AC 655.

[91] [2000] 2 AC 59.

[92] The House of Lords, making extensive use of American case law, held that these costs were not recoverable (though damages for pain and suffering and inconvenience were). The point was left open for the case of the birth of an impaired child.

[93] Sections 40 and 41 of the 1996 Constitution.

it was one which many judges – trained and accustomed to a very different regime – found difficult to adapt to.

In such instances foreign experience is particularly valuable. We have already seen that the outcome of *City of Cape Town v Ad Outpost* could have been different had the court utilised the wealth of German judicial experience and academic discussion concerning Art 12 BL. This material dates back as far as the *Pharmacy*-case of 1958,[94] and was clearly in the mind of Professor Etienne Mureinik when he proposed the German approach as a way to overcome the deadlock in the negotiations during the last stages of the Constitutional Assembly's work in 1996. The importance of comparative law in these situations has also been accepted by critics of the method. For instance, Johan Kriegler of the South African Constitutional Court thus stressed that

> where a provision in our Constitution is manifestly modelled on a particular provision in another country's constitution, it would be folly not to ascertain how the jurists of that country have interpreted their precedential provision.[95]

In other cases, national law is not based on a rule found in another *national* legal system but is rather modelled on provisions found in *international* law. The German *Bundesgerichtshof* has thus used the comparative method when dealing with rules which have their origin in international treaties or which are closely linked to international issues such as maritime disputes (an area highly influenced by English law). Here, the comparative approach is sometimes even explicitly prescribed by the German legislator.[96] The common denominator of these decisions – their subject proximity to internationally harmonised rules or the conflict of laws – clearly forces judges to look out of the window of their own system which otherwise can be obscured by the curtains of legal tradition.

It could be argued that in this type of legal dispute comparative law has established itself as an essential requirement in the evaluation of many cases. An analysis of German law by Professor Ulrich Drobnig thus shows that approximately 50 per cent of the decisions of the BGH and the German Courts of Appeal dealing with major international treaties such as the Warsaw Convention make use of foreign experience. Interestingly, the percentage of cases using such material is far lower (approximately 3 per cent) where the two conventions on Cheques and Bills of Exchange signed in Geneva in 1930/1931 are concerned. This can

---

94 A translation of this important case can be found on the website of the Institute of Global Law under www.ucl.ac.uk/laws/global_law/german-cases/constitutional-law/index.shtml?constitution_09.

95 *Bernstein and Others v Bester NO and others*, 1996 (4) BCLR 449 (CC).

96 See Arts 36 EGBGB and 7 CISG.

be explained by the fact that these two agreements were fully incorporated into German law, whereas other treaties analysed by Drobnig were merely ratified by Germany and thus remain distinctly international in character.[97]

Finally, a further area where we can expect European courts to look abroad is national legislation introduced in the wake of Community law and explicitly aimed, within more or less flexible boundaries, at harmonisation. The national courts of the Member States are 'Community courts' in the sense that they are bound to apply EU law. Judges may, of course, refer questions regarding the interpretation or validity of Community law to the ECJ if this is deemed necessary for the decision of the case at hand,[98] but by far most disputes are currently resolved solely on the national level. Courts applying this highly harmonised law without further guidance would do well in matching their own approaches with those chosen by the ECJ and other national courts confronted with the very same issues. More importantly, however, national courts continue to apply *national* law in areas where the Community has only identified a common *aim* by directive. Despite the greater flexibility of this tool (which allows Member States to adopt different means of achieving the common goal), and disregarding the special case where a directive may have direct effect, a comparative approach by judges seems particularly appropriate if Europe is to develop a coherent system of law. Thus far, however, national courts do not appear to have used in this context much comparative material.[99]

7. When a court is confronted with law regulating highly technical matters rather than value-laden issues

One of the recurring themes of this study is the distinction between different subject-matters regulated by the laws of a society and how the use of the comparative method in the courtroom could be more appropriate in some areas and less so in others.

Further research will again be necessary before exact boundaries can be drawn. Yet, even at this early stage it would seem that certain issues

---

[97] U. Drobnig, 'Rechtsvergleichung in der Deutschen Rechtsprechung' (1986) 50 *RabelsZ* 610 at 615.

[98] See Art 234 EC Treaty.

[99] For the German courts see Lutter, 'Die Auslegung angeglichenen Rechts' [1992] JZ 593 at 604; Mansel, 'Rechtsvergleichung und europäische Rechtseinheit' [1991] JZ 529 at 531; Odersky, 'Harmonisierende Auslegung und europäische Rechtskultur' [1994] ZEuP 1 at 2.

such as building regulations, rules on land development and zoning, norms regulating environmental questions such as noise levels or waste disposal, rules on public health and safety, data protection, or the labelling of products are matters which by virtue of their highly 'technical' content would, prima facie, belong to the category of topics where comparative work is less contentious.

This rough list of items might even be extended to constitutional matters. Proportionality, not as an underlying normative concept affecting the limitation of human rights by public authorities but rather as a structured approach to the judicial scrutiny of legislative or administrative decisions, might qualify for inclusion under this heading. Several South African judgments thus deal with the different aspects of the proportionality enquiry as developed in Canadian and German jurisprudence, while the initial decision to introduce the principle as such had already been taken by the legislator.[100] Similarly, courts dealing with the wider question of democratic legitimacy in the context of election issues could, for instance, gain insights from the approach other legal systems take when it comes to drawing the geographical boundaries of constituencies with regard to the number of votes needed to gain a seat in the legislature.[101]

Finally, wide areas of private and commercial law are 'technical' in the sense that particular values or policy considerations play, if at all, only a subordinate role.

In all of these situations, then, most of the objections raised against the comparative method would seem less convincing. In a world which is increasingly using the same technical equipment, produced and sold under very similar or even identical conditions, and involving the same potential hazards, the legal responses[102] – both by the legislator and the courts – to problems arising from such products should be quite similar. Though we are not advocating a far-reaching legal harmonisation, we believe that comparative law has much to offer in the judicial resolution of these less value-laden issues.

100 See s 33 of the 1993 Constitution and s 36 of the 1996 Constitution.

101 Election principles were thus one of the first issues where the German Federal Constitutional Court used foreign law; see BVerfGE 1, 208 ff (of 1952).

102 We are here, for instance, referring to the liability regimes but not the quantification of damages, for these are related to a variety of other factors (e.g. local earnings, presence or absence of social security, currency exchange rates, cost of living and the like) which may well justify a different size of awards. Some of these points are considered by Markesinis/et al., op. cit. note 59.

Chapter 4: Dangers and Obstacles in the Use of Foreign Law

1. General observations

Even those who favour the exchange of ideas and believe that, in a shrinking world, this practice may even be destined to become inevitable do not underestimate the difficulties (and the dangers) that accompany such intellectual exercises. Moreover, these problems can be magnified if one starts with the position that societies are very different[1] (which is true and even more so in days gone by before the advent of increased travel and communication) and then tries to give to these divergences a normative content. This is especially likely to happen if one ignores or underestimates, as we think adherents of this school tend to do, the growing assimilation in tastes, customs, and laws, which is greatly accelerated by modern ways of communication, enhanced travel, and the internet (which brings together practically every corner of the world where individuals have access to a telephone cable).[2] This trend towards assimilation is so important that it has affected even areas of the law (such as family law) which – not that long ago – comparatists[3] (and sociologists) of great distinction declared to be immune to such globalisation and assimilation forces.

These divergences are further enhanced if one is attempting the comparison of states which, for lack of a better term, one could prima

---

[1] See, for instance, William P. Alford, 'On the Limits of "Grand Theory" in Comparative Law' (1986) 61 *Wash. L. Rev.* 945 ff; George P. Fletcher, 'Constitutional Identity' (1993) 14 *Cardozo L Rev.* 737 ff; Frederick Schauer, 'Free Speech and the Cultural Contingency of Constitutional Categories' (1993) 14 *Cardozo L. Rev.* 865 ff.

[2] The examples of *how* the world is shrinking are as interesting to ponder over as is the *speed* in which it is shrinking. Thus, it was reported that after the recent Tsunami disaster in the Indian Ocean, some 33 per cent of American households responded with donations and more than half of these did so through the internet. National borders between countries, no longer able to stop the rapid movement of information and funds, will prove equally porous to ideas and tastes. The differences of geography are reduced by technology, which is equally minimising (it could be argued) those dictated by history and language – however much romantic spirits may regret this.

[3] See, e.g., Otto Kahn-Freund, 'On Uses and Misuses of Comparative Law' (1974) 37 *MLR* 1 at 15, declaring himself unable to see divorce ever being recognised in Ireland.

facie say belong to different cultural worlds. This is particularly likely to be the case if the views of some contemporary comparatists, advocating a redirection of comparative law towards other cultures, continents, or countries, were to gain acceptance.[4] But even this distinction should be treated with great caution. For it is, surely, becoming increasingly difficult to draw sharp lines and declare, for the purposes of the law, that country A belongs to a different culture than country B. Thus, we cannot treat Japan as belonging to a different culture for the purposes of the law,[5] not only because of its long dependence on German[6] (and to a lesser extent French) ideas but also because of its growing (and in the beginning enforced) association with American (especially public) law which followed the end of the Second World War. So even though in terms of culture, arts, music, and the like, the distinctiveness of its culture will be evident to any 'Westerner' who has attended such artistic performances (or simply enjoyed watching Hollywood films that have capitalised on the idea of distinctiveness),[7] in legal terms convergence is proceeding apace.

The same observation could be made in respect of all the former Communist block countries of Eastern Europe which, not that long ago, espoused an economic world very different to the free market model(s) of the West and were subject to institutional and constitutional regimes which would seriously hinder the importation of American or Western European models of law. Yet these, too, collapsed (more quickly and

---

[4] The first of us has expressed doubts as to whether this can really happen in the foreseeable future given the lack of linguistic expertise and serious lack of materials. To put it differently, if the borrowing from France, Germany, or Spain is, potentially, hampered for the above reasons how much more is this likely to be the case if the system studied belongs to one of the less developed countries (or areas) of the world?

[5] Though the Japanese (and one might even venture the generalisation 'Oriental') preference to conciliation instead of litigation may affect how different parts of the law (e.g. tort law) operate in practice.

[6] On the influence of German private law on Japan see Akira Ishikawa, 'Einflüsse des deutschen BGB auf das japanische Zivilrecht bzw die japanische Zivilrechtswissenschaft' in Staudinger, *Kommentar zum Bürgerlichen Gesetzbuch mit Einführungsesetz und Nebengesetzen, 100 Jahre BGB – 100 Jahre Staudinger, Beiträge zum Symposion* 1998, pp 201 ff. It is interesting to note that French private law, largely because of the crusading role of an individual – Professor Boissonade – initially exerted a much stronger appeal on the Japanese. The first draft of the Private Code (of 1890) thus drew heavily on the *Code civil*. German influence only started to become dominant after Japan decided to adopt a modern constitution based on the Prussian model in 1889. The Private Code of 1890, set to come into force in 1893, was scrapped. The subsequent Code of 1896/1898 was then dominated by German ideas. This influence, though diminished, has survived the influx of American legal ideas and culture after 1945.

[7] Even though the reverse may not be true, as attested by the fact that so many Japanese, Chinese, or Korean musicians can attain musical perfection in performing the works of Mozart and Beethoven.

more unexpectedly than any specialist could have expected), and their demise led to a sudden invasion of American intellectuals – especially from the Eastern Seaboard of the United States – anxious and eager to export their own model of constitutionalism to these newly liberated countries, often in (apparent) disregard of the fact that these exporters knew little about the cultures and most certainly the language of the targeted importers.[8] These very general observations are not meant to underestimate the obstacles placed before any transnational dialogue; but they are meant to warn the reader of the importance of the 'time factor' which, to us at least, seems to be dismantling barriers hitherto regarded as unmoveable. We thus shift our attention to some specific and worrisome hurdles which the internationalist will confront and must try to overcome.

2. Lack of precise information

In the post-War years comparative law was, mainly, in the hands of talented Central European Jewish émigrés. Though some branched out and taught different subjects in their host countries, transnational orientation was in most cases the only outlet for their talents.[9] The courses were, inevitably, general in nature; and indeed in some countries (such as France, where Professor David and his main book[10] seized the imagination of the scholars' interest in the subject) the generality of the works produced was linked to the idea that the main aim of teaching foreign law was its 'civilising' character. The disappearing breed of Roman lawyers took a not dissimilar line, arguing (in defence of the continued existence of their subject) that it 'taught young lawyers how to reason'. For years, the idea that the same educational purpose could be achieved by teaching modern German, French, or Italian law (and also give the student some *practically useful* knowledge) was thus carefully obscured from the new generation of lawyers. Tradition confers an aura of respectability but, alas, it can also lead to sclerosis.

Such a state of affairs increasingly became untenable as (a) the breed of émigrés begun to die or retire, (b) the needs of the new generation of

---

[8] It is, however, worth mentioning that continental constitutional thinking was not in all cases sidelined. The German–Austrian model of a specialised constitutional court was, for instance, adopted by many countries in Eastern Europe; see, e.g., Brunner, 'Die neue Verfassungsgerichtsbarkeit in Osteuropa' [1993] Verfassung und Recht in Übersee 819 ff. In areas of commercial and company law, too, the desire to join the European Union (involving a high degree of legal compatibility or even harmonisation) frequently led these new democracies to draft their laws on the basis of European models.

[9] The work of the late Professor Clive Schmithoff falls into this category, his considerable perspicacity and boundless energies being, on the whole, shamefully ignored by the British legal establishment.

[10] *Les Grands Systèmes de Droit Contemporain*, now in its 11th edn (2002).

students became increasingly determined by professional career demands, (c) the funding of law schools became more and more dependant on private support (which would be more forthcoming with funds if the subject taught had a practical significance) and finally, (d) the globalisation of business required the teaching of transferable skills (e.g. how to attempt comparisons) as well as *specific* knowledge of foreign law and not *generalities*. We return to these points below; here we limit our comments to a narrower but no less important question: 'How does one get hold of such information?' The question, more pressing in contemporary times as a result of the predilection of the past generation of comparatists towards matters of history or general culture,[11] can actually be split into two components. The first concerns 'access' and the second the 'form' in which it is made available to a potential foreign user.

Despite the often-voiced complaint that foreign material, especially 'raw' foreign material (i.e. statutes and leading decisions), is difficult to come by, the truth of the matter is the reverse. Thus, the Institute of Global Law of University College London and the Institute of Transnational Law of The University of Texas jointly run a website[12] which in the space of the last two and half years has reproduced in translated form nearly 1,000 leading German and French decisions, some of which are already accompanied by short notes indicating the subsequent history (acceptance, rejection, or modification) of the respective courts' rulings. Though it is difficult to be precise, we estimate that this material probably approaches one million words. The richness of the (growing) collection is surpassed only by the number of hits – over 350,000 in (as stated) approximately 30 months of operation – that the site has received. Other websites, within the United States and abroad, have similarly sprung up, providing access to important leading materials, while the number of books and articles written about foreign and comparative law have equally received a considerable boost in recent times.

Along with the above one finds numerous other projects (mainly launched under the aegis or the support of the European Union) openly considering projects of harmonisation and unification of the law and publishing their proposals from time to time. This is no place to go into a bibliographical kind of exercise by listing the growth of the available literature; but it would be entirely wrong not to say that the sources mentioned above, coupled with State-sponsored translations of the main

---

[11] The unwillingness of the classical comparatists of the second half of the twentieth century to bequeath a methodology for the practical use of foreign law in a national context is discussed (and criticised) by B. S. Markesinis, *Comparative Law in the Courtroom and Classroom. The Story of the last Thirty-Five Years* (2003), especially chapter 2.

[12] At www.ucl.ac.uk/laws/global_law (last accessed on 9 May 2006).

statutory materials, are daily transforming this landscape. Though full coverage can never be achieved (national lawyers are, indeed, themselves never able to command all of their own growing material), to suggest that access to foreign ideas, decisions, statutory material, and the like, is impossible in these days of electronic access to the legal world is an argument that wears thin and, more importantly, will continue to diminish in force with the passage of time. Paradoxically, therefore, what an Anglo-American researcher may often find difficult to discover will not be a translation of a leading foreign decision but material explaining foreign case law on the matter that interests him in English, making then recourse to foreign academic literature the only way of acquiring practically usable information about a foreign system.[13]

By way of conclusion we add that the electronic access to this material also means that it is no longer possible to argue that students studying in less wealthy institutions (with correspondingly weaker library facilities) or practitioners working in smaller urban areas are denied access to this information. Here, as indeed in law as a whole, we are thus very near the stage where the main concern is not access to material but the absence of time to reflect on it as well as the inability of practitioners to understand it without the help of experts. That is a very valid point and this is how Nicholas Underhill QC, Counsel for the defendants in the English blood contamination case, had to say on the matter:[14]

> Comparative law materials are not easy to use properly. If they are not in English, they have to be translated; even when translated, unfamiliar terminology, concepts, and procedures have to be explained if basic misunderstandings are to be avoided. There is no expert available to the court, which is accordingly dependant on Counsel (...). But the fact is that English lawyers cannot hope to educate either themselves or the court to a full understanding of the subtleties of foreign legal systems.

Important though this worry is, it is not unanswerable. For in that case both Counsel for the plaintiffs and the defendants employed the services of the retired draftsman of the EC Directive in question and an Australian expert in product liability law and, by their own admission, were greatly aided in their tasks. And for the present authors this supports their argument that persuading the judge and Counsel to have

---

[13] The point is obvious from the English 'contaminated blood' case discussed earlier. Nonetheless, in that decision authorities were cited from Australia, England, France, Germany, the Netherlands, the United States (Illinois and New Jersey), and the European Court of Justice.

[14] 'The Use of Comparative Law in *A & Others v National Blood Authority*' in Guy Canivet, Mads Andenas, and Duncan Fairgrieve (eds), *Comparative Law Before the Courts* (2004), p 79.

recourse to foreign law will also benefit the academic profession who can then be called upon to perform this task which neither of the key protagonists has the time or training to accomplish.

3. Is the information up-to-date?

But even allowing for such progress, is the available material always up-to-date? How difficult this task is can, for instance, be seen by glancing again at one of the early leading German cases on 'wrongful life' and 'wrongful birth' actions.[15] Earlier, we criticised the German court for quoting the decision of a California Court of Appeal in *Curlender v Bio-Science Laboratories*[16] even though it had been overruled by the decision of the Supreme Court of California in *Turpin v Sortini.*[17] Now, to be sure, *Turpin* was decided eight months *before* the BGH reached its decision.[18] But can a foreign court be expected to be so much up to speed with foreign case law?

The answer must be an emphatic 'no'. Our criticism was accurate though, perhaps, not fair. Yet, for our purposes, it must be coupled with the proviso that this may not always matter since what advocates of the exchange of ideas do *not* call for is a consideration or transplantation of specifics. In the instant case there was thus never any question of the German court granting the 'impaired' child any special damages for its extraordinary expenses since these, under German (and unlike American) law, are always to be borne by the parents. On the other hand, what matters (and mattered in that case) was to show that these (new) actions had to be met in a way that took care of the needs of the unfortunate victims and that they should not be defeated by metaphysical arguments such as the one often invoked in these cases, namely, that 'impaired life is preferable to non-life'. Finally, it was important to show that, notwithstanding the caution showed by the German court, mutual inspiration between two very different legal systems *was* possible since the outcome in the German case never really depended on the wording of a particular provision of the BGB.

So it is the *wider dialogue* we are advocating; and this, where circumstances specifically demand, can be expanded on an ad hoc basis more easily in our times than in days gone by. This is partly because, in the light of the above, the basic database is larger than ever before and,

---

15 BGHZ 86, 240 ff = JZ 1983, 447 ff.

16 106 Cal. App. 3rd 811, 165 Cal. Rptr. 477 (1980).

17 31 Cal. Rptr. 3rd 220, 643 P. 2d 954 (1982).

18 The decision in *Turpin* was published on 3 May 1982 while the decision of the BGH was published on 18 January 1983.

moreover, can easily be updated. It is also due to the fact that some of the prime innovators in the area of foreign and comparative law (such as the European Court of Justice, the Strasbourg Court on Human Rights, the Canadian Supreme Court, and the South African Constitutional Court) all publish their decisions in English. Finally, and here we speak from experience which (though localised) may reflect a potentially growing trend, we are aware of both judges and practitioners who turn to lawyers such as ourselves – not always for reward – seeking amplifications and updates to already published material. Our submission is that if to the above one adds the long-term effect which multi-national law firms are bound to have in the dispensing of multi-national legal advice, the so-called information gap will become smaller and the objection 'how do we find out about foreign law' will lose some of its (understandable) force.

4. Detailed consideration versus generalities

Readers of the old but continuing debate started by Professor John Langbein's 20-year old article on the German law of civil procedure will find in it an illustration for this heading. The preceding paragraphs may have in fact addressed this aspect; and in the Langbein context we shall add a few more words under the next sub-heading. Here, however, we address the point touched upon in the previous section, which concerns not only the *access* to foreign material but also its *presentation* in a way that makes it attractive and usable by the national lawyer.

We raise this point here even though one of us has made it a central theme of a book which, though published in England in 2003, has already appeared in a German and Italian edition.[19] One of the arguments there was that the use of foreign law was impeded by the fact that it was often merely translated into the language of the potential 'receiver' rather than packaged in a manner that made it useable by the judges and lawyers of the receiving system. There is no need to repeat here the many arguments put forward in that work; one example may suffice.

Take the often discussed question of liability for negligent certifications.[20] In American law it is dealt with through tort (or specific statutes, not here our concern) and, though one encounters the usual diversity of solutions between different State courts, the pivotal legal concept used to determine the outcome of the case is the presence or absence of a duty of care. As a generalisation, one could say that more

---

[19] Op. cit. note 11. The Italian edition appeared in 2004 under the title *Il Metodo della Comparazione* and the German in the same year as *Rechtsvergleichung in Theorie und Praxis. Ein Beitrag zur rechtswissenschaftlichen Methodenlehre.*

[20] Better known in the United States as 'accountants' liability for harm caused by negligent audits'.

often than not liability is *not* found, or it is restricted in various ways. In Germany the approach is through contract, which is extended (*over*-extended, one would be inclined to say) to cover persons other than the one initially commissioning and paying for the advice. Liability is often discovered and the need to explain this rather stark divergence from American law immediately becomes obvious, otherwise possible borrowing is out of the question (even not counting the language difficulty).

Yet, the German solution *can* become more relevant if presented against the background of the non-existence in that country of the 'class action' mechanism, which can (relatively easily) mobilise potential claimants in bringing a suit against a company showing signs of financial difficulty and – perhaps just as importantly – the existence of compulsory insurance coverage for such claims, which achieves some (though by no means complete in the most serious of cases) satisfaction of claims without leading to the bankruptcy of the maker of the statement. What the potential user of such information thus needs to have is (a) not the doctrinal discussion of the topic as it appears in German books (which is difficult to follow for all but the specialists in German law) nor, even, (b) decisions with factual equivalents similar to his own so that he can attempt his own comparison, but rather a sketch of the above-mentioned factors which can help place the system in a clearer setting and will then assist the potential borrower (litigant or legislator) in deciding whether he wishes to pursue this borrowing exercise further.[21]

The focused examination of foreign law (coupled, where possible, with a *functional* rather than *conceptual* examination of the foreign system) must in all but the most technical of cases be attempted against the wider background of the system used for inspiration.[22] This will often mean asking the question to what extent this can be fitted into the socio-economic environment of the potential borrower. This difficulty has been the subject of heated discussions in the United States during the last 15 years, and to these we must now turn our attention. From the outset, however, one must note that the American debate has mainly focused on

---

21 For further detail see Michael Coester (University of Munich) and B. S. Markesinis, 'Liability of Financial Experts in German and American Law: An Exercise in Comparative Methodology' (2003) 51 *The Amer. J. Comp. Law* 275 ff.

22 A point also made by Justice Breyer in his 'Constitutionalism, Privatization, and Globalization', 21 *Cardozo L. Rev.* 1045 (at 1060–1). This, incidentally, is not a task that judges can undertake on their own; but it is greatly facilitated if academics, in focused works, aid the judiciary (and, where called for, the legislator) in its task of understanding correctly the foreign ideas and solutions. This way of achieving the best possible co-operation between academics and practitioners is fully developed in B. S. Markesinins, op. cit. note 11, especially chapters 2, 4, and 5.

constitutional law matters, especially issues of judicial review, putting very much in a second place the analysis of the same issues in the private law context.

Generalised references to 'foreign law' or 'foreign systems' or 'world consensus' are not only liable to be less usable by a (potentially) importing court; they are also likely to create problems for those relying on such generalities.[23] To invoke, for instance, the English laws of 1933[24] and 1948[25] preventing execution of the death sentence on minors even before the general abolition of the death penalty is relevant and, we believe, instructive. But wider references to 'foreign systems' (such as one often finds in decisions of the German Constitutional Court) or allusions to the 'historic ties' – legal and cultural in general – that have existed between the United Kingdom and the United States could easily bring about plausible counterclaims that the position of the former has, especially in modern times, drifted apart from the latter on many issues. Justice Scalia was both quick and right to point this out in his dissenting judgment in *Roper v Simmons* – even though his examples had little to do with the dispute at hand. His concluding shot, therefore, that

> (T)o invoke alien law [and note, once again, the careful use of words to convey not only that the law is different but that its underlying values are also *alien*] when it agrees with one's own thinking and ignore it otherwise, is not reasoned decision-making, but sophistry.[26]

For one is not, nor indeed should be, comparing entire legal systems but the *answers* they provide – no doubt understood within their wider contexts – to the problem occupying the (potentially importing) court. What would be sophistry, or rather misleading practice, would be to use some views supported in a certain foreign system rather than others. But would that ever happen? The Common law 'adversarial' system should be able to expose this weakness, reveal (to the potentially importing court) the divergence of views, and thus put it 'on notice' of the dangers of using foreign law. This, however, is a problem we have warned against (and discussed) in several sub-sections of this chapter. Here, therefore, suffice it to say that we agree with the view (most recently expressed with force by Justice Scalia in *Roper*) that if foreign law is cited to a national

---

[23] The point is, rightly, made with some force by Professor Michael D. Ramsay in 'International Materials and Domestic Rights: Reflections on Akins and Lawrence', 98 *Am. J. Int'l L.* 69, especially at 77 ff.

[24] Children and Young Persons Act 1933, 23 Geo 5, chapter 12 (preventing execution of those aged under 18 on the date of sentence).

[25] Criminal Justice Act 1948, 11 and 12 Geo 6, chapter 58 (preventing execution of anyone under 18 at the time of the offence).

[26] 125 S. Ct. 1183, 1228 (2005).

court the judges of the latter, if inclined to use it as a source of inspiration, should first invite Counsel to express their views on it with regard to its reliability as well as its transplantability or inspirational value.[27] One has to admit at this point that in the United States the summary use of foreign material by the Supreme Court – a footnote in Atkins, three paragraphs in Lawrence – has certainly not satisfied this requirement whereas the House of Lords decision in *Fairchild v Glenhaven*[28] comes closer to the ideal we are advocating and which we believe the growing availability of foreign material in usable form nowadays makes possible.

5. The impact of the socio-economic and political environment

a) General observations

Much has been said about this topic as a serious inhibitor of using foreign ideas, and the value of these objections cannot be denied. But the discussion has not been focused; and to some extent this may be due to the vagueness of these terms and how they may operate in different parts of the law. Before we go into details, we wish to raise three preliminary points and restate our awareness of the fact that the best we hope to achieve is a contribution towards a debate which might, one day, lead to a more widely acceptable position.

First, one must ask the question 'are all *cultural*[29] factors strong – if not insurmountable – inhibitors to the use of foreign ideas?' To invoke culture in its various forms without more circumspection is tantamount to deciding in advance that national law lies beyond comparative criticism.

---

[27] A point made both by Justice Scalia in *Roper v Simmons* 125 S. Ct 1183 at 1222 ff. (2005) and, on the academic front and in more general terms, by Michael D. Ramsay, op. cit. note 23, at 78–9. In France, where amicus briefs are unknown and the 'gladiatorial discussion' of the law is extremely rare in the highest courts, an exception can be found in two instances where the *Cour de cassation*, itself, asked the *Société de Législation Comparé* to prepare a research report which was then sent to all parties to use in their briefs before the Court. On this see Guy Canivet, 'The Use of Comparative Law Before the French Private Law Courts', in Guy Canivet, Mads Andenas, and Duncan Fairgrieve (eds), op. cit. note 14, p 191.

[28] [2002] 1 AC 32.

[29] We have italicised 'cultural' in order to exclude, for present purposes, political factors which may openly oppose the introduction of foreign notions or values. That this can raise very sensitive issues can be seen from the history of the Hong Kong Bill of Rights, which suggests that political, not cultural, divergences (between East and West) gave human rights developments its very specific flavour there; see, among others, Yash Ghai, 'Sentinels of Liberty or Sheep in Woolf's Clothing? Judicial Politics and Hong Kong Bill of Rights' (1997) 60 *MLR* 459 ff.

This simply will not do for law – just as it does not in other areas either, for example, economics, politics, national security, or education (just to mention a few), where governments and other institutions and organisations refer to what is happening in other countries and try to learn from that experience. To give but two examples from a country, England, not particularly known for its willingness (especially during the latter half of the twentieth century) to use foreign experiences to reform its own institutions or ways of operating – this country is experiencing an unprecedented amount of discussion about using the French 'baccalaureate' system to change or adapt its own so-called A-level system, and changing its long-respected social security systems by increasingly toying with ideas that would 'privatise' some parts of it. Clearly, then, under this heading we may encounter topics (sodomy, death penalty, child chastisement, or homosexual marriages) where, say, the American public opinion holds views different from those found in European countries and, moreover, has expressed them in various democratic ways.

Second, as the late Sir Otto Kahn-Freund (among others) stressed a long time ago, we have structural (legal) reasons that may inhibit, indeed prohibit, the subversion of deeply held local value judgments through the introduction of foreign legal material into the adjudicatory process. We shall return to this point in later sections of this chapter; but we raise it here since it strikes us as being at the core of the current debate in the United States where there is a long and politically rooted tradition in some sectors to mistrust the subversion of constitutional ideas by means of judicial review.

Third, there is the time factor. What may appear as a deep cultural difference (inhibiting the influence of foreign ideas at one time) may cease to be so only a few years later. That these changes can occur despite the expectations of the most acute minds, and happen sooner than could ever have been imaginable, can be seen by reading Kahn-Freund's much cited 'On Uses and Misuses of Comparative Law'.[30] For there, referring to the inhibiting influence which non-legal institutions can exert on the reception of foreign law, he talked about the impact of the Catholic Church on Ireland and the resulting unwillingness to recognise divorce law or, we could add, abortion. The article was written in 1974. By the end of the century, both institutions were part of the Irish legal landscape (and, one might add, the change was to a large extent facilitated by the internationalisation of law and society). The point is thus raised merely to act as a warning against stereotyping countries and people and then using these vague images to inhibit all discussion about the advantages derived from the consideration of foreign experiences. Indeed, when one reflects on the 'reception' of American law in post-Second World War

---

[30] Op. cit. note 3.

Japan, German law in South Africa, or Canadian human rights law in Israel, one is forced to rethink the force of the inhibiting factor which differences in legal cultures can have *in times such as ours* when national borders have become so porous in so many respects. Incidentally, the importance of 'time' (or rather the passage of time) in facilitating the reception of a foreign idea which, a few years earlier, might have been inconceivable, has not been studied by scholars on either side of the Atlantic and yet it seems to us to be crucial to our chosen subject. Yet, as Sophocles put it in the mouth of Ajax, 'everything withers with time'.

As far as the United States is concerned one must add one further factor to those already mentioned; and this, too, shows the unpredictable nature of the time factor. Thus, when the first draft of this article was being composed, opinion polls across the United States seemed unable to predict the electoral outcome of the November 2004 general election. At the time of writing this outcome is now known; and the indications are that a series of 'conservative' nominations are likely to be made at the Supreme Court. At a stroke this could radically alter the persuasive force of the arguments for and against the use of foreign law in this country for a generation or more. Such a change could, of course, be justified by invoking the idea of democratic legitimacy. But that serious arguments can end up in the waste bin of history because a couple of hundred votes went one way rather than the other (which is what happened four years ago) is hardly a good way of deciding genuinely difficult intellectual issues, however much one may try to link them to theories of democratic legitimacy.

b) Two specific examples

The above observations, general though they are, prompt us to ask whether the question of the impact of the local environment on the consideration of foreign ideas might not be better considered by attempting, difficult though it is, a *gradation* of legal rules (and situations). Some of these rules may well reflect values so widely and deeply shared in one society that they could arguably make the consideration of foreign ideas and experiences unproductive in the context of a courtroom (though perhaps more welcome in the setting of a legislative assembly). Other rules, concerning, say, contract or tort problems, could be at the other end of the spectrum as, indeed, the American experience for the whole of the nineteenth century and the first quarter of the twentieth century suggests.[31] In between could lie a range

[31] See, for instance, Stefan Riesenfeld, 'The Impact of German Legal Ideas and Institutions on Legal Thought and Institutions in the United States' and James E. Herget, 'The Influence of German Thought on American Jurisprudence, 1880–1918', both in Mathias Reimann (ed), *The Reception of Continental Ideas in the Common Law World 1820–1920* (1993), at pp 89 ff and 203 ff respectively.

of topics which could be argued as falling within one side of the divide or the other, and are capable of a more nuanced consideration. Let us look briefly at two situations.

The first touches upon homosexuality, always an emotive issue.

Imagine a State in the United States voting in a referendum by a substantial majority to enact an amendment that bans any judicial or legislative legitimising of homosexual marriage (at the time of writing eleven States had this issue on ballot and it passed in all[32]). Imagine further a car accident involving two couples: one legally married, the other cohabiting in a homosexual union. Two out of the four are seriously injured and rushed to hospital while a few hours later the uninjured 'partners', having heard of the accidents, visit the hospital to find out about the state of health of their loved ones. The hospital rules authorise such disclosure to spouses (or other close relatives) but not to others, with the result that the lawfully wedded partner receives the desired information whereas the homosexual cohabitee is kept in the dark. Though the State in question may have expressed its disapproval towards homosexual marriages, is the above (hypothetical) example consistent with ideas of fairness, equality, and proportionality?[33] Would invoking the growing tendency among Western democracies (for better or worse) to improve the status of homosexuals in society be impermissible as undermining the earlier referendum result which showed its abhorrence to the idea of homosexual marriages? We called our example a 'hypothetical' because we are not aware whether a case with the kind of facts we have imagined has actually arisen in the United States. But the evidence one has from the recent expansion of statutory enactments that permit the establishment and registration of 'domestic partnerships'[34]

---

[32] And it may even have influenced the overall voting result in States such as Ohio, which was regarded to the very end as a so-called swing state.

[33] In Hamburg/Germany, State legislation (the *Hamburgisches Krankenhausgesetz*) introduced a right to information of same-sex partners about half a decade ago while the Federal Constitutional Court had still ruled that homosexuality was a clear violation of *bones mores* in 1959. Similar laws putting same-sex partners on par with married couples were enacted in the 1990s in many Scandinavian countries. For a more detailed comparative survey see Jürgen Basedow/Klaus Dopffel/Hein Kötz (eds), *Die Rechtsstellung gleichgeschlechtlicher Lebensgemeinschaften* (2000).

[34] California's Family Code s 297 subdivision (b)(6). In its 1999 form this provision only allowed the registration of domestic partnerships. But Statute 2001 chapter 893 s 2 amended s 377.60 subdivision (a) of the Code of Civil Procedure in a way which has enabled 'domestic partners' as defined by statutes – for which see *Holguin v Flores* 2004 WL 205166 (Cal. App. 2 Dist) 2004 – to make medical decisions for each other, adopt their partner's child, use sick leave to care for an ailing partner, and become recognised claimants for the purposes of wrongful death claims.

would suggest that such rights are being slowly established in a number of States.[35]

Though these situations may have been decided differently, both show that that a court decision at the most general level of a legal problem raising serious moral issues may go one way, while a court deciding a narrow (and, one might argue, more 'technical') question linked to the same wider issue may come to a different solution. Indeed, a series of statutes, executive orders, and other measures passed after the terrorist attacks on New York and Washington on 11 September 2001 resulted in a rapid increase of recognition of benefits given to surviving same-sex partners.[36] These hierarchically 'lesser' rules show that the legal system can tolerate at greater levels of specificity ideas which are repelled when phrased at a level of generality and abstraction that immediately provokes strong moral values and unreasoned opposition. If this assertion is correct, the room for manoeuvring with foreign ideas increases accordingly.

The second example is a 'dryer' one, on the surface of interest only to specialists. It comes from the area of civil procedure. Nearly 20 years ago, Professor John Langbein wrote an article commending the efficiency of the German civil procedure and contrasting its merits with the demerits, as he saw them, of the American trial process.[37] The proposal sparked off a heated and at times harshly phrased debate,[38] which (it may be safe to say) failed to budge the adherents of the two views from their respective

---

[35] A close parallel to our hypothetical can be found in England. This went the other way, even though homosexuality has been decriminalised for some time now in that country. In the case in point the court had to decide whether a railway company policy giving its married employees the right to obtain every now and again free tickets for their spouses could be availed by an employee for the benefit of his homosexual partner. The English court said no, and for reasons which need not be discussed here, the Court of the European Communities took the same view; see judgment of 17 February 1998, Case C-249/96.

[36] See, for instance, Shannon Minter, 'Expanding Wrongful Death Statutes And Other Death Benefits To Same-Sex Partners' (2003) 30 *SUM Hum. Rts* 6.

[37] 'The German Advantage in Civil Procedure' (1985) 52 *U. Chi.L Rev.* 823 ff.

[38] Thus see Ronald J. Allen, Stephan Kock, Kurt Reichenberg, and D. Toby Rosen, 'The German Advantage in Civil Procedure: A Plea for More Details and Fewer Generalities in Comparative Scholarship' (1988) 82 *NW. U. L. Rev.* 705 ff to which Professor Langbein replied 'The German Advantage' (1988) 82 *NW. U. L. Rev.* 763 ff. Allen's riposte, entitled 'Idealization and Caricature in Comparative Scholarship', appeared in (1988) 82 *NW. U. L. Rev.* 785 ff. Others joined the fray. Thus, see John H. Merryman, 'How Others Do It: The French and German Judiciaries' (1988) 61 *So. Cal. L. Rev.* 1865 ff and John C. Reitz, 'Why We Probably Cannot Adopt the German Advantage in Civil Procedure' (1990) 75 *Iowa L. Rev.* 987 ff. The articles mentioned in the next note show that the discussion is not abating but is now acquiring a new, sociological, dimension.

positions. More recently, however, Professor Chase[39] returned to the fray and, through extensive references to sociological literature,[40] attempted to suggest that cultural reasons prevented the transplantation of the German model to the United States. His views led us to reflect once again on the invocation of culture as an inhibitor of foreign borrowing.

Professor Chase's sources confirm (or are meant to confirm – personally we adopt an ambivalent position on the evaluation of the sociological evidence since we confess a certain mistrust towards the methods adopted and the meaningfulness of the conclusions for legal rules) the well-know stereotypes of German 'authoritarianism' and American 'individualism'. These characteristics, he argues, tend to make the Germans to value 'certainty' more than the Americans. It also leads them to wish to promote settlements at every conceivable opportunity. Leaving aside the fact that we both feel that certainty, predictability, and reduction of litigation are, in principle, desirable characteristics of any legal order,[41] the picture painted by Professor Chase of the German and American legal systems is not one which can be recognised with ease. Here are three reasons why we say this, though again they are mentioned only briefly because of lack of space.

First, it is the Anglo-American systems that have developed and used their legal devices (for instance the duty of care in their law of torts) or arguments such as that of floodgates *against* litigation, or phrases such as 'bright line rules' in order to ensure certainty (and rigidity) at the expense of flexibility and justice. While judges using the expression 'bright line rules' have in fact stressed that what is uppermost in their minds is administrative convenience and not justice, courts that have condemned this reasoning have exposed the true reasons behind them. These are not arguments or devices found in any civil law system.

Second, Professor Chase's article is based on a central theme which supports his contention that '(T)he German system (...) reflects a willingness to accept structures of authority that are inimical to the more individualistic Americans.'[42] If that is the case, one may be permitted to ask: are the Greeks or Italians, who essentially share the same model of

---

[39] 'Legal Process and National Culture' (1997) 5 *Cardozo J. Int' l & Comp. L.* 1 ff. For Professor Langbein's (somewhat intemperately phrased) reply see 'Cultural Chauvinism in Comparative Law' (1997) 5 *Cardozo J. Int'l & Comp. L.* 41 ff.

[40] The works most used were Geert Hofstede's *Culture and Orgnanisations. Software of the Mind* (1991), now available in a revised edition (1997), and his more substantive *Culture's Consequences* (now in its 2nd edn, 2001).

[41] Though one can always find authors arguing the opposite; see, for instance, Samuel R. Gross, 'The American Advantage: The Value of Inefficient Litigation' (1987) 85 *Mich. L. Rev.* 734 ff.

[42] Op. cit. note 39, p 1.

civil procedure as the Germans, also 'authoritarian' and any less 'individualistic' than the Americans? Since the answer must be negative, one is led to believe that there are other more important factors which make this transplantation of ideas and institutions possible.

Finally, if civil procedure rules 'must be placed in deep cultural context',[43] how does one explain the recent Woolf Reforms in England, which are based on a lengthy and comparative law exercise and led to the adoption of many rules and institutions that strengthen the managerial role of judges, accept the idea of court-appointed experts, and the like (all of which are features which Professor Chase does not treat as 'American')? Does this mean that the English are more like the Germans than the Americans? Or does it support Professor Chase's thesis that rules cannot be borrowed (not even ideas can be looked at) if some sociological model adopts a different way of classifying nations?

The problem with such an unadulterated sociological approach to law is not just that it does not sit well with what lawyers say and do; it also hides the real reason why such transplants are difficult. Professor Chase, himself, mentions it at the end of his article, though hardly gives it the prominence we think it deserves. In his words '(E)ven if American judges would try to expand their control of the trial we can predict a long and costly struggle with the trial bar (...).'[44] This may well be a valid prediction. We suspect that Professor Langbein would not deny such difficulties. But it is a pragmatic, not cultural (except in the loosest possible sense of the word) objection; and the acceptance of the changes made in England by the Woolf reforms suggests as much.

To sum up: First, the question of cultural differences *is* important, as is the need to adapt a foreign idea when introducing it in a different environment. But we entirely agree with Professor Langbein when he wrote '(I)t is all too easy to allow the cry of "cultural differences" to become the universal apologetic based upon comparative example.'[45] Moreover, the gradation approach we proposed shows that it does not work as an inhibitor. Second, legal practice proves that the 'cultural differences' card, though both important and delicate, can be overplayed. The impact of the Canadian Charter on the development of Israeli human rights law must, surely, attest to this. The *El Al Airlines Ltd. v Danilowitz*-decision[46] of a three-judge panel of the Israeli Supreme Court proves as much in one of the most sensitive of areas on which local religious feelings have clear-cut views (homosexual rights), Justice Dorner

---

43 Op. cit. note 39, p 6.

44 Ibid, p 8.

45 (1985) 52 *U. Chi. L. Rev.* 823, 855.

46 (1994) 48(5) P.D. 749.

indulging in an even more extensive use of comparative (mainly Canadian) material than Justice Barak (who in fact nearly lost his scheduled promotion to the post of President of the Court).[47]

The cultural factor is thus an important element that must be weighed carefully in any attempt to derive inspiration from another system. In many (but not all) cases, however, it may require little more than trying to understand the legal rule/solution within its wider context. In a limited sort of way we have attempted to do this in this book, for instance when trying to explain/discuss Justice Scalia's hostility (real or apparent) towards foreign ideas of justice within the political context in which his own ideas must be placed. Where this can be undertaken it has, in our view, the advantage of asking the judge to analyse a legal idea within the wider constitutional/political framework which he is capable of understanding without drawing him into the more 'murky' waters of sociology with which judges are less familiar.

6. Legal certainty

The use of the comparative method substantially expands the boundaries of a legal discourse. New arguments and perspectives found in foreign law can thereby impact on the outcome of a particular case and influence the further development of national law in general. Once the national gate to the 'world wide web of legal systems' is thrown open, however, the problem of *choice* arises – and with it the danger of 'cherry-picking' legal ideas from other systems when and where this seems appropriate to promote the judge's own cause. This, in itself, may not be so very different in disputes which are argued solely on the basis of national rules. If, however, foreign law can be introduced as persuasive authority, the parties will have to anticipate – and possibly counteract – a far larger range of legal materials than in the 'traditional' scenario in which the rules of the game are limited to well-known boundaries. Problems that already exist in the latter case (surprising changes of the law, the sheer number of legislative and judicial developments, and, subsequently, the increasing danger of liability for legal malpractice resulting from an insufficient evaluation of litigation risks) could increase. It would be wrong to deny this danger though it would seem equally wrong to overstate it in the absence of any hard evidence to that effect. We add this

[47] See 'An equal-rights decision that flies in the face of some beliefs', *Jerusalem Post* of 12 December 1994 at p 7 and the 1 December 1994 issue of the same publication at p 2. For a further discussion of the use of foreign law by Israel's Supreme Court see Segal, 'The Israeli Constitutional Revolution: The Canadian Impact in the Midst of a Formative Period', *Forum Constitutionnel* (1997) 8:3 and Dodek, 'The Charter in the Holy Land?', *Forum Constitutionnel* (1996) 8:1.

last point, for in today's world of increased international legal exchanges practitioners, especially those working in the multi-national law firms which handle most of this work, often have a working knowledge concerning at least the main features of other important legal systems in their respective areas of specialisation and, of course, close links with colleagues in other countries who can immediately assist in matters concerning problems with a transnational element.

7. Do courts have enough time to deal with other legal systems?

The cases we have discussed in the course of this study were decided by very different courts. Among them are a number of supreme or constitutional courts, specialised federal courts (such as the German *Bundesgerichtshof*), courts operating on a supra-national level (the European Court of Justice), and courts situated on lower tiers of a country's judicial system (such as the Cape Town Division of the High Court of South Africa). Not only do these forums operate in very different legal environments; judges sitting on theses bodies are also confronted with very different restraints as far as time, money, and research facilities are concerned. These are factors that have to be taken into account when advocating recourse to foreign law, even if it only be for the purposes of inspiration. One must also admit that the chances such a comparative law exercises being carried out are much greater and, one might add, even more appropriate, at courts of the highest level.[48] Yet, again, one must try to evaluate this danger; and if one is to do so on the basis of the space foreign arguments occupy in published judgments, or time spent arguing it in court, the answer would seem to be that this danger can easily be exaggerated.

There is another reason why this argument can be over-emphasised. For though judges across the spectrum have been quick to invoke it, the truth is that, as hinted at the beginning, they all work under very different circumstances.

Take for instance the judges at the European Court of Justice. Each will have three carefully selected and highly talented *referendaires* who will assist them greatly in the preparation of their judgments. Additionally, they can all have recourse – and Advocate Generals often do – to a department of the Court in charge of research and documentation. Its staff, composed of lawyers from all Member States, prepare so-called

---

[48] Yet if an issue of great importance presents itself and there is lack of local legal guidance a Court of First instance may be forced to undertake a comparative law exercise. *A & Others v National Blood Authority*, [2001] 3 All ER 289 is one such example and, to a lesser extent, so is *Greatorex v Greatorex* [2000] 1 WLR 1970.

notes de recherché on specific issues and how they are dealt with in the various systems. All of the above also enjoy excellent library and supporting technical facilities. The claim of lack of time or assistance in such a context seems very unconvincing.

The Strasbourg Court of Human Rights works somewhat differently. There, a legal committee composed of lawyers representing all Member States of the Council of Europe act as a collective source of aid and support for the Justices, and are also aided in their work by excellent library and technical facilities.

National supreme courts, like those of the United States and Canada, have for long enjoyed the help of judicial clerks drawn from the ranks of these country's top graduating lawyers and known for the exceedingly hard work they do. The same is true of the German supreme courts which receive assistance from junior but carefully selected judges who are assigned to these courts for a period of several years and both act as high-powered clerks and discharge other minor duties.

One could go on with this list but it would serve little purpose. For what is crucial about it is the contrast it reveals between such well-assisted courts (as the ones indicatively mentioned above) and many other Common law systems – especially English courts, which are known to operate in cramped (if historically and aesthetically attractive) premises, with limited library and computer facilities and hardly any clerkship system worth mentioning. Yet the English (and more, generally, Common law judges) have enjoyed an advantage not available to their civil law counterparts and that is the fact that Counsel do much of the research and gathering of authority for them; and, in a sense, that is equivalent to having some of the finest minds at your service (though, it must be admitted, not always up-to-date on matters of legal literature).

One last thought to conclude this sub-section and this is to say that no one asks for nor expects original legal and comparative research to take place in lower courts and the vast number of litigated cases. One's expectations, however, are different when it comes to the highest courts where the number of cases that have to be decided can be low and the time to reflect more widely makes this not only possible but, at times, also desirable given how the highest judges of the world are increasingly called upon to decide issues which are fairly common to us all, which all goes to show that though this 'argument' about lack of time has some merit, rarely is it really the true and decisive reason for the absence of any real use of foreign law.

8. The 'depth' of analysis of foreign legal ideas

This problem comes in two guises. In some systems, judges only give the barest of indications that foreign legal ideas may have influenced their reasoning. The ECJ's regular references to the fact that 'the Court draws inspiration from the constitutional traditions common to the Member States' often falls – when viewed in isolation – into this category. Similar phrases in German decisions show that judges have identified foreign law as similar, different, or otherwise meaningful, but the reader is left in the dark as to what these similarities and differences are in detail, how they compare to German law, and how they have influenced the judge in the instant case. Here, the use of the comparative method is not superficial; actually, the method is not used at all, and the reference to foreign legal systems is little more than a signal (others would say a fig-leaf) that courts are aware of the world outside. Indicative of their court's awareness that 'there is another world out there'[49] such 'mini-references' could also be seen as an individual judge's wish to demonstrate wider culture! Either way, from a scholarly point of view such references are of limited value and should be used with great caution.

The second variant may be more dangerous. In these cases, courts *do* embark on a more extensive analysis of foreign law and the insights that can perhaps be gained from the comparison. References to the text of a *single* statute, a *particular* case, or the writings of one or two foreign academics do not, however, always reveal the full picture of the law in practice. Many questions familiar to the professional comparatist arise. How does the legal system *as a whole* deal with a certain issue, and can answers perhaps be found in different (and sometimes surprising) parts of the law? How has the case law in question *developed*, and what were the alternatives? What is the view of *other* academics? And, more importantly, how does all of this impact on the 'local' question the court is called upon to resolve? In the United States these legitimate questions have been exploited by those who oppose the way foreign law has been used by the Supreme Court; but the complaint seems to us legitimate only in so far as the way this material has been used rather than in the value of consulting this material properly – which is what we are advocating in the belief that the growing availability of material makes this possible.

Justice Johan Kriegler of the Constitutional Court of South Africa addressed this issue in *Bernstein and others v Bester NO and others*[50] when he responded to the extensive comparative work presented by his colleagues on the bench and Counsel – a noteworthy contrast to the

[49] Sir Thomas Bingham, ' "There is a World Elsewere": The Changing Perspectives of English Law' in *The Business of Judging. Selected Essays and Speeches* (2000), pp 87 ff.

[50] 1996 (4) BCLR 449 (CC).

accusation levied against the use made by American courts – arguing the case with the following words:

> I agree with the identification and the logical analysis of the principle (...) but prefer to express no view on the possible lessons to be learnt from other jurisdictions. That I do, not because of a disregard for section 35(1) of the Constitution, or in a spirit of parochialism. My reason is twofold. First, because the subtleties of foreign jurisdictions, their practices and terminology require more intensive study than I have been able to conduct. Even on a superficial view, there seem to me to be differences of substance between the statutory, jurisprudential and societal contexts prevailing in those countries and in South Africa as to render ostensible analogies dangerous without thorough understanding of the foreign systems. For the present I cannot claim that degree of proficiency. (...) The second reason is that I wish to discourage the frequent – and, I suspect, often facile – resort to foreign 'authorities'. Far too often one sees citation by Counsel of, for instance, an American judgement in support of a proposition relating to our Constitution, without any attempt to explain why it is said to be in point. Comparative study is always useful, particularly where the courts in exemplary jurisdictions have grappled with universal issues confronting us. Likewise, where a provision in our Constitution is manifestly modelled on a particular provision in another country's constitution, it would be folly not to ascertain how the jurists of that country have interpreted their precedential provision. The prescripts of section 35(1) of the Constitution are also very clear: where applicable, public international law in the field of human rights must be considered, and regard may be had to comparative foreign case law. But that is a far cry from blithe adoption of alien concepts or inappropriate precedents.[51]

As stated, in the light of the enormous increase of comparative material on foreign legal systems readily available today, Kriegler J's criticism may seem a little harsh.

There is, however, a difference between the *availability* of knowledge, on the one hand, and the *use* of this knowledge on the other. Courts and practitioners work under heavy time constraints and will not always invest the necessary resources into the comparative exercise. Especially in systems where comparative law is currently *en vogue*, there will be a temptation to rely on only one or two readily accessible sources.

An example from South Africa proves the point. In *The State v Makwanyane and Mchunu*[52] on the constitutionality of the death penalty, President Arthur Chaskalson, delivering the unanimous decision of the Court, had recourse to German constitutional law in the context of (a) the use of legislative history as an interpretative tool in constitutional

---

51 At pp 506 ff.

52 Case No CCT/3/94 of 6 June 1995.

disputes;[53] (b) the right to human dignity;[54] (c) the limitation of fundamental rights;[55] and (d) section 33(1)(b) of the Interim Constitution, the so-called essential content clause.[56] The Court thereby referred to provisions of the German Constitution of 1949 and various judgements of the *Bundesverfassungsgericht*, but it is remarkable that it did so mainly by reference to two – American – sources: Professor Kommers' *The Constitutional Jurisprudence of the Federal Republic of* Germany (published in 1989) and Professor Currie's *The Constitution of the Federal Republic of Germany* (published in 1994). Professor Dieter Grimm (at the time a member of the German Constitutional Court) was also cited twice, but with an English publication.[57] Despite close linguistic ties between German and Afrikaans, original German sources (judicial and academic) were thus mostly referred to *indirectly*; the judgements of the *Bundesverfassungsgericht* were accessed by reference to the translations in Kommers and Currie, and one of the leading commentaries on the German Basic Law (by Maunz/Dürig) was cited by reference to the latter.

While the above example may have been influenced by the language barrier, the fact remains that comparative work should not rely on only one or two sources. Every author describing a legal system will inevitably make a selection of material (both cases and academic opinion); translations of court decisions will often be restricted to extracts; and summaries (such as the works of Kommers, Currie and Grimm) will, themselves, often lack detail due to restrictions in space. This does *not* mean that the comparative method cannot be utilised by judges; several other examples from South Africa show that courts *can* engage in a meaningful analysis of foreign law. The dangers highlighted by Kriegler J do, however, call for a cautious and, more importantly, *focused* approach. They also suggest that judges (in addition to their own work) should make more use of external expertise, which can easily be provided by academic institutions or even individuals specialising on the study and presentation of foreign and comparative law. In Germany, for instance, there is already a widespread practice of obtaining from such institutions written opinions (*wissenschaftliche Gutachten*) about the state of foreign law whenever such knowledge is required by the rules of private international law, and many court libraries have acquired extensive

---

53 At no [16].

54 At no [59].

55 At no [108].

56 At nos [132/133].

57 'Human Rights and Judicial Review in Germany' in Beatty (ed), *Human Rights and Judicial Review: A Comparative Perspective* (1994), pp 267 ff.

collections of such expert opinions. The same is true of the European Court of Justice, which (as explained above) makes use of its own research and documentation service. These sources should not, however, remain hidden behind the kind of generalised statements referred to in the first part of this sub-section but rather attached to the decisions and cross-referenced to in the relevant parts of the opinions.

9. Additional objections by American jurists

Judge Richard Posner, a jurist always willing to venture into ever-new areas of the law with an enviable sense of self-confidence, has adduced three additional arguments in expressing his doubts (if not outright hostility) towards the use of foreign law in the courtroom.[58]

First comes the extra cost, effort, and time 'wasted' on such exercises in an age when there is enough local law. Prima facie this is a serious objection; and though we call this an 'American' objection (mainly because it has been articulated most forcefully in that country[59]) it is an argument that could legitimately be raised in any jurisdiction. Yet, in practice its importance may have been seriously exaggerated. We offer three reasons for this scepticism.

First, one notes that the discussion of foreign law, at least in American decisions, has been *minimal* if one is to judge from the space these 'excursions' occupy in the published judgments and, even, the fact that they figure almost routinely only in footnotes. One also notes that much of the information on foreign law comes from briefs filed by *amicus* groups and thus do not burden directly (in terms of costs) either the court or the parties. Now, one could, of course, argue that this is precisely because American judges tend to display a hostile reaction to foreign law. But one could then respond that even if they were more receptive to it, the cost of assembling it for consideration would still be a mere fraction of the costs of litigation which, in any event, is wasteful in systems such as that of the United States if compared to other countries. To put it differently, one suspects (and in the absence of empirical data foreign commentators must be tentative in their reactions) that the big costs of litigation in the United States stem from other local features (e.g. class action characteristics, discovery rules, unnecessarily prolonged

[58] Posner, 'No thanks, we already have our own laws', 2004-AUG *Legal Affairs* 40.

[59] A point also raised by Counsel in *Bowers v Hardwick* 478 U.S. 186 (1986), upholding Georgia's sodomy statute and failing even to consider the earlier decision of the European Court of Human Rights in *Dudgeon v United Kingdom*, 45 Eur. Ct. H. R. (ser. A), reprinted in (1982) 4 *Eur. Hum. Rts. Rep*. 149 (holding that Art 8 of the European Convention on Human Rights accorded privacy protection to adult male homosexuals).

hearings, and – at least when compared to European models – the lack of an efficient supervisory role by the judge).

Second, we (tentatively) advance these concerns on the basis of some (limited) experience of the first of us before both American and British courts. Certainly in the latter situation, when the first of us appeared as 'junior counsel' in one of the early cases where foreign civil law was used in England, he can testify that the presentation of this material took less than one hour in a hearing that lasted five days before a panel of five law lords.[60] In short, the 'extra cost' argument, as a percentage of the total costs, seems more like a smoke-screen than a real objection. This personal experience would seem to be supported by those who have studied the sitting practices of great judges. Thus, the great Benjamin Cardozo who 'cited more authority in his opinions than did his colleagues on the New York Court of Appeals (…) wrote opinions which were no longer than average'.[61]

Third, we feel that the invocation, *in appropriate cases*, of foreign precedents can be useful even though there may be much 'internal' material (in the United States coming from, effectively, 51 jurisdictions). Yet, to paraphrase (slightly) Lord Justice Steyn (as he then was), '(…) it is arguments that influence decisions rather than the reading of pages upon pages from judgments'[62] which tend to echo the same basic philosophical position. And arguments are sharpened and refined if they are based on the consideration of differing positions rather than being formulated on the basis of decisions which represent variations on the same themes. Incidentally, this is a further reason why one should not be too concerned about the 'up-to-date' argument. For what can prompt reflection and reconsideration is not so much the recent vintage of a decision but the novelty of its perception of a problem and the originality of the proposed solution.

Second, Judge Posner objects to the 'undemocratic' nature of foreign judges. His concern could be understood in two very different ways.

The first is, possibly, the cruder of the two, implying that foreign judges do not undergo the same form of democratic legitimisation as most American judges do.[63] Anticipating the objection that this may not

[60] For further details see B. S. Markesinis, 'Five Days in the House of Lords: Some Comparative Reflections on *White v Jones*', in B. S. Markesinis, *Foreign Law and Comparative Methodology: A Subject and a Thesis* (1997), pp 329 ff. But (rare) exceptions do exist – *A & Others v National Blood Authority* (op. cit. note 48) being one of them.

[61] William H. Manz, 'Cardozo's Use of Authority: An Empirical Study' (1995) 32 *Calif. Wes. L. Rev.* 31. Those in the United States who have studied 'reputology' seem to argue that enduring reputation seems linked to high citation rates; see John H. Merryman, 'An Empirical Study of the Citation Practice of the California Supreme Court in 1950, 1960 and 1970', 50 *S. Cal. L. Rev.* 381 at 419.

[62] *White v Jones* (C.A.), [1995] 2 AC 207 at 235.

[63] We read Michael D. Ramsay's above-mentioned article (op. cit. note 23) as taking a similar line (at 80).

be real in the case of Federal judges, he alludes to the Senate confirmation hearings without much discussion of the fact – obvious to outside observers perhaps more than insiders – that they have, in recent times, become more of a show than a reality. But assuming that our reaction is too harsh and unjustified, so is Judge Posner's (possible) general implication that foreign judges are so *obviously* undemocratic. Judges of the German Constitutional Court, for example (and since we are talking about comparative law in a constitutional setting they are as good an example as any), have distinctly more democratic credentials than American Federal judges, the former having been appointed by the two German houses of parliament – the *Bundestag* and the *Bundesrat* – and, what is more, appointed for a restricted period of time.[64] Seen in this light, one might be forgiven for suggesting therefore that Judge Posner's argument is, in reality, more of a pyrotechnic than something that should leave a lasting impression on the debate.[65]

Judge Posner, however, may have been driving at another point. For what he may have meant when referring to the foreign judges not being 'democratically selected' is that their authority can (in our example) be traced to *German* voters, not to American ones. Posner's point is thus that no country's voters have any voice in the making of foreign law, so that importing that law is necessarily undemocratic. Posner, by the way, is no originalist. He famously rejected Scalia's effort to eliminate judicial discretion in an article entitled 'What Am I? A Potted Plant?'[66] But the objection derived from the notion of democracy is part and parcel of Scalia's model. Judges must confine themselves to enforcing only what was enacted by elected representatives of the people; unelected judges taking initiative or exercising discretion are behaving in an undemocratic manner – even if they are domestic judges, and even if they claim to be relying on domestic values. It follows from this a fortiori that if they are looking at or even relying on foreign judges (who have no claim whatever to authority derived from the American people or American voters) they are, again, acting in an undemocratic manner.

To us, the argument thus formulated seems to apply only to the United States – indeed, only to those judges who see dangers even in the use of foreign law as a source of inspiration or ascertainment of 'evolving ideas about justice and decency'. And we have seen in Chapter 1 that not

---

64 See Art 94(1) BL and §§ 5 ff. *Bundesverfassungsgerichtsgesetz* (Law regulating the Federal Constitutional Court).

65 Though, of course, one must admit that Posner has a point when it comes to the English system of appointing judges, a practice which only recently has become the subject of growing criticism.

66 First published in 197 *New Republic* 1987, No 23 and reprinted in David O'Brien (ed), *Judges on Judging. Views from the Bench* (2nd edn, 2004), pp 165 ff.

all American justices see themselves so circumscribed in performing the task of interpretation.

The argument, most recently resurrected by an academic colleague under the heading of accountability,[67] is also misleading in so far as it assumes that it is the foreign judge's view that shapes American law (in an undemocratic manner). In reality, of course, what has happened is that the foreign idea, where it has convinced an American judge of its true merit, then becomes part of *American* law because he – the democratically elected or confirmed judge – *chooses to formulate it as his own*. For anyone who believes in the exchange of ideas, nothing could be more attractive; and if there is a danger in the practice it lies in the fact that the 'importing' judge may misunderstand (or, less likely, deliberately misuse) foreign law, and not in the purported undemocratic nature of the latter.

Finally, Judge Posner expresses the fear that such (foreign) material would be yet another example of 'judicial fig leafing'. This need not occupy us for long, for, in essence, he provides his own answer: would that be any different to anything else the judge does? After all, with various degrees of intensity, we have been told since the Realist Movement first saw the light of day that judges decide first and justify afterwards.[68] Would recourse to foreign law really provide a distorting and reprehensible innovation to existing practice?

Yet it would be wrong to read too much into statements such as these since all theories can be exaggerated, especially by those who invent them. Mr Justice Burton's extra-judicial comments about the hearings in the blood contamination case[69] as well as the way he reached his own judgment thus repay quoting in full given the important role comparative arguments played in that case. He thus wrote:[70]

> The full and detailed oral argument was in my view essential both to ensure proper investigation of the issue and to put me in a position to arrive at an informed and reasoned decision. Bad ideas (...) can be tested and discarded. Good ideas can actually emerge in the course of discussion, but in any event can be tested and developed. (...) I had an entirely open mind and was very much swayed first one way and then the other as the argument and the evidence continued and developed. This meant that, once the case finished, I was able with a blank sheet of paper to reread not only my notes but, more importantly and more accurately, the transcripts of the forty-nine days of evidence and argument, and in particular to reconsider the bundles,

---

[67] David S. Law, 'Generic Constitutional Law', 89 *Minn. L. Rev.* 652 at 739 ff.

[68] Even British judges nowadays admit this; see, for instance, Lord Mustill, 'What do Judges Do?', *Särtryck ur Juridisk Tidskrift* 1996–97, Nr 3, 611 ff.

[69] *A & Others v National Blood Authority*, op. cit. note 48.

[70] 'Afterword' in Guy Canivet, Mads Andenas, and Duncan Fairgrieve (eds), op. cit. note 14, p 81.

> including the comparative law. I was given some five weeks' 'time off' to write the judgment, and I just about managed it in the dead-line, working the sort of hours which I had thought I had left behind at the Bar!

At 170 pages, the judgment in the blood contamination case is long even by English standards. But reading its carefully crafted text and the (subsequent) accounts provided by the main protagonists in that case not only reveals the English method of trial at its best; it also demolishes the argument that the use of foreign law would amount to little more than 'judicial fig-leafing'. It could, of course, be that; but if properly done it could also provide the core of the decision. So what matters, as always, is not just the provenance of the material but how it is presented and used.

10. Developing a neutral theory to determine which international materials are relevant

A number of American scholars have voiced the sensible objection that, at present, there is no transparently neutral theory that tells us how to select the materials which will be put before a court. Though the objection comes from scholars who, on the whole, seem opposed to the idea of foreign law becoming part of the canon of constitutional material, it is not without merit and must, therefore, be addressed. For the need is to ensure that the 'materials (...) used [are there] for their own merit, and not as a cover for other values'. The sentence is that of Professor Ramsay[71] of the University of Santiago Law School and is based on his objections, clearly articulated, that the amicus briefs submitted to the Court in the *Atkins*[72] and *Lawrence*[73] cases gave rise to concerns. In this he is not alone;[74] and to his raw data we can now add *Roper v Simmons* and Justice Scalia's analoguous (but not identical) objections[75] to the reliability of the *Roper* briefs.

In a stimulating analysis of the problem of learning from constitutional experience from other systems, Professor Mark Tushnet has considered three ways in which this can be done.[76] The first he calls *functionalism*. 'Comparative constitutional study', he writes, 'can help identify those functions and show how different constitutional provisions

---

[71] Michael D. Ramsay, 'International Materials and Domestic Rights: Reflections on Atkins and Lawrence', 98 *Am. J. Int'l L.* 69 at 72.

[72] *Atkins v Virginia*, 536 U.S. 304, 316 n 21 (2002).

[73] *Lawrence v Texas*, 123 S. Ct. 2472, 2483 (2003).

[74] Thus see Roger P. Alford, 'Misusing International Sources to Interpret the Constitution', 98 *Am. J. Int'l L.* 57 at 64.

[75] 125 S. Ct. 1183, 1225 ff.

[76] 'The Possibilities of Comparative Constitutional Law' (1999) 108 *Yale L. J.* 1225.

serve the same function in different constitutional systems. It might then be possible to consider whether the US constitutional system could use a mechanism developed elsewhere to perform a specific function, to improve the way in which that function is performed here.' The second he calls *expressivism*. It begins with the premise that 'constitutions help constitute the nation, (...) offering to each nation's people a way of understanding themselves as political beings.' Though it seems that 'comparative study could do little with respect to constitutional provisions or doctrine understood in this constitutive sense because each nation's constitution constitutes its people different', the author nevertheless proceeds to give his reasons why, even here, comparative study of the law can help. Finally, to his third category Professor Tushnet gives the most colourful term – *bricolage* – a term which he borrows from the work of Claude Lévi-Strauss, a famous French social thinker.[77] It is this method which has some bearing on this sub-section. Tushnet extends this notion to law by arguing that

> Constitution-makers and interpreters find themselves in an intellectual and political world that provides them with a bag of concepts 'at hand,' not all of which are linked to each other in some coherent way. As engineers, they would sort through concepts and assemble them into a constitutional design that made sense according to some overarching conceptual scheme. As bricoleurs, though, they reach into the bag and use the first thing that happens to fit the immediate problem they are facing.[78]

Tushnet thinks that, at times, this way of doing things reflects reality and may even have its uses, though he also admits that 'both randomness and playfulness [sic] seem incompatible with the justificatory obligations we ordinarily think judges have.'[79]

In this section we do not examine Professor Tushnet's theory as far as constitutional drafting is concerned. We accept, of course, that this process is 'eclectic' and that it also reflects political compromises; but the word 'bricolage' (at least in its French sense) invokes too much the ideas of 'random', 'haphazard', 'amateur', and almost 'casual'[80] to be acceptable

---

77 *The Savage Mind* (1966), pp 16–17.

78 Op. cit. note 76, at 1286.

79 Ibid, at 1237.

80 *Harrap's New Standard French & English Dictionary* defines 'bricolage' as pottering about, doing odd jobs, and 'bricoler' as (1) to put the breast-harness on a horse; (2) (fam.) 'bricoler une affaire' – to arrange a piece of (often shady) business; and (3) to do odd jobs; 'bricoler a la maison' – to potter, tinker, about the house. *The Oxford Hachette French Dictionary* defines the term as (1) do-it-yourself; fixing things and (2) makeshift job, and 'bricoler' as 'to tinker with; to throw together; to fiddle or tamper with'. For the purposes of law, at any rate, we regard all these renderings as unsatisfactory and, to the extent that they reflect judicial reality, as contributing to the complaints that wrong use is made of foreign law.

in the context of such a serious endeavour.[81] To an observer of the careful work of the framers of the South African Constitutions of 1993 and 1996, at least, these adjectives would not describe adequately the creation of new constitutional arrangements in that country – *despite* the fact that this process was overshadowed by numerous fundamental political disputes between the parties and, often, even serious violence between their followers out on the streets.

We are, on the other hand, concerned with the effect that the *bricolage*-theory would have on judicial decision-making, though we are not in a position to say to what extent actual practice in the United States can be said to support it. But to the extent that judges use this kind of approach as part of the justificatory process the practice must be seriously questioned. For, in our view, not only does it justify the concern that the use of foreign law is too personal, random, or unprincipled, it also helps to feed it and thus undermine what, at the end of the day, is for us (as well as Professor Tushnet) a desired objective, namely, to see comparative discourse increase not decrease. In any event, whatever the answer may be for the American judge, we seriously doubt that his Continental European counterparts would ever go down such a path of reasoning. Those concerned to address the worry that the use of foreign law is idiosyncratic and thus unreliable must try to find another way to justify the practice.

For us the role of the trained comparatist is to avoid, and also help the judge avoid, the haphazard (or wrongly motivated) use of foreign law. Recourse to foreign law is primarily a mind-broadening experience. It is meant to give the observer, here the judge, a new optic and show him how a common problem is solved by an equally qualified fellow judge. This it will do, not only if the rule is carefully selected but also clearly and 'properly'[82] presented to the judge for him to see its relevance. This is where the tasks of the academic and the advocate end and that of the judge begins. Depending on his observational powers, knowledge, experience, and intuition, *he* will then have to decide if the foreign idea is of use to him. This use may vary in content. It may lead him to understand the problem facing him better; it may encourage him to re-adjust his own law; or it may alert him to the kind of consequences that may follow if he adopts (or not) a particular solution. In other words, as

---

[81] To be told that a single paragraph in Hungary's 'accidental constitution' justifies this assertion (Tushnet, op. cit. note 76, at p 1293) is not, in our view, very convincing – not only because the circumstances under which this document was drafted were anything but ideal but also because we do not (with respect) see the document, itself, as being either a representative result of constitution-drafting endeavours the world over nor a paradigm of a text.

[82] By this we refer to the theory of 'packaging' which the first of us has developed at length (op. cit. note 11).

Guy Canivet, the First President of the French Cour de cassation, observed, he may be able to discern both the good and also the potentially harmful results of a particular rule.[83] For us, none of these endeavours leaves room for the haphazard, amateur, or random; on the contrary – it is (and should be seen to be) strictly scientific if it is to serve its purpose and allay the fears we are addressing in this sub-section.

These reactions to Professor Tushnet's wording do not mean, as we already stated above, that there is no merit in the basic demand for some kind of rational process of deciding what is chosen, how it is chosen, and then how it is used. The objections raised by colleagues (such as those mentioned at the beginning of this sub-section) must thus be addressed; and if what follows is far from perfect, it is because it represents, so far as we know, a first attempt to answer a question which has surfaced only recently thanks to American scholarship. Here then are some criteria we would like to advance for consideration and further elaboration. They are not meant to be read cumulatively; nor should one of them be seen as being more important than others. Often all may have to be weighed carefully, even if at the end of the day only one may prove to be decisive.

First, we must remember that the range of possible references/systems may be determined by the subject-matter, itself. If, for instance, the question before the court involves the understanding of a particular term found in an international convention or EU directive, the search would normally be limited to the countries that are signatories to that convention or bound by the directive. For it is from this usage and understanding that guidance should be sought and only rarely (and, for instance, for the purpose of comparison) will there be any need to go outside this 'closed' circle of systems. The contaminated blood case we discussed in Chapter 2, above, offers a good illustration;[84] the Vienna Convention on the International Sale of Goods or the UNCITRAL-model on international commercial arbitration (enacted by a number of States in the United States such as California and Texas) would be another.[85] No one could possibly object that such a limitation of the comparative exercise would be anything other than sensible.

---

83 See, inter alia, Guy Canivet, Le rôle du juge dans un monde en mutation in: Marie-Claire Belleau and Francois Lacasse (eds), *Claire L'Heureux-Dubé à la cour Suprême du Canada* 1987–2002, pp. 25 ff. (2003) and De Tous Horizons, *Mélanges Xavier Blanc-Jouvan*, pp 11 ff. (2005).

84 *A & Others v National Blood Authority*, op. cit. note 48.

85 For the interpretational difficulties which may flow from such conventions see, *inter alia*, Alan Scott Rau, 'The Culture of American Arbitration and the Lessons of ADR', (2005) 40 *Texas International Law Journal* 449 ff; Alan Scott Rau 'Integrity in Private Judging' (1997) 38 *South Texas Law Review* 485 ff.

Second, one must realise (and accept) that the search for inspiration must be justified by rational criteria – but this does not mean that it must be exhaustive. As Lord Steyn rightly, in our view, observed in a leading decision of the House of Lords,[86]

> (...) the discipline of comparative law does not aim at a poll of the solutions adopted in different countries. It has the different and inestimable value of sharpening our focus on the weight of competing considerations.

A similarity of the socio-economic environment will, for example, usually make the comparison more meaningful as well as facilitate (if so desired) the use or (even) transplantability of the foreign idea should it prove its worth in the eyes of the potential borrower.

But by placing the emphasis on the broad similarity in the socio-economic environment we are thus deliberately excluding the idea that comparison should be limited to systems that belong to the same legal family. This is partly because we do not find the divisions thus made of the various legal systems entirely convincing but mainly because this (old) concept was only based on their private laws (which dominated the legal scene when this division was devised) and ignores their public law rules (which can fall into entirely different categories).[87]

If this approach may end up by excluding a large number of countries/systems, it does not mean that the exercise has been either less useful or 'random' or 'playful' (to use some of Tushnet's expressions). On the contrary – it means that it is motivated by pragmatic considerations which include not only the potential 'transplantability' of the idea but also a realistic assessment of access to the relevant data as a result of linguistic considerations or library reasons.

This suggestion also reflects the idea that there is a difference between comparative law and comparative anthropology, and that the two may not always combine easily when, as is the case here, we are looking at our subject from a practical point of view. What one does in the ivory tower or cloister is, of course, another matter; but it is not our concern here. We stress this point, though some might find it unpalatable, because it also provides an answer to another (related) concern voiced by those colleagues who worry about the selective use of foreign material,[88] namely, that the search and use of foreign law should produce reliable facts and information about the other system.

Third, and it follows from the underlying premise of the previous observations, recourse to one (major) legal system may often, in itself, be both useful and legitimate. For instance, a legal system may in its rules

---

[86] *McFarlane v Tayside Health Board* [2000] 2 AC 59 at 81.

[87] In constitutional terms, the United States is thus much closer to (civilian) Germany than to its Common law 'family member' England.

[88] Ramsay, op. cit. note 71, at pp 77 ff.

reflect a traumatic period in its past and a concerted effort to address these experiences in its current phase. The German approach to informed consent in medical malpractice cases offers such an example; and it has proved its worth in countries which have been open-minded to the need of greater sensitivity towards all aspects of human dignity including the right to decide freely what is done with one's body. Thus, in the South African case of *Castell v De Greef*[89] Judge Ackermann (prior to his appointment to the Constitutional Court) wrote the judgment for the Cape High Court Full Bench in which the English solution (favouring doctors) was roundly rejected in favour of the German, the judgment making good use of the leading German (and comparative) treatise of that time written by the late Professor Dieter Giesen of the Free University of Berlin.[90] Despite the vast differences between South Africa and Germany – in terms of geography, size of the population, culture, economy, and (in general) the way of living – the fact that Germany had emerged from its dark years in 1949 with a new vision of human rights protection thus proved a powerful factor in the choice of German legal approaches not only in the area of constitutional law but private law, as well.

Fourth, the richness or maturity of a legal system and its related literature is also a factor militating in favour of a careful determination (and delimitation) of the range of the necessary research.[91] There may be some overlap between this factor and the previous one; yet they are not coterminous.

For a country and the system looked at for the purposes of inspiration may be more varied, ethnically mixed, and living under a 'variant' of the free economy model which pertains in the system of the potential borrower, but nonetheless have managed to develop a sophisticated jurisprudence worth a closer look. South Africa can, again, serve as an example that illustrates this point since in many ways – historically, ethnically, legally, and economically – it may present many differences with, say, England, France, or Germany. Yet its case law (especially, one is inclined to suggest, its constitutional case law) has more than earned its spurs during the last decade or so and, in our view at least, deserves to be considered.

Readers must not rush to misunderstand a distinction based on the belief that a more mature and sophisticated legal order will inevitably hold more in store for potential borrowers. Countries are not equal in size, wealth, or military terms. It would thus be wrong to assume that

---

[89] 1994 (4) SA 408 (C).

[90] See, in particular, pp 416–27.

[91] For the demand of an over-ambitious research may then play into the hands of those who argue that the process adds unnecessarily to the cost of the entire exercise.

their legal systems could hold out the same intellectual attraction. In our view, only rarely will it thus make sense to state that the 'whole world does this or that, and that should have a bearing on how a particular system, especially an advanced legal system, should react'. Though such statements may have influence on a national court (as, in fact, they did in *Lawrence v Texas* and *Roper v Simmons*) they are, in principle, too broad and too vague to carry the weight they appear to have at first sight. Though we favour the results reached in both of the above-mentioned American decisions, we do have some considerable sympathy for the methodological objections voiced against the way this raw data was presented to the US Supreme Court.

Fifth, the time and location of the potential borrower may, for pragmatic reasons, delimit the range of the comparative survey which his legislator or his courts may be realistically expected to undertake. Under this heading we are not envisaging the omni-present difficulty of access to foreign material[92] but a more political kind of difficulty. American constitutional law was thus an obvious 'choice' – and we deliberately put the words in inverted commas – for the Japanese when they were called upon to draw up a new constitution after the end of the Second World War. The dynamics of the current situation in Iraq are, by contrast, very different, as the second of us (acting as an advisor for the 'Democratisation Assistance Programme' of the German Foreign Office) has found out at many recent meetings with members of the Iraqi Parliament and political or religious groups involved in the search for a new constitutional settlement for the country. For, in this last instance, purely political reasons did *not* make the American model (despite its undisputable qualities) 'an ideal' choice in the search for inspiration. The German and South African variations did, on the other hand, offer intriguing and (more importantly) *politically acceptable* possibilities to an emerging nation desperately trying to come to grips with a model of federalism and human rights protection which best suits its troubled realities.

Thoughts such as the above can lead to three basic (albeit tentative) conclusions.

First, the choice of systems studied or used for the purposes of inspiration must not be undertaken randomly and solely because they help bolster an individual choice. The purpose of comparison is to help widen horizons and not to back already formed narrow and personal views.

---

[92] See, for instance, Justice Breyer's admission that neither he nor his clerks can easily find relevant foreign material (despite their close physical proximity to one of the world's top legal libraries): Keynote Address, 97 *Amer. Soc. of Intern. Law*, Proceedings (2003), p 265 (at pp 267–8).

Second, the choice of systems to be looked at must be made on the basis of pragmatic considerations which should include such matters as relevance, affinity, accessibility, and the like. In the preceding paragraphs we have advanced some suggestions which can, no doubt, be refined and adapted.

Third, the presentation should be primarily left to the attorneys (with or without the co-operation of academics) rather than UN Agencies or various interested groups acting through the medium of amicus briefs which, in our view, do not necessarily offer the best tool for undertaking this demanding task in a scholarly manner. Yet we accept that the practice is too well entrenched in the United States to be easily modified. The disputes about the reliability of the foreign material thus assembled will therefore continue to affect adversely the wider debate in America.

Finally, a wider observation – indisputably showing our preferences (or biases) – needs to be made. American academy is right in identifying these difficulties in the use of comparative law by the courts the world over. Yet, paradoxically, their discussions are 'academic' in the extreme. They are thus often keen to invent (or import) words, broaden the horizon of the search to include 'less developed' systems, and quick to confuse (we think) the bounds of comparative law and comparative anthropology – often lacing all of the above with a good dose of political ideology. All of these habits are to be expected in work done in academic cloisters; but they are also unlikely to give any real guidance to judges who are asked to conduct (or not to conduct) research into foreign law. These writings are thus likely to make other academics think but *not* likely to make judges follow. And, surely, this must be one of the aims these authors have in mind given that their academic work was, itself, born out of the activities of practitioners.

Chapter 5: Mental Disposition as a Factor Impeding Recourse to Foreign Law[1]

1. An unexplored subject

Those who object to the use of foreign law by national courts will invoke a series of well-rehearsed arguments in favour of their position. Some are ideological. In the United States, for instance, Justice Scalia recently stated[2] that he did not think it was right that 'approval by "other nations and peoples" should buttress our commitment to American principles any more than (...) disapproval by "other nations and peoples" should weaken that commitment.' His entire life at the bench has been to oppose even the dialogue with other systems;[3] and a number of academics would agree with this position. Other arguments, however, are more pragmatic; and in that sense, they can be surmounted only with technical and empirical evidence. They refer to the judge's lack of time, lack of expertise, lack of materials in his own language, inability to be up-to-date, deep differences in the background of each system (which make borrowing difficult if not dangerous), and so on. All of the above represent well-recognised dangers associated with the enterprise of comparative law and, as such, they have been stressed many times. Though not without some force all, we think, can be addressed if the will is there to look at them rationally on the basis of evidence, not unsubstantiated rumours or false images.

What has not been considered in a national (and even less so comparative) context is mentality, especially judicial mentality. As we will argue in this chapter this represents more of an obstacle *to* rather than a danger *of* using foreign ideas. In real life it *may* well be the most important inhibitor of the use of foreign material and the reason for

---

[1] This chapter reproduces a slightly adapted version of an essay written by the first of us under the title 'Judicial Mentality: Mental Disposition or Outlook as a Factor Impeding Recourse to Foreign Law' published in the Spring Issue 2006 of the Tulane Law Review, 80, Vol. 5, Tulane L. Rev. 1325 (2006).

[2] *Roper v Simmons* 125 S. Ct. 1183 at p 1229 (2005).

[3] In fact it took two years after his appointment to the Supreme Court in 1986 before he voiced his disapproval to a practice that had begun with a majority opinion 30 years earlier in *Tropp v Dulles* 356 U.S. 86. Thus, see his dissent in *Thompson v Oklahoma* 108 S. Ct. 2687 at 2711 and n 4 which, one year later, prevailed in *Stanford v Kentucky* 492 U.S. 361.

invoking (sometimes plausibly, in other instances as transparent excuse) the previously mentioned factors in order to avoid even looking at foreign law. Having said this with a fair measure of conviction we must do what all academics must do, namely, consider the opposing arguments. We must thus hasten to warn of the danger of forgetting that the factors that go into producing a judicial opinion (and, even more so, the decision of a court[4]) can be almost infinitely variable.[5] The way these variables coalesce can be so complex that one can, at best, only conjecture (as we have done) on these matters and not speak with the degree of certainty that we have manifested. Everything that follows must be read in this light.

Yet, be it *an* inhibitor or *the* most important inhibitor against the use of foreign law the fact is, as stated, that the role played by mentality has not been properly studied and, as a result, its importance may have been underestimated.[6] This is probably because it is such a difficult factor to define in a satisfactory manner (as psychological factors invariably are) and then link in a causative way to a particular decision. Even the term we have chosen to use may not capture accurately all of the points we shall make in this chapter. Just as importantly, it is very difficult to weigh and compare meaningfully with the other variables that go to make judicial choices.[7]

The reason for this neglect is not hard to discern. For the kind of information which this 'judicial psychobiography' – as it is sometimes known in the United States – requires in order to understand the outlook of the judge whose work is being examined calls for material coming from a combination of very different sources and disciplines. One must thus try to digest judicial biographies[8] and try to acquire an understanding of the historical times during which the objects of these biographies performed their functions, received their education and

---

[4] This is an important distinction for (in courts involving more than one judge) what matters is not individual opinions but final votes (though the strength of the former can influence the latter). This aspect of the topic is discussed by Walter F. Murphy, *Elements of Judicial Strategy* (1964).

[5] On which see, *inter alia*, J. Woodford Howard Jr., 'On the Fluidity of Judicial Choice', (1968) 62 *American Political Science Review* 43.

[6] By contrast, the study of character, personality, and other acquired factors have increasingly been used by a new 'breed' of scholars studying international relations. Among the pioneers of this *genre* of diplomatic history are the great French scholars Pierre Renouvin and Jean Baptiste Durosselle whose *Introduction à l' Histoire des Relations Internationales* (Armand Colin 1964) was among the first to make fascinating use of this kind of material.

[7] Woodford Howard (op. cit. note 5), p 50.

[8] Yet those who have studied judicial biographies warn us that 'the least satisfactory state of biographical knowledge concerns the relation of personality to judicial behaviour.' See, J. Woodford Howard Jr., 'Judicial Biography and the Behavioural Persuasion', (1971) 65 *American Political Science Review* 704 at 712.

training, felt the impact of their professional environment and ethnicity, delivered their extra-judicial (as well as judicial) pronouncements, and formed their allegiances (which includes political ideologies, more obvious in some systems than in others) and wider religious and societal beliefs, to mention but a few. Human character and psychology *may* be relevant as well, even though lawyers such as ourselves, trying to understand such psychological factors, 'lack the tools and daring to plumb the psychological roots of judicial behaviour'.[9] So, in the end, the 'investigating' author must combine knowledge with intuition born from experience if he is even to begin this kind of survey. But *if*, as the few studies that exist on this kind of topic[10] suggest, a link can be established – in the *national* context[11] – between outlook, character, and judgment, why cannot the same factors play a part in shaping the judge's attitude towards foreign law? If the possibility has not (yet) been explored in America it may be because the whole question of foreign law before American courts has only recently become a burning issue.

This chapter, therefore, represents our own effort to come to grips with a subject from the vantage point of foreign law and different legal systems. We do this not only because from this angle the enquiry is entirely virgin, but also because we believe that our own cosmopolite environment has sensitised us more to this factor than those who have grown up and worked in one environment only. Yet from the outset, we repeat our difficulty of linking judgments *conclusively* to individual personality traits

---

[9] As is rightly pointed out by Howard, op. cit. note 5 at p 712. Indeed, we confess a certain dislike of the American term 'psychobiography' (with all its Freudian connotations) since, we think, it can lead to the kind of 'sensational' enquiries made, for instance, about Cardozo and his relationship with his favourite sister Nellie. Another theory, in our view equally pseudo-psychological, has tried to link the moralistic tone of his judgments – e.g. *Meinhard v Salmon*, 249 N.Y. 458, 164 N.E. 545 (1928) – to the sense of guilt the learned judge felt for the 'disgrace' of his father. Such enquiries have led to nothing and, to our knowledge, have never provided even a partial explanation of the learned judge's opinions. More importantly, they create the risk of distracting us from searching more thoroughly the *educational and professional* environment of the judge for potentially more interesting clues of his attitude towards law in general and, what interests us here, foreign law in particular. For a general but, in our view, bland discussion of some of these issues (in connection with three anonymous trial judges) see Harold Dwight Lasswell, *Power and Personality* (1948), especially pp 65–88.

[10] For instance H. N. Hirsch, *The Enigma of Felix Frankfurter* (1981).

[11] See the previous note where, in our view, the author brings out very convincingly Frankfurter's insecurities and complexes, stemming from his Jewishness and personal looks, and shows how they affected his character and general outlook in life. According always to the same author (see, for instance, at p 148), the *accumulation* of Frankfurter's character traits can explain some of his leading opinions, e.g., his majority judgment in *Minersville School District v Gobitis*, 310 U.S. 586 (1940) and his dissent in *West Virginia State Board of Education v Barnette*, 319 U.S. 624 (1943).

and believe that the shape and content of the ultimate decision is the result of many factors including the one we investigate here.

This opening section must end with one further admission of weakness. In what follows we are conscious that our readers will experience some difficulty with our decision not always to identify the individual lawyers we have in mind when (tentatively) recording our thoughts on how mentality may condition a judge's (or jurist's) attitude towards foreign ideas. We have adopted this attitude in order to avoid becoming 'personal', especially where our statements and impressions are derived (as they often are) from long private talks with living judges and academics.

The 'anonymity' rule we have opted for brings in its wake risks, notably that such 'un-documented' or 'non-attributable' statements may weaken the persuasive value of our observations and ideas. Though this is inevitable if one is to avoid giving, even indirectly, the slightest ground for offence it would, in our view, also be regrettable if it also led to their hasty rejection on the grounds that they are either too fanciful or *appear* to be uncorroborated by hard evidence to warrant further consideration. The only exceptions we have made to this self-imposed rule is where the jurists we refer to are dead or where they have, themselves, expressed (judicially or extra-judicially) the kind of arguments that lend support to the present discussion.

2. Mentality – what does it mean and how do we find evidence that it has played a role in a judicial opinion?

Mentality, as the *Shorter Oxford English Dictionary* puts it, 'loosely' refers to 'mental disposition' or 'outlook'. These words would suggest to us that it is both inherited and conditioned by later life, education, professional environment, and experience, even though we suspect that few observers could, as a matter of general rule, rank these factors in order of importance in producing the final result – in this instance the rejection of foreign law. A mixture of deliberate and unconscious factors may thus lead an individual – a judge in this case – to be well- or ill-disposed towards allowing different or foreign ideas to enter his mind in the process of decision-making. On the whole we are inclined to think that, in many cases, a judge will not be conscious that he is excluding from his mental processes novel ideas simply because they are foreign. And even where he is, he is more likely not to admit this to others and, instead, choose to justify his rejection of the foreign ideas by invoking one of the previously mentioned difficulties or objections. (More about this later on.) Thus, the most one can hope to discover is a statement which will squarely support what we are saying here. More likely than not, this is likely to be uttered during an unguarded moment or during a social conversation during which the expectation will be that the remark will be forgotten and certainly not repeated in an attributable manner. Rarely, therefore, will such statements appear in writing.

In fact this last assertion must be qualified somewhat. For what is rare is the *explicit* formulation of such feelings. Yet the researcher can, plausibly, find evidence of them if he studies the language and style the judge uses to express his thoughts, which means seeking the thoughts *behind* his language. This may be difficult and call for self-restraint against discovering things which are not there but which the researcher, nonetheless, wishes to find; but it is not impossible. For language often conceals substance. A decision – by no means the only one – not involving foreign elements but, nonetheless, famously supporting the proposition in the preceding sentence of our text, is *Beswick v Beswick*,[12] a case raising the question of enforceability of a right given to a person (named in the contract) but providing no consideration for it. For the non-English readers of this text here are its facts.

The case concerned a sale of a business owned by Mr Beswick to his nephew in exchange for the latter paying of a small amount of money per week to Mr Beswick and a lesser amount to his widow if she survived him (which she did by about one year after the contract was concluded). After Mr Beswick's death, the nephew refused to honour his promise and the action by the widow (acting as administrate of her husband's estate) failed at first instance. On appeal, Lord Denning began his judgment as follows:

> Old Peter Beswick was a coal merchant in Eccles, Lancashire. He had no business premises. All he had was a lorry, scales and weights. He used to take the lorry to the yard of the National Coal Board, where he bagged coal and took it round to his customers in the neighbourhood. His nephew, John Joseph Beswick, helped him in the business.
>
> In March, 1962, old Peter Beswick and his wife were both over 70. He had had his leg amputated and was not in good health. The nephew was anxious to get hold of the business before the old man died.

As Professor Dennis R. Klinck has observed,[13]

> The simplicity [of the language] (...) is almost certainly part of a deliberate rhetorical strategy. (...) Lord Denning (...) win[s] over his audience. Most of the appeal is emotional, not intellectual. Thus, Peter Beswick is routinely called 'old Peter Beswick'. Which makes us both visualise him and pity him for his age (...). When 'old' is used to describe him in a context that suggests the nephew's point of view, the epithet takes on a pejorative colouring: we tend to dislike the person who would view Peter as 'old' in that way. John Joseph Beswick (note the formality of the tripartite name)

---

12 [1966] Ch 538.

13 'Criticising the Judges. Some Preliminary Reflections on Style', (1986) 31 *Revue de Droit de McGill* 655 at 680.

> becomes the 'the nephew' – depersonalised, unlike Peter; he is rendered unrelated to Peter by the use of the definite article instead of the pronoun ('his') which we might expect; he wanted to 'get hold of' the business. Peter is made more personal and familiar to us by the evocation of his life and circumstances: 'he had no business premises'; 'all he had ...'; he bagged the coal (himself, using his 'scales and weights'); he 'took it round' (not 'delivered it'); his customers were 'in the neighbourhood'. And, finally, he had his leg amputated.

Could anyone hearing these opening words read out in court have any doubt where Lord Denning was going? And was he not siding, as he invariably did during his long judicial career, with the weak, the needy, or the oppressed?[14] Only if our imagined observer was a lawyer would he need to wait to hear more to discover the ingenious way the former Master of the Rolls found in order to achieve this 'just' result. And there is no doubt that, for him at least, this was not just the fair but also the inevitable result. For, as he tells us a few lines further down,[15] '(I)f the decision of the Vice Chancellor truly represents the law of England, it would be deplorable.' Though good argument has been known to change a judge's views, we would be willing to take a bet that Lord Denning had made his mind up at a very early stage of this hearing; and this was in accord with the philosophy he manifested in all his judgments! The form of words he chose to use in his judgment supports, we think, our hunch.

Form thus communicates. Persuasion is often involved with stylistic choice; but so is concealment of something the judge may not wish to reveal in public. In the words of Felix Frankfurter, 'differences in style eventually may embody differences of content.'[16] Many judges have shared this idea. Mr Justice Holmes, we are thus told,[17] 'wanted to be read but not fully understood, inter[posing] his style between himself and the world' while Cardozo's latest biographer assures[18] us that the learned judge

> (...) cared about language and its relation to thought. His style was a striking feature of everything he wrote. Sometimes that style concealed problems. Sometimes it even created them. Most often it helped the reader along to a resolution of them. Certainly, it helped to keep the substance of his thought alive for future generations of lawyers, judges and scholars.

---

[14] For which he was often criticised by academics obsessed by doctrine and often unable to match the judge's sensitivity to changing times.

[15] [1996] Ch 538 at p 550E.

[16] Philip Elman (ed), *Of Law and Men. Papers and Addresses by Felix Frankfurter (1939–56)*, p 38.

[17] Yosal Rogat, 'Mr Justice Holmes: Some Modern Views', (1964) 31 *Univ. of Chicago L. Rev.* 213 at 238. Mr Justice Frankfurter probably captured this best when he wrote of his former idol that '(T)he significance of his genius would evaporate in any analysis of specific decisions.' See *Mr Justice Holmes and the Supreme Court* (1939), p 39.

[18] Andrew L. Kaufman, *Cardozo* (1998), pp 450–1.

Studying how the 'masters' set about reaching their desired result can thus be a fascinating exercise. His choice of 'old' English words (instead of their more contemporary equivalents)[19] is thus well known and had a purpose: to enhance the atmosphere of his narrative of the facts and, combining this with their often elliptical presentation and or subtle omissions, make the desired result look inevitable. Cardozo was, in fact, confident enough to say this himself in his classic essay *Law and Literature*[20] where he wrote, and the emphasis is ours,

> I often say that one [ie the judge writing the opinion] must permit oneself, and that quite advisedly and deliberately, a certain margin of *misstatement*.[21]

Modern writers, English as well as American, may have called his style 'contrived'. Beauty is in the eye of the beholder; what intrigues us about Cardozo's style is how it is used by him to achieve his aims or hide his true motives. Cardozo was never, to our knowledge, involved in a case which raised a major issue of comparative law; but if his complex personality would lead him to 'manipulate' the facts in a way that produced the desired result, why should not the same process be possible where foreign law is concerned? In any event, Cardozo conceded the 'inescapable relation between the truth without us and the truth within'.[22] We see this as a thought central to our thesis; and simply restate the main difficulty: discovering 'the truth within' and then linking it to a particular decision. But the difficulty of the exercise does not mean that the process is not there or that it is not worth studying.

We have no reason to believe that what happens in national law could also apply to foreign law. For a judge, as much as any other citizen, may feel discomfort, dislike, or even contempt for a foreign idea, value, or practice. In one sense, of course, we expect judges to rise above such attitudes and start with a clean slate. But we know that this does not happen at the level of national law, so why should it in those cases where

---

[19] His words in *People v Defore*, 242 N.Y. 13, 150 N.E. 585 (1926) – the criminal is to go free because the constable has blundered – offer a good example as Judge Posner, with equally exceptional clarity, shows in his biography of his great predecessor; see *Cardozo, A Study in Reputation* (1990), p 56.

[20] *Selected Writings*, pp 339, 341.

[21] We touch upon rather than draw any firm conclusions on these points because another great master of the American Common law – Karl Llewellyn – in a now forgotten but beautiful article shows the way Cardozo could, by embroidering the facts, help surface the solution he wished to achieve; see Karl Llewellyn, 'A Lecture on Appellate Advocacy', (1962) 29 *University of Chicago Law Rev.* 627, esp at 637, commenting on another of Cardozo's famous judgments: *Wood v Lucy, Lady Duff-Gordon*, 222 N.Y. 88, 118 N.E. 214 (1917). We are grateful to our colleague Professor Alan Rau of The University of Texas at Austin School of Law for drawing the article to our attention.

[22] *The Nature of the Judicial Process* (1921), p 174.

foreign law may somehow be relevant? Felix Frakfurter, himself a Justice of the United States Supreme Court,[23] admitted that a man (or now a woman) 'brings his whole experience, his training, his outlook, his social, intellectual, and moral environment with him when he takes a seat on the Supreme Court'.[24] To be sure, Frankfurter (a few lines further down) also qualified this statement – so much in line with what we are arguing here – by adding: 'But a judge worth his salt is in the grip of his function [and] his intellectual habits of self-discipline which govern his mind are as much part of him (...).'[25]

Yet, in our view, however powerful the 'self-discipline' may be, it cannot entirely tame all that is good (and bad) in the judge's character and outlook and has been acquired during the formative years of his life by which we (principally) mean the years of his professional training and career. Escaping from views inherited from his background and or deeply ingrained by his environment must thus be difficult to achieve, even assuming that this should be seen as desirable.[26] Endless statements from the law of defamation (and fair comment in particular) tell us how people reach conclusions on the basis of habit, tradition, prejudice, superficial judgment, or deep-rooted convictions, and accept that this is part and parcel of human nature. Few judges can *entirely* escape from these pressures themselves or lose habits and modes of thinking acquired from background and environment. To think of judges differently will be tantamount to looking at them through rosy spectacles.

An illustration of how misconceptions about foreign law, probably acquired at law school, can lead judges to make dismissive comments about

---

23 Described by Professor Vicki Jackson as 'probably the twentieth century's foremost US judicial practitioner of explicit comparative analysis as an aid to constitutional interpretation' in 'Narratives of Federalism: Of Continuities and Comparative Constitutional Experience', (2001) 51 *Duke L. J.* 223 at 248–9. A comparison of Frankfurter's frequent references to English historical rules with Scalia's list of differences (in *Roper v Stovin*, 125 S. Ct 1183 at pp 1227–8 of the judgment) between the criminal law rules of the two countries shows how the two 'related' systems have come to diverge. But while English and American law are less close than they were, some of the similarities between American and German law remain to be explored. But that is for another day!

24 Philip Elman (ed), op. cit. note 16 at p 40.

25 Ibid at p 41.

26 Authors might try to bring race into this group of factors which may determine a judge's attitude towards law and society. But the one attempt we have seen, centreing on the 'different' kind of 'Jewishness' of Justices Brandeis and Frankfurter, though not without interesting insights, did not strike us as very convincing. Thus, see Professor Robert A. Burt's *Two Jewish Justices: Outcasts in Promised Land* (1988) and the rather more convincing (and critical) review of Professor Eben Moglen in (1989) 89 *Columbia Law Review* 959 ff. By the way, both 'reviewer' and 'reviewed' are Jewish so it was particularly interesting to read their conflicting views about how race affected the work of the two judges who were the subject of the book.

the relevance of foreign law can be found in one of the early (but important) decision of the German Federal Supreme Court concerning wrongful life and wrongful birth actions.[27] At that time, these actions were still relatively novel for Germany though they had already received some attention in the United States. Though the BGH did, in fact, refer descriptively rather than analytically to Anglo-American law, it chose to precede its peremptory reference to this material with the sentence which, to me, carries with it the signs of earlier (intellectual) indoctrination. It thus said:

> Foreign judgments, which for the reasons alone that they are based on different laws are only of limited relevance for German law, appear to have been rendered in England and in the United States.

Now given that the problem there raised is, in many respects, a universal one; given that it is not linked to beliefs of a particular religious denomination (e.g. Protestantism or Catholicism); and, finally, given that they do not depend for their solution on a particular statutory text, one should have expected a greater willingness for an international dialogue. For, to put it differently, the problem and all its surrounding circumstances lent itself to comparative treatment as the *Cour de cassation* was to show in its subsequent famous (or infamous) *Perruche*-decision.[28]

In the previous paragraph we deliberately chose to cite a German illustration in order to suggest that our thesis is not limited to our own system but that, on the contrary, it is probably of universal value in the sense that comparable examples can be found – if one knows how to search – in all of the legal systems. Indeed, Professor Jutta Limbach, a former President of the German Constitutional Court, struck a very similar tone in a lecture given at the Humboldt University of Berlin in 1996[29] when she said that

> (I)f formally approached, it is of course the duty of the *Bundesverfassungsgericht* to answer authoritatively the question whether a certain provision is constitutional. The Court must, however, be aware of the fact that the answer to this question is the result of highly complex considerations involving a balancing of interests and values. There is no absolutely correct decision; at least such a decision cannot be achieved by us on this earth. The dissenting opinions of judges are, in many cases, proof of this fact. Conflicting views between judges do not materialise from thin air. *In addition to different historical and cultural perspectives which play a*

---

[27] BGHZ 86, 240 of 18 January 1983. The citation in the text comes from the English version reproduced in B. S. Markesinis and H. Unberath, *The German Law of Torts: A Comparative Treatise* (4th edn, 2002), p 160.

[28] Ass. Plén. 17 nov. 2000, JCP 13 déc 2000, no 50, pp 2293 ff (especially the conclusions of the *juge rapporteur* M. Sargos).

[29] *Das Bundesverfassungsgericht als politischer Machtfaktor* (1996). The emphasis is ours.

role, judges also have diverging opinions concerning social values. We know that individuals have an a priori understanding of certain issues which more or less affects the legal solutions they opt for. This has nothing to do with prejudice or bias. We are all determined by certain basic views which are independent of the process of applying the law and which are formed by intuition rather than by rational analysis. This is a mixture of moral, legal, philosophical, and political convictions, and it includes an individual's understanding of the world that we live in.

Not dissimilar views have been expressed by senior judges in the United States making it strongly arguable that these very same factors are at work in other courts even though they have not been admitted by the judges of these systems nor studied by their scholars. Judge Posner, writing most recently in the *Harvard Law Review*[30] observed that:

> It is no longer open to debate that ideology (which I see as intermediary between a host of personal factors, such as upbringing, temperament, experience, and emotion – even including petty resentments toward one's colleagues – and the casting of a vote in a legally indeterminate case, the ideology being the product of the personal factors) plays a significant role in the decisions even of lower court judges when the law is uncertain and emotions arrouded. It must play an even larger role in the Supreme Court, where the issues are more uncertain and more emotional and the judging less constrained.

'Foreignness' is thus part of the 'individual's understanding' (or misunderstanding) of the worlds that we live in, his 'upbringing', his 'temperament and experience', and it is difficult to believe that they do not have a part to play when issues involving immigration, asylum, extradition, death sentence, and homosexual rights, which are 'alive' in all systems, are being decided. Indeed, these are not just issues for lawyers; they are issues that concern us all and on which we all have (often very warped) views. The point thus is to what extent our collective views and discussions do not, beyond a certain point, also have a bearing on the judge's feelings, views, outlook, and decisions. Professor Limbach has done us a great service in admitting that these multiple, extra-judicial, factors affect the judge's perception of his world and can play a role in decision-making even in a system which tends to express its judicial opinions in a very abstract and conceptual manner, giving to outside observers the impression that such complex emotions do not exist behind the facade. A careful student of German decisions could, of course, reach such a conclusion himself (and we, ourselves, just gave one example). But, at the end of the day, this would be, mostly,

---

30 'The Supreme Court 2004 Term Foreword: A Political Court', 119 *Harvard Law Review* 32, at pp 48–9 (2005) and notes.

speculation or intuition by an outsider. The confirmation of such beliefs from a former President of the Constitutional Court carries a different weight and is thus of inestimable value. Our conviction thus remains that the ideas floated here can also be pursued in civilian legal systems despite the fact that they have not, thus far, shown any great interest in linking judicial decisions to their legal actors and studying them accordingly, and left it to the likes of President Limbach and Judge Posner to pioneer the debate (indeed, more than pioneer the debate, but also to show how broadly shared are these – rarely expressed – views and concerns).

The more one reflects on thoughts such as above, the more one wonders how these factors combine with others to produce the decisions we finally get. This is the problem of weighing the different variables alluded to in the first section which go to produce the final opinion and, what is even more complex in a plural bench, the decision of the court. For here, the personality of the judge may help or hinder him forge a majority around his preferred solution. In that sense this, too, is relevant to our enquiry for we know from history that judges with strong personalities – Frankfurter in the past, Scalia in our times – have not, despite their undoubted intelligence, managed to become consensus-builders in a plural court.[31] As a matter of common knowledge, one further suspects that one's views about 'foreignness' and 'foreigners' not only change with difficulty but also tend to veer more towards the negative rather than the positive. This must surely apply to the English as much as the French, Italian, or German judge. Worse still, more often than not, 'foreign' is instinctively equated with 'different' which, it has to be admitted, in many cases is or (more accurately) was true. And it is a small (but dangerous) step (but one also taken) from there to convince oneself that 'different' also really means 'bad' or (at least) 'not for us'. Such a drift of thinking is no less real because it often happens unconsciously or is not the result of logical thinking.

Of course, judges such as Frankfurter may be right about the judge's 'self-control' and 'grip' over his emotions. Certainly, in most cases this should lead him to reach his conclusion in a rational manner and express his views in measured tones, omitting statements, facts, or prejudicial hints to foreign elements in the case before him. Yet the judicial self-restraint cannot always be easy, especially if the wider contemporary climate is eager to find a slant in order to voice doubts – if not make unfriendly hints – about 'foreignness'.[32] We saw this in

[31] Likewise, *The New York Times*, 4 September 2005, p 12.

[32] *Palsgraf v Lord Island Ry Co.*, 248 N.Y. 339, 162, N.E. 99 (1928), another famous Cardozo decision, illustrates this point and shows how the learned Judge 'artfully' presented the facts of that case to fit in with the (non-liability) conclusion he clearly

Germany in the mid-1930s, and we also saw it in the United States during the War with Japan.[33] There is a real danger that we may see this again in the context of the present divergences – real or manufactured – between the so-called Western and Muslim worlds. The judge's views change in keeping with the times, especially when fear is stalking his land, though when calm returns he may later have to recant. Subconsciously if not consciously, judges may thus, in extreme cases, be swept along by this tide. For, as Walter F. Murphy observed,[34] '(A) Justice (...) cannot cavalierly toss off popular [views], (...) [for] public opinion, no matter how difficult to define or predict, can be a real political force.' Our observations about the importance of these 'factors' must have particular force in this day and age when terrorism places the legal system under huge strains and public views and perceptions are so easily fabricated and manipulated by sensation-seeking media (which can also be openly unpleasant towards judges who do not tow the line).

In this context, the negative impact of the tabloid Press (and populist television chancels) cannot be underestimated though we can well see how one could dispute any direct and immediate link between their message and the thinking processes of serious professionals. Yet in our view, based on our experience in England, we do believe that it helps perpetuate prejudices and, indirectly, undermine interest in a foreign country, its values, and its legal ideas.

To assume that the more educated English judge[35] is *entirely* immune of such stereotypical images would, we think, be wrong even though he

---

wished to achieve. Yet he refrained from even mentioning the apparently Italian origin of those carrying the fireworks which were nonetheless trumpeted by the national Press of the time and even appears in the pleadings. For further details on this see Posner, *Cardozo. A Study in Reputation* (1990), p 35.

[33] *Toyosaburo Korematsu v United States*, 323 U.S. 214 (1944). As Justice Roberts said in his dissent (65 S. Ct. 193 at 198), this is 'a case of convicting a citizen as a punishment for not submitting to imprisonment in a concentration camp, based on his ancestry, and solely because of his ancestry, without evidence or inquiry concerning his loyalty and good disposition towards the United States'.

[34] *Elements of Judicial Strategy* (1964), p 204.

[35] One might be tempted to add the word 'contemporary'; for English judges (and jurists) of the nineteenth and early twentieth centuries were much more interested in French and German law than those whom the first of the two authors of this book met when he was at University in the early 1960s. If a change (of sorts) has taken place, this has only manifested itself in the last 15 years or so. In a fascinating essay contributed to a volume published to honour the work of the great historian George Trevelyan, Lord Annan attributed the first to the 'confidence' of the Victorian era; see 'The Victorian Intellectual Aristocracy' in J. H. Plumb (ed), *Studies in Social History: A Tribute to G. M. Trevelyan* (1955), chapter 8. The change of heart in mid-twentieth-century England may be partly due to the decline in self-confidence but, in our view, is more due to the effect of the two Wars, especially the Second.

will externalise his mistrust of the foreign value in a moderate language and in a legally relevant way. Thus, one way of doing this would be to stress the German attachment to principle, or remind us of the excessive degree of abstraction found in German legal writing. Since there is truth in both of these ideas, the underlying indifference (or even hostility) has thus been plausibly concealed even though it is still there at the roots. So we find much value in Professor Harold Dwight Lasswell's pioneering work in which he claimed that[36]

> Political prejudices, preferences and creeds are often formulated in highly rational form, but they are grown in highly irrational ways.

Incidentally, though Lasswell, in the above passage, speaks of 'politicians' his conclusions are also based on case studies of individual (though anonymous) judges, so we found much of what he had to say in the third chapter of his book particularly instructive for our present project.

The rationalisation of the preference, creed, predilection, or prejudice, thus only affects its external appearance. Yet the harm is done by what lies hidden. For, in our case, the 'different' legal system and its solutions are never explored and independently evaluated; they are simply 'shut away'. And with this, the chance given to the national judge to test the validity of his own solution, or to find different angles to explore the common problem, are lost for ever. More importantly, in this day and age where so many of the international conventions forming the basis for international trade (such as the Vienna Convention on the International Sale of Goods, ratified by the United States and applicable to international sales) draw heavily on civil law notions, the failure to understand civil law and its thought processes represents a serious drawback for the lawyer engaged in this kind of international practice.

In reality of course such a judge, be he English or American, by stressing the negative aspects of a foreign system (typically a civilian system), is more likely to be demonstrating that the foreign ideas and thought processes all sit uncomfortably with his own pragmatic, casuistic, and incremental approach, acquired at law school and at the Bar over many decades. American lawyers in particular, nourished on a diet of Realist analyses of judicial opinions and 'laboriously trained (...) to debunk their explanatory power'[37] invariably find the French or German equivalents dry, uninformative, and not addressing the real issues. The fact that these same arguments may exist elsewhere will not even cross

---

[36] *Psychopathology and Politics* (Chicago 1930, Viking Press edition 1968), p 153. See also *Power and Personality* (1948), pp 65–88 (profiling three un-named trial judges).

[37] Alan Scott Rau, 'Integrity in Private Judging', (1997) 38 *South Texas L. Rev.* 485 at p 532.

his mind; and if it does, he will not know where to start looking for them. The chances are that he will think this way, even if these presuppositions are not applicable to the purpose at hand. In such circumstances, even an attempt to convince him otherwise with statistics or other empirical data must represent an uphill struggle if not actually being doomed to failure from the outset. The mind-set may simply not give such efforts a chance to prove even the plausibility of the alternative solution. Writing about the late Francis Mann, one of the greatest émigré jurists to settle in England, Sir Lawrence Collins, a rare example of an academic, practitioner and now a judge in the High Court, commented[38]

> What is perhaps most remarkable about Mann's practical influence is that it was achieved in a legal system whose Bar (and consequently whose judges) showed (although the position has now somewhat changed) little respect for legal scholarship, and even less respect for authority originating outside England.

The statement is entirely correct; and the use of the word 'respect' is, in our view, also noteworthy. If the result is very human, we personally think it is also to be regretted; and one draws some comfort from the fact that Sir Lawrence notes that nowadays there are, at last, some signs of a slow change.

What the above also suggest is that it is a characteristic of human ingenuity to find apparently logical excuses for not doing what one simply does not wish to do. It is thus for us to urge our readers to look at the reasons invoked for not looking at foreign law (if, indeed, any are given) and then decide if they are good reasons or merely excuses. Knowing something about the judge, his background, record, and what we have called 'mentality' can help understand him; perhaps, just perhaps, it might even help an advocate begin to shift him from his original position. Alternatively, it may persuade him that a particular judge will, from the outset, not have much faith in the use of comparative law. In such circumstances the prudent advocate may thus have to settle on a strategy that does not include recourse to foreign law and, instead, use his limited resources and time on other material. But, again, this 'advantage' comes at a price: the foregoing of the possibility 'to introduce new legal ideas from the outside world'[39] when they may be most needed. These are complex and finely balanced decisions and we are only alerting the reader to the possibility that these kinds of

---

[38] 'F. A. Mann (1907–1991)' in Jack Beatson and Reinhard Zimmermann (eds), *Jurists Uprooted. German-speaking Émigré Lawyers in Twentieth-Century Britain* (2004), p 380 (at p 438).

[39] See Carsten Smith (Chief Justice of the Norwegian Supreme Court), 'The Supreme Court in Present-Day Society', in Stephan Tschudi-Madsen (ed), *The Supreme Court of Norway* (1998), pp 134–5.

calculations may take place and, indirectly, result in courts and litigants missing the chance of benefiting from foreign experience all because a judge may be known (or suspected with good reason) to have a closed mind on foreign law.

3. Hints coming (extra-judicially) from the judge himself about his state of mind

The judges' extra-judicial writings and speeches might also help us determine the breadth of their culture and their willingness to look abroad for inspiration. A judge who has, for instance, said that he feels a 'certain personal ambivalence' towards comparative law 'because of its tendency in the past to attract away scholars from the field of Roman law'[40] is, in our opinion, unlikely to make use of it if he can help it. Whether we share this view or not we must, of course, try to understand it and also treat it as perfectly legitimate. For, after all, if he does not believe in its utility (for reasons which may be convincing or not) why should he go out of his way to cite it or otherwise try to promote its study?

Writings of this type can also give some indication of a particular judge's views on wider underlying issues of legal policy and this, in turn, might again give some hint of what his 'starting point' is when he later has to decide a case which touches upon these wider and deeper issues discussed in the earlier essay.

Finding evidence for this proposition has become easier in modern times given the contemporary trend of English (and French, Canadian, and American) judges to join the lecture circuit and talk and write about wider legal issues. In our view, these writings offer valuable clues into the underlying beliefs of the deciding judge.[41] Anyone who has read these judicial forays into the academic fields will, of course, have noticed how judges insert appropriately phrased provisos meant to safeguard their future freedom of action when wearing their judicial hat and deciding fact-sensitive disputes. There can be no doubt that writing these pieces is not meant to prejudge future judicial work just as it is beyond dispute that judges take great care on how they phrase these extra-judicial pronouncements.

Yet, as already stated, some of these writings are not only thoroughly researched pieces but contain *wide* and *carefully thought out* pronouncements about fundamental issues – for example, the

---

[40] Lord Rodger of Earlsferry, 'Savigny at the Strand', *John Maurice Kelly Memorial Lecture* (1995), p 23.

[41] See, for instance, Lord Mustill's 'Negligence in the World of Finance', (1992) 5 *The Supreme Court Journal* 1 ff (reproducing the text of a lecture given in Kuala Lumpur).

litigiousness of modern society, the insupportable insurance consequences of such or such an action, or the extent to which judicial interference is usurping the role of some other organ – which must be taken to reflect the judge's deeper beliefs. To put it differently, these are *reflective* writings embodying a life's beliefs and do not consist of a simple list of precedents reconciled (or not) with one another. To the extent that this is so, is it not safe to suppose that these beliefs will provide the judge's *starting* (if not also *ending*) *point* of reasoning in the next case he has to decide? For instance, if a judge believes, as many reasonable persons do, that litigiousness in our society is growing dangerously or that the level of damages is getting out of control, is it not likely that he will use one of the many vague notions of the law of tort as a possible peg on which to hang his decision that there is no liability or to fix the level of damages at a more modest level?

Such broadly phrased beliefs can, occasionally, even be found in judgments. For instance, in *Stovin v Wise*,[42] a case involving the potential tortuous liability of a local authority, Lord Hoffmann stated that

> The trend of authorities has been to discourage the assumptions that anyone who suffers loss is prima facie entitled to compensation from a person (...) whose act or omission can be said to have caused it. *The default position is that he is not.*

The opening words are meant to convey the impression that this is a general statement/conclusion emerging naturally from a shift of contemporary tort law towards the position of the defendant. With respect, tort law throughout its history – and, indeed, not just its recent history – has vacillated between 'plaintiff's' tort law and 'defendant's' tort law, so to formulate generalisations from shifting patterns of judicial behaviour is unconvincing.

On the other hand, for us much more significant are Lord Hoffmann's concluding words (italicised in the text above) for they have a programmatic ring about them and, indeed, have been followed by this judge in all his subsequent judgments. If this construction is plausible, it does not suggest that the judge is biased or prejudiced; but it does suggest that his subsequent judgments turn more on his starting philosophical point than on defining and redefining precedent. If this point is not adequately grasped by the interpreter, and this will happen if the key original phrase falls out of sight, he runs the risk of ignoring the extent of appreciation which a judge has when considering the binding nature of previous case law and failing to attribute to the judge's general

42 [1996] 3 WLR 388 at 411 (emphasis added).

appreciation of the world around him a crucial role in the result he actually reaches in court on the basis of his starting philosophical point.

For present purposes what follows from the above is crucial. For a judge who believes – for good reasons or bad – that tort law is running out of control is unlikely to look at foreign law on such a topic, even if it could help dispel his fears. To put it differently, his dislike of an expanded tort law will, subconsciously, force him to avoid even considering empirical evidence that dispels his deep-rooted fears. For him such exercise will be costly and wasteful while ignoring the 'trend of developing authorities' as he has constructed in his mind.

Further possible illustrations for all of the preceding propositions could be given; but they would destroy the anonymity rule adopted at the beginning of this chapter. Yet one thing must be re-stated again, even at the risk of repetition: what we are suggesting does *not* mean that our real or hypothetical judge is 'biased' or 'prejudiced'. All it means, in the words of Jutta Limbach cited earlier on, is that his judgments are made to fit in the world around him as he sees it. To that extent, of course, he is entitled to full latitude in expressing his views.

There is another variant to the above psychological factors. Occasionally, one can notice Common law jurists (i.e. judges, practitioners, and academics) with a Continental European background underplay or hide the extent of influence that a foreign source of law has had on their minds. One reason could be that openly associating a novel idea or approach with a 'foreign' system – with European or Roman law origins – might weaken its acceptance in the country of the borrowing judge. I am here thinking of the United Kingdom and of no lesser a person than Lord Atkin;[43] but I can also see instances where this could happen in the United States Professor Dr Ernest Stiefel, a distinguished German–Jewish émigré who played an important role in the industrial reconstruction of post-War Germany and practiced law in New York (and died there in the mid-1990s), always told the first of the two authors of this book that 'in the States, revealing the German origins of a legal idea is like giving it the kiss of death.' Professor Langbein had such an experience when in the 1960s he tried to advocate the reform of the American law of civil procedure along the lines adopted in Germany and provoked something of a legal storm. These examples, and many more could be cited, lend credence to the words of a German expert in comparative history when he said 'heard melodies are sweet, but those unheard are sweeter.'[44]

---

[43] The point is made by Professor Robin Evans-Jones in 'Roman Law in Scotland and England and Development of one Law for Britain', 115 (1999) *L.Q.R.* 605.

[44] Reinhard Zimmermann, 'Condicio tacita. Implied condition und die Fortbildung des eurapäischen Vetragsrechts', (1993) 193 AcP 212 ff. The notion of implied condition

Other reasons for such concealment of the source of inspiration may exist. A foreigner who is a voluntary or involuntary refugee, may feel inclined to be more 'royaliste que le roi' and proclaim the superiority of the rules and values and *modus operandi* of his adopted country. This should not be taken as hypocrisy but seen, instead, as a deep psychological need to adapt to the new environment. This may be less strongly felt in some countries than others (for instance, in the United States more than in England); but it has been widely observed nonetheless.

Yet, however intense the effort to conceal may be, the 'foreigner's' background can remain strong and even be obvious to those who know how to read his work. So, however ambivalent he may remain towards his 'old' law, what he writes and how he thinks in his new country remains influenced by his former 'existence'. The structure of his writing in particular remains, for instance, Germanic however much he may have mastered his second language. We repeat, our decision to float these ideas anonymously does not mean that we are not thinking of real people and real examples. All we are trying to do is to suggest reasons which may make some jurists more susceptible than others to look abroad for guidance while making others anxious to conceal such leanings.

Factors such as the above may be hard to isolate. The evidence is often circumstantial, and its evaluation very difficult. Recent books recording the life of Jewish (invariably Central European) émigré jurists have, as we stated, avoided shedding any real light on this aspect of their characters and work. Perhaps the nature of these factors was deemed too vague and uncertain for inclusion in mini-biographies; perhaps their authors thought them too 'hot' to handle. But their presence cannot be denied; and they can become even more powerful 'inhibitors' when one considers the fact that the judges who are most likely to have a realistic chance of using foreign law are the more senior in *standing* – which also means that, invariably, they are also likely to be the more senior in *age*. For, normally, it represents yet another obstacle to the study of foreign law if one is to ask older and well-established jurists with a set (or semi-set) state of mind, to revise (or even reconsider) their views because some academic invokes the availability of another way of doing things.

Finally, and this makes the picture we have tried to present in this chapter even more complex, personal characteristics or experiences which inevitably shape the mentality of judges and may lead some to ignore

---

very nearly got accepted in *Hall v Wright* (1858) El. Bl. & El. 746 at 765, decided only five years before *Taylor v Caldwel*. The interplay with foreign law was thus, at that time, more active than it is now, a point beautifully made by Professor Brian Simpson in his 'Innovation in Nineteenth Century Contract Law', (1975) 91 *L.Q.R.* 247 ff.

consciously the potential of foreign legal ideas are even more likely to keep *unconsciously* others from identifying comparative law as a useful technique in dealing with their task.[45] Concerns about the ability of predominantly white and male judges appointed in times of apartheid to embrace the new approach and values introduced by the South African Constitution of 1993 were thus one reason to create a new constitutional court (instead of retaining the court system inherited from the English) and to entrench comparative law as an accepted tool of human rights interpretation in that country.[46]

A decade later it is safe to say that the Court has achieved the task set by the framers of the South African Constitution but it is also interesting to note that judges in lower courts – though no doubt *willing* to adhere to the new constitutional standards – *did*, in fact, encounter some substantial difficulties which, eventually, had to be ironed out on appeal. The larger part of these problems must certainly be attributed to the fact that these jurists were faced with a new concept of constitutional law and thus needed some time to get accustomed to its principles. There is, however, no doubt that a substantial number of these decisions were guided by the old 'executive-mindedness' of a judiciary trained to apply laws enacted by a supreme legislature. Measuring legislative or administrative decisions by supreme human rights standards and finding an appropriate balance between public interests and individual freedom was obviously an extremely difficult exercise in this 'mental climate' – despite the unequivocal language of the constitutional text![47]

---

[45] Professor Ernst Kramer thus identifies a 'traditional introvertedness' of national judges, which is only slowly giving way to a more international outlook; see Ernst A. Kramer, 'Konvergenz und Internationalisierung der juristischen Methode', in Heinz-Dieter Assmann/Gert Brüggemeier/Rolf Sethe (eds), *Unterschiedliche Rechtskulturen – Konvergenz des Rechtsdenkens* (2001), p 31 at pp 39 f.

[46] The website of the South African Constitutional Court still acknowledges this today when it answers the question 'why did South Africa need a constitutional court?' in the following way:

> In 1994, the judiciary was overwhelmingly white (and male) and therefore limited in its legitimacy and its capacity to draw on the sense of justice of all communities and both sexes. It was agreed that a new court, more representative of South Africa's diverse population, should be established to protect the Constitution and the fundamental human rights it entrenches.

See the website of the Court at www.concourt.gov.za/site/thecourt/history.htm.

[47] For specific examples from the area of proportionality see J. Fedtke, *Die Rezeption von Verfassungsrecht. Südafrika 1993–1996* (2000), pp 156–68. It is interesting to note in this context that the judges of the German Constitutional Court – the model for its South African counterpart – were specifically accorded a different (and at that time highly unusual) formal status in their certificates of appointment. Instead of becoming, as all

4. The reasons for insular mentality: a paradox of our times

Ignorance, along with an introverted mentality, put countless instructive (and even beautiful) French, German, and Italian legal texts beyond the reach of English and American lawyers. The enduring English hostility towards Bonaparte has, for instance, coloured many a view on his Code,[48] besides effectively concealing from English legal eyes the mature wisdom found in the *Discours Préliminaire* of Portalis, the enactment's 'legal' father. We say nothing about that text's style, except to express our regret that current Anglo-Saxon critics of French culture in general are rarely given the opportunity to appreciate what elegance has been achieved by that language!

It is worth noting (and regretting) that 'intellectual unilateralism' has hit the Common law, especially the American Common law, more in our times of enhanced communication and travel than it did in the distant past. So, nowadays (more than, say, at the turn of the twentieth century), what is 'good' abroad somehow does not attract the headlines (or stay) in the legal mind – art, possibly, being the main exception, and 'trash' images another. Indeed, it is amazing to note how 'cheap' news reporting and denigrating political propaganda can slowly but steadily help decrease all interest in a foreign culture.

Combined with other factors, such image-making statements can, in the long run, affect students' interest in, say, French law and even weaken the presence of that subject in the law curriculum. It is thus interesting to see how Louisiana law schools seem these days to be divided as to whether they should retain a strong presence in the teaching of civil law or whether a re-orientation of resources towards the Common law would improve their standing in the Nations' consciousness and esteem. Being one among 49 does not help; but repeated negative sentiments about France cannot help, either. Though this cannot, of course, be linked solely to the political tensions of the very recent times, it does fit in with the current phase of American 'exceptionalism' which can help give the country that strange mixture of hubris and hypocrisy that those of us who belong to a different generation would have never recognised in days

---

other judges in that country, civil servants 'for life' (*Beamte auf Lebenszeit*) they were directly appointed 'Members of the Constitutional Court' to indicate their special and completely independent status. For the same – symbolic – reason the Court was located in Karlsruhe and not (as desired by Chancellor Konrad Adenauer) in Bonn, the former capital of Germany.

[48] See, for instance, B. S. Markesinis, 'The Enduring (Double) Legacy of the Code Napoleon', (2005) 121 *L.Q.R.* 80 ff.

gone by.[49] Critically, if this legal unilateralism is pursued to extremes, it will also deprive a community that 'lives off' globalisation the ability to understand a host of important international conventions which draw heavily on civilian – mainly French and German – conceptualism.[50] The 'Anglicisation process' runs the risk of thus being counter-productive rather than symbolic of a degree of legal self-sufficiency.

Though much of what was said in the preceding paragraphs has focused on England and America, neither of these countries have a monopoly of xenophobia. Naturally, it can be found elsewhere, as well. A different – and potentially more dangerous – variant of this narrow-mindedness emerged in South Africa during the drafting of the Constitution of 1996 when members of the Pan African Congress (PAC) attacked in the Constitutional Assembly what they perceived to be a 'copycat approach' by those looking at foreign law for inspiration.[51] Justice Albie Sachs of the Constitutional Court saw matters from a different angle and laid more emphasis on the synthesis that would be required. Writing extra-judicially in 1991 he thus argued that:

> An effective Bill of Rights in any country must relate to the culture, traditions, and institutions of that country, at the historic moment when the Bill of Rights is considered necessary. This is not to deny an educative and exemplary role for a Bill of Rights, nor to refuse it a capacity to take on new meanings in the course of time. But it is to insist that an effective Bill comes from inside the historical process, not outside, and that it reflects a set of values gained in the course of struggle and rooted in the consciousness of the people, not one imported from other contexts.[52]

In our times American legal and judicial knowledge about other systems has also decreased where once it was a sign of broader culture to follow what was happening in Europe. It would be wrong, we think, to see this as an example of growing internal self-sufficiency (though this is a real if inadequate reason) or as a realisation that there are other cultures, apart from the European, worth studying (which, in our view, when it comes to the major branches of law, is not true). Yet the growing neglect of the

---

[49] This point is brought out by some leading constitutional lawyers whose collected essays have been published by Professor Michael Ignatieff under the title *American Exceptionalism and Human Rights* (2005).

[50] The point is well made by Professor Alan Scot Rau in connection with the UNCITRAL Model Law on International Commercial Arbitration enacted by a number of American States (such as California and Texas) which is heavily influenced by Continental practice and even contains terms of art in French (such as 'amiables compositeurs') which cannot simply be translated into English without giving a false impression of what is really involved. See his 'The Culture of American Arbitration and the Lessons of ADR', (2005) 40 *Texas Intern. L. J.* 449 at 508 ff.

[51] See *Debates of the Constitutional Assembly* of 25 August 1995, col 321.

[52] See Albie Sachs, *Protecting Human Rights* (1991), p 14.

European culture, especially in law, is seen in some American academic circles as a sign of intellectual emancipation.[53] Talk about getting out of the European 'shadow'[54] indicates this, as well as suggesting that what happens in Europe is of no real interest or use to America and its lawyers. Both these ideas are unconvincing. For the future of European integration has provoked a flurry of intellectual activity in the legal field. Ignoring its outpourings can only contribute to an impoverishment of the general level of debate in the United States notwithstanding the huge intellectual resources of this country.

Reading Oliver Wendell Holmes' 'black book' – his private notebook recording the books he read in his lifetime – leaves one astounded at the speed with which he kept up-to-date with legal developments in Germany at a time when a book could easily take three to five months to reach him from Dresden (which could be six months or more after it has been published in Germany). Though one, naturally, finds in the United States of today highly cultured judges – Judges Calabresi and Posner offer obvious examples – one cannot but note with some embarrassment that the search for wider knowledge is more commonly evidenced in the writings of non-Common law judges than by their American counterparts. To be sure, there is something invidious in comparisons of this kind. Yet it is a humbling experience to read the writings of, say, the First President of France's Cour de cassation M. Guy Canivet, Israel's President of the Supreme Court Aharon Barak,[55] England's (or, we should say, Scotland's) Lord Goff of Chieveley, South Africa's former Constitutional Court Judge Laurie Ackermann, or Germany's Emeritus Constitutional Court Justice Dieter Grimm and note the extent to which they follow and utilise developments in the United States (and elsewhere). To our knowledge, all of the above (and many others besides) make a visible effort to remain abreast of what is happening in American constitutional law *and do so not because they have to but because of the*

---

[53] More sinister (but, in our view, equally unconvincing) reasons, advanced by the American neo-conservatives of our time, are the dangers and problems which the emerging European Union may be posing for the global influence of the United States. Characteristic of this genre are John R. Bolton, 'Should we Take Global Governance Seriously?', vol 1 no 2 (2000) *Chicago Journ. of Intern. Law* 205 ff and Jeremy Rabkin's 'Is EU Policy Eroding the Sovereignty of Non-Member States?', vol 1 no 2 (2000) *Chicago Journ. of Intern. Law* 273 ff.

[54] Matthias Reimann, 'Stepping out of the European Shadow: Why Comparative Law in the United States Must Develop its own Agenda', (1998) 46 *Amer. J. Comp. L.* 637 at 644.

[55] Interested readers might want to read both President Aharon Barak's *Purposive Interpretation in Law* (English translation by Sari Bashi, 2005) and Justice Breyer's *Active Liberty: Interpreting our Democratic Constitution* (2005), two books which appeared nearly simultaneously and cover broadly similar topics.

extent of their intellectual curiosity. But European writings, judicial and academic, are generally ignored by American judges.

This is something of a paradox here given that, especially in recent times, the American judiciary has made an effort to build stronger links with their European counterparts,[56] quite a few Supreme Court Justices even finding the time to travel to, say, England and France to demonstrate that not all of them share the 'originalist' beliefs and insularity.[57] The same is true of English judges who have, in recent times, increased their contacts with their European counterparts but otherwise still manifest a reluctance to look at foreign law.

In a shrinking world, such introvertedness is not just unwise; it can be unacceptable. In most cases ignorance of detail (and even of general matters) pertaining to another country lie at the bottom of the 'isolation mentality'. In one sense it is surprising that judges do not consciously make a greater effort to change it. Time (or lack of it) is, of course, an explanation; and we singled this out for special discussion earlier on since it is an important (and often genuine) factor. At the end of the day, however, one can always find time to do things one thinks are really worthwhile; and it is a well-known fact that it is the busy people of this world that always find the time to do more things! The examples of Lords Denning, Goff, Woolf, Bingham, Steyn are shining examples of what busy judges with the right mentality can do.

Yet, interest in foreign ideas does not come naturally, not at any rate in the contemporary world of the Common law. Training, habit, and lack of time may, as stated, often account for even the lack of effort to be exposed to different worlds (if indeed, they are as different as some think). Yet, in passing we wonder how, if this is really the case, those in America who oppose recourse to foreign law nevertheless expect their judges to find the time (and acquire the expertise) to undertake the kind of historical research which their originalist preferences dictate? For discovering the 'original understanding', when even the amateur student of American history knows how divided (and concerned) the Founding Fathers were with what they had produced, must be quite a task. Weighing such arguments in one's mind thus makes one return to the 'mentality' factor and place at its feet the blame for much of the

---

[56] See J. Clifford Wallace, 'Globalization of Judicial Education', (2003) 28 *Yale Journal of International Law* 355–64 (to some extent giving the theme a different slant to ours).

[57] Justice Ruth Bader Ginsburg being the latest to visit England and deliver a lecture at the University of Cambridge on 9 May 2005 entitled 'A decent Respect to the Opinions of [Human]kind: The Value of a Comparative Perspective in Constitutional Adjudication', to be published in the January 2006 issue of the *Cambridge Law Journal*. She gave a lecture under the same title on 1 April 2005 to the American Society of International Law; see www.asil.org/events/AM05/ginsburg050401.html.

contemporary indifference to foreign cultures. Originalism reinforces this tendency, also leading to a yet another paradox: a constitution born from internal as well as foreign reflection must, nonetheless, be henceforth interpreted as if it were destined to remain imprisoned within a time capsule.

5. Morality, religion, and wider societal beliefs

The judge's religious views and wider beliefs about family and society may also influence his opinions and lead him to give new meanings to concepts which do not accommodate these views. The Jewish origins of a number of leading American justices has thus been frequently analysed in an attempt to judge their work and understand their professional behaviour. That these works are of unequal quality[58] is only to be expected and says nothing of the value of undertaking this exercise in the first place. Our concern is that one day we do the same in a comparative as well as national context.

The attitude of the American 'right' towards what they perceive as Europe's current 'soft', 'leftist', or 'socialist' attitudes towards many issues – and the range is wide enough to include abortion, wrongful life claims, homosexuality in law, child chastisement, the death penalty as the correct retribution for the most heinous crimes, and the need for a more developed social welfare system – are all examples of how such beliefs can affect the judge's receptivity to foreign ideas. For instance, the language used by American judges when referring to European ideas leaves no doubt that not only do they not share them but also dislike the underlying culture that has produced them.[59]

In this context, it is interesting to note, as Professor Michelman of Harvard University has done,[60] how the 'inveterate resisters of the [United States] Supreme Court have not been very forthcoming [in giving their reasons for opposing the dialogue with foreign colleagues]' and continues:

> One has to search hard in their opinions for a single, cogent statement of a reason for resistance. It is as if they do not know how to name what is bothering them.

---

58 Thus, personally, we found H. N. Hirsch's *The Enigma of Felix Frankfurter* (1981) thought provoking but felt less convinced by the study of his life in parallel with that of Brandeis undertaken by Robert A. Burt, *Two Jewish Justices. Outcasts in the Promised Land* (1988).

59 'Foreign moods, fads or fashions (...)', taken from *Foster v Florida*, 537 U.S. 990, n.* (2002) per Justice Thomas, subsequently endorsed verbatim by Justice Scalia in *Lawrence v Texas*, 123 S. Ct. 2472.

60 In chapter one of Michael Ignatieff (op. cit. note 48), pp 260 and 264.

He thus concludes that:

> (...) when all is said and done, it is not beyond imagining that both the 'conservative' resisters to comparative analysis (Rehnquist, Scalia, Thomas) and the 'liberal' promoters (Breyer, Ginsburg, Stevens) believe that letting foreign sources in can only tend to tip American constitutional-legal discourse toward 'liberal' outcomes. Scalia's 'thankfully'[61] and Thomas's 'foreign moods, fads and fashions'[62] ring in our ears.

Now if this a plausible interpretation (and we believe it is), it suggests more than a political opposition to an outcome which is seen as the consequence of embarking on a dialogue with foreigners; it can also be seen as a hostile predisposition towards their law and values which, however, can only be known in very general terms. For all but the most specialist Americans, the European model is perceived in very simplistic terms as being 'left' as distinct to 'right'[63] and operating in a highly regulated rather than a free market economy. All intermediate gradations (and their impact on public as well as private law), passing from the English to the German or Italian models, are lost in a mist of simplifications.

Yet this unhappiness with certain 'consequences' as a reason for 'shutting out' any consideration of a legal system that might make them likely is found in other systems besides the American. Similar attitudes may also lie buried behind opaquely phrased European judgments and, likewise, account for the rejection of ideas which are seen to be either too liberal or too conservative to the deciding judge or flow from his deeply held moral or religious beliefs. In neither case, however, does the reasoning or the result have much to do with the proper interpretation of the text before him. Important and wide-ranging changes in the law can thus flow from decisions based on apparently very legalistic interpretations of (amorphous) concepts adopted simply in order to give effect to these underlying beliefs. To that extent the thesis that the result was dictated by the judge's wider but unexpressed (at least in the judgment) beliefs must, once again, become plausible. Indeed, it may take a very long time before this becomes apparent.

One example, from France this time, can show how this rich background can be hidden behind those opaque 'whereas' of the Cour de cassation.

A long series of decisions denying a 'mistress' (*concubine*) the right to claim fatal accident-type of damages (i.e. mainly loss of support) against

---

[61] *Atkins v Virginia*, 536 US 304, 347–8 (2002).

[62] *Foster v Florida*, 537 U.S. 990, n.* (2002).

[63] Which, again, is seen in simplistic terms ignoring the differences between traditional right, libertarianism, neo-conservatism (and the like), for which see the collection of essays edited by Peter Berkowitz, *Varieties of Conservatism in America* (2004).

the person who killed her paramour was thus established in 1936[64] when a former academic-turned-judge (Josserand) transplanted his deep religious objections to extra-marital cohabitation into the interpretation of Art 1382 CC in order to achieve the above result. In fact, the underlying beliefs ran all the way back to the French Revolution, the role of Church in French society during the nineteenth century,[65] and its view of the purpose of marriage. How extraneous to the text of the Code was this development was always known to legal specialists; but, for a long time, it was scarcely echoed in the legal literature. On the contrary, the discussion was invariably conducted in the form of concepts (*dommage légitime* or *dommage juridiquement protégé*) which are as open-ended and amorphous as our own 'duty of care'.[66] Yet this judicial 'fabrication', which caused considerable uncertainty as a result of the conflicting case law it gave rise to, was not exposed until nearly 40 years later when in 1970[67] the Court, itself, abandoned this reasoning. And, remarkably, the judge who composed the judgment, breaking with this recent tradition, wrote an eponymous case-note admitting the above![68]

The example in the preceding paragraph may strike some as very 'French'. Yet comparable reasoning can be found in other systems, geographically as well as legally far removed from France and its legal model. We are thinking of American cases such as *Elden v Sheldon*[69] which had to operate through concepts and notions (such as duty of care or policy) which, on the surface of things, are not replicated in French law. But these vacuous concepts have to be filled with the values developed by the professionals who operate the legal system as well as by individuals who cherish them. If the values change, or the judge deciding the case has a chance to inject his own in the decisional process, a result

64 Ch. Civ. 27 juil. 1937, S. 1938.1.321 and note Marty; D. 1938.1.5 and note Savatier.

65 For a very perceptive summary see Theodore Zeldin, *France 1848–1945*, vol I, chapters 11 and 13; vol II, chapter 20.

66 The French law of tort ignores this concept which, were it to know it, would have enabled the Court to deny the claim of the partner of a deceased man against the person who killed him for loss of support. But it does not, so the rejection of the claim had to be done by construing the notion of 'damage' in a normative and not factual sense by importing into the Code the requirement that the interest harmed should be 'juridically protected'.

67 Cass. 27 fév. 1970, D. 1970, 201.

68 For more on this see F. H. Lawson and B. S. Markesinis, *Tortious liability for unintentional harm in the Common law and the Civil law*, vol I (1982), pp 50 ff. Incidentally, these arguments (opposing recovery) were echoed, *almost identically*, in the decision of the Supreme Court of California in *Elden v Sheldon* 758 P. 2d 582 (1988) – a nervous shock case.

69 250 Cal. Rptr. 254, 758 P. 2d 582 (1988).

thought of as heretical only a few years earlier may suddenly become the new orthodoxy. In many ways *Edlen* is such a case, besides offering a strange parallel to the French cases just discussed.

In *Elden* the plaintiff was driven by his partner who was involved in a car accident caused by the defendant Sheldon. She was killed and he, sitting besides her, suffered physical injuries as well as serious emotional distress (or, as we nowadays call it in England, psychiatric injury). His claim for the psychiatric injury was denied even though his injury was not of the kind that is not recognisable in law (i.e. mere pain or grief) nor, indeed, because he was not in the danger zone (since, in fact, he was at the very epicentre of the accident) but because he pleaded the case on the 'by-stander' rule and failed to satisfy the Court of his 'close relationship' with the primary victim/deceased. For, as stated, though he had a stable and deep relationship with the deceased, he was not married to her and giving him compensation in such circumstances would, in the view of the Court, undermine the sanctity of marriage and was thus seen as being contrary to public policy. The views of the Court thus, essentially, replicate the old French debate. On the other hand, the moral/policy arguments 'entered' the American decision through the notion of public policy (never openly addressed in French decisions) and determined the existence of a 'duty of care', a concept not known in French law.

Elden can be seen as a departure from the earlier and more general decision of the same court in *Dillon v Legg*;[70] and to some extent exploited the allusion to policy made by the earlier judgment. Much more important, however, is the underlying religious/conservative switch which we find in Californian law of this period and which reflects two important factors – namely, first, the growing conservatism of the judiciary of the late 1980s (no doubt directly and indirectly reflecting the more conservative spirit of the Regan era) and, second, the fact that *Dillon*, itself, carefully phrased and well applied to begin with, was soon exploited by plaintiffs (and sympathetically inclined courts) to produce an excessively liberal thesis which then cried out for the conservative antithesis.

Now the point of mentioning this case is not in order to take sides on the morality of extra-marital cohabitation (which bothered the French in the 1930s and the Americans in the 1980s) and to what extent such relationships should generate legal entitlements, but the fact that this wider socio-religious debate can have an effect on what, on the surface, appears to be a legal argument concerning the application of value-neutral notions. In such a context, the room given for judicial outlook and predilection is considerable though, obviously, it will only prove durable if it is one that is also shared by a sizeable section of the judiciary

---

[70] 68 Cal. 2d 728, 441 P. 2d 912 (1968).

at a particular moment. In reality, however, the italicised words also suggest that this is not the end of the story but, on the contrary, a snapshot of the law in a legal continuum reflecting ever-changing views on moral and social issues.

In Germany, as well, the *Drittwirkung* doctrine, now at least beginning to captivate the English legal mind (under the longer phrase 'horizontal application of human rights'), also began its present life through a German judge (Carl Hans Nipperdey) who transferred into the judicial plane ideas which he had earlier canvassed[71] while still an academic and motivated by his dislike of the unequal treatment accorded by the law to men and women. Though the establishment of equality of treatment was mandated upon German private law by the Constitution of 1949, the conservative and predominantly male[72] Parliament of the time dragged its feet in the implementation of the required change.[73] So, in the end, it was judges with strong personal (and contrary) beliefs who forced the desired change in the law by refusing to apply the (dated) provisions of the Civil Code. Once again, however, reading the full Nipperdey judgment as President of the Supreme German Labour Court (where the new doctrine made its first appearance) does not reveal the details which one finds only when reading the earlier academic works of the judge and trying to reconstruct as best one can his complicated life and times.[74]

6. The impact of a stay abroad, a different education, and the professional environment

We have already mentioned ignorance (or partial knowledge), especially the kind which stems from the impoverishment of general culture in our times, as an important factor for the mistrust felt towards foreign law. Here we wish to focus more on the educational background of the judge – and by this we mean both his academic training as well as his 'formation' by his professional environment.[75]

---

[71] 'Gleicher Lohn der Frau für gleiche Leistung. Ein Beitrag zur Auslegung der Grundrechte', *Recht der Arbeit* 1950, 121 ff.

[72] Of the first 410 Members of Parliament there were only 28 women. Today, the percentage of women is nearly twice as high as in the United Kingdom or the United States.

[73] Max Rheinstein, 'The Law of Family and Succession' in A. Yiannopoulos (ed), *Civil Law in the Modern World* (1965), pp 25–7, reprinted in H. H. Leser (ed), *Gesamelte Schriften* (1972), pp 212, 219–20.

[74] For more (English and German readings) see B. S. Markesinis and Stefan Enchelmaier, 'The Applicability of Human Rights as between Individuals under German Constitutional Law' in B. S. Markesinis, *Protecting Privacy* (1999), pp 191 ff.

[75] In our enquiry we will exclude what we will call 'Freudian' explanations not only because we are unable to trace and evaluate them but also because in the area with which

We have already said something about how a judge (or, come to that, any jurist) has been taught to approach a case and how this can make him uneasy – to say the least – when reading a judgment or other legal text coming from a system which belongs to a different legal family. To these difficulties one must also add the judge's exposure (or lack of it) to foreign languages, culture, and life (e.g. as a student or émigré). For this, too, must be among the factors which will remain with him forever and affect his attitude towards a foreign country and its values.

Let us test this point by looking first at the Constitutional Court of Germany[76] in, say, the 1980s. Figures suggest that during this period the Court *appears*[77] to have been less interested in foreign law than it was during its formative years – that is, the 1950s. One could easily explain this by saying that in the intervening years the Court had grown in age and stature, had become less dependent on foreign guidelines and ideas, and thus no longer needed to look at foreign law.[78] To put it bluntly, one could argue that by the 1980s it had all the law it needed 'grown locally'.

Yet it could be argued with equal credibility that – in part at least – the change of attitude was due to a change of personnel. For more of the original justices of the *Bundesverfassungsgericht* had spent time as émigrés (and/or visiting professors) at American law schools than, proportionately speaking, their immediate successors.[79] This trend may

---

we are concerned – the use of foreign law – we see no link whatsoever. For the reasons explained in the text the emphasis is thus on education, professional environment, and, to some extent, the émigré or foreign status in the country where the judge (or academic) is working. Our list, especially when compared with the factors mentioned at the beginning of this essay, is obviously incomplete.

[76] A thorough study of the first 20 years was carried out by B. Aubin, 'Die Rechtsvergleichende Interpretation autonom-internen Rechts in der deutschen Rechtsprechung', (1970) 34 *RabelsZ* 458 ff.

[77] *Appears* is italicised because one knows from discussions with judges that the fact that a foreign idea was not cited in a judgment does not mean that it was not considered along with others.

[78] This is an argument which can also be invoked to 'explain away' the comparative hyper-activity of the South African Constitutional Court, and could be used to justify the reduced interest of American courts in English law. The same point could be made with respect to the European Court of Justice, which has by now developed a substantial corpus of 'own' judgments to draw upon and may feel less the need to indulge in comparative law than its first Advocates General did (e.g. Legrange and Romer).

[79] The highest share of émigrés is found in the Second Senate of the *Bundesverfassungsgericht* immediately after the creation of the Court in 1951. Four out of eight judges, among them the highly influential Justice Gerhard Leibholz, had spent time outside Germany during the National Socialist reign. One of them, Justice Rudolf Katz, had worked in Turkey, China, and the United States before joining the Court. Justice Walter Seuffert, elected Vice-President of the Court in 1967, was even born in the United States (Rahway/New Jersey) in 1907. Justice Willi Geiger, one of the initial members of the Second Senate, confirmed in an interview that the group of émigrés brought altogether

be changing yet again as many of the most recent recruits are fluent English speakers and have studied mainly in American law schools. For these older judges (and now the very newest ones, especially those with an academic background before they became judges), the use of American law came (and comes) more easily than for some of their intermediate successors/predecessors, not simply because they can access it more easily but mainly because it has for various reasons 'dazzled' them. This impact is perfectly evident in the extra-judicial writings of those with academic inclinations, even though, as stated, the need for open references to foreign material in the decisions themselves is no longer as great as it was.

If such information can be drawn from appropriate research and combined with comparable information from other countries, one could then begin to build a broader picture showing *if and how* these 'displacements' – of longer or shorter duration – can (a) influence and (b) 'show up' in the work of one's later life. Personally, through instinct and some knowledge, we believe this to be the case but, at present, do little more than raise it as a possibility worthy of deeper and wider investigation. And we do so because, as already stated, we believe that the importance of this side-effect of a 'stay abroad' will increase not decrease in the years to come, as student, academic, and judicial exchanges increase in intensity.[80] Recourse to foreign law will thus no longer be barred by the fact that local law has, in terms of volume, reached saturation levels, or linguistic difficulties. Rejection of such ideas will come only where they fail to convince.

The ethnic background of a lawyer appointed as a judge in a country other than that in which he was born (or first educated, or both) may also have a bearing on how his mind is set on a number of issues, the contours of which are largely shaped by religion, local politics, human rights disputes, and the like. We have certainly noticed this with numerous *academic* colleagues of Jewish Central European extraction even where they have spent as much as half their lives in a Common law country.

In many instances, they acclimatised superbly to the new environment. Max Rheinstein for instance, who has been dead now for long enough to appear eponymously, took to the Common law in a truly amazing manner. The late Harry Lawson and Jack Hamson, who shaped the mind of the

different perspectives into the work of the Court; see Dieter Preißler/Christian Peters, *Anfänge des Bundesverfassungsgerichts* (1992), a documentary produced by the Haus der Geschichte der Bundesrepublik Deutschland.

80 Under this heading one notes, in particular, the fact that eminent judges have been regular visitors to the United States. Included in this category are such eminent judges as Justice Barak (the President of the Israeli Supreme Court) and Professor Dieter Grimm (formerly a Justice at the German Constitutional Court).

first of the authors of this book through constant informal chats for over 20 years, always held him out as a superb example of a German jurist who truly understood the Common law. Despite his long 'displacement' and adaptability, his essential 'Germanness' was, however, never wiped out. Sir Michael Kerr, a friend and former Head of the first author's Chambers, could also be included in this category.

Francis Mann, also dead for long and thus mentionable by name, was known for constantly praising the law of his host country, especially the way it used precedent. He and others, by hitching their wagon to that of a major local jurist, often succeeded in overcoming the 'burden' of 'foreignness' and thus exploiting their undoubted talents to the full.[81] Yet he, too, retained to the end in his speech, his writing, and in his thinking processes many of the traits of his country of origin even though he remained highly ambivalent towards Israel, Judaism, and Germany.[82] Stephan Risenfeld at Berkeley is another example of this group, and so is the late Sir Otto Kahn-Freund who, unlike others (e.g. Professor Kurt Lipstein), also retained to the end a strong Germanic accent. Then you have the South African contingent in the House of Lords who brought to this great institution the different dimensions of a double legal culture, plus – in one case – a consistent attachment to liberalism which, one is strongly tempted to believe, is related to his own (difficult but highly successful) career. Canada and the United States could furnish examples of their own of how cultures mix and either produce jurists thirsting for cultural reconciliation or, by contrast, see it as impossible. Over the years, we have met so many jurists – academics, practitioners, and judges – who fall into this category to know (and not simply to think) that what we say

[81] And history suggests that the host country, certainly England, was quick to show its appreciation to those who 'flattered [their] new surroundings'. The words come from Professor Linda Colley's readable and thought-provoking monograph Britons. *Forging the Nation 1707–1837* (1994 paperback edition at p 33) and refer to George Fredric Handel. The famous artist Antonio Canaletto offers another example of a foreigner who understood perfectly the 'political symbolism' of the Venice of yesterday and contrived to reproduce it in paintings which bore little resemblance of the city in his time. On reflection, one can add others to the list (lawyers included) though, again, the semi-official biographies (sadly, we think) abstain from exploring this complex inter-relationship.

[82] Sir Lawrence Collins (op. cit. note 37) at p 440. From the personal knowledge of the first author of this book (for over 20 years) of Professor Kurt Lipstein the same could be said of him; yet none of this appears in his biography by Christopher Forsyth found in the same work at pp 463–81 nor in the more 'personal account' provided by Professor Christian von Bar at pp 749–60. Likewise missing from these biographies are the special, often tense, inter-relationships that these émigrés had among themselves, frequently leading to some of them receiving inadequate recognition during their lifetime. In our view Professor Clive Schmitthoff must be included in this category.

here has a strong element of truth.[83] It thus seems to us difficult to imagine that an academic or a judge who, say, started life in Nazi Germany would ever be able to shake off such a (traumatic) experience in later life. There are sufficient judicial give-aways to show that these experiences survive geographical displacements and become part of the individual's new professional culture.

The same is true of the reverse situation, namely, the German who is deciding a case in his own country and is conscious (and even guilty) of his own, recent past. Thus the briefest of glances over German cases dealing with such issues as wrongful life claims, involving a judgment on the value of life with impairments, or medical disputes dealing with the issues of informed consent, amply prove my point. In such cases, every concept and notion in the German Code has been used, twisted, and adapted to encourage the new reality and, at times, even openly condemn the political past. The same, we feel, can be said of contemporary South Africa and an academic or judge coming from that country and having experienced the apartheid regime.

What remains to be discussed is to what extent this phenomenon has affected the work of, say, South African, or German, or Jewish, or Greek, or Italian, jurists working in a Common law environment.[84] At the very least such 'jurists' – using the term here as an alternative to both academics and judges – cannot be expected to have banished from their minds ideas, knowledge, and information acquired elsewhere. Texts, notions, and precedents will not, in our view, easily be able to displace such mental predispositions, and these will show most clearly in human rights disputes. Mental predisposition, or mentality, will find a way to override most of the technical arguments or obstacles if they stand in the way in which the judge's outlook is pushing him to go. But this, we confess, is (at present at least) a hunch rather than a demonstrable fact. Nevertheless, let us add to what we have said so far a future hypothetical and allow the matter to rest at that until time proves it right or wrong.

Would it thus be unreasonable to assume that a jurist from a regime which has suppressed free speech but is now operating in England ever be psychologically able to give up a certain preference for free speech at the

---

[83] The first of the authors of this book met most of these 'great' heroes of the world of comparative law of yesterday when they were at an advanced age; and old men like reminiscing, thus revealing marvellous information about themselves, their colleagues, and their times. In two cases, he was also bequeathed personal papers which support many of the contentions made here, besides giving a unique picture of Cambridge (and his old College) in the 1950s and 1960s.

[84] We offer these nationalities indicatively but not randomly since we know that we have many lawyers who come from these backgrounds and operate in Common law jurisdictions.

expense of, say, reputation or privacy? The first of us discussed this issue once with a great judge (who is still alive) and, in our view, it would take a very clearly phrased constitutional text favouring a balancing of these often-competing values before such a mind-shift could even begin to take place. And such a clear text does not, arguably,[85] exist in contemporary England. And if that is true, would not such a judge be, understandably, less tempted to borrow ideas from Germany, the law of which differs so fundamentally from his well-formed beliefs even if he belongs to the select few who, in the past, have shown an interest in and knowledge of foreign law? Yet, and this is where matters become both complicated and interesting, we venture to think that such a judge would probably refuse to follow such a balancing process by arguing that the German experience was 'not relevant' or 'appropriate' to his own (new) environment. One phrase such judge could use to achieve this result and rebut Counsel's possible reference to foreign law could read as follows: 'The tour d'horizon of foreign jurisdictions given to us by Counsel was interesting but, ultimately, the case must be decided in the light of our legal policy and our Bill of Rights.' The 'our', of course, here refers to the legal policy of his new country; but he understands this policy of his 'new' country partly as a result of his experiences in his 'old' country. It would simply not be human to expect that such earlier experiences could be totally expunged from his mind and his reasoning process.[86]

This, of course, is not to say that either such a result – 'we do not use German law as inspiration' – or its justification – 'the system is too different to be copied' or 'our policy values prevail' – would be wrong. For, in abstract terms, all of these propositions are, after all, perfectly legitimate options. But if that same judge had, on an earlier occasion, himself resorted to foreign law, one would expect him to tell his audience why in this newer case the foreign experience was of no relevance. To assert in this day and age that our legal policy and our human rights are different would, it is submitted, be inadequate. And it would be intellectually unattractive to invoke the foreign system is one instance and reject its consideration in another because, for instance, 'it is based on a codal structure'or 'leads to a multiplicity of claims'. If these claims are made, they should also be explained and justified.

---

85 We say 'arguably' for this part of the law cannot, ultimately, escape the balance of values which Arts 8 and 10 of the European Convention of Human Rights requires.

86 Again, we base these views on long discussions with two eminent German émigrés, one dead, the other still alive, with whom the first of us discussed at length their experiences as 'émigrés' to this country. Incidentally, despite the number of books appearing on the lives and times of these quite amazing individuals who so enriched our intellectual life, none feels comfortable enough to discuss their mind-sets and disappointments in their new worlds.

Analysing why (and how) a judge really 'avoids using foreign law' can thus help us find out whether the notions he uses in his judgments are really nothing more than verbal devices which help him formulate his judgment but do not really explain them. The rejection of an idea found in a foreign system or, conversely, a certain openness towards it, may thus be determined by a subtly pre-conditioned mind.

The judge's wider culture and background – and we are not here thinking of social background – may also help 'open' or 'close' his mind to the ideas and laws of a particular legal culture. This is not only a matter of linguistic abilities (though it is that, as well); it is first and foremost the overall view and feelings he may have about the foreign culture which, in later life, he may be called upon to consider as a source of inspiration and guidance.

In this book we have given examples of how, since the mid-1990s, South African jurists turned to German public law for inspiration. Since the South African turn to German *public* law is not conditioned by the history of that country (as is the case with its private law), in our view more research needs to be done to examine this fascinating phenomenon.[87] And studies of this kind can become even more interesting when extended to cover other countries in an attempt to explain where and why systems are departing from their genealogical ancestors. This is a phenomenon that has been little studied even by those scholars who profess a special interest in mixed jurisdictions.

We raise this issue since we have had, in recent times, occasion to come into contact with various Brazilian and Argentinean colleagues and supervise students coming from these countries writing English or American theses. These works (and our correspondence) reveal, for instance, the extent to which the German Academic Exchange Service and its facilitation of studies of young South American students in Germany has 'paid off' in, ultimately, securing a presence of German legal culture in countries which otherwise were more open to ideas from the Romanesque family of legal systems. While clearly it would be wrong to treat such impressions as being correct and immutable we feel that long years of peripatetic teaching and researching should give these observations at least a prima facie reason for further investigation. This, incidentally, is not meant to weaken the view we subscribe to, namely, that the study of foreign law should be put primarily to the very practically oriented use of helping extend the international legal discourse by properly 'packaging' foreign ideas. But it does show that the practical aim we choose to treat as the prime purpose of our subject also carries with it the need to understand the legal systems in their wider context. To the extent that this

[87] For an in-depth analysis of the influence of German constitutional law on South Africa see J. Fedtke, op. cit. note 46.

can be acquired from wider and inter-disciplinary studies, it must also help calm the fears of those who believe that helping understand 'law in action' impoverishes the academic curriculum. It does not.

7. Other reasons for 'suspecting' foreign ideas and values

Judicial mentality can be shaped by many factors besides those hinted at already. Here are some more; and they tend to be linked to habits and practices picked up by judges from their professional environment as their careers developed over time.

Fear for the consequences of a judgment that disturbs established legal notions must be one of them. Maybe there is 'another world out there', as Lord Binhgam once urged us to consider;[88] but the one the practitioner or judge has learned how to operate invariably seems good enough, so why experiment with others? This is more than understandable; it is even very reasonable until, that is, one realises that the prevailing assumptions at the basis of a judgment – think, for instance, of the floodgates argument which the late and wise John Fleming called the 'flagship of the timorous' – are no longer as solid (or as acceptable) as one once thought. If foreign law can help prove this, should one avoid it by failing even to cite it in a judgment? In our view, the fact that one *does* find senior judges who are doing what we have just argued for, suggests that it can be done, and all that stops it from being done more frequently is mentality. Our example also suggests that such judicial efforts should be combined with academic work since they can make the use of such material and information not only more sophisticated but also more reliable. But for that to happen does not, ultimately, depend on academics but on judges being intellectually restless, often despite the passivity that old age brings, to realise that the world is changing, and accepting that in a changing world legal borders are becoming very porous. For the adoption of such foreign notions could usher in ways of reasoning with which the judge is not familiar (though how detrimental this would actually be has yet to be demonstrated). Additionally, a particular result may confront the economic interests of a pressure group which judges may be unhappy to take head on.[89]

---

[88] 'There is a World Elsewhere: The Changing Perspectives of English Law', in *The Business of Judging. Selected Essays and Speeches* (2000), pp 87 ff.

[89] Or, indeed, wish to protect. For the degree of protection given to defendants in negligent statement cases may be linked with the (unexpressed) wish to protect corporations and accounting or consultancy firms who thus benefit from a cleverly defended use of the notion of duty of care against the consequences of their negligence; see, for instance, *Billy v Arthur Young and Co.*, 834 P. 2d 745 (Cal 1992). A more sophisticated

The way English courts are, to put it bluntly, beating around the bush on the law of privacy in the post-Human Rights Act 1998 era may support both suppositions. These factors are, admittedly, not limited to foreign law and its possible adoption by national courts. They could arise just as well in a purely domestic dispute. Yet it is reasonable to argue that they can be compounded when the notions and thinking ways differ from those already established in a particular country.

The more traditionally oriented quarters of the legal community, especially the country's professional bodies, are likely to resent these changes and the uncertainty which they may bring to a system they have learnt how to operate, notwithstanding its drawbacks.[90] This may be true across the spectrum of legal subjects but is particularly likely to occur in matters concerning civil procedure and organisation of the courts. One should add that the concern felt in all these types of cases is legitimate; and academics should be slow in criticising habits which they, themselves, share in a different context. For it is a well-known fact that academics are slow to switch to new books used in their courses, one reason being that they have learnt their way around one author's book and method and are slow to do themselves what they may be willing to recommend to others: to change their approach. Arguments based on 'habit' are thus powerful ones even if they are only supported by 'superficial' logic.

This may also partly explain why English judges spend so much time manipulating old torts, devised for different times, to meet the challenges of our age instead of trying to develop legal guidelines which could help future courts determine which types of privacy cases deserve attention and which can be rejected outright. The decision of the Court of Appeal in *A v B plc*[91] may offer one of the few exceptions (even though what was said there has not met with the enthusiastic support of knowledgeable practitioners).[92]

(but as yet untested hypothesis) might be that the class action mechanism – not known in Continental European systems – may make such defendants more vulnerable to vast actions, often on the basis of unsubstantiated rumours which, nonetheless, can form the basis of demands that will end in costly settlements. Certainly, this is an area where the difference of legal rules between systems – e.g., the American and the German – requires something more than the mere analysis of the comparable technical rules in question.

[90] A good example can be found in the decision of *R v Wainwright* [2001] EWCA Civ. 2081 at para 42, where Lord Justice Mummery expressed his preference of approaching the new and complex issues of privacy by continuing to adapt mediaeval torts designed to cope with very different problems. The pros and cons of this approach are discussed by B. S. Markesinis, Colm O'Cinneide, Jörg Fedtke, and Myriam Hunter-Henin in 'Concerns and Ideas About the Developing English Law of Privacy (And How Knowledge of Foreign Law Might Be of Help)', (2004) 52 *The Am. Journ of Comp. Law* 133 at 135–7, 200 ff.

[91] [2003] QB 195.

[92] Matrix Media and Information Group, *Privacy and the Media* (2002).

Let us look at these points in greater detail.

The insistence to expand the notion of breach of confidence clearly cannot cover all cases of 'personality';[93] and it took the recent *Douglas*-case[94] to appreciate that even the term 'privacy' inadequately covers the second part of the *Douglas* claim. Yet, English judges, while gingerly enlarging the area of human privacy protected by the law, still prefer to put the breach of confidence on the Procrustean bed of litigated facts rather than use the notion they do not know: privacy.

So how do you avoid privacy as a notion? By attributing to it an 'open-endedness' that bodes badly for the legal system as a whole: the Press; the judges; the litigants. You make it, in other words, sound as if all concerned stand to lose from its fluidity. And yet has 'breach of confidence' not been shown to suffer from the same protean nature? Have not the elements of this tort been constantly re-interpreted since *Coco v A. N. Clark (Engineers) Ltd*[95] set them out clearly, thus encouraging not discouraging litigation?[96] Have not its origins – apparently in the notion of good faith – proved as elusive and as open-ended as anything that underlies the tort notion of 'duty of care'? And has not the judicial attempt to shoe-horn factual situations within the mould of the old equitable remedy in order to accommodate the Human Rights Act and the Strasbourg jurisprudence proved exasperating[97] and in some cases totally unable to produce a result? Sections of the Press can use such arguments to frustrate the creation of a new tort heading and go on making money out of sensationalism; judges, on the other hand, should have the courage to call a spade a spade. The alternative path that German courts have followed is both more rational and has been shown to work in practice. Being also essentially shaped incrementally by case law, it is also methodologically transplantable into English law. Mentality may thus be an important inhibitor from going down the German path.

Attachment to the notions you know rather than consideration of the ones you do not may also be combined with the 'fear' most judges have of the tabloid Press. Here, of course, one speculates – though one would prefer to describe it as 'informed speculation' since it is based on discussions one has had with many judges. Indeed, it came to us as a great surprise to discover that tenure and (high) prestige combined are, clearly, not enough to bolster a judge's confidence to stand up to the

[93] See, for instance, *Peck v U.K.*, (2003) E.H.R.R. 287 (App. No. 00044647/98).

[94] *Douglas and Others v Hello! Ltd and Others*, [2005] EWCA Civ. 595.

[95] [1969] PRC 41.

[96] Most recently in *Douglas and Others v Hello! Ltd and Others*, [2005] EWCA Civ. 595.

[97] *Von Hannover v Germany*, [2004] EMLR 21 thus invites comparison with some English decisions both in terms of conviction as well as style.

Press. But it seems they are not; and, intriguingly, a senior German Justice suggested to the first of us not that long ago at a conference attended while co-teaching in Texas that, in his opinion, the German law of privacy would have, likewise, been stalled in the late 1950s, and not developed by the courts in his country, had the German Press of that period had the powers it now has.

All of the above points can, of course, be subsumed under the various headings of 'difficulties and dangers' mentioned briefly at the beginning of this essay. Yet in our view this is, ultimately, a chicken and egg situation. For is the judge avoiding citing the foreign law because he dislikes a particular country, thinks lowly of its national characteristics, disparages its values, does not know or understand its system, has too much law of his own to consider, has no means of checking the veracity of information given to him about the foreign system? Or could it be that the above factors combine in his mind and, ultimately, lead him to the conclusion that the comparative law exercise is not worth the candle? It is thus much easier to stretch an old tort and describe its pliability and then, for good measure, add with a degree of satisfaction that this is a sign of the genius of the Common law.

And yet, what is so impossible to some is, nonetheless, undertaken with courage and conviction by others, no less affected by the above same factors. By studying the role of 'judicial mentality', however imperfectly, we may come closer to addressing the real problem; but that inevitably means getting to understand better the person under the wig! And that, we have been told, is what the wig was always meant to do: make the judge look remote and impersonal.

For, if the truth is to be told, most of the judges currently sitting in the highest courts have never been exposed to the internationalist environment which today's students (and tomorrow's judges) are. This is true, notwithstanding the increase of judicial contacts that seems to have taken place during the last 10 or 15 years. Thus, those who have shown a contrary interest in 'learning' foreign law are 'bold spirits' rather than 'timorous souls'.[98] For, by showing this interest, they are going outside the world in which they grew up, prompted by intellectual curiosity. One admires such intellectual restlessness, not least since those who display it must be aware that, like Lord Denning, they will have to wait long before their imagination is rewarded.

This picture, however, is bound to change – indeed it is already changing. For the contemporary British student, almost expected (and not just encouraged) to spend one of his three or four years of legal

---

98 The expressions come from Lord Denning's judgment in *Candler v Crane Christmans & Co.*, [1951] 2 KB 164 at 178.

studies in another European law faculty, will not experience such mental blocks towards a different way of doing things. This will eventually have consequences for the entire legal profession,[99] since the new generation of judges will have more material at their disposal, be more aware of solutions which would not occur to only 'locally' educated lawyers and, more importantly, will perhaps be less convinced of the undisputed superiority of their own system.

8. Some ways in which this hostile mentality is externalised

How then is this 'reserve' towards foreign law manifested by our judges? The externalisation of their 'suspicion' may take many forms. Here we shall mention by way of illustration three – the last and more dangerous being the attempt to pretend that foreign law does not even exist.

A usual refrain these days, hummed persistently in some 'floodgate'-type of cases[100] in order to explain why the German or the French judges can afford imposing liability more easily than we do in England, turns our thoughts to numbers: 'they (the foreign judges) are so many more than we are, they can afford to spend the time trying more cases.' Like the 'floodgates' argument, not looking at foreign law thus becomes an argument of administrative convenience and not one of justice. In this case it is made persuasive by comparing the size of the judiciary in England and Germany. The need to protect our own judges from potentially frivolous or vexatious claims is invoked with great conviction.[101]

At first blush this argument appears to be convincing. Certainly the size of the judiciary in Germany is huge compared to what one finds in England and Wales.[102] Yet, on closer analysis, the argument seems to be

---

[99] In theory, this may be even greater in Continental European countries where judges are recruited to the judiciary at a far earlier stage in their lives than is customary in the United Kingdom or the United States since these 'younger' minds will not yet have been 'hardened' by professional prejudices and pre-determined views. This speculation, however, may be premature, underestimating the (understandable) resistance of national professional bodies to ideas that emanate from outside.

[100] The floodgates argument is invoked in all kinds of cases. In some (e.g. pure economic loss) German and the Common law, take, on the whole, the same negative attitude. In others, however, German law takes (or appears to take) a much more liberal approach than the Common law. We are thinking here of cases involving psychiatric injury or tortious liability for breach of statutory duties.

[101] The validity of this argument has by no means met with universal approval. Thus see, for instance, Tobriner J in *Dillon v Legg*, 68 Cal. 2d 728, 69 Cal. Rptr. 72, 441 P. 2d 912 at pp 917 ff (1968), roundly condemning the so-called advantages of this approach.

[102] Though, of course, one never takes into account in these calculations the thousands of magistrates who, along with the legally trained clerks, resolve the vast number of criminal cases handled in Germany by professional (albeit often very young) judges.

given more force than it deserves since other elements, which point in a different direction, are not brought into the 'weighing exercise'. Lord Goff, a judge with greater sensitivity for foreign law than most, once gave some reasons why one should 'mistrust' this argument.[103] Others could be added to his list. For instance, one is not told anything about the fact that Continental judges in all cases have to do their own research and find the law themselves, and do not enjoy the unique privilege (as Common law judges do) of having expert Counsel do this for them. Also forgotten is the fact that litigation is cheaper on the Continent of Europe and that there is thus so much more of it around, adding to the judicial burden. Brushing aside the Civilian experience on the grounds of their numbers of judges – and we have heard English judges invoke it on more occasions than we care to mention – can thus be a very superficial way of evaluating foreign law and its practices and explaining a rule which throws out of court many potentially genuine complaints.

Another favorite way to dismiss Continental European law is to say that it is 'codal' in nature and thus of little use to us in the Common law. English judges, in the twentieth century (more so than in previous times) have been notoriously unable to understand how Continental codes work, and how they provide the starting point[104] of the reasoning process – but hardly all the answers.[105] There has even been the odd English judge who has seen the German Civil Code as an outgrowth of the Napoleonic Code. We say nothing of the old prejudice against the *Preussisches Allgemeines Landrecht* though the fact that this compilation covered private, administrative, criminal, *and* constitutional law must not be forgotten when stigmatising its indisputable hypertrophy. Compare it with all the French Codes on these subjects taken together, or the Digest of American Law, and it suddenly becomes more 'normal' in size. Yet, you can still make it sound bad (and we are not defending it here, not least because we do not like its basic assumption that the legislator can anticipate everything in advance) by intonating the word 'Prussian'. For, in England at least, the word can have multiple pejorative connotations just as the word 'Jew' once had and, when

---

[103] See his closing address for the Clifford Chance Millennium Lectures, published in B. S. Markesinis (ed), *The Coming Together of the Common Law and the Civil Law* (2000), pp 246–7.

[104] At best for one could argue that much case law, especially that based on the so-called general clauses of the BGB (such as § 242), has used these provisions as pegs on which to hang their policy value judgments – and nothing more.

[105] Thus, Lord Scarman in his 'Codification and Judge-made Law', a lecture delivered on 20 October 1966 to (and published by) the Law Faculty of the University of Birmingham, at p 19 claimed that codification encourages the 'planned' development of the law and can provide 'a compact, accessible, and complete [sic] formulation of the law.' This is not a picture any German or French lawyer looking at his civil code – the contract, tort, or unjust enrichment sections in particular – will easily recognise.

included in the Oxford English Dictionary in such a manner, led an offended litigant with a Jewish background to force the Oxford Press to remove this meaning of the word from its future editions.[106]

Refusing altogether to treat foreign ideas as a source of inspiration and assistance is another and the third way of giving effect to lack of interest in or showing hostility towards foreign law. This 'negation' of foreign law is the most dramatic and can take two forms.

The first consists of hiding the real source of inspiration. This may border upon intellectual dishonesty; but if it is foreign, disguising it might have the pragmatic advantage of helping it take root in foreign soil. To that extent, the concealment of the foreignness of the source may be justified by realistic considerations. But closing one's mind to foreign ideas altogether must, in intellectual terms at least, be seen as a sign of a closed and not a pragmatic mind. At times, it can even become bizarre, tempting one to search for the hidden motives which may not even be there.

Lord Blackburn's classic decision in *Rylands v Fletcher*[107] offers one example. For there he took great pains to make his innovation look as if it represented an application – at worst a simple analogical extension – of existing law. *Rylands* was, not, of course, a case which involved foreign law. But *Taylor v Caldwell*,[108] also decided by Blackburn some years earlier (though, again, an English case) gave him the chance to use his foreign (and Roman law learning) without any open attribution.[109]

The late Professor Grant Gilmore said the same thing about Cardozo, allowing us slowly to begin piecing together a wider picture, when he said of the great American judge that

> (T)he more innovative the decision to which he had persuaded his brethren on the court, the more the opinion strained to prove that no novelty – not the slightest departure from prior law – was involved.[110]

It is the personality of the judge, his culture, and the spirit of his age that, together, can give him the confidence and aplomb to achieve such innovation and yet conceal it from the public eye and thus make it less vulnerable to attack. So we, at least, do not subscribe to the view that judges are 'potted plants'[111] or, to use the more attractive metaphor

---

106 *Schloimovitz v Clarendon Press, The Times*, 6 July 1973.

107 (1866) LR 1 Ex 265 at 279–80.

108 (1863) 32 L.J.QB 164.

109 To his own *Treatise on the Effect of the Contract of Sale on the Legal Rights of Property and Possession of Goods, Wares and Merchandises* (1845) which the late C. H. S. Fifoot described as 'an early essay in comparative law'; see *Judge and Jurist in the Reign of Queen Victoria* (1959), p 16.

110 *The Ages of American Law* (1977), p 75.

111 As Judge Posner once asked rhetorically while (though conservative) rejecting the strictures of originalism; 197 *The New Republic* 23 (1987).

attributed to Montesquieu, merely act as the 'bouche de la loi'.[112] So how is the decision reached – 'how best to justify a result *already*[113] reached *on other grounds*?' And what are the 'other' grounds and how does the judge find them? Justice Frankfurter once argued that the judge must have 'antennae registering feelings and judgment beyond logical, let alone quantitative, proof'.[114] For a judge known for his persistent advocacy of judicial self-restraint this sounds puzzling, at least in so far as it suggests that his reasons may lie beyond the wording and the history of the text he is interpreting. The search for what is happening in the judge's mind thus becomes problematic.

The second way the judge may show his unwillingness to be drawn into the study of foreign law is by remaining silent or aloof. This is the case in those judicial disputes where one judge has broken out of this 'mold' and made an attempt to benefit from the experience of a foreign system by invoking its ideas and giving his views on them. If his colleagues in the same decision disagree with the use he has made of this material and wish to diverge from the conclusions which they have helped him reach, would it not be reasonable, constructive, and courteous to expect them to try and counter in a specific manner this material rather than pass it by in silence? The *Spiegel*-decision[115] of the German Constitutional Court of 1966 offers a good illustration of how judges should react in such cases. For there four judges put on record[116] their concerns regarding the way in which their other four colleagues had used foreign legal ideas. The litigant, posterity, and even the ordinary reader can better understand the factors which truly mattered in the judges' minds. This is an important point, so let us flesh it out somewhat.

So, if an 'internationalist'-minded judge cites foreign law which points towards a particular solution, *especially if this coincides with a solution which the citing judge feels is also reacheable under his own system*, would it not be logical for those who disagree with him to challenge this information, question the methodology used to gather it (or explain why its use is inappropriate), rather than assert that liability – and the case we have in mind here was a tort case – can be denied by using the notion of duty of

---

112 *De l'esprit des lois*. See the notes and explanation by Guy Canivet, in 'La convergence des systèmes juridiques par l'action du juge' in *De Tous Horizons. Mélanges Xavier Blanc-Jouvan* (2005), p 14, note 5.

113 On this see Lord Mustill's 'What do Judges Do?,' *Särtryck ur Juridisk Tidskrift*, 1996–96, Nr 3, 611 ff.

114 Felix Frankfurter in Philip Elman (ed), op. cit. note 16, pp 31, 39.

115 BVerfGE 20, 162 ff. In that case four judges referred to foreign material in answering the question whether members of the Press can refuse to give evidence in criminal proceedings involving treason and opted against such a right.

116 Ibid at pp 220–1.

care or its most fuzzy (English) ingredient 'fair, just and reasonable'?[117] Justice Scalia, with whom we have had much occasion to disagree in his various writings, nonetheless adopted the right posture in his dissenting judgment in *Roper v Simmons*[118] by voicing the kind of objections we think a judge who opposes foreign law and its solutions should externalise in his opinion. Disagreement does not mean losing respect for your intellectual opponent; but it does call for questioning the parts of his reasoning or the information which lead him, in your view, to the wrong decision.

The opposite of what we ask for (and praise in the Scalia dissent) is, however, what happened in the recent *Berkshire*-decision of the House of Lords.[119] For there Lord Bingham questioned in powerful but, naturally, moderate tones whether the use of the notion of duty of care was not an excessively blunt device in dealing with the problem of tort liability for breach of statutory duties. He also expressed a certain willingness to see the emphasis shift from duty to breach.[120] Yet his learned colleagues chose simply to re-assert old arguments – in our view bland and not very original – about the need to retain the duty device ignoring, *en passant*, the opposite view expressed not by 'biased comparatists' or 'foreigners' but by the Professor of *English* Law at the University of Oxford.[121] Moreover, they failed to probe the validity of Lord Bingham's observations that other systems coped whereas the English would crumble if the case in question was allowed to proceed to trial. Should not Counsel have been asked to address the Court on these fears as happened in *Fairchild*? Anyone who might argue that this would add cost and delay should give us an estimate – even a rough estimate – to support such a claim. In any event, even those who were not pleased with the *Fairchild*-decision have never, to our knowledge, raised this point about added costs incurred as a result of citing foreign law to their lordships. Our guess is that it represented a very small fraction of the overall costs of that dispute.

---

[117] 'Abandonment of the concept of duty of care in English law, unless replaced by a control mechanism which recognises this limitation [viz, that whatever concept was used to replace it would lead to uncertainty in the law]. The control mechanism has yet to be identified.' *Per* Lord Nicholls of Birkenhead in *JD (FC) v East Berkshire Community Health NHS Trust and others*, [2005] UKHL 23, at para 94. Compare the underlying thought (that duty stops potentially frivolous claims) with the doubts the same judge expressed about the fears that underlie the notion of duty of care when in *Phelps v Hillingdon London Borough Council* [2000] 3 WLR 776 at 804 he said: 'Denial of the existence of a cause of action is seldom, if ever, the appropriate response to defeat of its abuse.'

[118] 125 S. Ct. 1183.

[119] Op. cit. note 116.

[120] Ibid, para 49.

[121] Professor Paul Craig (writing together with Dr Duncan Fairgrieve), 'Barrett, Negligence and Discretionary Powers', [1999] PL 626 ff.

This is a crucial point; and the intelligent lawyer – academic or practitioner – should ask the question whether the systems that allow recovery in principle avoid financial disaster partly because they impose liability only in the most serious instances of fault but also, and mainly, because they do not go overboard on the question of damages. Is this not an intriguing new avenue worth exploring? Is ignoring such data and avoiding an open consideration of the foreign material not just a way of closing one's eyes to (instead of solving) the underlying problem and postponing the day of reckoning?

One ventures to suggest that to ignore such facts in a rapidly changing world, which also does not take kindly to neglect of human rights – the right to have one's legal suit properly heard (as Lord Bingham also pointed out in *East Berkshire*) – is not a practice that can last long. It could be tempting to attribute such omissions to simple ignorance, propped up by an arrogant belief that, in principle, the English Common law has nothing to learn from equally developed systems such as the German, the French, or the Italian (to mention but a few) but instead should go out and teach them.[122] But we must not yield to this temptation and adopt such a characterisation since we genuinely feel that the neglect of foreign law is largely the result of what we here call the 'mentality' factor; and this needs to be understood as much as, on occasion, it needs to be questioned.

9. More about *East Berkshire* and how foreign law might have aided their lordships

Before leaving this topic we wish to make one further point related to the possible utility of foreign law in the case of *East Berkshire.*[123] It switches the attention of the reader from 'duty' quantification of damages as a *possible* explanation of the difference in the *substantive* (rather than *compensatory*) rules of tort law. Since the point has not been raised before we touch upon it briefly here; and we will return to it in a longer piece we plan to write about this point in the near future.

Thus, if one looks at German *practice* during the years 1993–5 – roughly the time when the seminal decisions of *Bedfordshire*[124] and

[122] And cultured British judges with impeccable academic credentials (but who, otherwise, are best left anonymous) have come close to arguing such thesis.

[123] Op. cit. note 116.

[124] *M. v Newham London Borough Council and X (Minors) v Bedfordshire County Council*, [1995] 2 AC 633. Both these and the next case dealt with the issue of tortious liability for breach of statutory duties, discussed comparatively by B. S. Markesinis, Jean-Bernard Auby, Dagmar Coester-Waltjen, and Simon Deakin, *The Tortious Liability of Statutory Bodies* (1999).

Stovin v Wise[125] were casting their unimaginative shadows on this part of the law in England – one will find that the total number of writs issued against (German) municipalities and communes was approximately 23,000 per annum.[126] Of these, roughly 70 per cent 'collapsed' at an early stage, largely because of lack of evidence on causation or fault,[127] 20 per cent succeeded in part, while the remaining 10 per cent succeeded in full producing awards against municipalities totaling €30 million or, roughly speaking, £21 million (at today's rate of exchange).[128]

Now these figures, which we will scrutinise in our forthcoming article, must be seen against the following facts, namely: (a) the total number of tort writs issued in Germany (which is much higher than it is in England); (b) the total number of appeals decided by the Federal Supreme Court per annum (i.e. over 1,100 reasoned judgments); (c) the relative cheapness of litigation in Germany as compared to England; (d) the fact that the *Bedfordhsire-*, *Berkshire-*, and *Phelps*-type of cases form only a small part of the total number of suits brought against statutory bodies; and last (but by no means least) (e) the paltry amount of the total awards they produced in those comparatively few instances that actually succeeded (in part or in full).

Seen in this light, the German scene could suggest not only that the volume of this type of litigation, *as part of the wider number of litigated claims*, is small (despite the cheapness of litigation) but also that the size of awards (in their totality) is, in such cases, equally small. Together, these two points may explain why the consequences so feared by some English judges – for example, timid officials or bankrupt authorities unable to carry (or insure for) such losses – have not materialised in a country which economically and politically is not that different from our own and where, generally speaking, one finds the same level of damages for personal injury.[129] We hasten to add that this is by no means the end of the matter. But I also maintain that it is a preferable way of dealing with the issue (and

---

125 [1996] AC 923.

126 This includes awards for medical malpractice in hospitals and nursing homes owned or run by the *Länder* and municipalities.

127 The large figure of writs reflects the cheapness of litigation in Germany. The large number of failures shows that 'bad' cases collapse quickly once the claims of the plaintiffs can clearly not be substantiated.

128 The total size of awards, including awards for medical malpractice in hospitals and nursing homes owned or run by *Länder*, communes and municipalities, amounted to a mere DM88 million, i.e., €44 million (i.e. approximately £28 million). These figures come from Infratest Burke Rechtsforschung, *Zur Reform des Staatshaftungsrechts, Tabellarische Ergebnisse (1993–1995)*, Tables B 4.1, K 4, L 4.1, T 1.

129 On which see B. S. Markesinis, Michael Coester, Guido Alpa, and Augustus Ullstein, *Compensation for Personal Injury in English, German and Italian Law. A Comparative Outline* (2005).

the concerns) which the current English decisions raise by leaving litigants frustrated that their grievances, often involving horrendous facts (as the Strasbourg decisions in *Bedfordshire* revealed), are in England dismissed without anyone even ascertaining what actually went wrong.

10. Making a beginning

The essence of this chapter is that, at least in difficult cases, the judge does not come with an entirely open mind. As Professor Limbach, a former President of the German Constitutional Court, pointed out, this does not mean bias or favour. But it does suggest that judge like the rest of us has a certain view of the world which he has to fit in his judgment and this does not hinge only upon legal notions, precedents, and the like. Combined, these factors play a part in his final decision; the problem is that how they operate and how we find the evidence to study them is not an easy affair. We do not think many would diverge substantially from what we have just said; but our concern has been different – to see whether the same kind of analysis can be applied to the judge when he is looking (or not looking) at foreign law. Can this, too, be said to be influenced by these factors which, as we have repeatedly stressed, are difficult to identify but, we believe, are there nonetheless?

Our thesis has been that how quickly ideas 'leak' from one environment to another will, ultimately, depend on the mentality of the key actors. The political and technical arguments mentioned above are reasons which inhibit the use of foreign law. But they are not the only ones. Those that are less visible and certainly less studied may, one day, prove to be not only as important but also more interesting. A proper study remains to be done. This chapter has only tried to raise awareness that a huge subject remains out there waiting to be discovered.

Chapter 6: Conclusions

1. Heading towards a conclusion

a) *The use of foreign law as inspiration and as a cause of American doubts*

In recent times the interest shown by American academic writers in substantive rules of foreign, especially European, law appears to have diminished. Notable scholars[1] can, of course, be cited for expressing their deep unhappiness with this phenomenon, invariably referred to as 'American exceptionalism', which they have tried to explain. But their reaction has focused on American views towards foreign law rather than specific rules and why and how one could use them in the process of law making at the national level.

Intellectuals on the right of the American political spectrum – who, nowadays, like to call themselves 'Americanists' – are also on record for the strong language they have used against the so-called globalist. What makes this group notable is not any superior value in their arguments – how convincing the respective arguments ultimately are depends on one's political views – but the fact that they are, with the assistance of neo-conservative think tanks (such as the American Enterprise Institute and the Heritage Foundation), increasingly influencing the American political establishment and claiming 'plum' posts which are in its gift. John Bolton, recently appointed by President Bush as Ambassador of the United States to the United Nations, represents one such example.[2] Characteristically, each side in this divide claims to speak for the majority of Americans, though, to outsiders at least, the way the American electorate divides these days would suggest that there are no clear and permanent majorities in this dispute.

To be sure, this indifference to foreign law and hostility towards global developments (many of them created or, at least, encouraged by

---

[1] For instance those who have contributed to the *Ignatieff Essays* referred to in the Introduction and in Chapter 5. As elsewhere in the book, we shall use this abbreviated title to refer to the individual contributions found in this volume.

[2] See 'Should We Take Global Governance Seriously?', (Fall 2000) Vol 1, no 2 *Chicago Journal of International Law* 206 ff.

the United States), though a feature of the contemporary American scene, is not a universal phenomenon.[3] In almost all other countries, the interest in foreign developments has grown; and, as far as law is concerned, the impetus to this trend has often come from the courts. The South African Constitutional Court, for example, has attracted much attention as well as a measured degree of admiration for its open interest in what happens in other systems and its attempts to integrate any lessons that could be learnt from them into national law. And Canadian borrowings of American human rights law, used to shape their own human rights jurisprudence after the introduction of the 1983 Charter, have also been described by American writers in some detail, though frequently the aim of such commentaries has been to demonstrate the (real or alleged) superiority of the American version. Other systems, notably that of Israel, could be given as further examples of this trend to 'go global', largely under the influence of its current powerful President Aharon Barak, though, again, in the United States this work has had a mixed reception.

In the United States, if *academic* interest in foreign law *per se*[4] has been slender, *judicial* interest, especially in the domain of public law, has been even thinner, though some of the liberal judges of the Supreme Court *appear* to have recently launched a concerted campaign to prove to the world that America, politically as well as legally, does not speak with one voice when rejecting foreign law. More importantly, a handful of recent constitutional cases have made some use of foreign ideas in a way which has caused a storm of protest on the one side of the divide and excitement to those who see in these decisions the beginning of a possible re-orientation of the Supreme Court. As hinted already, and will be repeated several times in this chapter, we do not share this optimism.

Overall, this attitude towards foreign law must be seen as novel given how admiring American courts and judges were, in the past, towards foreign legal cultures, especially the English. In this respect it may also differ from American unilateralism in the political sphere where this attitude has had a long history (though, as we argue below, it may now have entered a new phase). But in the legal field, the hostility towards foreign law is not simply novel; it is surprisingly recent. For, though it is closely linked to 'orginalism' and can be seen as part and parcel of the rightist reaction against the liberty-enhancing decisions of the Warren Court, it did not really begin to manifest itself in the Supreme Court until

---

[3] For a study that tries to explain this divergence (between American and European attitudes but not the rest of the world) and does so with appropriate academic calmness and reason, see Jed Rubenfeld, 'Unilaterialism and Constitutionalism' (2004) 79 *N. Y. U. L. Rev.* 1971 ff.

[4] As distinct to discussing the obligations of American courts to consult it.

after the appointment of Justice Scalia in 1986. Thus, the opposition against recourse to foreign practices in the context of the Eighth Amendment, however peripheral, did not appear until *Thompson v Oklahoma* (1988),[5] two years after the learned justice took his seat at the Supreme Court, ending the judicial era which had begun exactly 30 years earlier with *Tropp v Dulles*[6] and which seemed to herald a certain openness to foreign ideas. Whether it ties in with the growing conservatism towards the end of the Regan years, or whether this conservatism found in Justice Scalia the pugnacious proponent it had lacked thus far, or both, is not something that need concern us at this stage of our enquiry.

The hostility towards foreign law is thus not only novel (in the sense suggested above); it also began confined to a narrow context. For the American judicial debate, passionate as it became, was, originally, focused on judicial review and on whether proper constitutional interpretation permits judges *even to look at* foreign law as a mere source of inspiration.[7] Whether there is any conceivable objection *in principle* to such empirical uses of information on foreign legal practice may be debated. But as Professor Michelman observes, '(Y)ou will look for it in vain in the history [of the cases since *Tropp*, which he recounted in his aforementioned essay].'[8] To foreign lawyers, however, orienting the discussion in this direction, though particularly illuminating of the inter-relationship of (American) politics and law, is of limited comparative value. The reason is clear since it becomes closely dependent on (indeed subordinate to) the American Constitution and American theories on 'orginalism' or 'textualism' and, above all, the political infighting between neo-conservatives and radical liberals. Indeed, many outside the United States would probably even find some of the more extreme of these writings distinctly odd![9]

Conclusions such as the above are disappointing to 'outsider' lawyers such as ourselves who have multiple links with the American legal world and who would like to see the considerable talents of

---

5 487 U.S. 815, at 869–70; and prevailed one year later in *Stanford v Kentucky*, 492 U.S. 361.

6 356 U.S. 86. In this context, the consistent recourse of the Supreme Court to foreign ideas up until 1988 is succinctly recorded by Professor Michelman's elegant contribution to the *Ignatieff Essays* (op. cit. note 1), pp 241, especially at 245 ff.

7 *Thompson v Oklahoma*, 487 U.S. 815, at 869–70 n 4.

8 *Ignatieff Essays* (op. cit. note 1), pp 257–8.

9 We are thinking for instance of the work of Professor Duncan Kennedy cited in Chapter 1.

American judges and academics *discuss*[10] more seriously a range of problems which are increasingly common to us all – stripped of the heavy layers of (competing) political ideologies. Thus, for a third time within a short space we find ourselves agreeing with and citing Professor Michelman when he argues that 'comparative analysis could almost certainly be managed by a Supreme Court jointly bent on doing so without jeopardising *legal-discursive integrity*' which, in his view, may be the real (but unexpressed) reason for the hostility towards using foreign law.[11]

The pre-occupation with the above issues has also meant that absent from these debates is all reference to *how* foreign law could or should be used by their courts and how the latter could guard against the risk of being misled by the misunderstanding of foreign law. All of these points are, in our view, important ones and have been obscured by the politically motivated arguments. For our part, we would thus like to hear more from our American colleagues about methodology – how to study and use what we find out about foreign law – for this could have some bearing on two major issues: first, how to introduce foreign law which is both reliably presented and usable by the potential borrower and, second, which parts of American law are the most suitable entry points for such 'foreign' ideas. Also noted in the first chapter was the fact that in the domain of constitutional theorising one finds a remarkable mirroring of interests between American and German

---

[10] And we at least have never argued (in this book or elsewhere) that foreign values should be enforced upon unwilling Americans (just as we resent American administrations telling Europeans what their foreign policy should be). Our book is premised on the idea that dialogue and exchange of ideas is mind-broadening and thus potentially useful.

[11] Op. cit. note 1, p 273. The italicised words refer to Professor Michelman's own explanation of the real concerns which judges have against the use of foreign law and which are elaborated on pp 264 ff of his essay. Professor Anne-Marie Slaughter, in her contribution to the *Ignatieff Essays* at pp 277 ff, summarises Michelman's explanation in the following way:

> Americans, in all their pluralist splendor, look to the Supreme Court to rescue them from their inevitable quarrels, some of which run very deep indeed. Whether or not the Court is actually as objective as it should or could be, its revered place in American political life derives from its supposed ability to hand down objective legal decisions that cut through moral disagreements. Theoretically at least, opening American constitutional discourse to a plethora of foreign sources could adulterate it to the point that it could undermine the court's vital legitimacy.

See pp 291–2. The elegance of this summary should not prevent the reader from reading Michelman's own, subtly phrased, formulation (in chapter 9 of the *Ignatieff Essays*) even though he ends up by refuting it himself on grounds which are often very similar to those advanced in this chapter.

scholars, a mostly spontaneous overlap which has not been explored adequately. Despite the richness of some academic writings,[12] the discussion of these issues has thus been sacrificed to the wider politico-legal quarrel alluded to in the earlier chapters of this book. If there is a definite loser from this, it is the science of comparative law and methodology.

So, in matters of law, Americans strike us as closed to foreign ideas in all sorts of ways and as never before even though the liberal judges seem, at the time of writing, to be scoring some heavy points in recent judgments and authors who, like us, favour the 'spirit of discourse' seem to be more optimistic than we are.[13] But this American 'introvertedness' or 'exceptionalism' is not only noteworthy, it is also odd for, as Professor Ignatieff aptly remarks, America 'under some administrations (...) has promoted human rights as if they were synonymous with American values. While under others, it has emphasized the superiority of American values over international standards.' This ambivalence is not only confusing; it can also be arrogant. Arguably, the whole attitude has also contributed to the impoverishment of America's own constitutional legal literature. Indeed, it is two Texan constitutionalists (not us) who have claimed that American constitutional literature 'has been deep, but not at all wide'.[14] When we read such statements we feel that there must be something we, the authors of this book, can give back to American law in exchange for what we have taken from it. Our aim has thus been not just to describe the richness of other legal cultures (that being one of the purposes of studying *foreign law*), but also to suggest realistic ways of making this knowledge useable (this being one of the aims of *comparative methodology*). Our appeal is, of course, directed to those who do not have their minds already closed to arguments.

To non-American lawyers in general and comparatists in particular, the most recent American literature presents the further drawback of having focused almost exclusively on public law and, there again, mostly

[12] We single out two American colleagues who have, in our view, made very significant contributions in the area of human rights and comparative law: Mary Ann Glendon and Anne-Marie Slaughter, whose work figure prominently in all these discussions. Significantly, both have anchored their 'American' work on a comparative law basis and, we add, argued their positions in appropriately modest tones.

[13] Anne-Marie Slaughter's contribution to the *Ingatieff Essays*, pp 277–303, in line with her earlier learned work, falls into this category.

[14] William Forbath and Larry Sager, 'Comparative Avenues in Constitutional Law: An Introduction' (2004) 82 *Texas L. Rev.* 1653 at 1669.

on the domain of judicial review.[15] In more recent times, and as a result of the same neo-conservative thinking, public international law has also been added to the list of 'suspect' subjects in an attempt to limit its reach over US courts. Further down, we shall explore a further possible extension of 'avoiding foreign law' to cover areas of pure private law where international trade makes this interaction with foreign ideas even more essential.

Generally speaking, therefore, the utility of the comparative method to national law as a whole, whether in the courtroom or the classroom, has not been systematically explored in the United States. The exceptions (so far as one can judge, given the vastness of the American legal literature) are sporadic; and they have mainly focused on the presence of the subject (never properly defined) in the legal curriculum. Worse still, and for the reasons we shall explore further down, the negative views that seem to dominate in the domain of public law about deriving any inspiration from foreign law seem likely to have *infected* (and we use the word advisedly) even the traditional area of Common law – what European lawyers usually call 'private law' – where cross-fertilisation was once a fact of life and where now globalised trading conditions make it a necessity. It would seem that only one subject provided a momentary deviation from this arid landscape. For in the United States in the 1980s and early 1990s aspects of comparative civil procedure tried to take root in this inhospitable environment. Yet, once again, even this debate fizzled out without having left anything to admire except some intemperately written articles (some, it must be added, of considerable scholarship).

Overall, it is thus difficult to avoid the conclusion that in matters of private law the more tolerant voices of yesterday have fallen silent, this silence engulfing English law as much as modern civil law. Further down we ask whether this decline may have, in part, been affected by the debates that have taken place in the domain of statutory interpretation, where opposition to foreign law has been at its most virulent. Whatever the answer, the fact is that for those seeking new ways to teach foreign law and, more importantly, to utilise good foreign ideas in the courtroom and in the drafting of legislation, the inspiration must be sought elsewhere

---

15 As we explained in the Introduction (and elsewhere in the book) this may also be a shortcoming of the *Ignatieff Essays*. By this we are not suggesting that the private law aspects of American 'self-sufficiency' should have been explored since this would, among other things, have meant a book double the original size. But, as we explain further down, the current 'exceptionalism', 'introvertedness', or 'self-sufficiency' (and we refrain at this stage from characterising the current state of affairs) may have the tendency of affecting legal practice even in the domain of private law.

than in the judgments of the United States Supreme Court.[16] Indeed, it is an irony of sorts to note that the most useful comments about the dangers of an ill-considered use of foreign law came from Justice Scalia, the man who would least wish us to deal with it in the first place!

To our knowledge only the South African, the Canadian, and, to a lesser extent, a small number of German, English, and Israeli judges (and academics) have shown a genuine interest in the above matters; and their work (though by no means always convincing), has the added advantage that it ranges over the whole area of law, namely public as well as private law.[17] This book has followed this tradition.

To be sure, in pursuit of these objectives we have been forced to take the risk of being too brief in our exposition (at some levels at least) in order to try to examine our topic from a wider angle than has hitherto been attempted by academic literature – that is, by discussing both public as well as private law. As stated, we have also tried to devote equal attention (if not space) to five – if we may call them 'major' – legal systems, namely (in alphabetical order) the American, Canadian, English, German, and the South African, partly because (as already stated) they seem to have generated the greatest interest, and compare them with the current and ambivalent (if we may so describe it) American position.

Absent from this list is the contribution of French legal thought, except in a somewhat cursory manner (though the Comment provided by the First President of the French Cour de cassation goes a long way in remedying our omission).[18] Even so, and despite the fact that the

---

[16] Though in the sparring between the justices in the recent death penalty decision of the Supreme Court in *Roper v Simmons*, 125 S. Ct. 1183, 1217ff (2005) one finds many useful tips about *how* to use or not to refer to foreign law.

[17] This generalisation may do injustice to the courts of other countries, some of which, such as Hungary (A Magya Köztárgaság Alketmánya Chapter XII, § 54, para 1: illegality of death penalty on the grounds of arbitrariness, discussed in (1992) 41 *BYU L. Rev.* 41), Zimbabwe (*State v Ncube* [1988] 2 SA 702: whether whipping of an adult male amounted to an inhuman or degrading punishment), or India (e.g. *Amar Nath v State A. I. R.* (38) 1951 Punjab 18; *Maneka Gandhi v Union*, 2 S.C.R. 621 (1978): the transferability of the principles of the First and Fourteenth Amendments *despite a different textual phrasing* of the Indian Constitution), have been known for courageous forays into the study and use of foreign law. For more details, ideas, and references see Lester, 'The Overseas Trade in the American Bill of Rights', 88 *Columbia L. Rev.* 537.

[18] And Israeli court decisions, largely because of our inability to access this literature in the original language. We note, however, that our own respect for the inventiveness shown by the Israeli Supreme Court is not shared by all in the United States; see, for instance, the views of Robert Bork who referred to it as 'the most activist, *antidemocratic* [sic] court in the world' in *Coercing Virtue: The World Wide Rule of Judges* (revised edn, 2003) at p 13, and contrast the view of the Israeli Supreme Court held by Professor Alexander Somek in (1998) 1 *U. Pa. J. Const. L.* 284 at 284 n 1 ('The most important comparative law institute of the world').

elegance and originality of the French legal mind are incontrovertible, the attention that French law has attracted from contemporary American scholarship and court practice (outside the State of Louisiana) is smaller than that of the other systems discussed in this book. For reasons of space, therefore, a fuller discussion of this system had to be deferred for another time. But should the present study ever be deemed worthy of further expansion to include a more in-depth analysis of contemporary Canadian tendencies, then this omission would no longer be tolerable and some attempt should be made to discover the true French picture despite the opaqueness of the judgments of the highest French courts. At present suffice it, therefore, to remind the reader of what was said in Chapter 2: that the interest in foreign law is being awakened in France, largely because of the efforts made by certain courts, indeed certain individuals. The same awakening can be noted in Italy, though here it is academics rather than the courts that have given the lead to these enquiries.

Finally, we should stress that being descriptive has not been our only aim. For when we started this research we were – and still remain – anxious to kick-start the process of formulating normative rules which could help clarify foreign practice and determine where and how this could be used by national courts. One of us has, indeed, already written about the need of 'packaging' foreign law before attempting to put it to some use in a purely national context.[19] Here, however, we wished to go a step back and talk about the wider and, in terms of time, *pre-existing* need to engage in such foreign dialogues. Thus, in attempting to formulate the normative guidelines which follow, we have drawn on the writings of others (especially the pioneering work and terminology of Sujit Choudhry,[20] on which we draw liberally, but not slavishly, in what follows). But we have gone beyond its aims for we have tried to suggest ways in which this discussion could be brought into the American scene with the minimum possible disruption of local sensibilities.

b) Choudhry's work

Like us, Choudhry takes the view that 'legal particularism[21] underlies most American theories of constitutional interpretation'.[22] This

---

[19] Basil Markesinis, *Comparative Law in the Courtroom and the Classroom. The Story of the Last Thirty-Five Years* (2003).

[20] 'Globalisation in Search of Justification: Toward a Theory of Comparative Constitutional Interpretation' (1998/1999) 74 *Indiana L. J.* 816 ff.

[21] Which he understands to emphasise '(T)hat legal norms and institutions generally, and constitutions in particular, both emerge from and reflect particular national circumstances, most centrally a nation's history and political culture.' Ibid, p 830.

[22] Ibid.

immediately puts the United States in the camp opposite from almost all major legal systems in the world. But Choudhry also notes that the globalisation of modern constitutionalism is also an undeniable fact of life which is not leaving even American judges and academics unmoved.[23] So, in order to deal with this phenomenon, he suggests three different modes of comparative constitutional interpretation.

The first he calls the 'universalist', which he believes 'posit[s] that constitutional guarantees are cut from a universal cloth'.[24] The second interpretative mode he calls 'dialogical'. This starts with the assumption that differences exist between the different legal systems, but also accepts that even in this context a dialogue with other systems is not only possible but useful in that it also 'furthers legal self-understanding'.[25] Finally, Choudhry sees a third interpretative mode, which he calls the 'geneological'.[26] This sees

> (...) constitutions [as being] often tied together by complicated relationships of genealogy and history, and that these relationships themselves offer sufficient justification to import and apply entire areas of constitutional doctrine.[27]

Choudhry explores this heading by references to specific cases taken mainly from the United States, South Africa, and Canada, and throughout admits that these interpretative modes are not mutually exclusive. Towards the end of his long paper, Choudhry sets out the different 'signals' that each of these interpretative modes may send to the citizens affected by the respective court decision as well as 'outside observers'.[28]

---

[23] For a selection of contradictory dicta see Chapter 2, above.

[24] Op. cit. note 20, p 833. Doctrinally, he supports this school of thought by citing the views of Zweigert and Kötz contained in the first edition of their *Introduction to Comparative Law* (1987) – which may not be advisable since this work deals almost exclusively with *private* law and may thus render the transposition of some of its ideas into the public law domain debatable. For present purposes, however, this point need not be considered further.

[25] Ibid, pp 835 ff.

[26] Ibid, p 838.

[27] Choudhry's discussion on this point seems to pay inadequate attention to the point made earlier on, namely that systems are often veering away from their genealogical ancestors. Studying the reasons for such shifts is important if one is to try to predict which system (and which case law) is likely to serve as a model in the future. Yet most American commentators (and some judges) wonder whether American constitutionalism can remain a model for exportation given its current introvertedness and also the fact that the phrasing of its Constitution does not tally easily with the wording of modern constitutional texts. Yet, it has to be admitted that this point cuts both ways. For, if the text of the US Constitution does not match that of most other constitutions, written much later in time and in a different political environment, then that is an obstacle not just to exporting, but also to importing foreign ideas.

[28] Op. cit. note 20, pp 885–92.

Thus, those using the 'internationalist mode' may have the international legal community in their sights, though they may also wish to internationalise their national legal culture in order to reform, revitalise, or re-orient it in a new direction. Though it could be argued that such formulations were (almost) devised with the South African experience in mind (or Hungary, whose Constitutional Court was, as already stated, early in its life willing to ban the death sentence[29]), to a large extent they can also be applied to Canada whose judges may not feel to be under similar pressures. The 'dialogical mode', on the other hand, may enable a court to learn from foreign experience without internationalising its domestic constitutional culture, at any rate not openly and drastically. To a very large extent this seems to us to have happened in Canada in the post-Charter era.

Choudhry's work is of great interest and value and, to our knowledge, it has been seen in this light by American academic writers. But he also seems more interested to 'describe' and 'classify' what happens than to come up with some kind of 'normative' set of rules that might help *guide* future judges and lawyers as to when recourse to foreign law is desirable or even necessary, and when one should back away from this task. We attempt this in the next sub-section in a tentative manner, desirous to 'start the ball rolling'. Before doing this, however, we must mention two of the main guidelines we have borne in mind throughout this endeavour.

In their writing, academics can be 'dreamers', presenting pure ideas to which they may be personally attached but also conscious of the fact that these may not be realisable in the immediate future. Our colleague Professor Larry Sager of The University of Texas Law School may well fall into this category when, in his most recent and stimulating monograph, he condemns the fact that American constitutional law has 'systematically' fallen short of addressing 'obvious requirements of a just political community'. These, in his view, can only be attained if economic arrangements that offer citizens 'minimally decent material lives', including health care, are put in place.[30]

This resembles in many respects the earlier campaign by Harvard Professor Frank Michelman to make welfare payments a constitutional right.[31] And to these proposed new entitlements one could add, as many

---

[29] Op. cit. note 17. For parallel tendencies in Zimbabwe see Lovemore Madhuku, 'The Impact of the European Court of Human Rights in Africa: The Zimbabwean Experience' (1996) 8 *African Journ. of Intern. and Comp. Law* 932 ff.

[30] Lawrence Sager, *Justice in Plainclothes. A Theory of American Constitutional Practice* (2004), especially chapter 6.

[31] Thus, see his 'In Pursuit if Constitutional Welfare Rights: One View of Rawls' Theory of Justice' (1973) 121 *U. Pa. L. Rev.* 962 ff and 'Welfare Rights in a Constitutional Democracy' (1979) *Washington U. L. Q.* 659 ff.

in Europe have, a new generation of human rights such as the right to education and the right to employment. With the number of Americans under the 'official' poverty line and the even larger numbers left totally without any health care coverage, these calls have a strong 'human' tone to them. But the political and economic history of the United States during the last 15 years or so has shown how hell-bent the American economic system – probably supported by the majority of electors, irrespective of party allegiance – is on not allowing this to happen. Much as we have agreed with Professor Michelman's analysis so far, on this score, we feel we part company with him. For, to attempt to achieve such major re-orientation of American thinking via judicial discretion is, in our view, more than utopian; it is also dangerous in so far as it illustrates precisely the kind of liberal attempt to subvert the democratic element of a constitution that conservative writers fervently resist. This, in other words, is a confrontational way of achieving a desired aim (and we are not disagreeing with the underlying 'human' aims but the way of implementing them); it is also likely to fail – and is, in fact, failing – except, perhaps, at the fringes. For what it is worth, comparative observation of the European scene, commonly seen by Americans as 'left'-inclined, shows that such attempts have failed there, as well. Thus, even in countries such as Germany[32] where the Basic Law, itself, defines the State as a Republic, devoted to the rule of law (*Rechtstaatprinzip*) and to social justice (*Sozialstaatsprinzip*), the latter concept, in *judicial* terms, has proved infinitely less important than the former;[33] and it has been particularly strongly denounced by private lawyers[34] on grounds which, philosophically, have not been that different to those found in America.

---

[32] And Japan where the *Ashai*-decision of the Japanese Supreme Court held that the right to enjoy at least the minimum standard of decent living enshrined in Art 25 of the Japanese Constitution was merely 'programmatic'. On this see Mary Ann Glendon, 'Rights in Twentieth-Century Constitutions' (1992) 59 *U. Chi. L. Rev*. 519 ff.

[33] It is mainly used as a notion that informs the interpretation of other provisions of the Basic Law. Two points must, however, be made. First, the two principles are *per se* different in content and thus difficult to compare when it comes to their respective practical relevance. The *Rechtsstaatsprinzip* contains, *inter alia*, human rights, judicial review, and the separation of powers principle, and *must* therefore be of higher importance in constitutional litigation. Second, it would be interesting to see what German courts would draw from the *Sozialstaatsprinzip* in the absence of an extensive social welfare network which, at its core, still dates back to the very best of times Germany has seen, in economical terms, since the Second World War. In the present economic climate this, however, is changing; and attempts to cut down on the system of social security and unemployment benefits might, eventually, prompt judges to use the *Sozialstaatsprinzip* as a constitutional yardstick by which to measure far-reaching reforms.

[34] For a general discussion see David Curry, *German Consitutional Law* (1994), pp 20 ff; for the (slender) impact of the principle on private law see Basil Markesinis, Hannes Unberath and Johnston, *The German Law of Contract. A Comparative Treatise* (2nd edn, 2006), chapter 1.

Other academics are realists. This does not mean that they lack ideas or agendas but know that incremental changes tend to work more smoothly because they cause less disruption. These academics are very much alive to the number one rule of 'real' politics – and we use the term 'real' to contrast it to 'judicial' politics (or even the lesser world of 'academic' politics where feelings can reach a high pitch because the stakes tend to be so low) – and that is the need not to forget that 'politics is the art of the possible'.

We have been very conscious of the force of this old adage; and while not letting it dilute our enthusiasm for transnational dialogue, we have endeavoured, both in what has preceded these pages and what follows, to devise compromises that would enable this dialogue to begin in a more serious way. This, we hope, has been shown by the fact that in this book version of an earlier lecture held at Tulane a number of corners have been 'smoothed' and greater sensitivity has been shown towards views with which we do not find ourselves in agreement. Equally, in what follows we remind both ourselves and our readers of that elegant warning by M. Canivet, the First President of the French Cour de cassation (reproduced at the end of Chapter 1). The essence of it was that the aim of comparatists is not to create synthetic rules on the basis of the minimum common denominator found in a number of legal systems but to try to engage with them in a way that broadens our angles of approach towards common problems. If, as a result of such efforts, we find an approach or a practice that presents some merits and if, moreover, this practice or approach seems to have gained wider acceptance, then we should consider learning from it – but in way that introduces it into one's system in a manner that makes sense 'locally'.

c) *Values and rules*

We again start with the system which nowadays seems most resistant to the use of foreign ideas in order to explore ways of bridging the gap that separates it from the other systems discussed in this book – the American. An additional aim is to try and explain the complexity of American law to foreign observers (sometimes too keen to copy it without understanding its wider setting and the passions it can raise) but also to give to our American readers an indication of how (well disposed) outsiders such as ourselves see it these days. To put it differently, those who wish to influence the American scene must learn to shape their proposals in a way that fits the environment they are trying to influence. They must also be prepared to accept that it is impossible to please everyone! The problem of 'packaging' thus acquires a new dimension. Of course, authors like Robert Bork, who would probably include us in his peremptual dismissal of 'faux intellectuals', are too hardened in their views to be persuaded. Others, however, might not be.

Our suggestions may be acceptable to those academics who, in one way or another, have followed the ideas launched (in exemplary moderate and stylistically attractive terms) some 40 years ago by influential thinkers such as Alexander Bickel[35] or John Hart Ely.[36] Indeed, in one sense, we see our ideas about the usability of foreign ideas as emanations of these moderate and liberal ripostes to originalism and textualism. For in the broadly phrased liberty-bearing provisions of the Constitution one may find 'entry points' for interesting ideas of foreign courts that might provide support for growing, indigenous trends. What is currently happening with the Eighth Amendment might provide further support for such a thesis and, possibly, grounds for expansion. The success of this exercise will be greater if one were to be willing to accept the line taken by English (e.g. Devlin) or French (e.g. Canivet) judges that their creative role is limited to 'updating' old texts in a creative manner but not 'leading' public opinion.[37]

For those who accept this as a starting point, and not all will, the question then becomes how does one present the foreign ideas before one can evaluate their persuasive force to a potentially receptive environment? For the fact is that the presentation of the foreign law, mainly through amicus briefs, has not escaped criticism by those opposed to its use on a variety of methodological grounds with the result that its effectiveness has been seriously weakened.[38] Likewise, as one of us tried to show in an earlier study,[39] presenting the foreign law in its full-blown conceptualism can only lead to it being ignored. Though meeting these concerns is unlikely to reverse the existing hostility of some members of the Supreme Court to foreign law and ideas, it could go some way towards producing a more reliable account of what the foreign practice really is on a particular problem. Though this will not be the end of the

---

[35] *The Least Dangerous Branch. The Supreme Court at the Bar of Politics* (2nd edn, 1982).

[36] *Democracy and Distrust. A Theory of Judicial Review* (1980).

[37] To be specific, our conception of the judicial role (for the purposes of comparative studies) does not go as far as Alexander Bickel's willingness to allow judges to 'anticipate but not by much' future evolution of societal views – see, for instance, *The Least Dangerous Branch. The Supreme Court at the Bar of Politics* (1962) at p 239 – and we certainly feel that siding with some of the most radically different theories which would like to see the Court 'lead the way' in socio-economic reform would be the kiss of death for any attempt to encourage comparative dialogue. Yet we do see some 'mileage' in using foreign law in cases such as *Roper* where internal evolution may suggest that the use of foreign ideas can help consolidate a reformative interpretation and even argue that this might be possible beyond the established 'entry point' of the Eighth Amendment.

[38] See the doubts expressed in *Roper* by Justice Scalia, citing an early opinion of the Chief Justice to the same effect: 125 S. Ct. 1187, at 1222 (2005).

[39] B. S. Markesinis (op. cit. note 19).

matter, nor can it be given that it is so intimately linked to the wider concerns about the limits of juridical review, it should make the debate more precise and, possibly, even more civilised. The question, as stated, is thus 'how to integrate the foreign idea into the very complex local fabric?'

Reducing the tension between the two schools[40] of constitutional interpretation would have other benefits besides those mentioned above. For it may be necessary not only for those who wish to understand what is *actually* happening in the United States at present; it may also reduce the 'destructive' effect which this constitutional theorising (especially in its various extreme forms) may be having on private law, as well. For, in our view, it is also, along with other reasons,[41] reversing a well-established contrary practice in this area of private law where transnational legal discourse (and even borrowing) has been quite usual for decades if not centuries. We shall return to this point further down where we suggest how the wider politico-economic debate could encourage such a development.

That the 'venom' which now exists in this constitutional debate is spreading to other areas of life and law cannot be doubted by many though it must also be regretted by those who dislike extremes as being disruptive and, eventually, destructive of social life. Yet it may also be aided and abetted by the belief, in the ascendancy at the moment among the governing political elites in the United States, that America is 'a city on the hill' (a) better than others *and* (b) morally bound to try to improve others who do not attain its own standards.[42]

---

[40] For a succinct account of the 'intermediary' schools that attempt to modify the excesses of the polar opposites, see Lawrence Sager, op. cit. note 30, chapter 2. The same task is undertaken in a lengthier manner and from a conservative optic by Robert Bork, *The Tempting of America. The Political Seduction of the Law* (1990) chapters 6–10.

[41] For instance the undoubted growing self-sufficiency in internal material. This does not mean that the thousands of local decisions will, necessarily, match in quality or inventiveness leading judgments of foreign courts, though it is of course difficult for the local attorney/judge to find these foreign exemplars. Indisputably, this leads us back to the difficulties associated with comparative law discussed in Chapter 4, above.

[42] These key words, coming from John Winthrop's address on the founding of the Massachusetts Bay Colony (and probably derived from Matthew 5:14), read as follows:

> For wee must Consider that wee shall be as a City upon a Hill, the eies of all people are uppon us; soe that if wee shall deale falsely with our God in this worke wee have undertaken and so cause Him to withdrawe His present help from us, wee shall be made a story and a byword through the world, wee shall open the mouthes of enemeis to speake evill of the wayes of god and all professours for Gods sake; wee shall shame the faces of many of God's worthy servants, and cause theire prayers to be turned into Cursses upon us till wee be consumed out of the good land whether wee are going.

As the phrase became 'politicised' over the ages, and certainly after the 'Reagan years' when it became often cited, it lost its cautionary note and became simply 'we are an example to the world'.

If the first proposition is tolerable (at the very least as a sign of justified self-satisfaction of the many achievements of this country) the second sounds like a tall order for both politicians and others in roles of power and influence. Yet, indisputably, there are many politicians (and not a few economists, journalists, and even lawyers) who see in the United States an example to the world. In law this takes the form of a series of beliefs: the United States is the first to have implemented democracy, protected human rights, recognised judicial review, and nowadays is re-proclaiming the merits of a property-owning nation, with its citizens taking their fate into their own hands. All these ideas are political, philosophical, economic; but they also translate into very specific legal rules.

Once seen as legal ideas one may debate to what extent these American claims are justified, exaggerated, or transplantable. Moreover, almost every idea (and policy aim) when taken to extremes can become unattractive, even dangerous. In any event, one must at least question whether America has any right to 'force' others[43] (through its foreign policy or otherwise) to adopt its values rather than merely rely on the superiority of its ideas and ideals to attract their own adherents. Harold Koh, the Dean of the Yale Law School (and formerly an Assistant Secretary in the Justice Department), has called this idea of 'imposed democracy' proclaimed after the invasion of Afghanistan 'oxymoronic';[44] and, in the same piece, rightly pointed out that it marked a departure from the time-honoured ideal of 'democracy promotion from the bottom up' to an objective of democracy 'imposed from the top down'.[45] This could be seen as an interference with the affairs of sovereign states, and thus as an abuse of international law, and is also deeply troubling in so far as it represents yet another manifestation of the new reality that contemporary American foreign policy is based on double standards.

Such beliefs thus form part of the current 'political climate' that we find in this great (in more ways than one) country. Moreover, we feel that they have been reinforced, even aggravated, in the minds of many Americans, by non-legal arguments contrasting their own beliefs with contemporary European reservations about the legality and wisdom of America's recent invasion of Iraq. Reason, pride, and sentiment – moral,

---

[43] The attempt to do this becomes even less convincing when one notes how 'offending' countries (Iraq or Serbia versus Saudi Arabia, Egypt, Jordan, Morocco, or, most recently, Uzbekistan) and leaders (Hussein or Milosevic versus Pinochet, Suharto, or the Shah of Iran) are treated differently depending on America's own politico-economic interests. Of course, as an example of *Realpolitik* this inconsistency is understandable; but as a reflection of the 'city on the hill' philosophy it requires much explaining.

[44] *Ignatieff Essays* (op. cit. note 1), chapter 5, at p 128.

[45] Ibid, p 127.

political, and economic – thus seem to have come together in the United States with legal concerns to produce an 'unstable' mix the likes of which neither of us has encountered in contemporary comparative constitutional law. Taken together they must account for the suspicions which a substantial proportion of the American population (including lawyers), aided and abetted by the kind of 'inflammatory and one-sided' reporting of news shown in some television channels, may nurture towards contemporary Europe, its values, its law, and its courts. A fear or dislike of foreign values nowadays thus comes with a very inadequate understanding of the 'rest of the world', its sensitivities, its institutional structures, its religious beliefs, and, of course, its law. We say nothing of foreign languages, for the neglect shown towards them by the American school curriculum is something which we think is little short of severely counter-productive to American cultural and economic interests abroad.

For us, thoughts such as the above may explain the Scalia or (more extremely phrased) Bork positions (even though we also accept that they can legitimately be seen as an extreme antitheses to some equally extreme positions promoted in the United States from the mid-1960s onwards[46] by the radical left (including branches of feminism). But in part the above may also explain something which we (as outsiders) see as a novel and strange trend.

Thus, one can nowadays find in American academe Jewish liberal constitutional theorists of distinction (such as, for instance, our Texas colleague Sanford Levinson) who are, nevertheless, able to 'sympathise' – our American colleagues might use the term 'empathise' – with Justice Scalia's ability to 'identify American values' – even though the latter is a Catholic by religion and, unhesitantly, a 'conservative' by conviction. Indeed, Professor Levinson has gone further in terms of the time continuum when he writes that

> (A)s a descriptive matter I certainly do not believe that the [US Supreme] Court has ever [sic] deviated in any truly significant way from the dominant [sic] sensibility.[47]

---

[46] Which are vividly described for those who did not live through them in Robert Bork's *Slouching Towards Gomorrah. Modern Liberalism and American Decline.* (revised paperback edition 2003), Part I.

[47] 'Looking Abroad When Interpeting the U.S. Consitution: Some Reflections' (2004) 39 *Texas Intern. L. Journ.* 353 at 359. It is invidious for outside observers to ask questions which insiders regard as *so obviously* settled, but academic debate requires us to try and consider issues in a more subtle way. Thus, on the basis of all Gallup polls conducted in the United States, we understand that anything between 65 and 75 per cent of those taking part seem to favour the death penalty when asked a simple straight question. These figures would, indeed, support Professor Levinson's use of the words 'dominant sensibility'. Yet the reality in the United States seems to suggest a more nuanced picture. Thus, at the time of writing, there exist twelve 'abolitionist' States, 24 'symbolic'

Significantly, he adds – which we feel is both important but also refers to what we call 'values' – that

> (...) I find it difficult to argue that the judge should ignore the dominant sensibility and declare that an inchoate notion of 'justice' requires something radically different (...).[48]

Notwithstanding the eminent status and experience of an important judge and a learned colleague, we find it difficult to understand 'how a judge can identify dominant sensibilities to the point of making them law' unless he has what Justice Frankfurter once described as 'antennae registering feelings and judgment[s] beyond *logical, let alone quantitative, proof*'.[49] We italicise the last few words for the raw material he is likely to use can, almost certainly, support a different conclusion by another judge evaluating it; and it is this degree of subjectivity that, we feel, leaves liberal thinkers open to the objection that their methods of adjudication are not really based on neutral rules and principles. But the truth of the matter is that no agreement can be reached on open-ended issues like that, hence the size and often repetitive nature of some of the literature. What, however, is less in doubt is that a tense/extreme *political* climate can not only polarise opinion; occasionally, it can produce strange bedfellows! The unusual revival of interest in the writings of Carl Schmitt, a brilliant constitutional theorist but a self-tainted apologist of the Hitler regime, must, surely, be somehow linked with this phenomenon unless, of course, the crises brought about by modern terrorism is suddenly making older appeals for a strong role of the state attractive again.

Be that as it may, one may have to – indeed must – concede that when such basic (national) sensitivities do, indeed, exist concerning certain values, institutions, or practices (and we are deliberately not being too specific in the term we use less we become bogged down with

---

States (recognising the death penalty but rarely practising it), and a further 14 States being 'executing' states. The result of these figures is an unprecedented 3,500 inmates currently sitting on death row. We have not seen convincing explanations for the reluctance of the States in the middle group to give effect to the laws on their statute books – only hypotheses of varying degrees of plausibility. But we feel it would take a bold gambler to assert (with such divided practices) that he knows what the 'dominant sensibilities' truly are and even more so to argue that these do not change! In any event, we wonder how Professor Levinson will treat *Roper v Simmons*. Will he (again) 'side' with Justice Scalia's dissent (in favour of the death penalty) on the grounds given in his text above? Or will he say that it is the Court which really identifies 'dominant sensibilities', in which case Justice Scalia has, on this count, now lost his touch of getting things right?

48 Ibid.

49 In P. Elman (ed), *Of Law and Men* (1956), pp 31–9. We considered how valid/acceptable this criterion may be under the section of mentality and intuition in Chapter 5.

details and dilute at this stage the main thrust of our argument), it would be difficult and unwise to argue that a judge should be able to by-pass them. The importation of notions, ideas, and practices originating from abroad cannot provide sufficient justification. The availability of the death penalty and the banning of homosexual marriages may fall into these categories of 'local realities', which foreign jurists cannot – *nor, perhaps, should* – attempt to dislodge.[50] The same, we think, could be said for claims (such as those made by Professor Sager) for greater social and economic justice coming into the system via the courts given the 'apparently' dominant political opposition to them. The fact that Europe, almost to a state, has done otherwise on both these issues thus seems irrelevant given the strength of American public opinion.

This, however, does not remove the difficulty of knowing what practices or what values are so essential and widely acknowledged in one society so as to be untouchable by the judges and which part of their content may lie at the fringes or borderlines where change could be acceptable. Merely relying on an academic's assertion that the judge (with or without the right kind of antennae) has 'got it about right' is not enough. And in the domain of statutory interpretation, the 'originalist' approach does not (in our view, as well as the views of those who do not adopt it in the United States) provide a conclusive answer either by being so fossilised in time, not to mention unable in all cases to give a 'correct' answer as to what the original understanding was at the crucial moment. To put it differently: what did the Founding Fathers of the US Constitution think about data protection or genetical engineering?

Moreover, as has been repeatedly stated in this book (perhaps for the first time in academic literature of this kind), one must always be aware of the effect that the time factor has on such issues. This is particularly true in an age such as ours when public opinion is constantly evolving and the 'stability' of the world of yesterday is no longer to be taken for granted today. The (rapidly) changing racial composition of the United States may also provoke in the not too distant future a reconsideration of values which at present seem to be fairly entrenched. Again, for the sake of completeness one must note how the 'originalists' seem to reject this argument; though we, with the temerity of outsiders, wonder whether the

---

[50] Others can be added to this list – notably child chastisement, on which Americans and Europeans may diverge significantly.

Founding Fathers (astute and experienced statesmen that they were) did, indeed, mean literally their assertion that their Constitution was 'intended to endure for ages to come'.[51]

In making this assertion we are not merely arguing that, in *appropriate* circumstances, foreign ideas might help buttress local views favouring the 'expansion' of constitutional rights but, by parity of reasoning, also their restriction – a point raised by some[52] but, to our knowledge, never extensively considered by the courts. Defining what is appropriate is, of course, difficult; but our suggestion, elaborated below, is that it may be possible not to interfere with the basic sensibility but to find consensus in modifying its edges. *Roper* might well be consolidating this kind of approach; and it might well contain the seeds of a compromise. That it might not please everyone does not matter in the least, since political compromises never do and that is why they tend to last so long!

The passage of time reveals gaps, even in revered constitutions; and they are filled by courts exercising discretion and judgment. Discretion cannot be banished from the judicial process, only disguised. For instance, the protection against unreasonable searches and seizures could not have envisaged wiretapping. Though it involves no trespass, and thus no violation to property, the US Supreme Court has included this last-mentioned activity in the Fourth Amendment.[53] Is this not a gap-filling exercise by a court? And does it not make sense? We think it does, because it was an 'up-dating creative interpretation' and not a 'society leading interpretation'.[54] Likewise, the Constitution was silent about sovereign immunity; yet the Supreme Court has incorporated the doctrine into American law.[55] As Judge Posner asks rhetorically, is this importation 'usurpative'?[56] We believe no European judge would think so.

---

[51] This well-known phrase forms a key part in Justice Black's dissent in *Bell v Maryland*, 378 U.S. 226, 341–2 (1964), warmly approved by Justice Scalia in his 'Assorted Canards of Contemporary Legal Analysis' (1989–90) 40 *Case Western Reserve Law Review* 581 at 596.

[52] Though it is almost unrealistic to mention the First Amendment under this heading, a good case could be made for nibbling at its fringes when it comes to such neglected rights as privacy.

[53] *Charles Katz v United States*, 389 U.S. 347, 88 S. Ct. 507. For an even bolder extension, ingeniously (or ingenuously?) presented by Justice Scalia, see *Kyllo v United States*, 533 U.S. 27 (2001).

[54] See our discussion in Chapter 1, s 3, where the distinction is looked at in a comparative way.

[55] *United States v Lee*, 106 U.S. 196, 1 S. Ct. 240; *United States v Shaw*, 309 U.S. 495, 60 S. Ct. 659.

[56] 'What Am I, A Potted Plant? The Case Against Strict Constructionism', in David M. O'Brien (ed), *Judges on Judging. Views from the Bench* (2004), p 165 at p 167.

Similar observations, arguably supporting our claim that judicial discretion can help mould the original text beyond what was envisaged at the outset, can be made by noting that its articles were sometimes drafted in very general terms whereas in others its provisions have been very specific. But if a clause is drafted widely, does it not (with the full intent of its framers) invite multiple interpretations and, to quote Judge Posner again (since he is a conservative lawyer, though not an originalist), is not 'this possibility an embarrassment for a theory of judicial legitimacy that denies judges have any right to exercise discretion'? And, conversely, have not 'specific provisions creating rights (...) proved irksomely (...) [or] dangerously anachronistic'?[57] This is particularly so when the interpretation is ensuring that the text is brought up-to-date with current societal beliefs and is not trying to shape them for this society.

Nor, finally, is it necessarily convincing to invoke popular votes or polls as a constant alternative to judicial review for, as Arthur Chaskalson, the President of the South African Constitutional Court, put it in the South African death penalty case:

> If public opinion were to be decisive there would be no need for constitutional adjudication. The protection of rights could then be left to Parliament, which has a mandate from the public, and is answerable to the public for the way its mandate is exercised, but this would be a return to parliamentary sovereignty,[58] and a retreat from the new legal order established by the 1993 Constitution. By the same token the issue of the constitutionality of capital punishment cannot be referred to a referendum, in which a majority view would prevail over the wishes of any minority. The very reason for establishing the new legal order, and for vesting the

---

[57] 'What Am I, A Potted Plant? The Case Against Strict Constructionism', in David M. O'Brien (ed), *Judges on Judging. Views from the Bench* (2004), pp 167–8. The examples given by Posner are the right to a jury trial in a federal court and the right to bear arms.

[58] Chaskalson's reference to the principle of parliamentary sovereignty has significance for other systems as well. Thus, influenced by the English doctrine, the drafters of the Canadian Charter of 1982 chose to give the legislature (Provincial or Federal) the last word on constitutional matters by allowing the suspension of Charter rights for up to five years. The basic idea behind this 'opt out' clause bears some resemblance to the regime now in force in the United Kingdom where, out of deference to the doctrine of sovereignty of Parliament, the Human Rights Act 1998 leaves the ultimate decision to the legislature. Such legislative supremacy is unknown both in the United States and Germany where judgments of the US Supreme Court and the FCC are a binding source of law. The balance of power between the legislature and 'unelected' judges is thus clearly tilted in favour of the legislator in England and Canada, while US, German, and South African judges wield substantial influence over the development of their respective constitutional systems. The only way to trump their will is by constitutional amendment. Yet here, too, one has to bear in mind the process allowing revision of the constitutional text in practice. Thus, whereas this has happened in less than 30 occasions in the United States, the German Basic Law has seen changes at a rate which (taking account of its shorter life span) is roughly nine times as high!

> power of judicial review of all legislation in the courts, was to protect the rights of minorities and others who cannot protect their rights adequately through the democratic process. Those who are entitled to claim this protection include the social outcasts and marginalised people of our society. It is only if there is willingness to protect the worst and weakest amongst us, that all of us can be secure that our own rights will be protected.[59]

Though there is much logical force (and humanity) in the above quotation which, for this purpose, we set out in greater length, we accept that such an approach may be difficult to transplant to an environment such as that of the United States where the constitutional text, itself (unlike that of South Africa), is so much more permissive of the death penalty (as Chaskalson, too, admitted in his judgment) and only seems to allow its occasional mitigation when the protection of the Eighth Amendment can be successfully invoked.

So, does foreign law have a place in the interpretative process where other values and a different textual background seem to prohibit it? Is there a hierarchy of international values which should prevail, in part if not entirely, over a possibly different internal set of rules? Cannot these (internal) values change with time? Are all constitutional provisions impermeable to solutions dictated by changes in society? And is recourse to foreign ideas prohibited in all of these instances? These are the kind of questions that arise from the preceding paragraphs and must now be addressed, albeit briefly.

d) The proposed 'gradation'

A partial answer to these undoubtedly difficult questions may lie in attempting a gradation which, to our knowledge, has never been undertaken in the domain of comparative law. This does not so much depend on the distinction between public and private law,[60] nor on whether the borrowing is attempted to enlarge or restrict local rights and entitlements as some American writers think. What to us is crucial are two things: (a) the 'importance' which the importing system ascribes to its own 'values' (and which may be threatened by the importation of the foreign idea), and (b) whether the idea considered for importation is universally (or just restrictively) valued.

---

[59] 1995 (3) SA 391, no 88 (CC).

[60] Even though, as Professor Alan Watson rightly observed, '(S)ocieties largely invent their constitutions, their political and administrative systems (…); but their private law is nearly always taken from others.' See Alan Watson, *Legal Transplants: An Approach to Comparative Law* (2nd edn, 1993), p 8.

This way of looking at things would first of all acknowledge that the injection of foreign thinking and arguments is always made more possible and more plausible where the local constitutional texts are ambiguous or silent or, as is the case with most modern constitutions, permit limitations of the enumerated and protected rights. But this is the (relatively) easy part of the answer. The real difficulty arises where the indigenous text is clearly phrased and prohibitive of foreign infiltration. Should, then, the attempt to look at foreign law for ideas be peremptorily halted? We think not, though here one should move with greater caution, paying due regard to local sensitivities. The influence/change may be easier at the fringes than at the core. It would also suggest asking the question: 'what is being affected – a value, especially a crucial one, or simply a technical legal rule?'

In such situations we would, therefore, suggest a tripartite distinction between cases which involve: (a) basic universal (or transcendent) values such as life, freedom from incarceration (subject to clear textual exceptions), or the presumption of innocence; (b) classic liberal values such as speech, freedom of movement, association, religion and the like; and (c) legal rules. Though we are mindful of the difficulty of pigeon-holing values or civil rights in one of the above categories, we nevertheless suggest this structure as being capable of accommodating more easily Choudhry's 'universalist' mode of interpretation at the one end of this scale (a) and the 'dialogical' mode of interpretation at the other (c), with both modes shading into each other in the middle ground (b).

We would be happy if this were to prove a good starting point and ask for nothing more. Yet even this statement needs some refinement as far as the first kind of values are concerned. For here, faced, as we are, with a universal value – the sanctity of life – and (in the United States) a clearly worded constitutional text that allows the State to take it away in certain circumstances, we must explore avenues of compromise in order to accommodate what are, indisputably, two American schools of thought. This is where we come to the idea of foreign law helping bring about changes in the margins, especially if such changes appear to be taking hold in the 'host' country, rather attempting to alter the core. How far down that road one can go is a matter of degree; and like all such issues, it is fact sensitive.

In our view the attempts to use the Eighth Amendment as a way of avoiding in some extreme cases the death penalty (e.g. for mentally retarded persons, now entirely accepted[61]) goes some way towards achieving this compromise between the incorporation of internationally

61 *Atkins v Virginia*, 536 U.S. 304, 122 S. Ct. 2242.

respected values in an apparently 'impermeable' national text.[62] We see this thesis receiving further support from the very recent decision of the US Supreme Court in *Roper v Simmons*. For here Justice Kennedy, delivering the majority opinion, relied on foreign practice to *bolster* the conclusion reached by himself and his colleagues in the majority on the basis of the 'internal' review of the changing pattern of State practices. He then proceeded to add:[63]

> Our determination that the death penalty is disproportionate punishment for offenders under 18 finds confirmation in the stark reality that the United States is the only country in the world that continues to give official sanction to the juvenile death penalty. *This reality does not become controlling*, for the task of interpreting the Eighth Amendment remains our responsibility. Yet at least from the time of the Court's decision in *Trop*,[64] the Court has referred to the laws of other countries and to international authorities as instructive for its interpretation of the Eighth Amendment's prohibition of 'cruel and unusual punishment'.

We emphasise the word 'bolster' since Justice Kennedy was eager to stress that while

> (T)he opinion of the world community, [*does not control the outcome*], [it] does provide respected and significant confirmation for our conclusions.

Yet in our view it is permissible to downplay the caveat indicated by the italicised words of the learned Justice in order to support our thesis and interpretation. And we advance this view because we feel that due regard must be had of the fact that the shift in State legislatures in favour of abolishing the death penalty for juveniles that took place between *Stanford v Kentucky*[65] and *Roper v Simmons* was much lower (namely four)[66] compared to that which justified the Court in *Atkins v Virginia* to

---

62 A similar 'gradation' can, incidentally, be found in the German Basic Law which protects some values more strongly than others. Thus, while most provisions are amendable by a two-thirds majority in both legislative chambers, Art 79(3) BL protects *absolutely* the division of the country into States, the participation of the States in Federal legislation, and the core principles enshrined in Arts 1 and 20 BL. This distinction is maintained when it comes to the process of European integration. Art 23 BL, a fairly unique provision which proclaims Germany's commitment to the European project, again emphasises the *absolute* protection given to these core values and principles of the Basic Law. In contrast, other – certainly important – notions such as free speech or the freedom of assembly (both part of the 'free democratic basic order' discussed in Chapter 2, above) *are* open to change in the context of European developments.

63 123 S. Ct. 1183, 1198 (2005).

64 *Trop v Dulles* 356 U.S. 86, 102–3, 78 S.Ct. 590 (plurality opinion).

65 492 U.S. 361, 109 S.Ct. 590.

66 Plus one State Supreme Court that had construed that State's death penalty statute as not to apply to the under-18 offenders; see *State v Furman*, 122 Wash. 2d 440, 458, 858 P.2d 1092,1103 (1993).

overrule *Penry v Lynaugh*[67] (16 states passing specific statutes). Justice Scalia may thus have been right when noting, in a similar vein (and, of course, criticising – which we do not do), *a shift* from previous practice because of the pressures of international opinion.[68]

We believe that Justice Scalia may be right in detecting such a 'shift' (which now makes it easier for the Court to detect such a change in national consensus) rather than search for the emergence of an 'overwhelming opposition to a challenged practice'[69] before abandoning it. Yet we also note that the members of the majority repeatedly stressed the 'supportive' rather than 'determinant' role which this (changed) international practice had in helping them alter their opinion. Not many, we suspect, will on reflection have difficulty in accepting such a carefully crafted formulation; and this certainly is consistent with the theory we are here advancing. In any event, good or bad, it would seem to provide a partial theoretical explanation for the changes taking place.

The proposed approach will not, of course, please originalists. Indeed, as already hinted, it drew a stinging attack from Justice Scalia in the *Roper* case[70] (which, however, also presents, for the reasons already given, a considerable – if, perhaps, unintended – contribution to the wider debate of how to use foreign law in the courtroom and the classroom). Yet we maintain that it is plausible, not least since the by now established (and accepted) phrase 'evolving standards of decency' itself sensitises us to the need to be alert that evolution is constantly taking place.

Yet at the end of the day, and as stated many times already, it remains a fact that such a shift *has* taken place (compatible with the views expressed extra-judicially by some of the Justices of the Supreme Court and referred to at the beginning of this book). And it is also noteworthy that the reference to international practice was the main point of the otherwise very short concurring opinion of Justices Stevens and Ginsburg. Finally, it also attracted the support of one of the dissenters – Justice Sandra Day O'Connor – who observed that

> (...) this Nation's evolving understanding of human dignity certainly is neither wholly isolated from, nor inherently at odds with, the values prevailing in other countries. On the contrary we should not be surprised to find congruence between domestic and international values, especially where the international community has reached clear agreement – expressed

---

67 492 U.S. 302, 109 S. Ct. 2934.

68 'Though the views of our own citizens are essentially irrelevant to the Court's decision today, the views of other countries and the so-called international community take center stage' (125 S.Ct 1183 at p 1125, per Justice Scalia).

69 See 125 S.Ct 1183, 1218 (2005).

70 125 S. Ct. 1183, 1217 (2005).

> in international law or in the domestic laws of individual countries – that a particular form of punishment is inconsistent with fundamental human rights.[71]

What remains to be seen is whether other, widely phrased provisions of the Constitution will act as entry points for foreign ideas in cases such as *Roper* where their invocation can help bolster an emerging local consensus without challenging truly dominant sensibilities. As we have already suggested, a path for doing this has been opened by the Eighth Amendment jurisprudence.

Turning now to what we called 'lesser' values (which, nonetheless, many of us would regard as the hallmarks of modern civilised society), the resistance of indigenous pressures to foreign ideas will be more understandable because, by their nature, these values leave room for more local variations. In looking at these cases, we are not thinking of extreme scenarios: free speech in Washington and Baghdad, for instance, for it is clear that however important it may be to introduce it in this long suffering part of the world it can never be done so *à l'Americain* at this historical moment.[72] England's or Germany's willingness not to subordinate unreservedly reputation and privacy to free speech is thus a better illustration of the dilemma we are envisaging and it would be a sad case to argue that the American preference for speech over dignity may in all cases be preferable. Because 'variation' here is more plausible (indeed, demanded by local sensibilities), the pressure to weaken the rigour of the First Amendment may be resisted. Indeed, it is not inconceivable to envisage that even in its own birthplace the First Amendment may be in for some modifications – though learned commentators on this subject seem to think that the institutional differences between, say, England and America are on this issue at least unbridgeable.[73]

The dialogical mode of interpretation can be applied 'constructively' even more easily in our last category of mere rules. This may be particularly worthy of doing whenever rules are or have become unclear, contradictory, or outmoded in a particular national context as a result of technological changes, streamlining of procedural rules, or growing

---

[71] 125 S. Ct. 1183, 1215 (2005). This citation is important. For, though the way foreign law was presented to the court and used by it may leave much to be desired, it does show that five out of nine judges were, in principle, not opposed to the idea of looking at it.

[72] Indeed, the post-9/11 climate of terror is already forcing 'liberal' countries to curtail traditional freedoms, which is illustrative of the fact that such rights cannot have a fixed contour but that their scope of protection may expand or constrict depending on a large variety of wider (and not necessarily legal) factors.

[73] See, for instance, Professor Schauer's comparative observation in 'The Exceptional First Amendment', *Ignatieff Essays* (op. cit. note 1), pp 29 ff.

international practices. We call this application of Choudry's mode 'constructive' because we feel that here it can go beyond the role assigned to it, that is, to make the national lawyer conscious of his own law and solutions but also to *encourage* him to use a foreign idea or solution in order to re-shape or change his own.[74]

We are, in this category, dealing largely with topics that traditionally fall under the heading of the Common law and we feel this is but one way of explaining past American practice[75] and sanctioning it for the future in the context of a more globalised economic and commercial world. For here the movement of ideas on technical matters that are regulated by the kind of rules we are envisaging should be facilitated and not impeded out of abstract notions of principle which may be relevant to the first group of cases but not this third category of disputes.

In making the above suggestion we do not, of course, delude ourselves in believing that it will stop opponents of all forms of foreign dialogue from trying to prevent it even in the case of a comparison of rules (and not values). For it does not take much ingenuity but only a minimum amount of disingenuousness to claim that, for instance, even ordinary contract or tort rules can be linked to 'values' held dear by some societies in order to preserve the status quo. Thus, any teacher of contract law in almost every country on the European Continent will be aware of the growing number of rules favouring consumer protection.[76] Almost all – certainly those which strive for greater employment protection – could be declared as incompatible with the American form of capitalism which (to us at least) seems hell-bent since the 1980s to unpick the New Deal revolution of the 1930s and return closer to the nineteenth-century ideal of *laissez faire*. Those who imagine European (including English) lawyers as being all 'socialists', 'anti-religious', or 'faux intellectuals' will certainly be tempted to try this tack.

The same could, likewise, be argued in the domain of tort rules,[77] which in Europe are, admittedly, fashioned against the reality of a safety

---

[74] And it is here that the topic of 'packaging' enters the equation, for the raw importation of the foreign solution or concept is often impossible.

[75] Which, in the past, succumbed to the intellectual appeal of foreign ideas. For an excellent collection of essays see Mathias Reimann (ed), *The Reception of Continental Ideas in the Common Law World 1820–1920* (1993).

[76] For a recent coverage of the German scene see Reinhard Zimmermann, 'Consumer Contract Law and General Contract Law. The German Experience', in the 2005 issue of *Current Legal Problems* at pp 415 ff.

[77] A host of tort rules – e.g., class actions suits, capping of damages, availability of punitives – could fall into this category. For restrictions imposed on any of them would, in Europe, be seen as reflecting tort choices whereas in the United States many would regard them as giving a free hand to enterprises to place profit before social responsibility.

net provided by a more developed system of social security. Finally, we remind our readers of a similar attempt to deny the possibility of considering foreign trial models which differ from the party-operated adversarial model found in American, especially State, court rules of civil procedure. For here, too, attempts were made to link these rules to deeply rooted cultural differences, though we have already expressed our reservations about the validity of such assumptions.

That the foundations of such objections are already being laid can be seen by looking at the writings of some of the 'Americanists' mentioned at the beginning of this chapter. John Bolton for instance has argued[78] that

> In substance field after field – human rights, labor, health, the environment, political–military affairs and international organisations -- the Globalists have been advancing while Americanists have slept. Recent clashes in and around the United States Senate indicate that the Americanist part is awakened.

This is a statement noted for its breadth, where subjects are listed indicatively, not exclusively, and which go beyond the traditional public law/human rights discussions and touch upon all branches of the law which can, effectively, have an impact on American economic and commercial life. In our view, it thus lays the foundations for future generations of Americanists, invoking politico-economic arguments of self-interest to scupper borrowings, or other attempts to provide the degree of legal harmonisation which modern commerce seems to require.

Yet, in our view, in all these instances there is room for more than just a dialogical discussion of foreign solutions, which can help identify the true reasons why such transplantation may be impossible. For if the dialogical mode helps identify the *true*[79] reasons for the opposition to foreign ideas it may also help find ways of addressing them. In this context we remind our readers of the many examples of imitation, inspiration, or even tansplantation which have taken place between two seemingly very different environments.

e) The United States: what is the real problem?

Can we then, in the light of the above, try to identify further (and then isolate) the real 'bug' that causes the American legal mind to 'crash' when it comes to consider the desirability of foreign law? If we combine what we said above with the essentials of the American literature we have

---

[78] Op. cit. note 2 at 206 ff.

[79] For instance, opposition from the American Bar may be a more realistic reason for not accepting civil procedure reform than the linking of the rules to alleged cultural differences.

used, we re-state our view that at the 'technical' level the problem can be located in one main area of American constitutional law – judicial review. This means for starters excluding from our work – whether it is in favour or against the use of foreign law – all references to public international law, traditionally governed by its own rules going back to the *The Paquete Habana*-decision,[80] which made customary international law part of American law.[81]

Where *foreign law* is used (or could have been used) to influence the outcome of a case, the fears that dominate the thinking of those who oppose it seem to us to be two. First, could foreign law end up being treated as having the force of binding authority? Second, could this facilitate the courts' power to invalidate majority decisions at Federal or State level in the name of the US Constitution?

To the first question the answer (already given above) is 'no'; and no advocate of the comparative method has, to our knowledge, ever suggested otherwise (except in the area of public international law). This book has eschewed this possibility completely.

The second issue has a particularly American flavour to it since it is linked to the fear of increasing judicial discretion through 'interpretation' – which, in the eyes of the more 'conservatively' inclined, is 'bad enough' now and would get worse if the interpretation were 'bastardised' through the importation of foreign notions of decency, morality, or legality. We have addressed this question, so here we merely venture the guess that to the conservative Justices of the US Supreme Court this belief is consistent with the view that restricting the sources of legal ideas and the ultimate authority of constitutional interpretation is essential in order to maintain a

---

80 175 US 677 (1900). This also makes it easier to exclude from the debate other statements of Justice Scalia which, again, reflect his internal optics as not being relevant to the issue which has been the subject of this book. See, for instance, the following statement in *U.S. v Alvarez-Machain*, 504 US 655, 669–70: 'In the U.S. resort to self-help, even if a "shocking" violation of international law, was not our concern, as it did not violate any U.S. law (...).'

81 Though even here the move to restrict the application of customary international law is growing in the United States. For more details consult Bradley and Goldsmith, 'U.N. Human Rights Standards and U.S. Law: The Current Illegitimacy of International Human Rights Litigation' (1997) *Fordham Law Review* 66; Jack Goldsmith, 'Should International Human Rights Law Trump U.S. Domestic Law?', (2000) Vol 1 no 2 *Chicago Journal of International Law* 327 ff. More generally, L Goldsmith and Eric A. Posner, *The Limits of International Law* (2005). The American literature is growing in size and confidence, while non-American experts in public international law are becoming increasingly critical of current American thinking towards international law; see, among others, Philippe Sands, *Lawless World: America and Making and Breaking of Global Rules* (2005).

coherent body of law.[82] Such a focus on limited sources and a defined structure of legal hierarchy ensure, it is believed, coherence in constitutional interpretation. To put it in the words of Professor Harding,[83]

> *coherence and thus legitimacy* under this model are secured through structural constraints rather than rational argumentation or persuasive reasoning. In short, ensuring coherence through the limiting of sources and participants, rather than persuasion through dialogue, is at the heart of the US Supreme Court's approach to judicial review.[84]

The fact that the experience in Canada, South Africa, or Israel does not seem to support such fears is unlikely to influence die-hard opponents of the 'foreign' method.

The threat to coherence and certainty is not the only concern that those who oppose the use of foreign law have. Coupled with it is the fear that 'foreign' (one also encounters the use of the word 'European' with the same sense of mistrust) values might water down the indigenous ones. We have alluded to these fears in several parts of the text and notes so we need not return to them here. Yet, is it justified to speak of a 'Europeanisation' of American (or any other) law? Is this a side effect that might follow the open approach we favour?

Ten years after the introduction of the Canadian Charter of Rights and Freedoms, the former Canadian Chief Justice Brian Dickson published an article with a title that posed this very question but with the emphasis being placed on the impact which American law had on Canadian law. His piece was entitled 'Has the Charter Americanized the Canadian Judiciary?'[85] His answer was an unequivocal 'no'. Can anyone seriously argue that what did not happen in Canada and, come to that,

---

[82] In the interests of completeness and consistency one must, again, admit that the distinction between 'binding' and inspirational' use of foreign law which, we think, can in some cases provide a workable answer to the American dilemmas, is not workable for those who subscribe to the Scalia approach. For if foreign law is treated as binding law it is illegitimate because it was not made by American voters. And if it is not binding but simply law that may be considered for the purposes of filling gaps or inspiration, it is still illegitimate because it involved judicial discretion and judicial lawmaking, which the followers of the school equally dislike.

[83] 'Comparative Reasoning and Judicial Review' (2003) 28 *Yale J. Int.'l. L.* 409.

[84] We italicise these words because we feel that, though true, they are understated. For coherence, to the Scalia school, is secondary – and legitimacy comes first. This is not to deny that both are important. For coherence, in itself, tends to constrain judicial discretion. But legitimacy depends on derivation from legitimate sources, and for the 'right', the list of legitimate sources is rather short. Nondiscretionary derivation from decisions of voters is the primary key to legitimacy; coherence is good, but not the key to legitimacy. 'Coherence *and thus* legitimacy' seems to get it backwards.

[85] (1995) *U. B. C. Law Rev.*

other countries that have used foreign law, would happen in the United States? Would judges like Scalia or Posner ever end up being 'Europeanized' by an exposure to the ideas of their (foreign) equals? Or would State judges succumb to European-type rules without more? Only those who fear the persuasive force of honest argument can really oppose such proposals from the very outset.

It goes without saying that the above does not mean that one is advocating the adoption of a foreign solution (or concept) without considering its transplantability, which can only arise as a possibility if it has been *preceded* by an attempt to 'package' it in any way that makes it intelligible to the potential foreign user. Bench, bar, and academe could easily thrash these out between them. And this will often mean not only citing a rule but also testing its accuracy and utility through the purifying ordeal of adversarial debate, something which has thus far been avoided in American courts altogether either because the consideration of foreign law was rejected outright or, if considered, has been done at a cursory level, more often than not in the form of footnotes.

2. Prophesying the future

Notwithstanding our efforts to find a common ground, *de lege lata* our study has ended by suggesting a division between the practice of US courts and those of other countries. This concluding section of the book may thus call for a similar division. We start with the internationalists and then turn to the isolationists.

a) Shades of internationalism

The courts of all major systems reviewed in this book display, or so it seems to us, a growing interest in the developments of legal ideas and solutions by sister courts and, occasionally, by foreign academics. To be sure, the interest varies in intensity, from the serious study of the foreign solution to the modest (but growing) amateurish curiosity to learn what others are doing. Further, this curiosity is often concealed rather than openly displayed. Except for countries such as, for instance, Canada, South Africa, Israel, and America, judges tend to hide their academic sources; and in some systems (France, Italy) they are positively expected to do so. So the full extent of the influence of foreign law may, often, only be a matter of speculation.

Our study also shows that the open use of foreign law ranges from the mere citation of foreign information as supporting material to the genuine attempt to take advantage of foreign experience for the sake of achieving the best possible solution to the national problem. One or two English judgments, discussed earlier on, provide some excellent illustrations of how this can be done. In between, we find instances which are, from an academic point of view, just as interesting and important and these include the cases where foreign law was considered but then rejected as inappropriate to national conditions. Canada provides illustrations, though because of lack of space we did not go into them in detail. These cases can even be the most interesting if the rejection of the foreign idea (or text) is justified and/or reveals the wider reasons why the national system cannot adopt it. For us, what is paramount is the *dialogue* (because of the intellectually stimulating advantages it brings with it) rather than the harmonisation or, even less, the unification of the law.

Whatever form it may take, the interest in foreign law may be prompted by different motives.

At one end of the spectrum national constitutions may permit or encourage it. South Africa may be the best illustration of this category. This approach finds, these days, continued support not only in s 39(1)(c) of the 1996 Constitution but also in the 'duty to promote the values that underlie an open and democratic society based on human dignity, equality, and freedom'.[86] Beyond this constitutional authorisation, it seems that comparative law was also particularly attractive due to the hybrid character of the legal system, which is rooted not only in Roman–Dutch but also in the English Common law, though originally this manifested itself mainly in the domain of private law.

In other cases, the nature of the court or the law it generates – transnational – can stimulate such interest and make mutual exchanges of varying intensity necessary. The European Court of Justice and the European Court of Human Rights in Strasburg fall into this category subject to the caveats expressed earlier on. A similar example can be found in cases where a national court has to interpret a European directive and, in the absence of a ruling from the European Court of Justice, will naturally strive towards reaching a common meaning of the law. The comparative exercise undertaken by the English High Court in the blood contamination case offers such an illustration.

Finally, a few words about another factor prompting interest in foreign law. The bulk of national courts seem to be developing this internationalist spirit because of enhanced contacts between judges, courts, universities, and, of course, the part of the legal profession that finds itself at the cutting edge of the globalisation phenomenon and deals with an array of commercially flavoured issues which have strong international elements.[87] Incidentally, though we use the plural and refer

---

[86] Section 39(1)(a) of the 1996 Constitution.

[87] For ample details on all this see Anne-Marie Slaughter in chapter 10 of the *Ignatieff Essays*, op. cit. note 1.

to judges, the truth of the matter is that innovation and experiment[88] has come from a few individual judges endowed with a broad culture and the courage to take what is good from wherever it comes. This is a topic that one must examine more closely at some future date for, as so often said, the history of the world can often be seen as the history of organised minorities or even individuals appearing at the 'right' historical moment. Here, suffice it to say that, individually and collectively, these factors will go on enhancing this trend, and we see no signs of a reverse movement developing that would push courts back to a state of intellectual self-sufficiency. The US Supreme Court *may* be the one major exception and we thus discuss this separately in the next sub-section. The same may be true of some of other countries, though the reasons for their insular tendencies may be different. Here the reason for avoiding foreign law may not be *over*-confidence in oneself but *lack* of confidence flowing from the danger that such contacts might weaken the internal culture. But these are bold comparative statements that must be amplified on another occasion[89] giving specifics to back them up. But we can look at one point here.

Is the majority trend we detect threatening to local pride, local history, cultural diversity, and the individuality of each traditional legal system? This is a question that is more likely to cause concern to old, major, and established legal orders than to new ones, or small ones, keen to learn from the experience of others. It is also often coloured by the views an individual observer or judge may hold about the political process of integration that may be taking place in a particular part of the world, notably modern Europe. Though we understand the fears, we dismiss them as essentially unfounded for two reasons.

First, the intellectual exchanges we have reviewed are not leading to one system absorbing the other but, at best, attempts to encourage organic harmonisation (not unification!) and, at worst, result in a mere exchange of ideas.[90] Thus, Israel has not, in our view, suffered any serious loss in the richness of its own intellectual and religious past by modernising its law, especially in the domain of human rights, by borrowing from Canada or the United States. South Africa has been catapulted into international legal prominence and gained almost universal praise by selectively using foreign law to transform what was once a legally discredited regime, and has often done so by invoking its own local, native traditions (and, indeed, shown them to be in many

---

[88] And also the resistance to foreign law.

[89] See Sir B. S. Markesinis, 'Auto-suffisance nationale ou arrogance internationale? Le droit étranger et les notions contemporaines de justicedevant le juge américain et le juge français', Lecture at the Institut de France, March 2006.

[90] See Guy Canivet (op. cit. note 5), p 45.

respects more human than those of the 'advanced' world[91]). Canada has not been Americanised (at least in its law) as it has been in other parts of its daily life. Germany has achieved in law, especially in the area of human rights law, a feat equivalent to its well-known and much vaunted post-War economic miracle (made possible by its own determination and hard work as much as by American money), though the modernisation of its legal system may be partly due to constitutional and statutory reform and partly to judicial activity, which has been both bold and pragmatic.[92] Guy Canivet of the French Supreme Court is on record for saying that[93]

> comparative law indisputably widens the horizons of a jurist as comparative law multiplies the approaches [one can take towards a particular problem] and enlarges the interpretative options.

Even England has attained a truly dominant position in the domain of international legal services by modernising (in spite of much internal foot-dragging) a legal profession which carries with it English professionalism wherever it goes. Romantics and prophets of gloom are the only ones who fear this internationalisation which, in the British Isles, takes the threatening shape of Europe. Their cries are often couched in patriotic language, their texts replete with literary references which make for attractive reading. But they are unable to stop the new world which is *ante portas* and this makes their calls more strident. Worse, still, they seem unable to appreciate the fact that Anglo-American legal cultures are the prime beneficiaries of the globalisation of law because of the importance of their language and because international and financial services are so dominated by Anglo-American institutions.

Who are the agents of these changes which 50 or even 30 years ago would have been unthinkable? Indisputably, it is the wider globalisation of trade and, to a secondary extent, the moves towards European integration, both of which have stimulated these developments and contributed enormously to the revival of comparative law literature the world over.

---

91 A good example is the famous death penalty case (CCT/3/94 of 6 June 1995) where several Justices invoked the customary notion of 'ubuntu' (meaning the possibility and, indeed, *necessity* of a reconciliation between the individual committing a crime and his or her tribal community) to show that the death penalty violates the values underlying South African society.

92 On this see the very useful observations of Justice Brun-Otto Bryde of the German Constitutional Court in 'Constitutional Courts in Constitutional Transition', in F. Van Loon and K. Van Aeken (eds), *60 maal recht en 1 mall wijn, Liber Amicorum Prof. Dr. Jean Van Houtte* (1999), pp 235 ff.

93 'Le role du juge dans un monde en mutation. The Role of the Judiciary in Times of Change' in Marie-Claire Belleau and François Lacasse (eds), *Claire Hereux-Dubé à la Cour Suprême du Canada 1987–2002* (2003), pp 25, 41.

Additionally, the flowering of international human rights, the growing linkage of financial aid with improvements in their status, and the painfully slow dismantling of beliefs in race superiority, have all contributed to this willingness to consider good ideas whatever their origin.

As already stated, it is not only events but also actors who bring about change. In the forefront here we must place the judges, aided and abetted by practitioners engaged in international practice. It is painful to assert (but nonetheless true) that in this movement academics have, mostly, followed not led. One of us has elsewhere given some reasons why this has been the case.[94] Pre-occupation with the past, more euphemistically referred to as interest in legal history or, at the other end of the spectrum, a newly acquired interest in trendy ideas most of which have little or no bearing on the law in action, have all played a part in securing to modern academic comparatists the third and last place in this race. This is not to imply that there is no talent at large but to suggest (emphatically) that it has, on the whole, been wasted. Being too clever at times is a drawback; what is much more difficult to muster is common sense.

Those are reasons that may explain a 'slump' in comparative initiatives in England, especially in the 1970s and 1980s. Since one of us has discussed them at length elsewhere,[95] they need not be repeated here. But similar or other (more local) reasons may explain the 'decline' – relative or absolute – of comparative law in the academic circles of other countries. Recently, for instance, one French comparatist, who also happens to be running one of the country's well-known centres for comparative law, attributed the 'crisis' in his country to the 'ethnocentricity' of many of his compatriots, their neglect of foreign languages, and the bureaucratic hand of the State-run underlying structures. These are phenomena which some French observers – and not only lawyers – regard as seriously affecting the progress of French society as a whole. That they have come into the fore because of the recent rejection of the (draft) European Constitution by the French (and Dutch) voters does not mean that the causes are found only in France. Yet, however important these reasons may be, for us they recede into the background when compared with judicial efforts to rekindle interest in the study of foreign law. It has been an important thesis of this book to note this phenomenon and urge its study more deeply than we have been able to do in the space available to us.

Our overall conclusion thus is that the situation we describe in this book will, in the systems bracketed under this heading, strengthen and not weaken with the passage of time. We regard this almost as an

---

[94] B. S. Markesinis, op. cit. note 19.

[95] B. S. Markesinis, op. cit. note 34, especially chapters 1 and 2.

historical inevitability and thus do not feel the need to defend it further even though in Chapter 4 we went to great lengths to stress the *indisputable* difficulties and dangers that come with this exercise. So we call colleagues to realise the trend and to work with one another to shape it in a controlled and systematic process rather than leave it happen in the piecemeal way it so often does when in the hands of practitioners alone rather than in conjunction with theoreticians co-operating in pursuit of a common aim. In other words, what we call for is a mix or collaboration of the different parts of the legal profession for the benefit of all.

b) Introspection or arrogant self-sufficiency?

How does one predict the future of the American model? Though (as we have seen) the Justices of the US Supreme Court do not speak with one voice, and some recent cases such as *Lawrence v Texas*[96] and *Roper v Simmons*[97] suggest (thanks to shifting alliances) a greater willingness to look abroad, our overall impression is that the isolationists still have the *louder* voice even if their opponents have been scoring some good points. But the balance on the Supreme Court may also be about to change during the next four years as two posts fall vacant, in which case the present trends could be reversed. The question thus arises, how does one characterise this trend and, more intriguingly, how does one explain it?

The frame of one's mind is crucial to matters as varied as dealing with adversity (including physical illness) or reaching a conclusion on a legal conundrum. The way we speak reflects the way we think; and this, in turn, is shaped not only by tools and arguments of our craft but by other factors including our wider culture at a particular moment of its historical evolution. We tried to address this point, albeit too briefly, at the end of Chapter 4. Whether a court uses foreign law as part of its arguments in justifying its decision, as occasionally it must in all democratic societies, will also be determined by such factors, including judicial mentalities. 'Isolationism', 'introverted attitudes', 'self-sufficiency', or 'arrogance' may all lead an individual judge to a denial of even a dialogue with a foreign system; and it is hardly necessary to remind the reader that we are *not* talking here of treating foreign law as binding precedent, but only as a source of *inspiration* which might prompt local change or adaptation.

Such a state of mind can be justified, or should we say 'disguised', by resorting to legal or legalistic arguments. Or, alternatively, it can be explained by exploring openly the above-mentioned notions – isolationism,

---

[96] 123 S. Ct. 2472 (2003).

[97] 125 S. Ct. 1183 (2005).

self-sufficiency, personal culture, and arrogance – and deciding whether they can explain the use or non-use of foreign law in general and the comparative method in particular. So which of these justifications is mostly relevant to America at the present juncture of its political and legal history? More likely, we need a combination of legal and legalistic reasons if we are to understand the complex American scene (as, indeed, we said we do if we try to understand other national scenes such as the French). The *Ignatieff Essays* have certainly provided this multi-causal explanation of the current state of affairs in the United States.

The second of these justifications is both more unusual to assert and more difficult to prove. For, though linking politics and law may not be fortuitous, especially these days, combining it with an attempt to understand the particular judge's mentality may be both crucial and difficult to do as one tries to understand which way America is going. As this attempt to understand these developments progresses, one has the inescapable feeling that one is moving away from what we have called the 'technical' (i.e. legal/constitutional) level of explanation and moving more and more into the realm of pure politics. If this is true, we are getting into deep rough waters.

There is little doubt that American law, especially constitutional law, is much more self-sufficient than, say, South African law, which has a relatively new presence in this field. But, as already stated, this does not help explain Canada which in the field of human rights may, arguably, have been a (relative) novice at the time of the enactment of the Charter and needed guidance, but can no longer be treated as an 'importer' only of ideas. For the Canadian experience shows that what may have started as a need – looking at foreign law – has now become a habit, and one which not only is accepted locally but also lends to Canadian case law an international aura and appeal. The importation of Canadian ideas into Israel surely illustrates how extended the reach can be, both in terms of distance travelled and cultures bridged. The same can, probably, be said of the South African Constitutional Court which can no longer be dismissed as a 'novice'. And just as success breeds success, internationalism breeds more internationalism.

If American law is (or sees itself as) self-sufficient these days, the United States as a political power is neither self-sufficient nor insular. It is, instead, a country that is enjoying a *phase* of political, military, and technological dominance which is unparalleled in historical terms and which is giving it the means and the excuse to express views (often externalised through the use of force thinly disguised behind rules of law) about events happening all over the globe. The way this power is exercised cannot always exclude the accusation that it is contradictory and even based on double standards. We mentioned in cursory way some examples of this inconsistency.

This political dominance is not our concern except to the extent that it can be linked to the *current* unilateralism of the Supreme Court. In one sense, it should not since (as Professor Henkin has not tired in saying) the American 'neglect' towards international law has, alas, a long tradition so it predates the present phase of unrestricted power. Yet this American attitude may be going through a new phase of acute paroxysm and, to that extent, it may not be un-linked to the wider climate of our times. The danger of personal political ideologies 'tarnishing' legal reasoning must be obvious from what has already been hinted; and, we repeat, it applies to us as authors of this book (and to our explanations) as much as to everyone else. But then law is not (and cannot be) removed from the wider political debate that is taking place around it at a given political time and place; and we note with some satisfaction that our views as 'outsiders' find counterparts among notable 'insiders' such as the eminent contributors to the *Ignatieff Essays*. When outsiders and insiders can broadly agree in the identification of some problem areas, the beginnings of a remedy may start to emerge.

If we differ from the general tenor of these *Essays* it is in the emphasis we place on what we (as 'outsiders') can see (more?) clearly, namely, the reality or appearance of American arrogance. We thus tentatively suggest that there are signs of 'world-wide hegemony'[98] in the American air, and that this tendency can be found in all forms of human endeavour – including law. The activities of neo-conservative think tanks such as the American Enterprise Institute or the Heritage Foundation offer a clear sign of the kind of thinking that prevails among the current ruling elites. The ideas are reflected in beliefs about American law, which is as good for exportation as are American ideas of government and Wall Street's unbridled version of capitalism.[99] This is the very same mentality which allows America the right to treat itself as being exempt from the Geneva Conventions and even to begin to formulate its own rules about detention, interrogation, and even torture (which in America can appear under different terms) even though the official condemnation of such practices has been restated by President Bush. The importation of foreign ideas – 'fads and fashions' says more about what some think of them – is, however, another matter.

---

[98] Professor Ackerman used the words (and asked the question) as far back as 1997; see (1997) 83 *Virginia L. Rev*. 771 at 772.

[99] Professor Rubenfeld (op. cit. note 3) suggests a subtler reason for the diverging views between American and Europe based on their respective understandings of constitutionalism. Intriguing (and at times attractive) though the thesis is we feel it pays inadequate attention to the current feeling of power experienced by the dominant elites. How real and durable this is may be another matter.

To the extent that we attribute so much significance to American unilateralism we must of course admit that it is not a new phenomenon – as many scholars have pointed out.[100] Yet, the way we see things, traditional American unilateralism was based on a deep conviction held by many senior political figures that, on the whole, it provided the best way of keeping America *out of war*. By contrast, American unilateralism of today is seen as giving the country, indeed the President, the power to decide on the basis of the country's interests (as he sees them) the right to use force (or political pressure) in an unprecedented way on an international level. One suspects that while America can, by virtue of its technological and military superiority, afford to practice such a doctrine, it will. Yet one must also note that by doing so it may not be fully conscious of the dangers – psychological as well as materialistic – of an over-reach.

Overall, therefore, we feel comfortable about placing the aspect of the debate which concerns us within this wider context. And if one is right in seeing things from such an optic, it is *almost* tempting to argue that the country's respected (but old) Constitution is not only a reason for an introverted interpretation; it is also a helpful pretext for not opening the country up to new ideas. By that we mean that constitutional/political analysis of law (especially constitutional law and public international law) is thus increasingly tainted by political thinking, so that much of it appears to be no longer legal–political but purely political. In making this assertion we stress, again, that the views we are floating are not new,[101] though new may be the strength of conviction that accompanies their presentation.

Yet, in looking at foreign events as a possible factor of internal legal attitudes we are careful not to forget the fact that the current (sometimes desperate) attempt to get constitutional interpretation under control is more fuelled by the intensity of the conflict between the religious 'right' and the secular 'left' over cultural issues such as abortion, gay rights, and the like, than it is determined by a suspicion or dislike of European ideas (and their progenitors) which are often seen by the American right as

---

[100] See, for instance, Jed Rubenfeld's comments (op. cit. note 3) but also compare Dean Harold Koh's 'Paying "Decent Respect" to World Opinion on the Death Penalty', (2002) 35 *U. C. Davis L. Rev.* 1085, arguing that international law has always been part of the American legal tradition. In our respectful opinion, there is in the history of American law enough material to support both views (indeed, almost any view one would like to put forward) so, ultimately, the way American unilateralism is resolved rests on the power politics of a particular era.

[101] We see germs of this thinking in Professor McCrudden's 'A Common Law of Human Rights? Transnational Judicial Conversations on Constitutional Rights', 20 *Ox. J. of Legal Studies* 499, especially at 520 ff, and (even earlier) in Louis Henkin's 'The U.S. and International Human Rights' in *Justice for a Generation* (papers presented in London on 15–19 July 1985 at the meetings of the ABA, the Senate of the Inns of Court, and the Law Society of England and Wales), p 377.

'woolly' and 'leftist'. What we are suggesting, however, is that in this wider context the post-9/11 climate and the European (if not world) reaction to America's current foreign policy may be fuelling further the in-built reasons for the self-sufficient approach to legal (especially statutory) interpretation.

We note, second (and with regret), that (contemporary) Americans find the notion that they 'should be governed by ideas from foreign sources [un]congenial'[102] is spreading to private law even though here history suggests different attitudes in days gone by – and even though in this case one is not faced with the textual constitutional obstacles one encounters in the area of human rights. We think it would be too facile to explain this 'neglect' of foreign (and mainly) European ideas by a surfeit of local law though, undoubtedly, this is a factor.

Take for instance, Professor Mathias Reimann, a German scholar with a substantial contribution to both comparative law and comparative (German/American) legal history. If his learning is not in dispute, some of his opinions deserve to be questioned. Thus, he has entitled one of his articles 'Stepping out of the European *Shadow*: Why Comparative Law in the United States *Must* Develop its Own Agenda.'[103]

That America should and, indeed, already has its own agenda is both understandable and reasonable. Yet to refer to the European cultural influence on American law as having cast (or still casting) a *shadow* strikes one as an unfortunate choice of word since (a) it neglects the past intellectual debt that America has towards Europe, and (b) seriously underestimates the intellectual vitality of modern European law, especially that generated during the last 20 years. To put it differently, we doubt whether the likes of Oliver Wendell Holmes, Benjamin Cardozo, Roscoe Pound, Karl Llewellyn, Jack Dawson, Fritz Kessler, Arthur Schlesinger, John Fleming, Arthur von Mehren, John Langbein, Mary Ann Glendon, Hans Baade, James Gordley, Richard Buxbaum, or Thanassis Yiannopoulos would have expressed themselves in such terms. On the contrary, like Goethe, who refused to condemn the French even when they invaded his own country (on the grounds that he owed too much to French culture), these giants of our subject would have refused to condemn the European (and, more precisely, German legal culture) to which they owed so much of their legal formation. And we doubt even more whether those who are no longer with us, had they been alive today, would have dared to ignore the outpourings from such European

---

[102] Louis Henkin, 'Constitutionalism and Human Rights', in L. Henkin and A. J. Rosenthal (eds), *Constitutionalism and Rights: The Influence of the US Constitution Abroad* (1990).

[103] (1998) 46 *Am. J. Comp. L.* 637 (our emphasis).

courts as those sitting in Luxembourg and Strasburg. But then, those were the days when legal culture was not influenced by notions of political correctness.

Reimann, however, is not alone in this, even though his undoubted learning makes him atypical. Strangely, to us at least, other American lawyers of recent European vintage have also adopted this anti-European stance, expressing themselves in language that touches on the verbose.[104] Judge Guido Calabresi is one of the relative few who have voiced in one of his judgments the opposite view and, of course, has done so in his usual restrained and elegant manner;[105] but then in him we find that mixture of cultures and breadth of knowledge that tends to dispose one towards the universal rather than the particular – a combination of European style with American dynamism; the complete that comes from the universal, not the simple that often is found in the insular.

Yet even in America, where cultures mix, the trend may be going in the other direction. Thus, a public lawyer of some repute has not only echoed thoughts similar to those we express here (with concern) but also indicated the reason why foreign ideas may be becoming less relevant to contemporary Americans. Quite simply, he feels indigenous ones are the ones that nowadays matter most. The idea makes much sense, though Professor Bruce Ackermann (the scholar we have in mind) may have expressed the thought in too extreme a manner (and one which misrepresents his own wide reading) when he wrote in the mid-1990s another of these 'prophetic' texts which show that America was getting ready for its 'intellectual imperialism' as the end of cold war deprived it of its only world competitor and in the trauma of 9/11 may have simply found the latest reason for expressing this confidence more openly.[106] Ackerman thus wrote:

> America is a world power, but does it have the strength to understand itself? Is it content, even now, to remain an intellectual colony, borrowing

[104] See, e.g., N. Demleiter, 'Challenge, Opportunity and Risk: An Era of Change in Comparative Law' (1998) 46 *The Amer. J. Comp. L.* 647 at 653: 'Colonialism and Social Darwinism were the primary contributors to the ethnocentric illusion of the superiority of (...) Western law. (...) Today, the presumption seems to be that legal systems (...) jostle with one another in a market place of possibilities.' Are we really talking of an 'illusion' of (intellectual) superiority of the European systems or a very actual reality? And are these systems not the progenitors of the American and Canadian systems (and still influence the latter)? And which systems are 'jostling' for the role of the 'inspirer' beyond the European, Canadian, and (contemporary) South African constitutional models (the latter precisely because it has proved itself so open to learning from the others)? This low regard for European ideas is also evident from the wording adopted by Professor Fletcher in his article 'Constitutional Identity', (1993) 14 *Cardozo L. Rev.* 737 ff.

[105] *U.S. v Then*, 56 Fed. Rep. (3rd) 464, 469 (1995).

[106] *We The People: Foundations* (1991), p 3.

> European categories, to decode the meaning of national identity? (...) To discover the Constitution, we must approach it without assistance of guides imported from another time and place. Neither Aristotle nor Cicero, Montesquieu nor Locke, Harrington nor Hume, Kant nor Weber will provide the key. Americans have borrowed much from such thinkers, but they have also built a genuinely distinctive pattern of constitutional thought and practice.

Such statements may, in some respects, sit uncomfortably with other writings by the same author who is known not only for his liberal views but also his impressive awareness of what other systems are doing in his own field of law.[107] They also seem to be unconvincing in a subject – constitutional law – where basic ideas such as justice, equity, equality, and liberty are not only the lawyer's daily tools but also tools deeply fashioned by the classics Ackerman seems to be asking his young (new?) readers not to bother to read. To our minds, the analysis of the different types of justice has thus not been bettered since Aristotle wrote his *Nichomachean Ethics*; and it will be a shame if new scholars, with the apparent blessing of their teachers, no longer feel the need to read such works. This is not about technicalities of Roman law but about the foundations of our legal culture.

Yet in this book we are not concerned in reconciling real or apparent contradictions in the published views of certain serious contemporary scholars such as Ackerman (nor, indeed, attempting to belittle the autochthonous contribution of the American legal and philosophical mind) but merely trying to detect and describe an emerging trend; and we are trying to do this by looking at it from as many angles as we can. And let us face up to it – as outsiders we may at times detect things in the American scene that internal commentators either take for granted or have become insensitised to.

So this, really, is our main concluding point. A system that wishes to inspire and influence others – indeed, even export its legal ideas (as many American academics and judges[108] openly say they do) – cannot do this in a *sustained* manner (however good these ideas may be) if it simultaneously expresses its newly found confidence in a manner which would strike potential 'importers' as bordering on the excessive.

Indeed, one might call this trend not merely excessive, but an *historically unprecedented arrogance* given that, in their heyday, neither the English jurists (nor, before them, the Romans) were so closed to

---

[107] See, for instance, 'The Rise of World Constitutionalism' (1997) 83 *Virginia L. Rev.* 771 ff.

[108] E.g., Sandra Day O'Connor, Keynote Address in Proceedings of the 96th *Annual Meeting of the American Society of International Law*, pp 348 ff.

foreign ideas when at the peak of their own power. To be sure, when making such comparisons one must remember that in both of these worldly and cultural 'empires' the perceived sources of law were different; and neither faced the kind of problems (and institutional strictures) which in the United States the founding document seems to generate.[109] But law and its interpretation is not entirely dependant on rules and structures. Imagination and confidence (or lack of it) can play a part in the shaping of the national or judicial mentality, especially in times of transition and change. And the Victorians, much more than the contemporary English, were a confident lot, riding on the crest of the industrial revolution and the belief that this made everything possible. They were thus willing not just to read foreign legal literature but also to say how much they admired the Germans, while the Roman debt to Greek thought was just as willingly acknowledged in public by Roman thinkers of the calibre of Cicero or, later, the Emperor Marcus Aurelius who wrote his *Meditations* in Greek. We find nothing strange in this since we believe that power, well entrenched and not ephemeral, can inspire the kind of confidence that tolerates, if not actively welcomes, new ideas, comparative discussion, and competition.[110] Yet this is not the kind of *confidence* that one encounters in the United States today. On the contrary, in a country constantly advocating the merits of free trade, we find the best example of protectionism in the realm of indigenous ideas through attempts to exclude in a blanket manner any active consideration of alternatives. Invoking the US Constitution when both its texts (and its Founding Fathers) are silent is unconvincing. Unconvincing it is and – to us at least – unrealistic to believe that if reform is to come it will come only through changing the Federal Constitution or State legislation. For would the States have acted on their own if there had not been *Brown v Board of Education*?[111] And has not the Constitution endured over its long life many silent or obscured revolutions?

Now we do not think it involves a great logical leap to argue that American academics and judges who think in this (introverted) way may, in some respects, be in tune with the political realities which have gripped the United States in the post-9/11 era. For this terrible date inaugurated a

---

[109] On this see the valid points of Professors Frederick Schauer and Andrew Moravcsik in chapters 2 and 6 of the *Ignatieff Essays* (op. cit. note 1) and, more generally, Professor Rubnefeld's views (op. cit. note 3).

[110] See Brian Simpson, 'Innovation in the Nineteenth Century Contract Law' (1975) 91 LQR 247 ff. Likewise C. H. S. Fifoot, *Judge and Jurist in the Reign of Victoria* (1959) passim. The theme of openness coming with confidence is explored in a wider context by the late Lord Annan, 'The Victorian Intellectual Aristocracy' in J. H. Plumb (ed), *Studies in Social History: A Tribute to G. M. Trevelyan* (1955), chapter 8.

[111] 347 U.S. 483 (1954), overruling *Plessy v Ferguson*, 163 U.S. 537 (1896).

new age in geopolitical strategy and military thinking. It has also set in motion the passing of a variety of statutes and regulations and the introduction of practices that have the laudable aim of protecting us against the scourge of terrorism – but also have the potential of being abused to intrude into domains not really related to this threat. Last but not least, through fear and other reasons these events have led scholars, even of a liberal predisposition, to come close to turning a blind eye to horrible practices such as torture,[112] the maintenance of unacceptable prison camps, and the waging of pre-emptive wars which the (few?) remaining adherents of classical international law may find difficult to comprehend. Ultimately, all this is possible since the ruling classes believe that America's technological might enables it to go alone on the world scene – be it in matters of war, the environment, and now, apparently, even justice. However, much American liberal thinkers may disagree with the conservative philosophies of the current ruling elites, the fact is that they do not seem – as yet – to have found a well-articulated voice on most of the matters discussed in this book.[113] We say that because we note that numerically judicial coalitions between left and moderate right may, in fact, be denting the conservative agenda. And the same judges, if to be measured by their writings (admittedly brief and often conclusionary in tone), seem closer to the view here presented than one might think. And yet, it is the right's position that comes across more articulated and more forcefully argued and may, with the help of some well-targeted judicial appointments, prevail in the foreseeable future. This is what we are singling out for discussion, for this is what we see happening in the law. And it is to this debate that this book (and the lecture on which it is based) aims to make a modest contribution.

Now, this new American thought (in politics often referred to as 'neo-conservatism') may well be the path to the future. Certainly, in its main characteristics it draws on features of American history, conservatism, and messianism which do not have parallels in Europe and thus make the country potentially less receptive to foreign ideas in general or – nowadays – European ideas in particular. The more an outsider familiarises himself with contemporary American literature (political as well as legal) the more he discovers glaring differences which are asserted by the American establishment in complete disregard to the reactions of this country's long-standing allies. But a confidence so blatantly based on power can evaporate when (rather than if) the power starts showing the signs of strain. Of course, it could be argued with some justification that

---

[112] For a collection of essays on this topic see Sanford Levinson (ed), *Torture. A Collection* (2004).

[113] Justice Scalia brings this point out clearly (and, we think, convincingly) in his article 'Originalism: The Lesser Evil', (1989) 57 *Cincinnati L. Rev.* 849, especially at 855 ff.

the writers of this piece represent – if not the 'old Europe' – the thinking of the world of yesterday (much as they proclaim their interest in the study of modern law and not the study of the law of past generations), and that their fears can be ignored even if their overall analysis is, if not accurate, at least plausible. In this case, the autochthonous ideas of contemporary America are sufficient (as undoubtedly they are often interesting and, occasionally, even inspiring) in that they do not need any cross-fertilisation from abroad. But in our view the case for such propositions has not yet been made out; and until it is, we at least feel much admiration for what our Canadian, South African, and, to a lesser extent, English, and German judges are doing – and hope that the growing globalisation of our universe will encourage them to re-double their efforts. Time, alone, will show how long we will have to wait before we see America enter the world of tolerance and real freedom which so many of its thinkers and citizens have done so much to create.

Constitutional Comparativism in South Africa

A Response to Sir Basil Markesinis and Dr Jörg Fedtke

Laurie W. H. Ackermann[1]

Ulpian's search for a philosophy underpinning the law is not surprising. Around AD 200 intellectuals were becoming dissatisfied with the view that whatever is traditional or customary in a society is automatically right. They were looking in both politics and religion for something more universal, rational, and philosophical (...) [but] (...) [p]hilosophically minded lawyers are not members of this or that school of philosophy. It is a mistake to attribute to a lawyer a system of philosophy rather than a set of values.

Tony Honoré[2]

The mere formulation of a problem is often far more essential than its solution, which may be merely a matter of mathematical or experimental skill. To raise new questions, new possibilities, to regard old problems from a new angle requires creative imagination and marks real advance in science.

Albert Einstein[3]

1. Disclaimer

This response to the book (the 'book') by Sir Basil Markesinis and Dr Jörg Fedtke (the 'authors') is written exclusively from the South African perspective. In the *Gay and Lesbian v Minister of Justice* case[4] the South African Constitutional Court (the 'Constitutional Court') declared the Common law offence of sodomy, as well as a number of

---

[1] SC; BA LLB LLD (hc) Stellenbosch University; MA (Oxon); Hon. Fellow Worcester College (Oxford), Emeritus Justice of the South African Constitutional Court.

[2] *Ulpian: Pioneer of Human Rights* (2nd edn, Oxford University Press 2002), pp 78, 80.

[3] A. Einstein and L. Infeld, *The Evolution of Physics* (Simon and Schuster, New York 1938), p 95, as quoted on a memorial pillar at the Nobel Museum, Stockholm.

[4] *National Coalition for Gay and Lesbian Equality v Minister of Justice and Others*, 1999 (1) SA 6 (CC); 1998 (12) BCLR 1517 (CC), para 106.

statutory provisions criminalising sexual conduct between adult males, to be constitutionally invalid. In argument extensive reference was made to comparative law in, amongst others, the United Kingdom, Ireland, Canada, Australia, New Zealand, Germany, and the European Union, and to the judgments of the United States Supreme Court (the 'US Supreme Court') in *Bowers v Hardwick* 478 US 186 (1986) and *Romer v Evans* 134 L Ed 2d 855 (1996). Reference was also made to the sustained criticism of *Bowers v Hardwick* in the United States. Despite being invited to do so, the Constitutional Court declined,[5] properly so, to express itself on such criticism or the current standing of *Bowers v Harwick* in the United States in the light of *Romer v Evans*.

I shall similarly, in this response, limit myself strictly to the validity and importance of comparative law for the interpretation and enforcement of the South African Constitution. I imply nothing for other jurisdictions. Those who look for something new out of Africa, must draw their own inferences.

In discussing comparative law in the South African context I shall limit myself (in the main) to the comparative discipline as applied to post-1994 constitutional and public law. I do not thereby distance myself from the comparative approach to private law; far from it. I merely indicate the (necessary) logistical limits of my contribution.[6] For similar reasons I shall focus on fundamental rights jurisprudence, without implying that a comparative approach is unsuitable for other areas of constitutional or public law. If I am to write honestly on the judge as comparative lawyer I shall, I fear, at times have to intrude my own personal experience. I write as one who has spent his legal life primarily[7] as an advocate (exclusive trial and appellate lawyer) and a judge.

2. Context

A proper understanding of the justification for and the importance and significance of a comparative jurisprudential approach to the interpretation and application of both the South African 1994 Interim Constitution (the 'Interim Constitution') and the 1996 Constitution ('the Constitution'), the latter being *preordained* and *controlled by* the former,

---

[5] *National Coalition for Gay and Lesbian Equality v Minister of Justice and Others*, 1999 (1) SA 6 (CC); 1998 (12) BCLR 1517 (CC), paras 53–6.

[6] For the influence of comparative methodology in South African private law, reference can be made, by way of example, to the following recent conttributions: D. Visser, 'Cultural Forces in the Making of Mixed Legal Systems', in [2003] 78 *Tulane L. R.* 41 ff and J. E. du Plessis, 'Common Law Influences on the Law of Contract and Unjustified Enrichment in Some Mixed Jurisdictions' [2003] 78 *Tulane* 219 ff.

[7] From 1987 to 1992 I was the inaugurating incumbent of the Harry Oppenheimer Chair in Human Rights Law at Stellenbosch University.

requires a fine understanding of the South African context. It is impossible, in a contribution such as this, to furnish such context satisfactorily, and in the brief sketch that follows I am guilty both of selectivity and over-simplification. For a fuller exposition, which explains, *inter alia*, what the concepts 'preordained' and 'controlled by' mean, and also describes the unique task of the Constitutional Court (imposed by the Interim Constitution) to 'certify' the validity of – and thereby give operative force to – the 1996 Constitution by evaluating it against, *inter alia*, the 34 so-called Constitutional Principles in the Interim Constitution (which constituted the key to unlocking the impasse in the constitutional negotiations), reference can be made to my published lectures 'The Legal Nature of the South African Constitutional Revolution'.[8] The legal revolution brought about by the above two Constitutions, although a substantive revolution, was not – in the Kelsen sense – a procedural one.[9] One of the consequences is that all law, common and statutory, in existence immediately prior to the Interim Constitution coming into force, continued with full force and effect thereafter, subject to its consistency with the Interim and later the 1996 Constitution.[10]

The South African Common law is not Anglo-Saxon but Roman–Dutch, introduced in 1652 by the Dutch East Indian Company's settlement in the Cape. The received Roman–Dutch law was the Common law of Holland prior to the latter's codification in the first decade of the nineteenth century. Neither the Cape, nor the united South Africa thereafter, codified its Common law in the Continental manner, and the Roman–Dutch Common law continued to be developed in South Africa through the judgments of the courts. Since 1806 English law, more particularly in the fields of company law, evidence and criminal procedure, has exercised considerable influence. But when difficult questions of substantive criminal law (which has remained Roman–Dutch) and private law arise that are not closely covered by South African precedent, regard is still had to the pre-codification Dutch and other European commentaries on Justinian's Digest, and even – where necessary – to the Digest itself.

The system of South African's Common law is currently regarded as mixed, with its tap-root in the deep soil of the Roman–Dutch law, and its side roots nourished by the Anglo-Saxon system. This enables us to benefit from the best of both worlds. The principled, deductive analysis

---

8 Published in [2004] *New Zealand Law Review* 633.

9 Ibid, p 646.

10 Section 229 of the Interim Constitution and item 2(1) of Schedule 6 to the 1996 Constitution.

of the Continent can be tested against the inductive, empirical, case-by-case methodology of the Anglo-Saxon system.

On the other hand, the constitutional law of South Africa, after unification in 1910, was closely modeled on that of the British Westminster system. The legislator was omni-competent and supreme; no supreme law (by way, for example, of an entrenched Bill of Rights) existed against which the validity of parliamentary legislation could be tested in the courts.[11] There was of course one serious flaw in the model. Even after the suffrage was extended to women, the vast (black) majority of the population remained unenfranchised. Before 1994 South Africa could be described as a white racial oligarchy in which whites enjoyed a form of parliamentary democracy. Even the civil rights of whites became seriously attenuated by the passing of draconian security legislation and the promulgation of successive states of emergency in the 1980s.

The judge's task of 'finding', 'developing', 'making'[12] the Common law in a mixed system of necessity requires a comparative legal approach. It was in fact the approach of the pre-codification Roman–Dutch academic writers[13] themselves. For well over a century our courts have, with a minimum of fuss – and mostly without specific mention that they were doing so – adopted a comparative law approach. For the most part[14] it has been done with care and discretion, particularly since 1910.

---

[11] It is interesting to note that the 1854 Constitution of the Orange Free State (one of the independent Boer states that was annexed by Britain in consequence of the Anglo-Boer War of 1899–1902 and subsequently became one of the four Provinces of the Union of South Africa in 1910) was significantly influenced by the United States Constitution. It was written, onerous procedures were prescribed for its amendment, the legislature was not supreme, certain rights – including equality before the law – were entrenched, and the power of judicial review accepted as a feature of the Constitution, following the US Supreme Court judgment in *Marbury v Madison*, 5 U.S. (1 Cranch) 137 (1803). 'This right, however, was of little assistance to Messrs. Cassim and Solomon in their dispute with the state [*Cassim and Solomon v S* (1892) 9 Cape L. J. 58], as judicial review was to Mr Dred Scott [in *Dred Scott v Sandford*, 60 U.S. (19 How.) 393 (1857)] some thirty-five years earlier on the other side of the Atlantic.' See L. W. H. Ackermann, 'Constitutional Protection of Human Rights: Judicial Review' [1989] 21 *Columbia Human Rights L. R.* 59, 61. For constitutional developments in South Africa prior to 1910 see also L. M. Thompson, 'Constitutionalism in the South African Republics', in 1954 *Butterworths South African Law Review* 49; Hahlo and Kahn, *South Africa: The Development of its Laws and Constitution* (Stevens and Sons/London and Juta/Cape Town 1960); and John Dugard, *Human Rights and the South African Legal Order* (Princeton University Press, Princeton, NJ 1978), pp 14–25.

[12] It is, for present purposes, unnecessary to debate the precise jurisprudential nature of the judicial function involved.

[13] Often referred to as 'the old authorities' (in Afrikaans: 'die ou skrywers').

[14] An exception to this was the period of several decades after 1815 when judges, from England or trained mainly in English law, would, at the drop of a hat, introduce English legal principles without any real attempt to satisfy themselves that they were compatible with the Roman–Dutch law.

A striking example of wholly appropriate cross-pollination has been the introduction from English law of the principles of repudiation (anticipatory breach) in the law of contract, a form of contractual breach unknown in Roman–Dutch law.[15] It has been expressed thus:

> [Repudiation as a species of breach of contract] is essential for the proper regulation of contractual relationships, and does not conflict with the fundamental principles of our law.[16]

The South African Supreme Court of Appeal[17] has since 1910 consistently sought guidance from the judgments of the higher courts and from academic writers in, amongst others, the United Kingdom and the rest of the Commonwealth, the United States of America, the Netherlands, and Germany; quite apart from relying on the 'old authorities' in Holland and the rest of Western Europe where reception of the Roman Law had taken place.

A unique contribution to analytical and comparative law methodology in South Africa was made by that colossus, Professor J.C. de Wet (1912–90). His genius encompassed the South African law of contract, criminal law, water law, and legal history, and his writings[18] exerted a remarkable influence on the jurisprudence of the Supreme Court of Appeal since 1950. There has never been an impediment to dialogue between the courts and living academics, although courts have not been consistently scrupulous in acknowledging the sources of their inspiration. JC (as he was affectionately known to all) 'has done more than anybody else in the course of the [twentieth] century to mould and invigorate the South African usus modernus of Roman-Dutch law',[19] and

---

[15] Reinhard Zimmermann, *The Law of Obligations: Roman Foundations of the Civilian Tradition* (Juta and Co. Ltd Cape Town 1990), note 228, p 816 and J. C. de Wet and A. H. van Wyk, *Die Suid-Afrikaanse Kontraktereg en Handelsreg* (4th edn, Butterworths, Durban 1978), Professor J. C. de Wet being responsible for s 1 (Law of Contract).

[16] J. C. de Wet, op. cit. note 15 at p 153 (my translation from the Afrikaans).

[17] From 1910 until 1994 the highest court in South Africa (known as the 'Appellate Division') and since 1994 the highest court in non-constitutional matters (now known as the 'Supreme Court of Appeal').

[18] His main writings include his work on the law of contract (op. cit. note 15), first published in 1947, his revolutionary and liberalising work on Criminal Law, *Die Suid-Afrikaanse Strafreg*, jointly authored – as far as specific offences are concerned – with H. L. Swanepoel (first published by Butterworths, Durban 1949), and in regard to legal history, *Die Ou Skrywers in Perspektief* (The Old Writers in Perspective) (Butterworths, Durban 1988).

[19] Reinhard Zimmermann in his dedication to Professor de Wet of 'Stipulatio Poena' in (1987) 104 *South African Law Journal* (*SALJ*) 399. See also the fuller appreciation by Zimmermann and Hugo, 'Fortschritte der Südafrikanischen Rechtswissenschaft im 20 Jahrhundert: Der Beitrag von J. C. de Wet (1912–90)', (1992) 60 *Tijdschrift voor Rechtsgeschiedenis* (*The Legal History Journal*), 157.

was 'the true pioneer of a critical comparative approach in South Africa'.[20] In the field of criminal law, in particular, he extrapolated, for the benefit of South African law, important new and humane developments in German law. He would not dream of lecturing or writing in a manner other than comparatively, and in his books he refers not only to the Roman–Dutch 'old authorities', but to modern law in the United Kingdom, the Netherlands, Switzerland, and Germany. Those of us who were fortunate to study under him did not at the time realise we were experiencing something unique; we naively thought (at least I did initially) that this was the way every good jurist taught criminal law and contract. But the comparative approach was imbibed by many of us.

I set out this comparative law background to counteract the possible misconception that the comparative law approach of the Constitutional Court has been due, in the main, to the provisions in the two Constitutions, alluded to in the main article, referring to the discretionary use of foreign law. I have not the slightest doubt that, because of the comparative law ethos in South Africa, the Court would have placed the same reliance on foreign law even had there been no such provision in the Constitutions. This emerges clearly from the judgment in *S v Makwanyane and Another* (the second judgment of the Constitutional Court and the one in which the death penalty was declared invalid)[21] where Chaskalson P,[22] delivering the judgment of the Court and after referring generally to the value of international and foreign authorities comments that '[f]or *this reason alone* they require our attention' and then observes that '[t]hey *may* also have to be considered because of their relevance to section 35(1) of the [Interim] Constitution.' (Emphasis supplied.)

For the same historical, normative, and analytical reasons it was natural, both in constitutional creation and adjudication, to turn for guidance also to Germany. In *Du Plessis v De Klerk*[23] the Court held, in a majority judgment, that the Interim Constitution's Bill of Rights applied

---

20 Barend van Niekerk in his brilliant and insightful 'J. C Noster: A Review and a Tribute to Professor J. C. De Wet' (1980) 97 *SALJ* 183, 187.

21 1995 (3) SA 391 (CC); 1995 (6) BCLR 665 (CC), para 34.

22 At the time the head of the Constitutional Court was designated 'President' and the head of the Supreme Court of Appeal was the Chief Justice. Subsequently, the position of Chief Justice was transferred to the head of the Constitutional Court. A corresponding transfer occurred with regard to the Deputy Chief Justice and the Deputy President of the Constitutional Court.

23 *Du Plessis and Others v De Klerk and* Another, 1996 (3) SA 850 (CC); 1996 (5) BCLR 658 (CC), referred to in the book.

vertically only. Kriegler J wrote for the minority. In a concurring majority judgment the following was said:[24]

> It is certainly true that our interim Constitution is textually unique and that the historical circumstances in which constitutions are adopted are never identical. In certain cases these circumstances may, for the most part, only differ in degree. Many constitutions, particularly those which come in the wake of rapid and extensive political and social change, are reactive in nature and often reflect in their provisions a response to particular histories and political and social ills.
>
> Kriegler J has, in his judgment, referred eloquently to the duration, acceleration and gravity of the human rights denials and abuses to which the interim Constitution is a response and which it seeks, amongst other things, to redress. Without wishing to over-simplify the nature and extent of these abuses and denials it is, I think, fair to say that they related in general to the core values of dignity, freedom and equality. There are other constitutions which have been a response to tragic histories or episodes in the national histories of particular countries during which gross abuses of human rights have occurred.
>
> I do believe that the German Basic Law (GBL) was conceived in dire circumstances bearing sufficient resemblance to our own to make critical study and cautious application of its lessons to our situation and Constitution warranted. The GBL was no less powerful a response to totalitarianism, the degradation of human dignity and the denial of freedom and equality than our Constitution. Few things make this clearer than Art 1(1) of the GBL,[2] particularly when it is borne in mind that the principles laid down in Art 1 are entrenched against amendment of any kind by Art 79(3).[3] (Emphasis supplied.)

3. The consideration of foreign constitutional law by South African courts

(a) Before considering the arguments in favour of such consideration it must be pointed out that the Constitutional Court has rejected any attempt to determine or rely on so-called original intent. The stage was

---

[24] Ibid, paras 90–2. Note 1 to the text has been omitted but notes 2 and 3 read:

> [2] 'The dignity of man is inviolable. To respect and protect it shall be the duty of all public authority.' (For English renderings of provisions of the GBL the official translation of June 1994 issued by the Press and Information Office of the Federal Government has been used.)
>
> [3] It is generally recognised that Art 1 constitutes an unmistakable rejection of totalitarianism and the ideology of national socialism ('you are nothing, your nation is everything'). See, for example, von Münch/Kunig *Grundgesetz-Kommentar* Band 1 (1992) 4 Aufl Art 1 Rn 6.

set in its first judgment, *S v Zuma and Others*, where Kentridge AJ said the following:[25]

> I am well aware of the fallacy of supposing that general language must have a single 'objective' meaning. Nor is it easy to avoid the influence of one's personal intellectual and moral preconceptions. But it cannot be too strongly stressed that the Constitution does not mean whatever we might wish it to mean.
>
> We must heed Lord Wilberforce's reminder that even a constitution is a legal instrument, the language of which must be respected. If the language used by the lawgiver is ignored in favour of a general resort to 'values' the result is not interpretation but divination. (...) I would say that a constitution 'embodying fundamental rights should *as far as its language permits* be given a broad construction'.

The Court has consistently adopted a purposive (teleological) approach to the interpretation of the Constitution and has approved[26] the following passage in the Canadian Supreme Court case of *R v Big M Drug Mart Ltd*:[27]

> The meaning of a right or freedom guaranteed by the Charter was to be ascertained by an analysis of the *purpose* of such a guarantee; it was to be understood, in other words, in the light of the interests it was meant to protect.
>
> In my view this analysis is to be undertaken, and the purpose of the right or freedom in question is to be sought, by reference to the character and larger objects of the Charter itself, to the language chose to articulate the specific right or freedom, to the historical origins of the concepts enshrined, and where applicable, to the purpose of the other specific rights and freedoms with which it is associated within the text of the Charter. The interpretation should be (...) a generous rather than a legalistic one, aimed at fulfilling the purpose of the guarantee and securing for individuals the full benefit of the Charter's protection.

In order to ascertain this purpose it is permissible to have regard to the background of the Constitutions and various materials in relation thereto,[28] but not to the subjective intentions or understandings of the persons who took part in the negotiations or in the enactment of the Constitution. In *S v Makwanyane*, the Court quoted with approval[29]

---

25 1995 (2) SA 642 (CC); 1995 (4) BCLR 401 (SA), paras 17–18 (emphasis original).

26 Ibid, para 15 and *S v Makwanyane and Another* (op. cit. note 21), para 9.

27 (1985) 18 DLR (4th) 321 at 395–6.

28 See *S v Makwanyane* (op. cit. note 21), paras 12–20.

29 Ibid, para 18.

the following passage from a Canadian Supreme Court judgment:[30]

> (...) the Charter is not the product of a few individual public servants, however distinguished, but of a multiplicity of individuals who played major roles in the negotiating, drafting and adoption of the Charter. How can one say with any confidence that within this enormous multiplicity of actors (...) the comments of a few federal civil servants can in any way be determinative,

and then itself observed as follows:[31]

> Our Constitution is also the product of a multiplicity of persons, some of whom took part in the negotiations, and others who as members of Parliament[32] enacted the final draft. The same caution is called for in respect of the comments of individual actors in the process, no matter how prominent a role they might have played.

The determination of a single collective original intention on the part of persons enacting a constitution is, in my view, a legal fiction and a dangerous one at that. A fiction, because the exercise is an impossible one. Logically, the moment for determining such intention is when the constitution is passed; not before and not after. In relation to constitutional enactment, memory is particularly deceptive, influenced (however genuine the recollection) by sanguine hopes of the period before enactment and the political disputes after enactment. But even if, hypothetically, it were possible to determine the true intention of each enactor at the time of enactment, this would be insufficient to rescue the fiction. It is simply impossible that all consenting minds would have a coherently similar understanding, particularly of those provisions that give rise to subsequent dispute. A dangerous fiction, because it permits (or tempts) subsequent interpreters of the constitution to inject their own subjective understanding of its meaning.

When a constitution, finally enacted, goes out into the world it acquires – in a manner of speaking – a meaning which results from a dialogue which the interpreter has with the constitutional text, taking into account the interpretative aids referred to above. There must be few judges who have not had this experience with the texts of their own judgments, once delivered. No matter how painstaking the efforts of judges may be to express as accurately as possible their meaning in judgments, such

---

[30] *Reference re s 94(2) of the Motor Vehicle Act (British Columbia)*, (1985) 18 CCR 30 at 49.

[31] Op. cit. note 29.

[32] It must be remembered that in *Makwanyane*'s case, it was the Interim Constitution that was being scrutinised. The Interim Constitution was enacted by the old pre-April 1994 Parliament, whereas the 1996 Constitution was enacted by the Constitutional Assembly provided for by and elected under the provisions of the Interim Constitution.

judgments are not understood by the reader in exactly the same manner as the author intended. One experiences this quite dramatically, and at first hand, on a collegiate court such as the Constitutional Court, where all 11 Justices sit *en banc* in all cases. Even where there is agreement on the outcome of a case and on the reasoning leading to such conclusion, careful attention has still to be given to the wording of the judgment in order to achieve agreement between colleagues as to its 'exact' meaning. Even when this has been achieved, subsequent disagreements still occur as to what individual members of the Court understood the judgment to mean at the time.

Moreover, in the case of a constitution, which is designed to last for (at least) a very substantial period of time, the meaning of values, rights, and norms cannot be fossilised in the form they may have been at the time of enactment. This is particularly so in the case of a Bill of Rights, no matter how all-embracing, and how extensive the formulation of these rights might be. Any attempt at such petrification would amount to an exclusion of the subsequent flow of the history of philosophy. Foundational constitutional concepts such as dignity, equality, and freedom are not self-defining. Even after all relevant historical materials and other legitimate aids to interpretation have been properly consulted and exhausted, there are innumerable questions which can still arise in the interpretation and application of these concepts, which cannot be solved (or fully or satisfactorily solved) by looking backwards.

Mahomed AJA (as he then was) was surely right when, delivering the judgment of the post-independence Namibian Supreme Court,[33] he said the following:

> The question as to whether a particular form of punishment authorised by the law can properly be said to be inhuman or degrading involves the exercise of a value judgment by the Court (...) which requires objectively to be articulated and identified, regard being had to contemporary norms, aspirations, expectations and sensitivities of the Namibian people as expressed in its national institutions and its Constitution, and further having regard to the merging consensus of values in the civilised international community (of which Namibia is a part) which Namibians share. It is a continually evolving dynamic. What may have been acceptable as a just form of punishment some decades ago, may appear to be manifestly inhuman or degrading today. Yesterday's orthodoxy might appear to be today's heresy.

How unfortunate it would be if one's understanding of dignity, equality, and freedom were locked into John Locke's views on these matters

33 *Ex Parte Attorney-General, Namibia: In re Corporal Punishment by Organs of State*, 1991 (3) SA 76 (NmS) 86 H-I and compare the judgment of the Constitutional Court in *S v Williams and Others*, 1995 (3) SA 632 (CC); 1995 (7) BCLR 861 (CC), para 22.

around 1689, no matter what falsification of them might have taken place in the nineteenth Century and thereafter. What an inestimable loss it would be if one were precluded from having regard to the views of the greatest moral philosopher of the past (at least) 200 years on such fundamental matters, simply because Immanuel Kant's *Groundwork of the Metaphysics of Morals* was published subsequent to the enactment of a (hypothetical) constitution or bill of rights.[34]

(b) The main article deals with a number of explanations for the influence of German constitutional law on the Interim and 1996 Constitutions. Mention is made in this context, quite rightly, of the contribution by Professor Francois Venter. It would be remiss of me not to mention two further names. The one is that of Professor Gerhard Erasmus of Stellenbosch University,[35] whose comprehensive knowledge of constitutional law (including comparative constitutional law) in general, and of German constitutional law in particular, was put to constructive use as an advisor in the drafting of the post-independence Namibian Constitution and subsequently as one of the expert advisors in the drafting of the Interim and 1996 South African Constitutions. The second is that of Professor Dr Jochen Frowein[36] who, together with other German lawyers, kept contact with South Africa throughout the 1980s and early 1990s and in a number of ways supported the move to a new constitutional democracy in South Africa.

---

[34] Hypothetical, and with no reference to the US Constitution or 'Bill of Rights', because one knows that Kant's work in question was published in 1785, whereas the US Constitution was adopted by the Constitutional Convention on 17 September 1787, was ratified by the States at the end of June 1788, and the first 10 Amendments were ratified and became part of the Constitution on 15 December 1791. It is, as an aside, a fascinating question whether this – or any other work – of Kant was known to anyone involved in the National Convention, the ratification process, or the adoption of the first 10 Amendments. In my limited reading on US constitutional history, I cannot recall any mention of Kant in the above context, but this is a matter on which one must (obviously) defer to the great US legal historians.

[35] Professor Erasmus was from 1993 to 2003 the second Harry Oppenheimer Professor of Human Rights Law at Stellenbosch University. During the early 1980s he had already introduced a course in comparative constitutional law in which the German Basic Law was one of the systems examined.

[36] Professor Frowein, apart from his German qualifications, also studied at the Michigan Law School, was for a number of years Vice-President of the European Human Rights Commission, and a director of the Max Planck Institute for Comparative Public and International Law, and could contribute this wide-ranging experience to the South African constitutional discussions.

4. The necessary circumspection which should accompany the use of comparative constitutional law

(a) Perhaps a discussion of the caution to be used when using foreign constitutional law logically follows, rather than precedes, a justification of its use, but from another perspective the two considerations are interdependent. Moreover, fear of the dangers often obfuscates discussion of the benefits of comparative legal usage. I believe it is conducive to greater clarity if one first deals with the care to be used in employing foreign constitutional law. Such caution (arising, amongst other things, from national differences relating to history, constitutional form, legal system, culture – legal and otherwise – and so forth) should itself be contextualised and not be used to discredit generally the use of foreign law. As I hope in due course to show, the main justifications for the appropriate use of foreign law have a value that transcends such national differences.

(b) In what follows, my argument assumes that constitutional law in the twentieth century – quite apart from the influence of binding international law – is not a wholly nationalistic and exclusively historical enterprise, but embodies a certain universally normative minimum core, or at least aspires thereto. There are, of course, limits to the impact of rationality and ethical persuasion that make further discourse impossible. As Isaiah Berlin points out, the acceptance of some irreducible minimum of common values was not only intrinsic to human communication but grounded our conception of a normal human being,[37] and that the possibility of understanding humans at any time depends on the existence of some common values; a person

> who (...) literally cannot grasp what conceivable objection anyone can have to (...) a rule permitting the killing of any man with blue eyes (...) would be considered about as normal a specimen of the human race as one who (...) thinks it probable that he is Julius Caesar.[38]

---

[37] 'Introduction' to *Four Essays on Liberty* (Oxford University Press 1969), pp xxxi–xxxii.

[38] Ibid, p xxxi.

One senses the same feel of weariness with absurdity in Bernard Williams,[39] when he points out that

> [t]he principle that men should be differently treated in respect of welfare merely on the grounds of their colour is not a special sort of moral principle, but (if anything) a purely arbitrary assertion of will, like that of some Caligulan ruler who decides to execute everyone whose name contained three 'R's.

(c) The Constitutional Court has been fully alive to the potential dangers in the use of comparative constitutional law. In considering the approach of the Constitutional Court one must throughout bear in mind the long-established use of comparative law in South Africa alluded to above. The fact that in a particular case, the caution which should accompany the use of foreign constitutional law is not explicitly repeated, does not warrant the inference that due care was not taken. The proper caution with which comparative law should be approached was explicitly recognised in one of the Court's early judgments, *Ferreira v Levin*.[40] One of the issues faced by the Court was what the constitutionality would be of a statutory provision that compelled the giving of self-incriminating evidence, if the only protection to be offered by the statute was an immunity against the direct use of such evidence in a subsequent criminal trial of the person compelled to give such evidence, but not an immunity against the derivative use of such evidence.[41] Immunity limited to direct use, subject to certain further safeguards, was sufficient in Canada but

---

39 'The Idea of Equality' in P. Laslett and W. G. Runciman (eds), *Philosophy, Politics and Society* (Second Series, Basil Blackwell, Oxford 1967), pp 110, 113. Williams further (at p 113) makes the following compelling points:

> This point is in fact conceded by those who practice such things as colour discrimination. Few can be found who will explain their practice merely by saying, 'But they're black: and it is my moral principle to treat black men differently from others.' If any reason at all is given, they will be reasons that seek to correlate the fact of blackness with certain other considerations which are at least candidates for relevance to the question of how a man should be treated: such as insensitivity, brute stupidity, ineducable irresponsibility, etc. Now these reasons are very often rationalizations, and the correlations claimed are either not really believed, or quite irrationally believed, by those who claim them. But this is a different point; the argument concerns what counts as a moral reason, and the rationalizer broadly agrees with others about what counts as such – the trouble with him is that his reasons are dictated by his policies, and not conversely. The Nazis' 'anthropologists' who tried to construct theories of Aryanism were paying, in very poor coin, the homage of irrationality to reason.

40 *Ferreira v Levin NO and Others*; *Vryenhoek and Others v Powell NO and Others*, 1996 (1) SA 984 (CC); 1996 (1) BCLR 1 (CC).

41 Ibid, paras 20 and 131–3.

not in the United States, which requires indirect use immunity as well. In the course of the judgment extensive reference was made, *inter alia*, to United Kingdom, Canadian, and Unites States jurisprudence, but the following was also stated:[42]

> In embarking on this enquiry regarding derivative use immunity, it is salutary to bear in mind that the problem cannot be resolved in the abstract but must be confronted in the context of South African conditions and resources – political, social, economic and human. The fact that a particular obligation may be placed on the criminal investigative and prosecutorial authorities in one country with vast resources, does not necessarily justify placing an identical burden on a country with significantly less resources. One appreciates the danger of relativising criminal justice, but it would also be dangerous not to contextualise it. The aphorism proclaims that it is better for ten guilty accused to go free than to have one innocent accused wrongly convicted. Does the same hold true if the proportion is stretched to a hundred to one or to a thousand to one? And must a system, which only produces one in a hundred wrong acquittals in one country, be maintained in another if it would consistently give rise to three in five wrong acquittals in the latter?

The Court, in deciding to follow the flexible Canadian approach, and holding that a direct use immunity, with the trial court having a judicial discretion to exclude derivative evidence – if that were necessary to ensure a fair trial – would pass constitutional muster, stated the following:[43]

> Although no statistical or other material was placed before us, it is quite apparent that the United States has vastly greater resources, in all respects and at all levels, than this country when it comes to the investigation and prosecution of crime, more particularly when regard is had to the particularly high crime rate, which one can take judicial notice of, currently prevalent in South Africa. This in my view gives added weight to the considerations of efficiency, economy of time and the most prudent use of scare resources, highlighted by La Forest J in *Thomson Newspapers* and to which I have already referred, and supporting the adoption of a flexible approach in dealing with the admissibility of derivative evidence. The flexible approach is narrowly tailored to meet important state objectives flowing from the collapse and liquidation of companies and the resulting duties of liquidators to protect the interests of creditors and the public at large, while at the same time interfering as little as possible with the examinee's right against self-incrimination. It is balanced and proportional and, in my view, fully justifiable in an open and democratic society based on freedom and equality.

---

[42] *Ferreira v Levin NO and Others*; *Vryenhoek and Others v Powell NO and Others*, 1996 (1) SA 984 (CC); 1996 (1) BCLR 1 (CC), para 133 (footnotes omitted).

[43] Para 152.

5. The justification for the use of comparative constitutional law in South Africa

(a) At the outset I emphasise what ought to be trite but, it seems, requires repetition – because of its use as a red herring in the debate about the use of foreign constitutional law – namely, that foreign law is not in any sense binding on the court referring thereto. There seems to be the fear that in referring to foreign law one is bowing to foreign authority and thereby endangering the national sovereignty of one's own legal system. This is manifestly not so. One may be seeking information, guidance, stimulation, clarification, or even enlightenment, but never authority binding on one's own decision. One is doing no more than keeping the judicial mind open to new ideas, problems, arguments, solutions etc.

(b) Einstein's views, in the header to this contribution, are relevant to the justification for comparative constitutional adjudication. Without the correct formulation of a constitutional problem, it is hardly possible to come up with the right constitutional answer. *Of course* the right problem must, in the end, be discovered in one's own constitution and jurisprudence, but to see how other jurisdictions have identified and formulated similar problems can be of great use. I say this both from personal experience and as a matter of epistemology.

In my own experience I have been struck by how often, when difficulties were experienced in finding the right answer in a case, this was caused by an incorrect or inadequate identification of the problem presented by the case. Recourse to foreign law often helped me (at least) to identify the correct problem, or to identify it properly, and I am at a loss to see what danger can lurk herein. There are, after all, few human and societal problems that are not, in their essence, universal. It is also useful to see how foreign courts have solved the problem, what methodology has been used to this end, what the competing considerations have been, and whether any potential dangers were identified in the process.

(c) The above approach and Einstein's observations are also epistemologically sound. Hume's 'problem with induction' arose from his discovery that it is impossible to justify a law by observation or experiment, and 'that there is no such logical entity as an inductive inference; or', differently put, 'that all so-called inductive inferences are logically invalid'.[44] Popper's well-known solution to Hume's problem points to a logical asymmetry between verification and falsification.

---

[44] Karl Popper, *Conjectures and Refutations* as quoted in David Miller (ed), *A Pocket Popper* (Fontana Paperbacks 1983), p 103. The validity of Hume's problem with induction has been shared by some of the other great thinkers of the past 100 years, including Bertrand Russel, Max Born, Peter Medawar, and John Eccles.

While accepting the validity of Hume's problem, as far as it goes, Popper contends that 'we *are* justified in reasoning [deductively] from a counter-instance to the falsity of the corresponding universal law (that is, of any law of which it is a counterinstance)'.[45] Popper's famous explanatory example is rendered thus by Bryan Magee:[46]

> [A]lthough no number of observation statements reporting observations of white swans allows us logically to derive the universal statement 'all swans are white,' one single observation statement, reporting one single observation of a black swan, allows us logically to derive the statement 'not all swans are white.'

Popper presents his four-stage model as follows:[47]

1. *the old problem*;
2. *formation of tentative theories*;
3. *attempts at elimination* through critical discussion, including experimental testing;
4. *the new problems* that arise from the critical discussion of our theories.

(d) I believe that the same, or a similar approach, is applicable to judicial reasoning. At some stage in a judge's reasoning process, which contains inductive as well as deductive elements, the judge will come to a preliminary conclusion (hypothesis) as to what the result should be and why. I suggest that the best way to test such preliminary conclusion is to attempt rigorously to falsify it. However, my experience – both of myself and other lawyers – has been that in judicial problem-solving one can easily become trapped into a sort of tunnel vision, from which it is difficult to escape, or to see other or lateral answers. One's thinking becomes unimaginative. One often ends up by rehearsing the same line of reasoning or – in a type of inductive process – by trying to find additional authority for the provisional conclusions one has already reached. It is in this context that foreign law can play a particularly valuable role. It may be that, when one commences the enquiry into foreign law one is (psychologically) hoping to find confirmation for one's hypotheses, but if one remains alive to falsifying possibilities, the foreign law can be of particular value. In any event foreign law may stimulate, in Einstein's

---

45 Karl Popper, *Conjectures and Refutations* as quoted in David Miller (ed), *A Pocket Popper* (Fontana Paperbacks 1983), p 103. The validity of Hume's problem with induction has been shared by some of the other great thinkers of the past 100 years, including Bertrand Russel, Max Born, Peter Medawar, and John Eccles, p 110 (and compare p 102).

46 *Popper* (Twelfth impression, Fontana Paperbacks, London 1985), p 22. This introduction by Magee to the work of Popper is the most accessible and lucid of which I am aware.

47 Popper, *All Life is Problem Solving* (Routledge, London and New York 1999), p 14.

words, 'creative imagination' by 'rais[ing] new questions, new possibilities, (...) regard[ing] old problems from a new angle'. In this context I should like to acknowledge my own great indebtedness to the American example and to American constitutional and human rights scholarship.

(e) In a recent judgment *K v Minister of Safety and Security* O'Regan J, writing for the Court, stated the following:[48]

> Counsel is correct in drawing our attention to the different conceptual bases of our law and other legal systems. As in all exercises in legal comparativism, it is important to be astute not to equate legal institutions which are not, in truth, comparable. Yet in my view, the approach of other legal systems remains of relevance to us.
>
> It would seem unduly parochial to consider that no guidance, whether positive or negative, could be drawn from other legal systems' grappling with issues similar to those with which we are confronted. Consideration of the responses of other legal systems may enlighten us in analysing our own law, and assist us in developing it further. It is for this very reason that our Constitution contains an express provision authorising courts to consider the law of other countries when interpreting the Bill of Rights. It is clear that in looking to the jurisprudence of other countries, all the dangers of shallow comparativism must be avoided. To forbid any comparative review because of those risks, however, would be to deprive our legal system of the benefits of the learning and wisdom to be found in other jurisdictions. Our courts will look at other jurisdictions for enlightenment and assistance in developing our own law. The question of whether we will find assistance will depend on whether the jurisprudence considered is of itself valuable and persuasive. If it is, the courts and our law will benefit. If it is not, the courts will say so, and no harm will be done.

(f) The main article has referred to certain observations by Kriegler J which may, possibly, create the impression that he was opposed in principle to the use of comparative law. While not referring to foreign law as frequently as other judges, his failure to do so – he made plain – was 'not in a spirit of parochialism' but because, on those occasions when he did not do so, or when he did not concur with such part of a colleague's judgment as referred to comparative law, he either felt that he had insufficient personal mastery of the foreign material, or that he could safely reach a conclusion, or concur in a colleague's conclusion, without reliance on the foreign material. Nor did he criticise the way in which a colleague had used comparative law.[49] While rightly condemning the

---

[48] *K v Minister of Safety and Security*, 2005 (9) BCLR 835 (CC), paras 34–5.

[49] See, e.g., *Bernstein and Others v Bester and Others NO*, 1996 (2) SA 751 (CC); 1996 (4) BCLR 449 (CC), paras 132–3.

uncritical use of foreign material by counsel, he supported the use of the comparative method by the courts[50] –

> Comparative study is always useful, particularly where courts in exemplary jurisdictions have grappled with universal issues confronting us. Likewise, where a provision in our Constitution is manifestly modelled on a particular provision in another country's constitution, it would be folly not to ascertain how the jurists of that country have interpreted *their* precedential provision

– and did not hesitate to employ it when he considered it appropriate.[51]

(g) Comparative law has proved instructive and helpful in the jurisprudence of the Constitutional Court in many different areas:

(i) The analysis of legal arguments, similar to those advanced in our courts.[52]

(ii) When dealing with unconstitutional punishment, whether such be described as 'cruel and unusual', or as 'inhuman or degrading', or as 'cruel, inhuman or degrading', because foreign law is instructive as it helps determine a common thread, namely 'the identification and acknowledgment of society's concept of decency and human dignity'.[53]

(iii) A review of the jurisprudence of both Commonwealth and non-Commonwealth countries, when considering the approach to be adopted in determining the competence of Parliament to delegate powers to the executive.[54]

(iv) Canadian (and sometimes United States) jurisprudence regarding the constitutionality of reverse onus (burden of proof) provisions in criminal cases and whether, and to what extent, such a provision could be justified under the Constitution's limitation provision.[55]

(v) The general rule in criminal matters that persons not at fault should not be deprived of their freedom by the state.[56]

---

50 See, e.g., *Bernstein and Others v Bester and Others NO*, 1996 (2) SA 751 (CC); 1996 (4) BCLR 449 (CC), para 133.

51 *S v Mamabolo*, 2001 (3) SA 409 (CC); 2001 (5) BCLR 449 (CC), dealing with the Common law offence of scandalising the court.

52 *S v Makwanyane* (op. cit. note 21), para 34.

53 *S v Williams and Others* (op. cit. note 33), para 35.

54 *Executive Council, Western Cape Legislature and Others v President of the Republic of South Africa and Others*, 1995 (4) SA 877 (CC); 1995 (10) BCLR 1289 (CC), paras 61–3.

55 See, e.g., *S v Bhulwana; S v Gwadiso*, 1996 (1) SA 388 (CC); 1995 (12) BCLR 1579 (CC), paras 12–24; *S v Coetzee and Others*, 1997 (3) SA 527 (CC); 1997 (4) BCLR 437 (CC), paras 32–46 and 91–8.

56 *S v Coetzee* (op. cit. note 55), paras 166–76.

(vi) The Court's consistent equality and unfair discrimination jurisprudence based on Kantian concepts and, *inter alia*, Canadian jurisprudence.[57]

(vii) The Court's conclusion, as a matter of fundamental jurisprudence, that the objective doctrine of constitutional invalidity should be adopted, following – at a basic analytical level – Canadian and German law.[58]

(viii) Adopting a particular form of constitutional interpretation, namely of giving a statutory provision a meaning in conformity with constitutional validity, if the provision in question is reasonably capable of bearing such meaning, rather than a construction leading to unconstitutionality, even if such latter construction is also reasonable.[59]

(ix) Distinguishing clearly between

(aa) giving a more limited meaning[60] or a more extensive meaning[61] to a provision, as a matter of constitutional *interpretation*; and,

(bb) the literal elimination of a provision, or part of a provision, as a constitutional *remedy*; or the literal reading in of words into an existing provision as a constitutional *remedy*; following on a declaration of constitutional invalidity.[62]

(x) The vitally important one of constitutional remedies –

(aa) generally;[63] and

(bb) the literal reading in of provisions.[64]

---

[57] For example, *Prinsloo v Van Der Linde and Another*, 1997 (3) SA 1012 (CC); 1997 (6) BCLR 759 (CC); *President of the Republic of South Africa and Another v Hugo*, 1997 (4) SA 1 (CC); 1997 (6) BCLR 708; *Harksen v Lane NO and Others*, 1998 (1) SA 300 (CC); 1997 (11) BCLR 1489 (CC); *City Council of Pretoria v Walker*, 1998 (2) SA 363 (CC); 1998 (3) BCLR 257 (CC); *National Coalition for Gay and Lesbian Equality and Others v Minister of Justice and Others*, 1999 (1) SA 6 (CC); 1998 (12) BCLR 1517 (CC); *National Coalition for Gay and Lesbian Equality and Others v Minister of Home Affairs and Others*, 2000 (2) SA 1 (CC); 2000 (1) BCLR 39 (CC); *Hoffmann v South African Airways*, 2001 (1) SA 1 (CC); 2000 (10) BCLR 1211 (CC); *Prince v President of the Law Society of the Cape of Good Hope and Others* 2002 (2) SA 794 (CC); 2002 (3) BCLR 231 (CC); *Volks NO v Robinson and Others* 2005 (2) BCLR 446 (CC).

[58] *Ferreira v Levin* (op. cit. note 40), paras 26–30.

[59] De Lange v Smuts NO and others, 1998 (3) SA 785 (CC); 1998 (7) BCLR 779 (CC), para 85; *The Investigating Directorate: Serious Economic Offences and Others v Hyundai Motor Distributors (Pty) Ltd and Others; In re Hyundai Motor Distributors (Pty) Ltd and Others v Smit NO and Others*, 2001 (1) SA 545 (CC); 2000 (10) BCLR 1079 (CC) paras 23–24.

[60] Sometimes, but misleadingly and confusingly, called 'reading down'.

[61] Sometimes, but even more misleadingly and confusingly, called 'reading in.'

[62] *National Coalition for Gay and Lesbian Equality and Others v Minister of Home Affairs and Others*, 2000 (2) SA 1 (CC); 2000 (1) BCLR 39 (CC), para 24.

[63] *Fose v Minister of Safety and Security*, 1997 (3) SA 786 (CC); 1997 (7) BCLR 851 (CC).

[64] *National Coalition for Gay and Lesbian Equality and Others v Minister of Home Affairs and Others* (op. cit. note 62), paras 64–82.

(xi) Privacy, in various aspects of its applications.[65]

(xii) The distinction between 'inconsistency' and 'invalidity' in a clash between the powers of Parliament and provincial legislatures.[66]

(xiii) Pornography.[67]

(xiv) The 'horizontal' or 'vertical only' application of a Bill of Rights. In *Du Plessis v De Klerk*[68] the German jurisprudence, in particular, was of great value in understanding the ways in which the horizontal operation of a Bill of Rights can operate and what potential problems inhere in a vertical application of its provisions.[69] The Court found that under the Interim Constitution the Bill of Rights had solely vertical application. The drafters of the 1996 Constitution, in a sense overruling the majority judgment in *Du Plessis v De Klerk*, made express provision in section 8(2), 8(3) and 9(4) for the Bill of Rights to have horizontal application as well.[70] Having regard to the innovative and nuanced way these provisions, and in particular section 8(3), are formulated, it is clear that the framers benefited from and relied on the Court's analysis in *Du Plessis v De Klerk*. Perhaps this can also be described as a form of constitutional 'dialogue'.

(xv) The care with which the principle of the separation of powers and checks and balances should be interpreted and given content in a particular constitution.[71]

---

65 *Bernstein*-decision (op. cit. note 49), paras 65 ff; *Case and Another v Min of Safety and Security and Others*; *Curtis v Minister of Safety and Security and Others*, 1996 (3) SA 617 (CC); 1996 (5) BCLR 609 (CC), paras 91–4.

66 *Speaker of the National Assembly, Ex Parte: In re Dispute Concerning The Constitutionality of Certain Provisions of the National Education Policy Bill 83 of 1995*, 1996 (3) SA 289 (CC); 1996 (4) BCLR 518 (CC), paras 13–20.

67 *Case v Curtis* (op. cit. note 65).

68 Op. cit. note 23. See also the text to notes 22 and 23.

69 Ibid, paras 39–4 and 93–108.

70 Section 8(2) and (3) declares:

> (2) A provision of the Bill of Rights binds a natural or a juristic person if, and to the extent that, it is applicable, taking into account the nature of the right and the nature of any duty imposed by the right. (3) When applying a provision of the Bill of Rights to a natural or juristic person in terms of subsection (2), a court – (a) in order to give effect to a right in the Bill, must apply, or if necessary develop, the common law to the extent that legislation does not give effect to that right; and (b) may develop rules of the common law to limit the right, provided that the limitation is in accordance with section 36 (1).
>
> Section 9(4) declares: 'No person may unfairly discriminate directly or indirectly against anyone on one or more grounds in terms of subsection (3). National legislation must be enacted to prevent or prohibit unfair discrimination.'

71 *Chairperson of the Constitutional Assembly, Ex Parte: In re Certification of the Constitution of the Republic of South Africa, 1996*, 1996 (4) SA 744 (CC), paras 106–13; 1996 (10) BCLR 1253 (CC); *Dodo v The State*, 2001 (3) SA 382 (CC); 2001 (5) BCLR 423 (CC), paras 15–17.

(xvi) The separation of powers issue, and the test of gross disproportionality in deciding whether a statutorily prescribed penal provision is unconstitutional.[72]

(xvii) The common law offence of scandalising the court.[73]

(xviii) Deportation or extradition and the death penalty,[74] where the discussion of foreign authority by the Court concludes as follows:[75]

> 'It is therefore important that the State lead by example. This *principle* cannot be put better than in the celebrated words of Justice Brandeis in *Olmstead et al v United States*: 'In a government of laws, existence of the government will be imperiled if it fails to observe the law scrupulously. (...) Government is the potent, omni-present teacher. For good or ill, it teaches the whole people by its example. (...) If the government becomes a lawbreaker, it breeds contempt for the law; it invites every man to become a law unto himself; it invites anarchy.'

(xix) Amnesty in respect of criminal liability.[76]

(xx) A father's consent to the adoption of an 'illegitimate' child.[77]

(xxi) The meaning of the concept 'no law may permit arbitrary deprivation of property' in section 25(1) of the Bill of Rights.[78]

(xxii) The concept of succession and the rule of male primogeniture in indigenous African law.[79]

(xxiii) The construction by the Constitutional Court (in a judgment delivered on 11 March 2005 that had not come to the attention of the authors when the book was drafted) of section 22 of the Constitution, guaranteeing the right to 'choose [a] trade, occupation or profession freely'.[80]

---

[72] *Dodo*-decision (op. cit. note 71), paras 22–34 and 35–41, respectively.

[73] *S v Mamabola* op. cit. 51).

[74] *National Director of Public Prosecutions and Another v Mohamed NO and Others, Another v President of the Republic of South Africa and Others*, 2002 (4) SA 843 (CC); 2002 (9) BCLR 970 (CC).

[75] Ibid, para 68.

[76] *Azanian Peoples Organisation (AZAPO) and Others v The President of the Republic of South Africa*, 1996 (4) SA 671 (CC); 1996 (8) BCLR 1015 (CC), paras 16–32.

[77] *Fraser v The Children's Court, Pretoria North and Others*, 1997 (2) SA 261 (CC); 1997 (2) BCLR 153 (CC), paras 31–43.

[78] *First National Bank of SA t/a Wesbank v Commissioner for the South African Revenue Services and Another; First National Bank of SA t/a Wesbank v Minister of Finance*, 2002 (4) SA 768 (CC); 2002 (7) BCLR 702 (CC). It is crucially important to have due regard to the comprehensive nature of s 25 which deals, *inter alia*, with expropriation against compensation and remedies for the dispossession of property after 19 June 1913.

[79] *Bhe and Others v Magistrate, Khayelitsha and Others; Shibi v Sithole and Others; SA Human Rights Commission and Another v President of the RSA and Another*, 2005 (1) SA 563 (CC); 2005 (1) BCLR 1 (CC), paras 156–211.

[80] *The Affordable Medicines Trust and Others v Minister of Health of the Republic of South Africa and* Another, 2005 (6) BCLR 529 (CC), paras 64–5; 87–93, Section 22 is almost identical to s 12(1) of the German Basic Law.

(xxiv) Fundamental normative principles of vicarious liability.[81]

(xxv) Whether a South African citizen has an enforceable right against the state for diplomatic protection.[82]

(xxvi) Whether prisoners can be excluded from voting.[83]

The above review is, perforce, selective and epigrammatic, and refers only to judgments of the Constitutional Court. It may, however, whet the appetite of some readers to investigate the cases further, and in so doing contribute to the debate on the use of comparative law.[84]

6. Conclusion

(a) A feature that I have, as yet, not referred to is one that has (possibly) wider applications than just to the South African context. Most, if not all, courts exercising extensive powers of review over the legislature and executive face problems of credibility (if not legitimacy) because of their above powers. It is of little avail to point to the transformation that the concept of democratic government has undergone over the past centuries; that bills of rights (and their enforcement by an independent judiciary) are essential to prevent majority tyranny; that comprehensive 'rule of law' constitutions, embodying the supreme law of the land, apply to such courts as well; that judges cannot be held 'accountable' *in the same way* as the legislature or the executive, without destroying their independence; or that the judges, by their judicial oath of office undertake, *inter alia*, to –

> uphold and protect the Constitution and the human rights entrenched in it, and will administer justice to all persons alike without fear, favour or prejudice, in accordance with the Constitution and the law.[85]

Suspicions nonetheless remain, despite attempts to devise appointment procedures for judges who seek to strike a balance between government, minority political parties, the judiciary itself, and the independent legal

---

[81] *K v Minister of Safety and Security* (op. cit. note 48), paras 34–43.

[82] *Kaunda & Others v The President of the RSA and Others*, 2004 (10) BCLR 1009 (CC).

[83] *Minister of Home Affairs v NICRO and Others*, 2004 (5) BCLR 445 (CC), paras 54–67.

[84] I trust that I will not be accused either of chauvinism or of incitement to treason if I mention the Constitutional Court's website www.constitutionalcourt.org.za on which all judgments of the Constitutional Court and the Supreme Court of Appeal, the text of the Constitutions, and much else, are available online.

[85] Constitution Schedule 2, item 6.

profession.[86] This is of course not surprising, given South Africa's apartheid history and all that went with it. But the problem is substantial in all pluralistic societies and will not disappear for as long as multi-party democracy continues to exist.

No judge is a 'Hercules'[87] or an 'Athena'. The best one can do is to strive consciously to become aware of *all* one's prejudices, to be aware that, this exercise notwithstanding, one will still have subliminal predispositions, and to toil as honestly as one can in the vineyard. I have, personally, found the comparative legal approach not only rewarding, but salutary – even admonishing – in the South African context, quite apart from all the benefits I have alluded to previously. The book refers to various types of dialogue. I should like to introduce a further one, the dialogue which judges have (or ought to have) with themselves. I exclude those who, through some form of genius or some oracular affiliation, are able to produce instant solutions, without having to engage in the intellectual wrestling process. It is in the course of this internal dialogue that hypotheses emerge; that intellectual, cultural, and other predispositions compete; that critical rationalism can come into play to test and adapt hypotheses. It is at this stage, consciously or not, that one's philosophical, economic, and jurisprudential *Gestalt* enters the picture. At this stage I have found comparative legal concepts to be most helpful. Is this, as part of one's *Gestalt*, any different from its other components? I believe that there is as little justification for proscribing comparative investigation, as there is for censuring a judge for reading Kant, or Rawls, or Dworkin, or law and economics, or going to church.

(b) Linked to the above is my belief in the constitution as a living reality, an objective normative corpus.[88] The answers to problems should, ideally, be found within this system; a dialogue with it should, eventually, produce the right constitutional answer; and the judge should intrude his own personality and predilections as little as possible. I am aware that this is a counsel of the impossible, but nevertheless a constant loadstar worth pursuing. An important way of testing one's hypotheses, of preventing the unwarranted intrusion of one's personal preferences, of dangerous intuitions, is the constant search for 'neutral principles of

---

[86] For South African attempts in this regard reference may be made to the composition (Constitution s 178) and role of the Judicial Service Commission in the appointment of Constitutional Court Judges; Constitution s 174(1)–(5).

[87] With apologies to Ronald Dworkin.

[88] Compare *Carmichele v The Minister of Safety and Security and the Minister of Justice and Constitutional Development*, 2001 (4) SA 938 (CC); 2001 (10) BCLR 995 (CC), para 54.

constitutional law'. This concept cannot be explicated here, but is one coined and fully developed by some of the finest US legal scholars.[89] It is in the search for such neutral principles that comparative law comes into its own, as a critical testing tool and a source of new solutions to old questions.

(c) Finally, I would justify the comparative enterprise for a more embracing reason. One is now, more than ever, haunted by the cry in the preamble to the Universal Declaration of Human Rights in 1948 that the 'inherent dignity' and the equality of 'all members of the human family' belong to those values and human rights that constitute 'the foundation of freedom, justice and peace in the world', whose contemptuous disregard has 'resulted in barbarous acts which have outraged the conscience of mankind'. The Declaration's appeal is that the protection of these rights by 'the rule of law' (which in my view includes the concept of the constitutional state or 'rechtsstaat') is essential, if humans are not 'to be compelled to have recourse, as a last resort, to rebellion against tyranny and oppression'. Human societies throughout the world have, in the nearly 60 years since the Universal Declaration, failed lamentably to turn this appeal into a reality. Any attempt to present fundamental human rights in terms that may lead to greater global understanding and acceptance of these core concepts and values, and that may contribute to the elimination of 'barbarous acts which (...) outrag[e] the conscience of mankind' is worthwhile. One should try, as far as is possible, to avoid these rights being rejected on the basis of cultural relativism, one of its arguments being that these rights are not universal, and the entitlement of all humankind, but relative to the cultures and political philosophies of only certain communities. I would suggest that by adopting a comparative laws approach, one would at least start a process of greater understanding of the fundamental values of other legal systems and, in the resulting dialogue, work towards a greater universalising of these values as enforceable rights. This may, in the long term, help diminish the continuing and widespread assault on human dignity, which appears no longer to outrage the conscience of humankind to the same extent as previously.

---

[89] I have in mind, *inter alia*, the following: Herbert Wechsler, 'Towards Neutral Principles of Constitutional Law', in (1959) 73 *Harv. L. Rev.* 1 ff and 'The nature of Judicial Reasoning', in Hook (ed), *Law and Philosophy* (2nd edn, 1970), p 290; Louis Henkin, 'Some Reflections on Current Constitutional Controversy' (1961) 109 *Univ. Pa. L. Rev.* 637 ff; 'Shelley v Kraemer: Notes for a Revised Opinion', in (1962) 110 *Univ. Pa. L. Rev.* 473 ff; and 'Infallibility Under Law: Constitutional Balancing' (1978) 78 *Colum. L. Rev.* 1023 ff; and Kent Greenawalt, 'The Enduring Significance Neutral Principles', in (1978) 78 *Colum. L. Rev.* 982 ff.

Comparison in Public Law

*Aharon Barak**

This book by Basil Markesinis and Jörg Fedtke may be a turning point. It will encourage generations of judges to try the path of comparative law. We may have here the beginning of an intellectual revolution. In the past we had the following phenomena: judges did not tend to rely on comparative law; lawyers did not cite comparative law to judges; law schools did not stress comparative law; scholars did not emphasise comparative law; judges did not tend to rely on comparative law; etc. This vicious circle is coming to its end. Judges *will* start to rely on comparative law; lawyers *will* tend to cite it to judges; law schools *will* start teaching comparative law; scholars *will* be encouraged to research in comparative law; judges *will* rely more and more on comparative law. And one of the important tools in breaking the vicious circle is this book of Markesinis and Fedtke. In what will follow, I am summarising my own experience in the use of comparative law in public law. I do hope it may encourage other judges to follow in this path, both in public law and in private law.

I. The importance of comparative law

I have found comparative law to be of great assistance in realising my role as a judge. The case law of the courts of the United States, Australia, Canada, the United Kingdom, and Germany have helped me significantly in finding the right path to follow. Indeed, comparing oneself to others allows for greater self-knowledge. With comparative law, the judge expands the horizon and the interpretive field of vision. Comparative law enriches the options available to us. In different legal systems, similar legal institutions often fulfil corresponding roles, and similar legal problems (like hate speech, privacy, and now the fight against terrorism)

---

* President of the Supreme Court, Israel. This contribution is a section in the forthcoming A. Barak, *The Judge in a Democracy* (2006).

arise.[1] To the extent that these similarities exist, comparative law becomes an important tool with which judges fulfil their role in a democracy ('microcomparison').[2] Moreover, because many of the basic principles of democracy are common to democratic countries, there is good reason to compare them ('macrocomparison').[3] Indeed, different democratic legal systems often encounter similar problems. Examining a foreign solution may help a judge choose the best local solution. This usefulness applies both to the development of the Common law and to the interpretation of legal texts.[4]

Naturally, one must approach comparative law cautiously, remaining cognizant of its limitations. Comparative law is not merely the comparison of laws. A useful comparison can exist only if the legal systems have a common ideological basis. The judge must be sensitive to the uniqueness of each legal system. Nonetheless, when the judge is convinced that the relative social, historical, and religious circumstances create a common ideological basis, it is possible to refer to a foreign legal system as a source of comparison and inspiration. Indeed, the importance of comparative law lies in extending the judge's horizons. Comparative law awakens judges to the potential latent in their own legal systems. It informs judges about the successes and failures that may result from adopting a particular legal solution. It refers judges to the relationship between a solution to the legal problem before them and other legal problems. Thus, comparative law acts as an experienced friend. Of course, there is no obligation to refer to comparative law. Additionally, even when comparative law is consulted, the final decision must always be 'local'. The benefit of comparative law lies in expanding judicial thinking about the possible arguments, legal trends, and decision-making structures available.

2. The influence of comparative law

Comparative law is a tool that aids in constitutional and statutory interpretation. This assistance may work on three levels. The *first*

---

[1] See *The Police v Georghiades* (1983) 2 C.L.R. 33, 50–4, 60–5, in which Justice Pikis compared different national and international legal systems to give content to the right of privacy. It was decided by the Supreme Court of Cyprus that the right of privacy applies not only vis-à-vis the state but also in the relationships between individuals.

[2] See Konrad Zweigert and Hein Kötz, *Introduction to Comparative Law*, Vol 1, p 5 (2nd edn, 1987, translation by Tony Weir).

[3] Ibid at pp 4/5.

[4] See T. Koopmans, *Courts and Political Institutions: A Comparative View* (2003), p 4.

concerns interpretive theory. Comparative law helps the judge better understand the role of interpretation and the role of the judge therein. To exemplify the point, consider the interpretative status of the intent of the creator in understanding constitutions and statutes. Before judges decide their own position on the issue, they would do well to consider how other legal systems treat the question. The *second* level on which judges rely on comparative law is connected with democracy's fundamental values. Democracies share common fundamental values. Democracy must infringe certain fundamental values in order to maintain others. It is important for judges to know how foreign law treats this question and what techniques it uses. Does it employ a technique of balancing or of categorisation? Why is one technique preferred over another? Every legal system grapples with the issue of constitutional limitations on human rights. What are these limitations, and what technique was used to reach them? What are the remedies for violating an unlawful order, and how can they be determined? The *third* level of aid provided by comparative law concerns the solutions it offers to specific situations: how protected is racist speech? Is affirmative action recognised? How does the foreign system deal with terrorism? Of course, the resolution of these issues is intrinsically local. However, in different legal systems, they have a common core in that they reflect the problems of democracy and the complexity of human relations. Again, I do not advocate adopting the foreign arrangement. It is never binding. I just advocate an open approach, one which recognises that for all our singularity, we are not alone. That recognition will enrich our own legal systems if we take the trouble to understand how others respond in situations similar to those we encounter.

3. Comparative law and interpretation of statutes

Comparative law is an important source from which the judge may learn the objective purpose[5] of a statute.[6] This is the case with regard

---

[5] On the objective purpose see A. Barak, *Purposive Interpretation in Law* (2005), p 148.

[6] For a discussion of comparative law and the courts see generally Ulrich Drobnig and Sjef van Erp (eds), *The Use of Comparative Law by Courts* (1999); Günter Frankenberg, 'Critical Comparisons: Re-thinking Comparative Law' [1985] 26 Harv. Int'l L. J. 411 ff; B. S. Markesinis, 'Comparative Law – A Subject in Search of an Audience' [1990] 53 *Mod. L. Rev.* 7 ff; Peter de Cruz, *Comparative Law in a Changing World* (1995); H. Patrick Glenn, 'Comparative Law and Legal Practice: On Removing the Borders' [2001] 75 *Tul. L. Rev.* 977 ff; Mathias Reimann, 'The Progress and Failure of Comparative Law

to both the specific purpose ('microcomparison') and the general purpose ('macrocomparison') of the statute. The comparison is relevant even if it is clear that the legislature was not inspired by foreign law. In looking for the specific statutory purpose, a judge may be inspired by a similar statute in a foreign democratic legal system. This is so when he wishes to learn of the purpose underlying legislation that regulates a legal 'institution' such as an agency or a lease. The judge does not refer to the details of the foreign laws. Rather, he examines the function that the legal institution fulfils in the two systems. If there is a similarity in the functions, he may find interpretive ideas about the (objective) purpose of the legislation. An example of this potential use is the principle of good faith in executing a contract. To the extent that this principle fulfils a similar function in different legal systems, it is possible to use the law of a foreign system to discern the purpose that underlies the principle of good faith in local law. Moreover, it is possible to use comparative law – from other national systems and from international law – to determine the general (objective) purpose that reflects the basic principles of the system. Again, however, this comparative analysis is possible only if the two legal systems share a common ideological basis.

4. Comparative law and interpretation of the constitution

Comparative law can help judges determine the objective purpose of a constitution. Democratic countries have several fundamental principles in common. As such, legal institutions often fulfil similar functions across countries. From the purpose that one given democratic legal system attributes to a constitutional arrangement, one can learn something about the purpose of that particular constitutional arrangement in another legal system. Indeed, comparative constitutional law is a good source of expanded horizons and cross-fertilisation of ideas across legal systems.[7]

---

in the Second Half of the Twentieth Century', [2002] 50 *Am. J. Comp. L.* 671 ff; Pierre Legrand and Roderick Munday (eds), *Comparative Legal Studies: Traditions and Transitions* (2003); Mary Ann Glendon, Michael Wallace Gordon and Christopher Osakure, *Comparative Legal Traditions* (1999); Anne-Marie Slaughter, *A New World Order* (2004), pp 65 ff.

[7] See Vicki C. Jackson and Mark Tushnet, *Comparative Constitutional Law* (1999); Norman Dorsen, Michael Rosenfeld, Andras Sajo, and Susanne Baer, *Comparative Constitutionalism: Cases and Materials* (2003); Sujit Choudhry, 'Globalization in Search of Justification: Toward a Theory of Comparative Constitutional Interpretation' [1999] 74 *Ind. L. J.* 819 ff; George P. Fletcher, 'Comparative Law as a Subversive Discipline'

This is clearly the case when the constitutional text of one country has been influenced by the constitutional text of another. But even in the absence of any (direct or indirect) influence of one constitutional text on another, there is still a basis for interpretative inspiration. An example is where a constitution refers expressly to democratic values or democratic societies.[8] But even without such a reference, the interpretative influence of comparative law is substantial.[9] This is the case with regard to determining the scope of human rights, resolving particularly difficult issues such as abortion and the death penalty, and determining constitutional remedies.

Nonetheless, as we have seen, interpretive inspiration is only useful if there is an ideological basis common to the two legal systems and a common allegiance to basic democratic principles. A common basis of democracy is, however, a necessary but insufficient condition for comparative analysis. As judges, we must also examine whether there are factors in the historical development and social conditions that make the local and the foreign system different enough to render interpretive inspiration impracticable.[10] But when there is an adequate similarity, interpretive inspiration is possible. This is the case with regard to inspiration from the law of another democratic country. It is also true with regard to interpretive inspiration from international law, as various

---

[1998] 46 Am. J. Comp. L. 683 at 695–6; Christopher McCrudden, 'A Common Law of Human Rights? Transnational Judicial Conversations on Constitutional Rights' in Katherine O'Donovan and Gerry R. Rubin (eds), *Human Rights and Legal History* (2000), pp 29 ff; Kathryn A. Perales, 'It Works Fine in Europe, So Why Not Here? Comparative Law and Constitutional Federalism', [1999] 23 *Vt. L. Rev.* 885 ff; Mark Tushnet, 'The Possibilities of Comparative Constitutional Law', [1999] 108 *Yale L. J.* 1225 ff; Lorraine Weinrib, 'Constitutional Conceptions and Constitutional Comparativism', in Vicki Jackson and Mark Tushnet (eds), *Defining the Field of Comparative Constitutional Law* (2002), 23; Francois Venter, *Constitutional Comparison: Japan, Germany, Canada and South Africa as Constitutional States* (2000).

[8] See, e.g., Canadian Constitution (Charter of Rights and Freedoms), § I; South African Constitution s 36(1); see also David M. Beatty, 'The Forms and Limits of Constitutional Interpretation' [2001] 49 *Am. J. Comp. L.* 79 at 102--9.

[9] See Donald P. Kommers, 'The Value of Comparative Constitutional Law' [1976] 9 *Marshall J. Pracs. & Procs.* 685 ff.

[10] See *R. v Keegstra* [1990] 3 S.C.R. 897, 740; *Rahey v The Queen* [1987] 1 S.C.R. 588 at 639 ('While it is natural and even desirable for Canadian courts to refer to American constitutional jurisprudence in seeking to elucidate the meaning of *Charter* guarantees that have counterparts in the United States Constitution, they should be wary of drawing too ready a parallel between constitutions born to different countries in

international conventions enshrine constitutional values.[11] These conventions influence the formation of the objective purpose of different constitutional texts.[12] The case law of international and national courts that interpret these conventions ought to serve as a basis for the interpretation of the constitutions of various nations.

5. Use of comparative law in practice

The use of comparative law for the development of the Common law and the interpretation of legal texts is determined by the tradition of the legal system. Israeli law, for example, makes extensive use of comparative law. When Israeli courts encounter an important legal problem, they frequently examine foreign law. Reference to law from the United States,[13] the United Kingdom, Canada, and Australia is commonplace. Those with the linguistic ability also refer to Continental European law, and sometimes we use English translations of Continental European (mainly German, French, and Italian) legal literature.

In countries of the British Commonwealth, there is much cross-fertilisation. Each such nation refers to UK case law. UK judges refer to Commonwealth case law, and Commonwealth judges, in turn, refer to each other's case law. The Supreme Court of Canada is particularly noteworthy for its frequent and fruitful use of comparative law.[14] As such, Canadian law serves as a source of inspiration for many countries around the world. Generous use of comparative law can be found in the

---

different ages and in very different circumstances.'); P. Hogg, *Constitutional Law of Canada* (4th edn, 1997), p 87.

[11] For the products of some of the most important international conventions see the International Covenant on Civil and Political Rights, 19 December 1966, 999 U.N.T.S. 171 (entered into force on 23 March 1976); the International Covenant on Economic, Social and Cultural Rights, 16 December 1966, 993 U.N.T.S. 3 (entered into force on 3 January 1976); the European Convention for the Protection of Human Rights and Fundamental Freedoms, 4 November 1950, Europ. T.S. No. 5, 213 U.N.T.S. 221 (entered into force on 3 September 1953); the American Declaration of the Rights and Duties of Man, O.A.S. Official Rec., OEA/Ser. L./V./II.23, doc. 21 rev. 6 (1948); the Universal Declaration of Human Rights, G.A. Res. 217A, U.N. GAOR, pt. 1, at 71, U.N. Doc. A/810 (1948).

[12] See, e.g., *Newcrest Mining (WA) Ltd. v Commonwealth*, (1997) 195 CLR 513, 655.

[13] See Pnina Lahav, 'American Influence on Israel's Jurisprudence of Free Speech', [1981] 9 Hastings Const. L. Q. 23 ff; Renee Sanilevici, 'The Use of Comparative Law by Israeli Courts', in Ulrich Drobnig and Sjef van Erp (eds.), op. cit. note 6, p 197.

[14] See Anne Bayefsky, 'International Human Rights Law in Canadian Courts', in Benedetto Conforti and Francesco Francioni (eds), Enforcing International Human Rights in Domestic Courts (1997), pp 295 ff at 310.

opinions of the South African Constitutional Court. In South Africa's Constitution, it is explicitly determined that:

> When interpreting the Bill of Rights, a court, tribunal, or forum –
>
> (a) must promote the values that underline an open and democratic society based on human dignity, equality and freedom;
>
> (b) must consider international law and,
>
> (c) may consider foreign law.[15]

Regrettably, until very recently, the US Supreme Court has made little use of comparative law.[16] Many democratic countries derive inspiration from this Court, particularly in its interpretation of the US Constitution.[17] By contrast, some Justices of the Supreme Court do not cite foreign case law in their judgments. They fail to make use of an important source of inspiration, one that enriches legal thinking, makes law more creative, and strengthens the democratic ties and foundations of different legal systems. Justice Claire L'Heureux-Dubé of the Canadian Supreme Court has rightly observed that '[i]f we continue to learn from each other, we as judges, lawyers, and scholars will contribute in the best possible way not only to the advancement of human rights but to the pursuit of justice itself, wherever we are.'[18] Of course, American law in general, and its constitutional law in particular, is rich and developed. American law is comprised of not one but 51 legal systems. Nonetheless, I think that it is always possible to learn new things even from other democratic legal systems that, in their turn, have

---

[15] Article 39(1) of the South African Constitution.

[16] See *Printz v United States*, 521 U.S. 898, 921 n 11 (1997) ('Justice Breyer's dissent would have us consider the benefits that other countries, and the European Union, believe they have derived from federal systems that are different from ours. We think such comparative analysis inappropriate to the task of interpreting a constitution.'); *Stanford v Kentucky*, 492 U.S. 361, 369 n 1 (1989) ('We emphasize that it is *American* conceptions of decency that are dispositive, rejecting the contention of petitioners and their various *amici* (...) that the sentencing practices of other countries are relevant.'); *Thompson v Oklahoma*, 487 U.S. 815, 868 n 4 (1988) (Scalia, J., dissenting) ('The plurality's reliance upon Amnesty International's account of what it pronounces to be civilized standards of decency in other countries (...) is totally inappropriate as a means of establishing the fundamental beliefs of this Nation.').

[17] See Gerald V. La Forest, 'The Use of American Precedents in Canadian Courts' [1994] 46 *Me. L. Rev.* 211 ff; Anthony Lester, 'The Overseas Trade in the American Bill of Rights' [1988] 88 *Colum. L. Rev.* 537 ff.

[18] See L'Heureux-Dubé, 'The Importance of Dialogue: Globalization, The Rehnquist Court, and Human Rights', in M. Belsky, *The Rehnquist Court: A Retrospective* (2002).

learned from American law. As Judge Guido Calabresi rightly said: 'Wise parents do not hesitate to learn from their children.'[19] There appears to be the beginning of a change in the US Supreme Court's attitude towards comparative law. In some recent cases, Supreme Court justices have cited case law from other jurisdictions.[20] Is the Court moving towards wider use of comparative law?

---

[19] *United States v Then*, 56 F.3d 464, 469 (2d Cir. 1995).

[20] See, e.g., *Lawrence v Texas*, 123 S. Ct. 2472 (2003).

The Constitutional Judge and the International Constitutionalist Dialogue*

Brun-Otto Bryde

Markesinis and Fedtke have made a convincing argument for an increased role of comparative law in the work of judges based on a broad survey of judicial practice. I will restrict myself to adding a few modest observations from my own field of experience. After some words about the practice of the German Constitutional Court (1), I will stress the importance of international human rights law for the internationalisation of constitutional law (2), and point out that we might underestimate the importance of foreign sources if we see their use only as inspirational (3).

Constitutional law is in many respects a special case.

On the one hand, there might be less incentive to look abroad. Constitutional law is more closely connected with national identity than any other field of law. It is extremely unlikely that reference to foreign private law by the Supreme Court would have incensed American legislators to the point of advocating a legal interdiction of referring to foreign sources.[1] The different private laws have a long common history. That foreign private or commercial law has an immediate impact on legal practice is evident in conflicts of law. The process of globalisation has been accompanied by a move towards uniform private and commercial law and has transformed large parts of the law into transnational law. There is no similar obvious practical relevance of foreign constitutional law.

On the other hand, however, methodologically the doors for inspiration from abroad are even more widely open in constitutional

---

* I would like to thank Andrea Kramer and Astrid Wallrabenstein for their helpful comments and critique.

[1] Cf. US house of Representatives, H.RES.97 of 2/15/2005, sponsored by not less than 65 Representatives:

> Expressing the sense of the House of Representatives that judicial determinations regarding the meaning of the Constitution of the United States should not be based on judgments, laws, or pronouncements of foreign institutions unless such foreign judgments, laws, or pronouncements inform an understanding of the original meaning of the Constitution of the United States.

adjudication than in private law. This is true both for the normative review standards and the subject matters of adjudication. The standards used by the constitutional judge are often open-ended, broad principles rather than norms that allow strict construction. The discourse about these principles is not restricted to a nation-state but is an international one. There can be no serious discussion of the concept of human dignity without reference to Kant and thinking about equality will usually start with Aristotle. When a constitutional court exercises judicial review of legislation it has to measure general policies against these principles. Again, such policies are often discussed internationally and as a result we can find relevant foreign experiences. Politicians adopting such legislation take a look at foreign inspiration and so can the constitutional judge.

I. Comparative law in the German Constitutional Court

Markesinis and Fedtke put Germany in the category 'Doing it openly' and include specifically the Constitutional Court in reaching this verdict.[2] To a certain extent this is correct. There are no fundamental objections against referring to international and foreign sources in German courts in general or the Constitutional Court in particular. A discussion like the one in the United States that forms the background of their argument is plainly unthinkable in Germany. Peter Häberle even advocates making comparative law 'the fifth method of interpretation' in constitutional law, alongside text, context, history, and policy.[3]

On the other hand, though, the German Constitutional Court has hardly been at the forefront of the internationalisation of constitutional law. Markesinis and Fedtke note that after a more frequent use of foreign law in the first years of its existence such a practice has declined.[4] Their thesis that the reliance on foreign experience is more frequent in young constitutional systems (like South Africa and Germany after 1949) and drops off with age might have some plausibility especially in the light of the extensive borrowing practice of the young constitutional courts in Eastern Europe. Judges like to justify their decisions by invoking precedents. In this perspective, drawing on persuasive precedents from international or foreign courts can add legitimacy to judicial decisions especially in new constitutional orders in which the courts cannot draw on a body of their own jurisprudence. An additional reason might be that in this way they can

---

2 Markesinis and Fedtke, in this volume, 4. b (II), pp 71 ff.

3 P. Häberle, 'Grundrechtsgeltung und Grundrechtsinterpretation im Verfassungsstaat', Juristenzeitung 1989, 913; supportive: Schulze-Fielitz, 'Verfassungsvergleichung als Einbahnstrasse', in Blankenagel *et al* (eds), *Liber Amicorum Häberle* (2004), pp 355 ff.

4 Markesinis and Fedtke, in this volume, 4. b (II), p 74.

justify judicial ideas that are unfamiliar, perhaps even unpopular, in their own country with an appeal to the authority of prestigious foreign sources.[5] In 1951 the German Court was in a similar position to today's constitutional courts in Eastern Europe. This might, indeed, explain the reference to foreign law in the early years. A prominent example is the leading case on freedom of speech and one of the Court's most important decisions overall (the *Lüth* case of 1958)[6] in which the Court cites both the French declaration of human rights in French (*un des droits les plus précieux de l'homme*) and Cardozo in English ('the matrix, the indispensable condition of nearly every other form of freedom').[7] Markesinis and Fedtke refer to additional examples.[8] But even for this early period the record is not comparable to today's practice in South Africa or Eastern Europe. Perhaps the German Court would have been similarly open to foreign experiences if there had been more foreign models. At this time, however, there was not much foreign material to borrow from.

That the need to rely on foreign precedents declines when a court develops its own case law, is plausible. In the case of the German Constitutional Court, though, the explanation might be much more mundane – and the actual importance of comparative law greater than appears on the record.

With the development of an extensive case law the German Constitutional Court has developed a style of reasoning where it basically cites only its own precedents. This is in striking contrast to the usual style of German legal writing and jurisprudence with its love of lengthy footnotes and references. The Court rarely cites scholarly opinions or other courts, much less so than other high courts in Germany. Nevertheless, it consults these sources extensively in reaching a decision. The result is a huge gap between the sources of the decision cited and those actually influencing the judges. The complete picture cannot be seen by the outsider[9] and therefore the reader will have to take my word for it.

---

[5] On the role of constitutional courts in constitutional transition cf. Bryde, 'Constitutional Courts in Constitutional Transition', in Van Loon/Van Aeken (eds), *60 maal recht en 1 maal wijn. Liber Amicorum Van Houtte* (1999), p 235 ff.

[6] There is an English translation in *Decisions of the Bundesverfassungsgericht*, Vol 2 Part I, Freedom of Speech (1998), pp 1 ff.

[7] BVerfGE 7, 198 [208].

[8] Markesinis and Fedtke, in this volume, 4. b (II), pp 75 ff; based especially on the research of J. M. Mössner, 'Rechtsvergleichung und Verfassungsrechtsprechung', (1974) AöR 193 ff.

[9] Not even after some time – the Constitutional Court refuses access to its internal papers even after the usual time under the law regulating German archives have lapsed. For a critique, cf. Th. Henne, 'Die historische Forschung und die Einsichtsnahme in Voten beim Bundesverfassungsgericht', in Henne/Riedlinger (eds), *Das Lüth-Urteil aus (rechts-) historischer Sicht*, 2005, p 19.

Every decision is prepared by a *Votum* which one judge, the rapporteur, prepares with the help of his staff. This *Votum* can be compared to the concluding observations of the Advocates General of the European Court of Justice or the *conclusions* of the *avocats généreaux* in France.[10] But regularly it is even lengthier – in important cases the *Votum* may reach the volume of a doctoral dissertation. The eight judges of the Senate will receive this *Votum* accompanied by voluminous folders of materials in which all the relevant case law and literature is collected. This collection will often include comparative material.

With this observation I do not claim that the Court regularly works on the basis of extensive comparative research. A constitutional court is not a comparative law institute and never will become one. Occasionally the Court specifically asks comparative law institutes for expert advice on foreign laws.[11] But this is a rare exception. Usually the inclusion of foreign law materials depends on their availability. When there is comparative literature (in German) relevant to the case the *Votum* will refer to it and such literature will be contained in the materials made available to the judges. To a certain degree, therefore, the extent to which the Court takes note of foreign law is decided by the productivity of German comparative law scholarship. In addition, the participants in the proceedings which in the Court's practice include not only the parties in a strict sense[12] but – by law – all state organs on the federal level and the *Länder* Governments, and – at the Court's discretion – interest groups and non-governmental organisations, are likely to bring foreign experiences to the knowledge of the Court in their briefs and pleadings when they can support their arguments.[13]

As already mentioned, compared to this hidden background influence, open references to foreign law are rare. When they appear they usually serve to provide additional legitimacy. Even an old court with much self-confidence can profit from pointing to persuasive foreign precedents. When the court decided against much popular opinion – both animal rights and xenophobic – for a Muslim halal-butcher it was helpful to point out that the Austrian Constitutional Court had reached the same

---

[10] Markesinis and Fedtke, in this volume, 4. a (ii), pp 65 f.

[11] For an example, cf. BVerfGE 83, 37 at pp 48/49 (alien suffrage); the report is published in Isensee/Schmidt-Jortzig (eds), *Das Ausländerwahlrecht vor dem Bundesverfassungsgericht* (1993), pp 284 ff. One may fairly say that it had no influence on the outcome of the case.

[12] Many types of proceedings have no 'parties' in a technical sense.

[13] As example I may point to my own pleading on behalf of the Schleswig-Holstein parliament in the aliens' suffrage cases; see Isensee/Schmidt-Jortzig (eds), op. cit. pp 238, 251 ff (brief); pp 522 ff (oral pleading).

result.[14] In another case the Court also referred to international human rights jurisprudence for the difficult task of reconciling the rule of law regarding retroactive penalisation with the avoidance of impunity for crimes committed in a non-democratic regime.[15] Finally, in establishing the constitutionality of same-sex unions it also made sense to put on the record in how many countries such unions have become accepted practice.[16]

2. The internationalisation of constitutional law under the influence of international human rights law

The usefulness of an internationalised interpretation is especially obvious if not imperative in the field of human rights. For this argument international law has to take a more prominent place than given to it by Markesinis and Fedtke.[17] If constitutional law is no longer a parochial subject, but has become an international one, the main reason is the development of international human rights law.

If we attempt – despite the obvious difficulties – to group constitutions in 'families' for comparative purposes a distinction between old and new constitutions turns out to be particularly fruitful, even if it might be unfamiliar. The decisive date for this distinction is not the turn of a century or a war, but the creation of the major instruments of international human rights law – the European Convention of Human Rights of 1950 and the International Covenants of 1966.

This distinction is important because after these dates, especially in the worldwide process of reform and democratisation in the 1980s and 1990s, international human rights treaties provided the main source of inspiration for the drafting of bills of rights. In Europe the new democracies tried to avoid any possible conflict between their new constitutional law and European human rights law by integrating Strasbourg law and jurisprudence into their own constitutional texts.[18] In other continents the UN Treaties were of major importance.[19]

---

14 BVerfGE 104, 337 at p 349.

15 BVerfGE 95, 96 at p 133.

16 BVerfGE 105, 313 at p 315.

17 Markesinis and Fedtke, in this volume, 1, pp 5f.

18 W. Kahl, *Das Grundrechtsverständnis der postsozialistischen Verfassungen* (1994), pp 69 ff.

19 Kabudi, 'Human Rights Jurisprudence in East Africa', VRÜ-Beihefte 15 (1995), pp 25 ff; Scholler, 'Die neue äthiopische Verfassung und der Schutz der Menschenrechte', VRÜ 1997, pp 166 ff; J. Dugard, 'International Human Rights', in van Wyk/Dugard/de Villiers/Davis (eds), *Rights and Constitutionalism: The New South African Legal Order* (1995), pp 193 ff; Bryde, 'Der Verfassungsstaat in Afrika', in Morlok (ed), *Die Welt des Verfassungsstaates. Kolloquium zum 65. Geburtstag von P. Häberle* (2001), pp 203, 212 ff.

But international human rights law influences national constitutional law not only by serving as a textual model. In constitutional systems without a bill of rights the international treaties are sometimes treated as constitutional law to fill this gap in the legal order. A good example is Austria, where the constitutional protection of human rights is guaranteed to a large extent through the ECHR.[20] But we find examples for the incorporation of international human rights law on all continents. In Tanzania, for example, the courts gave legal force to the invocation of the international human rights treaties in the constitution, which in the view of the drafters was probably mere rhetoric.[21]

Another way in which international human rights law influences national law is the interpretation of national law in conformity with international law. This method is especially popular in Common law jurisdictions.[22] Incorporation by interpretation has now been put into written law in the British Human Rights Act.[23]

Especially in those constitutional systems whose constitutional law has been influenced by the reception of international human rights law, the interpretation of constitutional law is internationalised because the law itself is internationalised. Legal doctrine and courts borrow freely from other countries. A leading case on the freedom of assembly by the Supreme Court in Zambia of 1995, for example, cites case law from Ghana, Nigeria, Tanzania, Zimbabwe, India, and the Strasbourg Court.[24]

This international process of receiving international human rights law has in turn influence on international law. In many countries constitutional texts that are identical or very similar to the international texts are now the law of the land. That helps to strengthen international law, because it leads to the creation of a body of case law and interpretative scholarship that could never have arisen on the international level alone.

International human rights law influences national law not only as a model but also because national courts have to take into account the possibility that international courts in regional human rights systems will declare their judgments unlawful when they deviate from international human rights standards. Especially for the highest tribunals this leads to an unfamiliar situation: to be no longer the highest authority.

---

[20] P. Pernthaler, *Österreichisches Bundesstaatsrecht* (2004), pp 627 ff; C. Grabenwarter, *Europäische Menschenrechtskonvention* (2nd edn, 2005), pp 15 ff.

[21] Kabudi, op. cit. note 19, pp 33, 94 ff.

[22] Ibid, pp 28 ff.

[23] Lord Irvine of Lairg, 'The Development of Human Rights in Britain under an Incorporated Convention on Human Right', (1998) Public Law 221 at 232 ff.

[24] Supreme Court of Zambia, *Christine Mulundika and 7 Others v. The People*, 1995/SCZ/25; Kabudi, op. cit. note 19, pp 122 ff.

This possibility of being overruled by international human rights courts has particularly influenced the development of constitutional control in countries without a tradition of judicial review. Obviously, the incorporation of the ECHR in Britain through the Human Rights Act was heavily influenced by the wish to stop those cases from reaching Strasbourg. In Scandinavia we also find the strengthening of control through the courts to be a result of a dialogue with international courts.[25] Similarly, as soon as France had opened the road for individual complaints reaching Strasbourg the French courts, especially the *Conseil d'État*, became much more ready to apply the Convention as part of the national law.[26]

While such internalisation is most prominent in the family of constitutional systems where international human rights and national bills of rights are more or less identical, it can also be observed in countries where this is not the case. Germany is a good example. The Basic Law (*Grundgesetz*) of 1949 is an 'old' constitution in my distinction. It does not belong to the family of constitutions that drafted their bill of rights with international human rights law serving as a model. In addition, the system of fundamental rights protected by the Basic Law is so comprehensive that there is less necessity than in other countries to fill gaps with the help of international documents. This might seem an exaggerated claim if you look only at the texts. Especially in the field of procedural law guarantees the European Convention of Human Rights is much more comprehensive. The German Constitutional Court has, however, developed very similar guarantees by judicial interpretation based on the principle of the rule of law enshrined in Art 20 GG.[27]

Yet German constitutional law is influenced by the European Bill of Rights. I already mentioned that the ECHR is much more differentiated and precise in providing for procedural guarantees. Here the influence is greatest. The Basic Law does not spell out, for example, the presumption of innocence. The Constitutional Court deduces it from the rule of law, but because it has no textual basis in the Basic Law it cited the words of the ECHR and drew heavily on the case law of the Strasbourg organs in its jurisprudence.[28] Similarly, the principle that court proceedings should be public is spelt out in the ECHR and not in the Basic Law, where it is deduced from the principle of rule of law and democracy. Again the Court cites the ECHR in a recent case.[29]

---

[25] Mors, *Verfassungsgerichtsbarkeit in Dänemark* (2002), pp 98 ff.

[26] C. Grewe, 'Die Grundrechte und ihre richterliche Kontrolle in Frankreich: Grundlagen und aktuelle Entwicklungen' (2002) EuGRZ 209 at 212.

[27] Right to a fair trial: BVerfGE 7, 250 at p 274; right for effective protection through the courts: BVerfGE 88, 118 at p 123.

[28] BVerfGE 35, 311 at p 320. BVerfGE 74, 102 at p 121; BVerfGE 74, 358 at p 370; BVerfGE 82, 106 at p 114.

[29] BVerfGE 103, 44 at p 64.

In addition (and similar to other countries), in Germany, too, there is an incentive to avoid defeats in international tribunals by bringing the national law into line with international standards from the outset. In Germany, the Convention does not have the quality of constitutional law.[30] Therefore, in case of conflict the judge would have to give precedence to the Constitution.[31] But by doing so he would violate Germany's international obligations. Thus there is a strong incentive to avoid such a conflict by interpreting German constitutional law in concordance with the Convention.

In Europe, the development towards a single space of human rights law has received additional input from European Community law. The European Court of Justice has developed unwritten fundamental rights from the principles common to the law of the Member States and the ECHR.[32] While these rights in principle limit the power of Community organs, not the Member States, this process has strengthened the assimilation of the three different sets of rights – ECHR, European Union, and Member States. With the adoption of the Charter of Fundamental Rights[33] the European Bill of Rights acquired a written form. In theory the Convention drafting the charter did not have a mandate for law-making, but had only the task to codify recognised principles within the meaning of Art 6 EU-Treaty, drawing on the jurisprudence of the Luxembourg and Strasbourg Courts and the national law of the Member States. Without – meanwhile unlikely – ratification of the European Constitution, of which it was to be an integral part, it has no binding force. But in practice the Charter is a systematic and innovative document that now also influences national constitutional law.[34]

3. The uses of foreign law

Regularly, the use of foreign law will be only inspirational. Markesinis and Fedtke concentrate on this aspect. But stressing the purely inspirational nature of the use of foreign law creates the danger of underestimating the

---

[30] On the different legal quality of the Convention in the Member States, cf. C. Grabenwarter (op. cit. note 20), pp 15 ff.

[31] A possibility overstressed by the 2nd Senate in BVerfGE 111, 307; in practice this situation is difficult to envisage.

[32] Developed in ECJ Case 29/69 (1969, 419) – *Stauder*; Case 11/70 (1970, 1125) – *Internationale Handelsgesellschaft*; now codified in Art 6 EU Treaty; Markesinis and Fedtke, in this volume, 5 a), pp 112, 115 ff.

[33] ABl 2000 Nr. C 364/1; Callies, 'Die Europäische Grundrechts Charta', in Ehlers (ed), *Europäische Grundrecht und Grundfreiheiten* (2003); A. Wallrabenstein, 'Die Grundrechte, der EuGH und die Charta', 2002 Kritische Jusitz 381 ff.

[34] It is cited by the constitutional courts of the Member States: BVerfGE 110, 339 at p 342.

challenge. Foreign law can also be used as a genuine legal argument suggesting a specific outcome of a case. Of course, this distinction is merely typological. In practice, every argument that is used in a legal dispute may be called 'legal' and where the foreign experience *prima facie* suggests that an interpretation of the national law is 'wrong' the judge will still find ways to justify a decision reaching the opposite solution. But typologically we can distinguish different degrees of persuasive power of foreign precedents.

a) Foreign law as an inspiration

If we consider only the inspirational use there should be little controversy about the usefulness to look to other countries. There is no *numerus clausus* of persuasive sources of law. If it is interesting what Professor X thinks of a problem so it should equally be of relevance what constitutional courts in other constitutional democracies have had to say in a similar case.

This only holds true, of course, when problems are indeed similar. Foreign precedents will be of little help where constitutional law contains very specific rules that are peculiar to the country in question. This is often the case when it comes to the organisation of state organs: there are hardly two countries that have exactly the same electoral laws or where the composition and functions of a second chamber are completely identical. Still, even in these cases international discussion about democracy, federalism, and the separation of powers might be of interest.

Much more typical for constitutional adjudication is the application of broad principles rather than the strict construction of rules.[35] The discourse on principles like equality and freedom, human dignity and democracy thereby is an international one, not a national one. There is no such thing like 'German' as opposed to 'French' human dignity. Therefore we find an international constitutional discourse, which we as judges can and should use to broaden our perspective and to better understand our own system. Often, what appears to be obvious according to national traditions becomes questionable if we submit it to the test of international experience and discussion.

For an inspirational use there are few normative or methodological requirements. While I do not want to encourage sloppy comparative research, one might even be fruitfully inspired by a foreign text which one misunderstood or has taken out of context. There are historical examples for outstanding contributions to constitutional theory that started from a misreading of foreign experience. Montesquieu used an

[35] On this distinction, cf. R. Alexy, *A Theory of Constitutional Rights* (2005), pp 44 ff.

idealised and completely unrealistic picture of the British Constitution to criticise French absolutism and to create the theory of separation of powers. Bagehot found an authoritative explanation of the British Constitution by contrasting it to the American Constitution despite the errors he made in understanding the American example.[36]

This argument in favour of productive errors should not be overdone: not everyone setting sail for India discovers America.[37] Obviously, misunderstanding the foreign experience might give the wrong inspiration for the interpretation of one's own law. Nevertheless, if one is aware of this danger, there is no fundamental objection against borrowing an idea from a foreign jurisdiction that for sociological or political reasons does not work there, but might work in one's own country.

b) Foreign law as a legal argument

It would be too narrow to see foreign law only as an inspiration. Instead, it can also become a genuine legal argument. In this case, of course, the methodology has to be more thorough: a judge may be inspired by a foreign idea which he misunderstood; he can use it as an argument only when he gets it right.

(i) Foreign experience in the application of national standards

Foreign experience may be used as an argument in the application of national constitutional standards. A simple illustration is the use of foreign examples in the application of the proportionality principle. This principle was developed by the German Constitutional Court as an unwritten boundary to the broad written competence of the lawmaker to limit guaranteed rights.[38] The principle of proportionality requires that all encroachments on fundamental rights – be they by the legislature the executive or the judiciary – pursue a legitimate purpose and are suited,

---

36 Richard Crossman, *The Myths of Cabinet Government* (1972), pp 10 ff.

37 I paraphrase a German author, Erich Kästner: 'Irrtümer haben ihren Wert, jedoch nur hier und da, nicht jeder der nach Indien fährt, entdeckt Amerika'.

38 BVerfGE 7, 377 at pp 397 ff; this jurisprudence has influenced European human rights law – see Grabenwarter, op. cit. note 30, pp 111 ff; European law – 'Proportionality' in *Oxford Encyclopedia of European Community Law* (1990), pp 433 ff – and many constitutional systems – cf. Zimmermann, 'Bürgerliche und politische Rechte in der Verfassungsrechtsprechung mittel- und osteuropäischer Staaten unter besonderer Berücksichtigung der Einflüsse der deutschen Verfassungsgerichtsbarkeit' in Frowein/Marauhn (eds), *Grundfragen der Verfassungsgerichtsbarkeit in Mittel-und Osteuropa* pp 89, 92 ff.

necessary and appropriate to achieve this purpose.[39] The argument that foreign experience shows that a law is ill-suited or unnecessary is in principle an argument which is able to establish the unconstitutionality of a legal provision. In practice this argument is more often invoked by parties than accepted by courts. If one uses the foreign situation not as an inspiration but as a legal argument, to show that a measure is unconstitutional because it is unnecessary, the methodological requirements in ascertaining the foreign situation are much higher than with an inspirational use of foreign law. One has to study not just the law in the books but also the law in action and establish that the alternative solution in another country is functioning properly. The lawmaker has a broad margin of appreciation in deciding what laws are necessary and practical. Conditions in another country are never exactly the same and therefore what works in one country might work differently in another. From the perspective of the lawmaker – vis-à-vis which the court has to use restraint – the situation might appear different enough to justify a differentiated solution. Even though in theory the reference to a foreign example might be a compelling legal argument showing that a course of action is ill-suited or unnecessary and therefore disproportional, in practice in this case, too, we will use the foreign experience rather as inspirational, as prima facie evidence that a law is questionable, but allow the lawmaker to show that his distinction is legitimate. Despite these difficulties I would maintain that foreign law in this context is used as a legal argument.

(ii) Appeal to international standards by text or implication

Foreign law is even more clearly used as a legal argument where the text of the national constitution itself refers to an international standard.

An example can be found in the 'family' of constitutional systems that have relied on international human rights law.[40] Here, one can commonly find a clause that allows only those limitations of guaranteed rights that are necessary in a 'democratic society'.[41] This is an abstract, transnational concept. In an international covenant it can hardly be otherwise, but this formulation does not necessarily lose its transnational content when transferred verbatim into the text of a national

---

[39] In detail BVerfGE 7, 377 at p 397 ff; see from the subsequent established case law only BVerfGE 17, 306 at pp 313–14; BVerfGE 30, 1 at pp 20–1; BVerfGE 44, 353 at pp 378 ff; BVerfGE 65, 1 at p 44; BVerfGE 70, 297 at p 311; BVerfGE 76, 1 at pp 50–1; BVerfGE 83, 201 at p 212.

[40] Cf. 2 supra.

[41] Cf. Grabenwarter (op. cit. note 20), pp 111 ff.

constitution. Therefore, I would consider evidence about the practice of other democratic countries with the same set of constitutional guarantees not as mere inspiration, but as a legal argument. The text of the national constitution cannot be understood without comparative analysis.

A more controversial example is the case that gave rise to the quarrel about the use of foreign law in the United States. In the death penalty cases the court had to decide what amounts to 'cruel and unusual punishment'. The question is: 'unusual' when and where? Originalists might answer: 'usual' punishment means punishment that was usual at the time of the drafting of the American Constitution. In view of penal practices in the eighteenth century most constitutionalists today would find this answer plainly unacceptable. Another possibility would be to base the judgment on what is 'usual' exclusively on national practice. But this would be very narrow and might also lead to circular arguments. If we take national practice as a standard, the constitution is in danger of losing its function to set limits to the lawmaker: the legal practice in place by definition would also be constitutional. This danger is avoided when one chooses a less parochial approach and interprets the term 'usual' in a way that takes international practice and evolving international standards of decency into account. The opposition from advocates of the death penalty is, however, understandable. They do not want to read in the judgment of their own Supreme Court evidence which shows that with regard to the practice of the death penalty the United States forms part of a 'family' of constitutional systems most other members of which belong to the 'axis of evil'.

(iii) Transnational constitutionalist principles as boundaries of constitutional lawmaking

Finally, we find an important field of a normative use of foreign law in constitutional systems where 'simple' constitutional law is limited by higher constitutional principles. This is the case where either constitution-making or constitutional amendments are bound to general principles of constitutionalism. These principles are established on a more abstract level than the 'ordinary' constitutional law of the country. This makes it attractive if not necessary to develop these principles from a comparative perspective.

1. Limits to constitution making

The Certification Judgments of South Africa's Constitutional Court, outstanding and much noted examples of comparative constitutional jurisprudence, fall into this category. South Africa's transitional constitutional law gave the Court a unique role. The Court itself describes this role in its First Certification judgment[42] where it points very precisely to the problem that led to this role, namely the question how to reconcile a negotiated transition with the concept of the constituent power of the people (para 13):

> [13] A national legislature, elected by universal adult suffrage, would double as the constitution-making body and would draft the new constitution. (...) But that text would have to comply with certain guidelines agreed upon in advance by the negotiating parties. What is more, an independent arbiter would have to ascertain and declare whether the new constitution indeed complied with the guidelines before it could come into force.

This arbiter was to be the Constitutional Court. It might seem astonishing that a judicial body was selected for this function. The judiciary had been too much part of the apartheid system to make judicial politics the obvious choice for the safeguarding of constitutional transition from a racist system to a multi-racial democracy. However, while for the black majority the system acted as an oppressive dictatorship, within the white judicial and political system vestiges of the values of liberal rule-of-law-traditions from English and Dutch legal heritage were retained. Abel has told us how this system contained just enough elements of the rule of law to be capable of being employed by the opposition as 'politics by other means'[43] and this more so the more the end of the apartheid system became visible. Without the story told by him I doubt that a judicial solution for the problems of constitutional transition could have been envisaged. More important for a comparative theory of constitutional jurisprudence, a specialised Constitutional Court could be constructed and staffed in a way so as to allow both sides to trust its judgement. This task could hardly have been entrusted to a Supreme Court staffed by senior career judges of the old regime.

The Constitutional Court approaches the difficult task of measuring constitutional law against constitutional principles with a comparative approach: it takes a worldwide survey of the realisations of the relevant constitutional principles and asks whether the South African solutions remain within this framework. This approach and the rich material gathered this way have made the judgment an instant classic in comparative constitutional law. The use of comparative law in this judgment is clearly not merely inspirational. The foreign materials are used to develop general transnational constitutional principles which are then used as standards against which the draft is measured.

---

[42] Constitutional Court CCT 23/1996 (Judgment of 6 September 1996), online at www.law.wits.ac.za/judgments/certsum.html (last accessed 23 May 2006).

[43] R. Abel, *Politics by other Means* (1995).

2. Limits to constitutional amendments

What holds true for constitution making should also be considered for constitutional amendments. Usually, in constitutional democracies the constitution limits the lawmaker but the democratic process retains the last word because judgments of courts holding laws unconstitutional can be overruled by changing the constitution if the necessary majorities are available. There are, however, constitutions that set limits to constitutional change.[44] Obviously, such restrictions of the amending power have to be used with special restraint by constitutional courts. For this task, again, a comparative approach similar to the one the South African Court used for the corresponding question of constitution-making appears to be the most fruitful.[45] When the constitution limits the amending power by enshrining general principles like democracy, federalism, the rule of law, or the principle of human dignity, the standard cannot be taken from the constitutional system itself. The amending power must be allowed to change the concrete form the principle has found in the respective country. A survey of the realisations of the relevant constitutional principles and an analysis whether the constitutional amendment remains within this framework appears to be the best solution. Here, too, the argument that the intended change is known in other constitutionalist democracies is a genuine legal argument.

To sum up – constitutional law is no longer a parochial subject but has become an international one. The main reason is the development of international human rights law. The ensuing international constitutional discourse has benefited all participants and will continue to do so. We should be inspired by foreign law to transcend a narrow-mindedness that has governed the development of constitutional law for too long and we should look to foreign experience in applying constitutional principles to the difficult problems which confront all societies in the twenty-first century.

---

[44] Survey by C. Grewe and H. R. Fabri, *Droits Constituionnels Europeens* (1995), pp 55 ff.

[45] On the interpretation of Art 79(3) BL, cf. Bryde in von Münch/Kunig, *Grundgesetzkommentar* (4/5th edn, 2003), Art 79 Rn. 28; Hain in von Mangoldt/Klein, *Grundgesetz Kommentar*, Art 79 Rn 58.

The Practice of Comparative Law by the Supreme Courts

Brief Reflections on the Dialogue Between the Judges in French and European Experience[1]

Guy Canivet

The laws, in their widest sense, are the necessary relations which derive from the nature of things.

Montesquieu, Esprit des Lois

Justice and injustice change in quality as they change in climate. (...) Amusing justice that a stream divides (...).

Pascal, Les Pensées

1. Introduction

As one often needs to do when treating a legal question, the introductory comments by Sir Basil Markesinis and Jörg Fedtke on 'The Judge as Comparatist' broach a theoretical issue expressed by the first quotation, followed immediately by a practical interpretation raised by the second.

From a theoretical point of view, if one admits with Montesquieu that the law is the product of the social order in which it is applied, then the difference between the rules of one country and another flow directly from the diversity between legal cultures.[2]

At the same time, the phenomenon of globalisation, resulting from the development of commercial relations and the spread of technologies and new means of communication, creates, as to the great questions facing society, a dialogue between civilisations and between currents of

[1] A Commentary upon the article of Sir Basil Markesinis and Jörg Fedtke, 'The Judge as Comparatist', published in Tulane Law Review (November 2005). The original French version was translated into English by Vernon Valentine Palmer, Thomas Pickles Professor of Law, Tulane University.

[2] See Eric Agostini, *Droit comparé* (1988), p 9 *et seq*.

opinion, tending to bring about convergence in the different legal systems, as Pascal urges in the second quotation. The convergence, however, derives from the first observation as to the existence of different systems of law which are the fruit of their cultures, of history, of geography, and economy. Thus, there are two movements: the incommensurability – irreducibility – of legal cultures, on the one hand, and convergence, on the other, set in motion contradictory movements between singularity and rapprochement in the legal systems.

The starting point of every comparative law inquiry consists in the study of the diversity that characterises the state of the law worldwide. This diversity is shown notably in the classification by category of the legal systems. Yet it cannot be reduced to that, alone. Borrowings are mixed together and interactions are reciprocal, to such an extent that it is effectively difficult in Europe to classify the legal systems of law according to exclusive zones of influence of Common law, French, Italian, or German law.[3]

The diversity found in legal systems, which is not a recent phenomenon, produces complex and indeed inextricable situations which are today as anachronistic as they are counter-productive. How can such wide differences in family status be admitted, even in Europe, while the flow of immigration continues to develop and to become the norm? What can be said of the variety of the commercial laws – the law of contracts, suretyship, business incorporation, credit transactions, competition law, the stock exchange – which differ from one economic area to another and which, in a world where the commercial exchanges and the economic structures overlap considerably, are a source of great complication if not confusion.

Moreover, even where texts regulating the same question are identical, it happens that the enforcement varies from one country to another. Such is, for example, the case of systems which practice the civil law derived from the Code Napoléon, such as France and Belgium. However close these countries may be culturally, geographically, historically, and legally, with the passage of time they have developed different – and sometimes opposite – interpretations of similarly phrased rules.[4]

On the one hand, since the ideological, religious, historical, economic, climatic, geographic, sociological, and cultural bases vary, it is understandable that their regulatory framework diverges in direct proportion to the extent of these variations and their respective objectives. On the other hand, business needs uniform rules to conduct its affairs, and at the same time citizens wish to move about freely without

---

[3] See Raymond Légeais, *Grands systèmes de droit contemporains – approche comparative* (2004), and particularly chapter I 'Peut-on classer les systémes de droit en groupe ou en familles?', pp 81 *et seq*.

[4] See for example, 'La responsabilité du fait des choses en France et en Belgique' in Raymond Légeais (op. cit. note 3).

seeing their personal or family status or their fundamental liberties vary from one country to another. Intuitively human beings have a universal conception of the idea of justice. They find it difficult to explain different solutions to the same questions, but they will not admit losing the national identity which underlies the institutions regulating their personal life.

From this contradiction arises the interest in comparative law. The object of this discipline consists in the reasoned study of systems and institutions of various States or groups of States; it permits the jurist to enlarge his or her field of research, to study, understand, and to explain the differences between the laws, and at the same time, it invites him or her to a deeper understanding of the foundations of his own legal order and, from there, to search for similarities and convergences.[5]

Moreover, certain systems are not simply important in themselves, but important for the influence they exert on others.[6] Knowledge of systems whose radiating influence is now or once was determinant for others is thus a necessary step in that it illuminates the 'juridical geography' of classifications and of invariables, helping to orient the jurist within diversity and to place in parallel the institutions under study. Such institutions as contracts and property law have no sense except through the tradition to which they are attached – Civil law or Common law – and are not comparable except within the context of that tradition.

Also worth emphasising is the fact that the existence of legal traditions should be seen in parallel with another phenomenon whose importance is increasingly felt these days. For there now exists a competition of laws in the world, which means that international affairs are dealt with by the legal regime which most efficiently produces and transfers economic wealth, and legal disputes are judged before the courts which seem the most adept at an optimal distribution of individual interests. It is, as a consequence, essential to know each of these laws to evaluate their economic efficiency, just as it is important to the States to make their legal systems adapt to this competition.

Originally, comparative law was spurred on by the utopia of legal unity, by the pursuit of a universal law, the impossible quest after a Common law of humanity.[7] Today, from a more realistic point of view, it

---

[5] See Roland Drago, 'Droit comparé' in Denis Alland et Stèphane Rials (eds) *Dictionnaire de la culture juridique* (2003), pp 453–7.

[6] See René David and Camille Jauffret-Spinosi, *Les grands systèmes de droit compare* (11th edn, 2002), pp 5 *et seq*.

[7] As Eric Agostini emphasises, 'At that time (nineteenth century) one made comparative law into a romantic conception bathed in the splendid dream of a universal law. However Portalis had said: "Uniformity is a type of perfection which, according to the words of a celebrated author, sometimes takes hold of great minds and infallibly astonishes the small ones.";' op. cit. note 2, p 22.

is oriented towards the understanding and the management of diversity. A great French comparatist, Professor Mireille Delmas-Marty, speaks of 'ordered pluralism'. The pluralist vision of the law is today uncontested. If the comparatists of yesterday considered diversity as a handicap, today they think that each nation ought to be faithful to its tradition and that the unity of law is neither feasible nor desirable. They see the future in a different light: law being a product of history, it changes continually, since no tradition can create fixed and immutable laws. Thus variety has a value in itself since, so far as it incites experimentation and efforts, it cannot be separated from evolution, hence from progress.

Developing in a competitive legal context, such experiments aim at efficiency and improvement, each system tending through incorporation or imitation to be inspired by the best in others in order to be the best performer. In this way one puts aside a static conception of laws in favor of a vision decidedly evolutionary. One knows, for example, that the so-called law on the Continent of Europe is open to Anglo-American models, such as the trust or accusatory procedure in penal matters. Seeing matters in this way means accepting that the law ceases 'to be' and is, instead, in a permanent process of 'becoming'. After all, the strength of a law may rest in its plasticity, in its ability to evolve, to adapt to social and economic necessities. It is not by accident that the renovated systems of the old socialist bloc seem more modern, hence more attractive, than those of the old democracies whose legal traditions are becoming paralysed. Cannot one thus explain the seductiveness of the laws of North America, the United States, and Canada, which have gone beyond the contribution offered by the English Common Law by modernising it in written form?

At the same time, legal science is enriched by the contributions of other disciplines. The modern theory of comparative law invites the use of other sciences: philosophy, history, sociology, economy, anthropology, ethics, and genetics, which is to say the human sciences as well as the natural sciences, all of which study life in all its manifestations. Law is thus open to the world and at the same time it enters the fields of science.

It should not be believed, however, that comparative law is merely an academic discipline, an object of (mere theoretical) study. On the contrary, it leads to tangible consequences and concrete applications, which is to say, to the influence of certain laws on others, either through imitation or by reception. Thus the act of comparison is interesting from two standpoints. On the one hand, it is a technique that permits the understanding of laws and the rational explanation of their respective identities. On the other hand, it offers practical aid in suggesting original models taken from foreign experience. It stimulates the circulation of models. The forces behind these exchanges, interpenetrations, and crossing influences are *doctrine* (i.e. academic writing), public authorities, and the judges.[8]

Comparative law being a scientific discipline, one easily sees the role that professors play in the area of research and teaching. Their studies are not, however, without effect upon the practitioners of law. These studies guide their action by furnishing information, incitation, and recommendation.

As to the public authorities, one increasingly observes that comparative law is the foundation of all reform. Before revising a system of law, the legislator or the administration observe the foreign solutions. Thanks to the comparative technique, the borrowing, imitation, or inspiration of a foreign legal rule is more conscious, more reasoned, better studied, and deliberate. Complete research and analysis of the foreign solution necessarily precedes its borrowing.

But how does the judge play a role in the circulation of legal ideas? In what way does comparative law commend itself to the practice of the courts? In what respect does its technique affect the interpretation of the law, or have an influence on the case law?

If one presumes that the judge is nothing but a totally neutral instrument in the application of law, then his study of other systems would be without reason or object. In reality, the influence of comparative law evidently varies according to the role attributed to case law as a source of law. One knows that under the system of precedent, the judge at Common law has a function of prime importance in the creation of law, whereas the case law in the systems of written law gives the appearance of being nothing but an accessory source of law. Here, the function of interpretation is in all cases the only recognised function of the judge. From the point of view of such a judge, it is the role of comparative law within the mechanism of interpretation which must be examined.

A movement of this kind is occurring within the judicial community. Nowadays, meetings among judges are multiplying. One can see the development of cooperative understanding, the creation of active, international organisations of judges and courts, the existence of means of exchange, and the fact that access to the different laws and the jurisprudence of the highest courts is now convenient, if not habitual.

As mediated by the judges, the legal systems communicate and correspond with one another, a process that Sir Basil Markesinis and Jörg Fedtke see as taking the form of a 'dialogue' and 'intellectual interaction' rather than that of direct borrowing. The foreign law is never in effect employed by the judges as a direct source or as a binding precedent but

---

[8] See Xavier Blanc-Jouvan, 'Prologues' in Société de legislation comparé (ed), *L'avenir du droit compare – un défi pour les jurists du nouveau* millénaire (2000), p 12.

rather as a secondary source, as a source of inspiration to apply, interpret, adapt, or complete the national law, particularly when that law is obsolete, unclear, or contradictory. The comparison broadens the horizon of the judge for the improvement of his or her own law.

The brilliant article of Sir Basil Markesinis and Jörg Fedtke invites us to reflect upon this opening up of judicial vision. As shown by their rigorous, scientific technique, for most of the great legal systems, this opening is of considerable significance and increasing frequency, due in particular to the rapid social changes which provoke new problems simultaneously in several countries and which incite the judges to reconsider older solutions. By way of example, one could cite, as they do, the liability of businesses which have exposed their employees to the risk of professional illness caused by the use of materials made of asbestos, and as added examples, the liability of the health systems brought about by the use of blood transfusions contaminated by the AIDS virus, the commercial or criminal activities which developed with the appearance of the internet, and the liability of the manufacturers of cigarettes with respect to smokers injured through addiction to tobacco, and so forth. It is evident that, confronted by social phenomena which produce cases of this sort and which arise in the same way in many countries, the judges do not fail to observe how these disputes are resolved abroad and to be inspired by them.

Without doubt, if we revert to the paradigm concerning the relationship between the affirmation of national legal identities and the convergence of international problems, the comparison of legal solutions by inter-judicial communication plays a role in the judicial practice of the supreme courts. To expand further the study of Sir Basil Markesinis and Jörg Fedtke, we will examine this phenomenon through the French jurisprudence, by examining first, the reasons which may make a judge decide to refer to extra-national legal sources, then the methods by which the judge integrates these elements into his or her judgement. To study the introduction of comparative law in judicial practice, we will thus follow the path which leads logically from reasons (2) to methods (3).

2. The reasons for recourse to comparative law

The reasons which lead the judge to refer to comparative law are multiple. Essentially, they vary according to the systems of law (a) and the interpretative techniques (b).

a) The recourse to comparative law varies according to the system of law

It is obvious that the greater the judge's freedom in interpreting law – here one speaks of judicial discretion – the more important recourse to elements external to the national law may become. Conversely, to the extent that judicial reasoning is narrow, purely deductive and centred on the literal application of the internal law, there will be less interest in looking at foreign systems. We know, from this point of view, that there is a characteristic difference between the Common law judge and the judges of the written law. In the one case the jurisprudence is an autonomous and primary legal source; in the other the written law is dominant, case law being an accessory and subordinated source that leaves but a passive role to the judge.

In its origins the Common law is, in effect, a structure composed of borrowings and mixed influences between courts belonging to the same system. After the conquest of England in the Middle Ages, the itinerant judges of the Norman kings had to resolve conflicts (initially on matters that concerned the Crown) between peoples of different origins, with different legal customs, who lived in the country: Celts, Saxons, and Normans. From these decisions arose a 'common' law which applied over and above all territorial practices and rules and which, by virtue of the growth of the English empire during the eighteenth and nineteenth centuries, spread to many countries on all continents. All of the systems within this very homogeneous legal family continue to influence and inspire each another (though this does not mean that they, nowadays, always follow the same rules or adopt the same interpretation). There is, thus, great communication between the jurisprudence of the high courts of these States whose law is inspired by the English Common Law: Great Britain, Canada, Australia, New Zealand, and even the United States.

Moreover, subject to several exceptions, notably that of the United States, the Common law retains an empirical and flexible character that is naturally open to the influence of other systems. Leading writers note that the highest courts in Canada, South Africa (especially the country's Consitutional Court), and, to some extent, England, appear to be adopting positions which are quite innovative in this regard.

Matters are considerably different in the systems inspired by Continental law. Here recourse to comparative law differs, depending upon the interpretative legal techniques and the extent to which they leave relatively more, or less, initiative or liberty to the judge.

b) Recourse to comparative law varies in accordance with the techniques of legal interpretation

One knows in effect that in the traditions of written law, there are diverse methods of interpretation, depending upon the historical period and the legal system in question. Certain methods, the so-called closed or intrinsic ones, do not authorise any reference except to the precise law to be applied internally, whereas more open methods, called extrinsic ones, may take into account elements outside of the internal norm to be applied.

(i) The slight use of comparative method in exegetical interpretation

The 'exegetical' school,[9] which controlled the interpretation of the Code Napoléon during the greater part of the nineteenth century, had the precise aim of leaving little initiative to the judge in the interpretation of the law. It confined him through grammatical, syntactical, and logical elements derived from the text itself to follow a central point of reference: the will of the legislator. The judge was only the passive expression of the law in a particular case. Obviously, such a doctrine left little space to judicial discretion and for the examination of or comparison with foreign law.

A question remains, however, when the written law is borrowed from foreign sources. In strict respect for the legislative will, can or should the judge refer back to the foreign interpretive case law of the transposed text? A typical example of this situation is found in the practice of francophone African States whose laws derived from French law but have evolved differently since decolonisation.

One observes that for historical, cultural, or academic reasons, the high courts of these countries continue to be inspired by the current jurisprudence of the Court of Cassation in the enforcement of their own codes even if these are no longer identical to the French law. This situation has justified the creation by all the francophone supreme courts of a jurisprudential base to which each court may refer.

Another example may be cited in the form of a question: French criminal law only recently incorporated a procedure inspired by the institution of 'plea bargaining' found in American criminal law.[10] Faced with the interpretation of these new texts, will the French judges be inspired by the American judicial practice regarding 'pleading guilty' or, on the contrary, will they reveal a tendency to 'deracinate the borrowing,' as the Minister of Justice invites them to do in an interpretive circular addressed to the prosecutors?

---

[9] See Jean Carbonnier, *Droit civil – introduction* (26th edn, 1999), pp 297 *et seq*; Henri Léon, Jean Mazeaud, and Francois Chabat, *Lecons de droit civil – introduction à l'étude du droit* (2000), pp 171 *et seq*.

[10] Loi no. 2004-204 of 9 March 2004 concerning the adaptation of justice to the evolutions of criminality.

(ii) The growing influence of comparative law within open methods of interpretation

From the end of the nineteenth century and under the influence of leading jurists, notably Gény, the founder of a new school of legal interpretration called 'free scientific research',[11] the French courts more or less managed to free themselves from the exegetical method by integrating in their reasoning certain elements external to the text to be applied. These could be purely juridical elements, such as the search for coherence and completeness in the legal system, or they might be factors external to national law or even law, itself (i.e. social or economic), thus permitting the law to evolve and to better adapt to the context of its application. Comparative law has a growing place among the elements taken into account, and besides, since the middle of the twentieth century, the supranational European courts are issuing new and original rulings dealing with national legal solutions that have an impact on the laws of other States.

In the French system, this modest and indeed insufficiently developed practice is not easily discerned since the French courts, in principle, cannot cite doctrinal authorities or jurisprudence in their judgments, whether it be national, supranational, or foreign. Additionally, the French decisions of the highest courts are particularly brief because by tradition and in principle they proceed by strictly deductive reasoning which prevents the elaboration of the true motives of the judgment. Indeed, so great is the fiction about the timeless meaning of the law that French judgments carry no internal reference to foreign laws and solutions.

Nevertheless, recently the French Court of Cassation has modified its practice in this respect by publishing the report presented by the member of the Court who wrote the draft of the decision submitted for discussion and collegial approval. The judgment of the Court of Cassation is thus published with this preparatory study which presents the different options made available to the court. These reports reveal more and more the consultation of foreign law that is taking place and give a glimpse of the type of case in which the judge allows himself to be exposed to such influences.

1. The recourse to comparative law in the enforcement of European rights

The most remarkable case of resort to comparative law is encountered when general legal principles common to many States are applied in the European courts. This arises in the enforcement of two treaties which

---

[11] See Jean Carbonnier (op. cit. note 9), pp 300 *et seq* and Henri Léon, Jean Mazeaud, and Francois Chabat (op. cit. note 9), pp 172 *et seq*.

integrate national rights within the European legal order. One is the Treaty of the European Union and the other is the European Convention on Human Rights.

Each treaty establishes a supranational court charged with enforcing it and with giving interpretations binding upon the State courts which have concurrent responsibility to enforce the treaties. The Treaty of the European Union creates the European Court of Justice and the European Convention on Human Rights establishes the European Court of Human Rights. Both of these treaties make reference, more or less, to the common legal tradition of the signatory States – in the one case, the members of the European Union, now 25 States, in the other, the States party to the European Convention on Human Rights, today numbering 46 States assembled in the Council of Europe. In applying these treaties, the two courts turn their attention to the laws of the Member States and in so doing they use the comparative method as a means of knowing and understanding these laws.

1) The law of the European Union

In the jurisprudence of the European Court of Justice, there are many indications of an interaction with the law of the Member States. In this respect an important role is played by the national jurisprudences in the construction of general principles common to the laws of these States, which, being legal sources themselves,[12] are common principles elevated to the rank of general principles of European Union law. In this case the European Court of Justice mobilises the resources of comparative law to discern, notably in the internal jurisprudence of the national courts, those rules which constitute the common legal patrimony of the European States.[13]

Sir Basil Markesiinis and Jörg Fedtke show this clearly through their analysis of the Algera,[14] Hauer,[15] and Internationale Handelsgesellschaft[16] decisions.

---

[12] CJCE, arrêt du 17 décembre 1970, *Internationale Handelsgesellschaft*, aff 11/70, Rec. p 1125, arrêt du 14 mai 1974, *Nold*, aff. 4/73, Rec. p 491.

[13] Yves Galmot, 'Réflexions sur le recours au droit compare par la Cour de justice des communautés européennes', RFDA, mars–avril 1990, pp 255–62.

[14] CJCE arrêt du 12 juillet 1957, *Mlle Dineke algera et autres contre Assemblée commune de la Communauté européenne du charbon et d l'acier*, aff. 7/56, 3/57 à 7/57.

[15] CJCE, arrêt du 13 décembre 1979, *Liselotte Hauer contre Land Rheinland-Pfalz*, aff. 44/79.

[16] CJCE, arrêt du 17 décembre 1970, *Internationale Handelsgesellschaft mbH contre Einfuhr- und Vorratsstelle fur Getreide und Futtermittel*, aff. 11–70.

For their part the judges of the Member States who are charged with the enforcement of the cases submitted to them use the same method in the contemplation of the laws and principles of the other countries of Europe. Thus, the technique of the European Court of Justice, in integrating a comparative approach to national laws, inevitably produces a kind of apprenticeship for the 'subordinate' courts.

The circulation of the principle of proportionality – the principle according to which a legal rule does not apply beyond the end pursued – is a characteristic example. A product of the German legal tradition, the principle of proportionality was brought into European Union law in the case of *Internationale Handelsgesellschaft*,[17] then taken up by a number of Member States, including France, which thereafter made general use of it even outside the field of application of European Union law. The Social Chamber of the Court of Cassation, for example, utilises this principle in the area of restrictions on individual liberties, as in defining the extent of the employer's power of control over his salaried workers.[18] Likewise, the Criminal Chamber applies proportionality as a control when an individual citizen makes use of force to apprehend someone presumed to have committed a flagrant breach of the law,[19] or in evaluating the compatibility of certain restrictions on liberty, such as the liberty of information, with the European Convention of Human Rights.

In Europe, the national courts are more and more inspired by the law and case law produced in other countries on the Continent, while at the same time the Charter of Fundamental Rights invites them to develop and preserve values of a common and universal character that constitute the common heritage of the States, such as human dignity, liberty, equality, and solidarity.

The national judicial decisions are just as important in the jurisprudence of the European Court of Human Rights where logically they occupy a primary place in the protective system established by the European Convention on Human Rights. The interpretative method of the European Court is founded first upon a consensus according to which the Convention is to be understood in the light of conceptions currently prevailing in the democratic States.[20] These common conceptions are obviously discovered in the law and jurisprudence of the courts of the States which are party to the Convention.

---

[17] Ibid.

[18] Cass. Soc. arrêt du 3 avril 2001, Bull. V no. 115.

[19] Crim, arrêt du 13 avril 2005, pourvoi no. 04-83.939

[20] CEDH, arrêt du 13 juin 1979, *Marckx contre Belgique*, Série A no. 31, S.58: the Convention 'ought to be interpreted in light of today's conditions'. See Frédéric Sudre, *Droit européen et international des droits de l'homme* (6th edn), pp 223 *et seq*.

An effort of this kind was clearly illustrated in the case of *Vô v France*, where the Court searched in vain the case law of the States for a common conception protecting the fetus within the framework of a right to life.[21]

In the same way, an interpretation of the Convention's evolution begins with an examination of the evolution of the national jurisprudence. The Court does this by taking into consideration the social changes perceived by the national judges, whether this refers, for example, the rights of natural children,[22] of transsexualism,[23] or of the structure of the family.[24] In this regard the Court emphasises that every evolution in the national jurisprudences is susceptible of moving the centre of gravity and to provoke in turn a change in the jurisprudence of the Court. This is what was articulated very clearly in 1989 in the Cossey-decision on the question of homosexual marriage.[25]

It is also the presence of common denominators in the national jurisprudences which constitutes the decisive element in the Court's control over the degree of discretion reserved to the States to place limits on guaranteed rights. The narrower the jurisprudential consensus, the narrower is the latitude afforded the States. Such, for example, was the reasoning followed by the European judges in connection with the equality among legitimate and natural children.[26] Conversely, the absence of convergence in the national jurisprudences leaves the States a greater margin of appreciation in the maintenance of measures restricting human rights, as in the *Fretté* case,[27] which upheld a refusal to accord parental rights to homosexuals as nonviolative of the prohibition against discrimination (Art 14 of the Convention) and respect for privacy (Art 8).

Finally, and above all, the European Court examines whether the national laws are sufficient to grant the level of protection required by the Convention and, in that event, the Court describes them very precisely.

As one can see, the comparison of the legal systems in force in the different countries of Europe is a habitual exercise for the European courts as well as for the judges of the Member States in the enforcement

---

21 CEDH, Grande Chambre, arrêt du 8 juillet 2004, *Vô contre France*, requite no. 53924/00, pp 84 *et seq*.

22 CEDH, arrêt du 1 février 2000, *Mazurek contre France*, Rec. 2000-II.

23 CEDH, arrêt du 25 mars 1992, *B. contre France*, Série A no. 232 and arrêt de Grande chambre du 11 juillet 2002, *Goodwin contre Royaume-Uni*, Rec. 2002-VI.

24 CEDH, arrêt *Marckx* (op. cit. note 20); arrêt du 18 décembre 1986, *Johnston et autres contre Autriche*, Série A no 112.

25 CEDH, arrêt du 27 septembre 1990, *Cossey contre Royaume-Uni*, Série A no. 184.

26 CEDH, arrêt *Mazurek* (op. cit. note 22).

27 CEDH, arrêt du 26 février 2002, *Fretté contre France*, requite no. 36515/97.

of the supranational legal order. It is equally a habitual method of perfecting the national laws.

2) The recourse to comparative law to perfect the national laws

The analysis of the jurisprudence of the Court of Cassation confirms in every way the trends revealed by Sir Basil Markesinis and Jörg Fedtke. The resort to comparative law is found, for example, each time that: the national law has the need to be completed or modernised; when the judge rules on the great societal issues; when the question is common to several countries; when the solution has an economic dimension that exceeds the limits of the legal system in which it applies; and, finally, when it is a question of deciding purely technical matters.

a) When the national law has a gap, an anachronism, or should be modernised

As to the modernisation of national law, recently the French Court of Cassation ruled on the compatibility of a 1977 law,[28] which prohibited publication in the Press of opinion polls about elections during the week preceding the vote, with Art 10 of the European Convention on Human Rights relative to the liberty to receive and communicate information. The preparatory materials of the case in the Criminal Chamber refer to positions adopted on this question by the Council of State of Belgium[29] and the Supreme Court of Canada,[30] and it was a position close to these foreign cases, and more respectful of a modern conception of freedom of expression, that the Court of Cassation adopted in ruling that the prohibition on publication of polls in the pre-electoral period was disproportionate.[31]

b) When the national judge rules on major social questions

Likewise, the solutions of the major foreign systems on sensitive questions involving ethical and religious considerations are a precious reference point for national courts confronting issues which trouble deeply a divided (internal) public opinion. Such was the case in a matter involving the very controversial question whether an infant born with a handicap due to an erroneous prenatal diagnostic could claim compensation

---

[28] Articles 11 and 12 of the loi du 19 juillet 1977.

[29] Arrêt du 17 février 1989.

[30] Arrêt du 29 mai 1998.

[31] Arrêt du 4 septembre 2001 (Bull.crim. no 170).

for his handicap from the doctor at fault.[32] In this case the Court of Cassation reached its conclusion after having considered the solutions given in similar cases in the major legal systems, notably in Germany and the United States, an exercise, however, which did not manage to shield it from a violent campaign in the Press led by the corporate interests affected by the decision.[33]

In a penal matter involving an equally difficult question the court was not protected any better from the violent criticisms of those favourable to a return to a ban on abortion. The case posed the question whether incrimination for involuntary homicide should be extended to a driver who caused an accident in which a married woman suffered a miscarriage and gave birth to a dead fetus.[34] The Court conducted a study of foreign law before reaching its decision.

In a case to be decided in the near future, the French high court has also engaged in research on the legislative and jurisprudential solutions adopted in North America and Europe on the equally sensitive question of homosexual parenting and the possibility of delegating parental authority over a child to a homosexual companion.

Already in 1997, before a law introduced the French contract of partnership which can be concluded between persons of the same sex (PACS), the Court of Cassation had to decide whether to recognise a homosexual companion as a 'notorious concubine'. A 1989 law[35] provided in effect that at the death of the lessee, a contract of lease could be transferred to a notorious concubine who lived with him for at least a year before his death. The conclusions of the *avocat général*[36] (a high magistrate but not a voting member of the Court) invited the judges of the Court of Cassation to endorse the same position taken by the law in Norway, The Netherlands, Belgium, and Finland which had already recognised for some, or were ready to recognise for others, an improved legal protection against discriminatory actions against homosexuals. The Court, however, concluded that the state of the positive law in France would not permit it to recognise a homosexual companion as a 'notorious concubine' since the statutory provisions were aimed expressly at concubinage resulting from a stable relationship between a man and a woman.[37]

---

32 Cour de Cassation, Ass. Plén., arrêt du 17 novembre 200, affaire 'Perruche', Bull no. 9, p 15.

33 Report of the Judge-Reporter Mr Sargos and conclusions of the Avocat général Mr Sainte-Rose (internet website of the Court of Cassation).

34 Court of Cassation, arrêt du 29 juin 2001, Bull. No. 8, p 17; see also the report of the Judge-Reporter Mr Sargos and conclusion of the Avocat général Mr Sainte-Rose (internet website of the Court of Cassation).

35 Loi no. 89-462 du 6 juillet 1989.

36 Mr Jean-Francois Weber.

37 Court of Cassation, 3ème Civil Chamber, arrêt du 17 décembre 1997.

On another disputed subject, the Court of Cassation has recently confirmed that the obligation imposed on religious ministers to keep secret information that they have acquired by virtue of their ministry does not impede the investigating judge from seizing all documents, objects, or pieces that may be useful in establishing the truth.[38] In his conclusions the *avocat général*[39] emphasised that the doctrine of the Criminal Chamber, which maintains that the duty of confidentiality does not in any way prohibit judicial access to an element of proof, is shared by the United States, Spain, Germany, the Czech Republic, and The Netherlands.

c) When a problem is common to several countries

Starting their analysis with the case of *Fairchild v Glenhaven*,[40] which dealt with the delicate question of liability of employers for workplace illness caused by the exposure of workers to asbestos dust, Sir Basil Markesinis and Jörg Fedtke show that in facing an identical problem, a common approach may gradually emerge that reduces, little by little, the traditional separation between the Common law and civil law.

In pursuing this point by using examples drawn from French jurisprudence, one can verify, however, that such a comparative exercise does not necessarily lead to similar results. In the area of transportation law, for example, the Commercial Chamber of the Court of Cassation recently ruled on the problem of the opposability of a jurisdiction selection clause inserted in the waybill sent to the consignee.[41] In the preparatory materials annexed to the judgment, reference is made to English and Italian authorities which, according to the reporting judge, follow a 'non-contractual conception' of the consignee's situation, according to which he 'succeeds' to the position of the shipper, a view which is contrary to that taken by Belgian law and the jurisprudence of the Commercial Chamber of the Court of Cassation which, instead, bring to light the necessity of consent, which may be presumed, on the part of the party to whom the clause is opposed. At the end of this examination of foreign solutions, the French judge kept to his prior reasoning, relying on the jurisprudence of the European Court of Justice in the area of international contracts and affirming that the consent of the consignee does not extend to a jurisdictional selection clause in a waybill. The latter is not part of the economic framework of the contract which, to bind the contracting parties, must be accepted, at least tacitly.

---

[38] Criminal Chamber, arrêt du 17 décembre 2002 (Bull. Crim. No. 231).

[39] Dominique Commaret.

[40] House of Lords, *Fairchild etc. v Glenhaven Funeral Services Ltd and others etc.*, 2002(3) WLR 89.

[41] Arrêt du 4 janvier 2005 (Bull. IV no. 5).

d) *When there is occasion to verify the effectiveness of jurisprudential evolutions suggested by foreign Law*

In a similar perspective, the Court of Cassation has examined, without however adopting the same position, the Anglo-Saxon practice of 'mitigation' in insurance claims, wherein the victim is obliged to minimise his own damage. In the area of tort liability, the Court has, in effect, considered that the tortfeasor ought to repair all the damage occasioned by his act and that the victim is not required to limit his losses in the interest of the responsible party.[42]

e) *When the solution has an economic scope that exceeds limits of the legal system in which it is applied*

A similar occurrence was presented to the French Court of Cassation in a series of cases where the Court needed to decide the validity of clauses disclaiming responsibility in contracts for delivery by courier. Since the operators carried on their postal activities in the entire European Economic Area and competed with foreign enterprises, it was indispensable to know what the governing rules were for the same clauses in the other States and in the international conventions in order not to burden the French operators with penalising indemnities vis à vis their European competitors.[43]

By extension, and based upon a particularly relevant demonstration, Sir Basil Markesinis and Jörg Fedtke consider that these convergent approaches are all the more easily brought about in purely technical matters devoid of all ethical, political or social considerations. Such, for example, are the cases of construction rights and town planning, environmental regulations, with respect, for example, to the level of noise, and waste treatment, health rules and public security. As to the environment in particular, it is remarkable that the Program of the United Nations for the Environment (PNUE), the organ of the United Nations specially charged with the protection of the environment, has facilitated comparative work by creating a data base of decisions rendered in all the States to serve as a guide for the judges in all countries.

Having attempted to show the diverse reasons why judges make recourse to comparative law, it is interesting to examine the methods by which the comparative technique is integrated into judicial reasoning.

3. The comparative method of courts

This involves an examination of the practical ability of the judge and the instruments at his disposal to introduce comparative law into the determination of the case.

---

[42] 2nd Civ., arrêt du 19 juin 2003 (Bull. II, no. 86).

[43] Cass, Ch. Mixte, arrêt du 22 avril 2005, pourvois no. 02-18.236 et 03-14.112.

a) The comparative law approach

To summarise in a few words the approach of the judge who proposes to use the resources of comparative law, one recommends that he or she act with prudence, conscious of the difficulty involved, and make the comparison with scientific precision and explicitness, bringing his or her sources and reasoning to the attention of the parties.

(i) Prudence

The first observation is that in acting within the sensitive domain of national cultural identities, the judge should doubtless act with prudence and discernment. Obviously the resort to comparative law does not seek what is vain and impossible – that is, a brutal and forced uniformity of laws on a worldwide basis – and it surely does not involve transposing foreign solutions without reflection.

In any event, comparative analysis does not necessarily lead to uniformity. On the contrary, it can explain the differences and reinforce national solutions. Such is, for example, the approach of the US Supreme Court, which (currently) does not eschew a comparative approach, but nevertheless seems very reluctant to base its decisions upon the influence of foreign texts or jurisprudence.

(ii) Consciousness of the Difficulty

The second observation is that the comparison of laws is a difficult exercise requiring a particular technique. A problem that quickly arises for those interested in comparative law is this: To know if an institution in a given legal system has an equivalent or several equivalents in another system which may authorise a comparison. To put it another way, the first problem to resolve is that of the comparability of laws.

The more the systems differ and rest upon civilisations with social and philosophical values far apart, the more difficult the question of comparability becomes. If there are reasons for one to be interested in very different systems that open up the field of possibilities, then at least this must reinforce the need for prudence in the approach.

Thus when the comparisons demonstrate the absence of unanimity, one should concentrate particularly on systems belonging to the same legal family or, alternatively, on deepening one's study of the major legal systems. In this respect, two types of institutions make comparisons difficult. In the first type, the institution belongs to a system in which the 'determining elements' are such that the technical reach of its institutions is far from being what one could legitimately believe at first glance. In the second type, the technical originality of its institutions renders it nearly impossible to discover equivalents in legal systems of a different family.

It is necessary in any event to avoid value judgments with respect to a foreign legal system founded on different philosophical or moral conceptions or on a different mode of social organisation. There is no moral hierarchy in the legal and judicial systems. Each is the expression of values appropriate to the civilisation to which it belongs.

Although the systems from which these institutions arise permits convergence for almost all of them, certain institutions or notions have a technical originality which is so conspicuous that it raises the question of their own comparability.

Yet if one admits there may be variable degrees in the comparative act according to the ends pursued by the research, then there is always an interest in the comparison of laws despite great differences. The goal of research is, in effect, far from being always the same. The comparative approach has its gradations, from general reflection with purely speculative ends, to technical comparisons aimed at practical application. Thus in the interpretation of his own law, the judge generally limits himself to a purely technical operation.

Thus, to give but one illsutration, despite the difficulty of understanding the English institution of trust, it is indispensable to proceed to a comparative analysis between it and the comparable institutions of French law. The technical qualities of the trust have given it such scope in international business relations that one has searched for ways to transpose it into various legal systems which do not belong to the Common law family. Precisely because of its utility in commercial law, the French courts have themselves completed this transposition. In doing so they have attempted, through their own case law, to adapt kindred French institutions so that they are made to produce legal effects comparable to those of the Anglo-Saxon trust.

In systems with determining elements which are true obstacles to technical comparisons, there is still room for comparison, either because these are areas where the examination of foreign law remains indispensable, such as the area of foreign trade, or because, even in a normal area, it is still possible to derive support from it. In the final analysis it is rare to find, after taking all precautions, that a parallel cannot be established between the most technically original institutions and the institutions of other legal systems, at least with regard to certain aspects.

(iii) Precision

Whatever the case may be, the comparison of laws is neither of interest nor relevance unless it is conducted with exactness. It is necessary to protect oneself against false resemblances and concealed identities, because the basis for convergence or for differentiation of certain institutions must often be sought in the expanses of the legal ensemble in which they are dispersed and, depending upon the case, more or less easily identified.

For this reason, the different methods of the social sciences – for example, case studies and statistics – can be utilised by the comparatists. It is a question of establishing the social function of an institution in order to discover another institution, sometimes very different, which fulfils the same function in the foreign legal order. For the same reasons, comparative law researchers have developed specific methods that are more and more perfected.

The difficulty of this endeavour leads to the conclusion that only supreme courts, the highest organs of legal interpretation, can proceed with its execution. Only they have the time, the resources, and the means for such a task.

(iv) Transparency

Since the methods of courts ought in all circumstances to be transparent, it is obvious that the comparative analysis which the judge intends to include among the elements under examination ought to be contradictory and explicit. In the first place it is indispensable that references to the foreign sources to which the judge resorts should be submitted to contradictory debate so that the parties can put forward their observations. This poses the question of the reliability of the instruments at the judge's disposal to establish proof of the reality and content of the foreign law that serves his reasoning. In the second place, the integration of the comparative law elements into the judicial reasoning ought to be explicit. Sir Basil Markesinis and Jörg Fedtke classify legal systems in terms of this important characteristic. Whether these elements are integrated in the opinions which constitute the decision, which is generally the case in courts of Common law, or in the documents annexed to the decision, as now practiced in France, it is essential to know the reasoning of the judge, even if only to verify its relevance.

b) The instruments of comparative law

Satisfaction of all these conditions leads to the examination of documentary sources from which the judge can examine the foreign law.

The article of Sir Basil Markesinis and Jörg Fedtke reveals that British judges employ very precise accounts of foreign law taken from specialised works which they cite and comment upon at length. In this case, the judge makes himself into a comparatist, which presupposes he has both the time and the qualifications to do so.

The French Court of Cassation proceeds in different manner. It identifies the legal question that it intends to examine in a comparative law perspective and consults a specialised research organ of the university and requests a study of the question. The report drawn up by the research unit is introduced into the debates in order to be discussed by the parties. Thus the exterior sources are used with utmost prudence and scientific rigour.

The French court can equally benefit from information communicated by French judges *de liason* who are on duty abroad. Thus, in the case mentioned pitting the professional secret of religious ministers against the needs of a criminal investigation, the *avocat général* informed himself as to foreign solutions in the case by means of this invaluable and efficient information network whose comparative function will no doubt increase.

4. Conclusion

I have tried to show that a Supreme Court in whatever legal family cannot live in a state of splendid isolation. It operates in effect within a global space. In one way or another, it shares responsibility with the legislature for the quality of the legal system in which it exists. In that respect, it is particularly a guarantor of the system's adaptation to economic and social realities, its efficiency, its attractiveness and international competitiveness. This tendency towards a global approach is only possible when the court's action stems from shared values between systems regarded as equals. In that respect Sir Basil Markesinis and Jörg Fedtke, with the open-mindedness and statesmanship which typifies great comparative scholars, regret the extent to which the Supreme Court of the United States is, in the present climate of American confidence, invited to shut itself off from the rest of the world. On the contrary, the emergence of common human values ought to incite the judge to examine other laws, whatever the degree of democracy in the State concerned, and a fortiori to examine those of the dominant political systems that are open to the outside world. It is evident that today judicial discourse is necessary more than ever. It may take diverse forms, for example, through bilateral relations. For a number of years the French Court of Cassation has been pleased to maintain privileged relations with numerous supreme Courts. It has thereby been better able to understand and appreciate their methods and their jurisprudence and to draw upon their teachings.

In the final analysis, by these means the judge brings his or her contribution to the dialogue between civilisations and contributes to the harmony of the world. In this endeavour, the profound reflection of a francophone black singer, known throughout the world, may be applied:

One cannot paint white upon white, or black upon black,
Each has need of the other to reveal itself.

Manu di Bongo

Comparative Law in Constitutional Adjudication

The South African Experience

Sir Sydney Kentridge, KCMG, QC

No one familiar with the writings of Sir Basil Markesinis needs to be persuaded of the value of the comparative approach in the judicial process. But comparative law in constitutional adjudication raises some peculiar issues. I shall try to illustrate them, particularly by reference to bill of rights jurisprudence in South Africa, following its post-apartheid emergence in 1994 as a constitutional state.

Why should the use of comparative law in constitutional cases differ from its use in other branches of law? Foreign comparisons may inform a national court of possible solutions to the problem before it, equally of the difficulties which might attend any solution. But comparison with law and practice of other jurisdictions is particularly appropriate in relation to some aspects of constitutional adjudication. I limit this to 'some aspects' because constitutional questions arising from the relationship between the different branches of government can seldom be the subject of useful international comparisons: the answers to such questions are to be found in the specific political arrangements embodied in the national constitution. While 'separation of powers' is an international catchphrase it means very different things in different countries. So the aspect of constitutional adjudication which I shall consider is the interpretation and application of human rights guarantees. There are a number of obvious reasons why in this field the comparative approach seems appropriate.

The first is the family relationship between modern domestic bills or charters of rights. The common ancestor is the Universal Declaration of Human Rights with descent through such instruments as the European Convention on Human Rights and the International Covenant on Civil and Political Rights. The Universal Declaration itself had drawn heavily on the Bill of Rights in the Constitution of the United States. There have also been other discernible borrowings – thus South Africa's new constitution took from Canada the two-stage process of adjudication of alleged infringements of rights, and took from Germany the emphasis on human dignity as a fundamental right.

Second, the use of comparative materials is virtually inescapable in countries introducing a justiciable bill of rights for the first time, such as

Hong Kong in 1991, South Africa in 1994, and the United Kingdom in 2000.

Many of the concepts found in typical bills of rights are broadly stated – for example, the right to life or to freedom from cruel or inhuman punishment or treatment. It is not easy to find objective standards by which to define the reach of these rights, and an entirely subjective approach is hardly a feasible alternative. As an American judge once warned, a constitution does not mean whatever we want it to mean. Comparative jurisprudence enables the judge to test his or her value judgment against the judgments of other courts which have grappled with similar provisions. Moreover, some bills of rights virtually mandate some degree of comparative approach. Thus Arts 9, 10, and 11 of the European Convention permit certain limitations on the rights therein stated provided that they are 'necessary in a democratic society'. The South African Constitution permits a limited derogation from the Bill of Rights 'to the extent (...) reasonable and justifiable in an open and democratic society based on human dignity, equality and freedom'. The Canadian Charter of Rights (s 1) has similar language as do many of the post-independence constitutions of the British Commonwealth. At least a glance at other open and democratic societies can hardly be avoided.

An illuminating example of the comparative method in practice is the first appeal heard by the South African Constitutional Court (a court of eleven judges, sitting *in banc*) in *The State v Makwanyane*.[1] The issue was the constitutionality of the death penalty for murder in light of the new Bill of Rights.[2] The Bill of Rights says nothing explicitly about the death penalty. In it one finds a right to life, a right to dignity, a right not to be subjected to cruel or inhuman punishment or treatment – all subject to limitation to the extent I have mentioned. Naturally, the starting point was a consideration of the meaning of those concepts. But the Court had put before it by counsel a mass of international rights instruments, constitutions, judgments, academic writings, and statistics from many parts of the world. How were these to be used? Some constitutions explicitly accept the death penalty (United States, India); others expressly prohibit it (Germany, Namibia). In nearly all countries where the death penalty had been abrogated that had been done by the legislature, not by judicial decision (an exception here was Hungary[3]). The largest body of case law was to be found in the United States. In some of the American cases death penalty statutes had been struck down because they resulted

[1] 1995 (6) BCLR 665 (BCLR stands for *Butterworths Constitutional Law Reports*).

[2] Contained in chapter 3 of the then Interim Constitution. See now the Constitution of the Republic of South Africa Act 1996, chapter 2.

[3] Decision No. 23/1990 of the Hungarian Constitutional Court.

in the infliction of the death penalty in an arbitrary, unequal, and often racially weighted manner. But persistent majorities in the Supreme Court of the United States had held that the death penalty could not in itself be regarded as a cruel and unusual punishment under the United States Constitution. How did the Constitutional Court in South Africa deal with this mass of conflicting authority? The judgments – eleven of them – are not easily summarised. In essence, the Court found that the death penalty was not compatible with the recognition of the dignity and worth of the individual which underlay the new Constitution. It negated the right to life and the right to dignity and was in itself cruel and inhuman. The judges noted that the US Constitution expressly recognised the existence of capital punishment, so they were particularly impressed by the fact that distinguished Supreme Court judges such as Brennan J.[4] and Blackmun J.[5] (albeit in dissent) had nonetheless felt driven to take a contrary view. In Brennan J.'s words (*Gregg v Georgia*):[6]

> The fatal constitutional infirmity in the punishment of death is that it treats members of the human race as non-humans (...). (It is) thus inconsistent with the fundamental premise of the clause that even the vilest criminal remains a human being possessed of common human dignity.

The South African judges also observed that dissenting judges in the US Supreme Court had said that notwithstanding the recognition of the death penalty in the US Constitution, it now had to be measured against standards of humanity and decency which had evolved since the far-off time when this document had been framed. They noted that the Supreme Courts of California[7] and Massachusetts[8] had struck down the death penalty in those states. A seminal decision of the European Court of Human Rights[9] barring or placing conditions on the extradition of murderers to the United States was regarded as persuasive. So too were judgments of the Privy Council in London[10] in appeals from Caribbean countries on the cruelty of what had been called the 'death-row phenomenon' and a similar judgment of the Supreme Court of Zimbabwe.[11] There was also reference to a number of judgments of the German Federal Constitutional Court.[12]

---

[4] In *Gregg v Georgia* 428 US 153 (1976).

[5] In *Callins v Collins* 114 S Ct 1127 (1994).

[6] At p 173.

[7] *People v Anderson* 493 P2d 880 (1972).

[8] *District Attorney for the Suffolk District v Watson* 381 Mass. 684 (1980).

[9] *Soering v United Kingdom* (1989) 11 EHRR 20.

[10] E.g., *Pratt v Johnson* [1994] 2 AC 1.

[11] *Catholic Commission for Justice and Peace v Attorney-General, Zimbabwe* 1994 (4) SA 329.

[12] Notably by Ackermann, J. See 1995 (6) BCLR at 730, n 16.

On the second stage enquiry – namely, whether the death penalty, although an infringement of the enumerated rights, could be justifiable in a democratic society – the Court considered statistical and other evidence from many countries in addition to South Africa, cited on the one side to prove that capital punishment was a real deterrent to would-be murderers or, on the other side, that it was not. Not surprisingly, the Court found that evidence inconclusive. It held, finally, that the Attorney-General had failed to show that the death penalty was justifiable in an open and democratic society, based on human dignity, equality, and freedom.

There were eleven judgments (one, I confess, was mine), but I would respectfully commend the main judgment, by the President of the Court, Justice Arthur Chaskalson. It shows an impressive mastery of the foreign materials, an appreciation of the differences between various bills of rights and of the differing legal, historical, and social backgrounds to the decisions of foreign courts.

And yet there are questions to be asked about all the judgments. The South African Court's use of the foreign materials was, I think, measured and careful. But some lawyers as well as those members of the public who disagree with the outcome in *Makwanyane* (as many in South Africa did and still do) may see the use of foreign precedents in a very different light. In using comparative materials the Court's freedom to select was unfettered. None of the foreign judgments referred to was binding on the Court. The judges were able to choose freely between the conflicting views of, say, Marshall J. and Brennan J. on the one hand, and Powell J. and Scalia J. on the other. It was open to them to endorse the judgment of the Hungarian Court and to distinguish a judgment in a contrary sense of the Supreme Court of Tanzania.[13] As to what was or was not justifiable in a democratic society, they attached greater weight to the abolition of capital punishment during the twentieth century in most Western democratic countries than to the fact that the two great democracies of the United States and India had not done so. Some members of the Court quoted the statement of Warren C.J. in *Trop v Dulles*[14] that the measure of permissible punishment under the Eighth Amendment to the United States Constitution was 'the evolving standards of decency that mark the progress of a maturing society'. But against that one must remember the warning of Scalia J.:

> Of course the risk of assessing evolving standards is that it is all too easy to believe that evolution has culminated in one's own views.[15]

---

13 *Mbushuu v The Republic*, Criminal Appeal No 142/1994.

14 356 US 86, 101 (1958).

15 *Thompson v Oklahoma* 487 US 815, 865 (1988). Both dicta were cited in *S. v Makwanyane*; see 1995 (6) BCLR para 199.

I believe that the South African Court avoided that risk (at least the other ten judges did). But while the *Makwanyane* case illustrates the depth which the judicious use of comparative material can give to constitutional adjudication, it also illustrates the constant need for objectivity when judges have the freedom to follow congenial authorities and reject inconvenient ones.

Professor Christopher McCrudden of Oxford has written on the problematical aspects of the use of comparative law in rights cases.[16] He quotes critics who have said that foreign authorities which may at the will of the judge be used or ignored are, when cited, no more than confirmation of the judge's opinion rather than a force which shapes that opinion. Foreign precedents on both sides of an argument are easy enough to find. The term 'cherry-picking' has been used. And it has been said that foreign authority is no more than a source of comfort for the judge who has to make a difficult or controversial decision.

There is also a very practical problem in the use of comparative law, and that is the limitations of language. In English-speaking countries, the great majority of counsel and (I respectfully venture to say) the great majority of judges cannot readily find their way into the rich jurisprudence of, say, Germany or France. Even when some of that material is translated the legal concepts used and their historical backgrounds are not always within the grasp of a foreign lawyer.

What conclusion does one draw? It is undoubtedly possible for a constitutional court to eschew foreign comparison. It is well-known that the US Supreme Court has not generally found it necessary to look at foreign authority. That approach may gradually be changing.[17] In any event, for courts without the benefit, or the burden, of 200 years of constitutional jurisprudence that is hardly a practical approach. On the contrary, and despite the risks and the criticisms to which I have referred, comparative human rights jurisprudence, carefully used, is at least informative, is often enriching, and at best can be inspiring.

Kriegler J. in one of the early judgments of the South African Constitutional Court[18] pointed out the danger of reliance on ostensibly analogous materials from another jurisdiction without some understanding

---

16 Christopher McCrudden, 'A Common Law of Human Rights?', *Oxford Journal of Legal Studies* Vol. 20 No. 4 (2000), 499.

17 See, e.g., the conflicting approaches of Stevens J. and Scalia J. in *Thompson v Oklahoma* 487 U.S. 815 (1988). There the majority held that to impose the death penalty on murderers younger than 16 was unconstitutional, Stevens J. noting that most Western democracies did not execute juveniles. Scalia J. rebuked this reference to foreign practice – '(...) the views of other nations, however enlightened the Justices of this Court may think them to be, cannot be imposed upon Americans through the Constitution.'

18 *Bernstein and Others v Bester NO and Others* 1996 (4) BCLR 449.

of the legal system of that jurisdiction. His views are worth quoting at length:

> I wish to discourage the frequent – and, I suspect, often facile – resort to foreign 'authorities'. Far too often one sees citation by counsel of, for instance, an American judgment in support of a proposition relating to our Constitution, without any attempt to explain why it is said to be in point. Comparative study is always useful, particularly where the courts in exemplary jurisdictions have grappled with universal issues confronting us. Likewise, where a provision in our Constitution is manifestly modelled on a particular provision in another country's constitution, it would be folly not to ascertain how the jurists of that country have interpreted their precedential provision. The prescripts of section 35(1) of the Constitutions are clear: where applicable, public international law in the field of human rights must be considered, and regard may be had to comparable foreign case law. But that is a far cry from blithe adoption of alien concepts or inapposite precedents.[19]

That surely strikes the right balance.

Let me give two instances of the application of comparative constitutional law. A recurring question in every jurisdiction where the presumption of innocence is constitutionally protected is the constitutionality of reverse onus provisions in criminal statutes. Nowhere, as far as I know, is it held that all reverse onus provisions must be struck down as unconstitutional. The individual's right must be balanced against the needs of society. But how is the balance to be struck? It is hard to believe that any court coming new to this problem would not be assisted by the systematic analyses developed by the US Supreme Court and by the Supreme Court of Canada.

In England, Lord Steyn in the House of Lords[20] has attempted to curb a too-easy justification of the transfer of the burden of legal proof by reference to judgments of both the Canadian Supreme Court and the South African Constitutional Court. He has quoted a passage from an eloquent (his word as well as mine) judgment of Sachs J. in the South African Constitutional Court[21] on the dangers inherent in any less rigorous analysis of the reverse onus provisions. I am sure that Lord Steyn was not simply seeking comfort: he was finding illumination.

In any event, if the use of comparative material gives comfort to the constitutional judge in a difficult case, what of it? Indeed, Chief Justice Barak of Israel, whose sophisticated use of foreign authority is the subject of general admiration, has himself said that comparative law 'grants

---

19 Para 133 of the judgment.

20 *R v Lambert* [2002] AC 545.

21 In *State v Coetzee* 1997 (4) BCLR 437 para 220.

comfort to the judge and gives him the feeling that he is treading on safe ground, and it also gives legitimacy to the chosen solution'.

If the use of material from other jurisdictions can be enriching, to avoid it can be improverishing. Let me illustrate that with my second instance.

In *Dudgeon v The U.K.*,[22] a case in the European Court of Human Rights, the applicant had complained that the police in Northern Ireland had entered his house and questioned him about his homosexual activities – activities conducted in private but for which he was liable to prosecution under the laws of Northern Ireland. The ECHR in a carefully reasoned judgment had held that the Northern Ireland legislation constituted an unjustifiable interference with the applicant's right to respect for his private life and thus infringed Art 8 of the European Convention. Four years later in *Bowers v Hardwick*[23] on virtually the same facts and the same domestic law, the issue came before the US Supreme Court in an appeal from Georgia. The majority held that the equivalent Georgia legislation was *not* unconstitutional. For the majority, in Justice White's succinct opinion, the US Constitution simply did not create a right to engage in homosexual sodomy. That was the end of it. Blackmun J. for the dissenters was equally terse. He said that civilised man's most valued right was the right to be let alone. In the words of a caustic American critic,[24] on the theory that two clichés are better than one, Blackmun J. added that a man's house was his castle. The *Dudgeon* case was not mentioned by either majority or dissenters nor, it seems, by Counsel.

The same critic, Mary Ann Glendon, said of these judgments:[25]

> Regardless of how one views the outcome of *Bowers v Hardwick*, it is hard to avoid a sense that the opinion writers in that case did not do justice to the gravity and complexity of the matter before them. This is not to insist that the result in *Bowers* was 'wrong' and certainly not that *Dudgeon* was 'authority' that American judges should have followed. The Supreme Court justices, however, and perhaps more especially plaintiff's counsel, did ignore a valuable (and readily available) resource. Crosslighting from other cultural and political contexts cannot solve American problems, but it can illuminate them (...). The six *Dudgeon* opinions (...) contained ideas and information that could have focussed issues, enlarged perspectives, improved the quality of reasoning, and ultimately helped to place our Court's decision – whichever way it went – on a sounder and more persuasive footing.

---

22 (1981) 4 EHRR 149.

23 478 U.S. 186 (1986).

24 Mary Ann Glendon, *Rights Talk* (The Free Press, New York 1993), p 151.

25 Ibid, p 152.

Possibly that criticism was noted. When the US Supreme Court revisited the same issue last year it refused to follow its own decision in *Bowers* and struck down the Texas law which made sodomy a criminal offence.[26] Justice Kennedy (for the majority) cited European precedents – in particular the *Dudgeon* case – and spoke of 'values we share with a wider civilisation' and of a right 'accepted as an integral part of human freedom in many other countries'. Whatever one's view of the outcome, the judgment of Justice Kennedy seems, in Professor Glendon's words 'sounder and more persuasive' than any of those in the earlier case. The comparative material has added substance and rigour to the legal reasoning.

Of course, the consideration of foreign precedents does not mean that one must follow them. On the contrary, they often stand as a warning. This has been the fate of repeated invitations by Counsel to persuade other courts to follow US precedents on freedom of speech in relation to 'hate speech' or defamation or contempt of court. The invitations have been declined by the European Court of Human Rights and by courts in Canada, England, Australia, New Zealand, and Hong Kong, and no doubt by other courts, too. This is not because freedom of speech is not valued by those courts. If I may again quote Kriegler J., in a case on the form of contempt of court known in English law as 'scandalising the court' he declined to follow US precedents on contempt of court[27] saying:

> The balance which our common law strikes between the protection of an individual's reputation and the right to freedom of expression differs fundamentally from the balance struck in the United States. The difference is even more marked under the two respective constitutional regimes. The United States Constitution stands as a monument to the vision and the libertarian aspirations of the Founding Fathers; and the First Amendment in particular to the values endorsed by all who cherish freedom. But they paint eighteenth century revolutionary insights in broad, bold strokes. The language is simple, terse and direct, the injunctions unqualified and they style peremptory. Our Constitution is a wholly different kind of instrument (...). The fundamental reason why the test evolved under the First Amendment cannot lock on to our crime of scandalising the court is because our Constitution ranks the right to freedom of expression differently. With us it is not a pre-eminent freedom ranking above all others. It is not even an unqualified right. The First Amendment declaims an unequivocal and sweeping commandment; section 16(1), the corresponding provision in our Constitution, is wholly different in style and significantly different in content. It is carefully worded and enumerating specific instances of the freedom and is immediately followed by a number of

---

26 *Lawrence v Texas* 539 U.S. 558 (2003).

27 In particular, the 'clear and present danger' test formulated in *Bridges v California* 314 U.S. 2542 (1941).

> material limitations in the succeeding subsection. Moreover, the Constitution, in its opening statement and repeatedly thereafter, proclaims three conjoined, reciprocal and covalent values to be foundational to the Republic: human dignity, equality and freedom. With us the right to freedom of expression cannot be said automatically to trump the right to human dignity. The right to dignity is at least as worthy of protection as is the right to freedom of expression. How these two rights are to be balanced, in principle and in any particular set of circumstances, is not a question that can or should be addressed here. What is clear though and must be stated, is that freedom of expression does not enjoy superior status in our law.[28]

That level of constitutional analysis ensures that there is more to comparative human rights law than mere cherry-picking.

A court's own constitutional text must undoubtedly be paramount. Yet, given a sensible understanding of the proper role of comparative law one must surely welcome its extended use. A transnational, even if not universal, rights culture has developed in the world in the 50 years or so since the Universal Declaration of Human Rights. In the words of Justice Kennedy we are part of a wider civilisation with shared values. If judges look out to the wider world when debating those values we can only applaud.

---

[28] *State v Mamabolo* 2001 (5) BCLR 449, 469–70 (paras 40 and 41).

The European Judge as Comparatist

*Christos L. Rozakis**

1. Some preliminary remarks

In their thorough and comprehensive study Sir Basil Markesinis and Jörg Fedtke scrutinise the role of national judges around the world when, in deciding certain cases in their docket, they act as 'comparatists', resorting to foreign law and alien legal experiences.[1] The authors present, in an exhaustive manner, a wide spectrum of possible parameters of this multifaceted phenomenon, where judges open a dialogue with laws and legal practices developed outside their jurisdictional confines in their effort to draw inspiration from them, and, as a consequence, to enrich, where appropriate, their administration of justice on the basis, *inter alia*, of principles and values which presumably have acquired ecumenical dimensions, or reflect societal or other changes which their own legal system is also ripe to undergo.

This phenomenon of interaction of national law with foreign law through the intermediary of judges is not, of course, a novel one, seen from a historical perspective. Yet it is becoming increasingly frequent in certain legal systems, owing to the evolution of interdependence of legal acts and situations, the close relationships of domestic societies between them, and the curtailment of national boundaries for certain human activities. All these matters have brought forward the acceptance of common values, morals, and aspirations easily applicable to all of them. Still, this phenomenon is distinguishable from another situation with which it bears some resemblance – that of the adoption of a legal system, or part of it, by another legal order, through the means of law-making activity undertaken by a national legislature. Indeed, this latter phenomenon, which again is not totally novel in the history of law creation, has recently acquired significant dimensions in the post-communist era of Central and Eastern Europe, where it is being applied as a means of adapting local societies to the western European traditions, and as a

---

* Professor of Public International Law, University of Athens; Vice-President, European Court of Human Rights; A. Member, Institut de droit international. The author wishes to thank Mr Panayotis Voyatzis (Legal Secretary, European Court of Human Rights) for his assistance in collecting material for this article and his comments, and Mr Nicholas Raveney for his linguistic corrections.

[1] See also the preceeding article by Sir Basil Markesinis and Jörg Fedtke, 'The Judge as Comparatist' in the Fall 2005 Issue of the Tulane Law Review.

tool for integrating the 'new' Europe into the 'old' one. Although the results may be similar, the first phenomenon – the dialogue of judges with foreign law – should not be confused with the second one – the adaptation, through the legislative process, of a legal order to the precepts of another legal system. First, because the repercussions of the legislative process on the legal order of a State is usually far wider than the influence judges can exert on it when they decide a specific case inspired by foreign law; and second, because the degree of democratic legitimacy is far higher when the legislature undertakes the task of transplanting foreign law into the domestic order than when judges undertake, in their own microcosm of settling specific disputes, to follow foreign law and decide accordingly. After all, if we follow the usual stereotypes, in the well-known tripartite division of power in modern democracies judges are supposed to apply law, not to create it; and they acquire their legitimacy (in most of the legal orders of the world) not through the regular consultation of a people's electoral body but through the people's consent, given once and for all, to the institution that they represent – rather than to the judges themselves. These elements undoubtedly demarcate the boundaries within which judges may act when determining the crucial questions relating to the applicable law and its interpretation.

International justice is also supposed to follow the same patterns: an international judge is, again according to stereotypes, bound to apply the law – most of the time international law, customary or conventional, general or particular – and not to create it. Yet the now long history of international justice – which has entered its second century of existence – has witnessed a substantial departure of the role of an international judge from the stereotypical approaches just described. International justice has acted, and is still acting, with formidable leeway, which many times has transgressed judicial restraint and has produced real, fresh law almost *ex nihilo*. The most characteristic examples of a 'law-making' pattern of an international judicial body can be found in the work of the International Court of Justice (hereinafter 'the ICJ' – and its predecessor, the Permanent Court of International Justice).[2] In certain fields of international law, such as the law of the sea, this international court has not only contributed to clarifying the law, but has also genuinely moulded legal rules which, in the end, have been adopted by States as part of their law. In this context, we should remind our reader of the law on continental shelf delimitation and the method of 'equitable' principles proposed by the ICJ, which can easily

[2] The ICJ is an organ of the United Nations, established under the Charter of the United Nations, while its predecessor was established, in the mid-war period, by the Covenant of the League of Nations.

be traced as judge-made law, later adopted by States through its inclusion in the 1982 Convention on the Law of the Sea.[3]

There is, of course, a plausible explanation to this practice of the ICJ which may equally apply to other international courts as well: the international legal order is still heavily decentralised and is lacking both a central legislature and a central executive power. It is also suffering (less than in the not so remote past, but still suffering) from considerable lacunae in its legal fabric, in the sense that, although international relations have become extremely complex and multifarious, legal rules have not always followed suit to cover in an effective manner all the legal exigencies of the new international realities. Hence the courts – and not only the ICJ – are almost obliged to assume the role of a legislator in situations where the law itself is incapable of providing adequate answers to the problems that they face when they deal with particular disputes.

2. The European Court of Human Rights and its interpretation techniques

This brings us to the core issue of our discussion: in this short paper we intend to focus our interest in one international court of a regional nature, the European Court of Human Rights.[4] Unlike the ICJ, the Court works on the basis of a conventional instrument which not only establishes it and determines the means of its functioning, but also provides the substantive legal rules on which its jurisdiction is founded: together with its additional Protocols, the European Convention on Human Rights contains a number of protected human rights which must be enjoyed without exception by all those who are under the jurisdiction of the European States which are parties to it.[5]

---

[3] The case law of the ICJ on matters of continental shelf delimitation has considerably evolved over the years and gradually been clarified through successive judgments. In construing customary international law, but also the Geneva Convention on Continental Shelf (1958), the ICJ gradually built its own 'law' on delimitation. This law, sometimes highly contested by certain legal writers, eventually found an echo in the 1982 UN Convention on the Law of the Sea, adopted by the great majority of the States of the international community.

[4] The European Court of Human Rights (hereinafter 'the Court') is established by the European Convention on Human Rights (see below note 5) through Art 19, which provides: 'To ensure the observance of the engagements undertaken by the High Contracting Parties in the Convention and the Protocols thereto, there shall be set up a European Court of Human Rights, hereinafter referred to as "the Court". It shall function on a permanent basis.'

[5] The European Convention on Human Rights (Convention for the Protection of Human Rights and Fundamental Freedoms, hereinafter 'the Convention') was adopted in Rome on 4 November 1950. Over the years it has been enriched by a number of additional

This difference between these two courts – which is not, of course, the only one – is still not very substantial. In reality the Court faces the same dilemmas and the same uncertainties that are common to most international courts, regardless of whether they work within the slippery field of general – or particular – international law, or are governed by conventional instruments providing them with substantive rules of law. The main reasons which make their difference rather insignificant are the fact that the Convention with which the Court works has now reached an age approaching 60 years, and that, having been conceived by the founding fathers to form a rudimentary text, it has proved – because of its rudimentary character – a long-living instrument, which has never been modified through legislative intervention, at least in so far as its substantive provisions are concerned. These two factors, namely, the rudimentary nature of its provisions and the age of the instrument, have acted as the main driving forces for an evolutive interpretation of its clauses by the Court. The very text of the Convention requires a specification of the concepts and notions contained therein, while the passing of time in a rapidly evolving world (and, with it, a rapidly evolving Europe) requires such specification in each instance to be given its current meaning, the one which is acceptable in European societies at the time of the application of a rule by the Court. To give but one example, it is clear that the concept of 'family life' contained in Art 8 of the Convention cannot be interpreted today by the Court as it was originally conceived by the drafters of its text in the late 1940s. Hence, in order to keep abreast of new developments in societal habits and morals, the Court is obliged to detect the new mentalities that have emerged, and to adapt the relevant concepts accordingly.

This interpretative latitude, which is dictated by the very nature of the Convention but also by the very nature of a judicial body which is called upon to apply a long-living instrument, has over the years been disciplined by the emergence of 'internal' principles, through the Court's case law, which delimit the Court's capacity to develop its own approach of what law is at a specific point in time. The case law also indicates the sources of inspiration to which the Court may have recourse in order to find assistance in the conceptual determination of the state of law in time and space. In this respect, 'foreign law' is a generic term covering the law of the European States parties to the Convention, judicial decisions of other 'brother' courts or influential domestic courts ranking high in the conscience of the legal

---

Protocols, which have added new substantive rights. Protocol No. 11 came into force on 1 November 1998 and contains the most recent amendment of the Convention to date by merging the two jurisdictional bodies originally existing under the Convention, the European Commission of Human Rights and the European Court of Human Rights, into a single Court.

world, and international conventions, or even acts of international bodies carrying weight at the level of international (or European) relations; in so far as they are pertinent to the interpretation of the Convention, they are taken into consideration by the European judge before deciding specific cases; and they may all contribute either to the creation of new case law, or to the preservation or modification of the existing case law.

3. The basic concepts governing interpretation

It seems that the paramount concept which permeates the whole case law of the Court and conceptually determines the evolution of the interpretation of the clauses of the Convention is that of the Convention as a 'living instrument'. In its judgment in the case of *Tyrer v United Kingdom*[6] the Court enunciated it for the first time when it stated:

> [t]he Court must also recall that the Convention is a living instrument which, as the Commission rightly stressed, must be interpreted in the light of present day conditions. In the case now before it the Court cannot but be influenced by the developments and commonly accepted standards in the penal policy of the Member States of the Council of Europe in this field.[7]

The finding in *Tyrer* not only stresses that the Court may adopt an evolutive interpretation to streamline its case law with current realities, but also indicates one of the possible sources to which it may resort in order to determine how to interpret the clauses of the Convention; in the context of *Tyrer* the sources of inspiration are the commonly accepted standards of the Member States of the Council of Europe (in other words the standards commonly applicable in the States parties to the Convention) in the field of penal policy.

The concept of a 'living instrument' allows judges of the Court to engage, in a number of cases, in judicial activism which does not seem common to most of the domestic jurisdictions.[8] As Paul Mahoney has rightly pointed out in one of his studies, 'the open textured language and the structure of the Convention leave the Court significant opportunities

---

[6] Judgment of 25 April 1978, Series A no 26.

[7] Ibid, para 31.

[8] Yet, one should not rush to the wrong conclusions. The Court does not act every day as a legislator constantly changing its case law and inventing new approaches to the European protection of human rights. Judicial restraint is usually the name of the game, and as the Court has rightly said in a number of instances, '(w)hile the Court is not formally bound to follow its previous judgments, in the interests of legal certainty and foreseeability it should not depart, without good reason, from its own precedents'. To continue: '(h)owever, it is of crucial importance that the Convention is interpreted and applied in a manner which renders its rights practical and effective, not theoretical and illusory. It is a living instrument which must be interpreted in the light of present-day conditions' (judgment in the case of *Mamatkulov and Askarov v Turkey*, 4 February 2005, para 121).

for choice in interpretation; and in exercising that choice, particularly when faced with changed circumstances and attitudes in society, the Court makes new law'.[9]

One of the jurisprudential peaks of the Court in applying the 'living instrument' technique is, undoubtedly, the adoption of the 'autonomous concepts' approach. Its appearance dates back to the early 1970s, when the Court in the case of *Engel and Others v Netherlands*[10] refused to accept that a sanction against the applicants, characterised by the domestic legal order as disciplinary, escaped the guarantees offered by the Convention under Art 6 (fair trial) only because, despite its serious repercussions on the applicants, the penalty and the relevant proceedings were not regarded by the State concerned as criminal in nature. In the question put by the Court in its analysis,

> Does Article 6 [dealing with criminal charges] cease to be applicable just because the competent organs of a Contracting State classify as disciplinary an act or omission and the proceedings it takes against the author, or does it, on the contrary, apply in certain cases notwithstanding this classification?

It gave this answer:

> If the Contracting States were able at their discretion to classify an offence as disciplinary instead of criminal (...) the operation of the fundamental clauses of Article 6 and 7 would be subordinated to their sovereign will.[11]

As a consequence of this answer, the Court applied Art 6 to the circumstances of that case, considering that where the repercussions of a sanction against an applicant are serious enough for an individual (for instance, a serious penalty of imprisonment), then the domestic characterisation of the proceedings is no longer a determining factor, and the guarantees offered by Art 6 in cases of criminal proceedings are applicable. This approach by the Court, which inaugurated a new phase in the applicability of Art 6 and the notion of 'criminal charge' contained therein, closely follows an earlier position taken by the European Commission of Human Rights in the case of *Twenty-One Detained Persons v Germany*,[12] in which it said that the Convention terms 'criminal charge' and 'civil rights and obligations' contained in Art 6

> cannot be construed as a mere reference to the domestic law of the High Contracting Party concerned but relate to an autonomous concept which

[9] Paul Mahoney, 'The Doctrine of the Margin of Appreciation under the European Convention on Human Rights: Marvellous Richness of Diversity or Invidious Cultural Relativism?' (1998) 19 *Human Rights Journal* 2 ff.

[10] Judgment of 1976, Series A no 22.

[11] Ibid, paras 80–1.

[12] European Commisson of Human Rights, Collection 29, at pp 97 ff.

> must be interpreted independently, even though the general principles of the High Contracting Parties must necessarily be taken into consideration in any such interpretation.[13]

In today's case law the 'autonomous concept' has been expanded to cover a great number of terms of the Convention such as the concepts of 'possessions' under Art 1 of Protocol No. 1, 'association' under Art 11, 'victim' under Art 34, 'civil servant' (linked to Art 6 case law), 'lawful detention' under Art 5, and 'home' under Art 8 of the Convention.[14] It is clear that the preference of the Court not to rely solely on the domestic characterisation of certain notions but to give its own independent definition of some terms contained therein is part and parcel of the 'living instrument' concept. In determining the autonomy of a term used in the Convention, the Court does not necessarily rely only on general trends in the States parties to the Convention but it may decide to 'autonomise' a term when it considers that the context of protection of human rights, the very purpose and object of its governing legal instrument, or, even, justice and moral values so require.

The concept of the 'living instrument' is also behind a great number of other jurisprudential achievements which have marked the case law of the Court. It is difficult to catalogue here all the cases which have ended in a judgment bearing such landmark characteristics. We may content ourselves to say simply that in the history of the development of the case law of the Court we may detect two categories of major jurisprudential trends which serve the concept of the 'living instrument': the first is wide interpretation of the rights and freedoms contained in the Convention, favouring the individual vis-à-vis the respondent State, or, at the other extreme of the same spectrum, restrictive interpretation of the Convention's clauses to the State's benefit, thereby limiting the rights and freedoms provided for by the Convention.[15] The second – not necessarily systematically different – category concerns the changes which occur in the case law of the Court, through its own initiative, and which usually follow

---

[13] European Commisson of Human Rights, Collection 29, para 4.

[14] See the very interesting article by George Letsas, 'The Truth in Autonomous Concepts: How to interpet the ECHR', in (2004) *European Journal of International Law* 281 ff.

[15] In the case of *Wemhoff v Germany* we find the famous dictum which has since influenced the Court in usually opting for a wide interpretation of the Convention favouring the protection of human rights. The Court held in that case that it was necessary 'to seek the interpretation that is most appropriate in order to realise the aim and achieve the object of the treaty, not that which would restrict to the greatest possible degree the obligations undertaken by the Parties' (judgment of 27 June 1968, Series A no 7, para 8). For a full discussion of this matter, with some criticism of the Court's position in its recent decision in *Bankovic and Others v Belgium and other States* and *Al Adsani v*

societal or other developments in Europe (or in the world), convincing the Court that it is time to adapt its position to these new situations.

With regard to the second category, among a great number of the Court's judgments we can indicatively cite two recent ones, showing how the judicial body has changed its own case law and conceded that its past decisions are no longer consistent with new developments which have occurred, on the one hand, in European social life, and, on the other, in the law applicable in the circumstances of a case. The first is the case of *Christine Goodwin v United Kingdom*,[16] which concerns the right of a post-operative transsexual applicant to enjoy her private life, and her right to marry. The settled case law of the Court, prior to this judgment, had been to refuse to secure to post-operative transsexuals the right, under Art 8, to regularise their new gender by asking the Government to alter the official register of births or to issue birth certificates whose content and nature differed from those of the original entries concerning the recorded gender of an individual at the time of his/her birth.[17] The Court had consistently held that there was no positive obligation on the United Kingdom to alter its existing system for the registration of births by establishing a new system or type of documentation to provide proof of current civil status, or a duty on the government to keep any annotations of the existing register of births secret from third parties. In *Christine Goodwin*, however, the Court made an impressive departure from its previous case law. In the crucial paragraph 92 of its judgment the Court, after having examined a number of changes or trends which had occurred in the meantime, both in UK society and in the European order, noted:

> In the previous cases from the United Kingdom, this Court has since 1986 emphasised the importance of keeping the need for appropriate legal measures under review having regard to scientific and societal developments. (...) Most recently in the *Sheffield and Horsham* case in 1998, it observed that the respondent State had not yet taken any steps to do so despite an increase in the social acceptance of the phenomenon of transsexualism and a growing recognition of the problems with which transsexuals are confronted. (...) Even though it found no violation in that case, the need to keep this area under review was expressly reiterated. Since then, a report has been issued in April 2000 by the interdepartmental working group [in the UK] which set out a survey of the current position of

United Kingdom, see Alexander Orakhelasshvili, 'Restrictive interpretation of human rights treaties in the recent jurisprudence of the European Court of Human Rights' (2003) 14 *European Journal of International Law* 1 ff.

16 *Christine Goodwin v United Kingdom*, judgment of 11 July 2002.

17 For a full account of the domestic law in the United Kingdom (including changes which have occurred in the meantime) and the previous case law of the Court see the text of the judgment in *Christine Goodwin v United Kingdom*, ibid.

> transsexuals in, *inter alia*, criminal law, family, and employment matters, and identified various options for reform. Nothing has effectively been done to further these proposals and in July 2001 the Court of Appeal noted that there were no plans to do so. It may be observed that the only legislative reform of note, applying certain non-discrimination provisions to transsexuals, flowed from a decision of the European Court of Justice of 30 April 1996 which held that discrimination based on a change of gender was equivalent to discrimination on grounds of sex (...).

On the basis of these findings the Court concluded that the respondent Government had failed to respect the right of the applicant under Art 8. Equally it concluded that the United Kingdom was in violation of Art 12, concerning the right to marry, where the Convention expressly refers to the right of a 'man and a woman' to marry. In this landmark decision the Court expanded this right to transsexuals when it held:

> It is true that the first sentence [of Article 12] refers in express terms to the right of a man and a woman to marry. The Court is not persuaded that at the date of this case it can still be assumed that these terms must refer to a determination of gender by purely biological criteria. (...) There have been major social changes in the institution of marriage since the adoption of the Convention as well as dramatic changes brought about by developments in medicine and science in the field of transsexuality. (...) The Court would also note that Article 9 of the recently adopted Charter of Fundamental Rights of the European Union departs, no doubt deliberately, from the wording of Article 12 of the Convention in removing the reference to men and women.[18]

To continue:

> It may be noted from the materials submitted (...) that though there is widespread acceptance of the marriage of transsexuals, fewer countries permit the marriage of transsexuals in their assigned gender than recognise the change of gender itself. The Court is not persuaded however that this supports an argument for leaving the matter entirely to the Contracting States [to the Convention] as being within their margin of appreciation. This would be tantamount to finding that the range of options open to a Contracting State included an effective bar on any exercise of the right to marry. The margin of appreciation cannot extend so far. While it is for the Contracting State to determine, *inter alia*, the conditions under which a person claiming legal recognition as a transsexual establishes that gender re-assignment has been properly effected or under which past marriages cease to be valid and the formalities applicable to future marriages (...), the Court finds no justification for barring the transsexual from enjoying the right to marry under any circumstances.[19]

---

[18] For a full account of the domestic law in the United Kingdom (including changes which have occurred in the meantime) and the previous case law of the Court see the text of the judgment in *Christine Goodwin v United Kingdom*, Ibid.

[19] Ibid.

In the case of *Christine Goodwin* the Court reversed its previous position, on the basis of a number of developments which have occurred in societal habits and morals, the evolution of science, and the approach taken by a more recent text (than the Convention) for the protection of human rights – the Charter of Fundamental Rights of the European Union – and by the European Court of Justice. In another case, *Mamatkulov and Askarov v Turkey*,[20] there is likewise a change in the case law, but this time the main incentive which persuaded the Court to change its approach was based on international law developments which had occurred between the time of its previous judgments and the new case before it.

In the case of *Mamatkulov and Askarov* the main issue of interest in terms of case law was whether the respondent Government had failed to comply with the interim measures indicated by the Court under Rule 39 of the Rules of Court. Previous case law had widely accepted that States parties to the Convention were not obliged to apply a request under Rule 39 since that request was only an indication, and had as its sole legal basis the Rules of the Court – an internal document of the judicial body setting out the procedures to be followed by it – and not the binding text of the Convention. This time the Court considered that it had enough material before it to reverse that position. Through a comparative study of different international procedures, such as those followed by the United Nations Human Rights Committee, the United Nations Committee against Torture, the Inter-American Court of Human Rights, and the International Court of Justice (more particularly with reference to the latter's change of case law in the *La Grand* case[21]) it observed:

> the International Court of Justice [and the other bodies referred to above], although operating under different treaty provisions to those of the Court, have confirmed in their reasoning in recent decisions that the preservation of the asserted rights of the parties in the face of the risk of irreparable damage represent an essential objective of interim measures in international law. Indeed it can be said that, whatever the legal system in question, the proper administration of justice requires that no irreparable action be taken while proceedings are pending.[22]

The Court, having solved through comparative analysis the question whether interim measures of protection are to be considered binding in the sphere of international legal relations within which it works, proceeded to the next step: how to legitimise the binding character of interim measures in a situation where the Convention itself was silent on

---

[20] Judgment of 4 February 2005.

[21] For the relevant parts of the judgment see *Mamatkulov and Askarov*, op. cit. note 8.

[22] Ibid, para 124.

this matter and the sole basis for their 'indication' were the Rules of Court. In addressing this question it adopted a technique which it had rejected in a previous case, and considered that the legal basis of the obligations on the parties was Art 34 of the Convention – with which Rule 39 is intertwined – which provides that the Contracting States are bound not to hinder in any way an individual application.[23]

4. The Court's sources of inspiration

The two instances of the Court's recent case law that we have just presented are illustrative of the way in which this judicial body works in deciding cases. It clearly transpires from these examples that the legal system of the Convention is not a watertight, self-sufficient system. It is in constant dialogue with other legal systems, including, of course, other courts (both domestic and international or, more particularly, regional). This dialogue basically serves two distinct purposes. The first, inherent in the function of the Court as determined by the Convention, is to detect the domestic legal parameters of a case before it – in other words, to have a close look at the legal system governing the facts of a case in order to be able to decide whether an applicant has exhausted domestic remedies, whether he/she has complied with the six-month rule, whether an interference by the State with an individual's right was duly provided for ('established') by domestic law, and, more generally, whether the legal treatment of an application by the bodies exercising power over him/her was consistent with the legal precepts of the State concerned. The second, of more importance for the discussion in this paper, is to construe the Convention taking into account its 'natural' legal environment, namely, first and foremost, the European legal order. At this juncture, it should be pointed out that the Court has recurrently referred in its case law to the Convention as an instrument of the European *ordre public*.[24] Moreover, the international legal order also constitutes part of its environment. The Convention is an international treaty and, as such, is bound to follow those rules of international law which determine the life of international conventions.[25] Admittedly, a human rights convention is not a common treaty, and as the European Commission of Human Rights affirmed as

---

[23] For the relevant parts of the judgment see *Mamatkulov and Askarov*, op. cit. note 8. For a different view see the joint dissenting opinion of Judges Caflisch, Türmen, and Kovler.

[24] See Alexander Orakhelashvili, op. cit. note 16, p 7. See also *Loizidou v Turkey*, judgment of 23 March 1995, para 75.

[25] See, *inter alia*, Lucius Caflisch and Antonio A. Cançado Trindade, 'Les conventions américaine et européenne des droits de l'homme et le droit international général' (2004) Revue générale de droit international public 5 ff.

long ago as the 1960s:

> Unlike international treaties of the classic kind, the Convention comprises more than mere reciprocal engagements between contracting States. It creates over and above a network of mutual, bilateral undertakings, objective obligations which, in the words of the Preamble, benefit from a 'collective enforcement'.[26]

Yet its particularity does not isolate it from the whole corpus of international law dealing with treaties. It simply requires those construing its clauses and those applying it to pay particular attention to its special nature and also to interpretations based on general international law that may be contrary to its object and purpose, which demand 'broader interpretation of individual rights on one hand and restrictions on State activities on the other'.[27] After all, the Convention is no longer the sole international treaty in the international legal system, and enough experience has been accumulated at the level of the international legal order concerning the ways in which these treaties should be interpreted and applied.

Finally, the Court has in certain instances opened a dialogue with extra-European jurisdictions, namely, courts or tribunals operating in domestic legal orders outside Europe, such as the US Supreme Court, or other judicial bodies of internationally recognised calibre.

a) The dialogue with the European legal order

The dialogue of the Court with the European legal order takes place in three distinct forms: (a) a dialogue with domestic legal systems of States parties to the Convention, to which the Court resorts in order to decipher the state of law prevailing at a particular moment on the European continent concerning a matter sub judice before the Court; (b) a dialogue with the European Union's legal system – and particularly the case law of its courts – whenever the Court realises that a matter before it requires an examination of the corresponding solutions already given by the former, in situations of 'overlapping' jurisdiction or competence, or when European Union's law is involved; (c) a dialogue with its immediate interlocutor, which is the Council of Europe, its bodies, and the law or the decisions they produce.

In so far as the dialogue with domestic legal systems of the States parties to the Convention is concerned, other than the respondent State in a specific case before it, the Court usually resorts to such dialogue whenever new issues are submitted to it for which no established case law

---

[26] *Austria v Italy* (1961) Yearbook of the European Convention on Human Rights 140.

[27] Bernhardt, 'evolutive Treaty Interpretation, especially of the European Convention of Human Rights' (1999) 42 *German Yearbook of International Law* 14 ff.

supports a secure solution, or when the Court feels that developments in the European continent call for a change to its established case law. There are an infinite number of cases where the Court has found assistance in interpreting the law of the Convention through recourse to the domestic solutions given by States parties to it: in matters concerning freedom of expression, the right to life, transsexuals and their right to private life, or the right of 'possession', the Court has recurrently relied on the domestic law of European States, with the understanding that this law mirrors the societal mentalities existing at a particular time in Europe.

Instead of interminable references to the rich arsenal of the case law of the Court on this matter, we shall merely present its recent decision in the case of *Stec and Others v United Kingdom*,[28] which effectively illustrates the techniques it applies in the interpretation of the law. In this case, the applicants complained that certain pension schemes in the United Kingdom, as applied to them, were discriminatory and in breach of Art 14 (prohibition of discrimination) taken in conjunction with Art 1 of Protocol No. 1 (protection of property).

The main issue which occupied the Court in this case, at the stage of admissibility, was whether these pension schemes, which were not contributory in nature, attracted the protection of Art 1 of Protocol No. 1. Previous case law had favoured the approach that non-contributory schemes did not enjoy the protection of Art 1, while an erosion of this attitude started to emerge in the recent case law of the Court's Chambers. Hence, the Court considered that it was its task – particularly because it was sitting as a Grand Chamber – to clarify its position on this matter, and to establish a clear and unambiguous position. In doing so it had regard to the legal rules of various European States. In paras 50 and 51 of the decision it held:

> 50. The Court's approach to Article 1 of Protocol No. 1 [whether non-contributory pension schemes are protected by this Article, as a 'possession'] should reflect the reality of the way in which welfare provision is currently organised within the Member States of the Council of Europe [all of them being at the same time States parties to the Convention]. It is clear that within those States there exists a wide range of social security benefits designed to confer entitlements which arise as of right. Benefits are funded in a large variety of ways: some are paid for by contributions to a specific fund; some depend on a claimant's contribution record; many are paid for out of general taxation on the basis of a statutorily defined status. (...) Given the variety of funding methods, and the interlocking nature of benefits under most welfare systems, it appears increasingly artificial to hold that only benefits financed by contributions to a specific fund fall within the scope of Article 1 of Protocol No. 1. Moreover, to exclude benefits paid for out of general taxation would be to disregard the fact that many claimants

---

[28] *Stec and Others v United Kingdom*, decision on admissibility of 6 July 2005.

> under this latter type of systems also contribute to its financing through the payment of tax.
>
> 51. In modern, democratic States, many individuals are, for all or part of their lives, completely dependent for survival on social security and welfare benefits. Many legal systems recognise that such individuals require a degree of certainty and security, and provide for benefits to be paid – subject to the fulfilment of the conditions of eligibility – as of right. Where an individual has an assertable right under domestic law to a welfare benefit, the importance of that interest should also be reflected by holding Article 1 of Protocol No. 1 to be applicable.[29]

The quest for the legal standards applied by the States parties to the Convention on issues raised in cases before the Court is primarily justified by the fact that its role is not solely to settle disputes between individuals and States, but also to construe the law of the Convention in a manner which may apply at pan-European level. In other words, the role of the Court is one of 'integration', in the sense that through its decisions and judgments it is attempting to create a coherent body of human rights rules applying equally and indiscriminately in the sphere of the legal relations of all of the States parties to the Convention. For this reason, and in order to avoid the risk of arbitrariness, the Court is obliged to consult the legal systems of the States parties to the Convention before announcing what the law is and to produce law which, if possible, is the common denominator of the existing law in the States involved. It goes without saying that this peculiarity of the Court's functioning, which makes it *par excellence* a comparatist court, contains some features of creating law, particularly if one takes into account the fact that the European judge retains, at the end of the day, the faculty to determine what the common denominator of European legal trends is, and to lean towards one or another solution accordingly.

There exists, nonetheless, a barrier against this otherwise unlimited capacity, and this is the judge-made concept of 'margin of appreciation'. Founded on the premise that a local society and its representative organs (mainly the domestic courts) are better equipped than the Strasbourg Court to determine what legal solution should be applied to the facts of a case, and that the Court, as a subsidiary organ for the protection of human rights, should not, as a matter of principle, have the primary duty of determining what is correct or what is wrong in all circumstances, the margin of appreciation has many times acted as a vehicle of judicial restraint, limiting the spectrum of the Court's interference, in certain matters, to an 'external' review of the compatibility of domestic acts with

---

[29] Ibid.

the Convention.[30] Still, it should be noted that the margin of appreciation does not apply uniformly and blindly, when applied at all. The rule is that a State party to the Convention has a wider margin of appreciation to construe its obligations under it whenever there is no established European consensus delimiting a right protected by the Convention. The more a consensus matures on a certain issue involving a right protected under the Convention, the smaller the margin of appreciation of the domestic authorities to determine freely the purview.

As far as the dialogue of the Court with the European Union and the Council of Europe are concerned, there are again abundant instances of regular exchanges. The Court has developed a dialogue with the European Union, and more frequently with its courts, as a result of the overlapping competence of the two mechanisms at European level.[31] The example that we have already given of the references made to the European Union's law in the Court's judgment in *Christine Goodwin v United Kingdom*[32] is characteristic. Another, equally characteristic, example may be found in the judgment of *Pellegrin v France*,[33] where the Court, in its search for new criteria to determine in what circumstances civil servants were covered by the protection of Art 6 of the Convention when they were parties to civil proceedings, 'borrowed' the tests applied by the European Union for the definition of the term 'civil servant' and provided for by Art 48(4) of the Treaty of Rome (1957) establishing the European Economic Community. A passing reference should also be made here to another interesting development which links the Court with the European Union's legal system. There is increasingly a tendency on the part of individual applicants to resort to the Court for protection of human rights allegedly violated by the European Union's institutions and bodies or by Member States of the

---

[30] The literature with regard to the margin of appreciation is indeed very extensive. See, *inter alia*, Paul Mahoney, op. cit. note 9, and Michael O'Boyle, 'The Doctrine of the Margin of Appreciation and the European Convention on Human Rights' (1998) 19 *Human Rights Law Journal* 23 ff (as well as the articles in the same issue of this periodical by Clare Ovey, Søren Prebensen, and others).

[31] The overlapping has become more extensive since the European Union started institutionalising its competence to deal with European human rights issues. The Charter of Fundamental Rights (2001) and its further inclusion in the draft European Constitution belong to the most recent vintage in this field. See, *inter alia*, Deny Simon, 'Des influences réciproques entre CJCE et CEDH: "je t'aime, moi non plus ?" ' (2001) Pouvoirs 31 ff; Dean Spielmann, 'Jurisprudence des juridictions de Strasbourg et de Luxembourg dans le domaine des droits de l'homme', in P. Alston (ed), *L'union européenne et les droits de l'homme* (Bruyant, Brussels 2001), pp 789 ff.

[32] Op. cit. note 16.

[33] Judgment of 8 December 1999.

European Union in applying the latter's law.[34] The Court has to date shown considerable restraint in interfering with the activities of the European Union but still the fact remains that another aspect of dialogue has been opened which enlarges the interdependence of those legal systems and their common fate.

The Council of Europe is, as we have already mentioned, a privileged interlocutor of the Court for obvious reasons: because the Court works under its auspices and is institutionally linked with it,[35] and because a number of activities of the Council of Europe, transformed into regional agreements, decisions or recommendations of its bodies, are interwoven with specific human rights issues. As has been rightly pointed out, the Court uses all this material with a certain degree of liberty, usually disregarding whether or not an instrument of the Council of Europe is binding on the respondent State concerned,[36] or, we could add, whether it has binding force at all. Yet, to be fair in regard to the way in which the Court assesses the value of these documents, reference to one of them does not automatically lead it to rely solely or exclusively on it in reaching its decisions;[37] the Court is free to consider all the material before it, in full knowledge of its legal value and validity, and to decide accordingly. Even trends showing societal reorientations or reappraisal of the status quo may have an impact on the Court, which is always open and sensitive to 'environmental' changes.

b) The dialogue with the international legal order

The international legal order is frequently reflected in the decisions and judgments of the Court in various forms: the law of treaties – as codified by the Vienna Convention on the Law of Treaties (1969) – appears recurrently in the Court's judgments and decisions when matters are

---

[34] See the recent judgment of the Court in the case of *Bosphorus Airways v Ireland*, 30 June 2005.

[35] The Convention was adopted by the Member States of the Council of Europe, and it is still linked with it institutionally (see, for example, Arts 22, 23, 46, 48, 50, 52, 54, 58, 59 of the Convention).

[36] Syméon Karagiannis, 'La multiplication des jurisdictions internationales: un système anarchique', in *La juridictionnalisation du droit international* (Editions Pedone, Paris), p 67, note 214.

[37] To mention but one example of the use of the Council of Europe's legislative instruments, the Court has made reference to – and sometimes relied heavily on – the clauses of the European Social Charter, adopted by the Member States of the Council of Europe (1961); see the judgments in the cases of *National Union of Belgian Police v Belgium* (Series A, no 19, para 38), *Swedish Engine Drivers' Union v Sweden* (Series A, no 20, paras 39–43), and *Schmidt and Dahlström v Sweden* (Series A, no 21, paras 34–7).

linked to procedural rules common to an international convention. Questions of interpretation of treaties or of reservations, for example, are regularly addressed by the Court, which in each case may (or may not) follow the general rules governing the life of treaties.[38] Substantive rules of customary or conventional law are also frequently mentioned by the Court, usually in situations where a pending case is inextricably intertwined with international law (in the sense that international law is part of the facts of the case), or where the Court has to resort to international law because the nature of the dispute before it requires reference to it as a condition for reaching a solution. As an example of the first category of cases, we may cite the case of *Bosphorus Airways v Ireland*.[39] In this case the Irish authorities impounded an aircraft in application of a United Nations Security Council decision, under the United Nations Charter (and a subsequent decision of the European Union), and this factor was duly taken into account by the Court. As an example of the second category of cases, we may mention the recent cases of *Bankovic and Others v Belgium and Others*[40] and *Ilaşcu and Others v Moldova and Russia*,[41] where the Court dealt with questions of jurisdiction linked closely with the more general question of State responsibility under international law.[42]

The dialogue of the Court with the international legal order is not limited to rules of general or particular international law. It also embraces decisions of international courts or tribunals, as well as pronouncements of international bodies carrying out activities of a semi- or quasi-judicial nature. We have already mentioned the impact that the change in the case law of the International Court of Justice concerning interim measures of protection – through the *La Grand*-decision – had on the Court's construction of the relevant term in its own Rules of Court.[43] We should also mention that the Court is in constant dialogue with all the international bodies – both of universal and regional calibre – which deal with human rights issues relevant to the rights protected by the Convention.[44] A prominent place in the Court's dialogue is given to the

---

[38] See, *inter alia*, Lucius Caflisch and Antonio A. Cançado Trindade, op. cit. note 25, pp 6 ff.

[39] Op. cit. note 34.

[40] Decision of 12 December 2001.

[41] Judgment of 8 July 2004.

[42] See also *Loizidou v Turkey*, op. cit. note 24.

[43] See note 21, above.

[44] The example given in the text of the judgment in *Mamatkulov* (op. cit. note 8) is illustrative. See also the judgment in the case of *Öcalan v Turkey* (12 May 2005), where the Court made reference to the case law of the United Nations Human Rights Committee. For a critical assessment of the Court's case law and the way it has used the case law of the latter body see Syméon Karagiannis (op. cit. note 36), p 111, footnote 375.

Inter-American Court of Human Rights, the closest 'ally' of the Court in the protection of human rights at a regional level, which has been a source of inspiration for the Court in many instances, mainly in cases which concern Arts 2 (the right to life) and 3 (prohibition of torture, inhuman or degrading treatment) of the Convention.[45] The focus of the Court on the case law of the Inter-American Court of Justice in relation to these latter issues is readily explainable; it is due to the fact that this 'brother' Court has extensively dealt with them as a result of the political conditions on the American continent, and its experience is easily transposable to analogous conditions in Europe.

c) The dialogue with foreign jurisdictions

The most interesting aspect of the Court's dialogue with judicial bodies and their case law (other than the domestic courts or tribunals which have ruled on the legal issues concerning a case submitted to it) is the interaction with high courts lying outside Europe and working under different legal systems – and, probably, different societal conditions from the ones existing in the majority of European States party to the Convention. We say 'the most interesting aspect' because this dialogue is contributing, more than the dialogue with the European or international legal orders, to a real 'globalisation' of the Court's functions in the sense that it brings within the Court's consideration laws and experiences relating directly to societies other than European ones, and, consequently, to mentalities, customs, and morals which are linked with conceptions not necessarily intended in the conscience of those applying them to operate as ecumenical principles or values.

In this situation, the most frequent interlocutor of the Court has been the US Supreme Court. In sharp contrast to the attitude of the latter, which had never mentioned the case law of the Court until 26 June 2003 (when the first express reference to it was made in the case of *Lawrence and Garner v Texas*[46]), the Strasbourg institutions have a tradition, however sparsely it may have been used, of resorting to a dialogue with the highest court of the United States. As early as May 1980 the European Commission of Human Rights made reference to the famous decision of *Roe v Wade* to justify its position that the right to life under

[45] See, *inter alia*, the judgments in the cases of *Akdivar v Turkey* (16 September 1996 – Reports of Judgments and Decisions 1996-IV, para 68) and *Ertak v Turkey* (9 May 2000, ECHR 2000-V, para 106).

[46] See Jean-François Flauss, 'La présence de la jurisprudence de la Cour Suprême des Etats-Unis d'Amérique dans le contentieux européen des droits de l'homme' (2005) 16 *Revue trimestrielle des droits de l'homme* 313 ff.

Art 2 of the Convention does not cover an unborn child.[47] Some years later, in 1988, in the case of *James and Others v United Kingdom*, the Court accepted certain arguments of the parties before it, based on their reference to a US Supreme Court decision in *Hawaii Housing Authority v Midkliff*.[48] Since then, and with increasing frequency, the Court has many times sought enlightenment from the American Court, by relating its case law to the facts of a case before it, or by referring to its case law in the part of a judgment covering the relevant law and domestic and international practice. In some cases reference to the American case law has also been made in the very reasoning of the Court's judgment, in support of its own position on certain matters.[49] It should also be noted that in a considerable number of cases, individual judges have appended separate (concurring or dissenting) opinions to the judgment of the majority in which they have wholly or partly relied on certain decisions of the US Supreme Court.[50]

The US Supreme Court is not, however, the only foreign court with which the Court has developed a dialogue. In some instances – albeit, admittedly, in a more limited number of cases – the Court has sought advice from the highest courts of South Africa, New Zealand, and Canada. South Africa appears in the already cited cases of *Christine Goodwin v United Kingdom and Öcalan v Turkey*,[51] New Zealand appears in the former case, while in the case of Canada reference to its case law is more extensive: in the recent cases of *Morris, Pretty, Appleby, Allan*, and *Hirst* (all against the United Kingdom) the Court has made extensive reference to the Canadian Supreme Court's case law, and in some of them it has relied on it to support its own reasoning and conclusions. In the case of *Pretty*, for instance, the Court held that its conclusion that States have the right to control, through their criminal laws, activities prejudicing the life and security of a third person, found support, *inter alia*, in the decision of the Canadian Supreme Court in the case of *Rodriguez v Prosecutor General*.[52]

5. Concluding remarks

The endeavour of this modest paper was to demonstrate – as a first, hasty attempt – that the European Court of Human Rights and its judges do not

---

[47] See Jean-François Flauss, 'La présence de la jurisprudence de la Cour Suprême des Etats-Unis d'Amérique dans le contentieux européen des droits de l'homme' (2005) 16 *Revue trimestrielle des droits de l'homme* 313 ff.

[48] Ibid.

[49] Ibid.

[50] Ibid.

[51] Op. cit. note 44.

[52] See Jean-François Flauss, op. cit. note 46.

operate in the splendid isolation of an ivory tower built with materials originating solely from the Court's interpretative inventions or those of the States parties to the Convention. The nature of the Court as an international court – working in a regional environment and aiming simultaneously to protect, provide for, and integrate human rights in Europe – is undoubtedly the main reason behind its cosmopolitan tendencies, which are gradually becoming a solid feature of its way of functioning and which seem to be influenced by the more general evolution of the protection of human rights around the world (at national and international level), the universal character of most of the protected rights enshrined in the Convention, and (why not?) the confidence that the Court now has as far as its place in the protection of human rights in Europe – and beyond that – is concerned.

We should, however, put a damper on this idyllic picture of the Court's cosmopolitanism. It would be an exaggeration to argue that the Court is working with constant vigilance to observe possible developments which may occur every day in its surrounding landscapes. Most of its cases are decided with reference to its established case law, which is impressively extensive after half a century of judicial accomplishments, and which is not lightly abandoned by a judicial body eager to prove that legal certainty is one of its merits. It should also be underscored that when the Court opens a dialogue with the 'external world' this dialogue does not automatically and indiscriminately lead to an adoption of 'foreign' preferences or choices in the Court's decisions. When we speak of a 'dialogue' we mean a 'dialogue'.

The Court may discuss 'foreign' law or experiences in analysing the facts of a case (in the 'relevant law' part of its judgment or even in its reasoning) but such a matter does not necessarily mean that its final conclusions will rely solely or even partly on them. It still retains sovereign power to use all the evidentiary material before it freely, and to assess it accordingly. Still, the fact remains that law extraneous to its own case law has gained ground, and is increasingly gaining ground, in the Court's mode of operating before it reaches a decision. This is a good sign for the founders of a court of law protecting values which by their nature are inherently indivisible and global.

The Judge as Comparatist

Konrad Schiemann

1. Introduction

The assertions by Markesinis and Fedtke[1] ('the authors') that 'in recent times the interest shown by American writers in foreign (and especially European) law appears to have diminished' and that 'if academic interest in foreign law has been slender, judicial interest, especially in the domain of public law, has been even thinner'[2] induced in me a feeling of regret.

The view, which I share, that a national judge can not in the vast majority of cases usefully spend much of his time looking abroad for inspiration is widely held and not just in the United States. This view tends in my experience to be based on the conviction that in general the results of such a search do not justify a judge devoting time to the exercise. Often foreign law is, at the end of the day, of no help to him in deciding the case before him and even where it could be of some help a little knowledge is a dangerous thing and he does not have much time to drink deeper from the spring.

But I am here not concerned with the vast majority of cases or indeed primarily with courts below the highest. What I find puzzling is an objection made by members of a supreme court on grounds of high principle to the reception of inspiration from abroad. That such an objection should come from the United States seems particularly strange given the nature of the history and outlook of that wonderfully welcoming country which has given the world so much. The United States, after all, is peculiarly distinguished by its absorption of foreigners and their ideas over centuries. Indeed the Native American might consider that it is a country run by foreigners. It is a country with a variety of legal systems within itself. The leaders of the United States are often to be heard advocating the adoption by other countries of the democratic ideals of the United States. They advocate – at any event from time to time – the abolition of barriers to free trade. Free speech is a primordial value. A deliberately fostered blinkered approach to life just does not seem in accord with much for which America stands.

---

[1] At p 220.

[2] Manifestly, in cases where that law is directly in issue the judge must take an interest in it and he will be helped if academics have done so too. But we are not concerned with those sorts of cases.

I am conscious that the strangeness may be in part the result of the fact that I have no great familiarity with American constitutional law and that I find the theoretical position of the originalists[3] a difficult one. But I would think it highly regrettable if the adoption of this theory in relation to the Constitution of the United States had the result of diminishing the study of foreign law from the intellectual diet of judges and academics.

Professor Markesinis has for some years been putting forward the thesis that for judges to refuse in principle to look abroad for inspiration is needlessly to clothe themselves in a restricting intellectual corset. He rightly stresses that there is no question of a national court being *bound* to adopt the analyses and solutions which appeal elsewhere. It is a question of being broadly educated and open to ideas which, although new in one country, have a history elsewhere.

If I find the general drift of the argument put forward by him appealing it may well have something to do with my personal background which, like his, lacks an exclusive attachment to a particular national order. For anyone who lives in Luxembourg – a country of half a million inhabitants whose boundaries have shifted many times over the centuries – the idea of having as a constitutional principle an isolationist theory that judges should never look beyond their national boundaries is simply inconceivable. But I do not understand the isolationists in the US Supreme Court to put forward any such universal theory. They speak only for the United States and are happy for their country to adopt such a policy and proceed on the basis that there is no need to take any interest in the world outside. I accept that there are precedents for such an approach to life's problems. As I understand it, China did just that for centuries.

I grew up in Luxembourg and the first court which I observed in action was the Court of Justice of the European Communities (ECJ) there. Although most of my professional life as a barrister and judge has been spent in England, I have now come full circle and sit in a court of judges from 25 different legal traditions in the ECJ. This paper is an attempt to share the perceptions which have come from that experience.

2. A national court

When I was at Cambridge in the 1960s the course leading to the first law degree made literally no mention of the United States, of current day law in France, Germany, or any other European country, or of the legal system evolving in what was then the European Economic Community. Although the student was encouraged to obtain a broader view by a study of Roman law as it evolved between 500 BC and 500 AD, the

3 As summarised on pp 7 ff.

course was based on a study of mediaeval English legal history, the feudal systems of land tenure, the ancient forms of writ, and the practice of the old courts of Chancery, the Exchequer, and the Kings Bench.

But this has all changed – witness, recently, the prolonged discussion of foreign practice in relation to limiting the retrospective effect of legal rulings in the House of Lords in *National Westminster Bank plc v Spectrum Plus Ltd* [2005] UKHL 41.

I myself have been accustomed as a national judge to analyse and resolve problems without feeling that the ways in which matters have been analysed in the past by the English courts are necessarily the only ways in which those problems can be satisfactorily analysed and resolved. Where I felt that the traditional approach led to a result which appeared to me unsatisfactory I would turn to foreign law to see whether my hesitations found any echo elsewhere[4] and whether some stimulus to my own thinking could be found.

I think the removal of nationalist blinkers in England has resulted in the adoption of some useful juridical tools for analysis, such as the doctrine of proportionality, and the improvement of our substantive law, for instance that affecting prisoners. The change has in part resulted from the results of the United Kingdom's ratification of the European Convention on Human Rights and of the constituent Treaties of the European Union. I now turn from English law to the practice of the ECJ.

3. The European Court of Justice

Situated at the crossroads of different, yet closely intertwined, legal cultures, the Community judicature is by nature a 'comparative' institution. In its daily activities it is permeated with the values of the legal systems of the constituent countries.[5] Since the judges of the ECJ are drawn from different legal traditions it is not surprising that each judge brings his mindset, ineluctably influenced by his heritage, to the deliberations of the Court. Clearly, so far as the individual judges are concerned a reluctance to look on anything other than their own national heritage would be absurd. The judges are obliged to work as a team since no dissenting or concurring judgments are allowed. No progress is possible unless one can come to some sort of agreement and no sort of agreement would be possible if one

---

[4] For instance, in *Gregory v Portsmouth City Council*, [2000] AC 419 in the context of a case dealing with the tort of malicious prosecution, both I in the Court of Appeal (as a result of research done after the close of the oral hearing) and Lord Steyn in the House of Lords looked at American case law and the *Restatement of the Law, Torts* 2d (1977).

[5] See Koen Lenaerts, 'Interlocking Legal Orders in the EU and Comparative Law', (2003) International and Comparative Law Quarterly 905 ff.

regarded the opinions of others with the sort of contempt which is evinced in some of the citations in this book.

When considering the ECJ, which lays down the law for a particular area comprising several nations ('the Union'), one must distinguish between the laws of the Member States and the law as laid down by sources outside the Union.

In practice I doubt whether the attitude of the judges of the ECJ to the laws of Member States of the European Union differs much from that of members of the US Supreme Court to the laws of the constituent states of that Union. The members of the ECJ think in a European context of which the national legal orders are part and to which those orders contribute. My experience is that the very fact of working together on a daily basis with judges from legal traditions other than one's own, of solving problems which emanate from one European country after another, of applying treaties and laws which have been adopted by the Union, and of being exposed to the lectures and writings of academics and judges from a number of different Member States leads one to regard the writings of jurists from those States as coming from within the family, so to speak, rather than as being foreign – even if they are written in a language which is not one's first. When we are faced with drafting a judgment and are looking for help we turn to whichever source we know of which we think might contain something useful. The national background of the writer is not remotely a determining factor.

This is the background not only to the process of the establishment of the general principles of Community law (which is well described in the book[6]) but to all of our work. It has to be borne in mind that the ECJ is always seeking a solution that does not risk encountering incomprehension or resistance in some Member States which could undermine the effectiveness and the uniform application of Community law.[7] For that reason alone it is seen as important that the judges have some awareness of the laws of the Member States other than their own. If it finds that those laws concur in the solution to the underlying problem then the ECJ will feel at ease in adopting the approach which the Member States have worked out. If, on the other hand, the national solutions reveal wide differences, the ECJ will usually try and avoid laying down any general rule.

But the ECJ does not pursue any policy of limiting its sources of stimulus to Member States.

Thus, the Court is also extremely concerned if possible to avoid any conflict with the judgments of the European Court of Human Rights

---

6 See pp 110–116.

7 See Koen Lenaerts, op. cit. note 5, pp 879–83.

(ECtHR). That court is charged with interpreting the European Convention on Human Rights and has a much wider membership than the ECJ. The Convention has played a huge, and in my judgment beneficial, role in restraining unbridled state power in Western Europe when dealing with various dissidents and in providing human rights guidelines and standards for the countries which have only recently emerged from Communist dictatorship and for others who wish to join the European Union. The ECJ has adopted an approach to fundamental human rights largely modelled on the ECtHR in part to meet the concern of Member States whose own laws incorporated the Convention or reflected the values in it. Those Member States were more at ease with the concept of the primacy of Community law once they had been assured that these fundamental values would be protected by the Community courts.

Similarly, the Community courts try and avoid conflicts with the World Trade Organisation.[8] They try and avoid friction in the international legal order where they can.

The Advocates General do not hesitate to draw on sources outside the Union to stimulate and guide their thinking. In so far as the Court uses the juristic writings and decisions of third states for inspiration – as it has done in competition cases, for instance, in which decisions from the United States have been regularly considered[9] – it feels itself free to make as much or as little use of them as seems good to it. As is indicated below, those sources are not usually cited in the judgments but that should not be taken as a reliable indication that the Court is ignorant of them.

4. What appears in judgments

It is common to find in academic writings, and there are traces of it sometimes in this book, an assumption that the whole of the court's thinking process appears in its judgment or judgments. That is not invariably the case in my experience. Not everything which has in fact helped shape a judgment will necessarily be mentioned in that judgment.

So far as foreign influences are concerned this may be because the judge has not recognised them as such. For it seems obvious that even the most rigorous isolationist – if I may use that term for those who as a matter of principle eschew all use of foreign material – will in fact have had foreign influences shaping his mind to a greater or lesser degree and will consciously or unconsciously have made greater or lesser use of that foreign input in coming to his conclusions. He may have used this input

---

[8] See Francis Jacobs, 'Judicial Dialogue and the Cross-Fertilisation of Legal Systems: the European Court of Justice', in (2003) 38 *Tex. International L.J.* at p 553.

[9] Ibid at p 555.

unconsciously but even where he has used it consciously he may not have registered its foreignness.

But even a judge who has deliberately investigated and drawn on foreign material may nevertheless consciously chose not to mention this fact in his judgment. There are a number of reasons for this, both in national and international courts, which can come into play.

For instance, in England intellectual exhibitionism is – or in any event was throughout much of the last century – widely regarded as socially unacceptable[10] even amongst those who are well read.

Moreover, in England the tradition is for the judgment not to contain matter which has not been canvassed with the advocates,[11] and most advocates will not be able without advance warning sensibly to take part in a discussion involving references to foreign law[12] let alone the writings of philosophers and others.

But even if he does feel certain of his ground, the judge will be mindful that his task in general is to solve the case in front of him and to explain in his judgment why the loser has lost. He may take the view that a proper academic treatise is out of place in a judgment and yet the citation of a mere snippet of foreign learning leaves him exposed to suggestions that he has not really grasped the whole context in which the citation is to be placed. So the simplest course for the judge is not to mention any foreign influences which may have played a part in shaping his ideas.[13]

The foregoing is written from the perspective of one coming from the Common law tradition which requires that each judge indicate his personal view and the reasons for coming to that view. This publishing of

---

[10] By contrast, in France it is generally taken as something which an intellectual is expected to bring to the party; to talk of the weather or how the ball was shot into the net last Saturday being regarded as inappropriate for those capable of discoursing on more demanding themes.

[11] Again, incidentally, not an approach invariably adopted on the Continent. In the ECJ two factors in particular militate against the adoption of such an approach. The first is that the working methods of the Court are, for reasons which it is not appropriate to explain here, such that the ideas which appear in the judgment will not have been hammered out at the time of the hearing with the advocates present and therefore can not be put to the advocates. The second is that it is all but impossible to have in a multi-lingual and multi-cultural setting the easy interchange of ideas between bench and bar which characterises the English court process.

[12] Giving such advance warning will result in extra work being undertaken by the advocates at the expense of their clients and a judge may reasonably hesitate before demanding this.

[13] This was the course adopted by me at first instance in *R. v Secretary of State for the Environment, ex parte Rose Theatre Trust Co.* [1990] 1 QB 504 in which the part of my (incidentally much criticised) judgment concerned with *locus standi* was significantly influenced by the rather restrictive German and European Community law approach to the question. However, it was the end of term and a lengthy disquisition on why the Continental approach might be regarded as preferable to the much more liberal view which has commended itself to the English courts did not seem appropriate.

individual judgments concentrates his mind, clearly fixes responsibility, makes it less easy just to row along with the majority rather than work further on a judgment, and is regarded as desirable in the interests of accountability, transparency, and democratic debate.

But there is a contrary view which also has merit. There is a strong tradition among many States which insists that the court must speak with one voice and declare the law. The law will be 'found' by anyone trained to find it. Confidence in the courts and the law will be shaken if the judges differ amongst themselves or betray any hesitations. While this view of the judicial process is generally accurate, anyone with a professional knowledge of the subject-matter knows that at times more than one solution may legitimately be open to the judge and that when this is the case the concept of 'finding the law' is inadequate. However, the single declaratory judgment has advantages. Not least of these is that it forces the judges who are responsible for producing the decision ('the formation'[14]) to try and agree, making use of their combined talents. A system which permits a judge, as it were, to walk away from further discourse with his fellows and simply say 'what I have written I have written' is sometimes less conducive to producing a first class result than one which forces the judges to work together and listen carefully to one another. Moreover, there is no denying that a plurality of judgments is not welcomed by the lawyer in the street who is seeking to advise his client. For him the oracular style has its attractions – provided, of course, that the oracle speaks clearly and that its words are not capable of being misunderstood.

This brings me to a point where I incline to differ from the authors on something which is an interesting and controversial theme in itself.[15] They express[16] the view that '(T)he understanding and acceptance of the Court's jurisprudence on the national level would improve substantially, we believe, if the ECJ were to discard the image of a 'unanimous oracle' and revealed the difficult – and often controversial – judicial dialogue which the identification of common principles and values must surely involve.'

Coming from my background I have of course considerable understanding for those who find many of the ECJ's judgments stylistically unattractive and unduly oracular. On a personal level moreover, I miss writing my own judgments. But then I also confess to some sympathy for those who find the judgments in a single appeal of an English superior court often unduly numerous and discursive in style.

---

14 This word of French origin is perhaps less confusing in the present context than 'constitution' which sounds more natural to the English judicial ear.

15 A recent excellent discussion can be found in Professor Mitchel de S.-O.-L'E. Lasser, *Judicial Deliberations. A Comparative Analysis of Judicial Transparency and Legitimacy* (Oxford University Press 2005).

16 At p 121.

I am not sure whether the authors when referring to judicial dialogue had in mind the judicial dialogue between the judges composing the formation. It is in the Common law tradition for the judge to say openly that he has hesitated between different solutions, that he has changed from his initial view, and for him to give his reasons for doing so. It is relatively easy to do this if the judge is sitting alone. It remains easy even when the judge is sitting in a larger formation provided that he is permitted, as he in general is in England,[17] to express a personal view concurring in the result for idiosyncratic reasons or to give a dissenting judgment. At present, the requirement in the ECJ of a single judgment, the express prohibition in the founding documents of the Union of revealing the contents of judicial discussions, and the strong tradition in the ECJ and many Member States that the Court speak with one voice, rule out revealing the dialogue (which can go on over months) between the judges involved in making a decision. Of course, given the required political will and decisions, the ECJ could move to a system, such as that which prevails in the ECtHR, which permits individual opinions but I detect no movement in that direction nor am I currently persuaded that on balance it would be desirable. The requirement of a single judgment coupled with a requirement of silence as to the judicial debate has the merit of removing, and being seen to remove, possible national pressures on a judge as well as encouraging, and in my experience producing, a team spirit amongst the judges which, judging by some of the acid comments one reads from time to time, seems singularly absent from members of the US Supreme Court. It would I think be possible, without legislative change, to draft judgments so as to indicate that the judges were divided but so as to conceal individual viewpoints, but several nations would I believe find the resultant overt dispute amongst the oracles of the law unacceptable. The Court, as I have already stressed, tries to avoid doing that which a significant number of Member States find unacceptable.

There is another judicial dialogue which is regularly going on in the ECJ and that is the dialogue between the national court which makes a preliminary reference and the ECJ which answers the question posed. Although the ECJ insists that the reference contain a clear explanation of the problem as it confronts the national judge and welcomes the considered opinion of that judge as to what the solution should be, an ECJ judgment does not in general spend much time (if any) on dealing with that opinion unless it be to approve it. This is partly because the Court sees itself as a specialist adviser to the national court on European law rather than as an appeal court but may also result from the need for a unanimous judgment. I return to this matter below.

[17] Though not in the Privy Council and the Court of Appeal (Criminal Division).

There is yet a third dialogue which may have been intended by the authors: that between those who have made representations to the Court and the Court itself. Here the judgment will refer to those representations and it often happens that the judgment will acknowledge that an argument which it sets out has force. However, a judgment will, as the authors suggest, sometimes deal with the argument in a magisterial manner with a thinly reasoned apophthegm or a blunt comment such as 'this argument should not be accepted'. As an advocate when I received this unadorned response from a court I found it infuriating and I can see that the same reaction may well come from an academic.

But consider the difficulties facing a court which has no option but to give a single judgment and which is unanimous in the final decision but for reasons which differ somewhat amongst the – often 13 and sometimes as many as 25 – judges. I take the simplest situation – the court is divided into three nearly equal camps. All agree on the result but, even after strenuous efforts to agree, or at least get a majority for, one line of reasoning, the reasoning adopted by each camp is inconsistent with the reasoning adopted by each of the other two camps. In those circumstances what will emerge from the court will inevitably be thin in its reasoning. Although the reasoning behind each of the camps may be perfectly respectable in itself, it can not be revealed.

Leaving such situations aside, the very fact that the Court is composed of many members obliged to issue one judgment expressing one opinion militates in favour of brevity. Every sentence of a draft judgment is scrutinised by many eyes and may give rise to disagreement. There is something seductive in drafting something which is sufficiently uncontentious as not to give rise to dissent even if it does not seek to resolve every arguable obstacle in the way of the solution adopted.[18]

In an international court there may,[19] moreover, be a number of reasons of delicacy which can lead a court to refrain from citing decisions or writings emanating from a particular nation. For instance, some nations will have contributed more than others to the juristic discourse. Yet regularly to cite from a few jurisdictions can leave the others feeling disadvantaged. The ECJ does not cite in its judgments individual national decisions or writings as having influenced its thinking although its Advocates General's opinions are full of them.

---

[18] If I am happy with my conclusion and my reasoning, even though on the way to it I may have undergone a period of doubt, I tend not to burden my draft and my colleagues with an explanation of those doubts and of what I regard as the answer to them. On the other hand, if I continue to have hesitations about a particular draft I signal these to my colleagues. Indeed I sometimes provide a draft with alternative endings or with alternative reasonings leading to the same ending. This, one hopes, will lead to a fruitful exchange of notes and discussion.

[19] As the authors point out at p 120.

5. The adoption of the isolationist theory requires justification

It is difficult to think of significant musicians, painters, architects, philosophers, scientists, novelists, or politicians who in a successful endeavour to improve their own work have not drawn sustenance from what their colleagues in other lands had to offer.

A judge might in his whole life adopt a policy of never looking abroad. However, in my experience they do not behave like this in the general way in which they conduct their lives. Anyone with an intimate knowledge of the higher judiciary and more distinguished law professors can see that the work of foreigners is ever present in their lives. If you consider their bookshelves and their music and artistic collections it becomes evident that they have grown up by choice or happenstance in internationally varied intellectual company. The Bible, Socrates, Aeschylus, Plato, Shakespeare, Milton, Wilde, Goethe, Schiller, Mann, Racine, Voltaire, Montesquieu, Balzac, Dante, Tolstoy, Solzhenitsyn, Bach, Schubert, Mozart, Berlioz, Verdi, Einstein, Wren, Kant, Marx, Benedict, Aquinas, Luther, Hume, Rembrandt, Picasso, Thoreau, Hemingway, Wilder and so on and so on – most of these could easily be found on a single judge's shelves or walls, accompanied by many others. Each of these of course in their turn will themselves have been shaped by innumerable others coming from many different countries.

Any examination of history shows that human societies change and that philosophical and religious and moral values change.[20] They change as a result of interaction of ideas. Ideas are exchanged daily between persons many of whom will have had their own ideas shaped by those outside their immediate societal background. When exercising discretion and judgment the judicial brain will inevitably first call upon whatever happens already to be there. Surely, in an ideal world the greater the amount of digested material in that brain the better. The decision as to how much of that material can be of use in any given situation one would expect to be a matter of judgment in the individual case rather than a matter governed by *a priori* rules which exclude any influence from abroad.

A person who has grown up surrounded by the products of major thinkers from many different countries finds without regretting it that his approach to many of life's problems and challenges has been influenced by the many foreign sources to which he has been exposed. His default setting, if I may express myself thus, is to make use of what the world, and not just his backyard, his town, or his country has to offer. That default setting seems to me as appropriate to judges in their general life as to anyone else.

---

[20] 'Progress' is a value laden word which it is not necessary to use in this context.

The question nevertheless arises whether in principle a judge should retain this default setting even in respect of his judicial activity or whether he should pursuant to an isolationist theory substitute in respect of his judicial work a different setting so as to exclude all foreign influences. Like the authors, instinctively I incline towards a negative response to this question.

Man in his attempt to live in society is everywhere faced with problems arising from mutually conflicting desires. Many of those problems will be similar in many different countries and settings. Selfishness is, alas, not a rare characteristic in mankind. The strong – physically, intellectually, or financially – often seek to dominate the weak. Those in power may seek to govern by every means to hand even if their right to adopt those means or pursue their chosen ends is not self-evident. Those not in power, but with strong political or religious convictions or who are just plain selfish, will often seek by fair means or foul to compel some or all of the rest of their society to bend to their will. Parties to contracts will not fulfil their obligations. Persons will, by accident, negligence, or design, harm others physically or financially or in their reputations. The persons harmed will often seek recompense from those whom they think responsible. Those persons in turn will often be reluctant to make recompense. All these are common problems with which all societies must cope. The law in any developed society is an established coping mechanism for resolving such tensions without violence. Any deliberate exclusion of any examination of how these conflicts are resolved in societies which one respects seems to me to require justification.

6. The justifications

But even if the *default* setting for the judge should be that he is open to persuasion that examination of some foreign law, experience, judgment, or writing would lead to a better judgment, it is only a default setting. So what are the justifications for adopting an isolationist approach?

a) Lack of time and resources

Most of the decisions which a judge has to take are ones in which it would pointlessly complicate his task to search to see whether any foreign writings and judgments might usefully be taken into account. Even a judge who gets as far as asking himself whether he should examine foreign law will often conclude that the resultant expense in time, energy, and money would be disproportionate to any benefit which can be expected to be received from the exercise. That conclusion, having necessarily been reached prior to any research, can inevitably from time to time be shown to be wrong by someone who has undertaken the work which the judge eschewed. But that regrettable fact does not justify the spending of time on such research in every case with the consequential lengthening of the time required to reach judgment in every case. It does, however, justify a bit of anticipatory extra-curricular reading by the judge in an attempt to make him more sensitive to those areas where foreign law might have something useful to contribute to his judicial activity.

In reaching the conclusion that the research exercise is not worth it the judge is doing much the same as when in the course of resolving an issue as to the validity of a will he excludes all consideration of the public health legislation. There are no real issues of principle involved here. I have the impression that academics tend not to be sufficiently conscious of the unremitting pressure a judge is under to produce an adequate judgment soon rather than a better judgment later. The lower down the judicial ladder a judge finds himself the greater that pressure is in general. But I was very conscious of it even in the Court of Appeal in England. It is not entirely absent even in the smaller chambers of the ECJ.

There is another point which is obvious but worth noting. The human brain can only absorb so much. All lawyers will have spent time investigating matters which might turn out to be relevant and important only to discover that the research was in the end not worth the time which had been spent on it. Life is about choices and one does not have the time to fill one's brain with all which would profitably furnish it, nor the time to investigate all matters which conceivably might provide a useful tool for decision making.[21] Thus the, on the face of it, eminently sensible suggestion by the authors[22] that judges and counsel dealing with Community law problems should investigate what has been done by courts in other Member States when faced by the same problem, is often just not financially and temporally possible.[23]

---

[21] A good example in a totally different context of the possible dangers has been shown in England where it used to be the law that any investigation of what was said in Parliament during the passage of a Bill leading to the Act which the judge had to construe was not regarded as permissible. The House of Lords in *Pepper v Hart* [1993] AC 593 relaxed that prohibition to a limited extent. I share the view expressed by Lord Hobhouse in *Wilson v First County Trustee Ltd (No.2)*, [2005] UKHL 40 at para. 140 that 'judicial experience has taught me (…) that the attempt by advocates to use parliamentary material (…) as an aid to statutory construction has not proved helpful and that the fears of the pessimists who saw it as simply a cause of extra expense in the context of litigation have been proved correct'. As Lord Bingham put it in *R v Secretary of State for the Environment, Transport and the Regions ex parte Spath Holme Ltd*, [2001] 2 AC 349: 'The worst of all worlds would be achieved if parties routinely combed through Hansard, and the courts dredged through conflicting statements of parliamentary intention (see p 631F), only to conclude that the statutory provision called for no further elucidation or that no clear and unequivocal statement by a responsible minister could be derived from Hansard.'

[22] See p 110.

[23] As indeed the authors recognise – see p 120.

b) Lack of knowledge

Particularly if he has limited time available for his task, the judge may well feel uncertain that his research has adequately equipped him to summarise accurately and comprehensively the foreign learning. He is very conscious of the dangers well described in the book. These dangers also are much greater lower down the judicial ladder and in jurisdictions, such as the English one,[24] where the judge is in principle expected to work without any assistance save that provided by counsel. They are least perhaps in a court such as the ECJ where there are to hand lawyers and judges from each of the Member States to help guide the Court away from egregious errors.

c) The originalist argument

It may be, for all I know, as the authors imply, that the originalist position has been adopted as a weapon in the fight to prevent certain ideas from triumphing in the US Supreme Court. The originalist argument discards contemporary judicial and political experience elsewhere on *time* grounds, not because it comes from outside the United States. Indeed, I would have thought that the proponents of the originalist position would accept foreign influences provided that they were among those many which had influenced the framers of the US Constitution in the eighteenth century. I say no more about the originalist argument save that as a judge I have never yet found it desirable or necessary to produce a result in judgment which I realised would be regarded as wholly unacceptable to contemporary society.[25] The originalist position seems to me likely to force a judge into that position.

d) Different value systems

As I understand it, the exclusionists rule out reference to opinions expressed abroad, in part because those foreigners live in societies which have different values from those which are widely held by the citizens of the United States alive today. Once one accepts that values can change

---

24 In recent years some attempt has been made to improve this situation in the House of Lords and the Court of Appeal but England still gives its judges nothing like the research services available to the US Supreme Court or the ECJ. Nor, except where foreign law is directly applicable, does the court in general have the benefit of academic assistance outside that provided in books or articles of which the court has knowledge.

25 I call to mind G. K. Chesterton's comment: 'Tradition means giving votes to the most obscure of all classes – our ancestors. It is the democracy of the dead. Tradition refuses to submit to the small and arrogant oligarchy of those who merely happen to be walking around.'

and that the court can take into account changed values, the mere fact that a particular change receives an impetus from what has happened abroad seems to me neutral. Of course not everything from abroad will attract and some will repel. But it seems self-evident that the value of the change should be judged on its perceived merits and that the evaluation of its merits or demerits may well be helped by looking at societies where that value has been given prominence.

History reveals that over a period of time the importance which a society gives to some values diminishes whilst that which it gives to others increases. I see no advantage whatever in excluding from the general debate which takes place at such time any experience or learning which may be gleaned from abroad. The courts, it seems to me, can usefully contribute to that debate because judges are skilled in analysis and in exposing arguments and have in general had the advantage before expressing their opinions of an ordered debate in a calm but adversarial context.

If one discards the temporal objection which constitutes the originalists' position and accepts that society's values change gradually and without legislation and that the court is in principle free to decide its cases in the light of values which have risen into prominence since the enactment of a constitution or its amendments, the court is then faced with deciding to what degree it should base its judgments on these values. The tensions are well known. Is the court in the business of declaring what always was the law or is it making the law? What constitutes general acceptance? Can the court lead or must it always follow? Must the court follow new values even if it does not share them? These are difficult questions beyond the scope of this contribution. But it does not seem to me that the presence of a foreign element significantly affects their difficulty.

7. Conclusion

The issues of principle arise in the context of what are sometimes called 'hard' cases where policy decisions have to be made by the judges if they are to fulfil their task of providing an answer for the litigant. The authors' contention[26] in relation to judicial activity that 'the passage of time reveals gaps, even in revered constitutions, and they are filled by courts exercising discretion and judgment' is manifestly right. For courts from which there is no appeal their hard cases consist in part of this work of filling gaps and in part of cases where one or other party is

[26] See p 237.

endeavouring to persuade the court to depart from a solution which it has in the past adopted.

Very few of us who take an interest in the world around us ever have an original thought of any general value. Very few of us in principle think it profitable to reinvent the bicycle. One inevitably turns to others for inspiration and stimulus. There are plenty of practical limitations as to what one can do but why exclude anything as a matter of principle? Why not follow the advice of St Paul to the Philippians[27]

> Whatsoever things are true, whatsoever things are honest, whatsoever things are just, whatsoever things are pure, whatsoever things are lovely, whatsoever things are of good report; if there be any virtue, and if there be any praise, think on these things.

In short, anything which furnishes the judicial mind with serious material should be a welcome addition. As a result of my experience both in a national and an international court I share the conclusion of the authors that keeping an eye open on what other legal systems are doing strengthens rather than weakens one's own. Moreover, international tensions are more easily avoided if a court when laying down the law has in mind how a particular pronouncement may be received by others in the international community. At times what is being done within a particular national legal order causes widespread international concern – witness Nazi Germany's treatment of Jews, apartheid South Africa's treatment of Blacks and Coloureds, Saddam Hussein's Iraq's treatment of Kurds, and French, British, Israeli, and American treatment of suspected terrorists – and may give rise to economic or other sanctions and indeed armed conflict. This concern will not always be a determinative factor for a court in the relevant national order but it surely is something of which it should be aware and of which it can sometimes take account in coming to its decisions.

[27] Chapter 4 v.10.

Postscript |

It is, in one sense, odd to touch upon a new idea at the end of a longish monograph; but then it is also not a bad practice – and one found in all kinds of literary products (such as the worthy but un-ending novels of yesterday and their less worthy contemporary successors, the television serials) – to end a story by planting the seeds for its sequel. And the companion topic we propose is *The Judge as Hero*. For though Carlyle did not include judges (or, come to that, lawyers of any kind) among those who deserved to be hero-worshiped (even though he lived at the time when the English judge was, arguably, reaching his apotheosis, as the late Mr Fifoot's elegant Hamlyn Lectures showed many years later), our suggestion could form a mighty subject. For though one normally ascribes to judges, if not anonymity, a low profile (and neither are attributes of heroism), the fact is that some of them can be shown to have been the catalysts for the adoption of foreign law in their own systems with consequences which are only now beginning to be grasped. So, along with political figures who, across the centuries, have been closely linked to major legal changes – Justinian, Napoleon, de Gaulle, and Mandela provide some obvious examples – why could we not explore the contribution made to our topic by judges such as Barak, Chaskalson, Kentridge, Bora Laskin, Canivet, Goff, or Bingham, or even the first two Advocates General of the Court of the European Communities, namely Lagrange and Roemer, whose broader cultures enabled them to apply a comparative method of interpretation, develop the law, and open our eyes to different worlds? The answer is – we must. For this seems to be another aspect of the contemporary discourse about judges and their role in society which seems to have escaped attention.

About the Authors of this Book

Sir Basil Markesins QC. Born in Athens of Venetian descent, he trained as a lawyer in Athens, Paris, and Cambridge (England). Sir Basil, who has a part-time practice as a barrister in London, held senior teaching positions in Cambridge (Fellow of Trinity College), Oxford (where he held, first, the Chair of European Law and, later, the Chair of Comparative Law) before being elected to the Chair of Common and Civil Law of University College London, a post he holds jointly with the Jamail Regents Chair at The University of Texas at Austin. In a career which spans nearly 40 years he has authored or co-authored 29 books and over 120 law articles published in major law journals all over the world. He has given named lectures in some 25 universities and has taught (in some instances several times) as Visiting Professor at the Universities of Athens, Cornell, Ghent, *Ecole Normale Superieure* (France), Leiden, Michigan, Munich, Paris I and II, Rome, and Siena. His work has been recognised by doctorates and honorary doctorates from (in alphabetical order) the Universities of Athens, Cambridge, Ghent, Munich, Paris (*Sorbonne*), and Oxford, and his election as Ordinary or Foreign Fellow of the Academies of Athens, Belgium, Britain, France (*Institute de France, Academie des Sciences Morales et Politques*), Netherlands, and Rome (*Academia dei Lincei*). He is also a Member of the American Law Institute. The Presidents of four European countries have honoured his work on comparative law and European integration by awarding him the insignia of Knight Grand Cross of the Order of Merit (Italy), Knight Commander of the Order of Merit (Germany), *Commandeur de la Legion d'honeur* (France), *Officier des Palmes Academiques* (France), and Commander of the Order of Honour (Greece). He was made Knight Bachelor by H. M. Queen Elisabeth II in the New Years Honours List of 2005 for 'Services to International Legal Relations'.

Sir Basil is married to Eugenie (*née* Trypanis), by birth half-American and half-Greek, and has two children, Julietta (who read history and languages) and Spyro George (who practices law in London as a Solicitor at the international law firm of Richards Butler Plc.).

Dr Jörg Fedtke was born in Tanzania, educated at schools in Zambia, the Philippines, and Germany, and went on to study law and political science at the University of Hamburg in Germany. He was awarded a PhD *summa cum laude* for a ground-breaking analysis of constitutional legal transplants in South Africa, written under the guidance of Professor Ingo von Munch in Hamburg, one of Germany's leading constitutional lawyers. Entitled 'Legal Transplants in Constitutional Law' and written largely at the Institute of Foreign and Comparative Law at the University of South Africa in Tshwane (then Pretoria), this project brought him in close contact with judges at the newly founded Constitutional Court of South Africa and academic experts involved in the drafting of the two South African Constitutions of 1993 and 1996.

Dr Fedtke joined the Institute for Foreign and International Private Law and Law of Procedure at the University of Hamburg in 2000, where he worked as a researcher and collaborator (with Professor Ulrich Magnus) for the Vienna-based European Group on Tort Law, which published its 'Principles of European Tort Law' in April 2005. He is a Fellow of the European Centre of Tort and Insurance Law in Vienna and the German reporter at the Centre's annual conferences on developments in European tort law.

Dr Fedtke joined University College London as Clifford Chance/DAAD Lecturer in German Law in September 2001. Promoted to a Readership in 2004, he is Director of UCL's prestigious Institute of Global Law. In 2005 he was invited to act as an external advisor in the constitutional negotiations in Iraq and participated in conferences and workshops organised in Amman/Jordan and Cologne/Germany within the framework of the 'Democratisation Assistance Programme' of the German Foreign Office. Dr Fedtke is also a Visiting Professor at The University of Texas at Austin since 2003, where he regularly teaches courses on comparative constitutional law and European Union law. Dr Fedtke, who specialises in both comparative public and private law, has written extensively in both areas. Most recently he edited and contributed to a volume on *Patterns of Federalism and Regionalism* (Hart Publishing, Oxford and Oregon).

Professor Laurie Ackerman was formerly Justice of the Constitutional Court of South Africa.

Professor Aharon Barak is President of the Supreme Court of Israel.

Professor Dr Otto Brun-Bryde is a Justice at the Constitutional Court of Germany.

Professor Guy Canivet is First President of the French Cour de cassation (Supreme Court).

Sir Sidney Kentridge KCMG, QC, is now practicing as a barrister in London, having previously served as a (part time) Justice of the Constitutional Court of South Africa.

Professor Christos Rozakis is currently Vice President of the Court of Human Rights in Strasbourg, having previously been Under-Secretary for Foreign Affairs in Greece and Professor of Public International Law.

The Rt. Hon. Judge Konrad Schieman PC, QC (whose great-great-grandfather was the first President of the German Imperial Court), was a Justice at the Court of Appeal in England before being nominated by the United Kingdom to become a Judge at the Court of the European Communites in Luxembourg.

Bibliography

A

Abel R., *Politics by other Means* (1995)
Ackerman B., *We the People: Foundations* (1991)
——— (1997) 83 *Virginia Law Review* 771 ff
——— 'The Rise of World Constitutionalism' (1997) 83 *Virginia Law Review* 771 ff
Ackermann L.W.H., 'Constitutional Protection of Human Rights: Judicial Review' (1989) 21 *Columbia Human Rights Law Review* 59 ff
——— 'The Legal Nature of the South African Constitutional Revolution' (2004) *New Zealand Law Review* 633 ff
Agostini E., *Droit comparé* (1988)
Alexy R., *A Theory of Constitutional Rights* (2005)
Alford R.P., 'Misusing International Sources to Interpret the Constitution' (2004) 98 *American Journal of International Law* 57 ff
Alford W.P., 'On the Limits of "Grand Theory" in Comparative Law' (1986) 61 *Washington Law Review* 945 ff
Allen R.J., Kock S., Reichenberg K., and Rosen D.T., 'The German Advantage in Civil Procedure: A Plea for More Details and Fewer Generalities in Comparative Scholarship' (1988) 82 *Northwestern University Law Review* 705 ff
Allen R.J., 'Idealization and Caricature in Comparative Scholarship', (1988) 82 *Northwestern University Law Review* 785 ff
Alpa G., *Tradition and Europeanization in Italian Law* (2005)
Andenas M. and Fairgrieve D., 'Introduction: Finding a Common Language for Open Legal Systems', in Canivet G., Andenas M., and Fairgrieve D. (eds), *Comparative Law before the Courts* (2004), pp xxvii ff
Annan Lord N., 'The Victorian Intellectual Aristocracy' in Plumb J.H. (ed), *Studies in Social History: A Tribute to G.M. Trevelyan* (1955)
Arndt A., *Das Bild des Richters* (1957)
Aubin B., 'Die Rechtsvergleichende Interpretation autonom-internen Rechts in der deutschen Rechtsprechung', (1970) 34 *RabelsZ* 458 ff

B

Basedow J., Dopffel K., and Kötz H. (eds), *Die Rechtsstellung gleichgeschlechtlicher Lebensgemeinschaften* (2000)
Barak A., *Purposive Interpretation in Law* (2005)
——— *The Judge in a Democracy* (2006)

Bayefsky A., 'International Human Rights Law in Canadian Courts' in Conforti B. and Francioni F. (eds), *Enforcing International Human Rights in Domestic Courts* (1997), pp 295 ff

Beatson J., *Anson's Law of Contract* (28th edn, 2002)

Beatty D.M., 'The Forms and Limits of Constitutional Interpretation' (2001) 49 *American Journal of Comparative Law* 79 ff

Bell D.A., *East Meets West* (2000)

Benda E., 'Constitutional Jurisdiction in West Germany' (1981) 18 *Columbia Journal of Transnational Law* 1 ff

Berkowitz P., *Varieties of Conservatism in America* (2004)

Berlin I., 'Introduction' to *Four Essays on Liberty* (1969), pp xxxi–xxxii

Bernhardt R., 'Evolutive Treaty Interpretation, Especially of the European Convention of Human Rights' (1999) 42 *German Yearbook of International Law* 14 ff

Bethge H. in Sachs M. (ed), *Grundgesetz Kommentar* (3rd edn, 2003), Art 5 GG

Bickel A., *The Least Dangerous Branch: The Supreme Court at the Bar of Politics* (1962; 2nd edn, 1982)

Bingham Lord T., 'The European Convention on Human Rights: Time to Incorporate', The Denning Lecture, reprinted in Gordon R. and Wilmot-Smith R. (eds), *Human Rights in the United Kingdom* (1996), pp I–II

——— 'Should there be a Law to Protect Rights of Personal Privacy?' [1996] *European Human Rights Law Review* 450 ff

——— ' "There is a World Elsewere": The Changing Perspectives of English Law' in *The Business of Judging. Selected Essays and Speeches* (2000), pp 87 ff

Blackburn Lord, *Treatise on the Effect of the Contract of Sale on the Legal Rights of Property and Possession of Goods, Wares and Merchandises* (1845)

Blanc-Jouvan X., 'Prologue' in *L'avenir du droit comparé – un défi pour les juristes du nouveau millénaire*, Sté de législation comparée (2000)

Bolton J.R., 'Should We Take Global Governance Seriously?', Vol 1 no 2 (2000) *Chicago Journal of International Law* 205 ff

Bork R., *The Tempting of America: The Political Seduction of the Law* (1990)

——— *Coercing Virtue: The Worldwide Rule of Judges* (revised edn, 2003)

——— *Slouching Towards Gomorrah: Modern Liberalism and American Decline* (revised paperback edn, 2003)

Bradley and Goldsmith, 'U.N. Human Rights Standards and U.S. Law: The Current Illegitimacy of International Human Rights Litigation', (1997) *Fordham Law Review* 66 ff

Brennan Jr. W.J., 'The Great Debate: Interpreting our Written Constitution', 11 *The Federalist Society* 1986

Breyer S., 'Constitutionalism, Privatization, and Globalization' (2000) 21 *Cardozo Law Review* 1045 ff

——— Keynote Address, 97 *American Society of International Law*, Proceedings (2003), 265 ff

——— *Active Liberty: Interpreting our Democratic Constitution* (2005)

Browne-Wilkinson Lord, 'The Infiltration of a Bill of Rights' [1992] *Public Law* 397 ff

Brugger W., 'Legal Interpretation, Schools of Jurisprudence, and Anthropology: Some Remarks from a German Point of View' (1994) 42 *American Journal of Comparative Law* 395

——— *Rundfunkfreiheit und Verfassungsinterpretation* (1991)

Brunner G., 'Die neue Verfassungsgerichtsbarkeit in Osteuropa' [1993] *Verfassung und Recht in Übersee* 819 ff

Bryde B.-O., *Verfassungsentwicklung* (1982)

——— 'Constitutional Courts in Constitutional Transition' in van Loon, F. and van Aeken K. (eds), *60 maal recht en 1 maal wijn. Liber Amicorum Prof. Dr. Jean van Houtte* (1999), pp 235 ff

——— 'Der Verfassungsstaat in Afrika', in Morlok (ed), *Die Welt des Verfassungsstaates. Kolloquium zum 65. Geburtstag von P. Häberle* (2001), pp 203 ff

———, von Münch I., and Kunig P., *Grundgesetzkommentar* (4/5th edn, 2003), Art 79

Bundesministerium der Justiz (ed), *Zur Reform des Staatshaftungsrechts* (1976)

Bundesverfassungsgericht (ed), *Decisions of the Bundesverfassungsgericht*, Vol 2 Part I, Freedom of Speech (1998)

Burt R.A., *Two Jewish Justices: Outcasts in Promised Land* (1988)

Burton Mr Justice M.J., 'Afterword', published in Canivet G., Andenas M., and Fairgrieve D. (eds), *Comparative Law Before the Courts* (2004), at pp 81 ff

C

Caflisch L. and Trindade A.A.C., 'Les conventions américaine et européenne des droits de l'homme et le droit international général' (2004) *Revue générale de droit international public* 5 ff

Callies C., 'Die Europäische Grundrechts Charta', in Ehlers (ed), *Europäische Grundrecht und Grundfreiheiten* (2003)

——— 'Grundlagen, Grenzen und Perspektiven europäischen Richterrechts' (2005) NJW 929 ff

Canivet G., 'La convergence des systèmes juridiques du point de vue du droit privé français' (2003) 11/1 *European Review of Private Law* 50 ff

——— 'Le role du juge dans un monde en mutation' in *Claire L'Heureux-Dubé à la cour suprème du Canada 1987–2002* (2003), 25 ff

Canivet G., 'L imagination du juge' in Canivet G. and Molfessis N. (eds), *Mélanges Jean Buffet* (2004)

——— 'The Use of Comparative Law before the French Private Law Courts', in Canivet G., Andenas M., and Fairgrieve D. (eds), *Comparative Law before the Courts* (2004), pp 181 ff

——— 'La convergence des systèmes juridiques par l'action du juge', *Mélanges Xavier Blanc-Jouvan* (2005), pp 11 ff

Carbonnier J., *Droit Civil – Introduction* (26th edn, 1999)

Cardozo B., *The Nature of the Judicial Process* (1921)

Chase O.G., 'Legal Process and National Culture' (1997) 5 *Cardozo Journal of International and Comparative Law* 1 ff

Choudhry S., 'Globalisation in Search of Justification: Toward a Theory of Comparative Constitutional Interpretation' (1998/1999) 74 *Indiana Law Journal* 816 ff

Coester M. and Markesinis B.S., 'Liability of Financial Experts in German and American Law: An Exercise in Comparative Methodology' (2003) 51 *American Journal Comparative Law* 275 ff

Colley L., *Britons: Forging the Nation 1707–1837* (1994 paperback edn)

Collins Sir L., 'F.A. Mann (1907–1991)' in Beatson J. and Zimmermann R. (eds), *Jurists Uprooted. German-speaking Émigré Lawyers in Twentieth-Century Britain* (2004), pp 380 ff

Conaghan J. and Mansell W., *The Wrongs of Tort* (1994)

Craig P. and Fairgrieve D., 'Barrett, Negligence and Discretionary Powers' [1999] *PL* 626 ff

Crossman R., *The Myths of Cabinet Government* (1972)

Currie D., *The Constitution of the Federal Republic of Germany* (1994)

D

Daig H.-W., 'Zu Rechtsvergleichung und Methodenlehre im Europäischen Gemeinschaftsrecht' in *Festschrift Zweigert* (1981), pp 395 ff

David R. and Jauffret-Spinosi C., *Les grands systèmes de droit comparé* (11th edn, 2002)

Dawson J., *The Oracles of the Law* (reprinted 1978)

de Cruz P., *Comparative Law in a Changing World* (1995, 2nd edn, 1999)

Decalo S., 'The Process, Prospects and Constraints of Democratization in Africa' [1992] *African Affairs* 7 ff

Devlin Lord, 'Judges and Lawmakers' (1976) 39 *MLR* 1 ff

Demleiter N.V., 'Challenge, Opportunity and Risk: An Era of Change in Comparative Law', (1998) 46 *American Journal of Comparative Law* 647 ff

de Búrca G., 'The Influence of European Legal Concepts on UK Law: Proportionality and Wednesbury Unreasonableness' (1997) *European Public Law* 561 ff de Waal J., 'A Comparative Analysis of the Provisions of German Origin in the Interim Bill of Rights' [1995] *South African Journal on Human Rights* 1 ff

de Wet E., 'A German Perspective on the Constitutional Enforceability of Children's and Labour Rights in the Interim Bill of Rights with Special Reference to *Drittwirkung*' [1996] *Tydskrif vir Hedendaagse Romeins-Hollandse Reg* 577 ff

de Wet J.C. and Swanepoel H.L., *Die Suid-Afrikaanse Strafreg* (1949)

de Wet J.C. and van Wyk A.H., *Die Suid-Afrikaanse Kontraktereg en Handelsreg* (4th edn, 1978)

de Wet J.C., *Die Ou Skrywers in Perspektief* (1988)

Dickson B., 'Has the Charter Americanized the Canadian Judiciary?' (1995) *UBC Law Review*

Dodek A.M., 'The Charter in the Holy Land?', *Forum Constitutionnel* (1996) 8:1

Doehring K., 'The Special Character of the Constitution of the Federal Republic of Germany as a Free Democratic Basic Order' in Karpen U. (ed), *The Constitution of the Federal Republic of Germany* (1988), 25 ff

Dölle H., 'Der Beitrag der Rechtsvergleichung zum deutschen Recht', in *Hundert Jahre Deutsches Rechtsleben (Festschrift Deutscher Juristentag), Band 2* (1960), 19 ff

Dorsen N., Rosenfeld M., Sajo A., and Baer S., *Comparative Constitutionalism: Cases and Materials* (2003)

Drago R., 'Droit comparé' in Alland D. and Rials St. (eds), *Dictionnaire de la culture juridique* (2003), 453–7

Drobnig U., 'Rechtsvergleichung in der Deutschen Rechtsprechung', (1986) 50 *RabelsZ* 610 ff

Drobnig U. and van Erp S. (eds), *The use of Comparative Law by Courts* (1999)

Dugard J., *Human Rights and the South African Legal Order* (1978)

——— 'International Human Rights', in van Wyk D., Dugard J., de Villiers B., and Davis D. (eds), *Rights and Constitutionalism: The New South African Legal Order* (1995), pp 193 ff

du Plessis J.E., 'Common Law Influences on the Law of Contract and Unjustified Enrichment in some Mixed Jurisdictions' (2003) 78 *Tulane Law Review* 219 ff

E

Einstein A. and Infeld L., *The Evolution of Physics* (1938)

Elman P. (ed), *Of Law and Men. Papers and Addresses by Felix Frankfurter* (1939–1956)

Elliott Sir J., *Richelieu and Olivares* (1984)

Ellwein T. and Jesse, *Der überforderte Staat* (1994)

Elster K., *Von der Mark zur Reichsmark* (1928)
Ely J., *Democracy and Distrust: A Theory of Judicial Review* (1980)
Errera R., 'The Use of Comparative Law before the French Administrative Law Courts', in Canivet G., Andenas M., and Fairgrieve D. (eds), *Comparative Law before the Courts* (2004), pp 153 ff
Evans-Jones R., 'Roman Law in Scotland and England and Development of One Law for Britain', (1999) 115 *LQR* 605 ff

F

Fedtke J., *Die Rezeption von Verfassungsrecht. Südafrika 1993–1996* (Nomos Verlagsgesellschaft, Baden-Baden 2000)
Fifoot C.H.S., *Judge and Jurist in the reign of Queen Victoria* (1959)
Flauss J.-F., 'La présence de la jurisprudence de la Cour Suprême des Etats-Unis d'Amérique dans le contentieux européen des droits de l'homme' (2005) 16 *Revue trimestrielle des droits de l'homme* 313 ff
Fletcher G.P., 'Constitutional Identity' (1993) 14 *Cardozo Law Review* 737 ff
——— 'Comparative Law as a Subversive Discipline' (1998) 46 *American Journal of Comparative Law* 683 ff
——— 'Three Nearly Sacred Books in Western Law' (2001) 54 *Arkansas Law Review* 1 ff
Forbath W.E. and Sager L., 'Comparative Avenues in Constitutional Law: An Introduction' (2004) 82 *Texas Law Review* 1653 ff
Frankenberg G., 'Critical Comparisons: Rethinking Comparative Law' (1985) 26 *Harvard International Law Journal* 411 ff
Frankfurter Mr Justice, *Mr Justice Holmes and the Supreme Court* (1939)
——— in Elman P. (ed), *Of Law and Men* (1956), pp 31 ff

G

Galmot Y., 'Réflexions sur le recours au droit comparé par la Cour de justice des communautés européennes', *R.F.D.A.*, mars-avril 1990, pp. 255–262
Gardbaum S., 'The "Horizontal Effect" of Constitutional Rights' (2003) 102 *Michigan Law Review*, 387 ff
Ghai Y., 'Sentinels of Liberty or Sheep in Woolf's Clothing? Judicial Politics and Hong Kong Bill of Rights' (1997) 60 *MLR* 459 ff
Giesen, *International Medical Malpractice Law* (1988)
Gilmore G., *The Ages of American Law* (1977)
Ginsburg R.B., 'Looking Beyond our Borders: The Value of a Comparative Perspective in Constitutional Adjudication', 40 *Idaho Law Review* 1 ff

——— 'A Decent Respect to the Opinions of [Human] kind: The Value of a Comparative Perspective in Constitutional Adjudication', Volume 64, Part 3, November 2005, pp 575 ff and January 2006 issue of the *Cambridge Law Journal*

Glendon M.A., 'Rights in the Twentieth-Century Constitutions' (1992) 59 *University of Chicago Law Review* 519 ff

——— *Rights Talk* (1993)

——— 'Comment', in Scalia A. (ed), *A Matter of Interpretation: Federal Courts and the Law* (1997), pp 95 ff

Glendon M.A., Gordon M.W., and Osakure C., *Comparative Legal Traditions* (1999)

Glenn H.P., 'Comparative Law and Legal Practice: On Removing the Borders' (2001) 75 *Tulane Law Review* 977 ff

Goethe, *Fust II*

Goff Lord, Closing Address for the Clifford Chance Millennium Lectures, published in Markesinis B.S. (ed), *The Coming together of the Common Law and the Civil Law* (2000), 246–247

Goldsmith J.L., 'Should International Human Rights Law Trump U.S. Domestic Law?' (2000) Vol 1, no 2 *Chicago Journal of International Law* 327 ff

Goldsmith J.L. and Posner E.A., *The Limits of International Law* (2005)

Grabenwarter C., *Europäische Menschenrechtskonvention* (2nd edn, 2005)

Grafton A., *The Footnote* (1997)

Graham, *Exchange, Prices and Production in Hyper Inflation: Germany, 1920–1923* (1930)

Greenawalt K., 'The Enduring Significance of Neutral Principles' (1978) 78 *Columbia Law Review* 982 ff

Grewe C. and Fabri H.R., *Droits Constituionnels Europeens* (1995)

Grewe C., 'Die Grundrechte und ihre richterliche Kontrolle in Frankreich: Grundlagen und aktuelle Entwicklungen', (2002) *EuGRZ* 209 ff

Griffith J. *The Politics of the Judiciary* (5th edn, 1997)

Grimm D., 'Human Rights and Judicial Review in Germany' in Beatty (ed), *Human Rights and Judicial Review: A Comparative Perspective* (1994), pp 267 ff

Gross S.R., 'The American Advantage: The Value of Inefficient Litigation' (1987) 85 *Michigan Law Review* 734 ff

Gündisch J. and Wienhues S., *Rechtsschutz in der Europäischen Union* (2nd edn, 2003)

H

Häberle P., 'Grundrechtsgeltung und Grundrechtsinterpretation im Verfassungsstaat', *Juristenzeitung* (1989), 913 ff

——— *Rechtsvergleichung im Kraftfeld des Verfassungsstaates* (1992)

Hahlo and Kahn, *South Africa: The Development of its Laws and Constitution* (1960)

Hain in von Mangoldt/Klein, *Grundgesetz Kommentar*, Art 79

Harding S., 'Comparative Reasoning and Judicial Review' (2003) 28 *Yale Journal of International Law* 409 ff

Hart Jr. H.M. and Sacks A.M. in Eskridge Jr. W.N. and Frickey P.P. (eds), *The Legal Process* (1994)

Henkin L., 'Some Reflections on Current Constitutional Controversy' (1961) 109 *University of Pennsylvania Law Review* 637 ff

——— 'Shelley *v* Kraemer: Notes for a Revised Opinion' (1962) 110 *University of Pennsylvania Law Review* 473 ff

——— 'Infallibility Under Law: Constitutional Balancing' (1978) 78 *Columbia Law Review* 1023 ff

——— 'The U.S. and International Human Rights' in *Justice for a Generation* (Papers presented in London on 15–19 July 1985 at the meetings of the ABA, the Senate of the Inns of Court, and the Law Society of England and Wales)

——— 'Constitutionalism and Human Rights', in Henkin L. and Rosenthal A.J. (eds), *Constitutionalism and Rights: The Influence of the US Constitution Abroad* (1990)

Henne T., 'Die historische Forschung und die Einsichtsnahme in Voten beim Bundesverfassungsgericht', in Henne/Riedlinger (eds), *Das Lüth-Urteil aus (rechts)historischer Sicht* (2005), pp 19 ff

Herget J.E., 'The Influence of German Thought on American Jurisprudence, 1880–1918', in Reimann M. (ed), *The Reception of Continental Ideas in the Common Law World 1820–1920* (1993), pp 203 ff

Hesse K., 'Der Gleichheitssatz in der neueren deutschen Verfassungsentwicklung' (1984) 109 *Archiv des offentlichen Rechts* 174 ff

——— Grundzüge des Verfassungsrechts der Bundesrepublik Deutschland 2 II 1 (20th edn, 1999)

Hirsch H.N., *The Enigma of Felix Frankfurter* (1981)

Hoffmann Lord, 'A Sense of Proportion' in F. Jacobs and M. Andenas (eds), *Community Law in English Courts* (1998)

Hofstede G., *Culture and Orgnanisations. Software of the Mind* (1991 / 1997)

——— *Culture's Consequences* (2nd edn, 2001)

Hogg P., *Constitutional Law of Canada* (4th edn, 1997)

Honoré T., *Ulpian: Pioneer of Human Rights* (2nd edn, 2002)

Howard Jr. J.W., 'On the Fluidity of Judicial Choice' (1968) 62 *American Political Science Review* 43 ff

——— 'Judicial Biography and the Behavioural Persuasion' (1971) 65 *American Political Science Review* 704 ff

I

Ignatieff M. (ed), *American Exceptionalism and Human Rights* (2005)

Infratest Burke Rechtsforschung, *Zur Reform des Staatshaftungsrechts, Tabellarische Ergebnisse (1993–1995)* (1999)

Ipsen J., *Staatsrecht II: Grundrechte* (8th edn, 2005)

Irvine of Lairg Lord, 'Judges and Decision-Makers: The Theory and Practice of *Wednesbury* Review' [1996] *Public Law* 59 ff

——— 'The Development of Human Rights in Britain Under an Incorporated Convention on Human Rights' [1998] *Public Law* 221 ff

Isensee J. and Schmidt-Jortzig E. (eds), *Das Ausländerwahlrecht vor dem Bundesverfassungsgericht* (1993)

Ishikawa A., 'Einflüsse des deutschen BGB auf das japanische Zivilrecht bzw die japanische Zivilrechtswissenschaft' in Staudinger, *Kommentar zum Bürgerlichen Gesetzbuch mit Einführungsesetz und Nebengesetzen, 100 Jahre BGB – 100 Jahre Staudinger, Beiträge zum Symposion* (1998), pp 201 ff

J

Jackson V.C. and Tushnet M., *Comparative Constitutional Law* (1999)

Jackson V.C., 'Narratives of Federalism: Of Continuities and Comparative Constitutional Experience' (2001) 51 *Duke Law Journal* 223 ff

Jacobs F., 'Judicial Dialogue and the Cross-Fertilisation of Legal Systems: The European Court of Justice', in (2003) 38 *Texas International Law Journal* 553 ff

Jarass H.D. and Pieroth B., *Grundgesetz für die Bundesrepublik Deutschland* (6th edn, 2002)

K

Kabudi, 'Human Rights Jurisprudence in East Africa', *VRÜ-Beihefte* 15 (1995), pp 25 ff

Kahl W., *Das Grundrechtsverständnis der postsozialistischen Verfassungen* (1994)

Kahn-Freund O., 'On Uses and Misuses of Comparative Law' (1974) 37 *MLR* 1 ff

Karagiannis S., 'La multiplication des jurisdictions internationales: un système anarchique', in *La juridictionnalisation du droit international* (Editions Pedone, Paris)

Karpen U., 'Auslegung und Anwendung des Grundgesetzes', *Hamburger Rechtsstudien Heft* 74 (1987)

Kaufman A.L., *Cardozo* (1998)

Klinck D.R., 'Criticising the Judges. Some Preliminary Reflections on Style', (1986) 31 *Revue de Droit de McGill* 655 ff

Koh D.H., 'Paying 'Decent' Respect' to World Opinion on the Death Penalty' (2002) 35 *UC Davis Law Review* 1085 ff

Koh H.H., 'America's Jekyll-and-Hyde Exceptionalism', in Ignatieff M. (ed), *American Exceptionalism and Human Rights* (2005), pp 111 ff

Kommers D.P., 'The Value of Comparative Constitutional Law' (1976) 9 *Marshall Journal of Practice and Procedure* 685 ff

——— *The Constitutional Jurisprudence of the Federal Republic of Germany* (1st edn, 1989 and 2nd edn, 1997)

Koopmans T., *Courts and Political Institutions: A Comparative View* (2003)

Kötz H., *Essays in Honor of John Henry Merryman* (1990), pp 183 ff

——— 'Der Bundesgerichtshof und die Rechtsvergleichung' in Heldrich and Hopt (eds), *50 Jahre Bundesgerichtshof, Festgabe der Wissenschaft, Band II* (2000), pp 842 ff

Kramer E.A., 'Konvergenz und Internationalisierung der juristischen Methode', in Assmann H.-D., Brüggemeier G., and Sethe R. (eds), *Unterschiedliche Rechtskulturen – Konvergenz des Rechtsdenkens* (2001), pp 31 ff

Kruger J., 'Towards a New Interpretative Theory', in Johan Kruger/Brian Currin (eds), *Interpreting a Bill of Rights* (1994), p 127

Kübler, 'Der deutsche Richter und das demokratische Gesetz', 162 *AcP* 1963, 114–15

Kühle K., NJW (1985) 2379 ff

L

La Forest G.V., 'The Use of American Precedents in Canadian Courts' (1994) 46 *Maine Law Review* 211 ff

Lahav P., 'American Influence on Israel's Jurisprudence of Free Speech' (1981) 9 *Hastings Constitutional Law Quarterly* 23 ff

Langbein J., 'The German Advantage in Civil Procedure' (1985) 52 *University of Chicago Law Review* 823 ff

——— 'The German Advantage' (1988) 82 *Northwestern University Law Review* 763 ff

——— 'Cultural Chauvinism in Comparative Law' (1997) 5 *Cardozo Journal of International and Comparative Law* 41 ff

Lasser M de S.-O.-L'E., *Judicial Deliberations: A Comparative Analysis of Judicial Transparency and Legitimacy* (Oxford University Press 2005)

Lasswell H.D., *Psychopathology and Politics* (Chicago 1930, 1968 Viking Press edn)

——— *Power and Personality* (1948)

Law D.S., 'Generic Constitutional Law', 89 *Minnesota Law Review* 652 at 739 ff

Laws Mr Justice, 'The Ghost in the Machine: Principle in Public Law' [1989] *Public Law* 27 ff

——— 'Is the High Court the Guardian of Fundamental Constitutional Rights?' [1993] *Public Law* 59 ff

——— 'Law and Democracy', [1995] *Public Law* 72 ff

Lawson F.H. and Markesinis B.S., *Tortious Liability for Unintentional Harm in the Common Law and the Civil Law* (1982)

Legeais R., *Grands systèmes de droit contemporains – approche comparative* (2004)

Legrand P. and Munday R. (eds), *Comparative Legal Studies: Traditions and Transitions* (2003)

Leibholz G., *Die Gleichheit vor dem Gesetz: Eine Studie auf rechtsvergleichender und rechtsphilosophischer Grundlage* (1959)

Lenaerts K., 'Interlocking Legal Orders in the EU and Comparative Law' (2003) *International and Comparative Law Quarterly* 905 ff

——— 'Interlocking Legal Orders or the European Union Variant of E Pluribus Unum' in Canivet G., Andenas M., and Fairgrieve D. (eds), *Comparative Law before the Courts* (2004), pp 99 ff

Henri, Léon H., Mazeaud J., and Chabat F., *Leçons de droit civil – introduction à l'étude du droit* (2000)

Leon P., 'A Personal Perspective on Etienne Mureinik's Contribution to South Africa's Final Constitution', (1998) 14 *South African Journal on Human Rights* 201 ff

Lester Lord A., 'The Overseas Trade in the American Bill of Rights', (1988) 88 *Columb. L. Rev.* 537 ff

Letsas G., 'The Truth in Autonomous Concepts: How to Interpet the ECHR', (2004) 2 *European Journal of International Law* 281 ff

Levinson S., 'Law as Literature' (1982) 60 *Texas Law Review* 373 ff

——— 'Looking Abroad when Interpreting the US Constitution: Some Reflections' in (2004) 39 *Texas International Law Journal* 353 ff

Levinson S. (ed), *Torture: A Collection* (2004)

Lévi-Strauss C., *The Savage Mind* (1966)

L'Hereux-Dubé C., 'The Importance of Dialogue: Globalisation and the International Impact of the Rehnquist Court' (1998) 34 *Tulsa Law Journal* 15 ff

——— 'The Importance of Dialogue: Globalization, The Rehnquist Court, and Human Rights' in Belsky M., *The Rehnquist Court: A Retrospective* (2002)

Limbach J., *Das Bundesverfassungsgericht als politischer Machtfaktor*, Humboldt Forum Recht 1996, Beitrag 12

Llewellyn K., 'A Lecture on Appellate Advocacy' (1962) 29 *University of Chicago Law Rev.* 627 ff
Lord Chancellor's Department and the Scottish Office, *Infringement of Privacy: A Consultation Paper* (1993)
Lutter, 'Die Auslegung angeglichenen Rechts' [1992] JZ 593 ff

M

MacCormick Sir N., *Legal Reasoning and Legal Theory* (1978)
Madhuku L., 'The Impact of the European Court of Human Rights in Africa: The Zimbabwean Experience' (1996) 8 *African Journal of International and Comprative Law* 932 ff
Magee B., *Popper* (12th impression 1985)
Magiera, 'The Interpretation of the Basic Law', in Starck C. (ed), *Main Principles of the German Basic Law* (1983), pp 89 ff
McCormick P., 'The Supreme Court of Canada and American Citations 1945–1994: A Statistical Overview', 8 *Supreme Court Law Review* 527 ff
——— 'What Supreme Court Cases Does the Supreme Court Cite?: Follow-up Citations on the Supreme Court of Canada, 1989–1993', (1996) *Supreme Court Law Review*, Vol. 7(2d), 451 ff
McCrudden C., 'A Common Law of Human Rights? Transnational Judicial Conversations on Constitutional Rights', 20 *Oxford Journal of Legal Studies* 499 ff
——— 'A Common Law of Human Rights? Transnational Judicial Conversations on Constitutional Rights' in Katherine O'Donovan K. and Rubin G.R. (eds), *Human Rights and Legal History* (2000), pp 29 ff
Mahoney P., 'The Doctrine of the Margin of Appreciation under the European Convention on Human Rights: Marvellous Richness of Diversity or Invidious Cultural Relativism?' (1998) 19 *Human Rights Journal* 2 ff
Mansel, 'Rechtsvergleichung und europäische Rechtseinheit' [1991] JZ 529 ff
Manz W.H., 'Cardozo's Use of Authority: An Empirical Study' (1995) 32 *California Western Law Review* 31 ff
Markesinis Sir B.S., 'Litigation-mania in England, Germany and the United States: are we so very different?' in Markesinis Sir B.S. (ed), *Foreign Law and Comparative Methodology. A Subject and a Thesis* (1977), pp 438 ff
——— 'Comparative Law – A Subject in Search of an Audience' (1990) 53 *Modern Law Review* 7 ff
——— 'Réflexions d'un comparatiste anglais sur et à partir de l'arrêt Perruche', *RTD civ.* (1), 77 ff

——— 'Five Days in the House of Lords: Some Comparative Reflections on White *v* Jones', in Markesinis Sir B.S. (ed), *Foreign Law and Comparative Methodology: A Subject and a Thesis* (1997), pp 329 ff

——— *Comparative Law in the Courtroom and the Classroom. The Story of the last Thirty-Five Years* (2003)

——— 'The Enduring (Double) Legacy of the Code Napoleon' (2005) 121 *L.Q.R.* 80 ff

——— 'Auto-suffisance nationale ou arrogance internationale? Le droit étranger et les notions contemporaines de justicedevant le juge américain et le juge français', Lecture at the *Institut de France*, March 2006

Markesinis Sir B.S., Auby J.B., Coester-Waltjen D., and Deakin S.F., *Tortious Liability of Statutory Bodies. A Comparative and Economic Analysis of Five English Cases* (1999)

Markesinis Sir B.S. and Enchelmeier S., 'The Applicability of Human Rights as between Individuals under German Constitutional Law', in Markesinis Sir B.S. (ed), *Always on the Same Path: Essays in Foreign Law and Comparative Methodology* (2001)

Markesinis Sir B.S. and Stewart A.R., 'Tortious Liability for Negligent Misdiagnosis of Learning Disabilities: A Comparative Study of English and American Law' (2001) 36 *Texas Internernational Law Journal* 427 ff

Markesinis Sir B.S., O'Cinneide C., Fedtke J., and Hunter-Henin M., 'Concerns and Ideas about the Developing English Law of Privacy (And How Knowledge of Foreign Law might be of Help)' (2004) 52 *American Journal of Comparative Law* 133 ff

Markesinis Sir B.S. and Deakin S.F., *Tort Law* (5th edn, 2003)

Markesinis Sir B.S., Coester M., Alpa G., and Ullstein A., *Compensation for Personal Injury in English, German and Italian Law* (CUP 2005)

Markesinis Sir B.S. and Unberath H., *The German Law of Torts: A Comparative Treatise* (4th edn, 2002)

Markesinis Sir B.S., Unberath H., and Johnson A., *The German Law of Contract: A Comparative Treatise* (2nd edn, 2006)

Matrix Media and Information Group, *Privacy and the Media* (2002)

Mattei H., 'An Opportunity not to be Missed: The Future of Comparative Law in the United States' (1998) 46 *American Journal of Comparative Law* 709 ff

Merryman J.H., 'An Empirical Study of the Citation Practice of the California Supreme Court in 1950, 1960 and 1970', 50 *Southern California Law Review* 381 ff

——— 'How Others Do It: The French and German Judiciaries' (1988) 61 *Southern California Law Review* 1865 ff

Michelman F.I., 'In Pursuit if Constitutional Welfare Rights: One View of Rawls' Theory of Justice', (1973) 121 *University of Pennsylvania Law Review* 962 ff

——— 'Welfare Rights in a Constitutional Democracy' (1979) *Washington University Law Quarterly* 659 ff

——— 'Integrity-Anxiety?', in Ignatieff M. (ed), *American Exceptionalism and Human Rights* (2005), p 241

Miller D. (ed), *A Pocket Popper* (1983)

Minter S., 'Expanding Wrongful Death Statutes and Other Death Benefits to Same-Sex Partners' (2003) 30 *SUM Human Rights* 6 ff

Moglen E., Book Review of Burt R.A., *Two Jewish Justices: Outcasts in Promised Land* (1988), (1989) 89 *Columbia Law Review* 959 ff

Montesquieu Baron de, *De l'esprit des lois*

Moravcsik A., 'The Paradox of U.S. Human Rights Policy', in Ignatieff M. (ed), *American Exceptionalism and Human Rights* (2005), pp 147 ff

Moréteau O., 'Ne tirez pas sur le comparatiste', *Dalloz* 2005, no 7, pp 452 ff

Mors W.-M., *Verfassungsgerichtsbarkeit in Dänemark* (2002)

Mössner J.M., 'Rechtsvergleichung und Verfassungsrechtsprechung', (1974) AöR 193 ff

Murphy W.F., *Elements of Judicial Strategy* (1964)

Mustill Lord, 'Negligence in the World of Finance' (1992) 5 *The Supreme Court Journal* 1 ff

——— 'What do Judges do?', *Särtryck ur Juridisk Tidskrift* 1996–97, Nr 3, 611 ff

N

Nipperdey C.H., 'Gleicher Lohn der Frau für gleiche Leistung. Ein Beitrag zur Auslegung der Grundrechte', *Recht der Arbeit* 1950, 121 ff

O

O'Boyle M., 'The Doctrine of the Margin of Appreciation and the European Convention on Human Rights' (1998) 19 *Human Rights Law Journal* 23 ff

O'Connor S.D., 'Broadening our Horizons: Why American Lawyers Must Learn About Foreign Law', 45 *Fed. Law* 20 and 'Keynote Address', Procedings of the 96th Annual Meeting of the American Society of International Law (2002) *American Society International Law* 348 ff

Odersky W., 'Harmonisierende Auslegung und europäische Rechtskultur' [1994] ZEuP 1 ff

Orakhelashvili A., 'Restrictive Interpretation of Human Rights Treaties in the Recent Jurisprudence of the European Court of Human Rights' (2003) 14 *European Journal of International Law* 1 ff

Ostberg C.L., Wetstein M.E., and Ducat C.R., 'Attitudes, Precedents and Cultural Change: Explaining the Citation of Foreign Precedents by the Supreme Court of Canada' (2001) 34 *Canadian Journal of Political Science* 377 ff

Oxford Encyclopedia of European Community Law (1990)

P

Perales K.A., 'It Works Fine in Europe, So Why Not Here? Comparative Law and Constitutional Federalism' (1999) 23 *Vermont Law Review* 885 ff

Pernthaler P., *Österreichisches Bundesstaatsrecht* (2004)

Popper K., *All Life is Problem Solving* (1999)

Posner R., 'The Constitution as Mirror: Tribe's Constitutional Choices', (1986) 84 *Michigan Law Review* 551 ff

——— 'What Am I, A Potted Plant? The Case Against Strict Constructionism', 197 *The New Republic* 1987, 23 ff – reprinted in O'Brien D.M. (ed), *Judges on Judging: Views from the Bench* (2nd edn, 2004), 165 ff

——— *Cardozo: A Study in Reputation* (1990)

——— 'No Thanks, We Already Have Our Own Laws' (2004-AUG) *Legal Affairs* 40 ff

Pound R., 'The Formative Era of American Law' in *The Life of the Law* (1964)

R

Rabkin J., 'Is EU Policy Eroding the Sovereignty of Non-Member States?', Vol 1 no 2 (2000) *Chicago Journal of International Law* 273 ff

Ramsay M.D., 'International Materials and Domestic Rights: Reflections on Atkins and Lawrence', 98 *American Journal of International Law* 69 ff

Rau A.S., 'Integrity in Private Judging' (1997) 38 *South Texas Law Review* 485 ff

——— 'The Culture of American Arbitration and the Lessons of ADR' (2005) 40 *Texas International Law Journal* 449 ff

——— 'Integrity in Private Judging' (1997) 38 *South Texas Law Review* 485 ff

Rautenbach I. and Malherbe E.F.J., *Constitutional Law* (2nd edn, 1998)

Rehnquist W., 'Constitutional Courts – Comparative Remarks' in Kirchhof P. and Kommers D.P. (eds), *Germany and Its Basic Law* (1993), p 412

Reimann M. (ed), *The Reception of Continental Ideas in the Common Law World 1820–1920* (1993)

Reimann M., 'Stepping out of the European Shadow: Why Comparative Law in the United States Must Develop its Own Agenda' (1998) 46 *American Journal of Comparative Law* 637 ff

Reimann M., 'The Progress and Failure of Comparative Law in the Second Half of the Twentieth Century' (2002) 50 *American Journal of Comparative Law* 671 ff

Reitz J.C., 'Why We Probably Cannot Adopt the German Advantage in Civil Procedure' (1990) 75 *Iowa Law Review* 987 ff

Rengeling H.-W. and Szczekalla P., *Grundrechte in der Europäischen Union* (2004)

Renouvin P. and Durosselle J.B., *Introduction à l' Histoire des Relations Internationales* (1964)

Rheinstein M., 'The Law of Family and Succession' in Yiannopoulos A. (ed), *Civil Law in the Modern World* (1965), reprinted in Leser H.H. (ed), *Gesamelte Schriften* (1972)

Riesenfeld S., 'The Impact of German Legal Ideas and Institutions on Legal Thought and Institutions in the United States' in Reimann M. (ed), *The Reception of Continental Ideas in the Common Law World 1820–1920* (1993), at pp 89 ff

Rodger Lord of Earlsferry, 'Savigny at the Strand', *John Maurice Kelly Memorial Lecture* (1995)

Rogat Y., 'Mr Justice Holmes: Some Modern Views' (1964) 31 *University of Chicago Law Review* 213 ff

Rubenfeld J., 'Unilaterialsim and Constitutionalism' (2004) 79 *New York University Law Review* 1971 ff

Ruck C., *Libel and Slander* (4th edn, 1992)

Rudden B., 'Courts and Codes in England, France and Soviet Russia' (1974) 48 *Tulane Law Review* 1010 ff

S

Sachs A., *Protecting Human Rights* (1991)

——— 'Constitutional Developments in South Africa' (1996) 28 *New York University Journal of International Law and Politics* 695 ff

Sager L., *Justice in Plainclothes: A Theory of American Constitutional Practice* (2004)

Sands P., *Lawless World: America and Making and Breaking of Global Rules* (2005)

Sanduli A., 'The Use of Comparative Law before the Italian Public Law Courts', in Canivet G., Andenas M., and Fairgrieve D. (eds), *Comparative Law before the Courts* (2004), pp 165 ff

Sanilevici R., 'The Use of Comparative Law by Israeli Courts' in Drobnig U. and van Erp S. (eds), *The Use of Comparative Law by Courts* (1999)

Savigny K.-F., *Das System des heutigen Romischen Rechts*, Vol. I, s 33 (1840)

Scalia A., 'The Rule of Law as a Law of Rules' (1989) 56 *University of Chicago Law Review* 1175 ff

——— 'Originalism: The Lesser Evil', (1989) 57 *University of Cincinnati Law Review* 849 ff

——— 'Assorted Canards of Contemporary Legal Analysis' (1990) 40 *Case Western Reserve Law Review* 581 ff

——— *A Matter of Interpretation. Federal Courts and the Law* (1997)

——— 'Commentary', 40 *St. Louis University Law Journal* 1119 ff

Scarman Lord, 'Codification and Judge-made Law' (lecture delivered on 20 October 1966), Law Faculty of the University of Birmingham

——— English *Law – The New Dimension* (1974)

Schauer F., 'Free Speech and the Cultural Contingency of Constitutional Categories' (1993) 14 *Cardozo Law Review* 865 ff

——— 'The Exceptional First Amendment', Ignatieff M. (ed), *American Exceptionalism and Human Rights* (2005), pp 29 ff

Schiemann J., 'Recent German and French influences on the development of English law' in Reiner Schulze and Ulrike Seif (eds), *Richterrecht und Rechtsfortbildung in der Europäischen Rechtsgemeinschaft* (2003), pp 189 ff

Schmitt C., *The Concept of the Political* (1932, translated 1976)

——— *Political Theology* (1985)

——— *The Crisis of Parliamentary Democracy* (1986)

——— *Political Romanticism* (1986)

Scholler, 'Die neue äthiopische Verfassung und der Schutz der Menschenrechte', VRÜ (1997), 166 ff

Scholz R., *Deutschland – In Guter Verfassung?* (2004)

Schulze-Fielitz, 'Verfassungsvergleichung als Einbahnstrasse', in Blankenagel et al (eds), *Liber Amicorum Häberle* (2004), pp 355 ff

Schwartz L.B., 'With Gun and Camera', (1984) 36 *Stanford Law Review* 413 ff

Scott S., 'Evaluation of Security by Means of Movables: Problems and Possible Solutions. Section C: Codification of the Law of Cession' (1997) *Tydskrif vir Hedendaagse Romeins-Hollandse Reg* 633 ff

Sedley Mr Justice, 'The Sound of Silence: Constitutional Law Without a Constitution' (1994) 10 *Law Quarterly Review* 270 ff

——— 'Human Rights: A Twenty-First Century Agenda' [1995] *Public Law* 386 ff

Segal Z., 'The Israeli Constitutional Revolution: The Canadian Impact in the Midst of a Formative Period', *Forum Constitutionnel* (1997) 8:3

Simitis S., NJW 1984, 398 ff

——— *KritV* 1994, 121 ff

——— 'Reviewing Privacy in an Informational Society', (1986) 135 *University of Pennsylvania Law Review* 797 ff

Simon D., 'Des influences réciproques entre CJCE et CEDH: 'je t'aime, moi non plus?' (2001) *Pouvoirs* 31 ff

Simon H., 'Verfassungsgerichtsbarkeit' in Benda/Maihofer/Vogel (eds), *Handbuch des Verfassungsrechts* (2nd edn, 1994), pp 1137 ff

Simpson B., 'Innovation in Nineteenth Century Contract Law', (1975) 91 *L.Q.R.* 247 ff

Slaughter A.-M., *A New World Order* (2004)

——— 'A Brave New Judicial World', in Ignatieff M. (ed), *American Exceptionalism and Human Rights* (2005), pp 277 ff

Smith C., 'The Supreme Court in Present-Day Society', in Tschudi-Madsen S. (ed), *The Supreme Court of Norway* (1998), 134 ff

Somek A., 'The Deadweight of Formulae: What Might Have Been the Second Germanization of American Equal Protection Review' (1998) 1 *University of Pannsylvania Journal of Constitutional Law* 284 ff

Somma A., *L'uso giursprudenziale della comparazione nel diritto interno e comunitario* (2001)

South African Law Commission (ed), *Project 58: Group and Human Rights – Interim Report* (1991)

Spielmann D., 'Jurisprudence des juridictions de Strasbourg et de Luxembourg dans le domaine des droits de l'homme', in Alston P. (ed), *L'union européenne et les droits de l'homme* (Bruyant, Brussels 2001), 789 ff

Stein E., *Staatsrecht* (16th edn, 1998)

Steinberger H., 'American Constitutionalism and German Constitutional Development' in Henkin L. and Rosenthal, A.J. (eds), *Constitutionalism and Rights* (1990), 199 ff.

Sudre F., *Droit européen et international des droits de l'homme* (6th edn)

Sunstein C.R., Book Review, *New Republic*, 11 March 1991, p 35

——— 'Why Does the American Constitution Lack Social and Economic Guarantees?' in Ignatieff M., *American Exceptionalism and Human Rights* (2005), pp 90–110

——— *The Second Bill of Rights* (2004)

T

Thompson L.M., 'Constitutionalism in the South African Republics', (1954) *Butterworths South African Law Review* 49 ff

Tridimas T., *The General Principles of EC Law* (2001)

Tushnet M., 'The Dilemmas of Liberal Constitutionalism', (1981) 42 *Ohio State Law Journal* 411 ff

——— 'The Possibilities of Comparative Constitutional Law', (1999) 108 *Yale Law Journal* 1225 ff

——— 'The Possibilities of Comparative Law', (1999) 108 *Yale Law Journal* 1225 ff

U

Underhill N., 'The Use of Comparative Law in *A & Others v National Blood Authority*' in Canivet G., Andenas M., and Fairgrieve D. (eds), *Comparative Law before the Courts* (2004), 79 ff

V

van Aswegen A., 'The Implications of a Bill of Rights for the Law of Contract and Delict' (1995) *South African Journal on Human Rights* 50 ff

van Gerven W. 'Community and National Legislators, Regulators, Judges, Academics and Practitioners: Living Together Apart?' in Markesinis B.S. (ed.), *Law Making, Law Finding and Law Shaping: The Diverse Influences* (1997), 13 ff

van Niekerk B., 'J.C. Noster: A Review and a Tribute to Professor J.C. De Wet' (1980) 97 *SALJ* 183 ff

Venter F., *Constitutional Comparison: Japan, Germany, Canada and South Africa as Constitutional States* (2000)

Visser D., 'Cultural Forces in the Making of Mixed Legal Systems' (2003) 78 *Tulane Law Review* 41 ff

von Beyme K., in *Der Gesetzgeber* (1997)

von Münch I., *Staatsrecht I* (6th edn, 2000)

——— Vorbemerkungen zu Art. 1–19, in von Münch I. and Kunig P. (eds), *Grundgesetz-Kommentar* (5th edn, 2000)

W

Wallace J.C., 'Globalization of Judicial Education' (2003) 28 *Yale Journal of International Law* 355 ff

Wallrabenstein A., 'Die Grundrechte, der EuGH und die Charta' (2002) *Kritische Jusitz* 381 ff

Warren and Brandeis, 'The Right of Privacy' (1890) 4 *Harvard Law Review* 193 ff

Watson A., *Legal Origins and Legal Change* (1991)

——— *Legal Transplants: An Approach to Comparative Law* (2nd edn, 1993)

Wechsler H., 'Towards Neutral Principles of Constitutional Law' (1959) 73 *Harvard Law Review* 1 ff

——— 'The Nature of Judicial Reasoning', in Hook (ed), *Law and Philosophy* (2nd edn, 1970), 290 ff

Weinrib L., 'Constitutional Conceptions and Constitutional Comparativism', in Jackson V.C. and Tushnet T. (eds), *Defining the Field of Comparative Constitutional Law* (2002), 23 ff

Weir T., 'Local Authority *v* Critical Ratepayer – A Suit in Defamation', (1972) *CLJ* 238 ff

Williams B., 'The Idea of Equality' in Laslett P. and Runciman W.G. (eds), *Philosophy, Politics and Society* (Second Series, Basil Blackwell, Oxford 1967), 110 ff

Wood G.S., 'Comment', in Scalia A. (ed), *A Matter of Interpretation: Federal Courts and the Law* (1997), 49 ff

Woolf Lord, *Protection of the Public: A New Challenge* (1990)
——— 'Droit Public – English Style' (1995) *Public Law* 57 ff

Z

Zeldin T., *France 1848–1945*
Zimmermann, 'Bürgerliche und politische Rechte in der Verfassungsrechtsprechung mittel- und osteuropäischer Staaten unter besonderer Berücksichtigung der Einflüsse der deutschen Verfassungsgerichtsbarkeit' in Frowein/Marauhn (eds), *Grundfragen der Verfassungsgerichtsbarkeit in Mittel-und Osteuropa,* pp 89 ff
Zimmermann R. and Hugo, 'Fortschritte der Südafrikanischen Rechtswissenschaft im 20 Jahrhundert: Der Beitrag von J.C. de Wet (1912–1990)', (1992) 60 *Tijdschrift voor Rechtsgeschiedenis* (*The Legal History Journal*), 157 ff
Zimmermann R., 'Stipulatio Poena', (1987) 104 *South African Law Journal* (*SALJ*), 399 ff
——— *The Law of Obligations: Roman Foundations of the Civilian Tradition* (1990)
——— 'Condicio tacita. Implied condition und die Fortbildung des eurapäischen Vetragsrechts', (1993) 193 *AcP* 212 ff
——— 'Consumer Contract Law and General Contract Law. The German Experience', in the 2005 issue of *Current Legal Problems*
Zweigert K. and Kötz H., *Introduction to Comparative Law* (3rd edn, 1998)

Name Index

Subject Index